T5-ADZ-273

Almanacs of the United States

Part II

compiled by

Milton Drake

The Scarecrow Press, Inc.
New York   1962

HUTCHINS' Revived Almanac for 1826. By David
Young. New-York: Caleb Bartlett. 18 ll. MWA; NjHi;
NjR. 6816

The KNICKERBOCKER Almanac for 1826. By David
Young. New-York: Caleb Bartlett. 18 ll. MWA. 6817

A MASONIC Register, and Pocket Magazine [for 1826].
By Henry Marsh. New-York: J. & J. Harper. 48 ll.
NHi. 6818

MING'S Hutchins' Improved; Almanac and Ephemeris
for 1826. New-York: Alexander Ming. 18 ll. MWA;
DLC; NB; NN. 6819

The NEW-JERSEY Farmer's Almanac for 1826. By
David Young. New York: Caleb Bartlett. 16 ll. MWA;
NjHi (15 ll.) 6820

NEW-YORK & New-Jersey Almanac for 1826. By David
Young. New-York: John Montgomery. 18 ll. MWA.
6821

The NEW-YORK Medical Almanac, and Repository of
Useful Science and Amusement for 1826. By David
Young. New-York: Samuel Marks. 18 ll. MWA; NjR
(17 ll.) 6822

PERMANENT Lodge Calendar. By Br. T. Tolman.
Rochester: Printed for the Publisher. 1826. 6 ll.
NNFM. 6823

PHINNEYS' Calendar, or Western Almanac for 1826.
Cooperstown: H. & E. Phinney. 18 ll. MWA; N; NN;
NHi; NCooHi; NRMA; NBuHi; DLC; NP; NRU; NUtHi;
CtHi; WHi; CLU; MnU; CtY; InU (16 ll); Drake. 6824

STATE of New-York Agricultural Almanack for 1826.
Albany: E. & E. Hosford. NbO (22 ll.) 6825

STEELE'S Albany Almanack for 1826. By Stephen Alexander. Albany: D. Steele & Son; Packard & Van Benthuysen, printers. 12 ll. N; NN; NCooHi (8 ll.); NR;
WHi. 6826

SWORDS'S Pocket Almanack, Christian's Calendar for
1826. New-York: T. & J. Swords. 40 ll. MWA; N;
NHi; NNS; NNG; NjR; DLC; MHi; PHi. 6827

The ULSTER County Farmer's Almanac for 1826. By
Andrew Beers. Kingston: S. S. Freer. 18 ll. NHi.
6828
The ULSTER County Farmer's Almanac for 1826. By
Andrew Beers. Kingston: John Tappen. 18 ll. MWA;
DLC; NHi. 6829

WEBSTER'S Calendar: or, the Albany Almanack for
1826. By Stephen Alexander. Albany: Websters &
Skinners. 18 ll. MWA; N; NN (two varieties); NHi;
DLC; NCooHi; NR; MiU-C; NjR (17 ll.); MnU; Pennypacker. 6830

WESTERN Almanack for 1826. By Oliver Loud. [np,
np] NR (10 ll.) 6831

WESTERN Almanack for 1826. By Oliver Loud.
Rochester: Everard Peck. 18 ll. NBuHi; NRHi; NRMA;
NRU (ntp) 6832

WOOD'S Almanac for 1826. By Joshua Sharp. New-
York: Samuel Wood & Sons. 18 ll. MWA; N; NHi;
NNA; InU (16 ll., ntp); DLC; OClWHi; RPB; CLU.
6833
YOUNG'S Ephemeris, or Almanack for 1826. By David
Young. Auburn: U. F. Doubleday. 18 ll. NAuT; NIC;
OClWHi; Drake. 6834

YOUNG'S Ephemeris, or Almanack for 1826. By David
Young. Auburn: T. M. Skinner. 18 ll. MWA; NN (10
ll.); OClWHi. 6835

YOUNG'S Ephemeris, or Almanack for 1826. By David
Young. Ithaca: Mack & Andrus. 18 ll. MWA; N; NN;
NHi (17 ll.); NBuG; MnM. 6836

ALMANACK, or Christian Calendar for 1827. Albany:
D. Steele & Son; Packard & Van Benthuysen, printers.
24 ll. N; MiD-B; WHi. 6837

BELL'S Almanac for 1827. New-York: J. W. Bell, &
S. Woodworth. 18 ll. CLU.   6838

C. BROWN'S, New-York State Almanac for 1827. By
Poor Old Richard. New-York: C. Brown. 18 ll. MWA
(impf); NN; OMC.   6839

The CHRISTIAN Almanack for 1827. Published at
Boston. Republished at Rochester by Everard Peck.
18 ll. N; NCooHi (6 ll.); NIC; NR; NRMA.   6840

The CHRISTIAN Almanack, for Connecticut and New
York for 1827. New-York: American Tract Society;
Hartford: Charles Hosmer. 18 ll. MWA; Ct; CtHi;
WHi.   6841

The CHRISTIAN Almanack, for New-York, Connecticut,
and New-Jersey for 1827. New-York: American Tract
Society. 18 ll. MWA; N; NN; NHi; NBLiHi; MBC;
OClWHi; CtNhHi; DLC; Mi; NjR; CtHT-W; CtY; MHi;
CtLHi; CLU; Ct; NR; MnM; ViU; NjP; WHi; NjMo;
MiD-B; CtB (impf); NRMA; NWhpHi; Bevier; Drake.
   6842

The CHRISTIAN Almanack, for New-York, Connecticut,
and New-Jersey for 1827. New-York: American Tract
Society; Hartford: Charles Hosmer. 18 ll. N; CtHi;
CtNhHi; NjR; Drake.   6843

The CHRISTIAN Almanack, for the Western District,
New-York for 1827. Utica: Hastings & Tracy, for the
American Tract Society. 18 ll. N; NN; NUt; NUtHi;
ICHi; CtHi; WHi.   6844

The COLUMBIAN Calendar, or New-York and Vermont
Almanack for 1827. Troy: Francis Adancourt. 24 ll.
MWA; N; NN; NHi; NR; NT; OClWHi; NbHi; MnU; NjJ;
MiGr; OMC; InU; CtLHi (impf); Pennypacker.   6845

DAY'S New-York Pocket Almanac for 1827. New-York:
M. Day. 12 ll. DLC; NHi.   6846

The DUTCHESS County Farmers' Almanac for 1827. By
David Young. Poughkeepsie: Isaac T. Doughty. 18 ll.

MWA; NHi; NRMA. 6847

The DUTCHESS County Farmer's Almanac for 1827.
By Charles Prindle. Poughkeepsie: P. Potter. 18 ll.
MWA; N (impf); NHi; NPV. 6848

The FARMER'S Almanac for 1827. By David Young.
New-York: Caleb Bartlett. 16 ll. MWA; NHi. 6849

FARMERS' Almanac for 1827. By David Young. Newburgh: Ward M. Gazlay. 18 ll. MWA; NHi. 6850

FARMERS' Almanac for 1827. By David Young. NewYork: John Montgomery. 18 ll. MWA; NWhpHi. 6851

FARMERS' Almanac for 1827. By David Young. NewYork: Daniel D. Smith. 18 ll. MWA; NN (impf);
NjHi (17 ll.) 6852

FARMERS' Almanack, and Astronomical Calendar for
1827. By Joshua Sharp. Rochester: Marshall &
Spalding. 12 ll. MWA; NBuHi; NR; NRHi; NRMA;
NRU. 6853

FARMER'S Calendar or the Buffalo Almanack for 1827.
By Edwin E. Prentiss. Buffalo: Lazell & Francis. 18
ll. Drake. 6854

FARMER'S Calendar; or the Utica Almanack for 1827.
Utica: William Williams. 18 ll. MWA; NHi; NUtHi;
Pennypacker; Drake. 6855

FARMER'S Calendar; or the Utica Almanack for 1827.
By Edwin E. Prentiss. Utica: Hastings & Tracy; W.
Williams, printer. 18 ll. N. 6856

FARMERS' Calendar, or Western Almanac for 1827.
By Edwin E. Prentiss. Fredonia: Hull & Snow, &
Burton & Spafford. 18 ll. MWA; N; NCooHi; NRMA;
NRU; OClWHi. 6857

The FARMERS' Diary, or Beers' Ontario Almanack for
1827. By Andrew Beers. Canandaigua: J. D. Bemis.

MWA (missing from shelves) 6858

The FARMER'S Diary; Or Ontario Almanack for 1827. By Oliver Loud. Canandaigua: Bemis, Morse and Ward. 18 ll. N (17 ll.); NN (impf); NCanHi; NRMA; PPeSchw. 6859

HOSFORD'S Calendar: or The New-York and Vermont Almanack for 1827. By Stephen Alexander. Albany: E. & E. Hosford. 12 ll. NHi; MB; NCooHi (10 ll.); N (10 ll.); NbO (6 ll.); Drake. 6860

-- Issue with 18 ll. NRMA; NN; MWA; DLC; NUtHi; NIC; VtHi. 6861

HUTCHINGS' Almanac for 1827. By David Young. New-York: James A. Burtus. 18 ll. DLC. 6862

HUTCHINGS' Almanac for 1827. By David Young. New-York: John Montgomery. 18 ll. MWA (17 ll.); NjR. 6863

HUTCHINGS' (Improved) Almanac for 1827. By David Young. New York: Samuel Marks. 18 ll. NP. 6864

HUTCHINGS' (Revived) Almanac for 1827. By David Young. New-York: James A. Burtus. 18 ll. Drake. 6865

HUTCHINGS' (Revived) Almanac for 1827. By David Young. New-York: N. B. Holmes. 18 ll. NBLiHi (impf); MSaE. 6866

HUTCHINGS' (Revived) Almanac for 1827. By David Young. New-York: John Montgomery. 18 ll. NN; MSaE. 6867

HUTCHINGS' (Revived) Almanac for 1827. By David Young. New-York: Daniel D. Smith. 18 ll. NWhpHi. 6868

HUTCHINS' Improved Almanac and Ephemeris for 1827. New-York: Caleb Bartlett. 18 ll. MWA; N; NN; DLC; Drake. 6869

HUTCHINS' Improved Family Almanac and Ephemeris

for 1827. New-York: Caleb Bartlett. 18 ll. NIC. 6870

HUTCHINS' Revived Almanac for 1827. By David Young. New-York: Caleb Bartlett. 18 ll. MWA (two varieties); NBLiHi. 6871

HUTCHINS' Revived Almanac and Ephemeris for 1827. New-York: Caleb Bartlett. 18 ll. NHi (17 ll.) 6872

KNICKERBOCKER Almanac for 1827. By David Young. New-York: Caleb Bartlett. 18 ll. MWA; NjR (two varieties); NjP. 6873

KNICKERBOCKER'S Almanac for 1827. By David Young. New-York: Caleb Bartlett. 16 ll. MWA; NN; MB; InU; NHi (15 ll.) 6874

-- Issue with 18 ll. Pennypacker. 6875

LOUD'S Almanack, or Connecticut, N. York and Vermont Calendar for 1827. [np:] Published by A. Prichard. 12 ll. MWA; NUtHi; Drake. 6876

MIDDLEBROOK'S Almanack for 1827. By Elijah Middlebrook. Ithaca: Augustin P. Searing; D. D. Spencer. 18 ll. MWA; DLC; NHi; NIC; NCH; NSyOHi (17 ll.); NBuG. 6877

MING'S Hutchins' Improved; Almanac and Ephemeris for 1827. New York: Alexander Ming. 18 ll. MWA; NN; NB. 6878

NEW-YORK and New-Jersey Almanac for 1827. By David Young. New-York: Daniel D. Smith. 18 ll. NBLiHi (impf) 6879

The NEW-YORK Medical Almanac, and Repository of Useful Science and Amusement for 1827. By David Young. New York: Samuel Marks. 18 ll. MWA; NHi; NWhpHi (15 ll.); NjR. 6880

The ORANGE County Farmers' Almanac for 1827. NRHi. 6881

PHINNEY'S Calendar, or Western Almanac for 1827.
By Edwin E. Prentiss. Cooperstown: H. & E. Phinney. 18 ll. MWA (two varieties); N; NN; NHi; NBuHi; NRMA; NIC; NHC; NSyOHi; NUtHi; DLC; ICN; PScrHi; InU; WHi; MnU; Drake. 6882

PHINNEY'S Calendar, or Western Almanac for 1827.
By Edwin E. Prentiss. Otsego: Niven & Co. 18 ll. [Severance] 6883

PHINNEYS' Calendar, or Western Almanack for 1827.
By Edwin E. Prentiss. Cooperstown: H. & E. Phinney. 18 ll. NCooHi. 6884

POOR Richard (Revived) Almanac for 1827. By David Young. New-York: James A. Burtus. 18 ll. [Sabin] 6885

POOR Richard (Revived) Almanac, and Ephemeris for 1827. By David Young. New-York: J. C. Totten. MWA (14 ll.) 6886

STEELE'S Albany Almanack for 1827. By Stephen Alexander. Albany: D. Steele & Son; Packard & Van Benthuysen, printers. 12 ll. N; NN; NHi; DLC; MnU. 6887

STODDARD'S Calendar, or The New-York and Vermont Almanack for 1827. By Stephen Alexander. Hudson: Ashbel Stoddard. 18 ll. MWA; NN; NHi; CtNhHi. 6888

SWORDS'S Pocket Almanack, Christian's Calendar for 1827. New-York: T. & J. Swords. 44 ll. MWA; NN; NHi; NNG; NNS; MHi; PHi; NjR; MBAt. 6889

The ULSTER County Farmer's Almanac for 1827. By Charles Prindle. Kingston: John Tappen. 18 ll. MWA (13 ll.); NHi; Hoes. 6890

WEBSTER'S Calendar: or, the Albany Almanack for 1827. By Stephen Alexander. Albany: Websters & Skinners. 12 ll. MWA; N; NN; NHi; NCooHi; NR; MH; NjR; NBuHi (10 ll.); NcD; MiU-C; MnU; WHi; ViU; Drake; NNSIHi (impf) 6891

WEBSTER'S Calendar: or the Albany Almanack for 1827. By Stephen Alexander. Albany: Websters & Skinners. (Second Edition) 12 ll. NN; DLC; MH; Drake. 6892

WESTERN Almanack for 1827. By Oliver Loud. [np, np] 12 ll. NR. 6893

WESTERN Almanack for 1827. By Oliver Loud. Rochester: Evered Peck. 12 ll. NR; NRMA; NRU; NBuHi; ICHi; WHi (impf) 6894

-- Issue with 18 ll. MH. 6895

WOOD'S Almanac for 1827. By Joshua Sharp. New-York: Samuel Wood & Sons. 18 ll. MWA; N (15 ll.); NN (impf); NNA; F; PPL; NHi. 6896

YOUNG'S Ephemeris, or Almanack for 1827. By David Young. Auburn: U. F. Doubleday. 18 ll. NAuHi; OClWHi. 6897

YOUNG'S Ephemeris, or Almanack for 1827. By David Young. Ithaca: Mack & Andrus. 18 ll. MWA; NN; DLC; OClWHi. 6898

ALMANACK for 1828. By David Young. Auburn: U. F. Doubleday. 18 ll. MWA; DLC. 6899

ALMANACK for 1828. By David Young. Ithaca: Mack & Andrus. 18 ll. MWA (16 ll.); NIC; NSyOHi; NBuG; PScrHi. 6900

ALMANACK for 1828. By David Young. Ithaca: A. P. Searing. 18 ll. MWA; NHi; NIC; WHi. 6901

The ANTI-MASONIC Almanack for 1828. By Edward Giddins. Rochester: Edwin Scrantom. 14 ll. MWA; N; NR (12 ll.); NRHi; NIC; NUt; MB; NRMA; NT; InU (ntp); NjR (12 ll., ntp) 6902

The ANTI-MASONIC Almanack for 1828. By Edward Giddins. Rochester: Edwin Scrantom. (Fifth Edition)

14 ll. N (13 ll.); NR; NRU. 6903

C. BROWN'S New-York State Almanac for 1828. By Poor Richard. New-York: C. Brown. 18 ll. NBuG. 6904

C. BROWN'S New-York State Almanac for 1828. By Uri Strong. New-York: C. Brown. 18 ll. MWA; NN. 6905

The CHRISTIAN Almanack for 1828. New-York: American Tract Society; Rochester: Re-Published by E. Peck & Co. 18 ll. N; NIC; NR; NRHi (17 ll.); NRMA; NT; NjP; MiD-B; OClWHi. 6906

The CHRISTIAN Almanac, For New-York, Connecticut, New-Jersey, and Pennsylvania for 1828. New-York: American Tract Society; Fanshaw, printer. 18 ll. MWA (two varieties); N; NN; NHi; CtLHi; OClWHi; Ct; NRMA; WHi; NBuG; CtNhHi; DLC; NjP; NBLiHi; CLU; NbHi; MnU; InU; NjR; PHi; PPL; PP; MH; NjMo; Drake (three varieties) 6907

The CHRISTIAN Almanac, for the State of New-York for 1828. Albany: American Tract Society, for the New-York State branch; Cornelius Gates. 18 ll. N; NNUT. 6908

The CHRISTIAN Almanac, For the United States for 1828. New-York: American Tract Society. 24 ll. DLC; NCooHi; NR; OClWHi; OMC; CtY; WHi; NjR; Drake. 6909

CHRISTIAN Almanack, For the Western District for 1828. Utica: American Tract Society; Western Sunday School Union; J. Colwell, printer. 18 ll. MWA; N; NN; NHi; NIC; NRU; OClWHi; NUt; IHi; MiD-B; CtHi; CLU; PHi (impf); MnU; NUtHi; WHi; NCooHi; NBuG; NCanHi; NSyOHi; Drake. 6910

COLUMBIA County Almanack for 1828. By Edwin E. Prentiss. Hudson: William E. Norman. 22 ll. N; Ct. 6911

The COLUMBIAN Calendar, or New-York and Vermont Almanack for 1828. Troy: Francis Adancourt. 24 ll. MWA; N; NN; NHi; NT (18 ll.); OClWHi; MnU; OMC;

VtHi. 6912

DAY'S New-York Pocket Almanac for 1828. New-York: M. Day. 12 ll. MWA; NHi. 6913

The DUTCHESS County Farmer's Almanac for 1828. Poughkeepsie: P. Potter. 18 ll. NHi (two varieties); NP; NjR (impf) 6914

The DUTCHESS County Farmers' Almanac for 1828. By David Young. Poughkeepsie: J. C. Meeks. 18 ll. MWA (17 ll.); N (impf); NP. 6915

FARMER'S Almanac for 1828. New-York: C. Brown. 18 ll. DLC; NB; NCooHi. 6916

FARMERS' Almanac for 1828. By David Young. Newburgh: Ward M. Gazlay. 18 ll. NHi. 6917

FARMERS' Almanac for 1828. By David Young. New-York: James A. Burtis. 18 ll. MWA; N; NWhpHi (17 ll.); F. 6918

FARMERS' Almanac for 1828. By David Young. New-York: John Montgomery. 18 ll. NN. 6919

FARMER'S Calendar or Utica Almanac for 1828. Utica: William Williams. [Williams] 6920

FARMERS' Calendar, or, Western Almanack for 1828. Fredonia: James Hull. 18 ll. NRU. 6921

FARMERS' Calendar, or, Western Almanack for 1828. Fredonia: Hull & Snow. 18 ll. MWA; DLC (17 ll.); ICHi. 6922

The FARMERS' Diary, or Ontario Almanack for 1828. By Oliver Loud. Canandaigua: Bemis, Morse & Ward. 18 ll. MWA; NN; NRMA; DLC; NCanHi. 6923

The FRANKLIN Almanac for 1828. By Charles Hoffman. New-York: Caleb Bartlett. 18 ll. DLC. 6924

GREENE County Almanack for 1828. By Edwin E.
Prentiss. Catskill: Samuel Wardwell; Hudson: A.
Stoddard, printer. 18 ll. NjR.   6925

HOSFORD'S Calendar; or The New York and Vermont
Almanack for 1828. Albany: E. & E. Hosford. 16 ll.
MWA; N; NHi (12 ll.); NIC; DLC; MiGr; Drake (12
ll., impf)   6926

HUTCHINGS' Revived Almanac for 1828. By David
Young. New-York: John C. Totten. 18 ll. Drake.
  6927
HUTCHINGS' Almanac for 1828. By David Young.
New-York: James A. Burtus. 18 ll. NHi.   6928

HUTCHINGS' Almanac for 1828. By David Young. New-
York: N. B. Holmes. 18 ll. NBLiHi (impf)   6929

HUTCHINGS' Almanac for 1828. By David Young.
New-York: Samuel Marks. 18 ll. MWA; NN (impf)
  6930
HUTCHINGS' Almanac for 1828. By David Young. New-
York: Daniel D. Smith. 18 ll. DLC.   6931

HUTCHINGS' Improved Almanac for 1828. By David
Young. New-York: John C. Totten. 16 ll. MWA;
NBLiHi (14 ll.)   6932

HUTCHINGS' (Revived) Almanac for 1828. By David
Young. New-York: John Montgomery. 18 ll. NHi;
CtB.   6933

HUTCHINS' Improved Almanac for 1828. New York:
C. Brown. 16 ll. MB.   6934

HUTCHINS' Improved. Almanac and Empheeris [sic]
for 1828. New-York: Caleb Bartlett. 18 ll. NBLiHi
(impf); NjR (16 ll.)   6935

HUTCHINS' Improved. Almanac and Ephemeris for
1828. New-York: Caleb Bartlett. 18 ll. NHi; NN (two
varieties); MnU.   6936

HUTCHINS' Revived Almanac and Ephemeris for 1828.
New-York: Caleb Bartlett. 18 ll. MWA; NBLiHi. 6937

KNICKERBOCKER'S Almanac for 1828. By David
Young. New-York: Caleb Bartlett. 18 ll. MWA (two
varieties); NHi; DLC. 6938

The LONG-ISLAND Almanack for 1828. By Thomas
Spofford. New-York: David Felt. 18 ll. NHi; Pennypacker. 6939

MING'S Hutchins' Improved; Almanac and Ephemeris
for 1828. New-York: Alexander Ming. 18 ll. NHi (17
ll.); NB; NBLiHi. 6940

The NEW-YORK Almanack for 1828. By Thomas Spofford. New-York: David Felt. 18 ll. MWA; NSyOHi
(17 ll.); MB. 6941

NEW York & New Jersey Almanac for 1828. By David
Young. New York: John C. Totten. 18 ll. MWA. 6942

The NEW-YORK Medical Almanac, and Repository of
Useful Science and Amusement for 1828. By David
Young. New-York: Caleb Bartlett. 18 ll. MWA; NN;
DLC (impf); NBLiHi; InU. 6943

PHINNEYS' Calendar, or Western Almanac for 1828.
By Edwin E. Prentiss. Cooperstown: H. & E. Phinney.
18 ll. MWA; N; NN; NHi; NIC; NCooHi; NUt; DLC;
NBuHi; NUtHi; NRMA; InU; WHi; PHi; CLU; Drake.
6944
PHINNEY'S Calendar, or Western Almanac for 1828.
By Edwin E. Prentiss. Little Falls: Sprague & Mc-
Kenster. 18 ll. [Severance] 6945

POOR Richard Revived. Almanac for 1828. By David
Young. New-York: John C. Totten. 18 ll. N (impf);
NN; NBLiHi (15 ll.) 6946

STEELE'S Albany Almanack for 1828. By Edwin E.
Prentiss. Albany: Oliver Steele. 12 ll. MWA; N; NN;
NHi; NR; DLC; CLU; ViU. 6947

STODDARD'S Diary; or Columbia Almanack for 1828.
By Edwin E. Prentiss. Hudson: A. Stoddard. 18 ll.
MWA (impf); N; NHi; NCooHi; CtNhHi; DLC; NbO
(14 ll.); Bevier. 6948

SWORDS'S Pocket Almanack, Christian's Calendar for
1828. New-York: T. & J. Swords. 48 ll. MWA; N;
NHi; NNS; NNG; NjR; MBAt; PPL; PHi. 6949

WEBSTER'S Calendar: or the Albany Almanack for
1828. Albany: Websters & Skinners. 18 ll. N; NN;
NHi (impf); NIC; NR; MnU; MiU-C; InU; WHi; PHi.
6950
WEBSTER'S Calendar: or the Albany Almanack for
1828. Albany: Websters & Skinners. 18 ll. MWA (11
ll.); N; NN (11 ll.); DLC; PHi. 6951

WESTERN Almanack for 1828. By Oliver Loud. Buffalo: Day, Follett & Haskins. 18 ll. NBuHi; WHi. 6952

WESTERN Almanack for 1828. By Oliver Loud. Rochester: Marshall & Dean. 12 ll. N; NRU (two varieties); NRMA; NRHi. 6953

WESTERN Almanack for 1828. By Oliver Loud. Rochester: E. Peck & Co. 18 ll. MWA; N; NR; NRMA; NRHi; CSmH. 6954

The WESTERN Farmer's Almanac for 1828. Auburn:
Oliphant & Skinner. OClWHi (missing from shelves)
6955
WILLIAMS' Calendar, or the Utica Almanack for 1828.
By Edwin E. Prentiss. Utica: William Williams. 18
ll. MWA (impf); N; NHi; NBuHi; NSyOHi; NUt; ICN;
ICHi; NBuG; WHi; MiD-B; Drake (17 ll.) 6956

WILLIAMS' Calendar, or the Utica Almanack for 1828.
By Edwin E. Prentiss. Utica: William Williams; Watertown: Knowlton and Rice. 18 ll. NHC; NWattHi.
6957
WOOD'S Almanac for 1828. By Joshua Sharp. New
York: Samuel Wood & Sons. 18 ll. MWA; NHi; NNA;
DLC. 6958

The ANTI-MASONIC Almanac for 1829. By Edward
Giddins. Rochester: E. Scrantom. 24 ll. MWA; N;
NN; NHi; PPFM; RPA (22 ll., ntp); NBuG; MnU;
NIC; NRHi; NRU; CLU; NUtHi; CL; NNA; NjR (23 ll.);
CtNhHi (impf); MB; Ct; MeP (impf); CoCC; InU; WHi;
NNFM; CtHi; Drake. 6959

The CHRISTIAN Almanack for 1829. New York: American Tract Society; Rochester: Re-published by E.
Peck & Co. 18 ll. DLC; NRU; NR; NIC; MnU;
MiD-B; NRMA. 6960

The CHRISTIAN Almanac, for New-York, Connecticut,
and New-Jersey for 1829. New-York: American Tract
Society. 18 ll. MWA; N; NN; NRMA; NBLiHi; WHi;
InU; MH; OMC; CLU; CtNhHi; DLC; OClWHi; NjHi;
NBuHi; NjR; IU; CtY; Ct; MiD-B; Drake. 6961

The CHRISTIAN Almanac, for New-York, Vermont, and
Massachusetts for 1829. Albany: American Tract Society; Oliver Steele. 18 ll. MWA; N; NN; NHi; MH;
NHC; NT; CtNhHi; VtHi. 6962

The CHRISTIAN Almanac, for the Western District for
1829. Utica: American Tract Society; Utica Auxiliary
Tract Society; George S. Wilson. 18 ll. NUtHi; MiD-B;
CtHi. 6963

The COLUMBIAN Calendar, or New-York and Vermont
Almanack for 1829. Troy: Francis Adancourt. 18 ll.
MWA; N; NHi; NT; MnU; OMC; PHi (impf); CLU.
6964
-- Issue with 24 ll. MWA; NN. 6965

The COLUMBIAN Calendar, or New-York and Vermont
Almanack for 1829. Troy: Francis Adancourt; Clark
& Hosford; J. Disturnell; E. S. Coon. (Third Edition)
12 ll. NN; NT; OClWHi. 6966

-- Issue with 24 ll. DLC. 6967

The COLUMBIAN Calendar, or New-York and Vermont
Almanack for 1829. Troy: Francis Adancourt, for

William S. Parker. 24 ll. MWA; NbHi. 6968

DAY'S New-York Pocket Almanac for 1829. New-
York: M. Day. 12 ll. NHi. 6969

FARMERS Almanac for 1829. New-York: C. Brown.
18 ll. MWA; DLC; Drake. 6970

FARMERS Almanac for 1829. By David Gomez. Peekskill: S. Marks & Son. 18 ll. [Hufeland] 6971

The FARMER'S Almanac for 1829. By David Young.
New-York: Caleb Bartlett. 24 ll. MWA; NjR; IU;
Drake. 6972

The FARMER'S Almanac for 1829. By David Young.
New-York: N. B. Holmes. 18 ll. WHi. 6973

FARMERS' Almanac for 1829. By David Young. New-
York: Daniel D. Smith. 18 ll. NN. 6974

FARMERS' Almanac for 1829. By David Young. Peekskill: S. Marks & Son. 18 ll. NHi. 6975

FARMERS' Almanac for 1829. By David Young.
Poughkeepsie: P. Potter. 18 ll. MWA; N (imprint
lacking); NHi (12 ll.); NP. 6976

The FARMER'S Almanack, and Annual Register for
1829. By Thomas Spofford. New-York: David Felt.
(For Long Island) 18 ll. MWA; NN; NHi; DLC;
NBLiHi; NSyOHi; MH; CtHT-W; OClWHi; InU (ntp);
Pennypacker. 6977

The FARMER'S Almanack, and Annual Register for
1829. By Thomas Spofford. New-York: David Felt.
(For New-York) 18 ll. NBLiHi. 6978

FARMER'S Calendar or Utica Almanac for 1829. Utica:
William Williams. [Williams] 6979

FARMER'S Calendar, or Western Almanac for 1829. By
Edwin E. Prentiss. Ithaca: Mack & Andrus; Coopers-

town: H. & E. Phinney, printers. 18 ll. MWA; N;
NIC; OClWHi; WHi; PScrHi. 6980

FARMER'S Diary; or, Catskill Almanack for 1829.
Catskill: C. Faxon. 12 ll. ViU. 6981

The FARMER'S Diary, or, Ontario Almanack for 1829.
By Oliver Loud. Canandaigua: Bemis & Ward. 18 ll.
DLC; NRMA. 6982

The FARMER'S Diary, or Ontario Almanack for 1829.
By Oliver Loud. Canandaigua: Morse & Willson. 18
ll. MWA; NN (impf); NHi; NSyOHi (impf); DLC;
NCanHi. 6983

GREENE County Almanack for 1829. By Edwin E.
Prentiss. Catskill: Nathan G. Elliott; Hudson: Rural
Repository. 18 ll. NCooHi (17 ll.); Drake. 6984

HUCHINGS' Improved Almanac for 1829. By David
Young. New-York: John C. Totten. 18 ll. NHi;
NWhpHi. 6985

HUCHINGS' Revived Almanac for 1829. By David
Young. New-York: John C. Totten. 18 ll. N; WHi.
6986
HUTCHINGS' Almanac for 1829. By David Young. New
York: James A. Burtis. 18 ll. MWA (impf); NjR. 6987

HUTCHINGS' Almanac for 1829. By David Young. New-
York: Daniel D. Smith. 18 ll. MWA; NBLiHi (16 ll.)
6988
HUTCHINGS' Almanac for 1829. By David Young.
Peekskill: S. Marks. 18 ll. Ct. 6989

HUTCHINGS' Almanac for 1829. By David Young.
Poughkeepsie: P. Potter. 18 ll. NN (ntp); NHi; NP;
DLC. 6990

HUTCHINGS' (Revived) Almanac for 1829. By Poor Old
Richard. New-York: C. Brown. 18 ll. NB (17 ll.)
6991
HUTCHINGS' (Revived) Almanac for 1829. By David

New York - 1829 687

Young. New-York: Daniel D. Smith. 18 ll. MWA; NN.
6992
HUTCHINGS' (Revived) Almanac for 1829. By David
Young. Poughkeepsie: P. Potter. 18 ll. MWA. 6993

HUTCHINS' Improved Almanac and Ephemeris for 1829.
New-York: Caleb Bartlett. 24 ll. MWA; N; NN; NHi;
NBLiHi; DLC; InU; CtHi; MB; NjMo; WHi. 6994

HUTCHINS' Improved Almanac and Ephemeris for 1829.
New-York: Caleb Bartlett; N. B. Holmes. 24 ll. NN.
6995
KNICKERBOCKER'S Almanac for 1829. By David
Young. New-York: Caleb Bartlett. 24 ll. MWA; N;
NN; CtY; CtHi (imprint lacking) 6996

KNICKERBOCKER'S Almanac for 1829. By David
Young. Poughkeepsie: Platt & Parsons. 24 ll. MWA;
NjR (23 ll.) 6997

MING'S Hutchins' Improved Almanac and Ephemeris for
1829. New York: Alexander Ming. 18 ll. MWA; N;
NN; NHi; DLC; Pennypacker; Drake. 6998

PHINNEY'S Calendar, or Western Almanac for 1829.
By Edwin E. Prentiss. Cooperstown: H. & E. Phinney.
18 ll. MWA; N; NN; NHi; DLC; NCooHi; NRMA;
NBuHi; NIC; NUt; NUtHi; NHC; CtY; InU; WHi; PHi;
FSpHi; NSyOHi (17 ll.) 6999

PHINNNEYS' Calendar, or, Western Almanack for 1829.
By Edwin E. Prentiss. Cooperstown: H. & E. Phinney.
18 ll. NCooHi; NNFM (impf) 7000

PHINNEY'S Calendar, or Western Almanac for 1829.
By Edwin E. Prentiss. Little Falls: J. C. Dann & Co.
18 ll. [Severance] 7001

PHINNEY'S Calendar, or Western Almanac for 1829.
By Edwin E. Prentiss. Utica: H. E. Phinney & Co. 18
ll. [Severance] 7002

POOR Richard's Almanack for 1829. By Poor Richard,

Jr. Rochester: Marshall & Dean. 12 ll. MWA; NUtHi (11 ll.); NRMA; NRU; MnM. 7003

STEELE'S Albany Almanack for 1829. By Edwin E. Prentiss. Albany: Oliver Steele. 12 ll. N; NN; NR; DLC; CLU; NcD. 7004

-- Issue with 13 ll. MWA; NCooHi. 7005

STODDARD'S Diary; or Columbia Almanack for 1829. By Edwin E. Prentiss. Hudson: A. Stoddard. 18 ll. MWA; N; NN; NHi; NjR; CtNhHi (17 ll.); PHi; InU. 7006

SWORDS'S Pocket Almanack, Christian's Calendar for 1829. New-York: T. & J. Swords. 48 ll. MWA; N; NHi; NNS; NNG; MBAt; PHi; NjR; MHi. 7007

WEBSTER'S Calendar: or the Albany Almanack for 1829. By Edwin E. Prentiss. Albany: Websters & Skinners. 18 ll. N; NN (12 ll.); NCooHi (impf); MiU-C; MnU; WHi. 7008

WEBSTER'S Calendar: or the Albany Almanack for 1829. By Edwin E. Prentiss. Albany: Websters & Skinners. (Second Edition) 18 ll. MWA; N; NN; NCooHi (17 ll.); DLC; OClWHi; PHi; Drake. 7009

WESTCHESTER and Putnam Farmers' Almanac for 1829. By David Young. Peekskill: S. Marks & Son. 18 ll. NjR. 7010

WESTERN Almanack for 1829. By Oliver Loud. Buffalo: Day, Follett & Haskins. 12 ll. WHi. 7011

WESTERN Almanack for 1829. By Oliver Loud. Fredonia: Henry C. Frisbee. 18 ll. DLC (10 ll.); ICHi. 7012

WESTERN Almanack for 1829. By Oliver Loud. Rochester: E. Peck & Co. 12 ll. MWA; N; NHi (11 ll.); NR; NRMA; NRU; NBuHi (ntp) 7013

WILLIAMS' Calendar, or the Utica Almanack for 1829. By Edwin E. Prentiss. Buffalo: Sargent & Wilgus.

18 ll. NBuHi; NRMA; CSmH.   7014

WILLIAMS' Calendar, or the Utica Almanack for 1829. By Edwin E. Prentiss. Utica: William Williams. 18 ll. MWA; N; NN; NHi; NIC; NBuHi; NUtHi; InU; CLU; CSmH.   7015

WILLIAMS' Calendar, or the Utica Almanack for 1829. By Edwin E. Prentiss. Watertown: Knowlton and Rice. 18 ll. NHC.   7016

WOOD'S Almanac for 1829. By Joshua Sharp. New York: Samuel Wood & Sons; Richard & George S. Wood, printers. 18 ll. MWA; N; NN; NHi; DLC; NNA; InU.   7017

The ANALETIC Calendar for 1830. By Oliver Loud. Lockport: E. A. Cooley. 18 ll. MWA (17 ll.)   7018

The ANTI-MASONIC Almanac for 1830. By Edward Giddins. Rochester: Edwin Scrantom. 18 ll. MWA (two varieties); N; NN; MB; CLU; CL; NR (two varieties); NRHi; NRU; IHi; NIC; NCanHi (impf); NRMA; CoCC; InU; CtHi; NBuG; WHi; PPFM; NNFM.   7019

The CHRISTIAN Almanac, for New-York, Connecticut, and New-Jersey for 1830. New-York: American Tract Society. 18 ll. MWA; N; NN; NHi; DLC; PHi; NBLiHi; CLU; NRU; IU; OClWHi; MH; NSyOHi; CtY; MnU; NjR; InU; NRMA; Drake.   7020

The CHRISTIAN Almanac for New York, Vermont and Massachusetts for 1830. Albany: American Tract Society; A. McKercher. 18 ll. MWA; N; NN; MH; MHi.   7021

The CHRISTIAN Almanac for the Western District for 1830. Utica: American Tract Society; Edward Vernon. 18 ll. MWA; N; NN; NHi; NUtHi; NCH; MiD-B; WHi; NUt.   7022

The CHURCHMAN'S Almanac for 1830. New-York: New-York Protestant Episcopal Press. 18 ll. MWA; N; IU; NNG; MSaE; PPL.   7023

The CHURCHMAN'S Almanac for 1830. Calculated for the Meridian of New York. By D. Young [and] F. R. Hasler. New-York: New-York Protestant Episcopal Press. 18 ll. MWA; N; NNA; NSyOHi; MB; MSaE; CLU; NcD; WHi. 7024

COLUMBIA County Almanack for 1830. By Edwin E. Prentiss. Hudson: Norman's; Rural Repository. 24 ll. MWA; NHi; CtB (12 ll., impf) 7025

The COLUMBIAN Calendar, or New-York and Vermont Almanack for 1830. Troy: Francis Adancourt. 12 ll. MWA (impf); NN; NHi; NT; PHi; OMC; MnU; VtHi; NjR (10 ll.); Drake. 7026

The COLUMBIAN Calendar, or New-York and Vermont Almanack for 1830. Troy: Francis Adancourt; William S. Parker; [etc]. 18 ll. N; OClWHi. 7027

DAY'S New-York Pocket Almanac for 1830. New-York: M. Day. 12 ll. NHi; NjR. 7028

DUTCHESS County Almanack for 1830. By Edwin E. Prentiss. Poughkeepsie: P. Potter. 12 ll. MWA; CtW (11 ll.) 7029

The FARMER'S Almanac for 1830. By David Young. New-York: Caleb Bartlett. 18 ll. MWA (17 ll.); InU (impf); OMC; OO. 7030

The FARMER'S Almanac for 1830. By David Young. New-York: Daniel D. Smith. 18 ll. MWA. 7031

The FARMER'S Calendar or Ontario Almanac for 1830. By Oliver Loud. Canandaigua: Bemis & Ward. 12 ll. NR. 7032

FARMERS' Diary; or Catskill Almanack for 1830. By Edwin E. Prentiss. Catskill: Faxon & Elliott. 16 ll. MWA; N; NN; NHi (impf); CLCM; ViU; CtNhHi (impf) 7033
-- Issue with 18 ll. Drake. 7034

The FARMER'S Diary, or Ontario Almanac for 1830.
By Oliver Loud. Canandaigua: Bemis & Ward. 12 ll.
MWA; N; NHi; NUtHi; NRMA; NRU. 7035

HUCHING'S Improved Almanack for 1830. By David
Young. New York: John C. Totten. 20 ll. MWA (18
ll.); N; NHi; DLC. 7036

HUTCHINGS' Almanac for 1830. [np, np] 18 ll. NP.
7037
HUTCHINGS' (Improved) Almanac for 1830. By David
Young. New-York: Daniel D. Smith. 18 ll. ICHi;
Drake. 7038

HUTCHING'S Improved Farmers' and Mechanics' Almanac for 1830. New York: Turner & Fisher. 18 ll.
NHi (17 ll.) 7039

HUTCHINS' Improved Almanac for 1830. New York:
C. Brown. 18 ll. NHi; CLU. 7040

HUTCHINS' Improved Almanac for 1830. New-York:
Christian Brown. 18 ll. NBLiHi. 7041

HUTCHINS' Improved Almanac and Ephemeris for 1830.
New-York: Caleb Bartlett. 18 ll. MWA; N; NN; NHi;
NBLiHi; PHi; NjP; OO; MSaE; Pennypacker; Drake
(17 ll.) 7042

HUTCHINS' Improved Almanac and Ephemeris for 1830.
New-York: Caleb Bartlett; N. B. Holmes. 18 ll. MWA;
MB. 7043

HUTCHINS' Revived Almanack for 1830. By David
Young. New-York: John C. Totten. 18 ll. DLC;
NWhpHi. 7044

KNICKERBOCKER'S Almanac for 1830. By David
Young. New-York: Caleb Bartlett. 18 ll. MWA; NNA;
DLC; PPL (13 ll.); NjR; CtY; NjHi. 7045

The LONG Island and Farmer's Almanack for 1830.
By Thomas Spofford. New-York: David Felt. 18 ll.

MWA (impf) 7046

MING'S Hutchins' Improved Almanac and Ephemeris for 1830. New York: Alexander Ming. 18 ll. MWA; NN; NHi (15 ll.); NjMo; PHi. 7047

NEW-YORK Almanack for 1830. By David Young. New-York: John C. Totten. 18 ll. N. 7048

The NEW-YORK and Farmer's Almanack for 1830. By Thomas Spofford. New-York: David Felt. 18 ll. MWA; N; NN; NHi; DLC; NCooHi; NjR; NB; OClWHi; ICHi; InU; PHi; WHi; NUtHi; Drake. 7049

NEW-YORK & New-Jersey Almanac for 1830. By David Young. New-York: Daniel D. Smith. 18 ll. NN (17 ll.); NjR. 7050

The NEW-YORK State Register [and Almanac] for 1830. By Roger Sherman Skinner. New-York: Clayton & Van Norden. 204 ll. N. 7051

PAUL Pry's Almanac for 1830. By David Young. New-York: C. Brown. 18 ll. MWA; Butterfield. 7052

PAUL Pry's Almanac for 1830. By David Young. New-York: Christian Brown. 18 ll. NjR. 7053

PHINNEY'S Calendar, or Western Almanac for 1830. By Edwin E. Prentiss. Cooperstown: H. & E. Phinney. 18 ll. MWA; N; NN; NHi; NBuHi; OClWHi; WHi; NSyOHi; IHi; CtHi (impf); DLC; NRMA; NR; CLU; NCooHi; MH; NIC; CtY; InU; ViU. 7054

PHINNEY'S Calendar, or Western Almanac for 1830. By Edwin E. Prentiss. Cooperstown: H. & E. Phinney; Ithaca: Mack & Andrus. 18 ll. MWA; NCooHi. 7055

PHINNEY'S Calendar, or Western Almanac for 1830. By Edwin E. Prentiss. Little Falls: J. C. Smith & Co. 18 ll. [Severance] 7056

POOR Richard (Revived) Almanac, and Ephemeris for

1830. New York: C. Brown. 18 ll. MWA. 7057

POOR Richard's Almanack for 1830. By Oliver Loud. Rochester: Marshall, Dean, & Co.; Waterloo: Chapin, Lucas, & Co. 12 ll. MWA; N; NN; NR; NRMA; NRU; CSmH. 7058

STEELE'S Albany Almanack for 1830. By Edwin E. Prentiss. Albany: Oliver Steele. 12 ll. MWA; N; NN; NHi; DLC; NSyOHi (impf); NR; MnU; OMC; NT; Drake (11 ll.) 7059

STODDARD'S Diary; or Columbia Almanack for 1830. By Edwin E. Prentiss. Hudson: A. Stoddard. 12 ll. MWA (11 ll.); NN; NP. 7060

SWORDS'S Pocket Almanack, Churchman's Calendar, and Ecclesiastical Register for 1830. New-York: T. & J. Swords; Edward J. Swords, printer. 50 ll. MWA; N; NHi; NjR; NNS; NNG; PPL; PHi; BritMus. 7061

WEBSTER'S Calendar: or the Albany Almanack for 1830. By Edwin E. Prentiss. Albany: Websters & Skinners. 12 ll. MWA; N; NHi; DLC; WHi; MB.
7062

WEBSTER'S Calendar: or, the Albany Almanack for 1830. By Edwin E. Prentiss. Albany: Websters & Skinners. (Second Edition) 12 ll. MWA; N; NN; NjR; MiU-C. 7063

WESTERN Almanack for 1830. By Oliver Loud. Buffalo: Day, Follett, & Haskins. 12 ll. NBuHi; NRU.
7064

WESTERN Almanack for 1830. By Oliver Loud. Rochester: E. Peck & Co. 12 ll. N; NR; NRHi; NRMA; NRU. 7065

WILLIAMS' Calendar, or the Utica Almanack for 1830. By Edwin E. Prentiss. Utica: William Williams. 18 ll. MWA; N; NN (13 ll.); NHi; NUt; NBuHi; NCooHi; NUtHi; MnU; WHi (ntp); Drake. 7066

WILLIAMS' Calendar, or the Utica Almanack for 1830.

By Edwin E. Prentiss. Watertown: Knowlton and Rice. 18 ll. MWA; DLC; Drake. 7067

WOOD'S Almanac for 1830. By Joshua Sharp. New York: Samuel Wood & Sons; R. & G. S. Wood, printers. 18 ll. MWA; DLC; NHi; NNA; NjHi; NPV; OClWHi. 7068

A. & C. A. WARREN'S Northern Almanack for 1831. Ballston Spa: A. & C. A. Warren. 12 ll. MWA; NHi. 7069

ALMANAC for 1831. Peekskill. Advertised in the "Westchester & Putnam Sentinel," October 14, 1830. 7070

ANTI Masonic Almanac for 1831. By Edward Giddins. Utica: William Williams. 36 ll. MWA; DLC; N; NN; NHi; MBFM; OClWHi; WHi; NCanHi (34 ll.); MnU; IaCrM; NEaa; MiD-B; MB; PHi; NRMA; PPFM; NBuG; NIC; NCooHi; NRU; PPiHi; NSyOHi (33 ll.); NNFM; Drake. 7071

BEERS'S (Revived) Almanac for 1831. By David Young. Poughkeepsie: P. Potter & Co. N (22 ll., ntp) Title from Wall. 7072

The CHRISTIAN Almanac, For New-York, Connecticut, and New-Jersey for 1831. New-York: American Tract Society. 18 ll. MWA; N; NN; NHi; NBLiHi; NjR; OMC; InU; NjHi; CtY; MH; CtHi; NRMA; NjP; CLU; OO; MnU; PPL; Drake. 7073

The CHRISTIAN Almanac, for New-York, Vermont, and Massachusetts for 1831. Albany: American Tract Society; Duncan McKercher. 18 ll. N; Drake. 7074

The CHRISTIAN Almanac for the Western District for 1831. Rochester: American Tract Society; Levi A. Ward. 18 ll. NR; NRU. 7075

The CHRISTIAN Almanac for the Western District for 1831. Utica: American Tract Society; Edward Vernon. 18 ll. N; NN (impf); NUtHi; NRU. 7076

The CHURCHMAN'S Almanac for 1831. By David Young.

New-York: New-York Protestant Episcopal Press. 18 ll. MWA; NHi; NR; NRHi; NNG; MB; CLU; PPL; ViW; WHi. 7077

The CHURCHMAN'S Almanac for 1831. By David Young [and] F. R. Hassler. New-York: New-York Protestant Episcopal Press. [Imprint ends with line of prices.] 18 ll. N; NNA. 7078

The COLUMBIAN Calendar, or New-York and Vermont Almanack for 1831. Troy: Francis Adancourt. 12 ll. MWA; N; NT; CLU; VtBennHi (impf); PHi; OClWHi; Vt; VtHi. 7079

DAY'S New-York Pocket Almanac for 1831. New-York: M. Day. 12 ll. NHi. 7080

DUTCHESS County Farmers' Almanack for 1831. By David Young. Poughkeepsie: W. M. Parsons. 18 ll. DLC; NBuG (impf) 7081

FARMER'S Almanack for 1831. Ithaca. 18 ll. private collection. 7082

FARMER'S Almanac for 1831. By David Young. New-York: Caleb Bartlett. 18 ll. NHi. 7083

FARMERS' Almanack for 1831. By David Young. New-York: Daniel D. Smith. 18 ll. NN; MHi. 7084

FARMERS' Almanack for 1831. By David Young. Poughkeepsie: P. Potter. 18 ll. MWA; NHi; NP; MB.
7085
FARMER'S Almanack, for the Middle States for 1831. By Thomas Spofford. New-York: David Felt; Boston: Willard Felt & Co. 18 ll. MWA; N; NN; MnM; MnU; NB; InU; PHi; MB; ViHi; NjR; Ct; CtLHi. 7086

FARMER'S Almanack for the Middle States for 1831. By Thomas Spofford. Utica: Hastings & Tracy. 18 ll. NSyOHi; AU. 7087

FARMERS' Diary; or Catskill Almanack for 1831. By

Edwin E. Prentiss. Catskill: Faxon & Elliott. 18 ll.
MWA; N; NN (12 ll.); NHi; NjR; NbO; WHi; Drake.
7088
The FARMER'S Diary, or Ontario Almanac for 1831.
Canandaigua: Bemis and Ward. 12 ll. N; NIC; NRU.
7089
The FARMER'S Diary, or Ontario Almanac for 1831.
Canandaigua: Morse & Harvey. 12 ll. NBuG; NCooHi
(11 ll.); NR; NRMA; NSyOHi. 7090

The FARMER'S Diary, or, Ontario Almanac for 1831.
By Andrew Beers. Canandaigua: Morse & Harvey.
12 ll. MWA; MiD-B; NCanHi; WHi. 7091

HUCHINGS' Improved Almanack for 1831. By David
Young. New-York: John C. Totten. 18 ll. MWA;
MnU (17 ll.); NBLiHi; NHi. 7092

HUCHING'S Revived Almanack for 1831. By David
Young. New-York: John C. Totten. 18 ll. MWA; NN
(17 ll.); MB. 7093

HUTCHING'S Almanack for 1831. By David Young.
New-York: Daniel D. Smith. 18 ll. NN; NHi (impf)
7094
HUTCHINGS (Revived) Almanac for 1831. New-York:
N. B. Holmes. Vail. 7095

HUTCHINS' Improved Almanac for 1831. By David
Young. New-York: C. Brown. 18 ll. NN. 7096

HUTCHINS' Improved Almanac and Ephemeris for 1831.
Albany: Tracy Doolittle. 18 ll. MWA. 7097

HUTCHINS' Improved Almanac and Ephemeris for 1831.
Newburgh: Sneden & Hathaway. 18 ll. DLC. 7098

HUTCHINS' Improved Almanac and Ephemeris for 1831.
New-York: Caleb Bartlett. 18 ll. MWA; NN; NHi;
NjMo; NjR; MH; Ct; OO. 7099

HUTCHINS' Improved Almanac and Ephemeris for 1831.
New-York: N. B. Holmes. 18 ll. CtHi (16 ll.) 7100

HUTCHINS' Improved Almanac and Ephemeris for 1831.
By David Young. New-York: Caleb Bartlett. 18 ll.
MWA; NBLiHi. 7101

The JUVENILE Almanac; or, series of monthly emblems [for 1831]. New-York: Mahlon Day. 12 ll. NIC.
7102

KNICKERBOCKER'S Almanac for 1831. By David
Young. New York: Caleb Bartlett. 12 ll. MWA; MB.
7103

KNICKERBOCKER'S Almanac for 1831. By David
Young. New-York: C. Brown. 18 ll. MWA; N; InU.
7104

LOOMIS' Calendar, or the New-York and Vermont Almanack for 1831. Albany: G. J. Loomis. 12 ll. MWA;
N; NHi; NT; MnU; CtHi; Drake. 7105

NEW-YORK Almanack for 1831. By David Young. New-York: John C. Totten. 18 ll. MWA; NHi; NjR. 7106

The NEW York Anti-Masonic Almanac for 1831. New
York: United States Anti-Masonic Book Store. 18 ll.
NHi; NjR; NjHi. 7107

NORMAN'S Columbia County Almanack for 1831. By
Edwin E. Prentiss. Hudson: Norman's. 12 ll. MWA.
7108

PAUL Pry's Almanac for 1831. By David Young.
New-York: C. Brown. 18 ll. MWA; NN (impf);
NBLiHi; DLC; RWe. 7109

PHINNEYS' Calendar, or Western Almanac for 1831.
By Edwin E. Prentiss. Cooperstown: H. & E. Phinney.
18 ll. MWA; N; NN; NHi; NIC; WHi; DLC; FSpHi;
NUtHi; PHi; OClWHi; NSyOHi; CtHi; CLU; NCooHi;
NBuHi; MH; MnU; InU; NUt; NRMA; Drake. 7110

PHINNEY'S Calendar, or Western Almanac for 1831.
By Edwin E. Prentiss. Oxford: George Hunt. 18 ll.
[Severance] 7111

POOR Richard's Almanack for 1831. Rochester: Marshall, Dean, & Co. 12 ll. MWA (impf); N; NN; NRU;

NBuHi; NRMA; MBAt; NCanHi (11 ll.); WHi. 7112

POOR Richard's Revised Almanac for 1831. New-York: Christian Brown. 18 ll. NN (17 ll.); NBLiHi. 7113

STEELE'S Albany Almanack for 1831. Albany: Oliver Steele. 12 ll. MWA; N; NN; NHi; NCooHi; NSchU. 7114

STODDARD'S Diary; or Columbia Almanack for 1831. By Edwin E. Prentiss. Hudson: A. Stoddard. 12 ll. MWA; PHi; NHi. 7115

SWORDS'S Pocket Almanack, Churchman's Calendar for 1831. New-York: T. & J. Swords; Edward J. Swords, printer. 50 ll. MWA; N; NHi; NNG; NNS; PPL; PHi; PP; MSaE; MHi; NjR; BritMus. 7116

TEMPERANCE Almanack for 1831. Rochester: Printed and published by E. Peck & Co. 18 ll. NR; NRMA. 7117

TEMPERANCE Almanac for 1831. Rochester: Printed and sold by E. Peck & Co. 12 ll. Butterfield. 7118

WEBSTER'S Calendar: or the Albany Almanack for 1831. By Edwin E. Prentiss. Albany: Webster & Skinners. 18 ll. MWA; N; NN; NHi; Ct (12 ll.); WHi; NBuHi; MiU-C; MnU. 7119

WEBSTER'S Calendar: or the Albany Almanack for 1831. By Edwin E. Prentiss. Albany: Webster & Skinners. (Second Edition) 18 ll. MWA; NHi; NSyOHi. 7120

WESTERN Almanack for 1831. Batavia: A. P. Parker. 12 ll. DLC; NRMA. 7121

WESTERN Almanack for 1831. Buffalo: Day, Follett, & Haskins. 18 ll. MWA. 7122

WESTERN Almanack for 1831. Fredonia: Henry C. Frisbee. DLC (11 ll.) 7123

WESTERN Almanack for 1831. Le Roy: Elisha Starr.

12 ll. NRMA. 7124

WESTERN Almanack for 1831. Rochester: E. Peck & Co. 12 ll. MWA (11 ll.); N; NRHi; NUtHi; NR; NRU. 7125

WESTERN Almanack for 1831. Watertown: Knowlton & Rice. 12 ll. MWA (impf) 7126

WOOD'S Almanac for 1831. By Joshua Sharp. New York: Samuel Wood & Sons; R. & G. S. Wood, printers. 18 ll. MWA; NHi; DLC; NWhpHi; NNA; OClWHi. 7127

ALMANAC for 1832. Peekskill. Advertised in the "Westchester & Putnam Sentinel," August 18, 1831.
7128

The AMERICAN Comic Almanac for 1832. New-York: David Felt. 24 ll. MWA (ntp); MnU; NT (23 ll.) 7129

ANTI Masonic Almanac for 1832. By Edward Giddins. Utica: William Williams, Publisher. 36 ll. N; NCooHi (35 ll.); NNFM; NjR. 7130

ANTI Masonic Almanac for 1832. By Edward Giddins. Utica: William Williams, Publishers [sic]. 36 ll. MWA; N; NN; NHi; CLU; NRU; IaCrM; NBLiHi; MiD-B; PPFM; PPL; MB; WHi; CL; NIC; ICHi; CtHi; NUt; OClWHi; NRMA; NBuG; KyU (35 ll.); MnU; Drake. 7131

BEERS'S (Revived) Almanac for 1832. By David Young. Poughkeepsie: P. Potter & Co. 24 ll. N; NP; CtB (22 ll.); CtY; MiD-B. 7132

BICKNELL'S Calendar, or Western Almanac for 1832. By Edwin E. Prentiss. Morrisville: B. Bicknell & Son. 12 ll. N; NN; NHi; NSyOHi (10 ll.); NCooHi (11 ll.) 7133

The CHRISTIAN Almanac, For New-York, Connecticut, and New-Jersey for 1832. New-York: American Tract Society. 18 ll. MWA; N; NN; NHi; IU; MB; NjR; NBuG; NBLiHi; NjP; CtY; CLU; MnU; CtNhHi; OClWHi;

OO; InU; NRMA; Drake (2 varieties) 7134

The CHRISTIAN Almanac, for the Western District for 1832. Geneva: American Tract Society; Rev. Warren Day. 18 ll. MWA; NN; NRMA. 7135

The CHRISTIAN Almanac, for the Western District for 1832. Rochester: American Tract Society; L. A. Ward. 18 ll. NRU. 7136

The CHRISTIAN Almanac, for the Western District for 1832. Utica: American Tract Society; Edward Vernon. 18 ll. MWA; NWattHi; MiD-B. 7137

The CHURCHMAN'S Almanac for 1832. By D. Young [and] F. R. Hassler. New-York: New-York Protestant Episcopal Press. 18 ll. MWA; N; NHi; NNA; NNG; InU; WHi; NRHi; PPL; MB; NR; NcD; OClWHi; Ct; MiD-B. 7138

CLARK & Hosford's New-York and Vermont Almanack for 1832. Albany: Clark and Hosford; George J. Loomis, printer. 12 ll. NN. 7139

The COLUMBIAN Calendar, or New-York and Vermont Almanac for 1832. Troy: Francis Adancourt. 12 ll. MWA; NN (6 ll.); NBuHi; PHi; MH; OMC. 7140

The COMMON Almanack for 1832. Watertown: Knowlton & Rice. 12 ll. MWA; NHi; DLC; NRMA. 7141

DAY'S New-York Pocket Almanac for 1832. New-York: M. Day. 12 ll. MWA; NN; NHi; MiU-C. 7142

The FARMER'S Almanack for 1832. Buffalo: R. W. Haskins. 12 ll. NBuHi. 7143

FARMERS' Almanac for 1832. Newburgh: Sneden & Hathaway. Vail. 7144

FARMERS' Almanac for 1832. New-York: S. Marks & Son. 18 ll. NjR. 7145

FARMERS' Almanac for 1832. Poughkeepsie: P. Potter & Co. 24 ll. N; NP; CtW. 7146

The FARMER'S Almanack for 1832. Utica: Hastings & Tracy. 12 ll. MWA; N; NRU; NIC; NUt; WHi; PScrHi. 7147

The FARMER'S Almanac for 1832. By David Young. Albany: Tracy Doolittle. 18 ll. NR. 7148

FARMER'S Almanac for 1832. By David Young. New-York: C. Brown. 18 ll. MWA (17 ll.); NjR. 7149

FARMER'S Almanac for 1832. By David Young. New-York: Christian Brown, No. 211 Water-Street. 18 ll. MWA (16 ll.); N; WHi; Drake. 7150

FARMERS' Almanac for 1832. By David Young. New-York: Christian Brown, No. 211 Water, Near Fulton Street. 18 ll. MWA; PHi. 7151

-- Cut of rooster on titlepage. 18 ll. MWA; N. 7152

The FARMERS' Almanac for 1832. By David Young. New-York: N. B. Holmes. 18 ll. MB. 7153

FARMERS' Almanac for 1832. By David Young. New-York: Daniel D. Smith. 18 ll. NN; DLC; MHi; NNSIHi. 7154

The FARMER'S Almanack for the Middle States for 1832. By Thomas Spofford. New York: David Felt; Boston: Willard Felt & Co. 18 ll. MWA; N; NHi; NB; NBLiHi; CtLHi; CtY. 7155

The FARMER'S Almanack for the Middle States for 1832. By Thomas Spofford. New York: David Felt; Boston: Willard Felt & Co.; William A. Mercien, printer. 18 ll. MWA (11 ll.); NN; NHi; NBLiHi; NSyOHi; NjR (12 ll.); RNHi; CtY; InU; PHi. 7156

FARMERS' Diary; or, Catskill Almanac for 1832. Catskill: N. G. Elliott. NbO (22 ll.) 7157

FARMERS' Diary, or Western Almanac for 1832.
Canandaigua: Bemis and Ward; Morse & Harvey,
printers.   N (10 ll.) 7158

The FARMER'S Diary or Western Almanac for 1832.
Canandaigua: Morse & Harvey. 12 ll. NR; NRMA.
7159
The FARMER'S Diary, or, Western Almanack for 1832.
Ithaca: Mack & Andrus. CtY. 7160

HUCHINGS' Improved Almanac for 1832. By David
Young. New-York: John C. Totten. 18 ll. NBLiHi;
NjR. 7161

-- Issue with 20 ll. NjMo; NjP. 7162

HUCHINGS' Revived Almanac for 1832. By David
Young. New-York: John C. Totten. 18 ll. DLC;
NBLiHi (17 ll.); PHi. 7163

HUCHINGS' Revived Almanac for 1832. By David
Young. Poughkeepsie: P. Potter & Co. 24 ll. MWA;
NP; NPV. 7164

HUTCHINGS' Almanac for 1832. By David Young. New-
York: Daniel D. Smith. 18 ll. Drake. 7165

HUTCHINGS Improved for 1832. New-York. Auction
catalog. 7166

HUTCHINGS' (Revived) Almanack for 1832. By David
Young. New York: C. Bartlett. 18 ll. CtY. 7167

HUTCHINGS' (Revived) Almanack for 1832. By David
Young. New-York: Wm. Beastall. 18 ll. NN; NjR (8
ll.) 7168

HUTCHINGS' (Revived) Almanack for 1832. By David
Young. New York: N. B. Holmes. 18 ll. MWA (17 ll.)
7169
HUTCHINGS' (Revived) Almanack for 1832. By David
Young. [New York:] John Langdon. 18 ll. N; MSaE.
7170

HUTCHINGS' (Revived) Almanack for 1832. By David Young. New-York: S. Marks & Son. 18 ll. NjR; NjHi. 7171

HUTCHINS' Improved Almanac for 1832. By David Young. New-York: C. Brown. 18 ll. MWA; N. 7172

HUTCHINS' Improved Almanac and Ephemeris for 1832. Albany: Tracy Doolittle. 18 ll. Drake. 7173

HUTCHINS' Improved Almanac and Ephemeris for 1832. New-York: Caleb Bartlett. 18 ll. NN; NHi; NBLiHi; MnU; MH; MB; NjR; Drake (17 ll.) 7174

The JUVENILE Almanac; or series of monthly emblems. New-York: Mahlon Day. 1832. 25 ll. N; MSaE. 7175

KNICKERBOCKER'S Almanac for 1832. By David Young. New York: Caleb Bartlett. 18 ll. DLC. 7176

KNICKERBOCKER'S Almanac for 1832. By David Young. New York: R. Bartlett and S. Raynor. 18 ll. DLC. 7177

KNICKERBOCKER'S Almanac for 1832. By David Young. New-York: Christian Brown. 18 ll. MWA; N; NHi; NBLiHi; OClWHi. 7178

LIVINGSTON'S Calendar, or Columbia Almanac for 1832. Hudson: C. Livingston. 12 ll. NHi. 7179

LOOMIS' Calendar or the New York and Vermont Almanack for 1832. Albany: Clark and Hosford; Troy: Clark & Hosford. 12 ll. MWA; N; InU. 7180

LOOMIS' Calendar or the New York and Vermont Almanack for 1832. Albany: G. J. Loomis. 12 ll. MWA; NHi; DLC; MnU; OMC. 7181

NEW Jersey and New York Almanac for 1832. By David Young. New-York: C. Brown. 18 ll. MWA; NHi; CtHi (impf) 7182

NEW-YORK Almanac for 1832. By David Young.
New-York: John C. Totten. 18 ll. MWA; NN; NBLiHi
(impf) 7183

The NEW-YORK Almanac, or the Merchants & Farmers
Calendar for 1832. New-York: William Minns & Co.
NHi (16 ll.) 7184

The NEW-YORK Western Pocket Almanac for 1832.
Auburn: H. Ivison & Co.; Oliphant's Press. 12 ll.
NN; Drake. 7185

N. YORK and N. Jersey Almanac for 1832. By David
Young. New-York: John C. Totten. 18 ll. MWA;
NjP. 7186

PAUL Pry's Almanac for 1832. By David Young. New-
York: C. Brown. 18 ll. Ct. 7187

PHINNEYS' Calendar or Western Almanac for 1832.
By Edwin E. Prentiss. Cooperstown: H. & E. Phinney.
18 ll. MWA; N; NN; NHi; NBuHi; MnU; CLU; DLC;
WHi; NIC; InU; NRMA; MBC (impf); NUtHi; CoD
(impf); NSyOHi; NHC; NCooHi. 7188

POOR Richard's Almanack for 1832. By Oliver Loud.
Rochester: Marshall & Dean. 12 ll. NR; NRHi; NRMA;
NRU; WHi. 7189

POOR Richard's Almanac for 1832. By David Young.
New-York: Christian Brown. 18 ll. NHi; MS (15 ll.)
7190
STEELE & Faxon's Buffalo Almanac for 1832. Buf-
falo: Steele & Faxon. 12 ll. MWA; NN; NBuHi;
NRMA. 7191

STEELE'S Albany Almanac for 1832. Albany: Oliver
Steele; Packard & Van Benthuysen, printers. 12 ll.
Drake. 7192

-- Issue with 18 ll. MWA; N; NHi; NBuG; Pennypacker. 7193

STODDARD'S Diary; or Columbia Almanac for 1832.
Hudson: A. Stoddard. 12 ll. N; NCooHi; PHi; NjR
(18 ll.) 7194

SWORDS'S Pocket Almanack, Churchman's Calendar
for 1832. New-York: T. and J. Swords; Edward J.
Swords, printer. 50 ll. MWA; N; NHi; NNS; NNG;
NRHi; NR; WHi; PHi; NjR; PPL; MHi; IU; BritMus.
7195

TEMPERANCE Almanac for 1832. Rochester: Hoyt,
Porter & Co. 18 ll. MWA (17 ll.); NR; NRHi; NRMA;
NIC; CtY. 7196

TEMPERANCE Almanac for 1832. Utica: Hastings &
Tracy; Rochester: Hoyt, Porter & Co. 18 ll. NHi;
NUtHi. 7197

TEMPERANCE Calendar for 1832. Sandy-Hill: Temperance Advocate Office. 12 ll. MWA; N; MH;
NbHi; CtY; MnU; ICHi; Drake. 7198

The UNITED States Temperance Almanac for 1832. By
Charles C. P. Crosby. New-York: Van Valkenburgh &
Crosby. 18 ll. MWA; N; MH; CLU. 7199

WEBSTER'S Calendar: or the Albany Almanack for
1832. By Edwin E. Prentiss. Albany: Webster &
Skinners. 18 ll. MWA; N; NHi; MnU; Drake. 7200

WEBSTER'S Calendar: or the Albany Almanack for
1832. By Edwin E. Prentiss. Albany: Webster &
Skinners. (Second Edition) 18 ll. MWA; N; NN (17
ll.); NNC; MiU-C. 7201

The WESTERN Almanac for 1832. Batavia: Sherman
Parker & Co. 12 ll. CSmH. 7202

The WESTERN Almanac for 1832. Geneva: J. Bogert.
12 ll. NN. 7203

The WESTERN Almanac for 1832. Rochester: Hoyt,
Porter & Co. 12 ll. MWA; NHi; NRMA; NRU; PHi;
MiD-B. 7204

WOOD'S Almanac for 1832. By Joshua Sharp. New York: Samuel Wood & Sons; R. & G. S. Wood, printers. 18 ll. MWA; NHi; NNA; OClWHi; PHi; PPL (16 ll.); Pennypacker. 7205

The AMERICAN Comic Almanack for 1833. New York: David Felt; Boston: Charles Ellms. 24 ll. MWA; NHi; NUtHi (23 ll.); NBuHi. 7206

The AMERICAN Miniature Almanac for 1833. New-York: William Minns & Co.; Boston: S. N. Dickinson, printer. (Allen's Edition) 16 ll. N; DLC; InU (14 ll.); MBC. 7207

The AMERICAN Temperance Almanac for 1833. New-York: Clinton Hall; L. D. Dewey. 18 ll. MWA. 7208

The AMERICAN Temperance Almanac for 1833. New-York: Clinton Hall; L. D. Dewey, and C. C. P. Crosby. 18 ll. MWA; N; NHi; NNA; NBLiHi; MnU; NjR; MH; OClWHi; NNC; NCooHi (15 ll.); NT; NjJ; DLC; RNHi; Drake. 7209

ANTI Masonic Almanac for 1833. By Edward Giddins. Utica: William Williams. 36 ll. MWA (two varieties); N; NN (impf); NHi; NjR (35 ll.); MBFM; PPFM; NSyOHi; MHi; MnU; WHi; NRU; NIC; NUt; Drake (30 ll.); NNFM (impf) 7210

An ASTRONOMICAL Diary for 1833. The New-York Farmer's Almanack for 1833. By Thomas Spofford. New-York: David Felt; Boston: Willard Felt & Co. 18 ll. NHi; CtY. 7211

CHAUTAUQUE County Almanac for 1833. Jamestown: A. Fletcher. NRU (11 ll.) 7212

The CHRISTIAN Almanac, For New-York, Connecticut, and New-Jersey for 1833. New-York: American Tract Society. 18 ll. MWA; N; NN; NHi; MSaE; NSchU; NR; NjR; DLC; NBLiHi; NjHi; MH; WHi; CLU; MiD-B; NbHi; CtNhHi; InU; IU; CtY; MnU; MBC; OMC; Drake. 7213

New York - 1833   707

The CHRISTIAN Almanac for the Western District for 1833. Rochester: American Tract Society; Levi A. Ward; Geneva: Rev. Warren Day. 18 ll. NR; NRMA; NRU; ICHi.   7214

The CHRISTIAN Almanac, for Western District for 1833. Utica: American Tract Society; Edward Vernon. 18 ll. MWA; NIC; CtY.   7215

The COLUMBIAN Calendar, or New-York and Vermont Almanac for 1833. Troy: Francis Adancourt; Wm. S. Parker; [etc] 12 ll. MWA; N; DLC; OClWHi; CLU; MnU; InU; VtHi.   7216

The COMMON Almanack for 1833. Buffalo: R. W. Haskins. 12 ll. NBuHi.   7217

The COMMON Almanac for 1833. Watertown: Knowlton & Rice. 12 ll. MWA (impf); N; NHi; DLC; NWattHi.   7218

DAY'S New-York Pocket Almanac for 1833. New-York: M. Day. 12 ll. MWA; NN; NHi; DLC; InU.   7219

The FARMER'S Almanac for 1833. New-York: R. Bartlett and S. Raynor. 18 ll. NHi; NNA; NBLiHi (17 ll.)   7220

The FARMER'S Almanac for 1833. Rochester: Hoyt, Porter & Co. 12 ll. NR; NRMA; NRU.   7221

FARMER'S Almanac for 1833. By David Young. New-York: C. Brown. 18 ll. ICU.   7222

FARMERS' Almanac for 1833. By David Young. New York: N. B. Holmes. 18 ll. NNC.   7223

FARMERS' Almanac for 1833. By David Young. N. York: Daniel D. Smith. 18 ll. NN; NjHi.   7224

FARMERS' Almanac for 1833. By David Young. Poughkeepsie: P. Potter & Co. 24 ll. MWA (20 ll.); NHi (22 ll.); DLC; NP.   7225

The **FARMER'S** & Mechanic's Almanac for 1833.
Montgomery: Thomas & Edwards. 12 ll. NHi; NBLiHi;
DLC. 7226

The **FARMER'S** Diary, or Western Almanac for 1833.
Canandaigua: Morse & Harvey. 12 ll. N (impf); NR;
CSmH. 7227

The **FARMER'S** Diary, or Western Almanack for 1833.
Ithaca: Mack & Andrus; Canandaigua: Morse & Harvey,
printers. 12 ll. MWA; NHi; NIC; NBuG; WHi; InU;
PScrHi. 7228

HUCHINGS' Improved Almanac for 1833. By David
Young. New-York: J. Dick. 18 ll. Pennypacker. 7229

HUCHINGS' Improved Almanac for 1833. By David
Young. New-York: John C. Totten. 18 ll. MWA;
NBLiHi (17 ll.); NjP; NjMo; NWhpHi. 7230

HUCHINGS' Revived Almanack for 1833. By David
Young. New-York: John C. Totten. 18 ll. NHi (two
varieties); NjR; Pennypacker. 7231

HUTCHINGS' Almanac for 1833. By David Young.
New-York: N. B. Holmes. 18 ll. NN (17 ll.) 7232

HUTCHINGS' Almanac for 1833. By David Young.
New York: S. Marks & Son. 18 ll. NBLiHi; DLC; Ct.
7233
HUTCHINGS' Almanac for 1833. By David Young.
New-York: D. D. Smith. 18 ll. MWA; NNSIHi. 7234

HUTCHINGS' Almanac for 1833. By David Young.
Poughkeepsie: Edward M'Whood. 18 ll. NP; CLU.
7235
HUTCHINGS' Almanac for 1833. By David Young.
Poughkeepsie: P. Potter & Co. 18 ll. N; NHi. 7236

HUTCHING'S Improved Almanac for 1833. By David
Young. New York: 177 Greenwich street. 18 ll. ICHi.
7237
HUTCHIN'S Improved Almanac for 1833. By David

Young. New-York: John C. Totten. 18 ll. NRMA.
7238

HUTCHINS' Improved Almanac for 1833. New-York:
R. Bartlett and S. Raynor. 18 ll. NN. 7239

HUTCHINS' Improved Almanac for 1833. New-York:
R. Bartlett and S. Raynor; Newburgh: Sneden & Hathaway. 18 ll. NN; NNA (16 ll.); MSaE. 7240

HUTCHIN'S Revived Almanac for 1833. By David
Young. New-York: John C. Totten. 18 ll. NN (impf);
Drake. 7241

KNICKERBOCKER'S Almanac for 1833. New York: R.
Bartlett and S. Raynor. 18 ll. PHi. 7242

MING'S Hutchins' Improved Almanac and Ephemeris for
1833. N. Y.: Alexander Ming. 18 ll. MWA; NHi; NjR.
7243

NEW-YORK Almanac for 1833. By David Young. New-
York: J. Dick. 18 ll. ICU. 7244

NEW-YORK Almanac for 1833. By David Young. New-
York: Daniel D. Smith. 18 ll. MH. 7245

The NEW-YORK Farmer's Almanack for 1833. By
Thomas Spofford. New-York: David Felt; Boston:
Willard Felt & Co. 18 ll. MWA; N; NN (16 ll.); NB;
DLC; MiD-B; ViHi; NjR; PHi; NR; OO; InU; NRMA;
CtLHi. 7246

PHINNEYS' Calendar, or Western Almanac for 1833.
By George R. Perkins. Cooperstown: H. & E. Phinney. 18 ll. MWA; N; NN; NHi; NUtHi; NRMA; NRU;
NR; DLC; PHi; NSyOHi; WHi; NHC; NCooHi; InU;
CLU; NBuHi; NIC; MnU; NBuG; NUt; Drake. 7247

POOR Richard's Almanack for 1833. Rochester: Marshall & Dean. 12 ll. MWA; N; NRHi; NR; NRU.7248

POOR Richard's Almanack for 1833. Rochester: C.
& M. Morse. NBuHi (7 ll.) 7249

New York - 1833

POOR Richard's Almanack for 1833. Rochester: Parsons & Phelps. 12 ll. NRMA; NRU. 7250

POOR Richard's Almanack for 1833. Utica: Gardiner Tracy. 12 ll. MWA; N; NSyOHi; NCooHi (11 ll.); WHi. 7251

POOR Richard's Almanack for 1833. Utica: Geo. Tracy. 12 ll. NR; NRHi. 7252

PRESTON'S Wallet Reckoner and Almanac [for 1833]. By Lyman Preston. Stereotyped by Conner and Cooke. New-York: R. & G. S. Wood, printers. 18 ll. MWA; NRMA. 7253

STEELE & Faxon's Buffalo Almanac for 1833. Buffalo: Steele & Faxon. 12 ll. NBuHi (ntp); OClWHi. 7254

STEELE'S Albany Almanac for 1833. Albany: O. Steele; Packard and Van Benthuysen, printers. 18 ll. N; NHi. 7255

STEELE'S Buffalo Almanac for 1833. Buffalo: O. G. Steele; Charles Faxon, printer. 12 ll. NHi. 7256

STODDARD'S Diary; or the Columbia Almanack for 1833. By Edwin E. Prentiss. Hudson: Ashbel Stoddard. 18 ll. MWA; PHi. 7257

SWORDS'S Pocket Almanack, Churchman's Calendar for 1833. New-York: Swords, Stanford, and Co. 56 ll. MWA; N; NHi; PHi; PU; NNS; NjR; NNG; MBAt; PPL; BritMus. 7258

The TEMPERANCE Almanac for 1833. Albany: Oliver Steele. 18 ll. MWA; MB; NbO (12 ll.) 7259

The TEMPERANCE Almanac for 1833. Rochester: Hoyt, Porter & Co. 16 ll. NRMA; NRU. 7260

The TEMPERANCE Almanac for 1833. Utica: Gardiner Tracy. 16 ll. NUt. 7261

WEBSTER'S Calendar: or the Albany Almanack for 1833. By Edwin E. Prentiss. Albany: Webster & Skinners. 18 ll. MWA; N; NN (16 ll.); NHi; DLC; InU; MiU-C; Drake (two varieties)   7262

WEBSTER'S Calendar: or the Albany Almanack for 1833. By Edwin E. Prentiss. Albany: Webster & Skinners. (Second Edition) 18 ll. N; MnU; MB. 7263

WESTERN Almanac for 1833. Rochester. MiD-B.
   7264

WILLIAMS' Calendar, or the Utica Almanac for 1833. Utica: William Williams. 16 ll. MWA; NN; NHi; InU; NUt; NUtHi; NSyOHi; WHi; NHC; NIC; MiD-B; Pennypacker.   7265

WOOD'S Almanac for 1833. By Joshua Sharp. New York: Samuel Wood & Sons; R. & G. S. Wood, printers. 18 ll. MWA; N; NHi; NNA; InU; PPL (16 ll.); DLC.   7266

The AMERICAN Comic Almanac for 1834. New-York: David Felt; Boston: Charles Ellms. 24 ll. MWA. 7267

The AMERICAN Miniature Almanac for 1834. New York: William Minns; Boston: Allen and Company; S. N. Dickinson, printer. 16 ll. MSaE; WHi; Pennypacker.   7268

The BUFFALO Almanac for 1834. Buffalo: Walter Rose; C. Faxon, printer. 12 ll. DLC (impf)   7269

The CHRISTIAN Almanac For New-York, Connecticut, and New-Jersey for 1834. [New York:] American Tract Society. 24 ll. MWA; N; NN; NHi; NSchU; MiD-B; CtY; MH; InU; CLU; IU; OClWHi; NjR (23 ll.); Drake.   7270

The CHRISTIAN Almanac for the Western District for 1834. Rochester: American Tract Society. 24 ll. N (titlepage impf)   7271

The CHURCHMAN'S Almanac for 1834. New-York:

New York - 1834

Protestant Episcopal Press. 18 ll. MWA; NHi; MBC;
CtW; OClWHi; NNG; MHi; MSaE.   7272

The CHURCHMAN'S Almanac for 1834. New-York:
Protestant Episcopal Press. (Fourth Edition) 18 ll.
MWA; N; NNA; PPL; RPB.   7273

COMMON Almanack for 1834. By Tobias Ostrander.
Watertown: Knowlton & Rice. 12 ll. N; NHi. 7274

DAY'S City and Country Almanac for 1834. By David
Young. New-York: Mahlon Day. 18 ll. MWA; NjMoW;
PPL; Ct.   7275

DAY'S New-York Pocket Almanac for 1834. New-York:
M. Day. 12 ll. MWA; NHi; DLC; MnU.   7276

ELTON'S Comic All-my-nack! for 1834. New-York:
R. H. Elton; Marsh & Harrison, printers. 18 ll. MWA;
NN; DLC; NT; ICU; MB; MnU.   7277

ELTON'S Comic All-my-nack! for 1834. New-York:
R. H. Elton; Marsh & Harrison, printers (Second Edition) 18 ll. MWA; N; NN; NHi; NjR. 7278

ELTON'S Comic All-my-nack! for 1834. New-York:
R. H. Elton; Marsh & Harrison, printers. (Third Edition) 18 ll. NRU.   7279

ELTON'S Comic All-my-nack! for 1834. New-York:
R. H. Elton; Marsh & Harrison, printers. (Fourth Edition) 18 ll. MWA.   7280

ELTON'S Comic All-my-nack! for 1834. New-York:
R. H. Elton; Marsh & Harrison, printers. (Fifth Edition) 18 ll. MWA.   7281

FARMER'S Almanac for 1834. Rochester: Hoyt, Porter
& Co. 12 ll. Barton.   7282

The FARMER'S Almanac for 1834. By G. R. Perkins.
Homer: Protestant Sentinel. 12 ll. NCooHi (impf);
NSyOHi.   7283

New York - 1834   713

The FARMER'S Almanac for 1834. By D. Spafford.
Kingston: C. W. & R. A. Chipp; Montgomery: Calvin
F. S. Thomas; C. F. S. Thomas, printer. 18 ll. MWA;
Hoes.   7284

The FARMER'S Almanac for 1834. By D. Spafford.
Montgomery: Calvin F. S. Thomas. 18 ll. DLC;
NCooHi (17 ll.)   7285

The FARMER'S Almanac for 1834. By D. Spafford.
Montgomery: Calvin F. S. Thomas; Sanford & Wheeler;
C. F. S. Thomas, printer. 18 ll. NHi.   7286

The FARMER'S Almanac for 1834. By D. Spafford.
Montgomery: Calvin F. S. Thomas; Goshen: Merriam
& Smith; C. F. S. Thomas, printer. 18 ll. NHi; CLU;
NjR.   7287

The FARMER'S Almanack for 1834. By Thomas Spofford. New-York: David Felt; Boston: Willard Felt &
Co. 18 ll. MWA; N; NN; NHi; NB; NBLiHi; DLC;
PHi; MBAt; NjR; CLU; NbO (16 ll.); MnU; CtY;
CtLHi; InU; Drake.   7288

The FARMER'S Almanac for 1834. By David Young.
New York: R. Bartlett and S. Raynor. NHi (missing
from shelves)   7289

FARMERS Almanac for 1834. By David Young. New-
York: D. D. Smith. 18 ll. NNSIHi.   7290

FARMER'S Almanac for 1834. By David Young. New
York: D. D. Smith. 18 ll. NHi (10 ll.); NN.   7291

The FARMER'S Almanac for 1834. By David Young.
Poughkeepsie: P. Potter & Co. 18 ll. MWA (17 ll.);
NP.   7292

The FARMER'S Diary, or Western Almanac for 1834.
By Tobias Ostrander. Canandaigua: Morse & Harvey.
12 ll. NRMA.   7293

The FARMER'S Diary, or Western Almanack for 1834.

By Tobias Ostrander. Ithaca: Mack & Andrus. 12 ll. MWA; NHi; DLC (impf); NBuG; NIC; IHi; PScHi.
7294

The FARMER'S Year Book of Useful and Entertaining Knowledge for 1834. New-York: David Felt. 24 ll. MWA. 7295

The GRAHAM Almanac for 1834. New-York: William Applegate. 18 ll. MWA (17 ll.); NHi; PPL; NjR (ntp) 7296

The GRAHAM Almanac for 1834. New-York: William Applegate. To be continued every year. 18 ll. MWA; N; NBLiHi (17 ll.) 7297

HOOD'S Komick Almanac for 1834. By Timothy Hood. Troy: J. Hosford. 16 ll. MWA (12 ll.); MB. 7298

HUTCHINGS' Almanac for 1834. By David Young. New-York: James A. Burtus. 18 ll. MWA; NBLiHi.
7299

HUTCHINGS' Almanac for 1834. By David Young. New-York: N. B. Holmes. 18 ll. WHi. 7300

HUTCHINGS' Almanac for 1834. By David Young. New-York: D. D. Smith. 18 ll. NjR; PHi. 7301

HUTCHINGS' Almanac for 1834. By David Young. Poughkeepsie: P. Potter & Co. 18 ll. MWA; NP. 7302

HUTCHIN'S Improved Almanac for 1834. By David Young. New-York: Thomas Cotrel; Benjamin Olds, printer. 18 ll. NN. 7303

HUTCHIN'S Improved Almanac for 1834. By David Young. New-York: J. Dick. 18 ll. NjR. 7304

HUTCHIN'S Improved Almanac for 1834. By David Young. New-York: D. D. Smith; Benjamin Olds, printer. 18 ll. NHi. 7305

HUTCHIN'S Improved Almanac and Ephemeris for 1834. By David Young. New-York: R. Bartlett and S. Raynor.

18 ll. MWA; NN; NHi; NRMA; MSaE; OO; NjR. 7306

KNICKERBOCKER'S Almanac for 1834. By David
Young. New York: R. Bartlett and S. Raynor. 18 ll.
MWA (impf); PPL (14 ll.); NjR; Drake. 7307

LOOMIS' Calendar, or the New-York and Vermont Almanack for 1834. Albany: W. C. Little, No. 67,
State Street. 12 ll. NCooHi; OMC. 7308

LOOMIS' Calendar, or the New-York and Vermont Almanack for 1834. Albany: W. C. Little, No. 67,
State street. 12 ll. N; Drake (8 ll.) 7309

LOOMIS' Calendar, or the New-York and Vermont Almanack for 1834. Albany: G. J. Loomis. 12 ll. MH
(7 ll.) 7310

LOOMIS' Calendar, or the New York and Vermont Almanack for 1834. Troy: W. S. Parker & Son. 12 ll.
MWA; N; NAlI; Drake. 7311

The METHODIST Almanac for 1834. By David Young.
New-York: B. Waugh and T. Mason, for the Methodist
Episcopal Church; J. Collord, printer. 18 ll. MWA;
NHi; CtHi; CtW; NIC; RPB; ICHi; MH; WHi; Ct;
ICU; MSaE; OClWHi; InU; BritMus; NjR; Drake. 7312

-- Issue with 24 ll. MiGr. 7313

The NEW-YORK State Pocket Almanac for 1834. Auburn: H. Ivison & Co.; Oliphant & Skinner, printers.
12 ll. NN. 7314

ONEIDA Almanac for 1834. By Tobias Ostrander.
Utica: Gardiner Tracy. 12 ll. MWA (impf) 7315

PACKARD & Van Benthuysen's Mercantile Almanack for
1834. Albany: Packard & Van Benthuysen. Broadside.
NHi. 7316

PARKER'S Almanac for 1834. By Tobias Ostrander.
Troy: W. S. Parker and Son. 18 ll. MWA (impf); NHi;

OClWHi; PHi (impf)   7317

The PEOPLE'S Almanac for 1834. New-York: David Felt. 24 ll. MWA; NHi; NbHi.   7318

PHINNEYS' Calendar, or Western Almanac for 1834. By George R. Perkins. Cooperstown: H. & E. Phinney. 18 ll. MWA; N; NN; NHi; NSyOHi; PHi; FSpHi; MBC (impf); NCooHi; NBuHi; NUtHi; DLC; MH; MnU; NBuG; WHi.   7319

POOR Richard's Almanack for 1834. By Tobias Ostrander. Rochester: Marshall & Dean. 12 ll. MWA; N; NR; NRHi; NRMA; NRU (impf); NBuHi.   7320

POOR Richard's Almanack for 1834. By Tobias Ostrander. Rochester: C. & M. Morse. 12 ll. MWA; NRMA; NRU.   7321

POOR Richard's Almanack for 1834. By Tobias Ostrander. Rochester: L. W. Sibley & Co. 12 ll. NRU.   7322

POOR Richard's Almanack for 1834. By Tobias Ostrander. Utica: Gardiner Tracy. 12 ll. MWA; NRU.   7323

The PROTESTANT Sabbath Almanack for 1834. Homer: John Maxson. 16 ll. MWA; NHi; NIC; InU; WHi; NRU; RPB; Drake.   7324

RICHARD Patten's Edition of the Nautical Almanac and Astronomical Ephemeris for 1834. Published.. London. New-York: Re-Published by Richard Patten. 58 ll. MWA.   7325

STEELE'S Albany Almanac for 1834. By Tobias Ostrander. Albany: Packard and Van Benthuysen. 18 ll. N; NR (19 ll.); NT; OMC.   7326

STEELE'S Buffalo Almanac for 1834. Buffalo: Oliver G. Steele; C. Faxon, printer. 12 ll. NBuHi (10 ll., impf); NRMA; WHi; MiD-B.   7327

STODDARD'S Diary; or Columbia Almanack for 1834.

By Tobias Ostrander. Hudson: A. Stoddard. 18 ll.
MWA; NHi; CtNhHi; PHi. 7328

SWORDS'S Pocket Almanack, Churchman's Calendar for
1834. New-York: Swords, Stanford, and Co. 48 ll.
MWA; NHi; NNS; NNG; PU; NjR; PHi; BritMus. 7329

The TEMPERANCE Almanac for 1834. New-York: L.
D. Dewey; N. Y. State Temperance Society; Albany:
Hoffman & White, printers. 24 ll. MWA; N; NN; NHi;
NjJ; KyU; RNHi; NbO; ICN; OClWHi; NR; NRHi;
NSchU; NRU; CLU; Ct; NRMA; MBC; MH; MHi;
CtHi; NBLiHi (impf); CtY; PPL; MSaE; CtW; RWe;
NNA; NjR; NNUT; MB; MBAt; RPB; NSyOHi; OMC;
Nh; CtLHi; ICHi; OC; InU; WHi; MiD-B; BritMus;
Drake. 7330

-- Line of prices at bottom of titlepage. 24 ll. MWA;
N; NjR; Drake. 7331

The TEMPERANCE Almanac for 1834. Philadelphia:
I. S. Lloyd; Albany: N. Y. State Temperance Society;
Hoffman & White, printers, Albany. 24 ll. PHi. 7332

The UNITED States Comic Almanac for 1834. New
York: William Minns; Boston: Allen & Company. 18 ll.
MWA. 7333

WEBSTER'S Calendar: or, the Albany Almanack for
1834. By Edwin E. Prentiss. Albany: Webster &
Skinners. 18 ll. MWA (16 ll.); N; NN (impf); DLC;
MiU-C; WHi; Drake. 7334

The WESTERN Farmers' Almanac for 1834. By Lyman Abbott, Jr. Auburn: Oliphant & Skinner, printers.
12 ll. MWA; OClWHi. 7335

The WESTERN Farmers' Almanac for 1834. By Lyman Abbott, Jr. Auburn: T. M. Skinner; Oliphant &
Skinner, printers. 12 ll. OClWHi; WHi (impf) 7336

The WESTERN or Independent Line Almanac for 1834.
By Tobias Ostrander. Bath: O. W. L. Warren. 12 ll.

NR; NRMA.   7337

WILLIAMS' Calendar, or The Utica Almanac for 1834.
Utica: William Williams. 12 ll. MWA (9 ll.); N;
NIC; NUtHi (6 ll.); WHi; InU (10 ll.); MiD-B; Drake.
                                                         7338
WOOD'S Almanac for 1834. By Joshua Sharp. New
York: Samuel Wood & Sons; R. & G. S. Wood, printers.
18 ll. MWA; NHi; NNA; PPL; WHi.   7339

The AMERICAN Comic Almanac for 1835. New-York:
D. Felt & Co.; Boston: Charles Ellms. 24 ll. MWA
(impf); MHi.   7340

The AMERICAN Family Almanac, or the Merchants &
Farmers Calendar for 1835. New-York: William
Minns; S. N. Dickinson, printer. 18 ll. MWA; CLU
(impf); MBC.   7341

The AMERICAN Miniature Almanac for 1835. New-
York: William Minns; Boston: Allen and Company; S.
N. Dickinson, printer. (Allen's Edition) 14 ll. NHi;
MHi; MSaE.   7342

The AMERICAN Temperance Almanac for 1835. Al-
bany: New-York State Temperance Society; Packard &
Van Benthuysen, printers; Stereotyped by G. J. Loomis.
18 ll. MWA; N; NN; NHi; CtY; NjJ; GU; NBLiHi;
KyHi; CLU; OMC; ICHi; CtHi; MiD-B; ViU; WHi;
NRMA; MBC; MHi; MB; MH; NjR; NNUT; OClWHi;
NIC; NCooHi; NR; NbO (17 ll.); NRU; NT.   7343

APPLEGATE'S Whig Almanac for 1835. New-York:
W. Applegate. 18 ll. MWA; NBLiHi (17 ll.); CtY
(impf); ICHi; IU.   7344

The CHRISTIAN Almanac, For New-York, Connecticut,
and New-Jersey for 1835. [New York:] American
Tract Society. 24 ll. MWA; N; NN; NHi; NSchU; IU;
CtY; NjMo; NjHi; NjR; NSyOHi; NBLiHi; NjP; MH;
InU; DLC; CtNhHi; Ct (impf); Drake.   7345

The CHRISTIAN Almanac, for Western District for

1835. Utica: American Tract Society; Edward Vernon; Geneva: Rev. Warren Day. 24 ll. N.   7346

The CHURCHMAN'S Almanac for 1835. New-York: Protestant Episcopal Press. 18 ll. MWA; NNA; NBLiHi; NNG; MBC; NRHi; NcD; OC; MHi; MiD-B.   7347

The CHURCHMAN'S Almanac for 1835. New-York: Protestant Episcopal Press. (Second Edition) 18 ll. N; NSyOHi; PPL.   7348

The CHURCHMAN'S Almanac for 1835. New-York: Protestant Episcopal Press. (Third Edition) Private collection (15 ll.)   7349

The CHURCHMAN'S Almanac for 1835. New-York: Protestant Episcopal Press. (Fourth Edition) 18 ll. NR.   7350

The COMIC Token for 1835. New-York: D. Felt & Co.; Charles Ellms. 24 ll. MWA; NHi; MDedHi. 7351

COMMON Almanack for 1835. By George R. Perkins. Watertown: Knowlton & Rice. 18 ll. N; DLC; NWattHi; WHi.   7352

DAY'S City and Country Almanac for 1835. By David Young. New-York: Mahlon Day. 18 ll. MWA.   7353

DAY'S Health Almanac for 1835. By David Young. New-York: Mahlon Day. 18 ll. NBLiHi.   7354

DAY'S New-York Pocket Almanac for 1835. New-York: M. Day. 12 ll. N; NN; NHi; PHi; MHi; CtHi.   7355

ELTON'S Comic All-my-nack for 1835. New-York: R. H. Elton. 18 ll. MWA (two varieties); N; NN; NHi; DLC; OClWHi (17 ll.); NjR; OMC.   7356

The FARMER'S Almanac for 1835. New-York: R. Bartlett and S. Raynor. 18 ll. NHi.   7357

The FARMER'S Almanac, for the Middle States for

1835. By Thomas Spofford. New-York: Charles Small; Boston: Samuel N. Dickinson, printer. 18 ll. MWA (impf); N; NN; NBLiHi; InU; NWhpHi; PHi; Pennypacker; Drake. 7358

The FARMER'S Diary, or Western Almanack for 1835. By William W. M'Louth. Canandaigua: Morse & Harvey. 12 ll. N; MB. 7359

The FARMER'S Diary, or Western Almanack for 1835. By William W. M'Louth. Ithaca: Mack & Andrus. 12 ll. N; NHi; NSyOHi (11 ll.); PScrHi; NBuG; IHi. 7360

HOOD'S Komick Almanac for 1835. New-York: Printed for the Purchaser. 18 ll. NT. 7361

HUTCHIN'S Improved Almanac for 1835. By David Young. New York: Collins & Henney. 18 ll. NRMA. 7362

HUTCHIN'S Improved Almanac for 1835. By David Young. New York: Thomas Cotrel. 18 ll. MWA. 7363

HUTCHINS' Improved Almanac and Ephemeris for 1835. New-York: R. Bartlett and S. Raynor, No. 76 Bowery. 18 ll. NHi; DLC; CtHi; NjR (ntp) 7364

HUTCHINS' Improved Almanac and Ephemeris for 1835. New-York: R. Bartlett & S. Raynor; James A. Burtus. 18 ll. NRMA; DLC. 7365

HUTCHINS' Improved Almanac and Ephemeris for 1835. By David Young. [New York:] R. Bartlett and S. Raynor, No. 76 Bowey [sic]. 18 ll. NBLiHi. 7366

JACKSON Almanack for 1835. New-York: Elton; Marsh & Harrison, printers. 18 ll. MWA (impf); DLC; ICN; OMC (17 ll.); Drake. 7367

KNICKERBOCKER'S Almanac for 1835. By David Young. New York: R. Bartlett and S. Raynor. 18 ll. MWA; NRU; CtY; InU. 7368

LOOMIS' Calendar, or the New York and Vermont Al-

manack for 1835. Albany: G. J. Loomis. 12 ll. N;
VtHi; Pennypacker. 7369

LOOMIS' Calendar, or the New York and Vermont Almanack for 1835. Troy: Z. Clark. 12 ll. MWA.
7370
LOOMIS' Calendar, or the New York and Vermont Almanack for 1835. Troy: A. A. Hill. 12 ll. MWA. 7371

The METHODIST Almanac for 1835. By David Young.
New-York: B. Waugh and T. Mason, for the Methodist
Episcopal Church; J. Collord, printer. 18 ll. MWA
(17 ll.); NHi; NBLiHi (16 ll.); NjR; OClWHi; Ct;
MiD-B; CtW; NCooHi. 7372

MINIATURE Almanac for 1835. New-York: David Felt
& Co.; S. N. Dickinson, printer. 18 ll. MWA. 7373

ONEIDA Almanac for 1835. Utica: Gardiner Tracy.
12 ll. NUt; NUtHi. 7374

ONEIDA Almanac for 1835. Utica: William Williams.
18 ll. NN; NUtHi. 7375

PARKER'S Almanac for 1835. By Tobias Ostrander.
Troy: W. S. Parker and Son. 18 ll. MWA; N; NHi;
NCooHi; MnU. 7376

The PENNY Almanac, and Repository of Useful Knowledge for 1835. New York: Thomas J. Crowen; Dean,
printer. 8 ll. N; DLC. 7377

PEOPLE'S Almanac for 1835. New-York: D. Felt &
Co.; Boston: Charles Ellms. 24 ll. N; NN (23 ll.);
MBAt; Pennypacker. 7378

PHINNEYS' Calendar, or Western Almanac for 1835.
By George R. Perkins. Cooperstown: H. & E. Phinney. 18 ll. MWA; N; NN; NHi; NR; NRMA; NUt;
NUtHi; MnU; NIC; InU; MBC; WHi; NBuHi; FSpHi;
NSyOHi; NCooHi. 7379

PHINNEY'S Calendar, or Western Almanac for 1835.

By George R. Perkins. Oxford: Ransom Rathbone. 18 ll. [Severance]   7380

PHINNEY'S Calendar, or Western Almanac for 1835. By George R. Perkins. Oxford: Williams & Hunt. 18 ll. [Severance]   7381

RENSSELAER County Almanac for 1835. Troy: N. Tuttle. 18 ll. MWA (17 ll.)   7382

STATIONERS' Hall Almanack for 1835. By Thomas Spofford. New York: David Felt & Co. 18 ll. MWA; N; NN; NHi; NB; DLC; NSyOHi; NjR; CtLHi; NBLiHi; Drake.   7383

STEELE'S Albany Almanac for 1835. By Tobias Ostrander. Albany: Packard and Van Benthuysen. 18 ll. MWA (impf); N; NHi; NBuG; NR; OClWHi; NjR (17 ll.); Drake.   7384

STEELE'S Buffalo Almanac for 1835. Buffalo: Oliver G. Steele; Charles Faxon, printer. 12 ll. MWA (11 ll.); NHi; NBuHi (impf); MiD-B.   7385

STODDARD'S Diary; or, the Columbia Almanack for 1835. By Edwin E. Prentiss. Hudson: A. Stoddard. 18 ll. N; NHi.   7386

SWORDS'S Pocket Almanack, Churchman's Calendar for 1835. New-York: Swords, Stanford, and Co. 40 ll. MWA; N; NHi; NNS; NNG; NjR; PHi; PPL; BritMus.   7387

WEBSTER'S Calendar: or the Albany Almanack for 1835. By Edwin E. Prentiss. Albany: E. W. & C. Skinner. 18 ll. MWA; N; NHi; DLC; CLU; NSchU; NN; MiU-C; MnU; WHi; Drake.   7388

WEBSTER'S Calendar: or the Albany Almanack for 1835. By Edwin E. Prentiss. Albany: E. W. & C. Skinner. (Second Edition) 18 ll. N; MiU-C; Drake.   7389

WESTERN Almanac for 1835. Rochester: William Alling & Co. 12 ll. MWA; N; NR; NRHi; NRMA; NRU;

NCanHi; NHC; NBuHi (11 ll.) 7390

The WESTERN Farmers' Almanac for 1835. Auburn: T. M. Skinner; Oliphant & Skinner, printers. 12 ll. MWA; NAuHi; NSyOHi; OClWHi; Drake. 7391

The WESTERN or Independent Line Almanac for 1835. By William W. M'Louth. Bath: O. W. L. Warren. 12 ll. NRMA. 7392

The WESTERN, Poor Richard and Farmer's Almanac for 1835. By John M'Lean. Geneseo: E. Clark. 12 ll. MWA; NRMA; NRU; Vail. 7393

The WHIG Almanac for 1835. New York: J. & G. Strong. 12 ll. MWA. 7394

WILLIAMS' Calendar for 1835. By Geo. R. Perkins. Auburn: H. Ivison & Co. 18 ll. OClWHi. 7395

WILLIAMS' Calendar, or the Utica Almanac for 1835. By George R. Perkins. Cazenovia: S. H. Henry & Co. 18 ll. MWA; NN; NIC; CLU. 7396

WILLIAMS' Calendar, or the Utica Almanac for 1835. By George R. Perkins. Utica: William Williams. 18 ll. MWA; N; NN; NUtHi; MiD-B; CtY; WHi; Drake. 7397

WOOD'S Almanac for 1835. By Joshua Sharp. New York: Samuel Wood & Sons; R. & G. S. Wood, printers. 18 ll. MWA; NN; NHi; DLC; InU; RNHi; Drake. 7398

The AMERICAN Anti-Slavery Almanac for 1836. New York: Executive Committee of the Am. Anti-Slavery Society. 24 ll. MWA; NN; OClWHi; Ct. 7399

AMERICAN Comic Almanac for 1836. New-York: D. Felt & Co.; Boston: Charles Ellms. 24 ll. MWA (22 ll., impf); MB. 7400

The CHRISTIAN Almanac For New-York, Connecticut, and New-Jersey for 1836. [New York:] American

Tract Society. 24 ll. MWA; NN; NHi; NjR; RPB;
IU; Ct; NjJ; CtY; OMC; InU; NBuG; MH; PPL;
VtHi; Drake. 7401

The CHRISTIAN Almanac for Western District for 1836.
[New York:] American Tract Society; Utica: Edward
Vernon; Geneva: Rev. Warren Day; Auburn: Henry
Ivison; Rochester: Levi A. Ward; Buffalo: J. C. Meek.
24 ll. MWA; Mi; NjR; Drake. 7402

The CHRISTIAN Register for 1836. By John Clark.
Union Mills: Printed by the Author. 12 ll. MWA; N;
NHi; CLU. 7403

The CHURCHMAN'S Almanac for 1836. New-York:
Protestant Episcopal Press. 18 ll. NR; NRHi; CtLHi.
7404

The CHURCHMAN'S Almanac for 1836. New-York:
Protestant Episcopal Press. (Second Edition) 18 ll.
NNG; Ct; NjR. 7405

The CHURCHMAN'S Almanac for 1836. New-York:
Protestant Episcopal Press. (Third Edition) 18 ll.
MWA; NSyOHi; PPL. 7406

The CHURCHMAN'S Almanac for 1836. New-York:
Protestant Episcopal Press. (Fourth Edition) 18 ll.
N; NHi; NjR; NcD; MBC; WHi. 7407

The CHURCHMAN'S Almanac for 1836. New-York:
Protestant Episcopal Press. (Fifth Edition) 18 ll.
NNA. 7408

CLARK'S Calendar, or the New-York Almanac for 1836.
Union Mills: R. P. Clark; John Clark & Co., printer.
12 ll. NN. 7409

-- Paged [pp 19 plus 5 ll.] MWA. 7410

COMMON Almanac for 1836. Watertown: Knowlton &
Rice. 12 ll. MWA (impf); NHi; DLC; WHi. 7411

CROCKETT'S Yaller Flower Almanac for 1836. Snagsville, Salt-River: Published by Boon Crockett, and Squire Downing, Skunk's Misery, Down East. N. Y.: Elton. 18 ll. MWA; DLC; MB; CtY; ICU. 7412

DAY'S City and Country Almanac for 1836. By David Young. New-York: Mahlon Day. 18 ll. MWA; N; NN; NHi; DLC. 7413

DAY'S New-York Pocket Almanac for 1836. New-York: M. Day. 12 ll. MWA; NN; NHi; CtHi; WHi. 7414

ELTON'S Almanac for 1836. New-York: R. H. Elton. [Phillips] 7415

ELTON'S Comic for 1836. Columbus, Ohio: Norman Tuttle; New York: Robert H. Elton. 18 ll. N. 7416

ELTON'S Comic All-my-nack for 1836. New-York: Sold at 76 Bowery. 18 ll. CtY. 7417

ELTON'S Comic All My Nack for 1836. New-York: Elton; David Felt & Co. 18 ll. MWA; NN (ntp); DLC; MB; InU; MDedHi; OMC; NBLiHi (ntp) 7418

ELTON'S Comic All My Nack for 1836. New-York: Elton; Owen Phelan. 18 ll. NHi. 7419

ELTON'S Comic All My Nack for 1836. New-York: Elton; C. Shepard; Marsh & Harrison, printers. 18 ll. MWiW. 7420

ELTON'S Comic All My Nack for 1836. New-York: Elton; Philadelphia: Turner & Fisher. 18 ll. MWA; N; NB. 7421

FARMER'S Almanac for 1836. By David Young. N. Y.: R. Bartlett & S. Raynor; Marsh & Harrison, printers. 18 ll. MWA; N; NP; CtW (13 ll.); WHi. 7422

The FARMER'S Diary, or Western Almanac for 1836. Canandaigua: Morse & Harvey. 12 ll. MWA; NN (11 ll.); NCanHi; NR; NRU. 7423

The **FARMER'S** Diary, or Western Almanack for 1836. Ithaca: Mack, Andrus & Woodruff. 12 ll. MWA; DLC; NBuG. 7424

HOSFORD'S Almanac for 1836. Troy: J. Hosford. 18 ll. MWA; N; NT. 7425

HUTCHINGS' Improved Almanac for 1836. By David Young. New-York: R. Bartlett & S. Raynor; Marsh & Harrison, printers. 18 ll. MB. 7426

HUTCHINS' [Improved] Almanac for 1836. By David Young. New-York: R. H. Elton; Marsh & Harrison, printers. 18 ll. MWA; NN. 7427

HUTCHINS' Improved Almanac for 1836. By David Young. New-York: R. H. Elton. 18 ll. NBLiHi. 7428

HUTCHIN'S Improved Almanac for 1836. By David Young. New York: Octavius Longworth. 18 ll. N; NN; NHi; NWhpHi (impf) 7429

HUTCHINS' Improved Almanac for 1836. By David Young. New-York: Robinson, Pratt & Co. 18 ll. MWA; NjR; CtB (16 ll.) 7430

HUTCHIN'S Improved Almanac for 1836. By David Young. New-York: N. & J. White. 18 ll. MWA; NHi; NSyOHi (impf) 7431

HUTCHINS' Improved Almanac and Ephemeris for 1836. By David Young. New-York: R. Bartlett & S. Raynor; Marsh & Harrison, printers. 18 ll. NHi; NBuG. 7432

JACKSON Almanac for 1836. New York: Elton. 18 ll. MWA; NHi; NBLiHi (17 ll.); OCHP. 7433

KNICKERBOCKER Almanac for 1836. By David Young. New York: R. Bartlett & S. Raynor. 18 ll. NN (16 ll.); NWhpHi; Vail. 7434

The **LUTHERAN** Almanac for 1836. Troy: Lutheran Revival Society; N. Tuttle. 18 ll. N. 7435

The METHODIST Almanac for 1836. By David Young.
New-York: B. Waugh and T. Mason, for the Methodist
Episcopal Church; J. Collord, printer. 18 ll. MWA;
NHi; NjR; ICU; NUtHi; InU; NcD; CtW; CLU; ICHi;
WHi. 7436

-- Issue for Boston. 18 ll. NjR. 7437

The NEW York Farmer's Almanac for 1836. By
Thomas Spofford. New-York: D. Felt & Co. 18 ll.
MWA; NB (titlepage impf); OClWHi; OMC; CtLHi;
Drake. 7437

The NEW York Farmer's Almanac for 1836. By
Thomas Spofford. New-York: David Felt & Co. 18 ll.
Drake (17 ll.) 7438

The NEW York Farmer's Almanac for 1836. By
Thomas Spofford. New York: David Felt & Co. ...
Sold also by... 18 ll. N; Drake. 7439

The NEW York Farmer's Almanac for 1836. By
Thomas Spofford. New York: Charles Small. 18 ll.
MWA; NBuG; PHi. 7440

The NEW York Farmer's Almanac for 1836. By
Thomas Spofford. New York: N. & J. White. 18 ll.
MWA (impf); NRU; CLU. 7441

The NEW-YORK State Pocket Almanac for 1836. Auburn: H. Ivison & Co.; Oliphant & Skinner, printers.
12 ll. NHi. 7442

ONEIDA Almanac for 1836. Utica: Gardiner Tracy.
12 ll. MWA; N; NSyOHi. 7443

PARKERS' Almanac for 1836. Troy: W. S. Parker &
Son. 18 ll. PHi (impf) 7444

The PEOPLE'S Almanac of Useful and Entertaining
Knowledge for 1836. New York: D. Felt & Co.; Boston: Charles Ellms. 24 ll. NHi (23 ll.) 7445

PETER Parley's Almanac for Old and Young for 1836.
New-York: Freeman Hunt, & Co. 48 ll. MWA; NN;
DLC; OClWHi; WHi (42 ll.); Drake. 7446

PETER Parley's Almanac for Old and Young for 1836.
New York: Freeman Hunt, & Co.; Philadelphia: Desilver, Thomas, & Co.; Boston: Samuel Colman. 48
ll. NjR. 7447

PHINNEYS' Calendar, or Western Almanac for 1836.
By George R. Perkins. Cooperstown: H. & E. Phinney. 18 ll. MWA; N; NN; NHi; NRMA; InU; NCooHi;
MBC (17 ll.); NBuHi (17 ll.); Ct (impf); NR; NBuG;
DLC; WHi; NIC; MiD-B; NUt; NSyOHi (17 ll.);
FSpHi. 7448

The SAILOR'S Temperance Almanac for 1836. New
York: Conner and Cooke. 14 ll. MWA; NN; NHi;
ViHi; InU; MSaE; NNUT; MBC; MH. 7449

SPOONER'S Long-Island Almanac, and Register for
1836. By Thomas Spofford. Brooklyn: Long-Island
Star. 18 ll. DLC; NBLiHi; NJQ; Drake. 7450

STEELE'S Albany Almanac for 1836. Albany: Packard
and Van Benthuysen. 18 ll. MWA; N; MnU; OMC.
7451
STEELE'S Buffalo Almanac for 1836. By William W.
M'Louth. Buffalo: T. & M. Butler. 12 ll. NRU. 7452

STEELE'S Buffalo Almanac for 1836. By William W.
M'Louth. Buffalo: Moorhead, Adams and Hosmer. 12
ll. MWA; WHi. 7453

STODDARD'S Diary, or Columbia Almanack for 1836.
By Tobias Ostrander. Hudson: A. Stoddard. 18 ll.
MWA; NHi. 7454

SWORDS'S Pocket Almanack, Churchman's Calendar for
1836. New-York: Swords, Stanford, and Co. 64 ll.
MWA. NHi; NjR; PU; PHi; PPL; NNG; MSaE; MNF;
BritMus. 7455

New York - 1836   729

The **TEMPERANCE** Almanac for 1836. Albany: Packard and Van Benthuysen; Henry H. Little. 12 ll.
MWA; N; NN; NHi; PP; MiD-B; OrU; InU; NBLiHi; CtY; ICHi; MeP; ABH; GA; MnU; OClWHi; Ct; NjMo; OC; OMC; NT; NBuHi; ViU; WHi; VtHi; CtHi; MBC; OCHP; MHi; RNHi; NIC; NRU; CLU; CtW; MH; NjR; MB; MBAt; Drake (two varieties)   7456

TUTTLE'S Almanac for 1836. Troy: N. Tuttle. 18 ll.
MWA; N; NHi; NjR; NjJ; VtHi; WHi; OClWHi; CLU; MnU.   7457

UNCLE Sam's Comic Almanac for 1836. New-York: R. H. Elton. Advertised in "Hutchins' Improved Almanac" for 1836.   7458

UNIVERSALIST Register and Almanac for 1836. By G. R. Perkins. Utica: O. Whiston and G. Sanderson. 24 ll. MWA (23 ll.); N; NUt; MiD-B.   7459

WEBSTER'S Calendar: or the Albany Almanack for 1836. By Edwin E. Prentice [sic]. Albany: E. W. & C. Skinner. 18 ll. MWA; N; NBuHi; NbO (12 ll.); MnU; MB; WHi; Pennypacker.   7460

WEBSTER'S Calendar: or the Albany Almanack for 1836. By Edwin E. Prentice [sic]. Albany: E. W. & C. Skinner. (Second Edition) 18 ll. MWA; N (15 ll.); MiU-C; OMC.   7461

WESTERN Almanac for 1836. Cazenovia: S. H. Henry & Co. 12 ll. MWA; ICHi; CtY; CoD; MiD-B.   7462

WESTERN Almanac for 1836. Rochester: William Alling & Co. 12 ll. NR; NRHi; NRU; NHC; OClWHi; WHi.   7463

WESTERN Almanac for 1836. Rochester: William Alling & Co., Successors to Marshall & Dean. 12 ll. N; NRHi.   7464

The **WESTERN** Farmers' Almanac for 1836. By Lyman Abbott, Jr. Auburn: Oliphant & Skinner; Oliphant

& Skinner, printers. 12 ll. NCH; OClWHi; WHi.
7465

WOOD'S Almanac for 1836. By Joshua Sharp. New York: Samuel Wood & Sons; R. & G. S. Wood, printers. 18 ll. MWA; NHi; DLC; PHi. 7466

The AMERICAN Anti-Slavery Almanac for 1837. New York: American Anti-Slavery Society; S. W. Benedict. 24 ll. MBAt; PP; OClWHi (impf) 7467

The AMERICAN Comic Almanac for 1837. Albany: Oliver Steele; Boston: Charles Ellms. 18 ll. MWiW; VtHi. 7468

The AMERICAN Comic Almanac for 1837. New-York: Collins, Keese, & Co.; Boston: Charles Ellms. 18 ll. MWA. 7469

The AMERICAN Comic Almanac for 1837. New York: Ins, Ellms, & Co. 18 ll. DLC (17 ll.) 7470

The AMERICAN Comic Almanac for 1837. New-York: Leavitt, Lord & Co.; Boston: Charles Ellms. 18 ll. Private collection. 7471

The CHRISTIAN Almanac, For New-York, Connecticut, and New-Jersey for 1837. [New York:] American Tract Society. 24 ll. MWA; N; NN; NHi; CtLHi; InU; CtY; MH; OMC; CLU; NjP; IU; In; OClWHi; CtNhHi; RPB; DLC; PPL; F (19 ll., ntp); Drake.
7472

The CHURCHMAN'S Almanac for 1837. New-York: Protestant Episcopal Press. (First Edition) 18 ll. MWA; MBC; NNG; NcD; MSaE. 7473

The CHURCHMAN'S Almanac for 1837. New-York: Protestant Episcopal Press. (Second Edition) 18 ll. MWA; N; NNA; PPL; NSyOHi; Ct; NcU. 7474

COMIC Texas Oldmanick for 1837. New York: Turner & Fisher; Philadelphia: Turner & Fisher. 12 ll. DLC; MWA. 7475

CROCKETT Awl-Man-Axe for 1837. New York:
Turner & Fisher. 12 ll. DLC. 7476

DAY'S City and Country Almanac for 1837. By David
Young. New-York: Mahlon Day. 18 ll. MWA; N;
NBLiHi; NjR; PHi. 7477

DAY'S New York Pocket Almanac for 1837. New-York:
M. Day. 12 ll. MWA; NN; CtY; MeWC. 7478

The DEVIL'S Comical Oldmanick for 1837. New-York:
Turner & Fisher; Philadelphia: Turner & Fisher. 12
ll. MWA; CSmH; NbO; DLC; ICU; Streeter. 7479

ELTON'S Comic All-my-nack for 1837. New-York: R.
H. Elton, 134 Division-St. 18 ll. MWA; NHi; MB;
OClWHi. 7480

ELTON'S Comic All-my-nack for 1837. New-York:
R. H. Elton, 134 Division-St. And sold also at 76
Bowery. 18 ll. MWA; DLC; InU (impf); PHi. 7481

EVERY Body's Comick Almanack for 1837. New-York:
J. & H. G. Langley. 18 ll. NN. 7482

EVERY Body's Comick Almanack for 1837. New York:
Turner & Fisher; Philadelphia: Turner & Fisher. 18
ll. MWA; NN; NHi; DLC. 7483

The FARMER'S Almanac for 1837. Cooperstown: Ivison & Phinney; Utica: William Williams, printer.
[Williams] 7484

The FARMER'S Almanac for 1837. By Thomas Spofford. [np, np] NR (15 ll.) 7485

The FARMER'S Almanac for 1837. By Thomas Spofford. New York: D. Felt & Co. (For the Middle
States) 18 ll. MWA; N; NN; NB; NBLiHi; NR; RNR;
PHi; InU; NjR. 7486

The FARMER'S Almanac for 1837. By Thomas Spofford. New York: D. Felt & Co.... Sold also by...

(For the Middle States) 18 ll. MWA; NN. 7487

The FARMER'S Almanac for 1837. By Thomas Spofford. New-York: N. & J. White. 18 ll. NSyOHi (impf); OClWHi; PScrHi. 7488

FARMER'S Almanac for 1837. By David Young. New-York: Mahlon Day, for the Booksellers. 18 ll. NN; NBLiHi; NjR. 7489

FARMER'S Almanac for 1837. By David Young. New-York: H. & S. Raynor; J. M. Marsh, printer. 18 ll. MWA. 7490

FARMER'S Almanac for 1837. By David Young. N.Y.: Daniel D. Smith; Peekskill: S. Huestis, printer. 18 ll. NjR. 7491

FARMER'S Almanac for 1837. By David Young. N.Y.: Doolittle & Vermilye; Peekskill: S. Huestis, printer. 18 ll. MWA; MB; NjP; NNSIHi (impf) 7492

FARMER'S Almanac for 1837. By David Young. Peekskill: James Brewster; S. Huestis, printer. 18 ll. MWA. 7493

The FARMER'S Diary, or Western Almanac for 1837. Canandaigua: C. Morse. 12 ll. NCanHi (11 ll.); WHi. 7494

The FARMER'S Diary, or Western Almanac for 1837. Ithaca: Mack, Andrus & Woodruff. 12 ll. NSyOHi. 7495

FARMER'S or Columbia Almanack for 1837. By Tobias Ostrander. Hudson: Samuel Wescott. 12 ll. MWA; N; NHi. 7496

FARMER'S or Dutchess County Almanack for 1837. Poughkeepsie: Potter & Wilson. NPV (6 ll.) 7497

GATES'S (Successor to Parker,) Almanac for 1837. By Tobias Ostrander. Troy: Elias Gates. 18 ll. MWA; N; PHi; Drake (17 ll.) 7498

New York - 1837

GATES'S Troy Almanac for 1837. By Tobias Ostrander. Troy: Elias Gates. 18 ll. MWA; N; PHi.
7499

HUTCHINGS' Almanac for 1837. By David Young. N.Y.: Daniel D. Smith; Peekskill: S. Huestis, printer. 18 ll. NN.
7500

HUTCHINGS' Almanac for 1837. By David Young. Poughkeepsie: George Nagell; S. Huestis, printer. 18 ll. DLC.
7501

HUTCHING'S Improved Almanac for 1837. By David Young. New-York: H. & S. Raynor; J. M. Marsh, printer. 18 ll. MWA (two varieties); MB.
7502

HUTCHING'S Improved Almanac and Ephemeris for 1837. By David Young. New-York: H. & S. Raynor; J. M. Marsh, printer. 18 ll. MWA; NWhpHi.
7503

HUTCHINGS' Improved Almanac and Ephemeris for 1837. By David Young. New-York: H. & S. Raynor; J. M. Marsh, printer. 18 ll. NBLiHi (17 ll.)
7504

HUTCHIN'S Improved Almanac for 1837. By David Young. New-York: Printed for the booksellers. 18 ll. NBuG.
7505

HUTCHIN'S Improved Almanac for 1837. By David Young. New-York: Mahlon Day, for the booksellers. 18 ll. NHi; NBLiHi; CtB.
7506

HUTCHINS' Improved Almanac for 1837. By David Young. New-York: Mahlon Day, for the booksellers. 18 ll. NjR.
7507

HUTCHINS' Improved Almanac for 1837. By David Young. New York: Collins, Keese & Co. 18 ll. NN (17 ll.); N; NHi.
7508

KNICKERBOCKER Almanac for 1837. By David Young. New-York: Mahlon Day, for the booksellers. 18 ll. MWA; NjP (17 ll.); NN; MH; MnU.
7509

KNICKERBOCKER Almanac for 1837. By David Young. New-York: H. & S. Raynor; J. M. Marsh, printer. 18 ll. MWA. 7510

MARRYATT'S Comic Naval Almanac [for 1837]. New-York: 134 Division-Street. 18 ll. MWA; N (impf); NHi; NCooHi; OMC. 7511

The METHODIST Almanac for 1837. By David Young. New-York: T. Mason and G. Lane, for the Methodist Episcopal Church; J. Collord, printer. 18 ll. MWA (two varieties); NHi; NjR; CtW; PPiHi; WHi. 7512

The NEW-YORK State Pocket Almanac for 1837. Auburn: H. Ivison & Co.; Oliphant & Skinner, printers. 12 ll. NN. 7513

The NEW-YORK State Pocket Almanac for 1837. Auburn: Oliphant & Skinner; Oliphant & Skinner, printers. 12 ll. NAuT. 7514

O'HARA'S Albany Almanac for 1837. By Tobias Ostrander. Albany: Packard and Van Benthuysen. 18 ll. MWA; N; NN (17 ll.); CLU. 7515

ONEIDA Almanac for 1837. Utica: Gardiner Tracy. 12 ll. MWA; NIC; NUt; CtY. 7516

OSWEGO Almanac for 1837. By David Young. Oswego: D. B. & A. A. Lane. 18 ll. NBuG; WHi. 7517

PEOPLE'S Almanac for 1837. New-York: Collins, Keese & Co. 24 ll. MWA; Pennypacker. 7518

PETER Parley's Almanac, for Old and Young for 1837. New-York: Freeman Hunt & Co. 40 ll. MWA; NN (impf); NjR; CtY; CtHT-W; OMC; NCooHi; DLC; WHi (32 ll.); NcA. 7519

PHINNEYS' Calendar, or Western Almanac for 1837. By George R. Perkins. Cooperstown: H. & E. Phinney. 18 ll. MWA; N; NN; NHi; NUt; NUtHi; ICHi; WHi; MiD-B; NSyOHi; NCooHi; MBC; CLU; NBuHi;

NR; CtY; InU; NIC; DLC. 7520

The **SAILOR'S** Temperance Almanac for 1837. Albany: Packard and Van Benthuysen; New York: Francis F. Ripley. 12 ll. MWA; NHi; NT; NUtHi; InU; MH; CtY; OC. 7521

SPOFFORD'S Pocket Almanac for 1837. By Thomas Spofford. New-York: D. Felt & Co. Advertised in "Farmer's Almanac" for 1837. 7522

STEELE'S Albany Almanac for 1837. By Tobias Ostrander. Albany: Packard and Van Benthuysen. 18 ll. MWA; N (impf); NHi; NjR; OClWHi; OMC. 7523

STEELE'S Western Almanac for 1837. By William W. M'Louth. Buffalo: T. & M. Butler. 12 ll. NBuHi. 7524

STEELE'S Western Almanac for 1837. By William W. M'Louth. Buffalo: O. G. Steele. 12 ll. NRU. 7525

STODDARD'S Diary, or Columbia Almanack for 1837. By Tobias Ostrander. Hudson: Ashbel Stoddard. 12 ll. N; NHi; CtNhHi; PHi. 7526

SWORDS'S Pocket Almanack, Churchman's Calendar for 1837. New-York: Swords, Stanford, and Co. 54 ll. MWA; N; NHi; NNG; NNS; PPL; PHi; MHi; NjR; MSaE; BritMus. 7527

The **TEMPERANCE** Almanac for 1837. Albany: Packard and Van Benthuysen; New York: Francis F. Ripley. 12 ll. MWA (three varieties); N; NN; NHi; Ct; MH; InU; OClWHi; WHi; CLU; NbHi; NSyU; NSyOHi; NBuHi; CtNhHi; RNHi; CtW; CtB; MBC; MHi; CtHi; CtY; MiD-B; ViU; NNUT; MB; MBAt; PPL; NjR (11 ll.); Drake. 7528

UNIVERSALIST Register and Almanac for 1837. By G. R. Perkins. Geneva: O. Whiston & G. Sanderson; Herald of Truth. 18 ll. N; NN; CLU; NRU; WHi. 7529

WEBSTER'S Calendar: or the Albany Almanack for 1837.

By Edwin E. Prentice [sic]. Albany: E. W. & C. Skinner. 18 ll. MWA; N; NN; NHi; NT; DLC; OMC; WHi; OClWHi; Drake (11 ll.) 7530

WEBSTER'S Calendar: or the Albany Almanack for 1837. By Edwin E. Prentice [sic]. Albany: E. W. & C. Skinner. (Second Edition) 18 ll. MWA; NN; MB; MiU-C. 7531

WESTERN Almanac for 1837. Cazenovia: S. H. Henry & Co. 12 ll. MWA (11 ll.); N (impf); NHi; NBuHi (11 ll.); NSyOHi. 7532

WESTERN Almanac for 1837. Rochester: William Alling & Co. 12 ll. N; NRHi; NRU; NR; NBuHi; WHi. 7533
WESTERN Almanac for 1837. Rochester: C. & M. Morse. 12 ll. NRU; CtY. 7534

WESTERN Almanac for 1837. Watertown: Knowlton & Rice. 12 ll. NHi; MB (impf) 7535

The WESTERN Farmers' Almanac for 1837. By Lyman Abbott, Jr. Auburn: Oliphant & Skinner; Oliphant & Skinner, printers. 12 ll. MWA; N; NUtHi; NAuHi; NSchU; NRHi; NBuG; DLC; NR; MnU; MiD-B. 7536

WOOD'S Almanac for 1837. By Joshua Sharp. New York: Samuel S. & William Wood; R. & G. S. Wood, printers. 18 ll. MWA; NHi. 7537

The AMERICAN Anti-Slavery Almanac for 1838. New-York: American Anti-Slavery Society; S. W. Benedict. [Phillips] 7538

The AMERICAN Comic Almanac for 1838. New York: D. Felt & Co.; Boston: Charles Ellms. 24 ll. MnU. 7539
The AMERICAN Pocket Almanack for 1838. New York: J. Disturnell and G. & C. Carvill & Co. 22 ll. DLC. 7540
CATSKILL Almanack for 1838. Catskill: Sturtevant & Austin; Hudson: Rural Repository Office. 12 ll. NHi. 7541

New York - 1838   737

The CHRISTIAN Almanac, For New-York, Connecticut, and New-Jersey for 1838. [New York]: American Tract Society. 24 ll. MWA; N; NHi; NN; NjR; CtY; MH; F; InU; PPL; NSyOHi. 7542

The CHURCHMAN'S Almanac for 1838. New-York: Protestant Episcopal Press. (First Edition) 18 ll. MWA; NNA. 7543

The CHURCHMAN'S Almanac for 1838. New-York: Protestant Episcopal Press. (Second Edition) 18 ll. MWA; NHi; NNG; MB; PPL; Ct; MBAt; ScC; NcD; InU; NjR. 7544

The CHURCHMAN'S Almanac for 1838. New-York: Protestant Episcopal Press. (Third Edition) 18 ll. MWA; NHi; Ct; ViHi; NSyOHi; NcU. 7545

The CHURCHMAN'S Almanac for 1838. New-York: Protestant Episcopal Press. (Fourth Edition) 18 ll. MWA; N; MHi. 7546

CLARK'S Troy Almanac for 1838. By C. H. Anthony. Troy: N. Tuttle. 12 ll. MWA; NN; NHi; NjR; InU; DLC. 7547

COMMON Almanack for 1838. Watertown: Knowlton & Rice. 12 ll. N; NHi; DLC; F; CLU. 7548

DAY'S City and Country Almanac for 1838. By David Young. New York: Mahlon Day. 18 ll. MWA; N. 7549

DAY'S New-York Pocket Almanac for 1838. New-York: M. Day. 12 ll. MWA (two varieties); NN; NHi; NBLiHi; CtLHi. 7550

The DUTCHESS and Ulster Farmer's Almanack for 1838. Poughkeepsie: George Nagell. 18 ll. CtW. 7551

ELTON'S Comic All-my-nack for 1838. New-York: Elton & Harrison. 18 ll. MWA; N; NN; NHi; NBLiHi; MB; OCHP; Drake. 7552

ELTON'S Comic All-my-nack for 1838. New York:
Elton & Harrison; Columbus, Ohio: G. W. Allen. 18
ll. OClWHi. 7553

The FARMER'S Almanac for 1838. By Thomas Spofford. New-York: D. Felt & Co. 18 ll. MWA; N;
NHi; NB; NBLiHi; CLU; NR; PHi; NjMo (12 ll.);
Drake; NjR. 7554

The FARMER'S Almanac for 1838. By Thomas Spofford. New-York: Robinson, Pratt & Co. 18 ll. MWA;
OClWHi. 7555

The FARMER'S Almanac for 1838. By Zadock Thompson. Whitehall: Y. D. S. Wright & Co.; Burlington:
H. Johnson & Co., printers. 12 ll. VtU. 7556

FARMER'S Almanac for 1838. By David Young. New-York: H. & S. Raynor. 18 ll. MWA; NHi; InU; NjR;
NjMoW; NjHi; MnU. 7557

FARMER'S Almanac for 1838. By David Young. New-York: H. & S. Raynor; Doolittle & Vermilye. 18 ll.
NN; NHi. 7558

FARMER'S Diary, and Western Almanac for 1838. By
William W. M'Louth. Canandaigua: Canandaigua
Bookstore. 12 ll. NRU. 7559

FARMER'S or Columbia Almanack for 1838. Hudson:
Samuel Wescott. CtNhHi (15 ll.) 7560

FARMER'S or Dutchess County Almanack for 1838.
Poughkeepsie: Potter & Wilson. 12 ll. NjR. 7561

FARMER'S or Greene County Almanack for 1838.
Catskill: H. Friar; Hudson: Rural Repository, printers.
14 ll. Drake. 7562

GATES' Troy Almanac for 1838. By C. H. Anthony.
Albany: Oliver Steele. 18 ll. MWA. 7563

GATES' Troy Almanac for 1838. By C. H. Anthony.

New York - 1838

Troy: Elias Gates. 18 ll. VtBennHi. 7564

GATES' Troy Almanac for 1838. By C. H. Anthony.
Troy: N. Tuttle. 18 ll. MWA; N; NT; OClWHi;
VtHi; PHi. 7565

HUTCHING'S Improved Almanac, and Ephemeris for
1838. By David Young. New-York: R. Elton. 18 ll.
NHi (17 ll.); NBLiHi; MnU; Drake. 7566

HUTCHING'S Improved Almanac, and Ephemeris for
1838. By David Young. New-York: H. & S. Raynor.
18 ll. MWA (two varieties); NN; PPL (16 ll.); IU;
NWhpHi; Drake. 7567

HUTCHING'S Improved Farmers' and Mechanics Almanac for 1838. New York: Turner & Fisher. 18 ll.
MWA; DLC; NBLiHi; CLU. 7568

HUTCHINS' Improved Almanac for 1838. By David
Young. New-York: Collins, Keese & Co. 18 ll. N.
7569

HUTCHINS' Improved Almanac for 1838. By David
Young. New-York: Robinson, Pratt & Co. 18 ll. NjR.
7570

HUTCHIN'S Improved Almanac for 1838. By David
Young. New-York: Charles Small. 18 ll. NHi. 7571

HUTCHIN'S Improved Almanac for 1838. By David
Young. New-York: Daniel D. Smith. 18 ll. NHi. 7572

KNICKERBOCKER Almanac for 1838. By David Young.
New-York: Mahlon Day. 18 ll. MWA (impf); NN;
NBLiHi (impf); OClWHi. 7573

KNICKERBOCKER Almanac for 1838. By David Young.
New-York: H. & S. Raynor. 18 ll. NHi. 7574

The METHODIST Almanac for 1838. Fitted to the horizon and meridian of New-York. By David Young.
New-York: T. Mason and G. Lane, For the Methodist
Episcopal Church; J. Collord, printer. 24 ll. MWA;
NHi; NjR; NBuHi (ntp); CtW; WHi; OClWHi. 7575

The METHODIST Almanac for 1838. Fitted to the horizon and meridian of Boston. By David Young. New-York: T. Mason and G. Lane, For the Methodist Episcopal Church; J. Collord, printer. 24 ll. MBAt. 7576

The METHODIST Almanac for 1838. Fitted to the horizon and meridian of Nashville. By David Young. New-York: T. Mason and G. Lane, For the Methodist Episcopal Church; J. Collord, printer. 24 ll. NcD.
7577

The NATIONAL Comic Almanac for 1838. [Wall] This is a Boston production. 7578

NEW-YORK [sic] State Pocket Almanac for 1838. Auburn: Oliphant & Skinner; Oliphant & Skinner, printers. 12 ll. N. 7579

ONEIDA Almanack for 1838. Ithaca: Mack, Andrus & Woodruff. 12 ll. NRU (11 ll.) 7580

ONEIDA Almanac for 1838. Utica: Gardiner Tracy. 12 ll. N. 7581

ONEIDA Almanac for 1838. Utica: Gardiner Tracy. (Late firm of Hastings & Tracy.) 12 ll. MWA; NUt; NUtHi. 7582

The PEOPLE'S Almanac of Useful and Entertaining Knowledge for 1838. New York: D. Felt & Co. 24 ll. MWA; MB; NBuG; OMC. 7583

PHINNEY'S Calendar, or Western Almanac for 1838. By George R. Perkins. Cooperstown: H. & E. Phinney. 18 ll. MWA; N; NN; NHi; DLC; MBC; NUtHi; MH; NBuHi; OClWHi; NSyOHi; FSpHi; NCooHi; NHC; WHi; NUt; NR; NIC; MnU; InU; CLU. 7584

POCKET Almanack for 1838. By Thomas Spofford. New York: David Felt & Co. 16 ll. NHi. 7585

The POUGHKEEPSIE Almanac for 1838. Poughkeepsie: George Nagell. 18 ll. NPV. 7586

The **POUGHKEEPSIE** Almanac for 1838. Poughkeepsie: Potter and Wilson. 18 ll. MWA; NHi; NP. 7587

The **SMALLER** Farmer's Almanac for 1838. By Thomas Spofford. New-York: D. Felt & Co. 12 ll. NBuHi. 7588

STEELE'S Albany Almanac for 1838. Albany: Packard and Van Benthuysen. 18 ll. MWA; N; NHi; TxDN.
7589
-- Issue with 42 ll. NjR. 7590

STEELE'S Western Almanack for 1838. By William W. M'Louth. Buffalo: Steele & Peck; Steele's Press. 12 ll. MWA; N; NBuHi; NRU. 7591

STEELE'S Western Almanack for 1838. By William W. M'Louth. Dansville: W. & J. Henderson; Steele's Press. 12 ll. NBuHi (10 ll.) 7592

STEELE'S Western Almanack for 1838. By William W. M'Louth. Fredonia: Frisbee; Steele's Press. 12 ll. NHi. 7593

STODDARD'S Diary, or Columbia Almanack for 1838. Hudson: Ashbel Stoddard. 18 ll. MWA; Drake. 7594

STODDARD'S Diary, or Columbia Almanack for 1838. Hudson: P. S. & R. G. Wynkoop. 18 ll. N; NSyOHi (impf) 7595

SWORDS'S Pocket Almanack, Churchman's Calendar for 1838. New-York: Swords, Stanford, and Co. 48 ll. MWA; NHi; NjR; PPL; PHi; NNS; NNG; MNF; MiD-B; BritMus. 7596

The **TEMPERANCE** Almanac for 1838. Calculated for meridian of Albany. By David Young. Albany: Packard and Van Benthuysen. 24 ll. MWA; N; NN; NHi; InU; NT; WHi; NSchU; NjR; MH; MHi; NBuHi; MnU; MB; MBC; CtY; OMC; ICHi; Drake (12 ll.) 7597

The **TEMPERANCE** Almanac for 1838. Calculated for

meridian of Buffalo. By David Young. Albany: Packard and Van Benthuysen. 24 ll. Drake. 7598

The TRIBUNE Almanac. New York. This series (1838 et seq) was actually issued later than 1850 and does not lie within the scope of this list. 7599

UNIVERSALIST Register and Almanac for 1838. Rochester: O. Whiston & G. Sanderson; Herald of Truth. 18 ll. MWA; N; NRU; MiD-B; WHi. 7600

WASSON'S Troy Almanac for 1838. By C. H. Anthony. Troy: N. Tuttle; Wasson's Book Store. 18 ll. MWA; CLU. 7601

WEBSTER'S Calendar: or the Albany Almanack for 1838. By Edwin E. Prentice. Albany: E. W. & C. Skinner. 18 ll. MWA (16 ll.); N (impf); NHi; MnU; MB; InU (fragment); DLC; CtHi; Drake (14 ll.) 7602

WEBSTER'S Calendar: or the Albany Almanack for 1838. By Edwin E. Prentice. Albany: E. W. & C. Skinner. (Second Edition) 18 ll. MWA; N; NN; NHi; MiU-C. 7603

WESTERN Almanac for 1838. Cazenovia: Henry & Severance. 12 ll. MWA; MiD-B. 7604

WESTERN Almanac for 1838. Ithaca: Mack, Andrus & Woodruff. 12 ll. MWA; NHi; DLC; NIC; NBuG; WHi. 7605

WESTERN Almanac for 1838. Rochester: William Alling. 12 ll. N; NHi; NR; NRHi; NRU. 7606

WESTERN Almanac for 1838. Rochester: Hoyt & Porter. 12 ll. NRU. 7607

WESTERN Almanac for 1838. Rochester: Clarendon Morse. 12 ll. NRU. 7608

The WESTERN Farmers' Almanac for 1838. By Lyman Abbot, Jr. Auburn: Oliphant & Skinner; Oliphant & Skinner, printers. 12 ll. MWA; N; NSyOHi;

OClWHi. 7609

The WHIG Almanac, and Politician's Register for 1838.
New York: George Dearborn & Co.; F. F. Ripley. 21
ll. MWA; N; NHi; MDedHi; InU; NBuG; NUtHi; ICHi;
NmU; MHi; Ct; WvU; NNCoCi; PHi; FTaSU; NPV;
In; LNHT; OO; PU; O. 7610

The WHIG Almanac, and Politician's Register for 1838.
New-York: H. Greeley; F. F. Ripley. 21 ll. N; NN;
IC (20 ll.); DLC; CtY; NSyOHi; NBLiHi; MnM; NjJ;
PU; WHi; CtW; PHi. 7611

The WHIG Almanac, and Politician's Register for 1838.
New-York: H. Greeley; F. F. Ripley. (Second Edition)
21 ll. N. 7612

The WHIG Almanac, and Politician's Register for 1838.
New-York: H. Greeley; F. F. Ripley. (Third Edition)
24 ll. MWA. 7613

WOOD'S Almanac for 1838. By Joshua Sharp. New
York: Samuel S. & William Wood; R. & G. S. Wood,
printers. 18 ll. N; NHi; DLC; NAlI; ViHi; NjR (ntp)
7614
ALLING'S Counting House Almanac for 1839. Rochester:
William Alling. Broadside. NN. 7615

ALMANAC for 1839. Rochester: William Alling. 12 ll.
NR. 7616

The AMERICAN Anti-Slavery Almanac for 1839. New
York: American Anti-Slavery Society. 24 ll. NjR. 7617

The AMERICAN Anti-Slavery Almanac for 1839. New-
York: American Anti-Slavery Society; S. W. Benedict.
24 ll. N; NN; NB; NSyOHi; F; NCooHi (16 ll.);
PPAmP; PPL. 7618

The AMERICAN Anti-Slavery Almanac for 1839. New-
York: S. W. Benedict. 24 ll. MWA; N; NHi. 7619

The AMERICAN Anti-Slavery Almanac for 1839. New

York & Boston: American Anti-Slavery Society. New
York: S. W. Benedict; Boston: Isaac Knapp. 24 ll.
MWA; N; NN; NHi; NjR; MB; PPL; MHi; In; OClWHi;
NSyOHi (ntp); CLU; NRU; PDoBHi; NBLiHi; MBAt;
NcD; IHi; MiU-C; KyU; Mi; CtHi; CtY; CoCC; InHi;
OMC; Nh; VtStjF; O; ICHi; InU; MdBJ; WHi; MSaE;
OCHP; PScHi; CtB (ntp); NUtHi; MBC; CtW; Drake.
7620

BROWN'S Improved Almanack, Pocket Memorandum, and Account Book for 1839. New York: Erastus Wilkins. (Third Edition) 35 ll. NHi. 7621

The CHRISTIAN Almanac, for New-York, Connecticut, and New-Jersey for 1839. [New York:] American Tract Society. 24 ll. MWA; N; NN; NHi; NjR; CtY; DLC; CtNhHi; CtW; NRU; IU; InU; Drake. 7622

The CHURCHMAN'S Almanac for 1839. New-York: Protestant Episcopal Press; Sherman and Trevett. 18 ll. MWA; NHi; NNC; MB; NNG; NcU; NcD; CtHi; CtHT-W. 7623

The CHURCHMAN'S Almanac for 1839. New-York: Protestant Episcopal Press; Sherman and Trevett; Philadelphia: Joseph Wetham. (Second Edition) 18 ll. NNA; NNC; PPL. 7624

The CHURCHMAN'S Almanac for 1839. New-York: Protestant Episcopal Press; Sherman and Trevett. (Third Edition) 18 ll. MWA; N; MHi. 7625

The CHURCHMAN'S Almanac for 1839. New-York: Protestant Episcopal Press; Sherman and Trevett. (Fourth Edition) 18 ll. MWA; NJQ; PPL. 7626

COMMON Almanac for 1839. Watertown: Knowlton & Rice. 12 ll. NHi; DLC. 7627

The COMMON School Almanac for 1839. N.Y.: The American Common School Society. 12 ll. MWA; N (two varieties); NHi; CtLHi; MB; CtY; CtHT-W; CtNhHi; CtHi; CtW; OClWHi; MSaE; NBLiHi; MBAt; MBC; IU; InU; NRMA; WHi; NBuHi (impf); CLU; MH;

MiD-B; NjR; RNHi; Pennypacker. 7628

CROCKETT Awlmanaxe for 1839. New York: Turner
& Fisher. 12 ll. MWA; DLC. 7629

CROCKETT'S Comic Almanac for 1839. N.Y.: Elton.
18 ll. MWA; NN (12 ll.); DLC; Drake. 7630

DAY'S City and Country Almanac for 1839. By David
Young. New-York: Mahlon Day. 18 ll. MWA (17 ll.);
N (impf); NBLiHi. 7631

DAY'S New-York Pocket Almanac for 1839. New-York:
M. Day. 12 ll. MWA; NN; NHi. 7632

The DEMOCRAT'S Almanac, and Political Register for
1839. New York: Evening Post. 30 ll. MWA; N;
NN; NHi; DLC; NIC; PHi; PPL; NBLiHi; InU; WHi;
MSaE; OO; NjR; IaU; MB; MnU; OClWHi; Drake.
7633
The DEMOCRAT'S Almanac, and Political Register for
1839. New York: Evening Post. (Second Edition) 30
ll. MWA; N; DLC; NjR; NbO; CtY; PPL. 7634

The DUTCHESS County Farmer's Almanack for 1839.
Poughkeepsie: Potter & Wilson. 12 ll. NHi; NP; NPV.
7635
ELTON'S Comic All-my-nack for 1839. N.Y.: Elton.
18 ll. MWA; NN; NHi; OClWHi; DLC; CtY; NjJ;
ICU; PHi; MB; NBLiHi; NRU; NIC. 7636

ELTON'S Comic All-my-nack for 1839. N.Y.: Elton;
Mitchell, printer. 18 ll. MWA; NN. 7637

FARMER'S Almanac for 1839. New-York: Mahlon Day.
18 ll. Private collection. 7638

FARMER'S Almanac for 1839. New-York: Turner &
Fisher. 18 ll. MWA; NHi (14 ll.); PHi. 7639

The FARMER'S Almanac for 1839. By Thomas Spofford. New York: D. Felt & Co. 18 ll. MWA; N;
NN; NHi; NB; NBuHi; NRMA; MBC; NCooHi; PHi;

DLC; NjR (17 ll.); NR; Ct; Drake. 7640

The FARMER'S Almanac for 1839. By Thomas Spofford. N.Y.: Robinson, Pratt & Co. 18 ll. MWA; NSyOHi (17 ll.); MnM (17 ll.); OClWHi. 7641

FARMERS' Almanac for 1839. By David Young. New-York: Collins, Keese & Co.; H. & S. Raynor. 18 ll. MWA; N; NRU. 7642

FARMERS' Almanac for 1839. By David Young. New-York: Octavius Longworth. 18 ll. MWA. 7643

FARMERS' Almanac for 1839. By David Young. New-York: H. & S. Raynor. 12 ll. NN. 7644

FARMERS' Almanac for 1839. By David Young. New-York: H. & S. Raynor, (formerly Bartlett & Raynor). 18 ll. MWA; NNA; NSyOHi; NBLiHi; NP; CtY. 7645

FARMERS' Almanac for 1839. By David Young. New-York: H. & S. Raynor; Poinier & Snell. 18 ll. NNSIHi (17 ll.) 7646

The FARMER'S Diary, and Western Almanac for 1839. Canandaigua: C. Morse. 12 ll. N; NRMA. 7647

FARMER'S or Greene County Almanack for 1839. Coxsackie: T. B. Carroll. 12 ll. MWA; N. 7648

GATES' Troy Almanac for 1839. Troy: Elias Gates; Belcher & Burton, printers. 18 ll. PHi; DLC; CLU; OMC; NRMA; NT. 7649

-- Paged. 18 ll. MWA; N. 7650

HUTCHING'S Improved Almanac, and Ephemeris for 1839. By David Young. New-York: Octavius Longworth. 18 ll. N. 7651

HUTCHING'S Improved Almanac, and Ephemeris for 1839. By David Young. New-York: H. & S. Raynor. 18 ll. NHi; NBLiHi; NWhpHi; CtHi; MB; MSaE. 7652

HUTCHING'S Improved Almanac, and Ephemeris for 1839. By David Young. New-York: H. & S. Raynor; Poinier & Snell. 18 ll. MWA. 7653

HUTCHING'S Improved Farmers' and Mechanics' Almanac for 1839. New-York: Turner & Fisher. 18 ll. MWA; NHi. 7654

HUTCHIN'S Improved Almanac for 1839. By David Young. New-York: Collins, Keese, & Co. 18 ll. MWA; NjR (17 ll.) 7655

HUTCHIN'S Improved Almanac for 1839. By David Young. New-York: Mahlon Day. 18 ll. NHi; NBLiHi (16 ll.) 7656

HUTCHINS' Improved Almanac for 1839. By David Young. New-York: Octavius Longworth. 18 ll. N; Drake. 7657

HUTCHINS' Improved Almanac for 1839. By David Young. New-York: Robinson Pratt, & Co. 18 ll. MWA; Drake. 7658

HUTCHIN'S Improved Almanac for 1839. By David Young. New York: Charles Small. 18 ll. NSchU. 7659

KNICKERBOCKER Almanac for 1839. By David Young. New York: H. & S. Raynor. 18 ll. NHi. 7660

KNICKERBOCKER Almanac for 1839. By David Young. New York: Turner & Fisher. 18 ll. MWA; CLU. 7661

The METHODIST Almanac for 1839. Fitted to... Cincinnati. By David Young. New York: T. Mason and G. Lane for the M. E. Church. 24 ll. NcD. 7662

The METHODIST Almanac for 1839. Fitted to... New-York. By David Young. New-York: T. Mason and G. Lane, for the Methodist Episcopal Church; J. Collord, printer. 24 ll. MWA (two varieties); NjP; NjR; MHi; MnU; CtHi; CtW; MiGr; KyU; InU; OC; NRMA. 7663

The NEW American Comic All-I-Make for 1839. New York: Elton. 12 ll. MWA; N; NN; DLC; InU; OClWHi. 7664

HEW-YORK [sic] State Pocket Almanac for 1839. Auburn: Oliphant & Skinner; Oliphant & Skinner, printers. 12 ll. Drake. 7665

ONEIDA Almanac for 1839. Utica: Gardiner Tracy. 12 ll. MWA; NUtHi; NRMA; MiD-B. 7666

PERPETUAL Counting-House Almanac. By Stephen V. R. Stewart. Rochester: J. T. Young. 1839. Broadside. Drake. 7667

PHINNEY'S Calendar, or Western Almanac for 1839. By George R. Perkins. Cooperstown: H. & E. Phinney. 22 ll. MWA (21 ll.); N; NN; NHi; DLC; NUt; NRMA; NUtHi; MBC; NSyOHi; MnU; MH; NCooHi; NBuHi; WHi; NIC; InU; Drake. 7668

POCKET Almanack for 1839. By Thomas Spofford. New York: David Felt & Co. 16 ll. MWA. 7669

The POLITICIAN'S Register for 1839. New-York: H. Greeley. 11 ll. IC; In; LNHT; OFH; ICHi; NBuG; InU; WvU. 7670

The POLITICIAN'S Register for 1839. New-York: H. Greeley. (Fourth Edition) 11 ll. [Sabin 63823] 7671

The POUGHKEEPSIE Journal Counting House Almanac for 1839. Poughkeepsie: Poughkeepsie Journal. Broadside. MWA. 7672

STEELE'S Albany Almanac for 1839. Albany: Packard, Van Benthuysen and Co. 18 ll. N; NN; NR; MnU; OMC; NCooHi (15 ll.); Drake. 7673

STEELE'S Western Almanack for 1839. By William W. M' Louth. Buffalo: Steele & Peck; Day & Steele's Press. 12 ll. NHi. 7674

STEELE'S Western Almanack for 1839. By William W. M'Louth. Dansville: W. & J. Henderson; Day & Steele's Press. 12 ll. NBuHi (impf); NRMA. 7675

STODDARD'S Diary, or Columbia Almanack for 1839. Hudson: Ashbel Stoddard. 12 ll. CtNhHi (impf) 7676

STODDARD'S Diary, or Columbia Almanack for 1839. Hudson: P. S. & R. G. Wynkoop; Rural Repository. 12 ll. NHi. 7677

SWORDS'S Pocket Almanack, Churchman's Calendar for 1839. New-York: Swords, Stanford, and Co. 72 ll. MWA; NHi; NNG; NNS; PHi; MHi; CtY; NjR; MSaE; PPL; BritMus. 7678

The TEMPERANCE Almanac for 1839. Albany: Packard, Van Benthuysen and Co. 18 ll. MWA; OClWHi; CtHi; CtHT-W; N; MH; CLU; Ct; WHi; NT; CtB; CtLHi. 7679

The THOMSONIAN Almanac for 1839. Poughkeepsie: Office of the Thomsonian; New York: F. F. Ripley. 18 ll. N; NHi; NT; NUtHi (17 ll.) 7680

The TOWN and Country Almanac for 1839. New York: Turner & Fisher. 18 ll. MWA; NRMA; NjMo. 7681

TROY Almanac for 1839. Troy: Z. Clark; Tuttle, Belcher & Burton, printers. 18 ll. MWA; N; NHi; NRU. 7682

TROY Almanac for 1839. Troy: Robert Wasson; Tuttle, Belcher & Burton, printers. 18 ll. MWA (impf); OClWHi. 7683

TURNER'S Comick Almanack for 1839. New York: Turner & Fisher. 18 ll. MWA; NN; DLC; PPL. 7684

The UNIVERSALIST Register, with an Almanac for 1839. Utica: Grosh and Hutchinson. 18 ll. Vi. 7685

The UNIVERSALIST Register, with an Almanac for 1839.

Utica: Grosh and Hutchinson; New-York: P. Price; [etc]. 18 ll. MWA; N; NRMA; NUt; NRU; CLU; WHi; Drake. 7686

WEBSTER'S Calendar: or the Albany Almanack for 1839. By Edwin E. Prentice. Albany: E. W. & C. Skinner. 18 ll. N; Drake (impf) 7687

WEBSTER'S Calendar: or the Albany Almanack for 1839. By Edwin E. Prentice. Albany: E. W. & C. Skinner. (Second Edition) 18 ll. MWA; N (impf); NN; NHi; PHi; MiU-C; MB; InU; NRMA; MH (impf); MnU. 7688

WESTERN Almanac for 1839. Buffalo: Edward Butler. 12 ll. MWA. 7689

WESTERN Almanac for 1839. Ithaca: Mack, Andrus & Woodruff. 12 ll. MWA; DLC; NBuG; WHi. 7690

WESTERN Almanac for 1839. Lockport: N. Leonard. 12 ll. WHi. 7691

WESTERN Almanac for 1839. Rochester: William Alling. 12 ll. MWA; N (two varieties); NHi; NCooHi; NRU (two varieties); NRHi (impf); NHC; NRMA; Drake. 7692

WESTERN Almanac for 1839. Rochester: Clarendon Morse. 12 ll. NBuHi; NR; NRHi. 7693

The WESTERN Farmers' Almanac for 1839. By Lyman Abbot, Jr. Auburn: H. Ivison, jr. NSyOHi (5 ll.) 7694

The WESTERN Farmers' Almanac for 1839. By Lyman Abbot, Jr. Auburn: Oliphant & Skinner; Oliphant & Skinner, printers. 12 ll. MWA; N; NN; NAuHi; NUtHi; OClWHi; CLU; MiD-B; OO; DLC. 7695

WOOD'S Almanac for 1839. By David Young. New York: Samuel S. & William Wood. 18 ll. DLC; NjR; OClWHi; MHi. 7696

YANKEE; or, Farmer's Almanac for 1839. By
Thomas Spofford. New-York: D. Felt & Co. 18 ll.
MoS. 7697

The AMERICAN Anti-Slavery Almanac for 1840. New
York: American Anti-Slavery Society. 24 ll. MWA; N;
NN; NHi; RNHi; NT; ICHi; NRMA; OClWHi; MBC;
OCHP; CoCC; InHi; InU; MdBJ; CLU; MSaE; NcD;
CtY; PPi; PPL; OHi; KyU; BritMus; Drake. 7698

The AMERICAN Anti-Slavery Almanac for 1840. New
York & Boston: American Anti-Slavery Society; J. A.
Collins. 24 ll. MWA; N; NjR; NSy; NSyU; CtHi;
MB; NRU; OMC; OO; MHi; OCl; ICHi; MdBJ; WHi;
Vt; ICU; Drake. 7699

The AMERICAN Pocket Almanac for 1840. New York:
Tanner & Disturnell. 42 ll. MWA; DLC. 7700

ASTRONOMICAL Diary for 1840. Pocket Almanac for
1840. By Thomas Spofford. New-York: David Felt &
Co. 16 ll. NHi. 7701

BLISS' Lansingburgh Almanac for 1840. Lansingburgh:
Luther Bliss; Troy: N. Tuttle, printer. 18 ll. MWA;
N; NHi (17 ll.) 7702

The CAROLINE Almanack, and American Freeman's
Chronicle for 1840. Rochester: Mackenzie's Gazette
Office. 60 ll. MWA; N; NHi; NBuHi (impf); VtU;
NRU; CLU; InU; PPAmP. 7703

-- Issue with 62 ll. MWA; MB; WHi. 7704

The CHRISTIAN Almanac, For New-York, Connecticut,
and New Jersey for 1840. [New York:] American
Tract Society. 24 ll. MWA; NN; NHi; PPL; CtY; IU;
WHi; CtW; InU; NjHi; NjMo. 7705

The CHRISTIAN Almanac, For New-York, Connecticut,
and New Jersey for 1840. New-York: J. C. Meeks.
24 ll. NCooHi; NRU. 7706

The CHURCHMAN'S Almanac for 1840. New-York:
Protestant Episcopal Press; John R. M'Gown. 18 ll.
MWA; NHi; NjR; NNG; PP; PPL; WHi; PHi; MB;
NcU; NcD. 7707

The CHURCHMAN'S Almanac for 1840. New-York:
Protestant Episcopal Press; John R. M'Gown. (Second
Edition) 18 ll. NNA. 7708

COMMON Almanac for 1840. Watertown: Knowlton &
Rice. 12 ll. MWA; NHi; DLC; Drake. 7709

CROCKETT'S Comic Almanack for 1840. Albany: A.
Skinflint [!]. 12 ll. MWA. 7710

DAY'S City and Country Almanac for 1840. By David
Young. New-York: Mahlon Day & Co. 18 ll. MWA.
 7711

DAY'S New-York Pocket Almanac for 1840. New-York:
M. Day & Co. 12 ll. NN. 7712

The DEMOCRAT'S Almanac, and Political Register for
1840. New York: Evening Post. 36 ll. MWA (two varieties); N; NN; NHi; WHi; VtHi; PP; PPL; PHi;
DLC; NBuG; NBuHi; MHi; MSaE; OClWHi; NSyOHi;
MB; OO; NCooHi; InU; InHi; CtY; CoCC; NjR; Drake
(two varieties) 7713

The DUTCHESS and Ulster Farmer's Almanac for 1840.
Poughkeepsie: George Nagell. 18 ll. NHi; CtW. 7714

The DUTCHESS County Farmer's Almanac for 1840.
Poughkeepsie: Potter & Wilson. 18 ll. NP. 7715

ELTON'S Comic All-my-nack for 1840. New York: 104
Nassau & 134 Division Sts. 18 ll. MWA; N; NHi; NIC;
NRMA; MB; NjR. 7716

The FARMER'S Almanac for 1840. By Thomas Spofford.
New-York: David Felt & Co. (For the Middle States)
18 ll. MWA; N; NHi; DLC; NR; NBuHi; OClWHi; WHi;
NCooHi; CtY (impf); PHi; NjR. 7717

New York - 1840

The FARMER'S Almanac for 1840. By Thomas Spofford. New-York: David Felt & Co., Stationers' Hall. (For the Middle States) 18 ll. NB.   7718

The FARMER'S Almanac for 1840. By Thomas Spofford. N.Y.: Robinson, Pratt & Co. (For the Middle States) 18 ll. NSyOHi; OClWHi.   7719

The FARMER'S Almanac for 1840. By Thomas Spofford. New-York: Charles Small. (For the Middle States) 18 ll. MWA; NBLiHi.   7720

The FARMER'S Almanac for 1840. By Thomas Spofford. New-York: [np] (For the Middle & Northern States) 18 ll. CRedl (17 ll.)   7721

The FARMER'S Almanac for 1840. By Thomas Spofford. Sag Harbor: O. O. Wickham & Co. (For Long Island) 18 ll. NN; NBLiHi; NRMA.   7722

The FARMER'S Almanac for 1840. By Thomas Spofford. Sag Harbor: O. O. Wickham & Co; New-York: David Felt & Co. (For Long Island) 18 ll. NRMA.   7723

The FARMER'S Almanac for 1840. By Thomas Spofford. Sag Harbor: O. O. Wickham & Co.; New-York: Robinson, Pratt & Co. (For Long Island) 18 ll. NRMA.   7724

FARMERS' Almanac for 1840. By David Young. New-York: Collins, Keese, & Co. 18 ll. MWA; NjP (17 ll.); NjHi; CtY.   7725

FARMERS' Almanac for 1840. By David Young. New-York: Mahlon Day & Co. 18 ll. MWA.   7726

FARMERS' Almanac for 1840. By David Young. New-York: Poinier, & Snell. 18 ll. WHi.   7727

FARMERS' Almanac for 1840. By David Young. New-York: H. & S. Raynor. 18 ll. MWA; NHi; NjR; NjHi; Drake.   7728

FARMER'S Diary, and Western Almanac for 1840.

New York - 1840

Canandaigua: C. Morse. 12 ll. NRU. 7729

The FRANKLIN Almanac, and Western New-York Calendar for 1840. Rochester: D. Hoyt. 12 ll. NR; NRHi; NRMA; NRU; NBuHi. 7730

GATES' Troy Almanac for 1840. Sandy Hill: G. Howland; Troy: N. Tuttle, printer. 18 ll. MWA; N; NHi; NIC; MH. 7731

GATES' Troy Almanac for 1840. Troy: Elias Gates; Tuttle & Belcher, printers. 18 ll. MWA; DLC; CLU; PHi (17 ll.); VtBennHi. 7732

GATES' Troy Almanac for 1840. Troy: Elias Gates; N. Tuttle, printer. 18 ll. NjR. 7733

GATES' Troy Almanac for 1840. Troy: N. Tuttle, printer. 18 ll. DLC; N. 7734

The HOUSEKEEPER'S Almanac, or the Young Wife's Oracle! for 1840. New-York: Elton. 18 ll. MWA; NHi; MB; MnU; NBuG; NjR (14 ll.) 7735

HUCHINS' Improved Almanac for 1840. By David Young. New York: R. H. Elton. 18 ll. MWA. 7736

HUTCHINGS' Improved Almanac, and Ephemeris for 1840. By David Young. New-York: H. & S. Raynor. 18 ll. MWA; NHi; NNA; NBLiHi (impf) 7737

HUTCHINGS' Revived Almanac for 1840. By David Young. New-York: H. & S. Raynor. 18 ll. NNSIHi (17 ll.) 7738

HUTCHIN'S Improved Almanac for 1840. By David Young. New-York: Mahlon Day & Co. 16 ll. N; NBLiHi. 7739

HUTCHINS' Improved Almanac for 1840. By David Young. New-York: R. H. Elton; Harrison, printer. 18 ll. DLC. 7740

HUTCHINS' Improved Almanac for 1840. By David Young. New-York: Poinier & Snell. 18 ll. MWA (17 ll.); MH. 7741

HUTCHINS' Improved Almanac for 1840. By David Young. New-York: Charles Small. 18 ll. NN. 7742

KNICKERBOCKER Almanac for 1840. By David Young. New-York: H. & S. Raynor. 18 ll. MWA; NN; NBLiHi (7 ll.) 7743

The METHODIST Almanac for 1840. Fitted to... Boston. By David Young. New-York: T. Mason and G. Lane, for the Methodist Episcopal Church; J. Collord, printer. 24 ll. Drake. 7744

The METHODIST Almanac for 1840. Fitted to... New-York. By David Young. New-York: T. Mason and G. Lane, For the Methodist Episcopal Church; J. Collord, printer. 24 ll. MWA; NIC; NjR; MiGr; OC; CtW; CtHi; MnU; OCHP; Drake. 7745

The METHODIST Almanac for 1840. Fitted to... Pittsburgh. By David Young. New-York: T. Mason and G. Lane, for the Methodist Episcopal Church; J. Collord, printer. 18 ll. NcD. 7746

MUTE'S Almanac for 1840. By Levi S. Backus. Canajoharie: L. S. Backus. 18 ll. MWA; NjR. 7747

NATIONAL Almanac, and Pocket Calendar for 1840. By J. W. Herschell. New-York: 100 Chatham Street; Cincinnati: S. C. Parkhurst; Louisville: 47 Wall Street. 18 ll. MWA; OO. 7748

PHINNEY'S Calendar, or Western Almanac for 1840. By George R. Perkins. Cooperstown: H. & E. Phinney. 18 ll. MWA; N; NN; NHi; NRMA; MiD-B; NCooHi; CLU; MBC (impf); NBuHi; WHi; Ct; FSpHi; InU; NUtHi; DLC; NSyOHi (17 ll.); NR; NIC; Drake.
7749

PHRENOLOGICAL Almanac for 1840. By L. N. Fowler. New-York Phrenological Rooms. 24 ll. MWA; N;

New York - 1840

NHi; ICN; WHi; CtW; CLU.   7750

POCKET Almanack for 1840. By Thomas Spofford. New York: David Felt & Co. 16 ll. MWA.   7751

The POLITICIAN'S Register for 1840. New York: H. Greeley. 18 ll. IC; In; LNHT; OFH; ICHi; NBuG; InU; WvU.   7752

The POLITICIAN'S Register for 1840. New York: H. Greeley. (Fifth Edition) 18 ll. CtHT-W; CtY.   7753

POOR Richard's Cent Almanac for 1840. New York: Elton. MWA (6 ll.)   7754

SAM Slick Comic All-my-nack for 1840. New-York: 104 Nassau & 134 Division Sts. 12 ll. MWA; N; DLC; MH; MWiW.   7755

SAM Slick Comic All-my-nack for 1840. New-York: Elton. 12 ll. WHi.   7756

STEELE'S Albany Almanac for 1840. Albany: Packard, Van Benthuysen and Co. 18 ll. MWA; NHi; NNC; OMC.   7757

SWORDS'S Pocket Almanack, Churchman's Calendar for 1840. New-York: Swords, Stanford, and Co. 48 ll. MWA; N; NHi; NjR; NNG; PP; PPL; PHi; NNS; MHi; WHi; BritMus.   7758

TEMPERANCE Almanac for 1840. By G. R. Perkins. Albany: Packard, Van Benthuysen and Co. 18 ll. MWA; N.   7759

TEMPERANCE Almanac for 1840. By G. R. Perkins. Albany: Packard, Van Benthuysen and Co. (Second Edition) 18 ll. MWA; N; NN; NHi; NCooHi (ntp); NRMA; F; PDoBHi (16 ll.); MBC; WHi; MiD-B; RNHi; NSyOHi; NRU; NBLiHi; MH; MnU; MHi; NB; OClWHi; Drake.   7760

TROY Almanac for 1840. Troy: Z. Clark; Tuttle &

Belcher, printers. 18 ll. MWA; N; NT; NjR. 7761

TROY Almanac for 1840. Troy: Robert Wasson; Tuttle & Belcher, printers. 18 ll. MWA; N; NHi; NR. 7762

TURNER'S Comick Almanack for 1840. New-York: Turner & Fisher; [and Philadelphia] 18 ll. MWA; N (impf); DLC; NBuG; PHi; OClWHi; InU; NjR; MBAt.
7763

The UNITED States' Almanac for 1840. New York: Collins, Keese, & Co.; Phil.: R. P. Desilver. 36 ll. MWA; NHi; NIC; NBuHi; MnU; PPL; NjR. 7764

UNITED States Thomsonian Almanac for 1840. Poughkeepsie: Lapham & Platt; Killey & Lossing, printers. 18 ll. MWA (impf); N; NHi (impf); DLC; NRU; F; CtNhHi; NjP; InU; CtB. 7765

UNIVERSALIST Register and Almanac for 1840. Utica: Grosh & Hutchinson; New-York: P. Price [etc]; C. C. P. Grosh, printer. 18 ll. MWA; N; NCanHi; MH; NCooHi; CLU; NRU; InU; NRMA; BritMus. 7766

WEBSTER'S Calendar: or, the Albany Almanack for 1840. By Edwin E. Prentiss. Albany: E. W. & C. Skinner. 18 ll. MWA; N; NN; PHi; CLU; MiU-C; MnU; WHi; Drake. 7767

WEBSTER'S Calendar: or, the Albany Almanack for 1840. By Edwin E. Prentiss. Albany: E. W. & C. Skinner. (Second Edition) 18 ll. MWA; N; NN; NHi; CtNhHi; MB; NT; DLC; NbO; NRMA; Drake. 7768

WESTERN Almanack for 1840. Ithaca: Mack, Andrus, & Woodruff. 12 ll. MWA; DLC; NIC; WHi (6 ll.)
7769
WESTERN Almanac for 1840. Rochester: William Alling. 12 ll. NRMA; NRU. 7770

The WESTERN Almanac for 1840. By David Young. New York: Collins, Keese & Co. 18 ll. DLC; NjR.
7771

The WESTERN Farmers' Almanac for 1840. Auburn: Oliphant & Skinner. 12 ll. MWA (11 ll.); N; NCH; WHi. 7772

The AMERICAN Anti-Slavery Almanac for 1841. New York: S. W. Benedict. 18 ll. MWA; N; MBAt; MBC; CoCC; CtB (impf); CtHi; KyU; BritMus. 7773

The AMERICAN Protestant Almanac for 1841. New York: Moses W. Dodd. 16 ll. NN. 7774

BLISS' Lansingburgh Almanac for 1841. Lansingburgh: Luther Bliss. 18 ll. MWA. 7775

BROWNE'S Banking and Mercantile Table and Counting-House Almanack, for 126 years, 1794-1920. New York: [np] 1841. Broadside. [Sabin] 7776

The CHURCH Almanac for 1841. New-York: Protestant Episcopal Tract Society. 18 ll. MWA; N; NHi; NCanHi; MiD-B; PHi; PPL; PP; CtY; NNA; NNG; CtW; OClWHi; MB; Ct; MHi; MSaE; NjR; NcU; PPAmP; NSyOHi; DLC; NcD; IU; WHi. 7777

CLARK'S Troy Almanac for 1841. Troy: Z. Clark. 18 ll. MWA (ntp); NjR (16 ll.); NT; CtLHi. 7778

COMMON Almanac for 1841. By George R. Perkins. Watertown: Knowlton & Rice. 18 ll. NHi (16 ll.); DLC. 7779

CROCKETT Almanac for 1841. New York: Turner & Fisher. [Dorson] 7780

CROCKETT'S Harrison Almanac for 1841. New-York: Elton; Vincent L. Dill. 12 ll. MWA; N; CtY; MoSM. 7781

DAY'S New-York Pocket Almanac for 1841. New York: M. Day, & Co. 12 ll. MWA. 7782

The DEMOCRAT'S Almanac, and Political Register for 1841. New York: Evening Post. 24 ll. MWA; N; NN; NHi; NBuHi; NIC; CtHi; NjR; NjP; RPB; WHi; DLC;

Drake. 7783

The DEMOCRAT'S Almanac, and Political Register for 1841. New York: Evening Post. (Second Edition) 18 ll. MWA; N; NBLiHi; NSy; NSyOHi. 7784

DUDLEY'S Almanac for 1841. Buffalo: T. J. Dudley. [Severance] 7785

DUTCHESS and Ulster Farmer's Almanac for 1841. Poughkeepsie: George Nagell. CtW (16 ll.) 7786

ELTON'S Comic All my nack for 1841. New-York: Book-sellers. 18 ll. MWA; DLC; PHi (17 ll.); MB; MBAt; NSyOHi; InU; WHi. 7787

ELTON'S Comic Sheet Almanac for 1841. New York: Elton. Broadside. Advertised in "Elton's Comic All my nack" for 1841. 7788

The FAMILY Christian Almanac for the United States for 1841. By David Young. New-York: American Tract Society. 18 ll. MWA; N (two varieties); NN; PPPrHi; GDC; MH; CLU; MHi; NjP; RPB; NSchU; MnU; Ct; MBC; CtHi; OMC; WHi; InU; MS; ICU; OClWHi; RNHi; CtW; CtY; NjR; PHi; MB; MBAt; NBLiHi (17 ll.); MdBE; BritMus. 7789

The FAMILY Christian Almanac for the United States for 1841. New York: American Tract Society; M. W. Dodd; D. Fanshaw, printer. 18 ll. NHi. 7790

The FARMER'S Almanac for 1841. Sag Harbor. [NN imprint catalog] 7791

The FARMER'S Almanac for 1841. By Thomas Spofford. New-York: David Felt & Co. 18 ll. MWA; NN; NBLiHi; InU; Drake. 7792

The FARMER'S Almanac for 1841. By Thomas Spofford. New-York: David Felt & Co. Stationers' Hall. 18 ll. MWA (two varieties); NSyOHi; NB; OClWHi; PHi; MnM (17 ll.); CtHi; IU; MBC; NjR. 7793

The **FARMER'S** Almanac for 1841. By Thomas Spofford. New-York: Robinson, Pratt & Co. 18 ll. MWA; N; NBuHi; NR (12 ll.)   7794

The **FARMER'S** Almanac for 1841. By Zadock Thompson. Whitehall: D. S. Wright. 12 ll. VtU.   7795

FARMER'S Almanac for 1841. By David Young. New York: Collins, Keese, & Co. 18 ll. MWA; Ct (impf); CtY.   7796

FARMERS' Almanac for 1841. By David Young. New-York: Poinier & Snell. 18 ll. MWA (impf); NN; NNSIHi.   7797

FARMERS' Almanac for 1841. By David Young. New-York: H. & S. Raynor. 18 ll. NWhpHi.   7798

FARMER'S Almanac for 1841. By David Young. New-York: H. & S. Raynor; O. Longworth. 18 ll. MWA; MB (17 ll.); NjMoW.   7799

FARMER'S Almanac for 1841. By David Young. New-York: Robinson, Pratt & Co. 18 ll. NRMA.   7800

The **FARMER'S** Diary, and Western Almanac for 1841. Canandaigua: J. D. Bemis & Son. 12 ll. NRMA; Drake.   7801

FISHER'S Comic Almanac for 1841. New York and Philadelphia: Turner & Fisher. 12 ll. ICN.   7802

The **FRANKLIN** Almanac [for 1841]. New-York: J. Pease & Son; P. Donaldson & Co., printers. 12 ll. MWA; PPL; PPAmP; PHi; ICU.   7803

The **FRANKLIN** Almanac, and Western New-York Calendar for 1841. Rochester: D. Hoyt. 12 ll. NRU.   7804

GATES' Troy Almanac for 1841. Troy: Elias Gates. 18 ll. MWA (17 ll.); N; NHi; InU; PHi; CLU.   7805

HARD Cider and Log Cabin Almanac for 1841. New

York: Turner & Fisher; [and Philadelphia]. 12 ll.
MWA; N; NHi; DLC; MBAt; PPL; NjJ; Drake. 7806

-- Head of cover-title: "Hurrah for old Tippecanoe."
Title on wrappers only; latter printed on one side only.
12 ll. NHi; InHi. 7807

The HARRISON Almanac for 1841. New-York: J. P.
Giffing. 18 ll. MWA (two varieties); NN; NHi; MB;
MoSM; NRU; PHi; CLU; NBLiHi; ICN; MHi; CtLHi;
MBAt; DLC; NCanHi; RNR; NUtHi; OMC; OC; OCHP;
NUt; NRMA; NCooHi (15 ll.); ICHi; InU; MNF; PP;
WHi; Ct; KyU; IU; IHi; O; NSyOHi; CtY; InHi (two
varieties); Drake. 7808

-- Improved Edition. 18 ll. MWA (two varieties); N
(two varieties); NHi; PHi; OClWHi; NBuHi; NBLiHi;
MoSHi; Ct; CtNhHi; NjR; NCooHi; InU; NSyOHi; (14
ll.); MeHi; InHi; MB; NRU; NcD; WHi; Drake. 7809

HUTCHIN'S Improved Almanac for 1841. By David
Young. New-York: Mahlon Day & Co. 18 ll. Drake.
7810
HUTCHINS' Improved Almanac for 1841. By David
Young. New York: Poinier & Snell. 18 ll. MH. 7811

HUTCHINS' Improved Almanac for 1841. By David
Young. New-York: H. & S. Raynor. 18 ll. MWA; N;
NP; NjMo; NjMoW; NjHi; MB; WHi. 7812

HUTCHINS' Improved Almanac for 1841. By David
Young. New-York: Charles Small. 18 ll. MWA; NHi.
7813
HUTCHINS' Improved Almanac, and Ephemeris for 1841.
By David Young. New-York: H. & S. Raynor. 18 ll.
MWA; NBLiHi; NSchU; CtHi; NjR; Pennypacker. 7814

HUTCHINS' Improved and [sic] Almanac, Ephemeris for
1841. By David Young. New-York: H. & S. Raynor.
18 ll. N. 7815

HUTCHINS' Improved Almanac, and Ephemeris for 1841.
By David Young. New-York: H. & S. Raynor; O. Long-

worth. 18 ll. MWA; NjR. 7816

HUTCHINS' Improved Almanac, and Ephemeris for 1841. By David Young. Poughkeepsie: William Wilson. 18 ll. NHi; NP. 7817

The MASONIC Register [for 1841]. New-York: Samuel Maverick, and William W. Nexsen. 28 ll. NNFM. 7818

The METHODIST Almanac for 1841. By David Young. New-York: T. Mason and G. Lane, For the Methodist Episcopal Church; J. Collord, printer. 18 ll. Ct; NcD. 7819

-- Issue with 24 ll. MWA; NBuHi; CtW; ICHi; WHi; TxAbH; NjR; Drake. 7820

The NEW-ENGLAND and Long Island Almanac, and Farmers' Friend for 1841. By Nathan Daboll. Sag Harbor: O. O. Wickham. 16 ll. MWA; NB; NJQ (15 ll.) 7821

NEW-YORK Almanac for 1841. By David Young. New-York: H. & S. Raynor. 18 ll. NHi; NjJ. 7822

NEW-YORK State Pocket Almanac for 1841. Auburn: Oliphant & Skinner. 12 ll. NN. 7823

PHINNEY'S Calendar, or Western Almanac for 1841. By George R. Perkins. Cooperstown: H. & E. Phinney. 18 ll. MWA; N; NN; NHi; DLC; MnU; NIC; NSyOHi; NCooHi; CLU; NBuHi (17 ll.); NUtHi; WHi; MBC (impf); CtY; InU; MiD-B; NRMA; ICU. 7824

The PHRENOLOGICAL Almanac for 1841. By L. N. Fowler. New-York: 135 Nassau-Street, and No. 60 Fulton-street; Philadelphia: No. 210 Spruce-street; Boston: Mr. Bartlett; W. J. Spence, printer. 24 ll. MWA (impf); N; PP; PHi; CtHi; CtW; OClWHi. 7825

POCKET Almanac for 1841. New-York: Robinson, Pratt & Co. Advertised in the "Farmer's Almanac" for 1841.

The POLITICIAN'S Register for 1841. New York: H. Greeley. 16 ll. IC; In; LNHT; OFH; ICHi; NBuG; InU; WvU.   7826

The POLITICIAN'S Register for 1841. New York: H. Greeley. (Sixth Edition) 16 ll. CtY.   7827

PRYNNE'S Almanac for 1841. By Arthur Prynne. Albany: Erastus H. Pease; J. Munsell, printer. 12 ll. MWA; N; NHi; DLC; NjR; NjHi; MHi; PHi; NCooHi; CLU; MnU; OMC; WHi; BritMus.   7828

STEELE'S Albany Almanac for 1841. Albany: C. Van Benthuysen. 18 ll. MWA; NCooHi.   7829

-- Issue with 22 ll. N; NHi; MnU; NSchU; NR.   7830

STEELE'S Almanack for 1841. By Geo. R. Perkins. Buffalo: W. B. & C. E. Peck; Steele's Press. 12 ll. N; NRU.   7831

SWORDS'S Pocket Almanack, Churchman's Calendar for 1841. New-York: Swords, Stanford, and Co. 48 ll. N; NNG; NNS; PHi; MHi; PPL; NHi; BritMus.   7832

TEMPERANCE Almanac for 1841. By G. R. Perkins. Albany: C. Van Benthuysen. 18 ll. MWA; N; NN; NNUT (16 ll.); PPL; MB; CLU; MBC; NjR; NRU; MnU; VtBennHi; Drake.   7833

TEMPERANCE Almanac for 1841. By G. R. Perkins. Albany: C. Van Benthuysen; New-York: Taylor & Clements. 18 ll. MWA; NjR; MH; CtY; WHi.   7834

TEMPERANCE Almanac for 1841. By G. R. Perkins. Albany: C. Van Benthuysen; Utica: G. Tracy's. 18 ll. N.   7835

The TIPPECANOE and Log Cabin Almanac for 1841. New York: H. A. Chapin & Co. 24 ll. MWA; NHi; DLC; InHi; PHi; NBLiHi; MB; NBuHi; O.   7836

The UNIVERSALIST Companion, with an Almanac, and

Register for 1841. By A. B. Grosh. Utica: Orren
Hutchinson; New-York: P. Price; Boston: A. Tompkins; T. Whittemore; C. C. P. Grosh; printer. 36 ll.
MWA; N; NHi; NBuG; CtHi; WHi; OClWHi; CLU;
NRMA. 7837

WEBSTER'S Calendar: or the Albany Almanack for
1841. By Edwin E. Prentiss. Albany: E. W. & C.
Skinner. 18 ll. MWA; N; NN; NHi; DLC; NSchU;
NT; PHi; MiU-C; InU; WHi; CtLHi; Drake. 7838

WEBSTER'S Calendar. Howland's Albany Almanac for
1841. Sandy Hill: G. & E. Howland. 12 ll. MWA;
InU (5 ll.) 7839

The WESTERN Almanac, and New-York Farmers' Calendar for 1841. Ithaca: Mack, Andrus, & Woodruff.
12 ll. MWA; NHi. 7840

The WESTERN Almanack, and New-York Farmers' Calendar for 1841. Rochester: William Alling. 12 ll.
MWA; NRMA (11 ll.); NRU; ICHi. 7841

The WESTERN Almanack, and New-York Farmers' Calendar for 1841. Rochester: Printed and Sold, at
wholesale and retail by William Alling. 12 ll. NR;
NRMA; NRU. 7842

-- Issue with 16 ll. MWA. 7843

The WESTERN Almanac, and New-York Farmers' Calendar for 1841. Rochester: H. Stanwood & Co. 12 ll.
N; NRU. 7844

WESTERN Farmers' Almanac for 1841. Auburn: Oliphant & Skinner. 16 ll. MWA; ICHi; F; CtY; InU.
7845

ALMANAC of the American Temperance Union for 1842.
New-York: American Temperance Union. 18 ll. MWA;
N; NHi; WHi; NRMA; NBLiHi; CtHi; CLU; Ct; CtW;
MH; NjJ; InU; OC; NNC; OClWHi; O; Drake. 7846

ALMANACH Franco-Americain pour 1842. New York:

Casserly & Sons. 16 ll. DLC. 7847

The AMERICAN Anti-Slavery Almanac for 1842. New York: S. W. Benedict. 18 ll. MWA; N; NHi; MB; MBAt; MBC; NSyU; Ct; MSaE; MHi; NRU; MnU; CtW; CtY; CtHi; CtNhHi; Mi; CoCC; OClWHi; OO; OMC; M; WHi; NRMA; BritMus; Drake. 7848

ANTI-MORMON Almanac for 1842. New-York: Health Book Store. 12 ll. MWA; NHi; DLC (impf); CtNhHi; CtY; CU-B (11 ll.) 7849

BEN Hardin's Crockett Almanac for 1842. New York: Turner & Fisher [and Philadelphia]. 18 ll. MWA; N; DLC; CtY. 7850

BLISS' Lansingburgh Almanac for 1842. Lansingburgh: Luther Bliss; N. Tuttle, printer. 18 ll. MWA; MnU. 7851

The CATSKILL Almanac for 1842. By David Young. Catskill: Austin & Doane. 12 ll. MWA. 7852

The CHURCH Almanac for 1842. New-York: Protestant Episcopal Tract Society. 18 ll. MWA; N; NHi; NNA; NNG; DLC; NcD; PP; NjR; MB; MBAt; CtW; NRHi; NSyOHi; PPL; NcU; NR; IU; Ct; WHi; OCHP; MiD-B; BritMus. 7853

The CHURCH Almanac for 1842. New-York: Protestant Episcopal Tract Society. (Second Edition) 18 ll. N. 7854

COMMON Almanac for 1842. By George R. Perkins. Watertown: Knowlton & Rice. 18 ll. MWA; DLC; InU. 7855

The COMMON School Almanac for 1842. By J. Orville Taylor. New York: Clement and Packard. 36 ll. MWA; MBU; MB; MH; RNHi; IU; CtY; PHi; CoCC; TxDN; OU; MiD-B. 7856

CROCKETT Comic Almanac for 1842. [New York:] Gotham: Published by Doleful Serious, and sold at 98 Nassau, and 18 Division Streets. 12 ll. NN; DLC;

TxU. 7857

DAY'S City and Country Almanac for 1842. By David
Young. New York: Mahlon Day & Co. and Baker,
Crane & Co. 18 ll. NBLiHi;CtB; Drake. 7858

DAY'S New York Pocket Almanac for 1842. [Wall]
7859
The DEMOCRAT'S Almanac and Political Register for
1842. New-York: Evening Post; Boston: E. Littlefield. 24 ll. MWA; DLC. 7860

The DEMOCRAT'S Almanac, and Political Register for
1842. New York: Evening Post; Boston: E. Littlefield. (Second Edition) 24 ll. PPL. 7861

The DEMOCRAT'S Almanac, and Political Register for
1842. New York: Evening Post; Boston: E. Littlefield. (Third Edition) 24 ll. MWA; N; NBLiHi; NBuHi;
DLC; NjR; WHi. 7862

DUDLEY'S Almanac for 1842. Buffalo: T. J. Dudley.
[Severance] 7863

The DUTCHESS and Ulster County Farmers' Almanac
for 1842. By David Young. Poughkeepsie: William Wilson. 18 ll. NP. 7864

DUTCHESS & Ulster Farmers' Almanac for 1842.
Poughkeepsie: George Nagell. 18 ll. MWA. 7865

ELTON'S Comic All-My-Nack for 1842. New York:
Elton; Vincent L. Dill. 18 ll. MWA (two varieties);
N; NN; MB; NBLiHi; NBuG; MBAt; DLC; InU; MWiW;
WHi; Drake (17 ll.) 7866

The FAMILY Almanac for 1842. By David Young.
New-York: 126 Fulton Street. 12 ll. MWA; NHi;
OClWHi; NjHi; CtB (11 ll.); CtLHi; Drake. 7867

The FAMILY Christian Almanac for the United States
for 1842. By David Young. New York: American Tract
Society. 18 ll. MWA; N; NN; NHi; OClWHi; NBuHi;

NBLiHi; MHi; CtY; CtW; RWe; CtNhHi; RNHi; NjHi;
GDC; RPB; CLU; NRU; MB; F; MH; Ct; MBC;
NRMA; NT; MiD-B; KHi; CtHi; ICHi (impf); NjMo;
WHi; MnU; OMC; InU; CRedl; PPPrHi; Drake (two
varieties)   7868

-- Philadelphia imprint on cover. 18 ll. PHi.   7869

The FARMERS' Almanac for 1842. By Thomas Spofford. Hudson: P. S. & R. G. Wynkoop. 18 ll. N. 7870

The FARMERS' Almanac for 1842. By Thomas Spofford. New-York: Baker, Crane & Co. 18 ll. N; NN;
NB; NjR; MB.   7871

The FARMERS' Almanac for 1842. By Thomas Spofford. New-York: Clement & Packard. 18 ll. MWA;
N; NR.   7872

The FARMERS' Almanac for 1842. By Thomas Spofford. New-York: David Felt & Co. 18 ll. MWA; N;
NHi; OClWHi; NRU; MnU; NT; CtLHi; Drake. 7873

The FARMERS' Almanac for 1842. By Thomas Spofford. New-York: F. J. Huntington & Co. 18 ll. ICU.
   7874

The FARMERS' Almanac for 1842. By Thomas Spofford. New-York: Charles Small. 18 ll. MWA (16 ll.);
NBLiHi; DLC; CtY.   7875

The FARMERS' Almanac for 1842. By Thomas Spofford. Sag-Harbor: O. O. Wickham. 18 ll. MWA;
CtNhHi.   7876

The FARMER'S Almanac for 1842. By Zadock Thompson. Plattsburgh: Vilas & Edsall. 12 ll. MWA. 7877

The FARMER'S Almanac [for 1842]. By David Young.
New York: Collins, Keese, & Co. 18 ll. MWA; N;
NHi; InU; NCooHi; CtY; CtNhHi; NRU.   7878

FARMERS' Almanac for 1842. By David Young. New-York: H. S. Raynor. 18 ll. NjR (16 ll.)   7879

The FARMER'S Almanac [for 1842]. By David Young.
New-York: H. & S. Raynor. 18 ll. MWA; WHi. 7880

The FARMER'S Almanac [for 1842]. By David Young.
Rochester: G. W. Fisher & Co. 18 ll. NHi; NRHi (17
ll.); NRMA; NRU. 7881

The FARMER'S Almanack, and Ephemeris for 1842.
By David Young. Ithaca: Mack, Andrus, & Woodruff.
18 ll. MWA; N; NHi; NIC; MB; OMC (16 ll.) 7882

The FARMER'S Diary and Western Almanac for 1842.
Bath: R. L. Underhill & Co. 12 ll. N; NHi. 7883

The FARMER'S Diary and Western Almanac for 1842.
Canandaigua: J. D. Bemis & Son. 12 ll. DLC; NCanHi;
NR; NRHi. 7884

The FRANKLIN Almanac, and New-York Farmers'
Calendar for 1842. Lockport: N. Leonard. 12 ll.
NjR. 7885

The FRANKLIN Almanac, and New-York Farmers' Calendar for 1842. Rochester: William Alling. 12 ll.
NBuHi; NRMA. 7886

The FRANKLIN Almanac, and Western New-York Calendar for 1842. Rochester: David Hoyt. 12 ll. NR;
NRU. 7887

The FRANKLIN Almanac, and Western New-York Calendar for 1842. Rochester: Clarendon Morse. 12 ll.
NR; NRMA; NRU. 7888

The FRANKLIN Almanac, and Western New-York Calendar for 1842. Rochester: H. Stanwood & Co. 12 ll.
MWA; N; DLC; CLU; WHi. 7889

GATES' Troy Almanac for 1842. Troy: Elias Gates;
N. Tuttle, printer. 18 ll. MWA; N; NHi; CLU; CtY;
NBuG; NT; PHi; NjR; OClWHi. 7890

The GENESEE Almanac and New-York Farmers' Calen-

dar for 1842. Batavia: William Seaver & Son. 12 ll.
NHi. 7891

The HEALTH Almanac for 1842. New-York: The
Health Depository. 24 ll. MWA; N; DLC; MB; MBC;
MSaE; NRHi; NBuG; OMC; CtHi; WHi. 7892

The HEALTH Almanac and Guide to Invalids for 1842.
By Samuel Sheldon Fitch. New York: The Health Depository. 24 ll. OClWHi. 7893

The HOUSE-KEEPER'S Almanac, or the Young Wife's
Oracle for 1842. New-York: Elton. 18 ll. MWA; N;
NHi; NIC; DLC; NjR. 7894

HUTCHING'S (Revived) Almanac for 1842. By David
Young. New-York: H. & S. Raynor. 16 ll. OMC. 7895

HUTCHINS' Improved Almanac for 1842. New-York:
Mahlon Day & Co. 18 ll. Private collection. 7896

HUTCHINS' Improved Almanac for 1842. By David
Young. New-York: Elton's Almanac Emporium. 12 ll.
MWA; MB; NjMoW. 7897

HUTCHINS' Improved Almanac for 1842. By David
Young. New York: Poinier & Snell. 18 ll. MH. 7898

HUTCHIN'S Improved Almanac for 1842. By David
Young. New York: Charles Small. 18 ll. MWA. 7899

HUTCHINS' Improved Almanac, and Ephemeris for
1842. By David Young. New-York: Elton's Almanac
Emporium. 12 ll. N; NBLiHi. 7900

HUTCHINS' Improved Almanac, and Ephemeris for 1842.
By David Young. New-York: H. & S. Raynor. 18 ll.
MWA; NHi; NT; DLC; CtY; NjR (16 ll.); Drake. 7901

HUTCHINS' Improved Almanac, and Ephemeris for 1842.
By David Young. New-York: H. & S. Raynor; A. & E.
Embree. 18 ll. WHi. 7902

HUTCHINS' Improved Almanac, and Ephemeris for 1842. By David Young. New-York: H. & S. Raynor; Newburgh: Odell S. Hathaway. 18 ll. N.   7903

HUTCHINS' Improved Almanac, and Ephemeris for 1842. By David Young. Poughkeepsie: William Wilson. 18 ll. NHi.   7904

HUTCHINS' Revived Almanac for 1842. By David Young. New-York: H. & S. Raynor. 18 ll. NWhpHi.   7905

KNICKERBOCKER Almanac for 1842. By David Young. New-York: Mahlon Day & Co. 18 ll. MWA; NHi; Ct.   7906

KNICKERBOCKER Almanac for 1842. By David Young. New-York: Elton's Almanac Emporium. 12 ll. MWA; N; CtHi.   7907

The KOMICAL Komic All-I-Make for 1842. [New York:] Gotham: Published by Doleful Serious, and sold at 98 Nassau and 18 Division Streets. MWA (11 ll.)   7908

The LADY'S Annual Register and Housewife's Almanac for 1842. New-York: Samuel Colman. 54 ll. OMC.   7909

MEGAREY'S Nautical Almanac and Astronomical Ephemeris for 1842. New York: Alexander Megarey. 64 ll. OMC.   7910

The METHODIST Almanac for 1842. By David Young. New York: G. Lane, For the Methodist Episcopal Church; J. Collord, printer. (Nashville edition) 24 ll. T.   7911

The METHODIST Almanac for 1842. By David Young. New-York: G. Lane, For the Methodist Episcopal Church; J. Collord, printer. (New York edition) 24 ll. MWA; NjR; MiGr; CtW; NBuG.   7912

The METHODIST Almanac for 1842. By David Young. New York: G. Lane, For the Methodist Episcopal Church; J. Collord, printer. (Rochester edition) 24 ll. NCooHi.   7913

NEW American Comic Almanac for 1842. [New York:]
Gotham: Doleful Serious. NN (12 ll.) 7914

The NEW Comic Almanack for 1842. New-York: S.
Colman. 16 ll. MWA; IU; OClWHi. 7915

The NEW-ENGLAND and Long-Island Almanac, and
Farmers' Friend for 1842. By Nathan Daboll. Sag-
Harbor: O. O. Wickham. 16 ll. MWA; NB; NJQ;
CtHi. 7916

The NEW-YORK City Calendar for 1842. By Edwin
Williams. New-York: Van Norden & King. 36 ll. NHi;
NNC. 7917

PARKER'S Medical Almanac for 1842. Fayetteville:
William Parker, Jr. 16 ll. WHi (impf) 7918

PARKER'S Medical Almanac for 1842. Fayetteville:
Parker & Hall; Methodist Reformer. 16 ll. N (15 ll.)
7919

PHINNEY'S Calendar, or Western Almanac for 1842.
By George R. Perkins. Cooperstown: H. & E. Phinney.
18 ll. MWA; N; NHi; IChi; WHi; NRMA; Ct (ntp);
NSyOHi; MBNEH; NCooHi; MBC (ntp); DLC; NBuHi;
NIC; NUtHi; NN; CtY; NSy; InU; MH; Drake. 7920

The PHRENOLOGICAL Almanac for 1842. By L. N.
Fowler. New-York: 135 Nassau Street and 126 Fulton
Street; [also Boston and Philadelphia]; Vincent L. Dill,
printer. 24 ll. MWA; N; NHi; InU; OClWHi; CtW;
CtHi; NjHi; CLU; DLC; IU; NRU; WHi; MiD-B; Drake.
7921

SAM Slick's Comic All-my-nack for 1842. New-York:
Elton. [The "n" in "Elton" is a reversed letter.] 12 ll.
Private collection. 7922

STEELE'S Albany Almanac for 1842. Albany: C. Van
Benthuysen. 18 ll. MWA; N; NN; NHi; NCooHi (17
ll.); MnU; NR; Pennypacker, Drake. 7923

STEELE'S Almanack for 1842. By Geo. R. Perkins.

New York - 1842

Buffalo: Edward Butler; Steele's Press. 12 ll.
OClWHi. 7924

STEELE'S Almanack for 1842. Fredonia: Winter &
Millet; Buffalo: Steele's Press. NHi (6 ll.) 7925

SWORDS'S Pocket Almanack, Churchman's Calendar for
1842. New-York: Swords, Stanford, and Co. 78 ll.
MWA; N; NHi; NNS; NNG; NjR; PHi; PPL; BritMus.
7926

TEMPERANCE Almanac for 1842. Albany: C. Van
Benthuysen. 18 ll. MWA; NN; NSchU; NUtHi; NHC
(12 ll.); MB. 7927

TEMPERANCE Almanac for 1842. Albany: C. Van
Benthuysen. (Fourth Edition) 18 ll. N; OMC; ViU.
7928

TOBACCO and Health Almanac for 1842. By John
Burdell. New York: Fowlers & Wells. Ct (9 ll.) 7929

The UNITED States Fuel Almanac for 1842. By Almond D. Fisk. New York: S. W. Benedict. 18 ll.
MWA. 7930

The UNIVERSALIST Companion, with an Almanac and
Register for 1842. By A. B. Grosh. Utica: O. Hutchinson; New York: P. Price; Grosh & Walker, printers.
32 ll. MWA; N; NHi; OClWHi; CLU; InU. 7931

WEBSTER'S Calendar: or the Albany Almanack for
1842. By Edwin E. Prentiss. Albany: E. W. & C.
Skinner. 18 ll. MWA; N; NN; NHi; DLC; PHi; NbO;
MoU; MB; MnU; InU; WHi; NRMA; Drake. 7932

WEBSTER'S Calendar - Howland's Albany Almanac for
1842. Sandy-Hill: G. & E. Howland. 12 ll. MWA;
PHi; InU. 7933

WESTERN Farmers' Almanac for 1842. By George R.
Perkins. Auburn: Henry Oliphant. 16 ll. MWA; N;
NN; NAuHi; NSyOHi; MiD-B. 7934

WILGUS' Farmers' Almanack for 1842. By George R.

Perkins. Buffalo: A. W. Wilgus. 12 ll. MWA. 7935

The YANKEE Farmers' Almanac for 1842. By Thomas
Spofford. New-York: David Felt & Co. 18 ll. NHi;
PHi. 7936

Z. CLARK'S Troy Almanac for 1842. Troy: Z. Clark;
N. Tuttle, printer. 18 ll. DLC. 7937

ALMANAC of the American Temperance Union for
1843. New-York: Office of the Am. Temperance
Union, Clinton Hall. 18 ll. MWA; N; NHi; InU; WHi;
MSaE; CtLHi; Ct; MBC; NjJ; NjR; NBLiHi; PPL.
7938
The AMERICAN Anti-Slavery Almanac for 1843. By
L. M. Child. New-York: American Anti-Slavery Socie-
ty; Samuel B. Eastman, printer. 24 ll. MWA (two va-
rieties); N; NN; NHi; CtHi; NCanHi; KyU; OClWHi;
OMC; InU; MSaE; WHi; ICU; OCHP; MBC; CLU;
PDoBHi; NjR; NSyU; MHi; NcD; Ct; CtY; BritMus.
7939
The AMERICAN Farmers' Almanack for 1843. New
York and Philadelphia: Turner & Fisher. 18 ll. PAnL
(16 ll.); PYHi. 7940

The ASTRO-MAGNETIC Almanac for 1843. Calculated
for Boston. By H. H. Sherwood [and] David Young.
New York: 138 Fulton St. 36 ll. N; NjR. 7941

The ASTRO-MAGENTIC Almanac for 1843. Calculated
for Montreal. By H. H. Sherwood [and] David Young.
New York: 138 Fulton St. 36 ll. MWA; WHi. 7942

The ASTRO-MAGNETIC Almanac for 1843. Calculated
for New York City. By H. H. Sherwood [and] David
Young. New York: 138 Fulton St. 36 ll. MWA (two
varieties); N; NHi; NSyOHi; OClWHi; MB; CLU;
CtHi; InU; CtLHi; PPL. 7943

BLISS' Lansingburgh Almanac for 1843. Lansingburgh:
Luther Bliss; N. Tuttle, printer. 18 ll. MWA. 7944

BLUE Beards Comic Almanac for 1843. New York:

Elton. 12 ll. MWA (impf); O. 7945

CAROLINA and Georgia Almanac for 1843. By Robert Grier. New York: Collins, Brother & Co. 18 ll. NcD. 7946

The CHURCH Almanac for 1843. New-York: Protestant Episcopal Tract Society; A. G. Powell, printer. 18 ll. MWA; N; NHi; DLC; NBLiHi; NcD; NcU; CtW; PPAmP; MiD-B; NNG; NNA; MHi; NjR; OClWHi; MB; PPL; WHi; BritMus. 7947

COLUMBIA Almanac for 1843. Hudson: S. Wardwell. 18 ll. MWA. 7948

COMMON School Almanac for 1843. By J. Orville Taylor. New-York: Clement & Packard. 18 ll. NN; NjR; CtHi; CtY; CLU; RNHi; MH. 7949

COMMON School Almanac for 1843. By J. Orville Taylor. New-York: Saxton & Miles. 18 ll. MWA (6 ll., impf); NjHi. 7950

The COOKERY Almanac for 1843. N. Y.: Robert H. Elton. 18 ll. MWA; N; NHi; CLU; OClWHi; WHi.
7951

DAY'S City and Country Almanac for 1843. By David Young. New-York: Mahlon Day & Co. and Baker, Crane & Co. 18 ll. MWA; OClWHi. 7952

DAY'S New York Pocket Almanac for 1843. New York: Mahlon Day & Co. [Wall] 7953

DAYTON & Newman's Almanac for 1843. New York: Dayton & Newman; S. W. Benedict, printer. 12 ll. MWA. 7954

The DEMOCRAT'S Almanac, and Political Register for 1843. New-York: Booksellers. 24 ll. MWA; NHi; NBLiHi; InU. 7955

The DEMOCRAT'S Almanac, and Political Register for 1843. New York: Wm. G. Boggs. 24 ll. PPL. 7956

New York - 1843   775

DUDLEY'S Almanac for 1843. Buffalo: T. J. Dudley.
[Severance]   7957

The DUTCHESS and Ulster County Farmers' Almanac
for 1843. By David Young. Poughkeepsie: William
Wilson. 18 ll. N; NHi; NP.   7958

DUTCHESS and Ulster Farmers' Almanac for 1843.
Poughkeepsie: George Nagell. 18 ll. MWA (impf) 7959

ELTON'S Comic All-my-nack for 1843. New-York:
Elton. 18 ll. MWA (17 ll.); NSyOHi (17 ll.); CtHT-
W; MH; NCooHi (16 ll.); NBuG; CtY; InU (impf) 7960

The FAMILY Almanac for 1843. By David Young.
New-York: C. W. Cornwell. 12 ll. NjR; PHi.   7961

The FAMILY Almanac for 1843. By David Young.
New-York: 156 Fulton Street, and 180 Pearl street. 12
ll. MWA; NBuHi; CtHi; MSaE.   7962

The FAMILY Christian Almanac for the United States
for 1843. By David Young. New-York: American Tract
Society. 18 ll. MWA (three varieties); N (two varie-
ties); NN; NHi; OClWHi; NBLiHi; PPPrHi; CtY; CtW;
RWe; CtNhHi; RNHi; MHi; WHi; CtHi; MB; NjR;
NNA; CLU; ABH; Ct; MBC; OMC; InU; MH; BritMus;
Drake.   7963

-- Philadelphia imprint on cover. 18 ll. PHi. 7964

FARMERS' Almanac for 1843. By Thomas Spofford.
New-York: David Felt & Co. 18 ll. NN; NHi; OClWHi.
                                               7965
The FARMER'S Almanack for 1843. By David Young.
Ithaca: Andrus, Woodruff & Gauntlett. 18 ll. MWA;
NHi.   7966

The FARMER'S Almanac for 1843. By David Young.
New-York: Collins, Brother & Co. 18 ll. MWA; N;
NHi; CtY; NjP; NjHi; WHi.   7967

The FARMER'S Almanac for 1843. By David Young.

New-York: Mahlon Day. 18 ll. CtY.   7968

FARMERS' Almanac for 1843. By David Young. New-York: H. & S. Raynor. 18 ll. MWA; NP; Drake.
   7969

The FARMER'S Almanack, and Ephemeris for 1843. By David Young. Ithaca: Mack, Andrus, & Woodruff. 18 ll. MWA; N; NIC.   7970

The FARMER'S Diary and Western Almanac for 1843. By Henry C. Frink. Bath: R. L. Underhill & Co. 12 ll. DLC; NCanHi; NR; NRHi; NRMA; NRU. 7971

The FARMER'S Diary and Western Almanac for 1843. By Henry C. Frink. Canandaigua: J. D. Bemis & Son. 12 ll. MWA; NHi; DLC.   7972

FISHER'S Crockett Almanac for 1843. By Ben Hardin. New York: Turner & Fisher. (Calendar for the Whole Country.) MB (16 ll.)   7973

FISHER'S Crockett Almanac for 1843. By Ben Hardin. New York: Turner & Fisher [and Philadelphia]. 18 ll. MWA; DLC; CtY; PPL; NjR.   7974

FISHER'S Temperance House-Keeper's Almanac for 1843. New York: Turner & Fisher [and Philadelphia]. 18 ll. MWA; NN; DLC; NSyOHi; NjR. 7975

The FRANKLIN Almanac and Western New-York Calendar for 1843. Rochester: Wm. Alling. 12 ll. NR; NRMA.   7976

The FRANKLIN Almanac, and Western New-York Calendar for 1843. Rochester: David Hoyt. 12 ll. MWA; N; NN; NHi; PHi; WHi; NBuHi; MB; NRMA (11 ll.); DLC; NRU; MiD-B; PPT.   7977

The FRANKLIN Almanac, and Western New-York Calendar for 1843. Rochester: Sage & Brother. 12 ll. NRMA.   7978

The FRANKLIN Almanac, and Western New-York Cal-

endar for 1843. Rome: Comstock & Johnson. 12 ll.
N.   7979

FREE Almanack for 1843. By Geo. R. Perkins. [np]
Steele's Press. 12 ll. MWA; NN; NHi; NBuHi;
NCanHi; CtY.   7980

The HEALTH Almanac for 1843. New York: Saxton &
Miles. 24 ll. CtY; IU.   7981

The HEALTH Almanac for 1843. Boston: Saxton &
Peirce; N. Y.: Vincent L. Dill. 24 ll. MWA (two va-
rieties); MSaE; IU.   7982

The HEALTH Almanac for 1843. Utica: Bennett,
Backus, & Hawley; New York: Vincent L. Dill. 24 ll.
MWA.   7983

HUTCHINS' Improved Almanac for 1843. By David
Young. New-York: Mahlon Day & Co. 18 ll. MWA.
                                                                            7984
HUTCHINS' Improved Almanac for 1843. By David
Young. New York: Poinier & Snell. 18 ll. MWA (no
imprint); NHi (17 ll.)   7985

HUTCHINS' Improved Almanac for 1843. By David
Young. New-York: Charles Small. 18 ll. NN; MB.
                                                                            7986
HUTCHINS' Improved Almanac, and Ephemeris for
1843. By David Young. New-York: H. & S. Raynor.
18 ll. MWA; N; NHi; DLC; NBLiHi; Ct; NjMo; NjR;
IU; Pennypacker.   7987

HUTCHIN'S Revived Almanac for 1843. By David
Young. N. Y.: Elton. 18 ll. MWA (12 ll.); NjR.
                                                                            7988
HUTCHINS' Revived Almanac for 1843. By David
Young. New-York: H. & S. Raynor. 18 ll. NjR (17
ll.)   7989

KNICKERBOCKER Almanac for 1843. By David Young.
New York: Elton's Almanac Emporium. 12 ll. MWA;
NHi; MB.   7990

New York - 1843

KNICKERBOCKER Almanac for 1843. By David Young.
New-York: H. & S. Raynor. 18 ll. NHi; NjR; NRU;
CtB (17 ll.) 7991

The MASONIC Register [for 1843]. By Sylvester Spencer. New-York: R. Tyrell. 36 ll. NNFM. 7992

MEGAREY'S Nautical Almanac for 1843. New York:
Alexander Megarey. 140 ll. MWA. 7993

The METHODIST Almanac for 1843. By David Young.
New-York: G. Lane & P. P. Sandford, for the Methodist Episcopal Church; J. Collord, printer. 29 ll. MWA
(two varieties); NjR (26 ll.); OC; OClWHi; CtW;
Drake (28 ll.) 7994

PHINNEY'S Calendar, or Western Almanac for 1843.
By George R. Perkins. Cooperstown: H. & E. Phinney. 18 ll. MWA (17 ll.); N; NN; NHi; MBC; DLC;
WHi; F (17 ll.); FNp; ICHi; NCH; NSyOHi; MnU; NR;
NRMA; NCooHi; NBuHi (17 ll.); MiD-B; NIC; NUt;
Drake. 7995

The PHRENOLOGICAL Almanac for 1843. By L. N.
Fowler. New York: O. S. & L. N. Fowler; Vincent L.
Dill. 24 ll. MWA; N; DLC; CtHi; CLU; WHi;
NSyOHi; NjHi; Drake. 7996

POUGHKEEPSIE Farmer's Almanac for 1843. Poughkeepsie: George Nagell. 18 ll. DLC; NP (16 ll.) 7997

STEELE'S Albany Almanac for 1843. Albany: C. Van
Benthuysen & Co. 18 ll. MWA; N; NHi; PHi; NjR;
NRMA; OMC; OClWHi; Drake. 7998

SWORDS'S Pocket Almanack, Churchman's Calendar for
1843. New-York: Swords, Stanford, and Co. 48 ll.
MWA; N; NNG; NNS; PHi; MHi; PP; PPL; IU; WHi;
BritMus. 7999

TEMPERANCE Almanac for 1843. By G. R. Perkins.
Albany: C. Van Benthuysen & Co. 18 ll. MWA; N;
NHi; NCooHi; NBLiHi; OClWHi; MHi; CLU; NR; MnU;

InU; MiD-B; BritMus; Drake. 8000

TRAGIC Almanack for 1843. New-York: C. P. Huestis. 18 ll. MWA; NHi; DLC; MSaE; OClWHi; WHi; MWiW; NUtHi; MH; MHi; CtHi. 8001

TRAGIC Almanack for 1843. New-York: Sun Office; C. P. Huestis. 18 ll. NHi; NNSIHi (17 ll.); NjR; NPV; CLU. 8002

The TROY Almanac for 1843. Troy: Stedman & Redfield; N. Tuttle, printer. 18 ll. MWA; DLC; PHi; OClWHi; NGlf; NjJ. 8003

The TROY Almanac for 1843. Troy: Young & Hartt; N. Tuttle, printer. 18 ll. MWA; N (17 ll.); NT; CLU; CtLHi. 8004

The UNITED States Farmers' Almanac for 1843. By Thomas Spofford. New-York: David Felt & Co. 18 ll. MWA; NN; NHi; NB; NBLiHi; NBuG; NCooHi (impf); OClWHi; PHi; NjR; InU; MH; MB. 8005

The UNITED States Farmers' Almanac for 1843. By Thomas Spofford. New York: Robinson, Pratt & Co. 18 ll. N (17 ll.); NSyOHi (17 ll.) 8006

The UNITED States Fuel Almanac for 1843. By Almond D. Fisk. New York: Robert H. Elton. 18 ll. MWA; MB; CtY. 8007

UNITED States Statistical & Chronological Almanac for 1843. By George R. Perkins. Utica: M. Miller; R. W. Roberts, printer. 28 ll. MWA; N; NHi; NCooHi; NRU; NbO; PPT. 8008

The UNIVERSALIST Companion, with an Almanac and Register for 1843. By Geo. R. Perkins. Utica: A. B. Grosh; Grosh & Walker, printers. 32 ll. MWA; N; NHi; InU; WHi; OClWHi; CLU. 8009

WEBSTER'S Calendar. C. M. Gilchrist & Co.'s Albany Almanac for 1843. Glens Falls: C. M. Gilchrist

& Co. 18 ll. CLU. 8010

WEBSTER'S Calendar. Howland's Albany Almanac for 1843. Glens Falls: C. M. Gilchrist & Co. 18 ll. [H. H. Hill] 8011

WEBSTER'S Calendar. Howland's Albany Almanac for 1843. Sandy-Hill: G. & E. Howland. 18 ll. MWA; N; NN (17 ll.); NHi; MH; NRMA; NjR; NCooHi; NR; MiU-C; MnU; Drake (17 ll.) 8012

WEBSTER'S Calendar. Huling's Albany Almanac for 1843. Saratoga Springs: B. Huling; Sandy Hill: G. & E. Howland, printers. 18 ll. N (17 ll.) 8013

WEBSTER'S Calendar: or the Albany Almanack for 1843. By Edwin E. Prentiss. Albany: E. W. & C. Skinner. 18 ll. MWA; N; NN; NHi; DLC; WHi; OClWHi; MnU; InU; Drake. 8014

WESTERN Farmers' Almanac for 1843. By Henry C. Frink. Auburn: H. Oliphant. 16 ll. MWA; NSyOHi; NSy; NRU; NAuHi; NCH; WHi. 8015

WESTERN Farmers' Almanac for 1843. By Henry C. Frink. Syracuse: I. A. Hopkins; Auburn: H. Oliphant, printer. 16 ll. DLC (impf) 8016

The WHIG Almanac and United States Register for 1843. New York: Greeley & McElrath. 32 ll. MWA; NjR.
8017
The WHIG Almanac and United States Register for 1843. New York: Greeley & McElrath (No. 160 Nassau Street). 32 ll. MWA; N; NN; NHi; KHi; NBuG; ODa; MiD-B; NjJ; ICHi; LNHT; WHi; MoKU; NIC; MiGr; WvU; Ct; OMC; OCl; InU; CtHT-W; PScrHi; PHi; CtHi; CtY; MHi; MH; DLC; RNHi; PU; NSyOHi; OSand; NCooHi; IC (26 ll.); ICN; Nh; NjR; NNCoCi; NBLiHi; OO; In; NR; I; AB; CoU; MoHi; MB; NPV; NBuHi (17 ll.); O; BritMus. 8018

WILGUS' Farmer's Almanack for 1843. By George R. Perkins. Buffalo: A. W. Wilgus. 12 ll. MWA;

NBuHi. 8019

The AMERICAN Agriculturist's Almanac for 1844. By
A. B. Allen. New-York: J. Winchester. 32 ll. MWA;
N; NHi; CtHi; MHi; MSaE; DLC; CLU; GU; PPiU
(35 ll.); MeHi; PPL. 8020

The AMERICAN Agriculturist's Almanac for 1844. By
A. B. Allen. New York: J. Winchester; New World
Press. 32 ll. NcD; NjR; Drake. 8021

The AMERICAN Anti-Slavery Almanac for 1844. By D.
L. Child. Calculated for...Boston. New York: American Anti-Slavery Society [also Boston and Philadelphia].
18 ll. N. 8022

The AMERICAN Anti-Slavery Almanac for 1844. By D.
L. Child. Calculated for... Cincinnati. New York:
American Anti-Slavery Society. 18 ll. N. 8023

The AMERICAN Anti-Slavery Almanac for 1844. By D.
L. Child. Calculated for... New York City. New York:
American Anti-Slavery Society, 143 Nassau Street. 18
ll. MWA; NHi; MB; NcD; NjHi; MBAt; PPi; OO;
OMC; OCHP; WHi; CtLHi; NBLiHi; NjR (16 ll.) 8024

The AMERICAN Anti-Slavery Almanac for 1844. By D.
L. Child. Calculated for... New York City. New York:
American Anti-Slavery Society at 143 Nassau street.
24 ll. MWA; NN; InU; OClWHi; MiU-C; NRU; MBC.
8025

The AMERICAN Farmer's Almanac for 1844. New York
and Philadelphia: Turner & Fisher. 18 ll. PHi. 8026

BELLINGER'S Almanac for 1844. New York: Comstock
& Co. 18 ll. Butterfield. 8027

BLACK Joke Almanac for 1844. New-York: 98 Nassau-
street. 12 ll. NHi; NN; CtY. 8028

BLISS' Lansingburgh Almanac for 1844. Lansingburgh:
Pelatiah Bliss; Troy: N. Tuttle, printer. 18 ll. MWA;
N; NHi; MnU. 8029

BRISTOL'S Free Almanac for 1844. By Lucas Seaver. Batavia: Lucas Seaver. 12 ll. MWA; N; NN; NHi; DLC; InU; OClWHi; O; NCH; NBuHi; NBuG; WHi; ICN. 8030

CAROLINA and Georgia Almanac for 1844. By Robert Grier. New York: Collins, Brother & Co. 18 ll. NcD. 8031

CAROLINA and Georgia Almanac for 1844. By Robert Grier. New York: Huntington & Savage. 18 ll. NcD. 8032

The CHURCH Almanac for 1844. New York: Protestant Episcopal Tract Society; Wm. H. Townsend, printer. 18 ll. MWA (two varieties); N; NHi; NRHi; CtW; NNA; NNG; NjR; CtY; IU; WHi; Ct; OClWHi; MB; PPL; NcU; CLU; NR; PP; PPAmP; MiD-B; BritMus. 8033

COMMON Almanac for 1844. By Geo. R. Perkins. Watertown: Knowlton & Rice. 18 ll. NHi (17 ll.); DLC (17 ll.) 8034

COMMON School Almanac for 1844. New York: Samuel S. & William Wood. 18 ll. N; NHi; MSaE; MB; OC (8 ll.) 8035

COMSTOCK'S Almanac for 1844. The General Family Directory. New-York: Comstock & Co. 18 ll. MWA; NcD. 8036

COPPUCK'S Almanac for 1844. New York: Comstock & Co. MWA (wrappers only) 8037

The CULTIVATOR Almanac, or rural calendar for 1844. By Willis Gaylor and Luther Tucker. Albany: L. Tucker. 16 ll. MWA; N. 8038

The CULTIVATOR Almanac, or rural calendar for 1844. By Willis Gaylor and Luther Tucker. Lansingburgh: Alex. Walsh. 16 ll. NR; CtY. 8039

The CULTIVATOR Almanac, or rural calendar for 1844.

By Willis Gaylord and Luther Tucker. New-York: M.
H. Newman. 16 ll. MWA; NSyOHi; MHi; MSaE;
OClWHi.   8040

DAVY Crockett's Almanac for 1844. New York:
Charles Small. 18 ll. ICN.   8041

DAVY Crockett's Almanac for 1844. New York:
Turner & Fisher. 18 ll. MWA.   8042

DAY'S New-York Pocket Almanac for 1844. New-York:
M. Day, & Co. and Baker & Crane. 12 ll. MWA; NHi;
InU.   8043

The DUCHESS and Ulster County Farmers' Almanac for
1844. By David Young. Poughkeepsie: William Wilson. 18 ll. MWA; NP; NjR.   8044

DUDLEY'S Almanac for 1844. Buffalo: T. J. Dudley.
[Severance]   8045

DUTCHESS and Ulster Farmers' Almanac for 1844.
Poughkeepsie: George Nagle. 18 ll. MWA.   8046

ELTON'S Comic All-My-Nack for 1844. New-York: 98
Nassau, 18 Division-Streets and 96 Bowery. 18 ll.
MWA; CtY; MnU; NjP (ntp); InU (impf); ICU.   8047

The FAMILY Almanac for 1844. Troy: W. & H. Merriam. 18 ll. MWA; N.   8048

The FAMILY Christian Almanac for the United States
for 1844. By David Young. New-York: American
Tract Society. 18 ll. MWA (two varieties); N; NN;
NHi; OClWHi; WHi; NjR; MB; NSyOHi; ICU; PPPrHi;
CtHi; OC; InU; NBuHi; CtW; CtY; NUtHi; MHi; ICHi;
MH; RPB; CLU; MnU; Ct; MeP; MBC; OMC;
BritMus; Drake.   8049

FARMER'S Almanac for 1844. New-York: Baker &
Crane. 16 ll. NjR.   8050

FARMER'S Almanac for 1844. New-York: Greeley &

McElrath; Robinson, Pratt & Co. 16 ll. MWA (14 ll.); NCooHi (15 ll.); MB. 8051

FARMER'S Almanac for 1844. New-York: Greeley & McElrath; Robinson, Pratt & Co.; [also Philadelphia and Cincinnati]. 16 ll. N. 8052

The FARMER'S Almanac for 1844. By Zadock Thompson. Plattsburgh: Vilas & Edsall. 12 ll. MWA. 8053

The FARMER'S Almanac for 1844. By David Young. New York: Collins, Brother, & Co. 18 ll. MWA; NHi; NjHi; CtY; NRU; MB. 8054

The FARMER'S Almanac for 1844. By David Young. New-York: Nafis & Cornish. 12 ll. Ct; NjMo. 8055

The FARMER'S Almanac for 1844. By David Young. New-York: H. & S. Raynor. 18 ll. MWA; NN; NjR (16 ll.); CtY. 8056

FARMERS' Almanac for 1844. By David Young. New-York: H. & S. Raynor. 18 ll. MWA; N; CtLHi. 8057

The FARMER'S Almanac, and Ephemeris for 1844. By David Young. Ithaca: Andrus, Woodruff & Gauntlett. 18 ll. MWA; NIC; WHi; NjR; OC. 8058

The FARMER'S Diary and Western Almanac for 1844. Canandaigua: J. D. Bemis & Son. 12 ll. MWA; DLC; NCanHi. 8059

The FARMER'S Diary and Western Almanac for 1844. By Horace Martin. Bath: R. L. Underhill & Co.; Richardson & Dow, printers. 12 ll. NCanHi; NBuHi (10 ll.); NUtHi; DLC; OFH. 8060

FISHER'S Comic Almanac for 1844. Buffalo: E. Hollidge. 18 ll. MWA. 8061

FISHER'S Comic Almanac for 1844. New York: Turner & Fisher. 18 ll. DLC; MoSHi. 8062

New York - 1844

The FRANKLIN Almanac, and Western New-York Calendar for 1844. Rochester: C. F. Crosman. 12 ll. MWA; NRU.   8063

The FRANKLIN Almanac, and Western New-York Calendar for 1844. Rochester: David Hoyt. 12 ll. NR.   8064

The FRANKLIN Almanac, and Western New-York Calendar for 1844. Rochester: Sage & Brother. 12 ll. NRMA.   8065

The FRANKLIN Almanac, and Western New-York Calendar for 1844. Rome: Comstock & Johnson. 12 ll. N.   8066

The HEALTH Almanac for 1844. New-York: Saxton & Miles; Vincent L. Dill. 24 ll. MWA; NHi; InU; CtLHi.   8067

The HEALTH Almanac for 1844. Rochester: C. F. Crosman. 24 ll. NCanHi.   8068

HEBREW and English Almanac for 1844-45. New-York: S. H. Jackson. 12 ll. CtY.   8069

The HENRY Clay Almanac for 1844. New York: Turner & Fisher [and Philadelphia]. 16 ll. MWA; MH; PPL; OClWHi.   8070

HUTCHIN'S Improved Almanac for 1844. By David Young. New-York: Baker & Crane. 18 ll. MWA; NjR (16 ll.)   8071

HUTCHINS' Improved Almanac for 1844. By David Young. New-York: Mahlon Day & Co. 18 ll. NHi; MB; Drake.   8072

HUTCHINS' Improved Almanac for 1844. By David Young. New-York: Charles Small. 18 ll. NN; NCooHi; Pennypacker.   8073

HUTCHINS' Improved Almanac for 1844. By David Young. New York: Isaac Snell. 18 ll. NHi; CtHi. 8074

HUTCHIN'S Improved Almanac for 1844. By David Young. Upper Aquebogue: G. O. Wells. 18 ll. MWA; MH; NJQ.   8075

HUTCHINS' Improved Almanac, and Ephemeris for 1844. By David Young. New-York: H. & S. Raynor. 18 ll. MWA; N; NN; NHi; NjR; NBLiHi; PHi; NbO; NNSIHi (16 ll.); Ct; NjJ; NjMo; NjMoW; WHi.   8076

HUTCHINS' Improved Almanac, and Ephemeris for 1844. By David Young. New-York: H. & S. Raynor; Albany: James Henry. 18 ll. MWA; N; MB.   8077

HUTCHINS' Improved Columbia County Almanac for 1844. By David Young. Hudson: R. D. & J. Van Deusen. 16 ll. CtNhHi.   8078

KEELER'S Almanack for 1844. New York: Comstock and Company. A-Ar (27 ll.)   8079

KNICKERBOCKER Almanac for 1844. By David Young. New York: Robert H. Elton. 18 ll. MWA.   8080

The LIBERTY Almanac for 1844. By J. N. T. Tucker [and] Geo. A. Perkins. Syracuse: I. A. Hopkins; J. Barber, printer. 18 ll. MWA; NHi; ICN.   8081

MARK H. Newman's Almanac for 1844. New-York: Mark H. Newman. 12 ll. [Sabin 55015]   8082

MEDICAL Almanac for 1844. New York: Samuel S. & William Wood. 18 ll. N; DLC; MSaE.   8083

The METHODIST Almanac for 1844. By David Young. [New York:] G. Lane for the Methodist Episcopal Church; J. Collord, printer. 18 ll. MWA; NRMA; ICU.   8084

The METHODIST Almanac for 1844. By David Young. New-York: G. Lane. & P. P. Sandford for the Methodist Episcopal Church; J. Collord, printer. 18 ll. MWA.   8085
-- Issue with 30 ll. MiGr; PPL; NjR.   8086

The METHODIST Almanac for 1844. Fitted to...Rochester. By David Young. New-York: G. Lane. & P. P. Sandford for the Methodist Church; J. Collord, printer. 18 ll. NjR (11 ll., ntp)   8087

The METHODIST Almanac for 1844. Fitted to...St. Louis. By David Young. New York: G. Lane and P. P. Sandford for the Methodist Episcopal Church; J. Collord, printer. 30 ll. NcD.   8088

MOFFAT'S United States' Almanac for 1844. By William B. Moffat. New-York: Published by the Editor. 16 ll. MWA; NHi.   8089

The OLD American Comic Almanac for 1844. New York: George F. Coolidge; Boston: Dickinson, printer. 16 ll. MWA; N; NjR; MHi.   8090

PAUL De Kock's Comic Almanac for 1844. New York: T. W. Strong. 12 ll. NHi; CtHT-W; CtY.   8091

The PEOPLE'S Temperance Almanac for 1844. By David Young. New York: Collins, Brother, & Co. 18 ll. N; CtY; OClWHi; Drake.   8092

PHINNEY'S Calendar, or Western Almanac for 1844. By George R. Perkins. Cooperstown: H. & E. Phinney. 18 ll. MWA; N; NN; NHi; NUtHi; DLC; NBuHi; NSyOHi; NCooHi; NR; NIC; NRMA; MiD-B; MBC; CLU; F (impf); MnU; ICHi; WHi; InU; Ct.   8093

The PHRENOLOGICAL Almanac for 1844. By L. N. Fowler. New-York: O. S. & L. N. Fowler; John Douglas, printer. 36 ll. MWA; N; InU; CtHi; CtW; OClWHi.   8094

The PHRENOLOGICAL Almanac for 1844. Calculated for...Ohio. By L. N. Fowler. New-York: O. S. & L. N. Fowler; John Douglas, printer. 36 ll. NjHi; Drake.   8095

The PIRATE'S Almanac for 1844. New York: Turner & Fisher. 18 ll. MWA.   8096

POCKET Almanack for 1844. By Thomas Spofford.
New York: D. Felt & Co. MoSHi (17 ll.) 8097

The POLITICIAN'S Register: being a Supplement to the Whig Almanac for 1844. New-York: Greeley & McElrath. 16 ll. NHi; InU; MnM; PHi; PP; PScHi. 8098

The POLITICIAN'S Register: being a Supplement to the Whig Almanac for 1844. New-York: Greeley & McElrath. (Fifth Edition) 16 ll. CtY. 8099

The POLITICIAN'S Register: being a Supplement to the Whig Almanac for 1844. New-York: Greeley & McElrath. (Seventh Edition) 16 ll. MWA. 8100

POUGHKEEPSIE Farmers' Almanac for 1844. Poughkeepsie: George Nagle. 18 ll. NHi. 8101

The SOLAR Almanac for 1844. New York: Sun Office. 12 ll. MWA; N; NBLiHi (11 ll.); NCooHi; CtY. 8102

STEELE'S Albany Almanac for 1844. Albany: C. Van Benthuysen and Co. 18 ll. MWA; NN; NHi (16 ll.); MiU-C (17 ll.); OMC. 8103

STEELE'S Almanack for 1844. By Geo. R. Perkins. Buffalo: O. G. Steele; Steele's Press. 12 ll. MWA; NHi; NBuHi; DLC. 8104

SWORDS'S Pocket Almanack, Churchman's Calendar for 1844. New-York: Stanford and Swords. 48 ll. MWA; N; NHi; NNS; NNG (impf); NjR; PHi; PP; PPL; BritMus. 8105

TEMPERANCE Almanac for 1844. New-York: Greeley & McElrath. 15 ll. MWA; OClWHi. 8106

TEMPERANCE Almanac for 1844. Rochester: Wm. Alling. 16 ll. NN. 8107

The TEMPERANCE Almanac for 1844. By G. R. Perkins. Albany: Ex. Com. of the New York State Temperance Society; J. Munsell, printer. 18 ll. MWA (two

varieties); N; NN; NHi; MHi; MB; OClWHi; NjHi;
CLU; MnU; BritMus. 8108

TEMPERANCE Lecturer and Almanac, of the American
Temperance Union for 1844. New York: American
Temperance Union; Philadelphia: A. Flint & L. Jewell.
18 ll.   MWA; NBLiHi; MH; MBC; CtLHi; CtHi; WHi
(17 ll.); NjR. 8109

The TERRIFIC Almanac for 1844. New York: No. 74
Chatham Street; Philadelphia: No. 15 North Sixth. 12
ll. MWA; PP. 8110

TRAGIC Almanac for 1844. New-York: T. W. Strong.
18 ll. MWA; NHi. 8111

The TROY Almanac for 1844. Troy: Stedman & Redfield; N. Tuttle, printer. 18 ll. MWA; NHi; NT; NjJ.
8112
The TROY Almanac for 1844. Troy: Young & Hartt;
N. Tuttle, printer. 18 ll. MWA; N (impf); NjR. 8113

TURNER'S Comick Almanack for 1844. New York:
Turner & Fisher. 18 ll. OClWHi. 8114

TURNER'S Improved House-Keeper's Almanac: and
Family Recipe Book for 1844. New York, and Philadelphia: Turner & Fisher. 18 ll. MWA (16 ll.); InU
(impf); DLC; PHi; PPL. 8115

The UNITED States Farmers' Almanac for 1844. By
Thomas Spofford. New-York: Baker & Crane. 18 ll.
NjR. 8116

The UNITED States Farmers' Almanac for 1844. By
Thomas Spofford. New-York: David Felt & Co. 18 ll.
MWA; NN; NHi; NB; MB; InU; PHi; CtW. 8117

The UNITED States Farmers' Almanac for 1844. By
Thomas Spofford. New-York: Huntington & Savage. 18
ll. N; NBLiHi. 8118

The UNITED States Farmers' Almanac for 1844. By

Thomas Spofford. New-York: Charles Small. 18 ll.
NR. 8119

UNITED States Statistical & Chronological Almanac for 1844. Rochester: Fisher & Co.; C. F. Crosman; R. M. Colton, printer. 28 ll. NRU; Barton. 8120

UNITED States Statistical & Chronological Almanac for 1844. Rochester: M. Miller; R. M. Colton, printer. 28 ll. MWA; NBuHi; DLC; NRMA (27 ll.) 8121

The UNIVERSALIST Companion, with an Almanac and Register for 1844. By Geo. R. Perkins. Utica: A. B. Grosh; Grosh & Walker, printers. 32 ll. MWA; N; NUt; OClWHi; Ct (34 ll.); InU; Drake. 8122

The WASHINGTONIAN Almanac for 1844. New York: E. Kearny. 18 ll. MWA; N; NN; MB; MHi; CLU; CtW; Drake (impf) 8123

WEBSTER'S Calendar. Howland's Albany Almanac for 1844. Sandy-Hill: G. & E. Howland. 18 ll. MWA (two varieties); N; NN; NHi; NSchU; NCooHi; CLU; Drake. 8124

WEBSTER'S Calendar, or the Albany Almanac for 1844. By G. R. Perkins. Albany: E. W. & C. Skinner; J. Munsell, printer. 18 ll. MWA (three varieties); N (three varieties); NN; NHi; MB; MHi; DLC; PHi; MoU; NSchU; NIC; MiU-C; MnU; InU; WHi; NCooHi (impf) 8125

The WESTERN Almanac and Franklin Calendar for 1844. Rochester: Fisher & Co.; C. F. Crosman; R. M. Colton. 12 ll. NR. 8126

The WESTERN Almanac, and Franklin Calendar for 1844. Rochester: M. Miller; R. M. Colton, printer. 12 ll. MWA (10 ll.); NRU; ICHi. 8127

The WESTERN and Oneida Almanac for 1844. By Geo. R. Perkins. Utica: Bennett, Backus & Hawley. 18 ll. MWA. 8128

The WESTERN and Oneida Almanac for 1844. By Geo.
R. Perkins. Utica: R. W. Roberts. 18 ll. MWA; N;
NN; NRMA; NSyOHi; CLU. 8129

The WESTERN and Oneida Almanac for 1844. By Geo.
R. Perkins. Utica: Roberts & Curtiss. 18 ll. MWA;
DLC; NUt; NUtHi; M (13 ll.); ICHi. 8130

WESTERN Farmers' Almanac for 1844. By Horace
Martin. Auburn: H. Oliphant. 16 ll. MWA (15 ll.);
NBuG; NSy (15 ll.); NCH; DLC. 8131

WESTERN Farmers' Almanac for 1844. By Horace
Martin. Syracuse: L. W. Hall & Co. 16 ll. Drake.
8132

The WHIG Almanac and Politicians' Register for 1844.
New York: Greeley & McElrath. 30 ll. IC. 8133

The WHIG Almanac and Politicians' Register for 1844.
New York: Greeley & McElrath. (Fifth Edition) 30 ll.
CtY. 8134

The WHIG Almanac and United States Register for 1844.
New York: Greeley & McElrath. 36 ll. MWA; N; NN;
NHi; PHi; NRHi; CtHT-W; MH; MHi; CtY; DLC;
MSaE; CtHi; PU; TxDN; I; NjT; MDedHi; InU; KHi;
NBuG; ICHi; MoS; OO; MeP; OSand; NNCoCi; NBLiHi;
MB; In; NjR; WvU; CoU; CLU; NPV; NCooHi; MiGr;
ICN; NRU; NR; AzU; ABH; Ct; ArU; CU; O; NjJ;
OMC; OCl; WHi; OCHP; MoHi; NIC; T; IU; MoKU;
LNHT; MiD-B; PScHi; ViU; PPL; Drake (two varieties) 8135

ALMANAC of the American Temperance Union for 1845.
New York: American Temperance Union. 18 ll. MWA
(two varieties); N; NRMA; InU; NjR; MBC; OClWHi;
WHi; Ct; CtLHi. 8136

ALMANAC of the American Temperance Union for 1845.
New York: American Temperance Union; Charleston:
J. W. Harrison. 18 ll. CtHi. 8137

ALMANAC of the American Temperance Union for 1845. New York: American Temperance Union; Pittsburg: Isaac Harris. 18 ll. N; CtHi. 8138

The AMERICAN Agriculturist Almanac for 1845. By A. B. Allen. New York: Saxton & Miles; [and Boston and Philadelphia]. 18 ll. MWA; N; NN; NHi; OClWHi (impf); MHi; MBC; DLC; MSaE; NjR; MB; MH; CLU; MnU; Ct; InU; Drake. 8139

The AMERICAN Agriculturist Almanac for 1845. By A. B. Allen. New York: Samuel S. & William Wood. 18 ll. MWA; NjR; OClWHi. 8140

The AMERICAN Farmers' Almanac for 1845. By David Young. New-York: Greeley & M'Elrath; Pratt, Woodford & Co. 16 ll. MWA; NHi; NSchU; ViW (14 ll.); WHi; CtB. 8141

The AMERICAN Mechanics' and Manufacturers' Almanac for 1845. New York: E. Kearney. 18 ll. MWA; MB; PPL. 8142

BELL & Goodman's T Almanac for 1845. Rochester: Bell & Goodman. 12 ll. N; NR. 8143

BLISS' Lansingburgh Almanac for 1845. Lansingburgh: Pelatiah Bliss; N. Tuttle, printer. 18 ll. MWA; NBuG; CLU; MnU; InU (ntp) 8144

BRISTOL'S Free Almanac for 1845. By George Perkins. Buffalo: Thos. Newell. 16 ll. MWA (two varieties); N; NRMA; DLC; OO; MnU; WHi; MB; NRU; InU; MiD-B. 8145

BRISTOL'S Free Almanac for 1845. By George Perkins. Buffalo: Thomas, General Job Printer. 16 ll. NBuHi. 8146

CAROLINA and Georgia Almanac for 1845. By Robert Grier. New York: Collins, Brother & Co. 18 ll. NcD. 8147

The CHURCH Almanac for 1845. New-York: Protestant

Episcopal Tract Society; Wm. H. Townsend, printer.
18 ll. MWA; N; IU; WHi; CtY; OClWHi; MB; PPL;
PP; MBAt; O; NcU; MiD-B. 8148

The CHURCH Almanac for 1845. New-York: Protestant Episcopal Tract Society; Wm. H. Townsend, printer. (Second Edition) 18 ll. MWA; N; NHi; NSyOHi; NNA; NNG; MHi; CtW; NcU; Drake. 8149

CLAY and Frelinghuysen Almanac for 1845. By F. B. Graham. New York: Turner & Fisher. 13 ll. MWA; NHi; NUt; DLC; PPL; MnU (12 ll.) 8150

COMIC Punchiana Almanac for 1845. N. York, and Phila.: Turner & Fisher. 12 ll. NHi; CtY. 8151

COMMON Almanac for 1845. By Geo. R. Perkins. Watertown: Knowlton & Rice. 18 ll. MWA; NHi. 8152

The CULTIVATOR Almanac for 1845. By Luther Tucker. Albany: Luther Tucker. 16 ll. MWA; N; NHi; NN; NBLiHi; Drake. 8153

The CULTIVATOR Almanac for 1845. By Luther Tucker. Albany: E. Van Schaack. 16 ll. PHi. 8154

The CULTIVATOR Almanac for 1845. By Luther Tucker. Auburn: J. C. Derby & Co. 16 ll. N; CtY; Drake. 8155

The CULTIVATOR Almanac for 1845. By Luther Tucker. Buffalo: Horton & Crane. 16 ll. NRU. 8156

The CULTIVATOR Almanac for 1845. By Luther Tucker. Lansingburgh: Alex. Walsh. 16 ll. N. 8157

The CULTIVATOR Almanac for 1845. By Luther Tucker. New York: Wm. H. Carey & Co. 16 ll. MWA; N; NHi; DLC; OClWHi; OMC. 8158

The CULTIVATOR Almanac for 1845. By Luther Tucker. New-York: M. H. Newman. 16 ll. MWA; NN.
8159

The CULTIVATOR Almanac for 1845. By Luther
Tucker. River Head: G. O. Wells. 16 ll. MWA. 8160

DAY'S New-York Pocket Almanac for 1845. New-York.
[Wall] 8161

DUDLEY'S Almanac for 1845. Buffalo: T. J. Dudley.
[Severance] 8162

DUTCHESS County Almanac, and Ephemeris for 1845.
By David Young. Poughkeepsie: William Wilson. 18
ll. NHi; NP. 8163

ELTON'S Comic All-my-nack for 1845. New York: 18
Division Street. 18 ll. MWA; NHi; MB; DLC; NBuG;
MWiW; CtY; Drake. 8164

The FAMILY Almanac for 1845. Troy: W. & H. Merriam. 18 ll. NHi. 8165

The FAMILY Almanac for 1845. By David Young.
New York: Collins Brother & Co. 16 ll. NN. 8166

The FAMILY Christian Almanac for the United States
for 1845. By David Young. New-York: American
Tract Society. 18 ll. MWA (three varieties); N (three
varieties); NN; NHi; OClWHi (two varieties); NBLiHi
(17 ll.); CtY; MoSHi; MH; CtW; MBAt; NjP; NjR;
MB; CLU; ICN; P; MHi; RPB; MeWC (impf); Ct;
VtHi; OMC; PDoBHi; PPPrHi; MBC; NBuG; WHi; InU;
MiD-B; BritMus; Drake (two varieties) 8167

The FARMER'S Almanac for 1845. By David Young.
New York: Collins, Brother, & Co. 16 ll. NCooHi.
8168

The FARMER'S Almanac for 1845. By David Young.
New York: William K. Cornwell. 16 ll. MWA (impf);
NjR; MB. 8169

FARMERS' Almanac for 1845. By David Young. New-York: H. & S. Raynor. 18 ll. N; NN; NHi; NjR; Ct;
CtNhHi; OClWHi; CtY (impf) 8170

FARMERS' Almanac for 1845. By David Young. New-York: H. & S. Raynor; Canandaigua: H. O. Hayes & Co. 18 ll. MWA. 8171

The FARMERS' Almanac, and Ephemeris for 1845. By David Young. Ithaca: Andrus, Woodruff & Gauntlett. 18 ll. MWA; NIC; NBLiHi; NRU; WHi (17 ll.); MiD-B. 8172

The FARMERS' Almanac, and Ephemeris for 1845. By David Young. Ithaca: Mack, Andrus, & Company. 18 ll. NSyOHi; WHi. 8173

FARMER'S Calendar, or Northern Almanac for 1845. Pulaski: Robinson, Wright & Co. 12 ll. ICHi (11 ll.) 8174

The FARMER'S Diary and Western Almanac for 1845. By Horace Martin. Bath: R. L. Underhill & Co. 12 ll. NCanHi. 8175

FISHER'S Comic Almanac for 1845. New York and Philadelphia: Turner & Fisher. 18 ll. NHi; CtY. 8176

FOSTER & Dickinson's Oneida Almanac for 1845. By Geo. R. Perkins. Utica: R. W. Roberts. 18 ll. MWA; NUtHi. 8177

FRANKLIN Almanac for 1845. Rochester: M. Miller & Co. 32 ll. NRU (tp impf) 8178

The GENERAL Family Directory [for 1845]. New York: Comstock & Co. 14 ll. MWA; N (12 ll.); VtHi. 8179

The HOUSE-KEEPER'S Almanac for 1845. New York and Philadelphia: Turner & Fisher. 18 ll. PPL. 8180

HOUSEKEEPERS Almanac: and the Young Wife's Oracle for 1845. New-York: 18 Division-Street; Nafis & Cornish. 18 ll. MWA; N; DLC (16 ll.); CLU. 8181

The HOUSEKEEPER'S Annual and Ladies' Register for 1845. New York: T. H. Carter & Company 48 ll. MeHi. 8182

HUTCHIN'S Improved Almanac for 1845. By David
Young. New York: Mahlon Day & Co. 18 ll. MWA;
NHi; NjR. 8183

HUTCHIN'S Improved Almanac for 1845. By David
Young. [New York:] Charles Small. 18 ll. NNSIHi.
8184

HUTCHIN'S Improved Almanac for 1845. By David
Young. Upper Aquebogue: G. O. Wells. 18 ll. MWA;
NJQ; NN; Pennypacker. 8185

HUTCHINS' Improved Almanac, and Ephemeris for
1845. By David Young. New-York: H. & S. Raynor.
18 ll. MWA; NN; NHi; Ct; DLC; NBLiHi; NjMoW;
NjMo; MB; NT; IU; WHi. 8186

IVISON'S Western Farmer's Almanac for 1845. By
Horace Martin. Auburn: H. Oliphant. 16 ll. Private
collection. 8187

KNICKERBOCKER Almanac for 1845. By David Young.
New York: Mahlon Day & Co. 18 ll. NHi. 8188

KNICKERBOCKER Almanac for 1845. By David Young.
New-York: H. & S. Raynor. 18 ll. MWA; NBuG.
8189

The LIBERTY Almanac for 1845. By J. N. T. Tucker.
Syracuse: Tucker & Kinney. 18 ll. MWA; N; NBuG;
NIC; NRU; CtHi; MH; MBAt; MBC; Ct; ICN; OMC.
8190

MANN & McKimm's Improved Almanac, and Guide to
Wealth and Comfort for 1845. By John Scroggins.
New York: Sold by the Proprietors. 12 ll. NHi. 8191

MARSH'S Masonic Register [for 1845]. By Br. J. M.
Marsh, Printer, New-York. 32 ll. NHi; NNFM. 8192

The METHODIST Almanac for 1845. Fitted to...Cincinnati. By David Young. New-York: G. Lane & C.
B. Tippett, For the Methodist Episcopal Church; J.
Collord, printer. 30 ll. NcD. 8193

The METHODIST Almanac for 1845. Fitted to...New-

York. By David Young. New-York: G. Lane & C.B. Tippett, For the Methodist Episcopal Church; J. Collord, printer. 18 ll. MWA; NHi; CtW; OClWHi; ICU; BritMus. 8194

-- Issue with 30 ll. MWA; CtLHi; MiGr; NjR. 8195

The METHODIST Almanac for 1845. Fitted to... Pittsburgh. By David Young. New-York: G. Lane & C. B. Tippett, For the Methodist Episcopal Church; J. Collord, printer. 30 ll. PPL (29 ll.) 8196

MOFFAT'S Agricultural Almanac for 1845. New-York: Dr. William B. Moffatt; S. W. Benedict & Co., printers. 24 ll. MWA; N; NHi; NWhpHi; NBLiHi; DLC; CLU; WHi; OClWHi; OMC (ntp); InU. 8197

The PEACE Almanac for 1845. New-York: Collins, Brother, & Co. 16 ll. MWA; NHi; NBLiHi; RNHi; MB; MSaE. 8198

PEOPLES' Comic Almanac for 1845. N. Y.: T. W. Strong. 12 ll. CtY. 8199

PHINNEY'S Calendar, or Western Almanac for 1845. By George R. Perkins. Cooperstown: H. & E. Phinney. 18 ll. MWA; N; NN; NHi; NIC; NUtHi; MBC; NRMA; MnU; InU; WHi; NUt; DLC; NCooHi; NBuHi; CLU; Drake. 8200

The PHRENOLOGICAL Almanac, and Physiological Guide for 1845. By O. S. & L. N. Fowler. New York: O. S. Fowler. 36 ll. MWA (two varieties); N; NN; NSyOHi; MB; CtHi; CtW; MHi; MS (24 ll.); WHi; InU; CLU; Drake. 8201

POUGHKEEPSIE Farmers' Almanac for 1845. Poughkeepsie: George Nagell; J. Munsell, printer. 18 ll. NP. 8202

PROPHETIC Almanac for 1845. By Orson Pratt. New York: Prophet Office. 12 ll. NN; CtY; USlC. 8203

The RIPSNORTER Comic Almanac for 1845. New-York: 18 Division-street. 12 ll. NHi; MWiW. 8204

SAILOR'S Almanac for 1845. New York: 148 Nassau street. 12 ll. MWA; NRMA; NcD; MH; MeHi. 8205

SERIOUS Almanac for 1845 & '46. New-York: T. W. Strong. 19 ll. MWiW. 8206

SPOFFORD'S United States Farmers' Almanac for 1845. By Thomas Spofford. New-York: Nafis & Cornish. 18 ll. NBLiHi; NjR; MB; MHi; ICHi. 8207

SPOFFORD'S United States Farmers' Almanac for 1845. By Thomas Spofford. New-York: Nafis & Cornish; G. B. Maigne, printer. 18 ll. N; NHi. 8208

SPOFFORD'S United States Farmers' Almanac for 1845. By Thomas Spofford. New-York: Charles Small; G. B. Maigne, printer. 18 ll. PHi. 8209

The SQUATTER'S Almanac for 1845. N. York and Phila.: Turner & Fisher. 12 ll. CtY; DLC. 8210

STEELE'S Albany Almanac for 1845. Albany: Daniel S. Durrie. OMC (17 ll.) 8211

STEELE'S Albany Almanac for 1845. Albany: Steele & Durrie; J. Munsell, printer. 18 ll. MWA (two varieties); N; NHi; NNC. 8212

STEELE'S Almanack for 1845. By Geo. R. Perkins. Buffalo: O. G. Steele; Steele's Press. MWA (11 ll.) 8213

STRONG'S Illustrated Knickerbocker Almanac for 1845. New-York: T. W. Strong. 12 ll. OMC. 8214

STRONG'S Illustrated Serious Almanac for 1845. New-York: T. W. Strong. 12 ll. PHi (10 ll.) 8215

SWORDS'S Pocket Almanack, Churchman's Calendar for 1845. New-York: Stanford and Swords. 88 ll. MWA; N; NHi; NNG; NNS; NjR; OClWHi; MHi; PHi; PPL;

MSaE; BritMus. 8216

The TEMPERANCE Almanac for 1845. Albany: Ex. Com. of the New York State Temperance Society; J. Munsell, printer. 18 ll. MWA; NjR. 8217

The TEMPERANCE Almanac for 1845. Troy: B. H. Boynton. 18 ll. MWA; N; NHi; MBC; MHi; PP; NjHi; MnU; NCooHi; OMC (14 ll.); InU; Drake. 8218

TRAGIC Almanac for 1845. New York: T. W. Strong. 12 ll. MWA. 8219

The TROY Almanac for 1845. Troy: Stedman & Redfield; N. Tuttle, printer. 18 ll. MWA; PHi (16 ll.); NR. 8220

The TROY Almanac for 1845. Troy: Young & Hartt; N. Tuttle, printer. 18 ll. N; NT; DLC (16 ll.) 8221

TURNER'S Comic Almanac for 1845. New York and Philadelphia: Turner & Fisher. 18 ll. MWA; N; NHi; PP; OMC; InU. 8222

TURNER'S Improved House-Keeper's Almanac; and Family Recipe Book for 1845. N. York, and Philadelphia: Turner & Fisher. 16 ll. MWA. 8223

The UNITED States Almanac, and Political Manual for 1845. New-York: J. Disturnell. 30 ll. NHi; NBLiHi; MSaE. 8224

The UNITED States' Constitution Almanac for 1845. New-York: 18 Division-st.; Nafis & Cornish. 12 ll. MWA; N; CtLHi; PPL; NjR; Drake. 8225

The UNITED States Farmers' Almanac for 1845. By Thomas Spofford. New-York: David Felt & Co. 18 ll. MWA; NHi; NB; NBLiHi; CtHi; CtNhHi (15 ll.) 8226

The UNITED States Farmers' Almanac for 1845. By Thomas Spofford. New York: Huntington & Savage. 18 ll. NN; OClWHi. 8227

The UNITED States Farmer's Almanac for 1845. By
David Young. New York: Greeley & McElrath; Pratt,
Woodford & Co. 12 ll. NHi; NjJ. 8228

UNITED States Statistical and Chronological Almanac
for 1845. By M. Miller. Rochester: M. Miller &
Co.; M. Miller, engraver; E. Shepard, printer. 24 ll.
NRMA; NRU; NBuHi; NUtHi. 8229

-- Issue with 32 ll. MWA; NR; NCanHi; Drake. 8230

The UNIVERSALIST Companion, with an Almanac and
Register for 1845. By Geo. R. Perkins. Utica:
Grosh & Walker. 32 ll. MWA; N; OClWHi; CLU; InU.
8231

The USEFUL Almanac for 1845. By George R. Perkins. Utica: Bennett, Backus & Hawley. 18 ll. NcA.
8232

VAN SCHAAK'S Pictorial Almanac for 1845. Albany:
E. Van Schaak. CtY. 8233

The WASHINGTONIAN Almanac for 1845. New York:
E. Kearny. 18 ll. MWA; NHi; MH; MoSHi. 8234

WEBSTER'S Calendar, or the Albany Almanac for 1845.
Albany: James Henry; J. Munsell, printer. 16 ll.
MWA; N; MB; MnU; MoU. 8235

WEBSTER'S Calendar, or the Albany Almanac for 1845.
Albany: W. C. Little; Joel Munsell, printer. 18 ll.
MWA; NN; PHi. 8236

WEBSTER'S Calendar, or the Albany Almanac for 1845.
Albany: Erastus H. Pease; Joel Munsell, printer. 18
ll. MWA; PHi (15 ll.) 8237

WEBSTER'S Calendar, or the Albany Almanac for 1845.
Albany: T. R. Richardson; J. Munsell, printer. 18 ll.
N. 8238

WEBSTER'S Calendar, or the Albany Almanac for 1845.
Albany: E. W. & C. Skinner... State and Pearl St. 18
ll. MWA; N; NHi; NjHi; NT; DLC; NSchU; PHi; MHi;

New York - 1845   801

MiU-C; NbO; MnU; InU (15 ll., ntp); WHi.   8239

WEBSTER'S Calendar, or the Albany Almanac for 1845.
Albany: E. W. & C. Skinner...State and Pearl sts.
18 ll.   MWA; Drake (14 ll.)   8240

WEBSTER'S Calendar, or the Columbia County Almanac
for 1845. Hudson: P. S. & R. G. Wynkoop; Albany: J.
Munsell, printer. 12 ll. N; CtNhHi (10 ll.)   8241

WEBSTER'S Calendar. Howland's Albany Almanac for
1845. Sandy Hill: G. & E. Howland. 18 ll. MWA; N;
NN; NGlf; NIC; NCooHi; CLU; CtY; OMC.   8242

The WESTERN Almanac, and Franklin Calendar for
1845. Dansville: N. Bradley & Sons. 12 ll. NBuHi.
                                                8243
The WESTERN Almanac, and Franklin Calendar for
1845. Rochester: C. F. Crosman; M. Miller; E.
Shepard, printer. 12 ll. DLC; NRMA.   8244

The WESTERN Almanac, and Franklin Calendar for
1845. Rochester: M. Miller & Co.; M. Miller; E.
Shepard, printer. 12 ll. MWA; NR; NRHi; NRMA;
MiGr.   8245

The WESTERN Clay Almanac for 1845. Rochester: J.
G. Reed. 12 ll. NN; NRMA; WHi.   8246

The WESTERN and Oneida Almanac for 1845. By Geo.
R. Perkins. Utica: R. W. Roberts. 18 ll. MWA; N;
NUtHi; NHC.   8247

WESTERN Farmers' Almanac for 1845. By Horace
Martin. Auburn: H. Oliphant. 16 ll. NCH; NSyOHi.
                                                8248
WESTERN Farmer's Almanac for 1845. By Horace
Martin. Rochester: David Hoyt. 16 ll. NR.   8249

WESTERN Farmer's Almanac for 1845. By Horace
Martin. Syracuse: J. R. Gilmore. 16 ll. MWA. 8250

WESTERN Farmer's Almanac for 1845. By Horace

Martin. Syracuse: I. A. Hopkins; Auburn: H. Oliphant, printer. 16 ll. Drake. 8251

The WHIG Almanac and United States Register for 1845. New York: Greeley & McElrath. 32 ll. MWA; N; NN; NHi; In; PHi; NBuHi; NRHi; CtHT-W; NPV; DLC; NCanHi; MBC; MH; MHi; Ct; CtY; PU; NRMA; NIC; CoU; NjR; MBAt (ntp); NNCoCi; PPL; MB; PPiHi; NR; CLU; NBLiHi; NSyU; NjHi; NCooHi; ICN; InU; KyLoF (ntp); IC; OSand; MoHi; NvHi; CU; MoKU; LNHT; ArU; MeP; NjJ; OO; OMC; Nh; OCl; MoS; I; ICHi; NBuG; KHi; WvU; WHi; OCHP; TxDN; IaDaM (31 ll.); VtBennHi; O; NT; MiD-B; PScHi; CtB; Drake. 8252

The YOUNG Hickory Almanac for 1845. Rochester: M. Miller. 16 ll. MWA; N; NN; NRU; MnU (15 ll.) 8253

The ALMANAC Comic for 1846. New-York: T. W. Strong. 12 ll. MWiW. 8254

ALMANAC of the American Temperance Union for 1846. By David Young. New-York: American Temperance Union. 18 ll. MWA (two varieties); F; NSyOHi; NBLiHi; OClWHi; CtHi. 8255

The AMERICAN Agriculturist Almanac for 1846. By A. B. Allen. New York: Saxton & Miles. 16 ll. MWA; MBU; MBC; MSaE; NjR (15 ll.); NjHi; InU; CtB. 8256

The AMERICAN Agriculturist Almanac for 1846. By A. B. Allen. New York: Saxton & Miles. (Boston edition) 16 ll. N. 8257

The AMERICAN Farmers' Almanac for 1846. By David Young. Kingston; Ulster Co., N. Y.: [np] NjR (15 ll.) 8258

AMERICAN Farmers' Almanac for 1846. New York and Philadelphia: Turner & Fisher. 16 ll. MWA. 8259

The AMERICAN Farmers' Almanac for 1846. By David Young. New York: Greeley & McElrath. 16 ll. MWA (two varieties); NCooHi; MB; OClWHi. 8260

The AMERICAN Protestant Almanac for 1846. New York: E. Walker. 14 ll. MWA; N; NN; NHi; Ct; InU; MBC; MB. 8261

ANSTICE'S Pocket Almanac for 1846. New-York: Henry Anstice. 12 ll. NN. 8262

ANTI-SLAVERY Almanac for 1846. New York: Finch & Weed. 16 ll. MWA; N; NBuG; NRU; MBC; MiD-B; CLU; OMC. 8263

BELL & Goodman's T Almanac for 1846. Rochester: Bell & Goodman. 16 ll. NR. 8264

BLISS' Lansingburgh Almanac for 1846. Lansingburgh: Pelatiah Bliss; Albany: J. Munsell, printer. 18 ll. MWA; N; NHi; MnU; InU (ntp); NBuG. 8265

BRINCKERHOFF'S Almanac [for 1846]. New-York: C. Brinckerhoff. 8 ll. MWA; MHi. 8266

BRISTOL'S Free Almanac for 1846. Buffalo: Thomas ... General Job Printer, Exchange Buildings, 3d Story, Main-st. 16 ll. N; NN; MHi; NCanHi; NRMA; NBuHi; InU; NbO; OO; ICHi. 8267

BRISTOL'S Free Almanac for 1846. Thomas - General Job Printer, Exchange Buildings, Buffalo, N.Y. 16 ll. MWA; MoHi. 8268

[CALENDAR] for 1846. N.Y.: John W. Oliver. Broadside. Drake. 8269

CAROLINA and Georgia Almanac for 1846. By Robert Grier. New York: Collins, Brother & Co. 18 ll. NcD (17 ll.) 8270

CAROLINA, Georgia, and Alabama Almanac for 1846. New York: Collins, Brother & Co. 16 ll. NcD. 8271

The CHURCH Almanac for 1846. New-York: Protestant

Episcopal Tract Society; H. Ludwig, printer. 24 ll. N;
PHi; NjR; PPB; NSyOHi; NcU; OC.   8272

The CHURCH Almanac for 1846. New-York: Protestant Episcopal Tract Society; H. Ludwig, printer. (Second Edition) 24 ll. MWA; N; NHi; CtY; CtW; NNG; NNA; MB; WHi; MiD-B; PP.   8273

COMMON Almanac for 1846. By Geo. R. Perkins. Watertown: Knowlton & Rice. 18 ll. MWA; NSyOHi; NWattHi; DLC.   8274

The CULTIVATOR Almanac for 1846. By Luther Tucker. Albany: Andrew Leighton. 16 ll. MWA. 8275

The CULTIVATOR Almanac for 1846. By Luther Tucker. Albany: Steele & Durrie. 16 ll. N.   8276

The CULTIVATOR Almanac for 1846. By Luther Tucker. Albany: Luther Tucker. 16 ll. MWA; WHi.
                                              8277
The CULTIVATOR Almanac for 1846. By Luther Tucker. New-York: Wm. K. Cornwell. 16 ll. MWA.
                                              8278
The CULTIVATOR Almanac for 1846. By Luther Tucker. New-York: Mark H. Newman. 16 ll. MWA (15 ll.); N; GA.   8279

The CULTIVATOR Almanac for 1846. By Luther Tucker. New-York: Payne & Burgess. 16 ll. MWA; NjP.   8280

The CULTIVATOR Almanac for 1846. By Luther Tucker. Rochester: William Alling. 16 ll. NRU.
                                              8281
The CULTIVATOR Almanac for 1846. By Luther Tucker. Rochester: Samuel Hamilton. 16 ll. NBuHi.
                                              8282
De DARKIE'S Comic All-me-nig for 1846. By David Young. Philadelphia, and New York: Turner & Fisher. 18 ll. NHi; DLC.   8283

DAY'S New-York Pocket Almanac for 1846. New-York:

Baker, Crane & Day. 12 ll. NN; NHi. 8284

DERBY'S Western Farmers' Almanac for 1846. By Horace Martin. Auburn: J. C. Derby & Co.; Oliphant's Power Press. 16 ll. NAuHi. 8285

DERBY'S Western Farmer's Almanac for 1846. By Horace Martin. Geneva: G. H. Derby & Co.; Oliphant's Power Press. 16 ll. NRMA. 8286

DUCHESS and Ulster Farmers' Almanac for 1846. By David Young. Poughkeepsie: William Wilson. 18 ll. MWA; NP. 8287

DUDLEY'S Almanac for 1846. Buffalo: T. J. Dudley. [Severance] 8288

DUTCHESS and Ulster County Farmers' Almanac for 1846. By David Young. Poughkeepsie: Arnold & Grubb. 18 ll. NP (17 ll.) 8289

ELTON'S Comic All My Nack for 1846. New York: Elton. 18 ll. MWA; DLC (impf); CtY; ICU; MWiW. 8290

ELTON'S Funny Almanack for 1846. New York: Elton. 18 ll. MWA; N; NHi; DLC. 8291

The FAMILY Almanac, and Franklin Calendar for 1846. Troy: W. & H. Merriam; Rochester: M. & J. Miller, printers. 16 ll. MWA; NHi. 8292

The FAMILY Christian Almanac for the United States for 1846. By David Young. New-York: American Tract Society. 18 ll. MWA; N; NN; NHi; OClWHi; MHi; PPPrHi; MoSHi; CtW; MBAt; NUtHi; MiD-B; CtHi; InU; OMC; WHi; MBC; IU; MeP; Ct; RPB; CLU; NSchU; NbHi; MH; ViHi; NNA; NjR; MB; NjP; GEU; MiEM; NBuHi (8 ll.); BritMus; Drake. 8293

The FARMERS' Almanac for 1846. New York: Collins, Brother, & Co. 16 ll. MWA; NHi. 8294

The FARMERS' Almanac for 1846. New-York: T. W.

New York - 1846

Strong. 12 ll. MWA; NjR. 8295

The FARMERS' Almanac for 1846. Stillwater: Samuel G. Eddy; Albany: J. Munsell, printer. 18 ll. N; NjHi; PHi; BritMus. 8296

FARMER'S Almanac for 1846. By David Young. New-York: Baker, Crane & Day. 18 ll. MWA; NBLiHi (impf); NjR. 8297

FARMERS' Almanac for 1846. By David Young. New-York: H. & S. Raynor, No. 76 Bowery. 18 ll. NN; NHi; NjR; CtNhHi; CtY; MB; WHi. 8298

FARMERS' Almanac for 1846. By David Young. H. & S. Raynor, No. 76 Bowery, New-York. 18 ll. MWA; N. 8299

The FARMERS' Almanac, and Ephemeris for 1846. By David Young. Ithaca: Mack, Andrus, & Company. 18 ll. MWA; NHi (17 ll.); NBLiHi; NIC; NPV; NRHi; NRMA; CLU. 8300

The FARMER'S Diary and Western Almanac for 1846. By Horace Martin. Bath: R. L. Underhill & Co.; G. B. Richardson, printer. 12 ll. NRU. 8301

The FRANKLIN Almanac for 1846. By George R. Perkins. Loccport [sic]: O. C. Wright. 16 ll. NRU.
8302

The FRANKLIN Almanac for 1846. By George R. Perkins. New York: Edward Kearny. 16 ll. MWA; NNA; MB; Ct. 8303

The FRANKLIN Almanac for 1846. By George R. Perkins. Rochester: E. Shepard & Co.; New York: E. Walker & Co. 16 ll. MWA; N; NCanHi; NWhpHi; NRMA; RPB; WHi. 8304

The FRANKLIN Almanac for 1846. By George R. Perkins. Utica: Benjamin F. Brooks. 16 ll. NUt. 8305

HUTCHINS' Improved Almanac for 1846. New-York: T.

W. Strong. 12 ll. NjR. 8306

HUTCHIN'S Almanac for 1846. By David Young. New-York: Daniel D. Smith. 18 ll. DLC; NjJ. 8307

HUTCHINS' Improved Almanac for 1846. By David Young. New-York: Baker, Crane & Day. 18 ll. NBLiHi; Pennypacker. 8308

HUTCHINS' Improved Almanac for 1846. By David Young. New-York: H. & S. Raynor. 18 ll. MWA; NHi; DLC; NB; MB; Ct; MH; PHi; PPL; PPAmP; NjMo; WHi. 8309

HUTCHINS' Improved Almanac for 1846. By David Young. New-York: H. & S. Raynor, for Jansen & Bell. 18 ll. NN. 8310

HUTCHIN'S Improved Almanac for 1846. By David Young. New-York: Charles Small. 18 ll. MWA; NN; NjR. 8311

HUTCHINS' Improved Almanac for 1846. By David Young. New-York: Isaac Snell. 18 ll. MSaE. 8312

HUTCHINS' Improved Almanac, and Ephemeris for 1846. By David Young. Newburgh: David L. Proudfit. 18 ll. N. 8313

HUTCHINS' Improved Almanac, and Ephemeris for 1846. By David Young. New-York: H. & S. Raynor. 18 ll. N; NBuG. 8314

HUTCHINS' Improved Almanac, and Ephemeris for 1846. By David Young. New-York: H. & S. Raynor; Kingston: C. W. & R. A. Chipp. 18 ll. Hoes. 8315

HUTCHINS Improved; being an Almanack and Ephemeris for 1846. By David Young. New-York: Charles Small. OMC (17 ll.) 8316

HUTCHIN'S Improved Farmer's Almanac for 1846. New York: Turner & Fisher. 12 ll. NSchU; NjR. 8317

New York - 1846

IVISON'S Western Farmer's Almanac for 1846. By
Horace Martin. Auburn: H. Oliphant. 16 ll. Private
collection. 8318

KNICKERBOCKER Almanac for 1846. New-York: T.
W. Strong. 12 ll. MWA. 8319

KNICKERBOCKER Almanac for 1846. By David Young.
New-York: H. & S. Raynor. 18 ll. MWA; NjR. 8320

The MAGNETIC Almanac for 1846. By George R.
Perkins. Albany: George Dexter. 20 ll. N (19 ll.);
NjR. 8321

The MAGNETIC Almanac for 1846. By George R. Perkins. Utica: Printed for the publishers. 16 ll. WHi.
8322

MARSH'S Masonic Register [for 1846]. New-York: By
Br. J. M. Marsh, printer. 32 ll. NHi; NNFM. 8323

The METHODIST Almanac for 1846. By David Young.
George Peck, Editor. New-York: Lane & Tippett, for
the Methodist Episcopal Church; James Collord, printer.
30 ll. MWA; ICU; NjR; CtW; MSaE; MBAt (24 ll.);
MHi; MiGr; PPL; WHi; OC; Nh; T; Drake. 8324

MOFFAT'S Medical and Agricultural Almanack for 1846.
New York: Dr. William B. Moffat; S. W. Benedict,
printer. 24 ll. MWA; N; NHi; DLC; MS (25 ll.);
MiD-B; InU; OClWHi; F (23 ll.); NRU; MSaE; WHi.
8325

NATIONAL Almanac for 1846. Rochester: M. Miller.
40 ll. NRU. 8326

NEW YORK [almanac for 1846]. New York: Gedney and
Bradley. 12 ll. NIC. 8327

The NEW YORK Pictorial Almanac, and Pocket State
Register for 1846. Rochester: M. Miller; New York:
Mark H. Newman; McConell & Curtis, printers. 31 ll.
MWA (two varieties); NBuHi; NUt. 8328

The NEW YORK State Statistical Almanac for 1846.

Rochester: E. Shepard. [McMurtrie, Rochester list]
8329

The NORTHERN Almanac for 1846. By J. G. Webb.
Pulaski: Tallmadge, Wright & Co. 12 ll. MWA. 8330

OLD Oaken Bucket Almanac for 1846. By David Young.
New York: Baker, Crane & Day. 18 ll. MWA. 8331

OLIPHANT'S Western Almanac for 1846. By Horace
Martin. Auburn: H. Oliphant; Oliphant's Power Press.
16 ll. NAuHi; NCH. 8332

OLIPHANT'S Western Farmer's Almanac for 1846. By
Horace Martin. Auburn: H. Oliphant; Power Press
Office. 16 ll. Drake. 8333

The PEACE Almanac for 1846. New-York: Collins,
Brother, & Co. 16 ll. MWA; N; MSaE; NjR. 8334

The PEOPLES' Almanac for 1846. Rochester: M.
Miller; Robinson & Brown. 8 ll. NRU. 8335

The PEOPLES' Almanac for 1846. Rochester: M.
Miller; Shelton & Co. 8 ll. NCanHi; NR (7 ll.) 8336

The PEOPLES' Almanac for 1846. Rochester: M.
Miller; Wilder & Gorton. 8 ll. NRMA. 8337

The PEOPLE'S Almanac, Complete for 1846 and 1847.
By David Young. New York: Piercy and Reed, printers.
8 ll. MWA (7 ll.); N; NBuG. 8338

PHINNEY'S Calendar, or Western Almanac for 1846.
By George R. Perkins. Cooperstown: H. & E. Phinney; [etc]. 18 ll. MWA; N; NN; NHi; NBuHi; MBC;
NUtHi; NR; DLC; ICHi; MiD; NCooHi; CLU; NIC;
NRMA; MnU; NUt; Drake. 8339

The PHRENOLOGICAL and Physiological Almanac for
1846. By O. S. & L. N. Fowler. New York: Fowler
& Wells. 24 ll. MWA; N; NN; CtHi; CtW; MHi; MB;
MBAt; NjHi; CLU; OC; WHi; Drake. 8340

New York - 1846

The PICTORIAL Almanac for 1846. New-York:
Baker, Crane & Day. 18 ll. MWA; NHi.   8341

POCKET Almanack for 1846. By Thomas Spofford.
New-York: E. Kearny; Maigne, printer. 16 ll. NN.
   8342

POUGHKEEPSIE Almanac for 1846. Poughkeepsie:
George Nagell. 18 ll. MWA; NP.   8343

The PROPHETIC Almanac for 1846. By Orson Pratt.
New York: New York Messenger Office. 12 ll. NN;
DLC; ICHi; USlC.   8344

REDFIELD'S Western Farmer's Almanac for 1846. By
Horace Martin. Syracuse: L. H. Redfield; Oliphant's
Power Press. 16 ll. ICHi; Drake.   8345

The RIP Snorter, or Everybody's Comic Almanack for
1846. New York: Elton. 12 ll. MWA; AU; MWiW.
   8346

SERIOUS Almanac for 1846. New York: T. W. Strong.
[Phillips]   8347

SPOFFORD'S United States Farmers' Almanac for 1846.
By Thomas Spofford. New-York: Nafis & Cornish. 18
ll. MH.   8348

STATISTICAL Companion [for 1846]. By Edwin Williams. New-York: William H. Graham; James Van
Norden & Co., printers. 81 ll. N.   8349

STEELE'S Albany Almanac for 1846. Albany: Steele
& Durrie; J. Munsell, printer. 18 ll. MWA; NHi;
OMC (17 ll.)   8350

SWORDS'S Pocket Almanack for 1846. New-York:
Stanford and Swords. 64 ll. MWA; N; NHi; NNS; NNG;
NjR; OClWHi; PHi; PPL; BritMus; Drake.   8351

TEMPERANCE Almanac for 1846. New-York: Tribune
Buildings. 8 ll. NjR.   8352

TRAGIC Almanac for 1846. New-York: T. W. Strong.

12 ll. MWA; MWiW. 8353

The TRAGICAL Calendar and Pirate's Own Almanac for 1846. New York: Turner & Fisher. 18 ll. MWA.
8354

The TROY Almanac for 1846. Troy: George Redfield. 18 ll. MWA; N; DLC; NjJ. 8355

The TROY Almanac for 1846. Troy: Young & Hartt. 20 ll. MWA; N; NT; CLU. 8356

TURNERS Comic Almanac for 1846. New York: Turner & Fisher. 18 ll. MWA; N; NBuG; DLC; MB; WHi. 8357

TURNER'S Improved House-Keeper's Almanac, and Family Receipt Book for 1846. N. York and Philadelphia: Turner & Fisher. 18 ll. MWA (17 ll.); NBLiHi (16 ll.); CtY; PP; PPL (ntp) 8358

TURNER'S Improved House-Keeper's Almanac, and Family Receipt Book for 1846. New York and Philadelphia: Turner & Fisher. (For the Middle and Western States) 18 ll. MWA; PHi; PPG. 8359

The UNITED States Almanac, and Political Manual for 1845 [sic; actually 1846]. New-York: J. Disturnell. (cover: The United States Almanac; 1846.) 30 ll. Drake. 8360

The UNITED States Almanac, and Political Manual for 1846. New-York: J. Disturnell. (cover: The United States Almanac and National Register) 30 ll. MWA; N; NBLiHi; DLC; PPL. 8361

The UNITED States Farmers' Almanac for 1846. New-York: David Felt & Co. 18 ll. NHi (12 ll.); CtY; MB; PHi. 8362

The UNITED States Fuel Calendar, and Almanac for 1846. By Almond D. Fisk. New-York: 209 Water Street; S. W. Benedict, printer. 12 ll. N; NHi. 8363

UNITED States National Almanac for 1846. Rochester: M. Miller. 41 ll. NN; NSyOHi (40 ll.); PHi (40 ll.)
8364

UNITED States Statistical & Chronological Almanac for 1846. Rochester: M. & J. Miller; McConnell & Curtis, printers. 24 ll. MWA; N; NSyOHi; PHi. 8365

UNIVERSALIST Companion, with an Almanac and Register for 1846. A. B. Grosh, Editor. By G. R. Perkins. Utica: A. Walker. 30 ll. MWA; N; OMC; InU; CtLHi (12 ll.); WHi. 8366

The USEFUL Almanac for 1846. By David Young. New-York: Elton. 12 ll. MWA; N; NN; NjR. 8367

The UTICA and Oneida Almanac for 1846. By George R. Perkins. Utica: R. W. Roberts. 18 ll. MWA (impf); NUt; NUtHi. 8368

WEBSTER'S Calendar, or the Albany Almanac for 1846. Albany: E. H. Bender, bookseller and stationer; J. Munsell, printer. 18 ll. OClWHi. 8369

WEBSTER'S Calendar, or the Albany Almanac for 1846. Albany: E. H. Bender, Bookseller and Stationer; J. Munsell, printer. 16 ll. MWA; MB; DLC; WHi. 8370

WEBSTER'S Calendar, or the Albany Almanac for 1846. Albany: James Henry; J. Munsell, printer. 18 ll. N; NRMA; PHi. 8371

WEBSTER'S Calendar, or the Albany Almanac for 1846. Albany: W. C. Little; J. Munsell, printer. 18 ll. MWA; NN; NCooHi; MiU-C. 8372

WEBSTER'S Calendar, or the Albany Almanac for 1846. Albany: Joel Munsell; J. Munsell, printer. 18 ll. MWA; PHi; CLU; MnU. 8373

WEBSTER'S Calendar, or the Albany Almanac for 1846. Albany: E. H. Pease; J. Munsell, printer. 18 ll. MWA; N; CtY. 8374

WEBSTER'S Calendar, or the Albany Almanac for 1846.
Albany: Thos. R. Richardson; J. Munsell, printer.
18 ll. NHi. 8375

WEBSTER'S Calendar, or the Albany Almanac for 1846.
Albany: Thos. R. Richardson, Paper Hangings and Variety Store; J. Munsell, printer. 18 ll. NjHi; MoU.
8376

WEBSTER'S Calendar, or the Albany Almanac for 1846.
Albany: E. W. & C. Skinner; J. Munsell, printer. 18 ll. NT. 8377

WEBSTER'S Calendar, or the Albany Almanac for 1846.
Albany: Steele & Durrie; J. Munsell, printer. 18 ll.
MWA; N; MHi; MnU. 8378

WEBSTER'S Calendar, or the Albany Almanac for 1846.
Catskill: C. Austin; Albany: J. Munsell, printer. 18
ll. N; NN. 8379

WEBSTER'S Calendar, or the Albany Almanac for 1846.
Catskill: James H. Van Gorden; Albany: J. Munsell, printer. 18 ll. MWA; PHi. 8380

WEBSTER'S Calendar, or the Albany Almanac for 1846.
Hudson: P. S. & R. G. Wynkoop; Albany: J. Munsell, printer. 18 ll. N. 8381

WELLMAN'S American Statistical Almanack for 1846.
By J. K. Wellman. New York: 118 Nassau street; S. W. Benedict, printer. 12 ll. MWA; NN. 8382

The WESTERN Almanac and Franklin Calendar for 1846.
Buffalo: W. B. & C. E. Peck; M. Miller, engraver.
12 ll. MWA; NRMA. 8383

The WESTERN Almanac and Franklin Calendar for 1846.
Rochester: G. W. Fisher & Co.; M. Miller. 12 ll.
NBuHi. 8384

The WESTERN Almanac and Franklin Calendar for 1846.
Rochester: M. Miller; M. & J. Miller; Isaac Butts.
16 ll. MWA; NR; NRHi (12 ll.) 8385

The WESTERN Almanac and Franklin Calendar for 1846. Rochester: M. Miller; M. & J. Miller; M⁽c⁾Connell & Curtis. 16 ll. NRMA. 8386

The WESTERN and Oneida Almanac for 1846. By George R. Perkins. Utica: R. W. Roberts; [etc]. 18 ll. MWA; N (impf); NN; NUtHi; NCooHi; Drake (17 ll.) 8387

-- Imprint ends with: "James Owens, Steuben." 18 ll. NCooHi; Drake. 8388

WESTERN Farmer's Almanac for 1846. Syracuse: L. H. Redfield. ICHi. 8389

The WHIG Almanac and United States Register for 1846. New York: Greeley & McElrath. 32 ll. MWA; N; NN; NHi; MH; MHi; DLC; CtY; PU; CoU; IC; MoHi; In; NIC; OMC; PEbCHi; O; Ct; NjJ; KHi; NNCoCi; PHi; NBLiHi; MB; CtLHi; NSyU; NjHi; OSand; NPV; ArU; NR; ICN; CU; LNHT; WHi; OO; OCl; ViAsR; Nh; ICHi; NBuG; InU; WvU; CtHT-W; NRMA; NT; MiD-B; Drake. 8390

-- After imprint: "For latest Election Returns, see Second Page of Cover." 32 ll. N; NCooHi; NjR. 8391

WILLIAMS'S Statistical Companion and Pictorial Almanac for 1846. New York: Homans and Ellis. 97 ll. MWA; NN; InU. 8392

AGRICULTURAL and Family Almanack for 1847. New-York: Dr. William B. Moffat. 24 ll. MWA; N; CtW; MBAt; MBC; RWe; DLC; NRMA; CtY; MSaE; NjR (23 ll.); OClWHi; CtLHi; CLU; NRU; OO; WHi; MiD-B; ICU. 8393

ALMANAC of the American Temperance Union for 1847. By David Young. New York: American Temperance Union. 18 ll. MWA; N; NBuG; MB; WHi; CtHi; CtW; MBC. 8394

The AMERICAN Anti-Slavery Almanac for 1847. By L.

M. Child. New-York: American Anti-Slavery Society
142 Nassau St. [paged] 24 ll. NHi; MHi; OO; MB;
OClWHi; WHi. 8395

The AMERICAN Anti-Slavery Almanac for 1847. By
L. M. Child. New York: American Anti-Slavery Society, 142 Nassau St. [unpaged] 24 ll. MWA; N; NHi;
PU; MBAt. 8396

AMERICAN Cultivator's Almanac for 1847. By H.
Martin. Albany: James Henry; Rochester: C. F. Crosman; M. Miller. 16 ll. MWA (impf) 8397

AMERICAN Cultivator's Almanac for 1847. By H. Martin. Rochester: Alling, Seymour & Co. 16 ll. MB
(14 ll.) 8398

AMERICAN Cultivator's Almanac for 1847. By H. Martin. Rochester: C. F. Crosman; M. Miller; Toronto:
Richard Brewer. 16 ll. NHi. 8399

AMERICAN Cultivator's Almanac for 1847. By H. Martin. Rochester: C. F. Crosman; M. Miller; D. D. T.
Moore; Troy: W. & H. Merriam; Buffalo: T. & M.
Butler. 16 ll. MWA; NIC; NSyOHi; InU. 8400

The AMERICAN Farmers' Almanac for 1847. New
York: A. S. Barnes & Co. 16 ll. NCooHi. 8401

The AMERICAN Farmers' Almanac for 1847. New
York: Saxton & Miles. 16 ll. MWA; NjR; CLU; MBC;
DLC; MnU. 8402

The AMERICAN Farmer's Almanac for 1847. By Seth
Smith. New York and Philadelphia: Turner & Fisher.
18 ll. MWA; PPeSchw. 8403

BLISS' Lansingburgh Almanac for 1847. Lansingburgh:
Pelatiah Bliss; Albany: J. Munsell, printer. 18 ll. NHi
(4 ll.); DLC; MnU. 8404

BREED'S Western Almanac for 1847. By George R.
Perkins. Buffalo: F. W. Breed. 18 ll. MWA; NRMA;

Drake. 8405

CAROLINA and Georgia Almanac for 1847. By Robert Grier. New York: Collins, Brother & Co. 18 ll. NHi; NcD. 8406

CHIPMAN & Remington's Almanac and Medical Advertiser for 1847. By George R. Perkins. Canandaigua: Chipman & Remington; Rochester: E. Shepard, printer. 16 ll. N. 8407

The CHURCH Almanac for 1847. New-York: The Protestant Episcopal Tract Society. 24 ll. MWA; N; NHi; CtHT-W; CtW; NNG; NjMhL; CtHi; MiD-B; RPB; CtY; NNA; MB; PPL; NSyOHi; NcU; WHi. 8408

COMMON Almanac for 1847. By Geo. R. Perkins. Watertown: Knowlton & Rice. 18 ll. NHi; NWattHi; NjR. 8409

The CULTIVATOR Almanac for 1847. By Luther Tucker. Albany: Cultivator Office; C. Van Benthuysen and Co., printers. 16 ll. Ct. 8410

The CULTIVATOR Almanac for 1847. By Luther Tucker. Albany: Erastus H. Pease; C. Van Benthuysen and Co., printers. 16 ll. MWA; N; DLC; PHi. 8411

The CULTIVATOR Almanac for 1847. By Luther Tucker. New-York: William K. Cornwell; Albany: C. Van Benthuysen and Co., printers. 16 ll. MWA; NHi; DLC; OClWHi. 8412

The CULTIVATOR Almanac for 1847. By Luther Tucker. New York: Mark H. Newman and Co.; Albany: C. Van Benthuysen and Co., printers. 16 ll. N; NBuHi.
8413

DAVY Crockett's Almanac for 1847. New-York: Turner & Fisher. 18 ll. MWA; N; DLC; WHi. 8414

DAY'S New-York Pocket Almanac for 1847. New-York: Baker Crane & Day. 12 ll. NHi. 8415

DUCHESS and Ulster Farmers' Almanac for 1847. By David Young. Poughkeepsie: Arnold & Grubb. 18 ll. MWA (impf) 8416

DUDLEY'S Almanac for 1847. Buffalo: T. J. Dudley. [Severance] 8417

DURYEE & Forsyth's Scale Almanac for 1847. [Rochester:] E. Shepard. 8 ll. NRU. 8418

DUTCHESS and Ulster Farmers' Almanac for 1847. Poughkeepsie: George Nagell; Albany: J. Munsell, printer. 18 ll. N. 8419

DUTCHESS and Ulster Farmers' Almanac for 1847. By David Young. Poughkeepsie: William Wilson. 18 ll. NHi; NP. 8420

ELTON'S Comic All-My-Nack for 1847. New-York: Elton. 18 ll. NHi; MB; MWiW. 8421

ELTON'S Funny Almanac for 1847. N. Y.: Elton. 18 ll. MWA; NHi; DLC; CLU. 8422

ELTON'S Tragical and Piratical Almanac for 1847. New-York: Elton. 18 ll. MWA. 8423

EMPIRE Almanac for 1847. By George R. Perkins. Rochester: Erastus Shepard. 8 ll. MWA; MH. 8424

The FAMILY Almanac, and Franklin Calendar for 1847. Buffalo: L. Danforth; Rochester: M. & J. Miller. 16 ll. NBuHi. 8425

The FAMILY Almanac, and Franklin Calendar for 1847. Buffalo: W. B. & C. E. Peck; Rochester: M. & J. Miller. 16 ll. MiD-B. 8426

The FAMILY Almanac, and Franklin Calendar for 1847. Lockport: James Scribner. 16 ll. NR. 8427

The FAMILY Almanac, and Franklin Calendar for 1847. Troy: Merriam, Moore & Co. 16 ll. NCanHi. 8428

New York - 1847

The FAMILY Almanac, and Franklin Calendar for 1847. Troy: Merriam, Moore & Co.; M. & J. Miller. 16 ll. N; NR; NRMA (8 ll.)   8429

The FAMILY Almanac, and Franklin Calendar for 1847. Troy: Robert Wasson. 16 ll. NHi.   8430

The FAMILY Christian Almanac for the United States for 1847. By David Young. New-York: American Tract Society. 18 ll. MWA; N; NN; NHi; OClWHi; MHi; CtNhHi; CLU; WHi; CtW; CtY; PU; MB; MdBE; Ct; MeP; NjHi; VtHi; PPPrHi; MNF; OMC; RPB; NcU; MH; MBC; InU; BritMus; Drake.   8431

The FARMER'S Almanac for 1847. New-York: Collins, Brother & Co. 16 ll. NN.   8432

FARMER'S Almanac for 1847. New York: T. W. Strong. Ct (15 ll.)   8433

FARMERS' Almanac for 1847. By David Young. Newburgh: Daniel Smith. 18 ll. N.   8434

FARMERS' Almanac for 1847. By David Young. New-York: Baker, Crane & Day. 18 ll. MWA.   8435

FARMERS' Almanac for 1847. By David Young. New-York: H. & S. Raynor. 18 ll. MWA; NHi; NBLiHi; NjR; WHi.   8436

FARMERS' Almanac for 1847. By David Young. New-York: H. & S. Raynor, for F. Punderson, Hudson. 18 ll. MWA; N; NHi (ntp)   8437

The FARMERS' Almanac, and Ephemeris for 1847. By David Young. Ithaca: Mack, Andrus, & Co. 18 ll. NIC (17 ll.); NPV.   8438

FARMER'S Calendar. The Albany Almanac for 1847. Glen's Falls: M. & T. J. Strong. 16 ll. MWA (impf); N.   8439

The FRANKLIN Almanac for 1847. By George R. Perkins. Canandaigua: L. C. Chenney & Co. 16 ll. MWA; NCanHi. 8440

The FRANKLIN Almanac for 1847. By George R. Perkins. Cazenovia: Henry & Sweetlands. 16 ll. NCooHi (15 ll.); NIC; CLU. 8441

The FRANKLIN Almanac for 1847. By George R. Perkins. LeRoy: R. L. Samson; Rochester: E. Shepard, printer. 16 ll. NRU. 8442

The FRANKLIN Almanac for 1847. By George R. Perkins. New York: Edward Kearney. 16 ll. MWA; NN; DLC; MB; PP. 8443

The FRANKLIN Almanac for 1847. By George R. Perkins. New York: Nafis & Cornish. 16 ll. MWA; CtY; Ct; NSchU; ICHi. 8444

The FRANKLIN Almanac for 1847. By George R. Perkins. Rochester: E. Shepard, printer. 16 ll. MWA; NRMA. 8445

The FRANKLIN Almanac for 1847. By George R. Perkins. Rochester: E. Shepard; New-York: E. Walker & Co. 16 ll. N. 8446

GENERAL Taylor's Old Rough and Ready Almanac for 1847. Buffalo: Eli Hollidge. 18 ll. Drake. 8447

HADLOCK'S Pulmonic Almanac for 1847. By David Young. New-York: James Wilson. 12 ll. NjR. 8448

The HOUSEKEEPER'S Almanac for 1847. By David Young. N. Y.: J. Slater. 18 ll. MWA; DLC. 8449

H. SCRANTON & Co.'s Almanac for 1847. By George R. Perkins. Rochester: H. Scranton & Co.; E. Shepard, printer. 16 ll. NBuHi. 8450

HUTCHINS' Improved Almanac for 1847. By David Young. New-York: Charles Small. 18 ll. Private collection. 8451

HUTCHINS' Improved Almanac for 1847. By David Young. New York: Isaac Snell. 18 ll. DLC. 8452

HUTCHINS' Improved Family Almanac for 1847. By David Young. New-York: Baker, Crane & Day. 18 ll. Pennypacker. 8453

HUTCHINS' Improved Family Almanac for 1847. By David Young. New-York: H. & S. Raynor. 18 ll. MWA; NN; NHi; NB; NBLiHi; MB; MH; NjJ; NjR; OClWHi; Ct; CtY; PHi. 8454

HUTCHINS' Improved Family Almanac for 1847. By David Young. New-York: H. & S. Raynor; Hudson: F. Punderson. 18 ll. MWA (17 ll.) 8455

HUTCHINS' Improved Family Almanac, and Ephemeris for 1847. By David Young. New-York: H. & S. Raynor. 18 ll. N. 8456

HUTCHINS' Improved Family Almanac, and Ephemeris for 1847. By David Young. New-York: H. & S. Raynor; Kingston: Rodney A. Chipp. 18 ll. NHi; NWhpHi; NjMoW; Hoes. 8457

IVISON'S Western Farmer's Almanac for 1847. By Horace Martin. Auburn: Ivison & Co. 16 ll. MWA. 8458

KNICKERBOCKER Almanac for 1847. By David Young. New-York: H. & S. Raynor. 18 ll. MWA; NHi; NjR; InU. 8459

The LIBERTY Almanac for 1847. New York: William Harned. 24 ll. MWA; N; NN; NHi; OClWHi; WHi; CtHi; MBC; MH; OCHP; ICN; CtY; MnU; OO; InU; NRU; TxU; NjR (23 ll.); MB; CLU; NcD; NIC; OMC (23 ll.); Drake. 8460

MAGNETIC and Health Almanac for 1847. By George R. Perkins. [np, np] 12 ll. NCooHi. 8461

MARSH'S Masonic Register [for 1847]. New-York: By Br. J. M. Marsh, printer. 36 ll. NHi; NNFM. 8462

The METHODIST Almanac for 1847. By David Young. George Peck, Editor. New-York: Lane & Tippett for the Methodist Episcopal Church; James Collord, printer. 30 ll. MWA; NRMA; NjR; PPiHi; OClWHi; CtW; MiGr (24 ll.); WHi; InU; BritMus; Drake. 8463

MOFFAT'S United States Almanac for 1847. By Dr. Moffat. [np, np] 24 ll. USlC (22 ll.) 8464

The NATIONAL Family Almanac for 1847. By Aaron Maynard. New York: William H. Graham. 24 ll. MWA; NjHi; CtY. 8465

NEW Year's Address by the Carriers of the Sun. January 1, 1847. [Calendar for 1847]. New York: M. Y. Beach & Sons. 4 ll. Private collection. 8466

NEW York Comic Almanack for 1847. [New-York:] T. W. Strong. 12 ll. N; MB; MWiW (10 ll.) 8467

The NEW York Dental Almanac for 1847. New York: Burgess, Stringer & Co. 12 ll. MWA; NjJ. 8468

The NEW York Pictorial Almanac, and Pocket State Register for 1847. Rochester: M. Miller; Troy: Merriam, Moore & Co.; New York: Mark H. Newman. 40 ll. MWA; NBuHi; NCanHi; NUtHi; MB; NR. 8469

The NORTH American Almanac for 1847. Saratoga Springs: George H. Fish. 18 ll. Pennypacker. 8470

NORTH-EAST Centre Farmers' Almanac for 1847. By David Young. North-East Centre: J. G. Caulkins & Co. 18 ll. CtB. 8471

OLIPHANT'S Western Farmer's Almanac for 1847. By Horace Martin. Auburn: Henry Oliphant; Oliphant's Power Press. 16 ll. Drake. 8472

PHINNEY'S Calendar, or Western Almanac for 1847. By George R. Perkins. Cooperstown: H. & E. Phinney. 18 ll. MWA; N; NN; NHi; NUtHi; DLC; NSyOHi; NHC; NCooHi; MnU; NBuHi; NIC; ICHi; InU; WHi;

NUt. 8473

The PHRENOLOGICAL and Physiological Almanac for
1847. By L. N. Fowler. New-York: Fowler and
Wells; Milwaukee: Ira A. Hopkins. 25 ll. WHi. 8474

The PHRENOLOGICAL and Physiological Almanac for
1847. By L. N. Fowler. New-York: Fowlers and
Wells; Wilson & Co. 24 ll. MWA; N; NN; NHi; NRU;
InU; OClWHi; CtW; MBAt; NjHi; NjR; NCooHi; CLU;
Drake. 8475

The PHRENOLOGICAL and Physiological Almanac for
1847. By L. N. Fowler. New-York: Fowlers and
Wells; Boston: Saxton & Kelt. 24 ll. MWA. 8476

RENSELLAER County Farmer's Almanac for 1847.
Troy: Robert Wasson. 16 ll. MWA; CLU. 8477

RIPSNORTER Comic Almanac for 1847. N. Y.: Elton.
12 ll. MWA; NN; MWiW. 8478

S. G. EDDY'S Calendar, or Family Almanac for 1847.
Stillwater Village: Stillwater General Store. 18 ll.
MWA; N. 8479

SPOFFORD'S United States Farmers' Almanac for 1847.
By Thomas Spofford. New-York: Nafis & Cornish. 18
ll. MWA; NHi; NBuG; MH. 8480

SPOFFORD'S United States Farmers' Almanac for 1847.
By Thomas Spofford. New York: Pratt, Woodford, &
Co. 18 ll. MWA; NHi; NBLiHi; WHi; Drake. 8481

STEELE'S Albany Almanac for 1847. Albany: Steele &
Durrie; J. Munsell, printer. 18 ll. MWA; N; NHi;
OClWHi; NjHi; DLC; NBuG; NNC; OMC; BritMus.
8482

STOUGHTON'S Western Farmer's Almanac for 1847.
By Horace Martin. Syracuse: C. H. Stoughton; Auburn: Oliphant's Power Press. 16 ll. NSyOHi. 8483

STRONG'S American Almanac for 1847. N. Y.: T. W.

New York - 1847

Strong. 18 ll. MWA. 8484

SWORDS'S Pocket Almanack for 1847. New-York: Stanford and Swords. 72 ll. MWA; N; NHi; MHi; NNS; NNG; CtY; PHi; PPL; NjR; Nh; BritMuS; Drake. 8485

The TROY Almanac for 1847. By George R. Perkins. Troy: George Redfield. 20 ll. MWA; N; NR (17 ll.) 8486

The TROY Almanac for 1847. By George R. Perkins. Troy: Young & Hartt. 20 ll. MWA; N; NT; NjJ; PHi. 8487

TURNER'S Improved House-Keeper's Almanac, and Family Receipt Book for 1847. New York & Philadelphia: Turner & Fisher. 18 ll. MWA; DLC; PPAmP. 8488

The UNITED States Farmers' Almanac for 1847. New-York: David Felt & Co. 18 ll. NN; NB; CLU; MB; CtY; PHi. 8489

The UNITED States Farmers' Almanac for 1847. By David Young. New York: H. & S. Raynor. 18 ll. NjJ. 8490

UNITED States National Almanac for 1847. Rochester: M. Miller. 32 ll. NRHi. 8491

The UTICA and Oneida Almanac for 1847. By George R. Perkins. Utica: R. W. Roberts. 18 ll. MWA (17 ll.); N; NN; NHi; F (ntp); CLU. 8492

The WATER-CURE and Health Almanac for 1847. By Joel Shew. New York: William H. Graham. 18 ll. DLC. 8493

WEBSTER'S Calendar, or the Albany Almanac for 1847. By J. Munsell [and] Geo. R. Perkins. Albany: E. H. Bender. 18 ll. MWA; MB; Drake. 8494

WEBSTER'S Calendar, or the Albany Almanac for 1847. By J. Munsell [and] Geo. R. Perkins. Albany: James Henry. 18 ll. MWA; N; NN; NBLiHi (impf); NRMA; MiU-C. 8495

WEBSTER'S Calendar, or the Albany Almanac for 1847.
By J. Munsell [and] Geo. R. Perkins. Albany: J.
Munsell. 18 ll. CtY; InU. 8496

WEBSTER'S Calendar, or the Albany Almanac for 1847.
By J. Munsell [and] Geo. R. Perkins. Albany: E. H.
Pease. 18 ll. MWA; N; NN; NHi; OClWHi; PHi;
MnU; MoU. 8497

WEBSTER'S Calendar, or the Albany Almanac for 1847.
By J. Munsell [and] Geo. R. Perkins. Albany: J. M.
Pierce. 18 ll. NCooHi; Drake (17 ll.) 8498

WEBSTER'S Calendar, or the Albany Almanac for 1847.
By J. Munsell [and] Geo. R. Perkins. Albany: Steele
& Durrie. 18 ll. MWA. 8499

WEBSTER'S Calendar, or the Albany Almanac for 1847.
By J. Munsell [and] Geo. R. Perkins. Catskill: C.
Austin. 18 ll. MWA; N; NIC; DLC; PHi; CtY; Drake.
8500

WEBSTER'S Calendar, or the Albany Almanac for 1847.
By J. Munsell [and] Geo. R. Perkins. Catskill: John
Doane. 18 ll. MWA; MHi. 8501

WEBSTER'S Calendar, or the Albany Almanac for 1847.
By J. Munsell [and] Geo. R. Perkins. Catskill: James
H. Van Gorden; Albany: J. Munsell, printer. 18 ll.
MBAt; Drake (16 ll.) 8502

WEBSTER'S Calendar, or the Columbia County Farmers'
Almanac for 1847. Hudson: P. S. & R. G. Wynkoop;
Albany: J. Munsell, printer. 12 ll. N; CtNhHi; NbO.
8503

The WESTERN Almanac and Franklin Calendar for 1847.
Buffalo: W. B. & C. E. Peck. 16 ll. MWA (15 ll.)
8504

The WESTERN Almanac and Franklin Calendar for 1847.
Buffalo: Titus & Miller; Rochester: M. & J. Miller.
16 ll. NRMA. 8505

The WESTERN Almanac and Franklin Calendar for 1847.
Cazenovia: Henry & Sweetland; M. & J. Miller. 16 ll. MWA
8506

The WESTERN Almanac and Franklin Calendar for 1847.
Rochester: Fisher & Co.; M. & J. Miller, printers. 16 ll.
MnU 8506a

The WESTERN Almanac and Franklin Calendar for 1847.
Rochester: M. Miller; Dansville: A. Bradley & Sons; M.
& J. Miller. 16 ll. DLC; NR; NRHi; NRMA; NRU. 8507

The WESTERN Almanac and Franklin Calendar for 1847.
Utica: O. & M. Gaffney; M. & J. Miller. 16 ll. NBuHi
(14 ll.); NRU. 8508

The WESTERN and Oneida Almanac for 1847. By George
R. Perkins. Utica: R.W. Roberts. 18ll. MWA; N; NRMA;
NUtHi; Drake. 8509

WESTERN Farmer's Almanac for 1847. By Norace Martin. Syracuse: Hall & Dickson; Auburn: Oliphant's Power
Press and General Book and Job Office. 18 ll. MWA; NBuG.
8510
WESTERN Farmer's Almanac for 1847. By Horace
Martin. Syracuse: B. R. Peck & Co.; Auburn: Oliphant's Power Press. 16 ll. MWA. 8511

The WHIG Almanac and United States Register for 1847.
New York: Greeley & McElrath. 32 ll. MWA; N; NN;
NHi; PHi; CtHT-W; Ct; MHi; NNCoCi; NBLiHi; IC;
CtY (two varieties); DLC; PPL; NjMhL; MBC; MH;
PU; NT; NSyU; MB; OSand; NCooHi; NPV; CoU; ICN;
In; CtB; I; MoHi; NIC; MoKU; CU; ArU; LNHT;
KyBgW; MiGr (31 ll.); MeP; NjJ; OO; OMC; OCl; Nh;
MoS; P; ICHi; NBuG; PYHi; KHi; InU; WvU; WHi;
MiD-B; NRMA; CtLHi; O; NjT; NjR; Drake. 8512

AGRICULTURAL and Family Almanac for 1848. [New-
York: Dr. Wm. B. Moffat] For Sale by... 24 ll.
MWA; N; NHi; WHi; MBAt; MB; CLU; NSchU; NRU;
NcD; InU; NIC; CtY; InRE; VtBennHi; MiD-B; NjR.
8513
ALMANAC of the American Temperance Union for 1848.
By David Young. New York: American Temperance
Union. 18 ll. MWA; NRMA; CtHi; ICHi. 8514

ALMANACH Francais pour 1848. New York: l'auteur;
S. W. Benedict, imprimeur. 22 ll. MWA; NjR;
Drake. 8515

The AMERICAN Almanac for 1848. N. Y.: T. W.
Strong. 18 ll. MWA; N; NN; NHi. 8516

AMERICAN Cultivator's Almanac for 1848. Rochester:
Miller & Crosman and D. D. T. Moore; Cazenovia:
Henry & Sweetlands; Syracuse: M. Cone. 16 ll. MWA;
N. 8517

AMERICAN Cultivator's Almanac for 1848. Rochester:
Miller & Crosman and D. D. T. Moore; Cleveland: J.
W. Watson. 16 ll. MWA (two varieties); NSchU; NT;
IaAS. 8518

AMERICAN Cultivator's Almanac for 1848. Rochester:
Miller & Crosman and D. D. T. Moore; Troy: Merriam, Moore & Co. 16 ll. MnU. 8519

The AMERICAN Farmers' Almanac for 1848. New
York: Clark & Austin. 16 ll. Drake. 8520

The AMERICAN Farmers' Almanac for 1848. New
York: William K. Cornwell. 16 ll. MWA. 8521

The AMERICAN Farmer's Almanac for 1848. New
York and Philadelphia: Turner & Fisher. 18 ll. MWA;
OClWHi; PHi; PYHi. 8522

The ANGLER'S Almanac for 1848. New York: John J.
Brown & Co.; R. Craighead, printer. 16 ll. MWA;
NHi; NjR; PPL. 8523

BELL & Goodman's Almanac for 1848. Rochester:
Bell & Goodman; Shepard & Reed, printers. 16 ll.
NRMA. 8524

The BENEFACTOR: An Annual for 1848. Sing Sing:
George E. Stanton & Co. 8 ll. MWA; InU. 8525

BLISS' Lansingburgh Almanac for 1848. Lansingburgh:

Pelatiah Bliss. 18 ll. NBuG; MnU (15 ll.) 8526

BREED'S Western Almanac for 1848. By George R. Perkins. Buffalo: F. W. Breed. 18 ll. [Severance] 8527

BRISTOL'S Sarsaparilla Almanac for 1848. By Horace Martin. Buffalo: C. C. Bristol. 32 ll. NBuHi. 8528

The BUFFALO Almanac for 1848. Buffalo: Ansel Warren. 17 ll. [Severance] 8529

BURNETT'S Western Farmers' Almanac for 1848. By Horace Martin. Skaneateles: R. M. & S. H. Burnett; Auburn: Oliphant Power Press and General Book and Job Office. 32 ll. NHi. 8530

CAROLINA and Georgia Almanac for 1848. By Robert Grier. New York: Huntington & Savage. 18 ll. InU; NcD. 8531

CENTRAL New York Family Almanac for 1848. By George R. Perkins. Little Falls: S. F. Bennett; Rochester: Benton & Fisher, printers. 16 ll. MWA; N; NRU (two varieties); CLU; Drake. 8532

CHIPMAN & Remington's Almanac for 1848. By George R. Perkins. Canandaigua: Chipman & Remington. 16 ll. MWA. 8533

The CHURCH Almanac for 1848. New-York: Protestant Episcopal Tract Society. 24 ll. MWA; N; NHi; NjMhL; CtW; NNG; MSaE; MiD-B; PPL; NcU; MB; IU; WHi; BritMus. 8534

The CHURCH Almanac for 1848. New-York: Protestant Episcopal Tract Society. (Second Edition) 24 ll. N. 8535

The CHURCH Almanac for 1848. New-York: Protestant Episcopal Tract Society. (Third Edition) 24 ll. MWA; NNA; NjHi; RNHi. 8536

COMMON Almanac for 1848. By Geo. R. Perkins.

Watertown: Knowlton & Rice. 16 ll. MWA; NWattHi; NWhpHi; DLC.   8537

The CULTIVATOR Almanac for 1848. By Luther Tucker. Albany: Erastus H. Pease & Co. 16 ll. N; NBuHi; WHi.   8538

The CULTIVATOR Almanac for 1848. By Luther Tucker. Albany: Luther Tucker. 16 ll. NCooHi (15 ll.)   8539

The CULTIVATOR Almanac for 1848. By Luther Tucker. Clyde: Isaac Miller. 16 ll. MWA; MBC.   8540

The CULTIVATOR Almanac for 1848. By Luther Tucker. New-York: Huntington & Savage. 16 ll. N.   8541

The CULTIVATOR Almanac for 1848. By Luther Tucker. New-York: M. H. Newman & Company. 16 ll. MWA.   8542

The CULTIVATOR Almanac for 1848. By Luther Tucker. New-York: Pratt, Woodford & Company. 16 ll. MWA; N; OClWHi.   8543

The CULTIVATOR Almanac for 1848. By Luther Tucker. New-York: E. Walker. 16 ll. NjR.   8544

The CULTIVATOR Almanac for 1848. By Luther Tucker. Norwich: Squire Smith. 16 ll. NbO.   8545

The CULTIVATOR Almanac for 1848. By Luther Tucker. Rochester: Alling, Seymour & Company. 16 ll. MWA; NRMA.   8546

DAY'S New-York Pocket Almanac for 1848. New-York: Stephen M. Crane. 12 ll. NN; NHi.   8547

The DEMOCRAT'S Almanac and Political Register for 1848. New York: Evening Post. 18 ll. MWA; DLC; CtW; OMC.   8548

DUCHESS and Ulster County Farmers' Almanac, and

Ephemeris for 1848. By David Young. Poughkeepsie:
Arnold & Grubb. 20 ll. NWhpHi. 8549

DUCHESS and Ulster Farmers' Almanac for 1848. By
David Young. Poughkeepsie: William Wilson. 18 ll.
NP. 8550

DUDLEY'S Almanac for 1848. By Geo. R. Perkins.
Buffalo: T. J. Dudley. 16 ll. MWA; NBuHi (15 ll.)
8551

DUTCHESS and Ulster Farmers' Almanac for 1848.
Poughkeepsie: George Nagell; Albany: J. Munsell,
printer. 18 ll. CtW (16 ll.); NP. 8552

ELTON'S Comic All-My-Nack for 1848. New-York:
Elton. 18 ll. MWA; MBAt; MWiW. 8553

ELTON'S Funny Almanac for 1848. New-York: Elton.
18 ll. MWA; DLC; MB; OMC; NjR. 8554

EMPIRE Almanac for 1848. By Geo. R. Perkins.
Rochester: Shepard & Reed. 32 ll. MWA. 8555

FAMILY Almanac, and Franklin Calendar for 1848.
By George R. Perkins. Buffalo: T. & M. Butler. 16
ll. MWA; N. 8556

FAMILY Almanac, and Franklin Calendar for 1848. By
George R. Perkins. Cazenovia: Henry & Sweetlands;
Miller & Fisher, printers. 20 ll. MWA; NBuG;
NSyOHi. 8557

FAMILY Almanac, and Franklin Calendar for 1848. By
George R. Perkins. Rochester: M. Miller. 16 ll.
MiD-B. 8558

FAMILY Almanac, and Franklin Calendar for 1848. By
George R. Perkins. Troy: Merriam, Moore, & Co. 16
ll. N; CLU. 8559

FAMILY Almanac, and Franklin Calendar for 1848. By
George R. Perkins. Troy: Merriam T. Moore. 16 ll

MWA; N. 8560

The FAMILY Christian Almanac for the United States
for 1848. By David Young. New York: American
Tract Society. 30 ll. MWA; N; NN; NHi; NBLiHi;
OClWHi; InU; CtHi; NjMo; NUtHi; CtW; CtNhHi;
MBAt; RNHi; MHi; WHi; Ct; CtY; NjP; NjR; DLC;
MB; MBC; MH; OMC; RPB; NSchU; CLU; NIC; MeP;
CoCC; PEbCHi; PPPrHi; TxU; CtB; MNF; NRMA;
CtLHi; ICU; BritMus; Drake. 8561

FARMER'S Almanac for 1848. New-York: Collins and
Brother. 16 ll. MWA; MnU; Drake. 8562

FARMER'S Almanac for 1848. New-York: T. W.
Strong. 12 ll. MWA. 8563

FARMERS' Almanac for 1848. New-York: Tribune
Buildings. 18 ll. MWA (two varieties); N. 8564

The FARMER'S Almanac for 1848. By Zadock Thompson. Plattsburgh: Vilas & Crosby. 12 ll. MWA. 8565

The FARMER'S Almanac for 1848. By David Young.
New-York: Collins and Brother. 16 ll. CtLHi. 8566

FARMERS' Almanac for 1848. By David Young. New-York: Stephen M. Crane. 18 ll. MWA (impf) 8567

FARMERS' Almanac for 1848. By David Young. New-York: Isaac Snell. 18 ll. MB. 8568

FARMERS' Almanac for 1848. By David Young. New-York: Samuel Raynor. 18 ll. MWA; NHi; CtY (impf);
InU; WHi. 8569

The FARMERS' Almanac, and Ephemeris for 1848. By
David Young. Ithaca: Mack, Andrus, & Co. 18 ll. NIC
(17 ll.); NPV. 8570

GEN. Zachary Taylor's Old Rough & Ready Almanac for
1848. New York & Philadelphia: Turner & Fisher. 18
ll. KyBgW; PYHi; NjR; Drake. 8571

GRATUITOUS Almanac for 1848... and Dr. Lucius S. Comstock & Co.'s Family Physician. By Geo. R. Perkins. New-York: Comstock & Co. 16 ll. MWA; NHi; CLU; F (15 ll.) 8572

HADLOCK'S Pulmonic Almanac for 1848. By David Young. New York: James Wilson. 14 ll. N; Drake. 8573

HARPER'S United States Almanac for 1848. By David Young. New York: Harper & Brothers. 13 ll. MWA; NHi; MBAt; DLC; MSaE; MB; CtY; MnU. 8574

-- Issue with catalogue. 32 ll. MWA; N; NN; CtHi; MiD-B; InU; OC. 8575

HARPER'S United States Almanac for 1848. By David Young. New York: Harper & Brothers; Philadelphia: Stokes & Brother. 32 ll. PPL. 8576

HUTCHINS' Improved Almanac for 1848. By David Young. New-York: Stephen M. Crane. 18 ll. MWA; CLU; PPL (16 ll.) 8577

HUTCHINS' Improved Almanac for 1848. By David Young. New-York: Charles Small. 18 ll. N (impf); NB; Ct. 8578

HUTCHINS' Improved Almanac for 1848. By David Young. New-York: Isaac Snell. 18 ll. NNSIHi (impf); MSaE. 8579

HUTCHINS' Improved Almanac for 1848. By David Young. Upper Aquebogue: G. O. Wells. 18 ll. MWA; NN; NBLiHi; Pennypacker. 8580

HUTCHINS' Improved Family Almanac for 1848. By David Young. New-York: Samuel Raynor. 18 ll. MWA; NN; NHi (17 ll.); MB; DLC; NjMoW; CtY; NjR; NjJ; NBLiHi. 8581

HUTCHINS' Improved Family Almanac for 1848. By David Young. New York: John C. Riker. 18 ll. MWA. 8582

HUTCHINS' Improved Family Almanac, and Ephemeris for 1848. By David Young. New-York: Francis & Loutrel. 18 ll. ViHi. 8583

HUTCHINS' Improved Family Almanac, and Ephemeris for 1848. By David Young. New-York: Samuel Raynor. 18 ll. NBLiHi; NBuG. 8584

HUTCHINS' Improved Family Almanac, and Ephemeris for 1848. By David Young. New-York: Samuel Raynor; Kingston: Rodney A. Chipp. 18 ll. MWA; Hoes. 8585

HUTCHINS' Improved Family Almanac, and Ephemeris for 1848. By David Young. New-York: Samuel Raynor; Newburgh: James S. Brown. 18 ll. N. 8586

KNICKERBOCKER Almanac for 1848. New-York: T. W. Strong. 12 ll. MWA; NHi; DLC; MB; MBAt; MHi; MnU; WHi. 8587

KNICKERBOCKER Almanac for 1848. By David Young. New York: Samuel Raynor. 18 ll. MWA. 8588

The LIBERTY Almanac for 1848. New York: William Harned, For the American and Foreign Anti-Slavery Society. 24 ll. MWA; N; NN; NHi; OClWHi; CtY; MH; MeBa; MBC; MSaE; MB; NcU; RPB; CLU; ICN; InU; OCHP; MDedHi; OO; MnU; NIC; CtLHi. 8589

MARK H. Newman & Co.'s Useful Almanac for 1848. New York: Mark H. Newman & Co. 24 ll. DLC; MB (14 ll.) 8590

MARSH'S Masonic Register [for 1848]. New-York: Br. J. M. Marsh, printer. 48 ll. NHi; MSaE. 8591

MEGAREY'S Nautical Almanac, and Astronomical Ephemeris for 1848. New-York: Alexander Megary; John Gray, printer. 70 ll. OClWHi. 8592

The METHODIST Almanac for 1848. By David Young. George Peck, Editor. New-York: Lane & Tippett, for the Methodist Episcopal Church; Joseph Longking,

printer. 30 ll. MWA; CtW; NjR; CLU; NR (31 ll.);
NRMA; KyHi; MiGr; Nh; ICU; Drake. 8593

NATIONAL Almanac [for 1848]. Rochester: M. Miller.
32 ll. NBuHi; NUtHi. 8594

The NATIONAL Almanac and Astronomical Ephemeris
for 1848. New York: E. & G. W. Blunt; J. M. Elliott, printer. 134 ll. PPL. 8595

NATIONAL Reform Almanac for 1848. New-York:
Office of Young America. 24 ll. MWA; NcD. 8596

NEW-YORK Comic Almanac for 1848. New-York: T.
W. Strong. 12 ll. MWiW. 8597

The NEW York Pictorial Almanac for 1848. By George
R. Perkin [sic]. Rochester: M. Miller; Troy: Merriam, Moore & Co. 48 ll. MWA; N; NCooHi (30 ll.);
NRU. 8598

ONEIDA Almanack & Franklin Calendar for 1848. By
George R. Perkins. Utica: O. & M. Gaffney. MWA.
8599

The PEOPLE'S Illustrated Almanac and Ephemeris for
1848. Buffalo: E. Hollidge. 14 ll. NR. 8600

The PEOPLE'S Illustrated Almanac and Ephemeris for
1848. New York: Clapp & Townsend. 16 ll. MWA;
NCooHi; NWhpHi; CtY; Drake. 8601

The PEOPLE'S Illustrated Almanac, and Ephemeris for
1848. New York: Clapp & Townsend... Sun Building;
Vincent Dill, Jr., printer. 16 ll. MWA; N; NN; NHi;
NBLiHi (15 ll.); MSaE; CtNhHi; MH; WHi; DLC; CtY;
NjR; MiD-B; NSyOHi; Ct; InU; NCanHi. 8602

-- Issue with 20 ll. MWA; NWhpHi. 8603

PHINNEY'S Calendar, or Western Almanac for 1848.
By George R. Perkins. Cooperstown: H. & E. Phinney. 18 ll. MWA; N (impf); NN; NHi; NUtHi; PHi;
NUt; NRMA; NSyOHi; CLU; WHi; NcA; MnU; NIC;

InU; NBuHi (17 ll.); NCooHi; Drake. 8604

PHRENOLOGICAL and Physiological Almanac for 1848. By L. N. Fowler. New York: Fowlers and Wells; Burns & Baner, printers. 30 ll. MWA (three varieties); N; NN; NHi; OO; OClWHi; CtHi; MBC; MBAt; WHi; ICU; InU; OC; Ct; NSyOHi; MB; CLU; NRU; P (7 ll.); Drake. 8605

-- Issue with 24 ll. CtW; CtLHi; NjR. 8606

PHRENOLOGICAL and Physiological Almanac for 1848. By L. N. Fowler. New York: Fowlers & Wells; Pratt, Woodford, & Co.; J. S. Redfield; Burns & Baner, printers. 24 ll. NjR. 8607

POUGHKEEPSIE Almanac for 1848. Poughkeepsie: George Nagell; Albany: J. Munsell, printer. 18 ll. NP; OO; MHi. 8608

RIPSNORTER Comic Almanac for 1848. New York: Elton. 12 ll. MWiW; NjR (11 ll.) 8609

ROUGH and Ready Almanac for 1848. New-York: Elton. 12 ll. MWA; NHi; CtY; OMC. 8610

ROUGH and Ready Almanac for 1848. New York: Tribune Buildings. 20 ll. MWA; NSyOHi; CLU (18 ll.); Ct (two varieties) 8611

ROUGH & Ready Almanac for 1848. By David Young. New-York: Stephen M. Crane. 18 ll. N. 8612

SONS of Temperance Almanac for 1848. Ballston Spa. [Sabin 87104] 8613

SPOFFORD'S United States Farmers' Almanac for 1848. By Thomas Spofford. New-York: Nafis & Cornish. 18 ll. MWA; CtW; NSyOHi; WHi; Drake. 8614

STEELE'S Albany Almanac for 1848. Albany: Steele & Durrie; J. Munsell, printer. 18 ll. MWA; N; NN; NHi; DLC. 8615

New York - 1848   835

STODDARD'S Diary, or Farmers' Almanac for 1848.
Hudson: Punderson & Ham. 18 ll. MWA; N.   8616

SWORDS'S Pocket Almanack for 1848. New-York:
Stanford and Swords. 100 ll. MWA; N; NNG; PHi;
PPL; OClWHi; MSaE; NNS; WHi; BritMus.   8617

The TRAGIC Almanac for 1848. New York: T. W.
Strong. 10 ll. MWA; InU (impf)   8618

The TROY Almanac for 1848. Troy: George Redfield.
16 ll. NR.   8619

The TROY Almanac for 1848. Troy: Young & Hartt;
Albany: J. Munsell, printer. 18 ll. NHi; NT; WHi;
MHi; DLC; CLU; BritMus.   8620

TROY Almanac, and Franklin Calendar for 1848. Troy:
Merriam, Moore & Co.; Albany: J. Munsell, printer.
18 ll. N (impf)   8621

TURNER'S Improved House-Keeper's Almanac for 1848.
New York and Philadelphia: Turner & Fisher. 18 ll.
MWA; MSaE.   8622

The UNITED States Constitution Almanac for 1848.
New-York: Elton. 12 ll. MWA.   8623

The UNITED States Farmers' Almanac for 1848. New-
York: David Felt & Co. 18 ll. MWA; NHi; RNHi; MB.
   8624
The UTICA and Oneida Almanac for 1848. By George
R. Perkins. Utica: R. W. Roberts. 18 ll. MWA; N;
NUt; NRMA; NHC (ntp); NjR.   8625

The VICTORY Almanac for 1848. New-York: T. W.
Strong. 12 ll. MWA; NHi; PHi.   8626

WASSON'S Troy Almanac for 1848. Troy: Robert Wasson. 18 ll. DLC.   8627

WEBSTER'S Calendar, or the Albany Almanac for 1848.
By J. Munsell. Albany: E. H. Bender. 16 ll. N;

NHi; MnU; DLC; CtY; PHi. 8628

WEBSTER's Calendar, or the Albany Almanac for 1848.
By J. Munsell. Albany: B. Blakeman. 18 ll. N; NHi; MnU.
8628a
WEBSTER's Calendar, or the Albany Almanac for 1848.
By J. Munsell. Albany: R. Garrett. 18 ll. NCooHi (17 ll.)
8629
WEBSTER's Calendar, or the Albany Almanac for 1848.
By J. Munsell. Albany: James Henry, bookseller and stationer. 18 ll. MWA; N; NN; OClWHi; MnU; PHi; MiU-C.
8630
WEBSTER'S Calendar, or the Albany Almanac for 1848.
By J. Munsell. Albany: James Henry, Bookseller and Stationer. 18 ll. MWA; NN; NRMA; MB. 8631

WEBSTER'S Calendar, or the Albany Almanac for 1848.
By J. Munsell. Albany: W.C. Little & Co. 18 ll. MWA;
WHi; Drake. 8632

WEBSTER'S Calendar, or the Albany Almanac for 1848.
By J. Munsell. Albany: Joel Munsell. 18 ll. NNC; NIC;
InU; MHi; CtY. 8633

WEBSTER'S Calendar, or the Albany Almanac for 1848.
By J. Munsell. Albany: E.H. Pease & Co. 18 ll. MWA;
N; MoU. 8634

WEBSTER'S Calendar, or the Albany Almanac for 1848.
By J. Munsell. Albany: Steele & Durrie. 18 ll. MWA; PHi.
8635
WEBSTER'S Calendar, or the Albany Almanac for 1848.
By J. Munsell. Catskill: J. Doane. 18 ll. MWA;
MBAt; NjHi. 8636

WEBSTER'S Calendar, or the Albany Almanac for 1848.
By J. Munsell. Troy: L. Willard. 18 ll. MWA; N.
8637
WEBSTER'S Calendar, and Wynkoop's Columbia County
Almanac for 1848. Hudson: Rossman & McKinney; J.
Munsell, printer. 18 ll. N (impf) 8638

WEBSTER'S Calendar, and Wynkoop's Columbia County

Almanac for 1848. Hudson: P. S. Wynkoop, Jr. 18 ll.
N.   8639

The WESTERN and Oneida Almanac for 1848. By
George R. Perkins. Utica: R. W. Roberts. 18 ll.
MWA; NUt; NRMA.   8640

WESTERN Farmers' Almanac for 1848. By Horace
Martin. Auburn: J. C. Derby & Co.; Oliphant's Power
Press. 32 ll. NCH.   8641

WESTERN Farmers' Almnaac [sic] for 1848. By Horace Martin. Auburn: Henry Oliphant; Oliphant's Power
Press. 32 ll. NCH.   8642

WESTERN Farmers' Almanac for 1848. By Horace
Martin. Skaneateles: R. M. & S. H. Burnett; Auburn:
Oliphant's Power Press. 32 ll. NHi.   8643

WESTERN Farmers' Almanac for 1848. By Horace
Martin. Trumansburg: Charles Nicholson. 18 ll.
MWA.   8644

The WHIG Almanac and United States Register for 1848.
New York: Greeley & McElrath. 32 ll. MWA; N; NN;
NHi; IC; KyHi; MoKU; CU; O; NjJ; OMC; PHi;
NBuHi; Ct; MHi; Nh; NjP; CtY; DLC; PPL; MBC;
MH; PU; PPiU; NSyU; NNCoCi; NBLiHi; MB; OSand;
NCooHi; NPV; CLU; NR; I; ICN; MoHi; In; NIC; IU;
OO; LNHT; KyBgW; OCl; MoS; ICHi; NBuG; KHi; InU;
WHi; WvU; PYHi; NT; CtHT-W; MiD-B; P; NjR;
Drake.   8645

AGRICULTURAL and Family Almanac for 1849. [New
York: Dr. Wm. B. Moffat] 24 ll. MWA; NN (23 ll.);
NBuHi; USlC (21 ll.); ICHi; ICU; InU; NHi; NCanHi;
MBC; OClWHi; IHi.   8646

AGRICULTURAL and Family Almanac for 1849. For
Gratuitous Distribution. [New York: Dr. Wm. B. Moffat] 24 ll. N; NWhpHi; NCooHi; NRMA; DLC; CLU;
CtY; NjR; WHi; MiD-B; MBAt; MH.   8647

AGRICULTURIST'S Guide, and Almanac for 1849. By
M. M. Rodgers, M.D. [and] Samuel H. Wright. Rochester: Shepard & Reed. 55 ll. NBuHi; NCanHi.
8648

ALBANY Annual Register for 1849, with an Almanac.
By Joel Munsell. Albany: E. H. Pease & Co. 91 ll.
InU. 8649

ALMANAC of the American Temperance Union for 1849.
New York: American Temperance Union. 18 ll. MWA;
NHi; MBC; CtHi. 8650

-- Issue with 24 ll. OMC. 8651

ALMANACH Francais des Etats-Unis pour 1849. New-York: l'Auteur; D. Fanshaw, imprimeur. 26 ll. NSchU;
MH; PHi; NjR (23 ll.) 8652

-- Issue with 44 ll. PPL. 8653

AMERICAN Cultivator's Almanac for 1849. New York:
Cady & Burgess. 16 ll. MWA (15 ll.); CtHi. 8654

AMERICAN Cultivator's Almanac for 1849. New-York:
Nafis & Cornish. 16 ll. MiD-B. 8655

AMERICAN Cultivator's Almanac for 1849. Rochester:
Benton & Fisher. 16 ll. NRMA; Drake. 8656

AMERICAN Cultivator's Almanac for 1849. Rochester:
Benton, Fisher & Miller. 16 ll. NBuHi; NR. 8657

AMERICAN Cultivator's Almanac for 1849. Rochester:
Miller, Benton & Fisher; Benton & Fisher, printers.
16 ll. IaAS (13 ll.) 8658

AMERICAN Cultivator's Almanac for 1849. Troy: Merriam, Moore & Co. 16 ll. MWA. 8659

AMERICAN Family Almanac for 1849. By George R.
Perkins. Little Falls: S. F. Bennett; Rochester: Benton & Fisher, printers. 16 ll. NHi; NBuHi (10 ll.);
NRU. 8660

AMERICAN Farmers' Almanac for 1849. Auburn: J. C. Iveson & Co.; Oliphant's Power Press. 16 ll. N.   8661

The AMERICAN Farmers' Almanac for 1849. New York: C. M. Saxton. 16 ll. MWA.   8662

The AMERICAN Farmers' Almanac for 1849. New-York: Spalding and Shepard. 16 ll. MWA; Drake. 8663

The AMERICAN Farmers' Almanac for 1849. New-York: Spalding & Shepard. 16 ll. Drake.   8664

AMERICAN Farmer's Almanac for 1849. By Horace Martin. Syracuse: L. W. Hall; Auburn: Oliphant's Power Press. 32 ll. NCanHi.   8665

The AMERICAN Water Cure Almanac for 1849. New York. [Phillips]   8666

The ANGLER'S Almanac for 1849. New York: John J. Brown & Co.; R. Craighead, printer. 16 ll. MWA; NN; NjR.   8667

BELL & Goodman's Almanac for 1849. Rochester: Bell & Goodman; Shepard & Reed, printers. 16 ll. MWA; NR (15 ll.); NRMA.   8668

BEMIS Farmers' Almanac for 1849. By Horace Martin. Canandaigua: G. W. Bemis. 32 ll. NCanHi.   8669

BENDER'S Family Almanac for 1849. Albany: E. H. Bender; J. Munsell, printer. 18 ll. MWA; N.   8670

BENDER'S Farmer's Almanac for 1849. Albany: E. H. Bender; J. Munsell, printer. 18 ll. N; NCooHi. 8671

The BENEFACTOR: An Annual for 1849. Sing Sing: George E. Stanton & Co. 18 ll. MWA.   8672

BLISS' Lansingburgh Almanac for 1849. Lansingburgh: Pelatiah Bliss; N. Tuttle, printer. 16 ll. MWA; MnU.   8673

The BOSTON Book-Store, Almanac for 1849. By

George M. Perkins. Rochester: M. T. Gardner; Benton & Fisher, printers. 12 ll. MWA. 8674

BREED'S Western Almanac for 1849. By George R. Perkins. Buffalo: F. W. Breed. 18 ll. NBuHi; NRMA; DLC; WHi. 8675

BUFFALO Almanac for 1849. By Samuel H. Wright. Buffalo: [np] 16 ll. MWA; NBuHi (14 ll.) 8676

BURNETT'S Farmers' Almanac for 1849. By Horace Martin. Skaneateles: R. M. & S. H. Burnett; Auburn: Oliphant's Power Press and General Book and Job Office. 32 ll. NHi. 8677

CANANDAIGUA Almanac for 1849. By Samuel H. Wright. Canandaigua: Cheney & Sons. 16 ll. NCanHi. 8678

CAROLINA & Georgia Almanac for 1849. By Robert Grier. New York: Collins & Brother. 18 ll. GU. 8679

CHIPMAN & Remington's Almanac for 1849. By Samuel H. Wright. Canandaigua: Chipman & Remington; Rochester: Shepard & Reed, printers. 16 ll. MWA. 8680

The CHURCH Almanac for 1849. New-York: The Protestant Episcopal Tract Society. 24 ll. MWA; N; NcU; OC; PPL. 8681

The CHURCH Almanac for 1849. New-York: The Protestant Episcopal Tract Society. (Second Edition) 24 ll. MWA; N; NSyOHi; NcU; OCHP. 8682

The CHURCH Almanac for 1849. New-York: The Protestant Episcopal Tract Society; (Pudney & Russell, printers). (Third Edition) 24 ll. MWA; N; NHi; MHi; CtW; NNG; NjMhL; IU; MSaE; DLC; WHi; MiD-B; Wv-Ar; NNA; MB; MBAt; BritMus. 8683

COMMON Western Almanac for 1849. By George R. Perkins. Watertown: Knowlton & Rice. 18 ll. MWA; NWattHi; DLC; InU. 8684

DANFORTH & Co.'s Almanac for 1849. By Samuel H.

New York - 1849   841

Wright. Buffalo: L. Danforth & Co. MWA (15 ll.)
8685

DAY'S New-York Pocket Almanac for 1849. New-York: Stephen M. Crane. 12 ll. MWA; NHi.   8686

DUCHESS and Ulster County Farmers' Almanac, and Ephemeris for 1849. By David Young. Poughkeepsie: John Grubb. 18 ll. NWhpHi.   8687

DUCHESS and Ulster Farmers' Almanac for 1849. By David Young. Poughkeepsie: William Wilson. 18 ll. MWA; NP (17 ll.)   8688

ELTON'S Comic All My Nack for 1848-1849. New-York: Elton. 16 ll. MWA; N; NSyOHi; NCooHi (7 ll.); MWiW; ICU.   8689

ELTON'S Farmers' Almanac for 1849. By David Young. New York: Elton. 12 ll. MWA; MH; MBC; NHi; MB; MHi; MiD-B.   8690

FAMILY Almanac, and Franklin Calendar for 1849. By Geo. M. Perkins. Rochester: E. Darrow; Benton & Fisher, printers. 16 ll. NR; NRHi; CtY.   8691

FAMILY Almanac, and Franklin Calendar for 1849. By Geo. M. Perkins. Troy: Priest, Allendorph & Co.; Rochester: Benton & Fisher, printers. 16 ll. N. 8692

FAMILY Almanac, and Franklin Calendar for 1849. By Geo. M. Perkins. Troy: Young & Hartt; Rochester: Benton & Fisher, printers. 16 ll. MWA.   8693

FAMILY Almanac, and Franklin Calendar for 1849. By George R. Perkins. Buffalo: Wm. B. & Charles E. Peck; Rochester: Benton & Fisher, printers. 16 ll. NHi.   8694

FAMILY Almanac, and Franklin Calendar for 1849. By George R. Perkins. Rochester: Benton, Fisher & Miller. 16 ll. NBuHi; NRU.   8695

FAMILY Almanac, and Franklin Calendar for 1849. By

George R. Perkins. Rochester: M. Cone; Benton & Fisher, printers. 16 ll. MWA.   8696

FAMILY Almanac, and Franklin Calendar for 1849. By George R. Perkins. Troy: Merriam, Moore & Co. 16 ll. MWA (13 ll.); NN; NBuG.   8697

The FARMER'S Almanac for 1849. New York: Isaac Snell. CtY.   8698

The FARMER'S Almanac for 1849. By David Young. Newburgh: Daniel Smith. 18 ll. MnU.   8699

FARMERS' Almanac for 1849. By David Young. New-York: Samuel Raynor. 18 ll. MWA (two varieties); NHi; NBLiHi.   8700

The FARMERS' Almanac and Ephemeris for 1849. By David Young. Ithaca: Mack, Andrus, & Co. 18 ll. MWA; NIC; MB; Ct (17 ll.); Drake.   8701

FARMERS' Almanac, and Ephemeris for 1849. By David Young. New-York: Samuel Raynor. 18 ll. MWA; N.   8702

FISHER'S Comic Almanac for 1849. New York [and] Philadelphia: Turner & Fisher. 18 ll. MWA; NN; DLC; MBAt.   8703

The FRANKLIN Almanac for 1849. By Samuel H. Wright. Buffalo: Parmelee & Hadley. 16 ll. NRMA; NRU.   8704

The FREE Soil Almanac for 1849. Rochester: D. M. Dewey; Shepard and Reed, printers. 16 ll. MWA; NR.   8705

GAFFNEY'S Oneida Almanac for 1849. By George R. Perkins. Utica: O. & M. Gaffney. 18 ll. MWA; N; NCooHi; NUtHi; DLC; OFH.   8706

The HERALD Almanac for the United States for 1849. New York: James Gordon Bennett. 24 ll. MWA; N; InU; PP; PPL (23 ll.); CtY.   8707

HOWLAND, Harvey & Co.'s Farmers Almanac for 1849.
Sandy Hill: Howland, Harvey & Co. 12 ll. MWA; N;
NCooHi (11 ll.); CLU; PHi. 8708

HULING'S Saratoga Almanac for 1849. Saratoga
Springs: E. J. Huling. 12 ll. N. 8709

HUTCHINS' Improved Almanac for 1849. By David
Young. New York: Stephen M. Crane. 12 ll. MWA;
NBuG. 8710

HUTCHINS' Improved Almanac for 1849. By David
Young. New-York: Isaac Snell. 18 ll. MSaE. 8711

HUTCHIN'S Improved Almanac for 1849. By David
Young. River Head: G. O. Wells. 18 ll. NN (17 ll.);
NHi; NJQ (impf) 8712

HUTCHINS' Improved Family Almanac for 1849. By
David Young. New-York: Samuel Raynor. 18 ll. MWA;
NN (impf); NHi; MB; DLC; NjR; NjJ; NjMo; NjMoW;
CtHi; NNSIHi. 8713

HUTCHINS' Improved Family Almanac and Ephemeris
for 1849. By David Young. Kingston: Rodney A.
Chipp. 18 ll. Hoes. 8714

HUTCHINS' Improved Family Almanac and Ephemeris
for 1849. By David Young. New-York: Samuel Raynor. 18 ll. NBLiHi (17 ll.) 8715

HUTCHINS' Improved Family Almanac and Ephemeris
for 1849. By David Young. New-York: Samuel Raynor; Newburgh: James S. Brown. 18 ll. N. 8716

HUTCHINS' Improved Family Almanac and Ephemeris
for 1849. By David Young. New-York: J. C. Riker.
18 ll. N; NN; NjR; CtHi. 8717

The ILLUSTRATED Family Christian Almanac for the
United States for 1849. By David Young. New-York
[and] Boston: American Tract Society. 30 ll. MWA; N;
NN; NHi; OClWHi; NBLiHi; FSpHi; MHi; MBC; Ct;

CtY; PPL; NUtHi; CtW; MH; CtNhHi; MBAt; PHi;
DLC; NjR; PU; ScU-S; MB; NSyOHi; NBuG; NcA;
LNHT; NbHi; MnU; CLU; IU; RPB; NIC; CoCC; WHi;
ICU; NjP; NjHi; NCooHi; MeP; OMC; CtHi; InU; ViU;
CtHT; RU; PPPrHi; MiD-B; MNF; NRMA; CtLHi;
BritMus; Drake. 8718

KNICKERBOCKER Almanac for 1849. By David Young.
New-York: Samuel Raynor. 18 ll. MWA; NHi (17 ll.)
8719
KNICKERBOCKER Almanac for 1849. By David Young.
River Head: G. O. Wells. NBLiHi (15 ll.) 8720

The LIBERTY Almanac for 1849. New-York: Am. &
For. Anti-Slavery Society; William Harned. 24 ll. MWA;
N; NN; NHi; OClWHi; CtNhHi; MiD-B; CtHi; CtY; MH;
OO; MB; MBC; RPB; OCHP; NcD; ICN; NIC; InU;
MdBJ (23 ll.); WHi; TxU; P. 8721

MARSH'S Masonic Register [for 1849]. New York: Br.
J. M. Marsh, printer. 63 ll. NHi; NNFM. 8722

The METHODIST Almanac for 1849. By David Young.
George Peck, Editor. New-York: Lane & Scott; Joseph
Longking, printer. 30 ll. MWA; NjR; InU; Ct; CtW;
MiGr; Drake. 8723

The METHODIST Almanac for 1849. By David Young.
George Peck, Editor. New-York: Lane & Tippett. 30
ll. NR. 8724

MIDDLEBROOK'S New England Almanac for 1849. By
Elijah Middlebrook. River Head: G. O. Wells. 16 ll.
CtHi. 8725

NATIONAL Almanac for 1849. Rochester: Benton,
Fisher & Miller. 32 ll. NBuHi; NR. 8726

NATIONAL Reform Almanac for 1849. New-York: Office of Young America. 24 ll. MWA; NN; MH. 8727

NORTH-EAST Centre Farmers' Almanac for 1849. By
David Young. North-East Centre and South Canaan: J.

G. Caulkins & Co. 18 ll. NN. 8728

The OLD Rough and Ready Almanac for 1849. Philadelphia [and] New York: Turner & Fisher. 18 ll. NHi (17 ll.) 8729

The PEOPLE'S Illustrated Almanac for 1849. New-York: Clapp & Townsend. 16 ll. NCooHi. 8730

The PEOPLE'S Illustrated Almanac for 1849. New-York: Clapp & Townsend... Sun Building. 16 ll. MWA; N; NN; NHi; InU; MiD-B; OClWHi; WHi; MH; MHi; MSaE; DLC; NjR; CLU; MBC. 8731

PHINNEY'S Calendar, or Western Almanac for 1849. By George R. Perkins. Cooperstown: H. & E. Phinney. 18 ll. MWA; N; NN; NHi; NRMA; PHi; NSyOHi; MBC; NCooHi; NUtHi; NBuHi; InU; MiD-B; MH; MnU; WHi; Drake. 8732

PHRENOLOGICAL and Physiological Almanac for 1849. By L. N. Fowler. New York: Fowlers and Wells. 24 ll. MWA (three varieties); N (two varieties); NBLiHi; CtHi; MBC; PPAmP; NRMA; CLU; Ct; NP (impf); PPL; WHi. 8733

RIPSNORTER Comic Almanac for 1849. New York: Elton. 12 ll. MWA; MH. 8734

ROUGH and Ready Almanac for 1849. By David Young. River Head: G. O. Wells. 18 ll. NBLiHi. 8735

SPOFFORD'S United States Farmers' Almanac for 1849. New-York: Nafis & Cornish. [Phillips] 8736

STEELE'S Albany Almanac for 1849. Albany: Daniel S. Durrie; Joel Munsell, printer. 18 ll. N. 8737

SWORDS'S Pocket Almanack for 1849. New-York: Stanford and Swords. 82 ll. MWA; NHi; NNG; NjR; PHi; PPL; BritMus. 8738

TOBACCO and Health Almanac for 1849. By John Burdell. New York: Fowlers & Wells. 24 ll. MWA (two varieties); N (two varieties); NHi; InU. 8739

TROY Almanac, and Franklin Calendar for 1849. By Geo. M. Perkins. Troy: Young & Hartt. 16 ll. N. 8740

The UNITED States Farmers' Almanac for 1849. New-York: D. Felt & Co. 18 ll. MWA; NHi; NB; NBLiHi (impf); NBuG. 8741

The UNITED States Farmers' Almanac for 1849. New York: Charles Small. 18 ll. MWA. 8742

The UTICA and Oneida Almanac for 1849. By George R. Perkins. Utica: Roberts & Sherman. 18 ll. MWA; N; NN (17 ll.); NUtHi; NUt; NSyOHi (impf) 8743

V. B. PALMER'S Business-Men's Almanac for 1849. New York: V. B. Palmer. 34 ll. MWA; N; NN; NHi; MeP; NBuG; InU; NjT; WHi; OClWHi; NBLiHi; CtHi; DLC; MBAt; PPL (36 ll.); MBC; MH; MHi; NjR; NjHi; NNC; M; IU; MoKU; CtY; Drake. 8744

WANZER'S Farmers' Almanac for 1849. By Horace Martin. Auburn: R. M. Wanzer; Oliphant's Power Press. 32 ll. NCH (31 ll.) 8745

WATER-CURE Almanac for 1849. By Joel Shew. New York: Fowlers and Wells. 24 ll. MWA (two varieties); Ct; InU (impf); DLC (two varieties); WHi; NRMA.
8746

WEBSTER'S Calendar, and Wynkoop's Columbia County Almanac for 1849. Hudson: P. S. Wynkoop; Albany: J. Munsell, printer. 18 ll. MWA; N. 8747

WEBSTER'S Calendar, or The Albany Almanac for 1849. By J. Munsell. Albany: E. H. Bender. 18 ll. NRMA.
8748

WEBSTER'S Calendar, or The Albany Almanac for 1849. By J. Munsell. Albany: B. Blakeman. 18 ll. N; NN; NRMA.
8749

WEBSTER'S Calendar, or The Albany Almanac for 1849.

By J. Munsell. Albany: Peter Cooke. 18 ll. MWA;
NHi. 8750

WEBSTER'S Calendar, or The Albany Almanac for
1849. By J. Munsell. Albany: Garrett & Gilbert. 18
ll. MWA; NbO. 8751

WEBSTER'S Calendar, or The Albany Almanac for
1849. By J. Munsell. Albany: James Henry. 18 ll.
N; NcD; OClWHi; PHi; MiU-C. 8752

WEBSTER'S Calendar, or The Albany Almanac for 1849.
By J. Munsell. Albany: W. C. Little & Co. 18 ll.
NN; MB; OClWHi; PHi; NjR. 8753

WEBSTER'S Calendar, or The Albany Almanac for 1849.
By J. Munsell. Albany: Joel Munsell. 18 ll. MWA;
N; NN; MBAt; DLC; CtY; WHi; NIC; PHi; NNC; InU
(16 ll., ntp); CLU; MnU; CoCC. 8754

WEBSTER'S Calendar, or The Albany Almanac for 1849.
By J. Munsell. Albany: E. H. Pease & Co. 18 ll.
MWA; N; NR; NjR; CtHi; CtNhHi; MHi; MoU; Drake.
8755
WEBSTER'S Calendar, or The Albany Almanac for 1849.
By J. Munsell. Albany: William Richardson's Paper
Hanging Store. 18 ll. MWA; N. 8756

WEBSTER'S Calendar, or The Albany Almanac for 1849.
By J. Munsell. Albany: C. R. & G. Webster; E. W.
Skinner & Co. 18 ll. NSchU. 8757

WEBSTER'S Calendar, or The Albany Almanac for 1849.
By J. Munsell. Catskill: J. H. Van Gorden. 18 ll.
Drake. 8758

WEBSTER'S Calendar, or The Albany Almanac for 1849.
By J. Munsell. Coxsackie: J. H. McCoy. 18 ll. MWA.
8759
The WESTERN and Oneida Almanac for 1849. By
George R. Perkins. Utica: Roberts & Sherman. 18 ll.
NRMA. 8760

WESTERN Farmers' Almanac for 1849. By Horace Martin. Syracuse: B. R. Peck & Co.; Auburn: Oliphant's Power Press. 32 ll. MWA. 8761

WESTERN Farmers' Almanac for 1849. By Horace Martin. Syracuse: Stoddard & Babcock; Auburn: Oliphant's Power Press. 32 ll. NCooHi; ICHi. 8762

The WHIG Almanac and United States Register for 1849. New York: Greeley & McElrath. 32 ll. MWA; N; NN; NHi; PHi; NBuHi; Ct; NBuG; NBLiHi; MHi; NjP; CtY; DLC; PPL; OSand; MBC; CtHi; PU; NSyU; NCooHi; AzU; NRMA; ICN; NNA; NjR; NNCoCi; CoCC; MeP; TxDN; NjT; MDedHi; MiD-B; TxAbH; OCHP; KyBgW; CtHT-W; InU; WHi; OMC; KHi; NIC; P; In; MoHi; CoU; IC; CLU; OCl; ICHi; NPV; MB; F; MoKU; CU; MiGr; LNHT; NT; MnM; O; I; NjJ; OO; Nh; MoS; WvU; PYHi; CtB; ViW; Drake. 8763

WILLARD'S Troy Almanac for 1849. Troy: L. Willard; Albany: J. Munsell, printer. 18 ll. MWA; NHi. 8764

The YANKEE Doodle Comic All-My-Nack for 1849. N. Y.: Elton. 8 ll. MWA; NHi; ICU. 8765

AGRICULTURAL and Family Almanac for 1850. [New-York: Dr. William B. Moffat] 24 ll. MWA; N; NHi; NCooHi; NWhpHi; DLC; CtY; MSaE; CLU; ICHi; WHi; NjR (23 ll.); Drake. 8765

The AGRICULTURISTS' Guide and Almanac for 1850. By David Young. [np, np] 46 ll. MWA; N; NHi; NRMA; CtLHi (41 ll.); CtHi. 8766

-- Issue with 60 ll. MWA; NjR; Drake. 8767

ALMANACH Francais des Etats-Unis pour 1850. New-York: l'Auteur; D. Fanshaw, imprimeur. 19 ll. PHi. 8768

The AMERICAN Family Almanac for 1850. By George R. Perkins. Little Falls: Lorenzo O. Gay; Utica: R. Northway & Co., printers. 18 ll. MWA; N (impf); NBuHi; NRMA; NSyOHi (6 ll.) 8769

The AMERICAN Family Almanac for 1850. By George R. Perkins. Oriskany: D. C. Balis; Utica: R. Northway & Co., printers. 18 ll. Drake.   8770

The AMERICAN Family Almanac for 1850. By George R. Perkins. Utica: Harrison & Hale; R. Northway & Co., printers. 18 ll. NCooHi.   8771

AMERICAN Farmers' Almanac for 1850. By Horace Martin. Auburn: H. Oliphant; Oliphant's Power Press. 32 ll. Drake.   8772

AMERICAN Temperance Almanac for 1850. New York: American Temperance Union. 18 ll. Drake.   8773

ASTROLOGICAL Almanac for 1850. By C. W. Roback. New York. [Sabin 71720]   8774

BELL & Goodman's Almanac for 1850. Rochester: Bell & Goodman. 16 ll. MWA; NR (15 ll.)   8775

BENDER'S Farmers' Almanac for 1850. Albany: E. H. Bender; J. Munsell, printer. 18 ll. NHi.   8776

The CHURCH Almanac for 1850. New-York: The Protestant Episcopal Tract Society; Pudney & Russell, printers. 24 ll. MWA (two varieties); N; NHi; NBLiHi; RNHi; CtW; NNG; NNA; DLC; MBAt; WHi; MB; NcU; IU; NSchU; NRMA; MiD-B; OCHP; BritMus.   8777

-- Issue with 36 ll. PPL.   8778

COMMON Almanac for 1850. By Geo. R. Perkins. Watertown: Knowltown, Rice & Co. 18 ll. MWA; NHi; NWattHi; DLC.   8779

CROCKETT'S Almanac for 1850. New York [and Philadelphia and Boston]: James Fisher. 18 ll. MBAt.   8780

CROCKETT'S Almanac for 1850. New York [and Philadelphia and Boston]: Fisher & Brothers. 18 ll. MWA; CtY; WHi; TMC.   8781

DISTURNELL'S United States Almanac and National Register for 1850. New York: J. Disturnell. 51 ll. NHi; DLC; MHi; ViHi; NBuHi.   8782

DISTURNELL'S United States National Register for 1850. New York: J. Disturnell; George W. Wood, printer. Broadside. DLC.   8783

DR. BLAKE'S Calendar of Health, or Family Almanac for 1850. New York: Dr. Thomas Blake. 18 ll. MWA; PPL.   8784

DUTCHESS and Ulster County Farmers' Almanac for 1850. By David Young. Poughkeepsie: John Grubb. 18 ll. NHi; NP.   8785

ELTON'S Californian Comic All-my-nack for 1850. N. Y.: Elton. 18 ll. MWA; PPL; CHi; MWiW.   8786

ELTON'S Comic All-My-Nack for 1850. New York: Elton. 18 ll. MWA; N; NSchU; CLU; CtY (ntp); MWiW; Drake.   8787

ELTON'S Funny Almanac for 1850. New-York: Elton. 18 ll. CLU.   8788

ELTON'S Ripsnorter Comic Almanac for 1850. N. Y.: Elton. 12 ll. DLC; OMC; MWiW.   8789

FAMILY Almanac. The American Hebrew and English Almanac for 1849-50. New-York: J. M. Jackson. 12 ll. MWA.   8790

FARMER'S Almanac for 1850. By David Young. New York: Samuel Raynor. 18 ll. MWA; NBLiHi; NRMA; CtY (impf)   8791

FARMERS' Almanac and Ephemeris for 1850. By David Young. Ithaca: Andrus, Gauntlett & Co. 18 ll. MWA; NIC; NPV; CLU; InU; Drake.   8792

FARMERS' Almanac, and Ephemeris for 1850. By David Young. New York: Samuel Raynor. 18 ll.

NjR. 8793

FARMERS' Almanac, and Ephemeris for 1850. By
David Young. New York: Samuel Raynor; Newburgh:
James S. Brown. 18 ll. N. 8794

FELT'S Pocket Almanac for 1850. New-York: David
Felt & Co.; D. Felt & Co. & Hosford. 12 ll. NHi.
8795
GAFFNEY'S Family Almanac for 1850. By George R.
Perkins. Utica: M. Gaffney. 18 ll. DLC. 8796

The GENESEE Valley Almanac for 1850. Rochester:
J. & T. Hawks. 16 ll. NRMA. 8797

The GENESEE Valley Almanac for 1850. Utica: J. E.
Warner & Co. 16 ll. N (15 ll.) 8798

The GOOD Samaritan Almanac for 1850. New York:
M. A. F. Harrison. 8 ll. NRMA. 8799

GRATUITOUS Almanac for 1850. New York: Comstock
& Co., Brothers. 16 ll. N. 8800

HOWLAND, Harvey & Co.'s Farmers Almanac for 1850.
Sandy Hill: Howland, Harvey & Co. 12 ll. MWA. 8801

HULING'S Saratoga Almanac for 1850. Saratoga Springs:
E. J. Huling; Auburn: Oliphant's Power Press and General Book and Job Office. 32 ll. MWA (missing from
shelves) 8802

HUTCHINS Improved Almanac for 1850. New York:
Bartlett. [Phillips] 8803

HUTCHINS' Improved Family Almanac for 1850. By
David Young. New-York: Samuel Raynor. 18 ll. MWA;
N; NN; NHi; CtHi; DLC; MB; NjMo; ICU; NB;
NWhpHi; WHi; NNSIHi. 8804

HUTCHINS' Improved Family Almanac for 1850. By
David Young. New-York: J. C. Riker. 18 ll. CtHi.
8805

HUTCHINS' Improved Family Almanac and Ephemeris for 1850. By David Young. Kingston: Rodney A. Chipp. 18 ll. Hoes. 8806

HUTCHINS' Improved Family Almanac and Ephemeris for 1850. By David Young. New-York: J. C. Riker. 18 ll. NjR. 8807

HUTCHINS' Improved Family Almanac and Ephemeris for 1850. By David Young. New-York: Samuel Raynor. 18 ll. NBLiHi; NjR; Drake (13 ll.) 8808

ILLUSTRATED Family Almanac for 1850. By David Young. Troy: Merriam, Moore & Co. 16 ll. MnU.
8809

The ILLUSTRATED Family Christian Almanac for the United States for 1850. By David Young. New-York: American Tract Society. 30 ll. MWA; N; NN; NHi; OClWHi; NBuHi; MBAt; NBLiHi; Ct; PPL; NUtHi; CtW; RWe; OU; CtNhHi; MHi; CtY; PDoBHi; CtB; CtLHi; NUt; PPeSchw; MNF; PPAmP; ICU; IU; MH; TxU; ViU; InU; MBC; MeBa; PPPrHi; WHi; MnU; NjMo; OMC; CoCC; NBuG; NcA; CtHT; TxAbH; PAtM; MDedHi; MiD-B; MB; RPB; IHi; NbO; MoSM; MeP; NbHi; ViHi; DLC; NNA; PHi; MBu; NSyOHi; NPV; CLU; NjHi; NCooHi; NSchU; NcD; BritMus; NjR; Drake.
8810

The ILLUSTRATED Family Recipe and Medical Almanac for 1850. New-York: A. B. & D. Sands. 12 ll. MWA; NN; NRMA; OClWHi; MHi (ntp); NSchU; InU.
8811

The ILLUSTRATED Phrenological Almanac for 1850. By L. N. Fowler. New-York: Fowlers and Wells. 24 ll. MWA; N; NN; NHi; OClWHi; CtW; NBLiHi; MBAt; MBC; CLU; NSyOHi; NjHi; NP; WHi; InU; Drake (23 ll.) 8812

The ILLUSTRATED Phrenological Almanac for 1850. By L. N. Fowler. New York: J. S. Redfield. 24 ll. MWA. 8813

The ILLUSTRATED Water-Cure and Health Almanac for 1850. New York: Fowlers and Wells. 24 ll. MWA;

NHi; NT; OHi; Ct; OMC; WHi; DLC; MBAt; MSaE;
F; OClWHi. 8814

ILLUSTRIRTER Deutsch-Amerikanischer Volkskalender
für 1850. Von Martin Hammer. New-York: G. & B.
Westermann Brothers, printers. 49 ll. MWA. 8815

KNICKERBOCKER Almanac for 1850. By David Young.
Newburgh: Daniel Smith. 12 ll. MWA. 8816

KNICKERBOCKER Almanac for 1850. By David Young.
New York: Samuel Raynor. 18 ll. MWA; NjR (17 ll.)
8817
KNICKERBOCKER'S Almanac for 1850. By David
Young. New York: Samuel Raynor. 18 ll. DLC. 8818

The LIBERTY Almanac for 1850. New York: Am. &
For. Anti-Slavery Society; William Harned. 24 ll.
MWA; N; NN; NHi; OClWHi; CtY; CtHi; MBC; MH;
TxU; MB; ICN; NIC; WHi. 8819

M'ALISTER'S All-Healing Almanac, and Family Friend
for 1850. New York: James M'Alister. 8 ll. N. 8820

A MASONIC Register for 1850. By R. R. Boyd. New-
York: Br. Jas. Narine, printer. 44 ll. NNFM. 8821

MESSER'S Western Farmers' Almanac for 1850. By
Horace Martin. Penn Yan: Marsena Messer; Auburn:
Oliphant's Power Press. 32 ll. NRMA. 8822

The METHODIST Almanac for 1850. By David Young.
New-York: Lane & Scott; Joseph Longking, printer. 30
ll. MWA; NHi; N; InU; NR; NBuHi; WHi; MiGr; NcD;
NBuG; MBAt; MH; NjR; OClWHi; CtW; Drake. 8823

MORTLEY'S Family Almanac for 1850. By George R.
Perkins. Utica: A. B. Mortley; R. Northway & Co.,
printers. NRMA (17 ll.) 8824

NEW-YORKER Volks-Kalender auf 1850. New-York:
Magnus u. Bach. 18 ll. N. 8825

OLIVER & Brother's Pictorial Temperance Almanac
for 1850. New-York: Oliver & Brother. 24 ll. MWA.
8826

The PEOPLE'S Illustrated Almanac for 1850. New
York: Clapp & Townsend. 16 ll. MWA (three varieties);
N; NN; NHi; InU; RWe; CLU; WHi; NRMA; NCanHi;
NjR. 8827

PHINNEY'S Calendar or Western Almanac for 1850.
Buffalo: Phinney & Co.; [etc] 18 ll. MWA; N; NN;
NBuHi; DLC; MBC; MnU; NBuG; InU; NRMA; NIC;
NSyOHi; FSpHi; MH; CLU; NCooHi; Drake. 8828

"POOR RICHARD." Poor Richard's Almanac for 1850.
By Prof. Benj. Peirce. New-York: John Doggett Jr.
30 ll. MWA; N; NN; NHi; MH; CLU; CoU; PPiU; P;
MeHi; OMC; InU; OClWHi; NjHi; CtY; ViW; NBLiHi;
RNR; PPL; MBAt; MBC; CtHi; MHi; CtNhHi; MSaE;
DLC; PHi; NNUT; MB; NRMA; IU; NBuG; MDedHi;
PDoBHi; WKenHi; WHi; MiD-B; PPAmP; MS; CtLHi;
BritMus; NjR; Drake. 8829

ROCHESTER Almanac for 1850. By David Young.
Rochester: Wm. Alling. 14 ll. NR; NRHi; NRMA;
NRU. 8830

SAXTON'S American Farmers' Almanac for 1850. New
York: A. B. Allen & Co. 16 ll. MWA. 8831

SAXTON'S American Farmers' Almanac for 1850. New
York: C. M. Saxton. 16 ll. MWA; NHi; CtLHi (14 ll.);
NCanHi (15 ll.); DLC; NRMA. 8832

SAXTON'S American Farmers' Almanac for 1850. New
York: Spalding & Shepard. 16 ll. NjR; Drake. 8833

STRONG'S Comic Almanac for 1850. New York: T.
W. Strong. 18 ll. MWA. 8834

SWORDS'S Pocket Almanack for 1850. New-York:
Stanford and Swords. 80 ll. MWA; N; NHi; OClWHi;
NNG; CtY; MSaE; PHi; PPL; BritMus. 8835

New York - 1850

SYRACUSE Almanac for 1850. By David Young. Syracuse: L. W. Hall; J. G. Reed & Co., printers. 16 ll. NCooHi; NSyOHi.   8836

The TRAGIC Almanac for 1850. [np, np] MWiW (6 ll.)   8837

The TROY Almanac for 1850. By George R. Perkins. Troy: Hart & Jones. 18 ll. MWA.   8838

TROY Almanac and Franklin Calendar for 1850. Troy: Merriam, Moore & Co. 18 ll. MWA; DLC; CLU; WHi.   8839

TROY Almanac and Franklin Calendar for 1850. By Geo. R. Perkins. Troy: Young & Hartt. 18 ll. N.   8840

TURNERS Comic Almanac for 1850. New York: Fisher & Brothers; James Fisher. 18 ll. MWA; NN (impf); NHi; DLC; MSaE; NBuG; MWiW.   8841

The UNITED States Family Almanac for 1850. By David Young. New York: Collins and Brother. 12 ll. MWA.   8842

The UNITED States Farmer's Almanac for 1850. New York: David Felt & Co. 18 ll. MWA; NHi.   8843

The UNITED States Farmer's Almanac for 1850. By David Young. New York: Samuel Raynor. 18 ll. NjJ.   8844

The UNITED States Farmer's Almanac for 1850. New York: Charles Small. 18 ll. NBLiHi.   8845

The UNITED States Farmers' Almanac for 1850. New York: Charles Small. 18 ll. NjR.   8846

The UTICA and Oneida Almanac for 1850. By George R. Perkins. Utica: Roberts & Sherman. 18 ll. MWA; N; NCooHi; Drake.   8847

VAN Gorden's Diary, or Farmers' Almanac for 1850. Catskill: J. H. Van Gorden; Hudson: Rural Repository. 26 ll. Drake.   8848

New York - 1850

V. B. PALMER'S Business-Men's Almanac for 1850.
By S. H. Wright. New York: V. B. Palmer. 32 ll.
MWA; N; NN; NHi; NBLiHi; OClWHi; MiD-B; MBC;
MH; MHi; DLC; MBAt; NNC (impf); MnU; PPL (36
ll.); MoKU; CtY; ICU; OMC; KHi; NjR. 8849

WEBSTER'S Calendar, or the Albany Almanac for 1850.
By J. Munsell. Albany: Daniel S. Durrie. 16 ll. N;
OClWHi. 8850

WEBSTER'S Calendar, or the Albany Almanac for 1850.
By J. Munsell. Albany: James Henry. 18 ll. MWA;
N; NN; MB; PHi; MiU-C. 8851

WEBSTER'S Calendar, or the Albany Almanac for 1850.
By J. Munsell. Albany: Aaron Hill. 18 ll. N; NHi;
NRMA; DLC; PHi; CtY. 8852

WEBSTER'S Calendar, or the Albany Almanac for 1850.
By J. Munsell. Albany: P. L. Gilbert. 18 ll. NjR
(16 ll.) 8853

WEBSTER'S Calendar, or the Albany Almanac for 1850.
By J. Munsell. Albany: Little & Co. 18 ll. N; NjR.
8854
WEBSTER'S Calendar, or the Albany Almanac for 1850.
By J. Munsell. Albany: Joel Munsell, printer. 18 ll.
MWA; NIC; ICN; InU; MHi. 8855

WEBSTER'S Calendar, or the Albany Almanac for 1850.
By J. Munsell. Albany: E. H. Pease & Co. 18 ll.
MWA; N; NR; MoU; NjR; Drake (16 ll.) 8856

WEBSTER'S Calendar, or the Albany Almanac for 1850.
By J. Munsell. Catskill: C. Austin. 18 ll. N. 8857

WEBSTER'S Calendar, or the Albany Almanac for 1850.
By J. Munsell. Schenectady: G. Y. Van de Bogert.
18 ll. MWA; N; NcD; WHi. 8858

WESTERN Family Almanac for 1850. Auburn: J. C.
Iveson & Co. 32 ll. N. 8859

WESTERN Farmers' Almanac for 1850. By Horace Martin. Auburn: James M. Alden. 32 ll. NHi; NCH; CtY. 8860

WESTERN Farmers' Almanac for 1850. By Horace Martin. Auburn: J. C. Ivison & Co.; Oliphant's Power Press. 32 ll. MWA; N. 8861

WESTERN Farmers' Almanac for 1850. By Horace Martin. Manchester: N. K. Cole. 32 ll. NCanHi. 8862

WESTERN Farmers' Almanac for 1850. By Horace Martin. Syracuse: L. W. Hall; Auburn: Oliphant's Power Press. 32 ll. MWA. 8863

WESTERN Farmers' Almanac for 1850. By Horace Martin. Syracuse: B. R. Peck & Co.; Auburn: Oliphant's Power Press. 32 ll. WHi. 8864

WESTERN Farmers' Almanac for 1850. By Horace Martin. Syracuse: Stoddard & Babcock; Auburn: Oliphant's Power Press. 32 ll. NCooHi. 8865

The WHIG Almanac and United States Register for 1850. New York: Greeley & McElrath. 32 ll. MWA; N; NN; NHi; In; PHi; NBuHi; LNHT; MHi; MH; ICN; NNCoCi; NSyU; MB; OSand; NCooHi; IU; NIC; NjP; CtY; DLC; I; PU; PPL; MBC; NNA; NBLiHi; NPV; CoU; MoHi; IC; CLU; MoSW; MoKU; CU; CHi; Ct; NjJ; OO; OMC; OCl; NBuG; KHi; MiD-B; P; NT; NjT; InU; WvU; WHi; CtB; CtHT-W; TxDN; NCanHi; Nh; ICHi; O; NjR; Drake. 8866

WILLARD'S Troy Almanac for 1850. Troy: L. Willard. 18 ll. MWA; NHi. 8867

WYNKOOP'S Diary, or Farmer's Almanac for 1850. Hudson: P. S. Wynkoop. 24 ll. MWA. 8868

NORTH CAROLINA

ALMANACK for 1784. Newbern: R. Keith. Advertised in imprint of broadside (in DLC) headed "Twenty Pounds Reward," dated December 10, 1783.   8869

The NORTH-CAROLINA Almanack for 1790. By William Thomas. Fayetteville: Sibley & Howard. Advertised in the "North-Carolina Chronicle," February 1, 1790.   8870

The NORTH-CAROLINA Almanac for 1791. Fayetteville: George Roulstone for John Sibley & Co. Advertised in the "North-Carolina Chronicle," October 4, 1790.   8871

The NORTH-CAROLINA Almanack for 1792. Newbern: François-Xavier Martin. Advertised in the "North-Carolina Chronicle," November 5, 1791.   8872

HODGE'S North-Carolina Almanack for 1795. By William Thomas. Halifax: Abraham Hodge. 20 ll. MWA; DLC (15 ll.); NcU.   8873

HODGE'S North-Carolina Almanack for 1796. By William Thomas. Halifax: Abraham Hodge. 24 ll. MWA; DLC; PHi; CSmH; NcU.   8874

HODGE'S North-Carolina Almanack for 1797. By William Thomas. Halifax: Abraham Hodge. 24 ll. MWA; DLC; NcD; NcU.   8875

The NORTH-CAROLINA Almanack for 1797. Newbern: François X. Martin. 18 ll. NcU.   8876

HODGE'S North-Carolina Almanack for 1798. By William Thomas. Halifax: Abraham Hodge. 24 ll. MWA;

North Carolina - 1799   859

DLC; NcD; NcU.   8877

HODGE'S North-Carolina Almanack for 1799. By William Thomas. Halifax: Abraham Hodge. 24 ll. MWA; NcD (ntp); NcHiC (impf); NcU; KyHi (23 ll.)   8878

The NORTH-CAROLINA Almanack for 1799. Newbern: John C. Osborn & Co. 18 ll. NcU (impf)   8879

The NORTH-CAROLINA Almanack for 1799. Salisbury: Francis Coupee. 20 ll. DLC; Cotten.   8880

HODGE & Boylan's North-Carolina Almanack for 1800. By William Thomas. Halifax: Abraham Hodge. 24 ll. MWA; NcU.   8881

The NORTH-CAROLINA Register, and Almanac for 1800. Wilmington: Gazette Office. Advertised in the "Wilmington Gazette," March 3, 1799.   8882

HODGE & Boylan's North-Carolina Almanack for 1801. By P. B. Halifax: Abraham Hodge. 24 ll. MWA (ntp); NcD; NcU.   8883

The NORTH-CAROLINA Almanac for 1801. Salisbury: Francis Coupee. 24 ll. DLC (21 ll., ntp; title presumed)   8884

HODGE & Boylan's North-Carolina Almanack for 1802. By P. Brooks. Halifax: Abraham Hodge. 24 ll. MWA (23 ll.); NcU.   8885

The NORTH & South-Carolina Almanac for 1802. By Philip Brooks. Salisbury: F. Coupee. 26 ll. NcD; ViW (14 ll.)   8886

GALES'S North-Carolina Almanack for 1803. Raleigh. 24 ll. MWA (ntp)   8887

HODGE & Boylan's North-Carolina Almanack for 1803. By P. Brooks. Halifax: Abraham Hodge. 24 ll. NcD; NcU; InRE.   8888

North Carolina - 1803

The NORTH-CAROLINA Almanack for 1803. By Alexander B. Silliman. Wilmington: A. Hall. 25 ll. NHi.
8889

GALES'S North-Carolina Almanack for 1804. By P. Brooks. Raleigh: J. Gales. 24 ll. MWA; NN. 8890

HODGE & Boylan's North-Carolina Almanack for 1804. By P. Brooks. Halifax: Abraham Hodge. 24 ll. NcD; NcU. 8891

GALES'S North-Carolina Almanack for 1805. By P. Brooks. Raleigh: J. Gales. 24 ll. MWA; NcU (impf) 8892

HODGE & Boylan's North-Carolina Almanack for 1805. By P. Brooks. Halifax: Abraham Hodge. 24 ll. MWA (20 ll.); NcHiC (22 ll.); NcU. 8893

BOYLAN'S North-Carolina Almanack for 1806. By P. Brooks. Raleigh: William Boylan. 18 ll. NcU. 8894

GALES'S North Carolina Almanack for 1806. By P. Brooks. Raleigh: J. Gales. 24 ll. NcD (ntp) 8895

BOYLAN'S North-Carolina Almanack for 1807. By P. Brooks. Raleigh: William Boylan. 24 ll. MWA (22 ll.); NcU. 8896

GALES'S North-Carolina Almanack for 1807. By P. Brooks. Raleigh: J. Gales. 24 ll. NcD; NcU (impf) 8897

BOYLAN'S North-Carolina Almanack for 1808. By P. Brooks. Raleigh: William Boylan. 24 ll. NcU. 8898

GALES'S North-Carolina Almanack for 1808. By P. Brooks. Raleigh: J. Gales. 24 ll. MWA (21 ll., ntp); NcD; NcU (impf) 8899

WATSON & Hall's North-Carolina Almanac for 1808. By P. Brooks. Newbern: Watson & Hall. 26 ll. PHi.
8900

BOYLAN'S North-Carolina Almanack for 1809. By P. Brooks. Raleigh: William Boylan. 24 ll. MWA (23 ll.); NcU; T (23 ll.) 8901

North Carolina - 1809   861

COUPEE'S North-Carolina Almanac for 1809. By
Philip Brooks. Salisbury: Francis Coupee. 18 ll. NcU.
8902

GALES'S North-Carolina Almanac for 1809. By P.
Brooks. Raleigh: J. Gales. 24 ll. NcD; InRE. 8903

WATSON and Hall's North-Carolina Almanac for 1809.
By P. Brooks. Newbern: Watson and Hall. 24 ll.
NcU.   8904

BOYLAN'S North-Carolina Almanack for 1810. By P.
Brooks. Raleigh: William Boylan. 24 ll. NcU; ICHi.
8905

COUPEE'S North-Carolina Almanac for 1810. [np, np]
ViW (17 ll.)   8906

GALES & Seaton's Almanac for 1810. Raleigh: Gales
& Seaton. 24 ll. MWA (22 ll., ntp); NcD.   8907

BOYLAN'S North-Carolina Almanack for 1811. By P.
Brooks. Raleigh: William Boylan. 24 ll. NcD. 8908

HENDERSON'S Almanack for 1811. By Jno. Beasley.
Raleigh: Thomas Henderson, jun'r. 24 ll. MWA; NN
(4 ll.); NcU.   8909

The NORTH-CAROLINA, South-Carolina and Georgia Almanack for 1811. By Elijah Middlebrook. [np, np] 18
ll. Nc; GA.   8910

COUPEE and Crider's North & South-Carolina Almanac
for 1812. By P. Brooks. Salisbury: Coupee and Crider. 18 ll. MWA.   8911

GALES & Seaton's Almanack for 1812. By P. Brooks
[and] John Beasley. Raleigh: J. Gales. 24 ll. NcD;
NcU (ntp)   8912

HENDERSON'S Almanack for 1812. By Joshua Sharp.
Raleigh: Thomas Henderson. 24 ll. NcU (23 ll.) 8913

LUCAS and Abraham H. Boylan's North-Carolina Almanack for 1812. By Philip Brooks. Raleigh: Lucas &

A. H. Boylan. 16 ll. NcU. 8914

MIDDLEBROOK'S Almanack, for Georgia and the Carolinas for 1812. By Elijah Middlebrook. [np, np] MWA (16 ll.) 8915

GALES & Seaton's Almanack for 1813. By P. Brooks [and] John Beasley. Raleigh: J. Gales. 24 ll. MWA; NcD. 8916

GALES & Seaton's North-Carolina Almanack for 1813. By P. Brooks [and] John Beasley. Raleigh: J. Gales. 24 ll. NcD; MH. 8917

HENDERSON'S Almanack for 1813. By Joshua Sharp. Ralegh [sic]: Thomas Henderson. 24 ll. MWA; NcD; NcU; InRE. 8918

GALES'S North-Carolina Almanack for 1814. By P. Brooks [and] John Beasley. Raleigh: J. Gales. 18 ll. MWA (ntp); NcD (17 ll.); NcU (impf) 8919

HENDERSON'S Almanack for 1814. By Joshua Sharp. Ralegh [sic]: Thomas Henderson. 18 ll. MWA; NcU.
8920

GALES'S North-Carolina Almanack for 1815. By J. Beasley. Raleigh: J. Gales. 18 ll. MWA; NcD (ntp); NcU; InU. 8921

No entry. 8922

No entry. 8923

No entry. 8924

No entry. 8925

HENDERSON'S Almanack for 1815. By Joshua Sharp. Ralegh [sic]: Thomas Henderson. 18 ll. MWA (17 ll.); NcD.   8926

The NORTH-CAROLINA Almanack for 1815. By Philip Brooks. Raleigh: A. Lucas. 18 ll. NcU.   8927

GALES'S North-Carolina Almanack for 1816. Raleigh: J. Gales. 18 ll. MWA (ntp); DLC (impf); NcHiC (17 ll.); NcU (impf)   8928

HENDERSON'S Almanack for 1816. By Joshua Sharp. Ralegh [sic]: Thomas Henderson. 18 ll. MWA (17 ll.); NcU.   8929

The NORTH-CAROLINA Almanack for 1816. By Philip Brooks. Raleigh: A. Lucas. 16 ll. NcD.   8930

GALES'S North-Carolina Almanack for 1817. By John Beasley. Raleigh: J. Gales. 16 ll. NcD; NcU.   8931

HENDERSON'S Almanack for 1817. By Joshua Sharp. Raleigh: Thomas Henderson. 18 ll. MWA; DLC; NcD (ntp); TKL.   8932

The NORTH-CAROLINA Almanack for 1817. By Philip Brooks. Salisbury: 18 ll. ViW (17 ll., tp impf)   8933

GALES'S North-Carolina Almanack for 1818. By John Beasley. Raleigh: J. Gales. 18 ll. DLC; NcD; NcU (impf)   8934

HENDERSON'S Almanack for 1818. By Joshua Sharp. Raleigh: Thomas Henderson. 18 ll. NcD; NcU; TKL.   8935

GALES'S North-Carolina Almanack for 1819. By John Beasley. Raleigh: J. Gales. 18 ll. MWA; DLC; NcD.   8936

HENDERSON'S Almanack for 1819. By Joshua Sharp. Raleigh: Thomas Henderson. 18 ll. NcD; NcU; TKL.   8937

GALES'S North-Carolina Almanack for 1820. By J.

Beasly. Raleigh: J. Gales. 18 ll. NcD (17 ll.);
NcHiC (17 ll.)   8938

HENDERSON'S Almanack for 1820. By Joshua Sharp
[and] J. Beasly. Raleigh: Thomas Henderson. 18 ll.
MWA; Nc; NcD; NcU; TKL.   8939

GALES'S North-Carolina Almanack for 1821. By John
Beasley. Raleigh: J. Gales. 18 ll. MWA (ntp); DLC;
Nc; NcD; NcU.   8940

HENDERSON'S Almanack for 1821. By Joshua Sharp.
Raleigh: Thomas Henderson. 18 ll. MWA (ntp); NcU.   8941

GALES'S North-Carolina Almanack for 1822. By John
Beasley. Raleigh: J. Gales. 18 ll. DLC; NcD;
NcHiC (12 ll.); NcU.   8942

HENDERSON'S Almanack for 1822. By John Beasly.
Raleigh: Thomas Henderson. 18 ll. MWA; Nc; NcD;
NcU.   8943

LAWRENCE & Lemay's North Carolina Almanac for
1822. Raleigh: Lawrence & Lemay. 18 ll. NcHiC (17
ll.)   8944

D. HEARTT'S North-Carolina Almanac for 1823. By
H. M. Cave. Hillsborough: D. Heartt. 18 ll. DLC (17
ll.)   8945

GALES'S North-Carolina Almanack for 1823. By John
Beasley. Raleigh: J. Gales & Son. 18 ll. MWA (17
ll.); Nc (13 ll.); NcD (ntp); NcU.   8946

HENDERSON'S Almanack for 1823. By John Beasley.
Raleigh: Thomas Henderson. 18 ll. MWA (17 ll.);
NcD (11 ll.); NcU; TKL.   8947

The NORTH Carolina Register and United States Calendar for 1823. By Rev. Colin M'Iver. Raleigh: J.
Gales & Son. 77 ll. NcU.   8948

BELL & Lawrence's Almanack for 1824. By William

Collom. Raleigh: Bell & Lawrence. 14 ll. MWA
(impf); NcD; OClWHi (12 ll.)   8949

GALES'S North-Carolina Almanack for 1824. Raleigh:
J. Gales & Son. 18 ll. MWA; DLC; NcU; InU (ntp)
    8950

HENDERSON'S Almanack for 1824. Raleigh:
MWA (15 ll., ntp)   8951

GALES'S North-Carolina Almanack for 1825. By Hudson M. Cave. Raleigh: J. Gales & Son. 18 ll. MWA
(17 ll.); NcD (ntp); NcHiC; NcU.   8952

GALES'S North-Carolina Almanac for 1826. By Dr.
Hudson M. Cave. Raleigh: J. Gales & Sons. 18 ll.
MWA; DLC; Nc (14 ll., ntp); NcU; NBuHi; InU. 8953

BELL and Lawrence's Almanack for 1827. By William
Collom. Raleigh: Bell and Lawrence. 18 ll. NcU.
    8954

GALES'S North-Carolina Almanac for 1827. By Dr.
Hudson M. Cave. Raleigh: J. Gales & Son. 18 ll.
DLC; NcD; NcHiC (17 ll.); NcU.   8955

The CHRISTIAN Almanac for North Carolina for 1828.
Raleigh: American Tract Society. 18 ll. NcU.   8956

The FARMERS' and Planters' Almanac for 1828. Salem:
J. C. Blum. [Paschal]   8957

GALES'S North-Carolina Almanac for 1828. By Dr.
Hudson M. Cave. Raleigh: J. Gales & Son. 18 ll.
DLC; NcD (ntp); NcHiC (16 ll.); MH.   8958

LAWRENCE & Lemay's North Carolina Almanac for
1828. By William Collom. Raleigh: Lawrence & Lemay. 18 ll. NcD; NcHiC; NcU.   8959

The CHRISTIAN Almanac for North Carolina for 1829.
Raleigh: American Tract Society; North Carolina Book
Company. 18 ll. DLC; NcU.   8960

GALES'S North-Carolina Almanac for 1829. By Dr.

Hudson M. Cave. Raleigh: J. Gales & Son. 18 ll.
NcD (ntp); NcHiC (17 ll.); NcU; TKL. 8961

LAWRENCE & Lemay's North-Carolina Almanack for
1829. By William Collom. Raleigh: Lawrence & Lemay. 18 ll. MWA; NcD; NcHiC; Drake. 8962

The CHRISTIAN Almanac for North Carolina for 1830.
Raleigh: American Tract Society. 18 ll. NcD; NcU.
8963

GALES'S North-Carolina Almanac for 1830. By Dr.
Hudson M. Cave. Raleigh: J. Gales & Son. 18 ll.
NcD; NcU (impf); TKL. 8964

LAWRENCE & Lemay's North Carolina Almanac for
1830. By Dr. Hudson M. Cave. Raleigh: Lawrence
& Lemay. 18 ll. NcHiC. 8965

GALES'S North-Carolina Almanac for 1831. By Dr.
Hudson M. Cave. Raleigh: J. Gales & Son. 18 ll.
NN; NcU. 8966

LAWRENCE & Lemay's North Carolina Almanack for
1831. By Dr. Hudson M. Cave. Raleigh: Lawrence
& Lemay. 18 ll. MWA (5 ll.); NcD; MH; Drake (12
ll.) 8967

GALES'S North-Carolina Almanac for 1832. Raleigh:
J. Gales & Son. 18 ll. NcU (impf) 8968

LAWRENCE & Lemay's North Carolina Almanac for
1832. Raleigh: Lawrence & Lemay. 19 ll. NcD;
NcHiC; NcU. 8969

FARMERS' and Planters' Almanac for 1833. Salem.
18 ll. NcD (ntp) 8970

GALES'S North-Carolina Almanac for 1833. Raleigh:
J. Gales & Son. 18 ll. MWA; NcD; NcU. 8971

LAWRENCE & Lemay's North Carolina Almanac for
1833. By William Collom. Raleigh: Lawrence & Lemay. 20 ll. NcHiC; NcU. 8972

FARMERS' and Planters' Almanac for 1834. Salem.
16 ll. NcD (ntp)   8973

GALES'S North-Carolina Almanac for 1834. By William Collom. Raleigh: J. Gales. 18 ll. NcU.   8974

LAWRENCE & Lemay's North Carolina Almanac for 1834. By William Collom. Raleigh: Lawrence & Lemay. 20 ll. NcD; NcHiC (19 ll.)   8975

NORTH Carolina Temperance Almanac for 1834. Fayetteville: William Whitehead. 24 ll. NcU.   8976

GALES'S North-Carolina Almanac for 1835. Raleigh: J. Gales & Son. 18 ll. NcD; NcU (17 ll.); MH.   8977

LAWRENCE & Lemay's North Carolina Almanac for 1835. Raleigh: Lawrence & Lemay. 20 ll. NcD; NcHiC; NcU.   8978

GALES'S North-Carolina Almanac for 1836. By William Collom. Raleigh: J. Gales & Son. 18 ll. NcD; NcU (17 ll.)   8979

GALES'S North-Carolina Almanac for 1837. By William Collom. Raleigh: J. Gales & Son. 18 ll. NcD (17 ll.); NcU (17 ll.)   8980

LEMAY'S North Carolina Almanack for 1837. By William Collom. [Raleigh:] Thos. J. Lemay. 20 ll. NcD; NcU.   8981

The FARMERS' & Planters' Almanac for 1838. Salem. MWA (13 ll., ntp)   8982

GALES'S North-Carolina Almanac for 1838. By William Collom. Raleigh: J. Gales & Son. 18 ll. NcD; NcU.   8983

LEMAY'S North Carolina Almanack for 1838. By William Collom. [Raleigh:] Thos. J. Lemay. 18 ll. NcU.   8984

TURNER & Hughes's North Carolina Almanac for 1838.

Raleigh: Turner & Hughes. 18 ll. NcHiC; CtY.   8985

TURNER & Hughes's North Carolina Almanac for 1838.
Raleigh: Turner & Hughes. (Second Edition) 18 ll.
MWA; DLC; Nc; NcD; NcU.   8986

FARMERS' and Planters' Almanack for 1839. Salem:
John C. Blum. TKL.   8987

TURNER & Hughes's North Carolina Almanac for 1839.
Raleigh: Turner & Hughes. 18 ll. MWA; DLC; Nc;
NcD; NcHiC; NcU; CtY.   8988

TURNER & Hughes' North Carolina Almanac for 1840.
Raleigh: Turner & Hughes. 18 ll. MWA; DLC; Nc;
NcD; NcHiC; NcU; CtY; Drake (12 ll.)   8989

The FARMERS' & Planters Almanac for 1841. Salem:
Blum & Son. MWA (17 ll.); NcD (17 ll.)   8990

TURNER & Hughes' North Carolina Almanac for 1841.
Raleigh: Turner & Hughes. 18 ll. MWA; DLC; Nc;
NcD; NcHiC; Nc-Ar; NcU.   8991

FARMERS' and Planters' Almanac for 1842. Salem:
Blum & Son. 18 ll. NcD (17 ll.)   8992

TURNER & Hughes' North Carolina Almanac for 1842.
Raleigh: Turner & Hughes. 18 ll. MWA; DLC; Nc;
NcD; NcU; CtY; Drake.   8993

FARMERS' and Planters' Almanac for 1843. Salem:
Blum & Son. 15 ll. NcD; NcGW.   8994

TURNER & Hughes' North Carolina Almanac for 1843.
Raleigh: Turner & Hughes. 18 ll. MWA; NHi; DLC;
NjR (17 ll.); CtY; NcD; Nc (6 ll.); NcU.   8995

FARMERS' and Planters' Large Almanac for 1844.
Salem: Blum & Son. 18 ll. MWA; NcD; NjR (17 ll.)
    8996
TURNER & Hughes' North Carolina Almanac for 1844.
Raleigh: Turner & Hughes. 18 ll. DLC; NcD; NcU. 8997

FARMERS' and Planters' Almanac for 1845. Salem: Blum & Son. 18 ll. Nc; NcD. 8998

TURNER & Hughes' North Carolina Almanac for 1845. Raleigh: Turner & Hughes. 18 ll. Nc; NcD; NcU; CtY. 8999

TURNER & Hughes' North Carolina Almanac for 1845. Raleigh [and] New York: Turner & Hughes. 18 ll. DLC; NHi; NcHiC (17 ll.); MH. 9000

FARMERS' and Planters' Almanac for 1846. Salem: Blum & Son. 18 ll. Nc (impf); NcA-S; NcD. 9001

TURNER & Hughes' North Carolina Almanac for 1846. Raleigh: Turner & Hughes. 18 ll. DLC; NHi (12 ll.); NcD; NcU; CtY; MTaHi. 9002

-- Issue with 24 ll. Nc (22 ll.); NcHiC. 9003

FARMERS' and Planters' Almanac for 1847. Salem: Blum & Son. 18 ll. MWA (17 ll.); Nc; NcD. 9004

TURNER'S, Late Turner & Hughes' North Carolina Almanc for 1847. Raleigh: Henry D. Turner. 18 ll. MWA; NHi (12 ll.); DLC; Nc; NcD; NcU; MBAt; CtY. 9005

FARMERS' and Planters' Almanac for 1848. Salem: Blum & Son. 18 ll. Nc (impf); NcD; NcGW; NcU. 9006

TURNER'S North Carolina Almanac for 1848. Raleigh: Henry D. Turner. 18 ll. MWA; NHi (13 ll.); NcD; NcHiC; NcU; MBAt; MH; CtY. 9007

-- Issue with 24 ll. Nc. 9008

The FARMERS' & Planters' Almanac for 1849. Salem: Blum & Son. 18 ll. Nc; NcD; NcU; KyU (17 ll.) 9009

TURNER'S North Carolina Almanac for 1849. Raleigh: Henry D. Turner. 18 ll. MWA; NHi; Nc; NcD; NcU; CtY; WHi; MBAt; Drake. 9010

The FARMERS' and Planters' Almanac for 1850. Salem: Blum & Son. 18 ll. Nc (17 ll.); NcD; NcU; KyU (17 ll.)
9011

TURNER'S North Carolina Almanac for 1850. Raleigh: Henry D. Turner. 18 ll. MWA; Nc; NcD; NcU; CtY; Drake.
9012

OHIO

BROWNE'S Western Calendar; or the Cincinnati Almanac for 1806. By William M'Farland. Cincinnati: John W. Browne. 18 ll. MWA (17 ll.); DLC; MHi; OCHP; OClWHi (ntp)   9013

The OHIO Almanac for 1806. By Robert Stubbs. Cincinnati: Joseph Carpenter. 18 ll. OC; OCHP; CSmH; Lindley.   9014

BROWNE'S Western Calendar; or, the Cincinnati Almanac for 1807. By Robert Stubbs. Cincinnati: John W. Browne and Company. 18 ll. CSmH; NN; OCHP; OClWHi; RPB; MiU-C; ODa (17 ll.); Lindley.   9015

The OHIO Almanac for 1807. By Robert Stubbs. Cincinnati: David L. Carney. 14 ll. MWA; OCHP (ntp)   9016

BROWNE'S Western Calendar, or the Cincinnati Almanac for 1808. By Robert Stubbs. Cincinnati: John W. Browne. 18 ll. MWA; DLC; OCHP; OClWHi; ODa (17 ll.); OMC.   9017

TEUTSCHER Calender auf 1808. By Robert Stubbs. Rendered into German by Edward H. Stall. Cincinnati: John W. Browne. Advertised in "Liberty Hall," October 6, 1807.   9018

BROWNE'S Western Calendar, or the Cincinnati Almanac for 1809. By Robert Stubbs. Cincinnati: John W. Browne. 18 ll. MWA; MHi; MiU-C; OC; OCHP; OClWHi; OCM; ODa (16 ll.); OMC.   9019

BROWNE'S Cincinnati Almanac for 1810. By Robert Stubbs. Cincinnati: John W. Browne & Co. 18 ll. MWA (ntp); DLC; CSmH; ICN; MHi (14 ll.); InU (ntp); OCHP; ODa (12 ll., ntp); OMC.   9020

The OHIO Almanac for 1810. By Robert Stubbs. Cincinnati: Carney & Morgan. 18 ll. ICN; OC (17 ll.); OCHP; OClWHi.   9021

BROWNE'S Cincinnati Almanac for 1811. By Robert Stubbs. Cincinnati: John W. Browne and Company. 18 ll. MWA; CSmH; MHi; NbHi; MiU-C; OC; OCHP; ODa (16 ll.); OMC.   9022

The OHIO Almanac for 1811. By Robert Stubbs. Cincinnati. [Sabin 56965]   9023

BROWNE'S Cincinnati Almanac for 1812. By Robert Stubbs. Cincinnati: J. W. Browne & Co. 18 ll. MWA; MHi; InHi (two varieties); OC; OCHP; OClWHi. 9024

The MIAMI Calendar, or Lebanon Almanac for 1812. By Matthias Corwin, Jun. Lebanon: M'Clean & Hale. 12 ll. OC (11 ll.); OClWHi (10 ll.)   9025

The OHIO Almanac for 1812. By Robert Stubbs. Cincinnati: J. Carpenter & Co. 18 ll. OC; OCHP.   9026

BROWNE & Co's. Cincinnati Almanac for 1813. By Robert Stubbs. Cincinnati: J. W. Browne & Co. 16 ll. MHi; ICN; OCHP; OClWHi; Lindley (impf)   9027

The OHIO Almanac for 1813. By Robert Stubbs. Cincinnati: Browne & Looker, for George Strowhuver. 18 ll. OC.   9028

The OHIO Almanac for 1813. By Robert Stubbs. Cincinnati: J. Carpenter. 18 ll. OCHP.   9029

The OHIO Almanac for 1814. By Robert Stubbs. Cincinnati: Browne & Looker, for George Strowhuver. 18 ll. MWA (16 ll.); DLC; InU (impf); OCHP; OClWHi; OHi.   9030

KEEN and Stewart's Almanac for 1815. Hamilton: Keen & Stewart. Advertised in the "Hamilton Miami

Intelligencer," September 12, 1814. 9031

The OHIO Almanac for 1815. By Robert Stubbs. Cincinnati: Looker & Wallace, for Strowhuver & Stevens. 24 ll. MWA; DLC; CSmH; ICN; InRE; OCHP; OClWHi; OFH. 9032

ALMANAC for 1816. Hamilton: 'Intelligencer' Office. 18 ll. OCHP. 9033

The OHIO Almanac for 1816. By Robert Stubbs. Cincinnati: Looker & Wallace. 24 ll. MWA; DLC (21 ll.); OCHP (22 ll.) 9034

The WESTERN Calendar; or, Cincinnati Almanac for 1816. By Robert Stubbs. Cincinnati: Morgan, Williams & Co. 18 ll. MWA (impf); N; ICN; InHi; O (16 ll.); OClWHi. 9035

The WESTERN Reserve Magazine Almanac for 1816. By John Armstrong. Warren: James White & Co. 30 ll. OClWHi. 9036

The OHIO Register, and Western Calendar for 1817. By William Lusk. Columbus: P. H. Olmsted and Co. 36 ll. MWA; NN; NHi; OClWHi (34 ll.) 9037

The WESTERN Almanac for 1817. By Robert Stubbs. Cincinnati: Williams & Mason. 18 ll. MWA (17 ll.); DLC; ICN; NHi; In; O; OC; OCHP; OClWHi. 9038

The COLUMBUS Almanac for 1818. By William Lusk. Columbus: Office of the Intelligencer; P. H. Olmsted, printer. 50 ll. Lindley. 9039

The COLUMBUS Magazine Almanac for 1818. By William Lusk. Columbus. [Briggs] 9040

The EDUCATION Almanac for 1818. Nathan Guilford, editor. Cincinnati. cf "North American Review," Vol. XLVII, page 48, July 1938. 9041

GANZ Neuer Westlicher, für die Staaten von Ohio, Kentucky und Indiana auf 1818. Lancaster: Johann Herman. 18 ll. OHi; Lindley (17 ll.) 9042

The OHIO Register, and Western Calendar for 1818. By William Lusk. Columbus: Register Office; P. H. Olmsted, printer. 48 ll. MWA; DLC (43 ll.); InHi; NHi; InU (11 ll.); OCHP (47 ll.); OClWHi; OHi. 9043

The WESTERN Almanack for 1818. By James R. Stubbs. Cincinnati: Williams & Mason and Morgan, Lodge & Co. 18 ll. MWA; DLC; N; InU; ICN; OC (20 ll.); OFH; OClWHi (10 ll.); OCHP; InHi; KyLoF (17 ll.); Lindley. 9044

The CHILLICOTHE Almanac for 1819. Chillicothe: Geo. Nashee. 24 ll. MWA (22 ll.); RPB (ntp); OClWHi; OHi. 9045

The COLUMBUS Almanac for 1819. By William Lusk. Columbus: Gazette Office; P. H. Olmsted, printer. MWA (13 ll.) 9046

The FARMER'S Almanac for 1819. By Samuel Burr & Oner R. Powell. Cincinnati: Ferguson & Sanxay; Looker, Reynolds & Co., printers. 18 ll. MWA (impf); OCHP. 9047

Der NEUE Ohio Calender auf 1819. Lancaster: Johann Hermann. 18 ll. OHi (17 ll.); Lindley. 9048

The OHIO Register, and Western Calendar for 1819. By William Lusk. Columbus: Gazette Office; P. H. Olmsted, printer. 48 ll. DLC; NHi (impf); InHi; OClWHi (42 ll.); OHi. 9049

The WESTERN Almanac for 1819. By Samuel Burr & Oner R. Powell. Cincinnati: Morgan, Lodge & Co. 18 ll. OCHP. 9050

The WESTERN Almanac for 1819. By Samuel Burr & Oner R. Powell. Cincinnati: Morgan, Lodge and Co.; Williams, Mason and Co. 18 ll. MWA; DLC; ICN; OC; OClWHi; InHi; InRE; O (17 ll.) 9051

The CHILLICOTHE Almanac for 1820. By Samuel Burr. Chillicothe: Geo. Nashee. 24 ll. OClWHi; OHi.
9052

The CINCINNATI Almanac for 1820. By Samuel Burr. Cincinnati: Mason and Palmer. 27 ll. MWA; DLC; ICN; OHi; OC; OClWHi; OFH; OCHP. 9053

The CINCINNATI Directory [and Almanac for 1820]. [Cincinnati:] Oliver Farnsworth; Morgan, Lodge and Co., printers. 78 ll. MiU-C. 9054

The COLUMBUS Almanac for 1820. Columbus: P. H. Olmsted. 14 ll. O. 9055

The FARMER'S Almanac for 1820. By Samuel Burr. Cincinnati: Phillips & Speer; Looker, Reynolds & Co., printers. 18 ll. MWA (impf); DLC; Or; OCHP; OClWHi; OHi. 9056

Der NEUE Ohio Calender auf 1820. Lancaster: Johann Herman. 18 ll. OHi (17 ll.); Lindley. 9057

The OHIO Register, and Western Calendar for 1820. By William Lusk. Columbus: Monitor Office; David Smith, printer. 42 ll. MWA; DLC; O. 9058

An ASTRONOMICAL Diary, and Almanac for 1821. By Paul Brown. Columbus: P. H. Olmsted. OHi (10 ll.)
9059

The CHILLICOTHE Almanac for 1821. By Samuel Burr. Chillicothe: Geo. Nashee. 18 ll. O; OClWHi; OFH.
9060

The COLUMBUS Almanac for 1821. By William Lusk. Columbus: Monitor Office; David Smith, printer. 12 ll. OClWHi; OMC. 9061

The FARMERS' Almanac for 1821. By Samuel Burr. Cincinnati: Morgan, Lodge & Co. 18 ll. MWA (impf); DLC; O; OCHP; InRE. 9062

The FARMERS' Almanac for 1821. By Samuel Burr. Cincinnati: Phillips and Speer; Looker, Palmer & Reynolds, printers. 18 ll. MWA; ICN; OC; OCHP;

OClWHi; OHi (17 ll.) 9063

The FARMER'S Almanac for 1821. By Andrew Foster.
Lebanon: Van Vleet & Co. 18 ll. O; OC. 9064

The OHIO Register, and Western Calendar for 1821.
By William Lusk. Columbus: Monitor Office; David
Smith, printer. 30 ll. OC; OClWHi; WHi; Lindley.
9065
The CHILLICOTHE Almanac for 1822. By Samuel
Burr. Chillicothe: Geo. Nashee. 18 ll. OClWHi; OHi;
Lindley. 9066

The COLUMBUS Almanac for 1822. By William Lusk.
[Worthington:] Ezra Griswold, Jun. & Co. 12 ll.
MWA; OClWHi. 9067

The FARMER'S Almanac for 1822. By Samuel Burr.
Cincinnati: Morgan, Lodge & Co. 18 ll. O. 9068

The FARMERS' Almanac for 1822. By Samuel Burr.
Cincinnati: Phillips & Speer; Looker & Reynolds,
printers. 18 ll. MWA; DLC; In (impf); InHi; InRE;
O; OC; OCHP; OClWHi. 9069

The FARMERS' Almanac for 1822. By Samuel Burr.
Cincinnati: Phillips & Speer; Looker & Reynolds,
printers. (Second Edition) 18 ll. DLC. 9070

The OHIO Register and Western Calendar for 1822. By
William Lusk. Worthington: Ezra Griswold, jun. & Co.,
printers. 24 ll. OCHP; OClWHi. 9071

The FREEMAN'S Almanack, or, Complete Farmer's
Calendar for 1823. Cincinnati: Oliver Farnsworth and
Co. 28 ll. MWA; NN (23 ll.); InRE; O; OCHP; OHi;
OClWHi. 9072

The FREEMAN'S Almanack, or Farmer's Calendar for
1823. By Samuel Burr. Cincinnati: Oliver Farnsworth & Co. 15 ll. MWA (14 ll.); DLC (14 ll.); IU
(14 ll.); InHi; InU; OC; OClWHi. 9073

Der NEUE für den Staat von Ohio eingerichtete Calender auf 1823. Von Carl Friedrich Egelmann. Canton: Eduard Schaeffer. 18 ll. MWA. 9074

The OHIO Almanac for 1823. Canton: Edward Schaeffer. 18 ll. MWA; DLC (impf); OMans. 9075

The OHIO Register, and Western Calendar for 1823. By William Lusk. Ripley: James Finley, & Co., printers. 20 ll. NN. 9076

The FARMER'S Almanac for 1824. By Samuel Burr. Cincinnati. 18 ll. OClWHi (ntp) 9077

The FREEMAN'S Almanack, or, Complete Farmer's Calendar for 1824. Cincinnati: Oliver Farnsworth & Co. 24 ll. MWA; DLC; NN; MH; N; O (23 ll.); OClWHi; OMC (23 ll.); Drake. 9078

The FREEMAN'S Almanack, or Farmer's Calendar for 1824. By Samuel Burr. Cincinnati: Oliver Farnsworth & Co. 12 ll. MWA; ICN; MnU; In; InHi; InU; Wv-Ar (4 ll.); OC; OCHP; OFH; OHi. 9079

Der NEUE für den Stat von Ohio eingerichteter Calender fur 1824. Canton: Eduard Schaeffer. 16 ll. OHi. 9080

The OHIO Almanac for 1824. By Charles F. Egelmann. Canton: Edward Schaeffer. 18 ll. MWA. 9081

The FREEMAN'S Almanack, or, Complete Farmer's Calendar for 1825. By Samuel Burr. Cincinnati: Oliver Farnsworth & Co. 24 ll. MWA (two varieties); DLC (23 ll.); ICN; O (23 ll.); OClWHi; OHi. 9082

The FREEMAN'S Almanack, or Farmer's Calendar for 1825. By Samuel Burr. Cincinnati: Oliver Farnsworth and Co. 12 ll. MWA (two varieties); In; InU; OC (15 ll.); OCHP; OClWHi. 9083

The WESTERN Reserve Almanac for 1825. By Ansel Young. Painesville: E. D. Howe. 18 ll. MWA (17 ll.); OClWHi. 9084

The COLUMBUS Almanac for 1826. By William Lusk.
Columbus: Geo. Nashee & Co. 12 ll. MWA.   9085

The FREEMAN'S Almanack; or, Complete Farmer's
Calendar for 1826. By Samuel Burr. Cincinnati: O.
& W. M. Farnsworth & Co. 24 ll. MWA; DLC (impf);
NjR; ICN; InHi; InU; O; OClWHi; OHi; OMC.   9086

The FREEMAN'S Almanack, or, Farmer's Calender
[sic] for 1826. By Samuel Burr. Cincinnati: O.
Farnsworth & Co. 12 ll. In (ntp); OCHP; OClWHi.
                                              9087
The FRIENDS' Almanac for 1826. By Samuel Burr.
Cincinnati: Oliver Farnsworth; Richmond: Edmund S.
Buxton. 18 ll. InHi; InRE.   9088

Der NEUE Für den Staat von Ohio eingerichtete Calender auf 1826. Von William Lusk. Canton: Eduard
Schaeffer. 16 ll. MWA; N.   9089

The OHIO Almanac for 1826. By William Lusk. Canton: Edward Schaeffer. 15 ll. OHi.   9090

The WESTERN Reserve Almanac for 1826. By Ansel
Young. Painesville: E. D. Howe. 18 ll. DLC; OClWHi.
                                              9091
The COLUMBUS Almanac for 1827. By William Lusk.
Columbus: Geo. Nashee & Co. 12 ll. MWA; InU; OHi
(11 ll.)   9092

The COLUMBUS Magazine Almanac for 1827. By William Lusk. Columbus: Geo. Nashee & Co. 24 ll.
MWA; OClWHi.   9093

The FREEMAN'S Almanack for 1827. By Samuel Burr.
Cincinnati: N. & G. Guilford; Oliver & Wm. M. Farnsworth. 12 ll. MWA (10 ll., tp impf); ICN; In (ntp);
InU (impf)   9094

-- Issue with 24 ll. MWA; DLC; WHi; MoSM; ICU;
InHi; InU; O; OCHP; OClWHi; OFH; OHi; OMC. 9095

The FRIENDS' Almanac for 1827. By Samuel Burr.

Richmond: Burton & Walling; Cincinnati: O. & W. M. Farnsworth. 18 ll. InRE. 9096

The WESTERN Almanack for 1827. Portsmouth: Western Times. 12 ll. OClWHi. 9097

The CHRISTIAN Almanac, for Ohio, Kentucky, and Indiana for 1828. Cincinnati: Auxiliary Tract Society of Cincinnati. 20 ll. MWA; IHi; OCHP (18 ll.) 9098

The COLUMBUS Magazine Almanac for 1828. By William Lusk. Columbus: P. H. Olmsted & Co. 24 ll. OClWHi. 9099

The FREEMAN'S Almanack for 1828. By Samuel Burr. Cincinnati: N. & G. Guilford; Oliver Farnsworth; W. M. & O. Farnsworth, Jr., printers. 12 ll. MWA; WHi (impf); In; InHi; InU; InRE; Wv-Ar, ICN; OClWHi; OCHP; OMC; Lindley. 9100

-- Issue with 24 ll. MWA; DLC (23 ll.); NN; Ct (18 ll.); OCHP; OClWHi; OC; OHi (23 ll.); O; OFH; CLU. 9101

STATE of Ohio Agricultural Almanac for 1828. By John Armstrong. Zanesville: William Davis. 18 ll. OHi; Smith. 9102

WESTERN Almanack for 1828. By Oliver Loud. Cleaveland [sic]: Henry Bolles. 18 ll. OClWHi. 9103

The CHRISTIAN Almanac, for Ohio, Kentucky & Indiana for 1829. Cincinnati: American Tract Society; Auxiliary Tract Society of Cincinnati; George T. Williamson. 18 ll. O; OC; OCHP; WHi. 9104

The COLUMBUS Almanac for 1829. By William Lusk. Columbus: P. H. Olmsted. 12 ll. MWA. 9105

-- Issue with 24 ll. O (23 ll.); OHi; Wv-Ar (21 ll.)
9106

The FREEMAN'S Almanack for 1829. By Samuel Burr. Cincinnati: N. & G. Guilford; Oliver Farnsworth;

William M. Farnsworth, printer. 12 ll. MWA; InRE
(10 ll.) 9107

-- Issue with 24 ll. MWA; DLC; OClWHi; In (18 ll.,
ntp); OC (18 ll.); OHi; OMC (23 ll.); InU; WHi. 9108

OHIO Magazine Almanack for 1829. By John Armstrong. Zanesville: William Davis. 28 ll. MWA; NHi;
OHi (21 ll.) 9109

The CHRISTIAN Almanac, for Ohio, Kentucky, & Indiana for 1830. Cincinnati: American Tract Society;
George T. Williamson; Robert Boal. 20 ll. MWA; In;
KyHi; KyLoF; O; OC; OClWHi. 9110

The COLUMBUS Almanac for 1830. By William Lusk.
Columbus: Olmsted and Bailhache. 12 ll. MWA;
OClWHi. 9111

The COLUMBUS Magazine Almanac for 1830. By William Lusk. Columbus: Olmsted & Bailhache. 25 ll.
MWA; OHi (24 ll.) 9112

The FREEMAN'S Almanack for 1830. By Samuel Burr.
Cincinnati: N. & G. Guilford; Oliver Farnsworth;
William M. Farnsworth, printer. 12 ll. MWA (impf);
In; InRE; InU; OCHP; OClWHi (10 ll.); OFH; OHi;
Lindley. 9113

The FREEMAN'S Almanack for 1830. By Samuel Burr.
Cincinnati: N. & G. Guilford; Sentinel Office, printers.
24 ll. NN (21 ll.); DLC (23 ll.); OCHP; OClWHi
(two varieties); OMC (22 ll.) 9114

OHIO Magazine Almanack for 1830. By John Armstrong. Zanesville: William Davis. 28 ll. MWA; NN
(27 ll.); Wv-Ar (24 ll.) 9115

The WESTERN Almanac for 1830. By Oliver Loud.
Cleveland: Henry Bolles. 12 ll. OClWHi. 9116

The WESTERN Almanack, for the State of Ohio, Kentucky, and Indiana for 1830. By Oner R. Powell. Cin-

cinnati: G. T. Williamson. 24 ll. MWA; InHi; OC.
9117

ALMANAC, for the States of Ohio, Kentucky, and Indiana for 1831. By Oner R. Powell. Cincinnati: William Conclin. 12 ll. OClWHi (11 ll.) 9118

Der Bauern Calender auf 1831. Von Samuel Burr. Cincinnati: N. und G. Guilford; Oliver Farnsworth; Lancaster: Johann Herman, printer. 18 ll. PPL (15 ll.) 9119

The CHRISTIAN Almanac for the States of Ohio, Kentucky, and Indiana for 1831. Cincinnati: American Tract Society; George T. Williamson. 18 ll. OCHP; OHi. 9120

The CHRISTIAN Almanac, for the Western Reserve for 1831. Cleaveland [sic]: American Tract Society. 18 ll. MWA; OClWHi; Applegate. 9121

The COLUMBUS Almanac for 1831. By William Lusk. Columbus: Olmsted & Bailhache. 12 ll. MWA (11 ll.); OHi. 9122

-- Issue with 24 ll. [covertitle: "Magazine Almanac for 1831"] N. 9123

The FARMER'S Almanack for 1831. By Samuel Burr. Cincinnati: N. & G. Guilford; Oliver Farnsworth; O. & P. M. Farnsworth, printers. 18 ll. DLC (16 ll.); OClWHi. 9124

The FREEMAN'S Almanack for 1831. By Samuel Burr. Cincinnati: N. & G. Guilford; Oliver Farnsworth; O. & P. M. Farnsworth, printers. 12 ll. In; OCHP; OClWHi. 9125

-- Issue with 24 ll. MWA; NN; WHi; ICN; KyHi; O; OClWHi; OHi; OMC. 9126

WESTERN Almanac for 1831. By Oliver Loud. Cleveland: Henry Bolles. 12 ll. OClWHi. 9127

The WESTERN Almanack, for the States of Ohio, Kentucky, and Indiana for 1831. Cincinnati: George T. Williamson. 12 ll. MWA; OClWHi; KyBgW. 9128

-- Issue with 24 ll. OMC. 9129

The WESTERN Almanac, for the States of Ohio, Kentucky, and Indiana for 1831. By Oner R. Powell. Cincinnati: W. Conclin. 12 ll. MWA; OClWHi. 9130

The CHRISTIAN Almanac, for the States of Ohio, Kentucky, and Indiana for 1832. Cincinnati: John H. Wood; John Finley. 18 ll. In; OHi. 9131

The CHRISTIAN Almanac, for the Western Reserve for 1832. Hudson: American Tract Society; Prof. Elizur Wright. 18 ll. MWA; DLC; WHi; OClWHi; OMC.
9132

The COLUMBUS Almanac for 1832. By William Lusk. Columbus: Jenkins & Glover. 12 ll. MWA; InU; O.
9133

The COLUMBUS Magazine Almanac for 1832. By William Lusk. Columbus: Jenkins and Glover. 26 ll. MWA. 9134

The FARMER'S Almanac for 1832. By Samuel Burr. Cincinnati: N. & G. Guilford; Oliver Farnsworth. 18 ll. OClWHi (16 ll.) 9135

The FREEMAN'S Almanack for 1832. By Samuel Burr. Cincinnati: N. & G. Guilford; O. & P. M. Farnsworth, printers. 12 ll. MWA; CU; In (10 ll.); InU; OCHP.
9136

The FREEMAN'S Almanack, or, Complete Farmer's Calendar for 1832. By Samuel Burr. Cincinnati: N. & G. Guilford; O. Farnsworth. 24 ll. CLU; InRE; WHi (22 ll.); OClWHi; OHi (22 ll.) 9137

The OHIO Antimasonic Almanack for 1832. Columbus: Jenkins & Glover. 24 ll. NN; OClWHi. 9138

Der OHIO Bauern Calender auf 1832. Cincinnati: N. und G. Guilford. 16 ll. MWA. 9139

The WESTERN Almanac, for the States of Ohio, Kentucky, and Indiana for 1832. Cincinnati: J. H. Wood. 24 ll. MWA; OMC (22 ll.) 9140

The WESTERN Reserve Almanack for 1832. Cleveland: Bolles & Kelley. 16 ll. NHi (9 ll.); OCl (ntp) 9141

The CHRISTIAN Almanac, for the States of Ohio, Kentucky, and Indiana for 1833. Cincinnati: Cincinnati Branch of the American Tract Society; Silas Woodbury. 18 ll. In; OCHP. 9142

The COLUMBUS Almanac for 1833. By Wm. Lusk. [Columbus:] David Smith, printer. 24 ll. OHi. 9143

The FARMER'S Almanack for 1833. By Samuel Burr. Cincinnati: N. & G. Guilford; Oliver Farnsworth & Son. 18 ll. DLC. 9144

The FREEMAN'S Almanack for 1833. By Samuel Burr. Cincinnati: N. & G. Guilford; Oliver Farnsworth & Son. 24 ll. MWA (two varieties); DLC; NcD; In (10 ll.); InHi; InRE; InU; ICU; WHi; OHi (12 ll.); OClWHi; OMC (23 ll.); OCHP. 9145

HAMBURGER Familien Kalender auf 1833. Fremont: Stausmyer's Park Drug Store. 16 ll. OFH. 9146

The OHIO Antimasonic Almanack for 1833. By William Brown. Columbus: Jenkins & Glover. 24 ll. OMC. 9147

Der OHIO Bauern Calender auf 1833. By Samuel Burr. Lancaster: N. & G. Guilford. 18 ll. OClWHi. 9148

The OHIO Farmers' Almanack for 1833. By William Brown. Columbus: Jenkins and Glover. 14 ll. MWA (8 ll.); OFH. 9149

POOR Richard's Almanac for 1833. By Joseph Ray. Cincinnati: Roff & Young. 24 ll. MWA (19 ll.); ICN; OC. 9150

UNITED States' Calendar of the Nineteenth Century. By

Jno. S. Williams. 1833. Cincinnati: J. A. James.
Broadside. Drake. 9151

The WEST Country Almanac for 1833. Cincinnati: Hubbard and Edmands. 18 ll. InHi (16 ll.); OCHP. 9152

WESTERN Almanack for 1833. By Henry Bolles.
Cleveland. [Briggs] 9153

The WESTERN Reserve Almanac for 1833. By Ansel Young. Cleveland: Madison Kelley. 16 ll. MWA; OClWHi. 9154

Der WESTLICHE "Vaterlandsfreund" und Cantoner Calender auf 1833. Von Carl F. Egelmann. Canton: Peter Kaufmann. 14 ll. MWA. 9155

The COLUMBUS Almanack for 1834. By William Lusk.
Columbus: E. Glover & Co. 12 ll. OClWHi. 9156

The COLUMBUS Magazine Almanac for 1834. By Wm. Lusk. Columbus: E. Glover & Co. 25 ll. MWA; InU; OClWHi; OHi (22 ll.) 9157

The FARMER'S Almanack for 1834. By Elisha Dwelle.
Cincinnati: N. & G. Guilford. 18 ll. OHi. 9158

The FARMER'S Almanack for 1834. By Elisha Dwelle.
Cincinnati: N. & G. Guilford; Oliver Farnsworth. 18 ll.
OCHP. 9159

The FREEMAN'S Almanac for 1834. By Elisha Dwelle.
Cincinnati: N. & G. Guilford & Co.; Hubbard and Edmands. 12 ll. OHi (11 ll.); InU (fragment); OC; OCHP. 9160

-- Issue with 24 ll. MWA; DLC (23 ll.); In (20 ll., ntp); OFH; WHi. 9161

The WESTERN Almanac, for the States of Ohio, Kentucky, and Indiana for 1834. Cincinnati: Josiah Drake.
24 ll. MWA; OMC. 9162

Ohio - 1834

The WESTERN Comic Almanac for 1834. Cincinnati:
N. & G. Guilford & Co.; Hubbard & Edmands. 24 ll.
OClWHi. 9163

The WESTERN Reserve Almanac for 1834. By Ansel
Young. Cleveland: M. Kelley. 12 ll. OCl; OClWHi.
9164

The CHRISTIAN Almanac, for the Western Reserve for
1835. Hudson: American Tract Society. 24 ll. MWA;
WHi; OClWHi; PPL; OMC. 9165

The FARMER'S & Mechanic's Almanac for 1835. Cincinnati. OClWHi (12 ll. tp impf) 9166

The FARMERS' & Mechanics' Almanac for 1835. Columbus: John Gilbert & Co. 16 ll. OClWHi. 9167

The FREEMAN'S Almanac for 1835. By Elisha Dwelle.
Cincinnati: N. & G. Guilford and Co. 12 ll. OHi; In
(4 ll.) 9168

-- Issue with 24 ll. MWA; DLC; OClWHi; OMC (20
ll.); O; WHi; OCHP (23 ll.) 9169

The MAGAZINE Almanack for 1835. By William Lusk.
[Columbus:] E. Glover & Co., printers. 24 ll. OC;
OClWHi; OFH (23 ll.); OHi. 9170

The OHIO Annual Register for 1835. By John A. Bryan. Columbus: J. Gilbert & R. C. Bryan. 64 ll. NN;
NHi; OClWHi. 9171

POOR Richard's Almanac for 1835. By Joseph Ray.
Cincinnati: Truman and Smith. 12 ll. MWA; OC (10
ll.); OClWHi. 9172

The WESTERN Almanac for 1835. Cincinnati: John
Gilbert & Co. 12 ll. MWA. 9173

The WESTERN Almanac for 1835. Columbus: John
Gilbert & Co. 12 ll. MWA (6 ll.); OClWHi. 9174

The WESTERN Comic Almanac for 1835. Cincinnati:

N. & G. Guilford & Co.   24 ll.   MWA (23 ll.); O;
OCHP.   9175

The WESTERN Magazine Almanack for 1835.   By William Lusk.   Columbus: E. Glover & Co. 24 ll.   MWA.
                                                                     9176

The WESTERN Reserve Almanac for 1835.   By Ansel Young.   Cleveland: M. Kelley.   12 ll.   OCl; OClWHi.
                                                                     9177

The WESTERN Temperance Almanac for 1835.   Cincinnati: Truman & Smith.   12 ll.   O (11 ll.); OCHP;
OMC.   9178

Der WESTLICHE "Vaterlandsfreund" und Cantoner Calender auf 1835.   Von Carl F. Egelmann.   Canton: Peter Kaufmann.   14 ll.   MWA; OClWHi.   9179

BARNES' Cincinnati Pocket Almanac for 1836.   By Joseph Ray.   Cincinnati: Barnes.   12 ll.   Private collection.   9180

The CHRISTIAN Almanac for the Western Reserve for 1836.   Hudson: American Tract Society.   24 ll.
OClWHi; WHi.   9181

The COLUMBUS Almanac for 1836.   By William Lusk.
Columbus: E. Glover.   MNF (11 ll.)   9182

ELTON'S Comic Almanac for 1836.   Columbus: Norman Tuttle; New York: Robert H. Elton.   18 ll.   N.
                                                                     9183

The FREEMAN'S Almanac for 1836.   By Elisha Dwelle.
Cincinnati: N. & G. Guilford.   12 ll.   MWA; N; ICN;
In (11 ll.); OC; OHi.   9184

-- Issue with 18 ll.   O; OCHP; OMC; WHi (16 ll.)
                                                                     9185

WESTERN Comic Almanac for 1836.   Cincinnati: N. & G. Guilford.   16 ll.   OCHP.   9186

The WESTERN "Patriot" and Canton Almanac for 1836.
By Charles F. Egelmann.   Canton: Peter Kaufmann.
14 ll.   MWA; CLU; OClWHi; OHi (13 ll.)   9187

The WESTERN Reserve Almanac for 1836. By Ansel
Young. Cleveland: J. Kellogg & Co. 16 ll. MWA
(15 ll.); OCl; OClWHi.   9188

Der WESTLICHE "Vaterlandsfreund" und Cantoner Calender auf 1836. Von Carl F. Egelmann. Canton:
Peter Kaufmann. 15 ll. MWA.   9189

The AMERICAN Anti-Slavery Almanac for 1837. By
N. Southard. Cincinnati: The Ohio Anti-Slavery Society. 24 ll. InHi; OCHP (20 ll.); OClWHi.   9190

The CHRISTIAN Almanac, for the Western Reserve for
1837. Cleaveland [sic]: American Tract Society. 24
ll. MWA (21 ll.)   9191

The FARMER'S Almanack for 1837. By Elisha Dwelle.
Cincinnati. 16 ll. OCHP (tp impf)   9192

The FREEMAN'S Almanac for 1837. By Elisha Dwelle.
Cincinnati: Guilford and Taylor. 12 ll. MWA; OClWHi;
CLU; O; OMC; OC.   9193

-- Issue with 18 ll. MiU-C; WHi; OCHP (16 ll.) 9194

The MAGAZINE Almanac for 1837. By William Lusk.
Columbus: E. Glover. 24 ll. MWA; OCHP.   9195

The WESTERN Comic Almanac for 1837. Cincinnati:
Guilford & Taylor. 18 ll. O; OClWHi (17 ll.)   9196

The WESTERN "Patriot" and Canton Almanack for 1837.
By Charles F. Egelmann. Canton: Peter Kaufmann.
16 ll. MWA; CLU; OHi.   9197

The WESTERN Reserve Almanac for 1837. By Ansel
Young. Cleveland: W. W. Strong & Co.; F. B. Penniman, printer. 16 ll. OCl; OClWHi.   9198

AMERICAN Anti-Slavery Almanac for 1838. By N.
Southard. Cincinnati: Anti-Slavery Society. 24 ll.
MWA; OClWHi; OC; OCHP.   9199

Ohio - 1838

The FARMER'S Almanack for 1838. By Joseph Ray.
Cincinnati: N. & G. Guilford. 19 ll. DLC (15 ll.);
ODa.   9200

The FREEMAN'S Almanac for 1838. By Joseph Ray.
Cincinnati: N. & G. Guilford; T. Surguy, printer. 18
ll. MWA; DLC; NN; O; OC (14 ll.); OClWHi; InRE;
WvU.   9201

The MAGAZINE Almanac for 1838. By William Lusk.
Columbus: E. Glover. 18 ll. MWA; OClWHi; OHi.
   9202

TAYLOR'S Western Farmer's Common Almanac for
1838. By Rev. John Taylor. Steubenville: James
Turnbull. 18 ll. OHi.   9203

The WESTERN Farmer's Almanac for 1838. By Rev.
John Taylor. Steubenville: James Turnbull; Pittsburgh: G. W. Holdship; Anderson & Loomis, printers.
30 ll. MWA; PPi; OMC (21 ll.)   9204

The WESTERN "Patriot" and Canton Almanack for 1838.
By Charles F. Egelmann. Canton: Peter Kaufmann.
16 ll. MWA; OHi (15 ll.)   9205

The WESTERN Reserve Almanac for 1838. By Ansel
Young. Cleveland: Younglove & Wetmore. 12 ll. OCl;
OClWHi (11 ll.)   9206

The WESTERN Reserve Almanac for 1838. By Ansel
Young. Cleveland: Younglove and Wetmore; Penniman
and Bemis, printers. 12 ll. N; OHi.   9207

The CHRISTIAN Almanac for Northern Ohio for 1839.
Cleveland: American Tract Society. 24 ll. OClWHi;
PPL.   9208

The CINCINNATI Almanac for 1839. Cincinnati: Glezen & Shepard. 45 ll. MWA; OClWHi; NN; NHi (44
ll.); OHi; OMC; OCHP.   9209

The CINCINNATI Almanac for 1839. Cincinnati: Robinson & Jones. DLC.   9210

EVERY Body's Komick Almanack for 1839. Cincinnati:
U. P. James. 18 ll. MWA; NN. 9211

-- Another issue. O (31 ll.) 9212

The FREEMAN'S Almanac for 1839. Edited by Solomon
Thrifty. By Elisha Dwelle. Cincinnati: G. Guilford
and Ely & Strong. 18 ll. MWA; NN; N; OClWHi; CLU;
In (ntp); OC; OMC (17 ll.); ICHi; WHi; OCHP (10 ll.);
OU. 9213

The LIBERAL Almanac for 1839. By Isaac Pillsbury.
Cleveland: James S. Underhill. 12 ll. OClWHi. 9214

TAYLOR'S Western Farmer's Magazine Almanac for
1839. By Rev. John Taylor. Steubenville: James
Turnbull. 30 ll. MWA. 9215

TURNER'S Comick Almanack for 1839. Cincinnati: N.
G. Burgess & Co. 18 ll. OCHP. 9216

The WESTERN Almanac for 1839. By R. Falley.
Columbus: E. Glover. 16 ll. MWA. 9217

The WESTERN Farmer's Almanac for 1839. By Rev.
John Taylor. Steubenville: James Turnbull; Wilson &
Worstell, printers. 18 ll. PPi. 9218

The WESTERN Farmer's Magazine Almanac for 1839.
By Rev. John Taylor. Steubenville: James Turnbull.
30 ll. OClWHi (29 ll.); OMC. 9219

The WESTERN Patriot and Canton Almanack for 1839.
By Charles F. Egelmann. Canton: Peter Kaufmann &
Co. 16 ll. MWA (15 ll.); OHi. 9220

The WESTERN Reserve Almanac for 1839. By Ansel
Young. Cleveland: M. C. Younglove; Penniman &
Bemis, printers. 12 ll. OCl; OClWHi. 9221

The CHRISTIAN Almanac for Northern Ohio for 1840.
Cleveland: American Tract Society. 24 ll. OClWHi.
9222

The CINCINNATI Almanac for 1840. Cincinnati: Glezen & Shepard. 41 ll. OCHP; OClWHi; OMC; PPPrHi.
9223
-- Issue with 47 ll. NN; NHi. 9224

The CINCINNATI Almanac for 1840. Cincinnati: Robinson & Jones. DLC; ICU. 9225

The DEMOCRATIC Harrisonian Almanack for 1840. [Medina: Joseph W. White] 15 ll. N. 9226

The FARMER'S Almanac for 1840. By David Young. Cleveland: Sanford & Lott. 18 ll. OClWHi. 9227

The FREEMAN'S Almanac for 1840. By Elisha Dwelle. Cincinnati: G. Guilford and Ely & Strong. 18 ll. MWA; DLC; NN; OClWHi; OMC; CLU; O; OC; KHi (12 ll.); WHi; OCHP; OU. 9228

The LAKE County Almanac for 1840. Sandusky: David Campbell & Sons. 12 ll. OClWHi. 9229

NATIONAL Almanac, and Pocket Calendar for 1840. By J. W. Herschell. [np, np] [Cincinnati] 18 ll. OCHP. 9230

The OHIO Almanack for 1840. By Seth Pratt. Cleveland: Sanford & Lott. 16 ll. OClWHi. 9231

TURNER'S Comick Almanack for 1840. Cincinnati: C. & F. Cloud. 18 ll. DLC. 9232

TURNER'S Comick Almanack for 1840. Cincinnati: U. P. James. 18 ll. OC. 9233

The WESTERN Farmer's Almanack for 1840. Medina: Joseph W. White. 18 ll. MWA (16 ll.); InHi. 9234

The WESTERN Patriot and Canton Almanack for 1840. By Charles F. Egelmann. Canton: Peter Kaufmann & Co. 16 ll. MWA; CLU; OHi. 9235

The AMERICAN Anti-Slavery Almanac for 1841. Cin-

cinnati: Ohio Anti-Slavery Society. 18 ll. NHi; OClWHi;
MBAt; KyHi; InHi; OMC; WHi; OCHP.   9236

The COLUMBUS Almanack for 1841. By William Lusk.
Columbus: E. Glover. 12 ll. OClWHi.   9237

The FREEMAN'S Almanac for 1841. By Joseph Ray.
Edited by Solomon Thrifty. Cincinnati: G. Guilford
and J. W. Ely. 18 ll. MWA; NN; OClWHi; OHi (12
ll.); O; OC; WvU; WHi; OU; OCHP (17 ll.)   9238

The LOG Cabin Almanac for 1841. By John B. Russell. Cincinnati: Truman & Smith. 24 ll. MWA; DLC;
IU; O; OFH; InU; WHi; Drake.   9239

The LOG Cabin Almanack for 1841. By William Lusk.
Columbus: E. Glover. 24 ll. InHi; OHi.   9240

NATIONAL Whig Almanac and Log Cabin Political and
Statistical Register for 1841. Cincinnati: James D.
Taylor. 18 ll. MWA (impf); KyU; O; OClWHi.   9241

The WESTERN Almanack for 1841. By William Lusk.
Columbus: E. Glover. 12 ll. MWA; OCHP; OClWHi;
OHi (10 ll.)   9242

The WESTERN Comic Almanac for 1841. Edited by
"Quiz." [Cincinnati: np] 18 ll. MWA; OClWHi.   9243

The WESTERN Patriot and Canton Almanack for 1841.
By Charles F. Egelmann. Canton: Peter Kaufmann &
Co. 14 ll. MWA (impf); OClWHi; CLU; OHi.   9244

The WESTERN Reserve Almanac for 1841. By Ansel
Young. Cleveland: Sanford & Co. 16 ll. MWA; OCl;
OClWHi.   9245

-- Issue with 26 ll. OHi.   9246

Der WESTLICHE "Vaterlandsfreund" und Cantoner Kalender auf 1841. Canton: Peter Kaufmann und Co. 16 ll.
OC.   9247

Der CINCINNATIER Hinkende Bote, ein Calender auf 1842. Von Carl Friedrich Egelmann. Cincinnati: Louis Meyer & Co. 18 ll. NHi. 9248

The COLUMBUS Almanack for 1842. By William Lusk. Columbus: E. Glover. 12 ll. MWA; OHi. 9249

The FARMER'S Almanac for 1842. By Joseph Ray. Cincinnati: G. Guilford & J.W. Ely. 18 ll. OCHP; OClWHi. 9250

The FARMER'S Western Reserve Almanac for 1842. By David Young. Cleveland: M. C. Younglove. 18 ll. OClWHi. 9251

The FREEMAN'S Almanac for 1842. By Joseph Ray. Cincinnati: G. Guilford and J. W. Ely. 18 ll. MWA; DLC; NN; OClWHi; OHi; O (17 ll.); OMC; InU; OC; OU; WvU; WHi. 9252

The MORAL Almanac for 1842. By Isaac N. Pillsbury. Cleveland: Sanford & Co. 16 ll. MWA; OClWHi; WHi. 9253

NATIONAL Whig Almanac for 1842. By John H. Wood. Cincinnati: [np] 12 ll. MWA; OCHP. 9254

TURNER'S Comic Almanac for 1842. Cincinnati: W. R. Fisher. 18 ll. OClWHi. 9255

The WESTERN Farmer and Gardener's Almanac for 1842. By Thomas Affleck. Illustrated by Charles Foster. Cincinnati: Edward Lucas. 71 ll. MWA; DLC; NHi; In (ntp); InU; TxU; ODa (61 ll., ntp) 9256

The WESTERN Patriot and Canton Almanack for 1842. By Charles F. Egelmann. Canton: Peter Kaufmann & Co. 16 ll. MWA; CLU; OHi. 9257

The WESTERN Reserve Almanac for 1842. By Ansel Young. Cleveland: A. W. North; Sanford & Co. 16 ll. MWA (8 ll.); OClW (12 ll.); OClWHi. 9258

The WESTERN Reserve Almanac for 1842. By Ansel Young. Cleveland: Sanford & Co. OCl; OHi (11 ll.) 9259

Ohio - 1842

Der WESTLICHE "Vaterlandsfreund" und Cantoner Calender auf 1842. Von Carl Friedrich Egelmann. Canton: Peter Kaufmann und Co. 16 ll. MWA; PPG; PPL. 9260

WHITE'S Farmer's and Mechanic's Almanack for 1842. By Sanford C. Hill. Chardon: Thomas J. White. 16 ll. MWA; InU; OClWHi; OHi. 9261

WILSON'S Western Pocket Almanac for 1842. By David Young. Cincinnati: Weed & Wilson; Kendall & Henry, printers. 12 ll. MWA. 9262

The BUCKEYE Almanac for 1843. Cincinnati: Shepard & Co. 16 ll. OCHP (ntp); OClWHi; ODa. 9263

The BUCKEYE Almanac for 1843. Dayton: B. F. Ells. 16 ll. MWA; CLU; InHi; OC (8 ll.); OClWHi; ODa; OMC; OHi. 9264

COUNTING-HOUSE Calendar for 1843. [Cincinnati: The Cincinnati Enquirer] [Heading: The Carrier's Address ...] Broadside. NHi. 9265

The FARMER'S Almanac for 1843. By Joseph Ray. Cincinnati: J. W. Ely. 18 ll. OClWHi; OHi. 9266

FISHER'S Temperance Housekeeper's Almanac for 1843. Cincinnati: W. R. Fisher. 18 ll. OCHP. 9267

The FREEMAN'S Almanac for 1843. By Joseph Ray. Edited By Solomon Thrifty. Cincinnati: J. W. Ely. 12 ll. DLC. 9268

-- Issue with 18 ll. OU; WvU. 9269

The FREEMAN'S Almanack or Complete Farmer's Calendar for 1843. By Joseph Ray. Edited by Solomon Thrifty. Cincinnati: G. Guilford & J. W. Ely. 18 ll. MWA; OClWHi; O; OHi; OMC; InU (impf); OC; OCHP (14 ll.) 9270

HUTCHINS' Farmers Almanac for 1843. By a Western Lady. Cincinnati: G. F. Thomas & Co. 18 ll. OC (16 ll.); OCHP; OMC. 9271

The MORAL Almanac for 1843. By Isaac N. Phillsbury [sic]. Cleveland: Sanford & Co. 16 ll. OCl; OClWHi (15 ll.); WHi. 9272

The WESTERN Almanack for 1843. By William Lusk. Columbus: E. Glover. 16 ll. MWA (15 ll.); OCHP.
9273

The WESTERN Farmer and Gardener's Almanac for 1843. Cincinnati: Chas. Foster. 48 ll. DLC; O; OCHP (45 ll.); OClWHi. 9274

The WESTERN Patriot and Canton Almanack for 1843. By Jacob Blickensdorfer, Jr. Canton: Peter Kaufmann, & Co. 15 ll. OC; OHi. 9275

The WESTERN Reserve Almanac for 1843. By Ansel Young. Cleveland: Sanford & Co. 16 ll. OCl; OClWHi.
9276

WESTLICHE Vaterlands-freund und Cantoner Calender auf 1843. Von Charles F. Egelmann. Canton: Peter Kaufmann und Co. 16 ll. OClWHi. 9277

WILSON'S Western Pocket Almanac for 1843. By David Young. Cincinnati: Wilson & Drake; Kendall & Barnard, printers. 12 ll. OC. 9278

The BUCKEYE Almanac for 1844. Dayton: B. F. Ells; Cincinnati: Shepard and Co. 18 ll. MWA; NHi; CLCM (17 ll.); OClWHi; ODa; OHi; OMC. 9279

CINCINNATIER Hinkende Bote auf 1844. Von Lewis Meyer. Cincinnati: Lewis Meyer. 18 ll. OC; OClWHi.
9280

The FARMER'S Almanac for 1844. By Joseph Ray. Cincinnati: J. W. Ely. 18 ll. OClWHi. 9281

The FREEMAN'S Almanac for 1844. By Joseph Ray. Edited by Solomon Thrifty. Cincinnati: J. W. Ely. 18 ll. MWA; NN; IU; OHi (12 ll.); OC; OMC; OU; OCHP. 9282

The MORAL Almanac for 1844. By Isaac N. Pillsbury. Cleveland: Sanford & Hayward. 16 ll. OCl; OClWHi; WHi. 9283

The OHIO Almanack for 1844. By William Lusk. Columbus: Chas. Scott. 12 ll. OClWHi; PHi. 9284

The THRIFTY Almanac for 1844. Cincinnati: A. Randall. 18 ll. MWA; MnU. 9285

UNCLE Ben's Farmers' and Mechanics' Ohio Almanac for 1844. Columbus: Whiting & Huntington. 30 ll. MWA; OClWHi; CLU; O; PP. 9286

WESTERN Almanac for 1844. By P. Johnson. Cincinnati: A. Randall. OC (10 ll.) 9287

The WESTERN Almanack for 1844. By William Lusk. Columbus: E. Glover. 15 ll. MWA; OHi (14 ll.); OCHP. 9288

The WESTERN Farmer and Gardener's Almanac for 1844. By A. Randall. Cincinnati: E. Morgan & Co. 78 ll. OCHP (57 ll.); OClWHi. 9289

WESTERN Liberty Almanack for 1844. By W. B. Jarvis. Columbus: E. Glover. 19 ll. IHi. 9290

The WESTERN Patriot and Canton Almanack for 1844. By Jacob Blickensderfer, Jr. Canton: Peter Kaufmann & Co. 16 ll. MWA; DLC (15 ll.); CLU; OHi; WHi. 9291

The WESTERN Reserve Almanac for 1844. By Ansel Young. Cleveland: Sanford & Hayward. 16 ll. OCl; OClWHi. 9292

The WESTERN Whig Almanac for 1844. By Charles Whittlesey. Cincinnati: Wm. H. Moore & Co. 24 ll. MWA; OCHP; OClWHi. 9293

Der WESTLICHE "Vaterlandsfreund" und Cantoner Calender auf 1844. Von Carl Friedrich Egelmann. Canton: Peter Kaufmann & Co. 16 ll. MWA; OClWHi. 9294

Ohio - 1844

W. H. MOORE & Co.'s Almanac for 1844. Cincinnati: W. H. Moore & Co.; S. W. Benedict & Co., printers. 12 ll. OC.   9295

Der CINCINNATIER Hinkende Bote auf 1845. Cincinnati: Louis Meyer u. co. 18 ll. OHi.   9296

The COLUMBUS Almanack for 1845. By William Lusk. Columbus: Thrall & Glover. 12 ll. O.   9297

EVERYBODY'S Almanac for 1845. Dayton: Ells & Claflin. 16 ll. ODa.   9298

The FARMER'S Almanac for 1845. By David Young. Cleveland: M. C. Younglove. 16 ll. OClWHi.   9299

The FREEMAN'S Almanac for 1845. By Joseph Ray. Edited by Solomon Thrifty. Cincinnati: J. W. Ely. 18 ll. DLC; OClWHi; OMC; WHi; OCHP (17 ll.); OU.   9300

The OHIO Almanack for 1845. By William Lusk. Columbus: Chas. Scott. 12 ll. PHi.   9301

The PLOW Boy's Almanac for 1845. By A. Randall. Cincinnati: H. Huxley. 57 ll. OCHP; WHi.   9302

The THRIFTY Almanac for 1845. Cincinnati: A. Randall. 24 ll. MWA.   9303

UNITED States Liberty Almanack for 1845. By W. B. Jarvis. Columbus: Thrall & Glover. 18 ll. MWA; NHi; IHi; InU (impf); OCHP; OClWHi.   9304

The WESTERN Almanac for 1845. By P. Johnson. Cincinnati: A. Randall. 12 ll. MWA; OCHP.   9305

The WESTERN Patriot and Canton Almanack for 1845. By Charles F. Egelmann. Canton: Peter Kaufmann, & Co. 16 ll. MWA; NHi; OHi (15 ll.); WHi.   9306

The WESTERN Reserve Almanac for 1845. By Ansel Young. Cleveland: Sanford & Hayward. 16 ll. MWA; OCl (15 ll.); OClWHi.   9307

Der WESTLICHE "Vaterlandsfreund" und Cantoner Calender auf 1845. Von Carl Friedrich Egelmann. Canton: Peter Kaufmann und Co. 16 ll. NHi; OCHP; OClWHi.   9308

ALLEN'S Land Bill Almanack for 1846. Columbus: E. Glover. 12 ll. MBAt; OHi.   9309

The AMERICAN Farmer's Almanac for 1846. Columbus: Joseph H. Riley. 18 ll. ICU.   9310

The BOTANICO-MEDICAL Almanac for 1846. By A. Curtis. Cincinnati: Sparhawk and Lytle. 12 ll. OCHP.
  9311

The CINCINNATI Almanac for 1846. Cincinnati: Robinson & Jones. 84 ll. DLC; NHi; MB; MH; OCHP.
  9312

-- Errata leaf tipped in. 85 ll. OMC.   9313

Der CINCINNATIER Hinkende Bote auf 1846. Von Lewis Meyer. Cincinnati: Lewis Meyer. 18 ll. OClWHi.
  9314

CITY Book Store Almanac for 1846. Dayton: Ells, Claflin & Co. 16 ll. OCHP.   9315

The COLUMBUS Almanack for 1846. By William Lusk. Columbus: E. Glover. MWA (15 ll.)   9316

EVERYBODY'S Almanac for 1846. Dayton: Ells & Claflin. 14 ll. KHi.   9317

The FARMER'S Almanack for 1846. By Joseph Ray. Cincinnati: J. W. Ely. 18 ll. OCHP.   9318

FARMER'S Almanac for 1846. By David Young. Cleveland: M. C. Younglove. 16 ll. MWA; OClWHi.   9319

The FARMERS' and Mechanics' Almanac for 1846. Columbus: C. Scott & Co. 16 ll. OHi.   9320

The FARMER'S & Mechanic's Almanac for 1846. By J. W. White. Cincinnati: J. W. White. OClWHi (15 ll.)
  9321

The FARMER'S & Mechanic's German-English Almanac for 1846. Cincinnati: J. W. White. OClWHi (15 ll.)
9322

The FREEMAN'S Almanac for 1846. By Joseph Ray. Edited by Solomon Thrifty. Cincinnati: J. W. Ely. 18 ll. DLC; MH; OCHP; OClWHi; OMC; OU. 9323

FRIENDLY Monitor Almanac, and Repository of Useful Knowledge for 1846. By H. N. Robinson. Cincinnati: Bartlett Baker. 16 ll. OHi. 9324

The OHIO Almanack for 1846. Columbus: Chas. Scott & Co. 16 ll. OHi; OMC; WHi. 9325

The OHIO Meteorologist Almanac for 1846. By A. C. Richard. Columbus: E. Glover. 19 ll. MWA; O (18 ll.) 9326

The PEOPLES Almanac for 1846. By H. N. Robinson. Cincinnati: Derby, Bradley & Co.; Louisville: Derby, Anthony & Co. 16 ll. OClWHi. 9327

The PIONEER Almanac, and Repository of Useful Knowledge for 1846. By H. N. Robinson. Cincinnati: Derby, Bradley & Co. 12 ll. OMC. 9328

The PIONEER Almanac, and Repository of Useful Knowledge for 1846. By H. N. Robinson. Cincinnati: J. A. James. 12 ll. MWA (11 ll.) 9329

The TRAVELLER'S Register, and River and Road Guide [Almanac for 1846]. Cincinnati: Robinson & Jones. 36 ll. CtY. 9330

TURNER'S Comic Almanac for 1846. Cincinnati: J. G. Hanzsche. 18 ll. OCHP. 9331

The WESTERN Patriot and Canton Almanack for 1846. By Charles F. Egelmann. Canton: Peter Kaufmann & Co. 16 ll. MWA; CLU; OClWHi; OHi. 9332

The WESTERN People's Almanac for 1846. By H. N. Robinson. Cincinnati: J. A. James. 18 ll. MWA (two varieties); OC (17 ll.); OHi (17 ll.)   9333

The WESTERN Reserve Almanac for 1846. By Ansel Young. Cleveland: Sanford & Hayward. 16 ll. OClWHi.   9334

Der WESTLICHE "Vaterlandsfreund" und Cantoner Calender auf 1846. Von Carl Friedrich Egelmann. Canton: Peter Kaufmann & Co. 16 ll. MWA; PPL (12 ll.)   9335

WHITE'S Farmer's & Mechanic's Almanac for 1846. Chardon: J. W. White. 16 ll. MWA.   9336

WHITE'S Farmer's & Mechanic's Almanac for 1846. Painesville: Thomas J. White. 16 ll. MWA; OClWHi.   9337

Der CINCINNATIER Hinkende Bote, ein Kalender für 1847. Cincinnati: Louis Meyer & Co. 18 ll. OC. 9338

CITY Book Store Almanac for 1847. Dayton: Ells, Claflin & Co. 15 ll. KHi; WHi.   9339

The COLUMBUS Almanack for 1847. By William Lusk. Columbus: E. Glover. 12 ll. MWA; OClWHi.   9340

The COLUMBUS Almanack for 1847. By William Lusk. [Columbus:] E. Glover. 24 ll. OHi.   9341

EVERYBODY'S Almanac for 1847. Cleveland: A. S. Sanford. 16 ll. OClWHi.   9342

The FARMER'S Almanac for 1847. By David Young. Cleveland: M. C. Younglove. 16 ll. OClWHi.   9343

FARMERS and Mechanics' Almanac for 1847. Dayton: Ells, Claflin, & Co. 18 ll. MWA; InLP.   9344

FARMERS and Mechanics' Almanac for 1847. Dutch-English. Dayton: Ells, Claflin & Co. ODa (17 ll.)   9345

The FREEMAN'S Almanac for 1847. By Joseph Ray. Cincinnati: J. W. Ely. 12 ll. MWA; OClWHi.   9346

-- Issue with 18 ll. OC; OCHP; OMC; WHi.   9347

The OHIO Almanack for 1847. By William Lusk. Columbus: Charles Scott & Co. 24 ll. NN; OClWHi.
9348

The PIONEER Almanac, and Repository of Useful Knowledge for 1847. By H. N. Robinson. Cincinnati: J. A. James. 12 ll. OC.
9349

PLOW Boy's Almanac for 1847. Cincinnati: Robinson & Jones. 49 ll. OCHP.
9350

The ROUGH and Ready Almanac for 1847. Cincinnati: Robinson & Jones. 24 ll. DLC.
9351

The WESTERN Almanac for 1847. Cincinnati: Robinson & Jones. 12 ll. OHi.
9352

The WESTERN Almanack for 1847. By William Lusk. Columbus: E. Glover. 15 ll. MWA; OCHP (ntp); OHi.
9353

The WESTERN Patriot and Canton Almanack for 1847. By Charles F. Egelmann. Canton: Peter Kaufmann & Co. 16 ll. MWA; OClWHi; OHi (14 ll.)
9354

The WESTERN Reserve Almanac for 1847. By Ansel Young. Cleveland. 16 ll. OClWHi (10 ll., ntp)
9355

The YOUNG Vermont Mathematician's Almanac for 1847. By Truman H. Safford. Jun. Cincinnati: J. A. James. 24 ll. MWA; MB; MHi; O; OC; OCHP.
9356

The BUCKEYE Almanac for 1848. Dayton: B. F. Ells. 16 ll. MWA; OC; OMC.
9357

Der CINCINNATIER Hinkende Bote für 1848. Cincinnati: Louis Meyer & Co. 18 ll. CLU.
9358

The COLUMBUS Almanack for 1848. Columbus: E. Glover. 12 ll. OClWHi; OMC (11 ll.)
9359

The COUNTRY People's Almanac for 1848. Dayton: B. F. Ells. 15 ll. ODa.
9360

The CULTIVATOR Almanac for 1848. By Luther Tucker.

Cleveland: Stephens & Hitchcock. 16 ll. OClWHi; N.
9361

The FARMER'S Almanac for 1848. Elyria: Orrin
Cowles. OClWHi (8 ll.) 9362

The FARMER'S Almanac for 1848. By David Young.
Cleveland: M. C. Younglove. 16 ll. OClWHi. 9363

FARMERS & Mechanics' Almanac for 1848. Dayton:
Ells, Claflin & Co.; John Wilson & Co., printers. 16
ll. In; InLP; ODa; OHi. 9364

The FREEMAN'S Almanac for 1848. By Solomon
Thrifty. Cincinnati: J. W. Ely. 18 ll. MWA; OC;
OCHP; OMC; WHi. 9365

The NU Speling and Nu Lejislashun Aulmanak for 1848.
Bi Bartlet Baker. Sinsinati: J. A. & U. P. Jamz. 12
ll. MWA; InU; OHi. 9366

The PEOPLES' Illustrated Almanac for 1848. Cleveland: Gaylord & Co. OClWHi (13 ll.) 9367

The PIONEER Almanac, and Repository of Useful
Knowledge for 1848. By H. N. Robinson. Cincinnati:
J. A. & U. P. James. 12 ll. MWA; OC; OClWHi;
OMC. 9368

The TRAVELER'S Register, and River and Road Guide
[Almanac for 1848]. Cincinnati: Robinson & Jones. 34
ll. ICN. 9369

The WESTERN Almanac for 1848. Columbus: E.
Glover. MWA (15 ll.) 9370

WESTERN Patriot and Canton Almanac for 1848. By
Charles F. Egelmann. Canton: Peter Kaufmann. 16 ll.
OCHP; OClWHi; OHi. 9371

The WESTERN Reserve Almanac for 1848. By Ansel
Young. Cleveland: A. S. Sanford; W. H. Hayward,
printer. 16 ll. OClWHi. 9372

The AMERICAN Cultivator's Almanac for 1849. Cleveland: William Fisk; Rochester: Benton, Fisher & Miller. 16 ll. OClWHi. 9373

CINCINNATIER Hinkende Bote für 1849. Von Lewis Meyer. Cincinnati: Lewis Meyer. 18 ll. OClWHi. 9374

The FARMER'S Almanac for 1849. Zanesville: H. G. O. Cary. 16 ll. OClWHi. 9375

FARMERS & Mechanics Almanac for 1849. Cincinnati: E. D. Truman. 8 ll. OCHP. 9376

FARMERS' & Mechanics' German English Almanac for 1849. Dayton: Ells, Claflin & Co. 16 ll. ODa. 9377

The FARMER'S Free Soil Almanac for 1849. By E. L. Gibbs. Ashtabula: George Ray & Co. 16 ll. MWA. 9378

The FARMER'S Western Reserve Almanac for 1849. By E. L. Gibbs. Ashtabula: Root, Barnes, & Co. 16 ll. OHi. 9379

The FARMER'S Western Reserve Almanac for 1849. By E. L. Gibbs. Cleveland: M. C. Younglove & Co. 16 ll. MWA; OClWHi. 9380

The FREEMAN'S Almanac for 1849. By Joseph Ray. Cincinnati: J. W. Ely. 18 ll. MWA; DLC; O; OCHP; OClWHi; OMC; WHi. 9381

JAMES' Farmer's Almanac for 1849. By Horatio N. Robinson. Cincinnati: J. A. & U. P. James. 16 ll. MWA; In; OCHP; OMC (14 ll.) 9382

The OHIO Almanack for 1849. By William Lusk. Columbus: Chas. Scott. OHi (11 ll.) 9383

OHIO Cultivator Almanac for 1849. By M. B. Bateham. Columbus: Ohio Cultivator. 16 ll. MWA (15 ll.); N; OCHP; OClWHi; OMC. 9384

The OLD Rough and Ready Almanac for 1849. Cincin-

nati: G. Hanzsche; New York and Philadelphia: Turner
& Fisher. 18 ll. Mi. 9385

The PIONEER Almanac and Repository of Useful Knowledge for 1849. By H. N. Robinson. Cincinnati: J. A.
and U. P. James. 12 ll. OC; OMC. 9386

The PIONEER Almanac and Repository of Useful Knowledge for 1849. By Horatio Nelson Robinson. Cincinnati: U. P. James. 12 ll. OCHP. 9387

RESOR'S Stove Almanac for 1849. Cincinnati: J. A. &
U. P. James. 18 ll. OC. 9388

The WESTERN Reserve Almanac for 1849. By Ansel
Young. Cleveland: A. S. Sanford. 12 ll. OClWHi. 9389

The AMERICAN Family Almanac for 1850. By George
R. Perkins. Cincinnati: Lorenzo O. Gay; Utica: R.
Northway & Co. 18 ll. NRU. 9390

The BOSTON Store Almanac for 1850. By Horace Martin. Painesville: Holmes & Benson; Sandusky: D.
Campbell & Son. 16 ll. OClWHi. 9391

Der CINCINNATIER Hinkende Bote für 1850. Cincinnati:
Louis Meyer & Co. 18 ll. CLU; OC. 9392

The DELAWARE Almanac for 1850. By William Lusk.
[Delaware:] Wm. W. Fay. 12 ll. MWA. 9393

The FARMER'S Almanac for 1850. Dresden: H. G. O.
Cary. 12 ll. OClWHi. 9394

The FARMER'S & Mechanic's German-English Almanac
for 1850. Dayton: L. F. Claflin & Co. 16 ll. OClWHi.
9395
The FARMER'S Western Reserve Almanac for 1850.
By E. L. Gibbs. Cleveland: M. C. Younglove & Co.
16 ll. OHi. 9396

The FARMER'S Western Reserve Almanac for 1850. By
E. L. Gibbs. Warren: W. N. Porter. 16 ll. OClWHi. 9397

GIBBS' Western Reserve Almanac for 1850. By E. L.
Gibbs. Cleveland: [np] 16 ll. OClWHi. 9398

JAMES' Farmer's Almanac for 1850. By Horatio N.
Robinson. Cincinnati: J. A. & U. P. James. 18 ll.
OCHP; OClWHi (17 ll.); In (ntp) 9399

JAMES' Farmer's Almanac for 1850. By Horatio N.
Robinson. Madison: Dutton & Adams. 16 ll. OMC.
9400

The PIONEER Almanac, and Repository of Useful
Knowledge for 1850. By H. N. Robinson. Cincinnati:
J. A. & U. P. James. 12 ll. OMC. 9401

The PIONEER Almanac, and Repository of Useful
Knowledge for 1850. By H. N. Robinson. Cincinnati:
E. D. Truman. 12 ll. MWA; OC; OClWHi. 9402

TRESCOTT'S German-English Almanac for 1850. By
Horatio N. Robinson. Salem: J. Trescott & Co. 15 ll.
OHi. 9403

TRESCOTT'S Pioneer Almanac for 1850. By H. N.
Robinson. Salem: J. Trescott & Co. 12 ll. OClWHi.
9404

WILLIAMS' Cincinnati Almanac, Business Guide and Annual Advertiser for 1850. Cincinnati: C. S. Williams.
100 ll. MWA; MH; MiD-B; OClWHi; Drake. 9405

OKLAHOMA

CHAHTA Almanac for 1836. Union: Mission Press; John F. Wheeler, printer. 8 ll. MWA.   9406

CHEROKEE Almanac for 1836. Calculations from the Temperance Almanac. Union: Mission Press; John F. Wheeler, printer. 8 ll. MBAt; WHi; MBACFM; ICN; MHi; OkTG; Hargrett.   9407

CHAHTA Almanac for 1837. Calculations copied from The Louisiana and Mississippi Almanac. Union: Mission Press; John F. Wheeler, printer. 12 ll. MWA.   9408

The CHEROKEE Almanac for 1838. Fitted to the meridian of Fort Gibson. Park Hill: Mission Press; John F. Wheeler, printer. 12 ll. NN (11 ll.); ICN; MBACFM; OkTG; Hargrett.   9409

CHAHTA Almanac for 1839. Park Hill: Mission Press; John F. Wheeler, printer. 12 ll. ICN.   9410

CHEROKEE Almanac for 1839. Park Hill: Mission Press; John F. Wheeler, printer. 18 ll. DLC; CSmH; DSI-E; ICN; OkTG.   9411

CHEROKEE Almanac for 1840. Park Hill: Mission Press; John Candy, printer. 12 ll. NN; NHi; ICN; MBAt; OkHi; OkTG; PPAmP; Hargrett.   9412

CHEROKEE Almanac for 1842. Park Hill: Mission Press; John Candy, printer. 18 ll. MWA; NN; NHi; DLC; MH; OkTG; MBACFM.   9413

CHAHTA Almanak for 1843. Park Hill: Mission Press; John Candy, printer. 22 ll. MH.   9414

CHEROKEE Almanac for 1843. Park Hill: Mission Press; John Candy, printer. 18 ll. OkTG; Hargrett.
9415

CHAHTA Almanak for 1844. Park Hill: Mission Press; John Candy, printer. 12 ll. MWA. 9416

CHEROKEE Almanac for 1844. Park Hill: Mission Press; John Candy, printer. 18 ll. NN; MH; MBACFM; ICN; VtU; Hargrett. 9417

CHEROKEE Almanac for 1845. Park Hill: Mission Press; John Candy and John F. Wheeler, printers. 18 ll. NSyOHi; Nc; NcWsM; OkTG; VtU; BritMus; Hargrett. 9418

CHEROKEE Almanac for 1846. Park Hill: Mission Press; John Candy and John F. Wheeler, printers. 18 ll. NN; MBAt; MH; GHi; VtU; BritMus. 9419

CHEROKEE Almanac for 1847. Park Hill: Mission Press; Edwin Archer, printer. 18 ll. NN; NHi; MBAt; DLC; MH; CtHT-W; OkHi; OkU; VtU. 9420

CHEROKEE Almanac for 1848. Park Hill: Mission Press; Edwin Archer, printer. 18 ll. NN; DLC; MB; MH. 9421

CHEROKEE Almanac for 1849. Park Hill: Mission Press; Edwin Archer, printer. 18 ll. NN; DLC; MBACFM; MBAt; MH; OkHi; VtU; Hargrett. 9422

CHEROKEE Almanac for 1850. Park Hill: Mission Press; Edwin Archer, printer. 18 ll. NN; DLC; MBACFM; MH; MHi; OkU; VtU; Drake. 9423

CHEROKEE Almanac for 1851. Park Hill: Mission Press; Edwin Archer, printer. 18 ll. NN; MBACFM; MH; OkU; Hargrett. 9424

CHEROKEE Almanac for 1852. Park Hill: Mission Press; Edwin Archer, printer. 18 ll. NN; MBACFM; MH. 9425

CHEROKEE Almanac for 1853. Park Hill: Mission Press; Edwin Archer, printer. 18 ll. NN; DLC; MBACFM; MH; MdBP; CtHT-W. 9426

CHEROKEE Almanac for 1854. By Benjamin Greenleaf. Park Hill: Mission Press; Edwin Archer, printer. 18 ll. NN; DLC; MH; NHi; OkTG; OkU; VtU; Hargrett. 9427

CHEROKEE Almanac for 1855. By Benjamin Greenleaf. Park Hill: Mission Press; Edwin Archer, printer. 18 ll. NN; MBACFM; MH; CtY; DSI-E; NjHi; OkTG; OkHi. 9428

CHEROKEE Almanac for 1856. By Benjamin Greenleaf. Park Hill: Mission Press; Edwin Archer, printer. 18 ll. NN; DLC; MBACFM; MH; MHi; OkTG. 9429

CHEROKEE Almanac for 1857. By Benjamin Greenleaf. Park Hill: Mission Press; Edwin Archer, printer. 18 ll. NN; ICN; MBACFM; MBC; MH; CSmH; OkToU; OkTG; PPL. 9430

CHEROKEE Almanac for 1858. By Benjamin Greenleaf. Park Hill: Mission Press; Edwin Archer, printer. 18 ll. MWA; NN; ICN; MBACFM; MH; MHi; CtHT-W; MiD-B; VtU. 9431

CHEROKEE Almanac for 1859. By Benjamin Greenleaf. Park Hill: Mission Press; Edwin Archer, printer. 18 ll. MWA; NN; MBACFM; MH; ICN; OkTG; VtU. 9432

CHEROKEE Almanac for 1860. By Benjamin Greenleaf. Park Hill: Mission Press; Edwin Archer, printer. 18 ll. MWA (impf); NN; DLC; CSmH; MBACFM; MH; MBAt; NBLiHi; OkHi (13 ll.); OkTG; WHi; VtU. 9433

CHEROKEE Almanac for 1861. By Benjamin Greenleaf. Park Hill: Mission Press; Edwin Archer, printer. 18 ll. MWA; NN; MBACFM; MHi; MH; InU; WHi; OkHi; OkU; ICN. 9434

OREGON

The OREGON Almanac for 1848. By Henry H. Everts. Oregon City: Spectator Office; W. P. Hudson. 12 ll. NN; CtY; CU-B (11 ll.); CSmH; Or; OrFP; OrHi; OrP.   9435

The OREGON and Washington Almanac for 1855. By W. Mix, [and] S. J. M'Cormick. Portland: S. J. M'Cormick; Democratic Standard Print. 12 ll. CtY; CSmH; Or; OrHi; OrP.   9436

The OREGON and Washington Almanac for 1856. By S. H. Wright [and] S. J. M'Cormick. Portland: S. J. M'Cormick. 24 ll. CtY; CSmH; OrHi; OrP.   9437

The OREGON and Washington Almanac for 1856. Being the fourth year after Bissextile [sic]. By S. H. Wright [and] S. J. M'Cormick. Portland: S. J. M'Cormick. 24 ll. MWA; OrHi; WaSp.   9438

The OREGON and Washington Almanac for 1857. Portland: S. J. M'Cormick. 24 ll. CtY; OrHi; WaSp.   9439

The OREGON and Washington Almanac for 1857. Portland: S. J. M'Cormick. (Second Edition) 24 ll. DLC; OrHi; OrP; Drake.   9440

The OREGON and Washington Almanac for 1858. Portland: S. J. M'Cormick. 24 ll. CtY; CSmH; OrHi; OrP; WaSp.   9441

The OREGON and Washington Almanac for 1859. Portland: S. J. McCormick. 25 ll. MH; CtY; OMC (24 ll.); OrHi; OrP; OrU (24 ll.); WaSp.   9442

The OREGON and Washington Almanac for 1860. Port-

land: S. J. McCormick. 24 ll. MH; CtY; OrHi; OrP;
OrU; WaSp. 9443

The OREGON and Washington Almanac for 1861. Portland: S. J. McCormick. 12 ll. CtY; OrHi; OrP;
WaSp. 9444

The OREGON and Washington Almanac for 1862. Portland: S. J. McCormick. 24 ll. MH; CtY; CU-B;
CSmH; Or; OrHi; OrP; OrU; WaSp. 9445

The OREGON and Washington Almanac for 1863. Portland: S. J. McCormick. 28 ll. MH; CtY; CSmH;
OrHi; OrP; OrU; WaSp. 9446

McCORMICK'S Almanac for 1864. Portland: S. J. McCormick. 28 ll. MH; CtY; CU-B; CSmH; OrHi; OrP;
OrU; WaSp. 9447

McCORMICK'S Almanac for 1865. Portland: S. J. McCormick. 28 ll. MH; CtY; CU-B; OrHi; OrP; OrU;
WaSp. 9448

McCORMICK'S Almanac for 1866. Portland: S. J. McCormick; Oregon Farmer Book and Job Office. 32 ll.
MH; CtY; CU-B; CSmH; OrHi; OrP; OrU; WaSp. 9449

McCORMICK'S Almanac for 1867. Portland: S. J. McCormick; A. G. Walling & Co., printers. 30 ll. MH;
CtY; CSmH; OrHi; OrP; OrU (29 ll.); WaHi; WaSp;
WaSpHi; WaU. 9450

McCORMICK'S Almanac for 1868. Portland: S. J. McCormick; A. G. Walling & Co., printers. 29 ll. MWA
(23 ll.); DLC; CtY; CU-B; CSmH; MH; Or; OrHi (28
ll.); OrP; OrU (23 ll.); WaSp; WaU. 9451

McCORMICK'S Almanac for 1869. Portland: S. J. McCormick; A. G. Walling, printer. 36 ll. MH; CtY;
CU-B; OrHi; OrP; OrU; WaSp; WaU; CSmH; Drake.
9452
McCORMICK'S Almanac for 1870. Portland: S. J. McCormick. 33 ll. MH; CtY; NBuG; CSmH; OrHi; OrP;

OrU; WaSp; WaU. 9453

McCORMICK'S Almanac for 1871. Portland: S. J. McCormick; A. G. Walling, printer. 36 ll. NN; MH; CtY; PPL; OrHi; OrP; OrU; WaSp; WaU; CSmH. 9454

McCORMICK'S Almanac for 1872. Portland: S. J. McCormick. 35 ll. NN; MH; OrP; OrU (36 ll.); WaSp; Drake. 9455

McCORMICK'S Almanac for 1873. By S. J. McCormick. Portland: S. J. McCormick. 36 ll. OrP (34 ll.); OrU; WaSp. 9456

BENTON County Almanac for 1874. Corvallis: Wm. B. Carter; Gazette Office. 20 ll. CU-B. 9457

McCORMICK'S Almanac for 1874. By S. J. McCormick. Portland: S. J. McCormick. 36 ll. CU-B; MH; OrP; OrU; WaSp. 9458

OREGON Farmers' Year-Book for 1874. Portland: Geo. H. Himes. 32 ll. CtY; OrP. 9459

PENNSYLVANIA

KALENDARIUM Pennsilvaniense, or America's Messinger, being an Almanack for 1686. By Samuel Atkins. Philadelphia: William Bradford. 20 ll. PPRF.   9460

KALENDARIUM Pennsilvaniense, or, America's Messinger, being an Almanack for 1686. By Samuel Atkins. [Philadelphia:] William Bradford; Philadelphia: Author; H. Murrey; New-York: Philip Richards. 20 ll. PHi; PPL; CSmH.   9461

An ALMANACK for 1687. By Daniel Leeds. near Philadelphia: William Bradford. Broadside. PHi; PPL (impf); BritMus (fragment)   9462

An ALMANACK for 1687. Particularly respecting the meridian and latitude of Burlington. By Daniel Leeds. [np, np] Broadside. MB (impf)   9463

An ALMANAC for 1688. By Edward Eaton. Philadelphia: William Bradford. [Morrison]   9464

An ALMANACK for 1688. By Daniel Leeds. Philadelphia: William Bradford. [Evans]   9465

An ALMANACK for 1689. By Daniel Leeds. Philadelphia: William Bradford. [Morrison]   9466

An ALMANACK for 1690. By Daniel Leeds. Philadelphia: William Bradford. [Morrison]   9467

An ALMANACK for 1691. By Daniel Leeds. Philadelphia: William Bradford. [Morrison]   9468

An ALMANACK for 1692. By Daniel Leeds. Philadelphia: William Bradford. [Morrison]   9469

An ALMANACK and Ephemerides for 1693. By Daniel Leeds. [Philadelphia:] William Bradford. 28 ll. PHi (24 ll.); CSmH (impf); Garrett (20 ll.) 9470

An ALMANACK for 1700. By Jacob Taylor. Philadelphia: Reiner Jansen. PPL (tp only) 9471

An ALMANACK for 1702. By Jacob Taylor. Philadelphia: Reynier Jansen. [Morrison] 9472

An ALMANACK for 1703. By Jacob Taylor. Philadelphia: Reynier Jansen. [Morrison] 9473

An ALMANACK for 1704. By Jacob Taylor. Philadelphia: Reynier Jansen. [Morrison] 9474

An ALMANACK for 1705. By Jacob Taylor. Philadelphia: Tiberius Johnson. 16 ll. PPAmP. 9475

EPHEMERIS Sideralis. A Mathematical Almanack for 1706. By Jacob Taylor. Philadelphia: For the Author. 16 ll. PPAmP. 9476

EPHEMERIS Sideralis or, An Almanack for 1707. By Jacob Taylor. Philadelphia: Tiberius Johnson. 16 ll. DLC; RPJCB. 9477

An ALMANACK for 1708. By Jacob Taylor. Philadelphia: Jacob Taylor. [Morrison] 9478

An ALMANACK for 1709. By Jacob Taylor. Philadelphia: Jacob Taylor. 12 ll. PPAmP. 9479

An ALMANACK for 1710. By Jacob Taylor. Philadelphia: Jacob Taylor. [Morrison] 9480

An ALMANACK for 1711. By Jacob Taylor. Philadelphia: [np] 12 ll. PPAmP. 9481

An ALMANACK for 1712. By Jacob Taylor. Philadelphia: [np] 14 ll. PPAmP. 9482

An EPHEMERIS for 1713... or an Almanack. By Jacob

Pennsylvania - 1714   913

Taylor. Philadelphia: [np] PHi (17 ll., 5 are fragments) 9483

An ALMANACK for 1714. By Jacob Taylor. Philadelphia: Andrew Bradford. [Morrison] 9484

The AMERICAN Almanack for 1714. By Titan Leeds. Philadelphia: A. Bradford. [Sabin 39826] 9485

An ALMANAC for 1715. By Jacob Taylor. Philadelphia: Andrew Bradford. [Morrison] 9486

LEEDS, 1715. The American Almanack for 1715. By Titan Leeds. Philadelphia: A. Bradford. 14 ll. PHi. 9487

An ALMANAC for 1716. By Jacob Taylor. Philadelphia: Andrew Bradford. [Morrison] 9488

LEEDS, 1716. The American Almanack for 1716. By Titan Leeds. Philadelphia: A. Bradford. 12 ll. PHi; DLC (8 ll.) 9489

An ALMANAC for 1717. By Jacob Taylor. Philadelphia: Andrew Bradford. [Morrison] 9490

LEEDS, 1717. The American Almanack for 1717. By Titan Leeds. Philadelphia: A. Bradford. 12 ll. MWA; PHi. 9491

An ALMANACK for 1718. By Jacob Taylor. Philadelphia: Andrew Bradford. [Morrison] 9492

LEEDS, 1718. The American Almanack for 1718. By Titan Leeds. Philadelphia: Andrew Bradford. 12 ll. PHi; PPAmP. 9493

LEEDS, 1719. The American Almanack for 1719. By Titan Leeds. Philadelphia: Andrew Bradford. 12 ll. MWA; DLC; PHi. 9494

PENSILVANIA. An Almanack for 1719. By J. T. Philadelphia: Andrew Bradford. 15 ll. MWA; PPAmP. 9495

An ALMANACK for 1720. By J. T. Philadelphia: Andrew Bradford. 12 ll. PPAmP. 9496

LEEDS, 1720. The American Almanack for 1720. By Titan Leeds. Philadelphia: Andrew Bradford. 12 ll. PHi. 9497

An ALMANACK for 1721. By Jacob Taylor. Philadelphia: Andrew Bradford. [Morrison] 9498

An EPHEMERIS for 1721; or, an Almanack. By John Jerman. Philadelphia: Andrew Bradford. 12 ll. PHi; PPL (8 ll.) 9499

LEEDS, 1721. The American Almanack for 1721. By Titan Leeds. Philadelphia: Andrew Bradford. PPAmP (11 ll.) 9500

An ALMANACK for 1722. By Jacob Taylor. Philadelphia: Andrew Bradford. [Morrison] 9501

LEEDS, 1722. The American Almanack for 1722. By Titan Leeds. Philadelphia: Andrew Bradford. 12 ll. DLC; PHi; PPAmP; PPL (impf) 9502

An ALMANACK for 1723. By John Jerman. Philadelphia: Andrew Bradford. 12 ll. PPL. 9503

An ASTRONOMICAL Diary, or an Almanack for 1723. By B. A. New-York and Philadelphia: William & Andrew Bradford. 16 ll. DLC. 9504

An EPHEMERIS, of the Planetary Motions and Aspects for 1723. By Jacob Taylor. Philadelphia: Andrew Bradford. 16 ll. DLC (ntp); PPAmP. 9505

LEEDS, 1723. The American Almanack for 1723. By Titan Leeds. Philadelphia: Andrew Bradford. PPAmP (11 ll.) 9506

An ALMANACK for 1724. By John Jerman. Philadelphia: Andrew Bradford. [Morrison] 9507

An ALMANACK for 1724. By Jacob Taylor. Philadelphia: Andrew Bradford. [Morrison] 9508

LEEDS, 1724. The American Almanack for 1724. By Titan Leeds. Philadelphia: Andrew Bradford. 12 ll. DLC; NHi; PPAmP; PPL. 9509

An ALMANACK for 1725, or an Ephemeris. By John Hughes. Philadelphia: Andrew Bradford. 16 ll. PHi (tp impf); PPAmP. 9510

An ALMANACK for 1725. By John Jerman. Philadelphia: Andrew Bradford. 12 ll. PHi; PPL (4 ll.) 9511

An ALMANACK for 1725. By Jacob Taylor. Philadelphia: Andrew Bradford. [Morrison] 9512

LEEDS 1725. The American Almanack for 1725. By Titan Leeds. Philadelphia: Andrew Bradford. 12 ll. NHi; PPAmP; PPL (fragment) 9513

An ALMANACK for 1726. By John Jerman. Philadelphia: 1725. [Morrison] 9514

An ALMANACK for 1726. By Jacob Taylor. Philadelphia: Andrew Bradford. [Morrison] 9515

An EPHEMERIS for 1726, or an Almanack. By John Hughes. Philadelphia: Andrew Bradford. 16 ll. PHi. 9516

LEEDS. The American Almanack for 1726. By Titan Leeds. Philadelphia: Andrew Bradford. MWA (9 ll.); NN (4 ll.); NHi (9 ll.); RPJCB (10 ll.) 9517

TAYLOR, 1726. A Compleat Ephemeris for 1726. By Jacob Taylor. Philadelphia: Samuel Keimer; Mary Rose; Sara Read; Jacob Shoemaker; Nath. Edgecome; Charles-Town: Eleazer Philips. 24 ll. DLC; NN (22 ll.); PHi (15 ll., ntp); PPAmP. 9518

An ALMANACK for 1727. Philadelphia: S. Keimer. 12 ll. PHi (8 ll.) 9519

An ALMANACK for 1727. or an Ephemeris. By John Hughes. Philadelphia: Andrew Bradford. 12 ll. PHi.
9520

An ALMANACK for 1727. By John Jerman. Philadelphia: Andrew Bradford. 12 ll. PHi. 9521

An ALMANACK for 1727. By Jacob Taylor. Philadelphia: PPAmP. 9522

The AMERICAN Almanack for 1727. By Felix Leeds. Philadelphia: Andrew Bradford. 12 ll. MWA; MWiW-C (4 ll.); PPAmP; CSmH (10 ll.) 9523

LEEDS, 1727. The American Almanack for 1727. By Titan Leeds. Philadelphia: Samuel Keimer; Flushing: David Humphry's; Charles-Town: Eliezar Phillips. 16 ll. MWA; NN (10 ll.); PHi (15 ll.); PPRF. 9524

An ALMANACK for 1728. By John Jerman. Philadelphia: 1727. [Morrison] 9525

An ALMANACK for 1728. By Jacob Taylor. Philadelphia: Samuel Keimer. [Morrison] 9526

The AMERICAN Almanack for 1728. By Titan Leeds. Philadelphia: S. Keimer; New-York: W. Huertin Goldsmith; Flushing: David Humphreys. (Beware of the Counterfeit One.) 16 ll. MWA (impf); NN; NHi; PHi; PPAmP. 9527

LEEDS. The American Almanack for 1728. By Felix Leeds. Philadelphia: Andrew Bradford. 12 ll. DLC; PHi. 9528

An ALMANACK for 1729. By William Birkett. Philadelphia: Andrew Bradford. 12 ll. PHi (impf) 9529

An ALMANACK for 1729. By John Jerman. Philadelphia: Andrew Bradford. 12 ll. PPL. 9530

An ALMANACK for 1729. By Jacob Taylor. Philadelphia: 1728. [Morrison] 9531

The AMERICAN Almanack for 1729. By Felix Leeds. Philadelphia: Andrew Bradford. 12 ll. PPAmP. 9532

The AMERICAN Almanack for 1729. By Titan Leeds. Philadelphia: S. Keimer; New-York: W. Huertin Goldsmith; Flushing: David Humphreys. (Beware of the Counterfeit One.) 16 ll. DLC (12 ll.); NN (13 ll.); CtY (impf); PHi; PPAmP; RPJCB. 9533

An ALMANACK for 1730. By William Birkett. Philadelphia: Cornelia and Andrew Bradford. 14 ll. PPAmP. 9534

An ALMANACK for 1730. By Thomas Godfrey. Philadelphia: Franklin and Meredith. Broadside. [Morrison] 9535

An ALMANACK for 1730. By John Jerman. Philadelphia: David Harry. [Morrison] 9536

An ALMANACK for 1730. By Felix Leeds. Philadelphia: Andrew Bradford. [Morrison] 9537

An ALMANACK for 1730. By Jacob Taylor. Philadelphia: Andrew Bradford. [Morrison] 9538

The GENUINE Leeds Almanack for 1730. By Titan Leeds. Philadelphia: D. Harry. 14 ll. MWA; DLC (12 ll.); NN; PHi; PPL; RPJCB. 9539

LEEDS, 1730. The American Almanack for 1730. By Titan Leeds. Philadelphia: Printed; Newport: Edward Nearegreas, and Daniel Arnot. 16 ll. MWA; PPL (4 ll.) 9540

An ALMANACK for 1731. By William Birkett. New-York: William Bradford; Philadelphia: Andrew Bradford. PPAmP. 9541

An ALMANACK for 1731. By Thomas Godfrey. Philadelphia: Franklin and Meredith. [Morrison] 9542

An ALMANACK for 1731. By Felix Leeds. Philadelphia: Andrew Bradford. [Morrison] 9543

Pennsylvania - 1731

The **AMERICAN** Almanack for 1731. By John Jerman. Philadelphia: B. Franklin and H. Meredith. 12 ll. DLC; CtY; PHi; PPRF.   9544

PENNSYLVANIA 1731. An Almanack for 1731. By Jacob Taylor. Philadelphia: Andrew Bradford. [Morrison]   9545

Der **TEUTSCHE** Pilgrim: Mitbringende Einen Sitten-Calendar auf 1731. Philadelphia: Andreas Bradfordt. 14 ll. NBLiHi.   9546

An **ALMANACK** for 1732. By William Birkett. Philadelphia: Andrew Bradford. [Morrison]   9547

An **ALMANACK** for 1732. By Jacob Taylor. Philadelphia: 1731. [Morrison]   9548

The **AMERICAN** Almanack for 1732. By John Jerman. Philadelphia: Franklin and Meredith. [Morrison] 9549

The **AMERICAN** Almanack for 1732. By Titan Leeds. New-York: William Bradford; Philadelphia: Andrew Bradford. 14 ll. PPAmP; CSmH.   9550

The **GENUINE** Leeds Almanack. The American Almanack for 1732. By Titan Leeds. Philadelphia: Andrew Bradford. 12 ll. NN; CSmH; PHi; PDoBHi.   9551

The **PENNSYLVANIA** Almanack for 1732. By Thomas Godfrey. Philadelphia: Franklin and Meredith. [Morrison]   9552

A **SHEET** Almanac for 1732. By Thomas Godfrey. Philadelphia: Franklin and Meredith. Broadside. [Morrison] 9552a

Der **TEUTSCHE** Pilgrim: Mitbringende Einen Sitten-Calender auf 1732. Philadelphia: Andreas Bradford. 14 ll. NBLiHi.   9553

An **ALMANACK** for 1733. By William Birkett. Philadelphia: Andrew Bradford. [Morrison]   9554

An **ALMANACK** for 1733. By John Jerman. Philadelphia:

Andrew Bradford. [Morrison] 9555

An ALMANACK for 1733. By Jacob Taylor. Philadelphia: 1732. [Morrison] 9556

LEEDS 1733. The American Almanack for 1733. By Titan Leeds. New York: William Bradford; Philadelphia: Andrew Bradford. 12 ll. DLC; NHi (impf); PDoBHi.
9557

The PENNSYLVANIA Almanack for 1733. By T. Godfrey. Philadelphia: A. Bradford. 12 ll. DLC; NN (9 ll.); PHi. 9558

POOR Richard, 1733. An Almanack for 1733. By Richard Saunders. Philadelphia: B. Franklin. 12 ll. PPRF. 9559

POOR Richard, 1733. An Almanack for 1733. By Richard Saunders. Philadelphia: B. Franklin. (Second Edition) 12 ll. PU. 9560

POOR Richard, 1733. An Almanack for 1733. By Richard Saunders. Philadelphia: B. Franklin. (Third Impression) 12 ll. PHi. 9561

SHEET Almanack for 1733. Philadelphia: B. Franklin. Broadside. Advertised in the "Pennsylvania Gazette," December 19, 1732. 9562

Der TEUTSCHE Pilgrim: Mitbringende Einen Sitten-Calender auf 1733. Philadelphia: Andreas Bradford. NBLiHi (11 ll.) 9563

An ALMANACK for 1734. By William Birkett. Philadelphia: Andrew Bradford. [Morrison] 9564

An ALMANACK for 1734. By John Jerman. Philadelphia: B. Franklin. [Morrison] 9565

An ALMANACK for 1734. By Jacob Taylor. Philadelphia: 1733. [Morrison] 9566

The AMERICAN Almanack for 1734. By Matthew Boucher. Philadelphia: Andrew Bradford. [Morrison] 9567

The GENUINE Leeds Almanack. The American Almanack for 1734. By Titan Leeds. Philadelphia: Andrew Bradford. 12 ll. DLC; NN (6 ll.); CtY (11 ll.); PDoBHi; PHi.   9568

The PENNSYLVANIA Almanack for 1734. By T. Godfrey. Philadelphia: Andrew Bradford. 12 ll. DLC; PHi.   9569

POOR Richard 1734. An Almanack for 1734. By Richard Saunders. Philadelphia: B. Franklin. 12 ll. MWA; MBC; CtY.   9570

POOR Richard, 1734. An Almanack for 1734. By Richard Saunders. Philadelphia: B. Franklin. (Second Edition) 12 ll. PPAmP.   9571

An ALMANACK for 1735. By William Birkett. Philadelphia: Andrew Bradford. [Morrison]   9572

An ALMANACK for 1735. By Thomas Godfrey. Philadelphia: Andrew Bradford. Broadside. [Morrison]
                                                              9573
An ALMANACK for 1735. By Theophilus Grew. Philadelphia: B. Franklin. [Morrison]   9574

An ALMANACK for 1735. By Jacob Taylor. Philadelphia: 1734. [Morrison]   9575

The AMERICAN Almanack for 1735. By Matthew Boucher. Philadelphia: Andrew Bradford. [Morrison]
                                                              9576
The AMERICAN Almanack for 1735. By John Jerman. Philadelphia: B. Franklin. 12 ll. PPL (ntp); PU (11 ll.)   9577

The GENUINE Leeds Almanack. The American Almanack for 1735. By Titan Leeds. Philadelphia: Andrew Bradford. 14 ll. N (tp impf); PDoBHi; PHi; PPAmP.
                                                              9578
The PENNSYLVANIA Almanack for 1735. By Thomas Godfrey. Philadelphia: Andrew Bradford. [Morrison]
                                                              9579

POOR Richard 1735. An Almanack for 1735. By Richard Saunders. Philadelphia: B. Franklin. 12 ll. MWA (tp only); CtY; PPAmP (impf); Gimbel.   9580

The AMERICAN Almanack for 1736. By William Birkett. Philadelphia: Andrew Bradford. [Morrison] 9581

The AMERICAN Almanack for 1736. By Matthew Boucher. Philadelphia: Andrew Bradford. [Morrison] 9582

The AMERICAN Almanack for 1736. By John Jerman. Philadelphia: Benjamin Franklin. 12 ll. MWA (9 ll., ntp)   9583

The GENUINE Leeds Almanack. The American Almanack for 1736. By Titan Leeds. Philadelphia: Andrew Bradford. 14 ll. MWA; DLC; NHi (impf); InU; PDoBHi; PHi; PPAmP; PPL (12 ll., ntp)   9584

PENNSYLVANIA 1736. An Almanack for 1736. By Jacob Taylor. Philadelphia: B. Franklin. [Morrison] 9585

The PENNSYLVANIA Almanack for 1736. By T. Godfrey. Philadelphia: Andrew Bradford. 12 ll. MWA; NN (10 ll.); PHi.   9586

POOR Richard, 1736. An Almanack for 1736. By Richard Saunders. Philadelphia: B. Franklin. 12 ll. MWA; NN; CtY; MdBJ-G; CSmH; PHi; PPAmP (impf); PU (11 ll.)   9587

A SHEET Almanack for 1736. By T. Godfrey. Philadelphia: Andrew Bradford. Broadside. [Morrison] 9588

ALMANACK for 1737. Philadelphia: Andrew Bradford. Broadside. [Morrison]   9589

An ALMANACK for 1737. By John Jerman. Philadelphia. [Morrison]   9590

The AMERICAN Almanack for 1737. By William Birkett. Philadelphia: Andrew Bradford. MWA (10 ll.)   9591

The **AMERICAN** Almanack for 1737. By Matthew Boucher. Philadelphia: Andrew Bradford. [Morrison]
9592

The **GENUINE** Leeds Almanack. The American Almanack for 1737. By Titan Leeds. Philadelphia: Andrew Bradford. 15 ll. MWA (three varieties); DLC; NHi (impf); CSmH; PDoBHi; PHi; PPL. 9593

PENSILVANIA, 1737. An Almanack or Ephemeris for 1737. By Jacob Taylor. Philadelphia: Andrew Bradford; Concord: John Taylor. 16 ll. PPAmP. 9594

The **PENNSYLVANIA** Almanack for 1737. By Thomas Godfrey. Philadelphia: Andrew Bradford. [Morrison]
9595

POOR Richard, 1737. An Almanack for 1737. By Richard Saunders. Philadelphia: B. Franklin. 12 ll. MWA; NN; CtY; CSmH; PHi; PPAmP; PPPrHi (impf); PPRF (impf); PU; Woodward (impf) 9596

An **ALMANACK** for 1738. By William Birkett. Philadelphia: Andrew Bradford. [Morrison] 9597

An **ALMANACK** for 1738. By John Jerman. Philadelphia: Andrew Bradford. [Morrison] 9598

The **AMERICAN** Almanack for 1738. By Matthew Boucher. Philadelphia: Andrew Bradford. [Morrison]
9599

The **GENUINE** Leeds Almanack. The American Almanack for 1738. By Titan Leeds. Philadelphia: Andrew Bradford. 12 ll. MWA; NN (11 ll.); NHi (impf); PDoBHi; PHi. 9600

-- Issue with 14 ll. PPL. 9601

PENSILVANIA. An Almanack for 1738. By Jacob Taylor. Philadelphia: Andrew Bradford. 16 ll. MWA; PPAmP. 9602

PENSILVANIA, 1738. An Almanack for 1738. By Jacob Taylor. Philadelphia: Andrew Bradford; Concord: John Taylor. 16 ll. PPL. 9603

POOR Richard, 1738. An Almanack for 1738. By Richard Saunders. Philadelphia: B. Franklin. 12 ll. NN; NBLiHi; MB; MH; CtY; DeWint; CSmH; PU; PPL (impf); PHi; PPRF (impf)   9604

The AMERICAN Almanack for 1739. By John Jerman. Philadelphia: Andrew Bradford. 12 ll. MWA (two varieties); InU; PHi.   9605

The GENUINE Leeds Almanack. The American Almanack for 1739. By Titan Leeds. Philadelphia: Andrew Bradford. 12 ll. MWA; NHi (impf); InU; PDoBHi; PHi.   9606

Der HOCHDEUTSCH Americanische Calender auf 1739. Germantaun: Christopher Sauer; Philadelphia: Johann Wister. 12 ll. PP-F.   9607

PENSILVANIA. An Almanack for 1739. By Jacob Taylor. Philadelphia: Andrew Bradford. [MWA has photostat copy of tp; Proud copy ?]   9608

POOR Richard, 1739. An Almanack for 1739. By Richard Saunders. Philadelphia: B. Franklin. 12 ll. MWA; DLC; MB; CtY (impf); CSmH; PPF; PU; PPAmP (impf); PPL (9 ll.); PHi (5 ll.); PPRF; Cooke.   9609

POOR William's Almanack for 1739. By William Birkett. Philadelphia: Andrew Bradford. 12 ll. NN; NBLiHi; DeWint; CSmH.   9610

The AMERICAN Almanack for 1740. By John Jerman. Philadelphia: Andrew Bradford. 12 ll. NHi.   9611

The GENUINE Leeds Almanack. The American Almanack for 1740. By Titan Leeds. Philadelphia: Andrew Bradford. [Morrison]   9612

The GENUINE Leeds Almanack. The American Almanack for 1740. By Titan Leeds. Philadelphia: Andrew Bradford. (Second Edition) 12 ll. MWA; PDoBHi; PHi.   9613

Der HOCH-DEUTSCH Americanische Calender auf 1740. Germanton: Christoph Saur. 12 ll. PHi. 9614

PENSILVANIA, 1740. An Almanack, or Ephemeris for 1740. By Jacob Taylor. Philadelphia: Andrew Bradford. 16 ll. DLC (15 ll.); PPAmP; PPL (13 ll.) 9615

POOR Richard, 1740. An Almanack for 1740. By Richard Saunders. Philadelphia: B. Franklin. 12 ll. MWA (impf); DLC (impf); NN; CtY; NhD; CSmH; PPAmP; PPL; PHi; PU (10 ll.); PPRF. 9616

POOR Richard, 1740. An Almanack for 1740. By Richard Saunders. Philadelphia: B. Franklin. (Second Edition) 12 ll. [Morrison] 9617

POOR Richard, 1740. An Almanack for 1740. By Richard Saunders. Philadelphia: B. Franklin. (Third Edition) 12 ll. [Morrison] 9618

POOR Will's Almanack for 1740. By William Birkett. Philadelphia: Andrew Bradford. 12 ll. MWA; CSmH; PHi. 9619

An ALMANACK for 1741. Philadelphia: B. Franklin. Broadside. [Morrison] 9620

The AMERICAN Almanack for 1741. By John Jerman. Philadelphia: B. Franklin. 12 ll. PHi; PPL. 9621

The GENUINE Leeds Almanack. The American Almanack for 1741. By Titan Leeds. Philadelphia: Andrew Bradford. 12 ll. MWA (fragment); DLC; NjMoW; CSmH; PHi; PDoBHi; PPL. 9622

Der HOCH-DEUTSCH Americanische Calender auf 1741. Germanton: Christoph Saur. 12 ll. PHi. 9623

-- Printed in red and black. 12 ll. [Morrison] 9624

The NEW-YEAR'S Gift; or A Pocket Almanack for 1741. Philadelphia: B. Franklin. 16 ll. CtY. 9625

PENSILVANIA. An Almanack for 1741. By Jacob
Taylor. Philadelphia: Andrew Bradford. 16 ll. MWA;
DLC; InU; OClWHi; PPAmP; PPL. 9626

POOR Richard, 1741. An Almanack for 1741. By
Richard Saunders. Philadelphia: B. Franklin. 12 ll.
MWA (9 ll.); DLC (impf); CtY; CSmH; PHi (9 ll.);
PPAmP; PU (11 ll.) 9627

POOR Will's Almanack for 1741. By William Birkett.
Philadelphia: Andrew Bradford. 12 ll. NBLiHi; PHi.
9628

The AMERICAN Almanack for 1742. By John Jerman.
Philadelphia: B. Franklin. [Morrison] 9629

The GENUINE Leeds Almanack. The American Almanack for 1742. By Titan Leeds. Philadelphia: Andrew
Bradford. 12 ll. PHi. 9630

Der HOCH-DEUTSCH Americanische Calender auf 1742.
Germanton: Christoph Saur. 12 ll. DLC (10 ll.); PHi
(11 ll.) 9631

-- Larger issue. PDoBHi (15 ll.) 9632

The NEW-JERSEY Almanack for 1742. By William
Ball. Philadelphia: B. Franklin. Advertised in the
"Pennsylvania Gazette," October 22, 1741. 9633

PENSILVANIA. An Almanack for 1742. By Jacob Taylor. Philadelphia: Andrew Bradford. 16 ll. MWA;
PPAmP; PPL (13 ll.) 9634

A POCKET Almanack for 1742. By R. Saunders.
Philadelphia: B. Franklin. 8 ll. DLC; PHi; PPL.
9635

POOR Richard, 1742. An Almanack for 1742. By
Richard Saunders. Philadelphia: B. Franklin. 12 ll.
MWA (impf); DLC (impf); CtY; CSmH; PU; PHi; PPL;
PPRF (impf) 9636

POOR Robin's Almanack for 1742. Philadelphia: William Bradford. DLC (4 ll., ntp) 9637

POOR Will's Almanack for 1742. By William Birkett.
Philadelphia: Andrew Bradford; New-York: William
Bradford. 12 ll. MWA; DLC (11 ll.); NN (11 ll.)
9638

The AMERICAN Almanack for 1743. By William Birkett. Philadelphia: Andrew Bradford. 12 ll. MWA
(impf) 9639

The AMERICAN Almanack for 1743. By John Jerman.
Philadelphia: W. Bradford. 12 ll. PHi. 9640

The GENUINE Leeds Almanack. The American Almanack for 1743. By Titan Leeds. Philadelphia: Andrew
Bradford. 12 ll. DLC (10 ll.); NjMoW. 9641

Der HOCH-DEUTSCH Americanische Calender auf 1743.
Germantown: Christoph Saur. 12 ll. MWA (11 ll.);
InU; PHi (8 ll.) 9642

The NEW-JERSEY Almanack for 1743. By William
Ball. Philadelphia: B. Franklin. Advertised in the
"Pennsylvania Gazette," November 11, 1742. 9643

PENSILVANIA, 1743. An Almanack, or Ephemeris for
1743. By Jacob Taylor. Philadelphia: Isaiah Warner.
16 ll. MWA; DLC; NN; NHi; NjMoW; PHi; PPAmP;
PPL. 9644

A POCKET Almanack for 1743. By R. Saunders.
Philadelphia: B. Franklin. 8 ll. DLC; CtY; PPL.
9645

POOR Richard, 1743. An Almanack for 1743. By
Richard Saunders. Philadelphia: B. Franklin. 12 ll.
MWA (impf); DLC; CtY; CSmH; PHi; PU. 9646

POOR Robin's Almanack for 1743. Philadelphia: William Bradford. [Morrison] 9647

POOR Will's Almanack for 1743. By William Birkett.
Philadelphia: Andrew Bradford. 12 ll. MWA; DLC;
ScC. 9648

An ALMANACK for 1744. By John Jerman. Philadel-

phia: Isaiah Warner and Cornelia Bradford. [Morrison]
9649

The AMERICAN Almanack for 1744. By William Birkett. Philadelphia: Andrew Bradford. 12 ll. MWA (10 ll., ntp) 9650

BOUCHER 1744. The Pennsylvania Almanack for 1744. By Matthew Boucher. [Philadelphia:] W. Bradford. 12 ll. PHi. 9651

The GENUINE Leeds Almanack. The American Almanack for 1744. By Titan Leeds. Philadelphia: I. Warner and C. Bradford. 12 ll. DLC; PHi. 9652

Der HOCH-DEUTSCH Americanische Calender auf 1744. Germantown; Christoph Saur. 15 ll. MWA; PHi. 9653

The NEW-JERSEY Almanack for 1744. By William Ball. Philadelphia: I. Warner and C. Bradford. 16 ll. MWA (impf); PHi. 9654

PENSILVANIA, 1744. An Almanack, or Ephemeris for 1744. By Jacob Taylor. Philadelphia: I. Warner and C. Bradford. 16 ll. MWA; DLC; NN; InU; PHi; PPAmP; PPL; Drake (impf) 9655

A POCKET Almanack for 1744. By R. Saunders. Philadelphia: B. Franklin. 12 ll. DLC (11 ll.); CtY; PU. 9656

POOR Richard, 1744. An Almanack for 1744. By Richard Saunders. Philadelphia: B. Franklin. 12 ll. PU. 9657

POOR Richard, 1744. An Almanack for 1744. By Richard Saunders. Philadelphia: B. Franklin at the New Printing Office on Market Street. 12 ll. MWA.
9658

POOR Richard, 1744. An Almanack for 1744. By Richard Saunders. Philadelphia: B. Franklin; Annapolis: Jonas Green. 12 ll. MH; CtY; CSmH; PHi; PPRF. 9659

POOR Robin's Almanack for 1744. Philadelphia: William Bradford. 16 ll. DLC (ntp) 9660

POOR Will's Almanack for 1744. By William Birkett. Philadelphia: I. Warner & C. Bradford. 12 ll. MWA; DLC; NHi (impf); PHi. 9661

The AMERICAN Almanack for 1745. By William Birkett. Philadelphia: Andrew Bradford. MWA (tp only) 9662

The AMERICAN Almanack for 1745. By John Jerman. Philadelphia: I. Warner and C. Bradford. 12 ll. MWA; DLC (11 ll.); PPL. 9653

The GENUINE Leeds Almanack. The American Almanack for 1745. By Titan Leeds. Philadelphia: Cornelia Bradford. 12 ll. MWA (ntp); DLC (ntp); PHi. 9654

Der HOCH-DEUTSCH Americanische Calender auf 1745. Germantown: Christoph Saur. 16 ll. MWA (2 ll.); NBLiHi; PHi. 9655

The NEW-JERSEY Almanack for 1745. By William Ball. Philadelphia: 18 ll. MWA (imprint lacking) 9656

PENNSYLVANIA, 1745. An Almanack, and Ephemeris for 1745. By Jacob Taylor. Philadelphia: William Bradford. 16 ll. MWA; DLC; InU; NjMoW; TxU; PPL (15 ll.) 9657

The PENNSYLVANIA Almanack for 1745. By Matthew Boucher. Philadelphia: I. Warner and C. Bradford. 12 ll. MWA; DLC; NjMoW; PHi. 9658

A POCKET Almanack for 1745. By R. Saunders. Philadelphia: B. Franklin. 12 ll. DLC; Ct; CtY; PHi; PU. 9659

-- Printed in red and black. 12 ll. CtY. 9660

POOR Richard, 1745. An Almanack for 1745. By Richard Saunders. Philadelphia: B. Franklin. 12 ll. MWA; NN (11 ll.); MH; InU (7 ll., ntp) 9661

POOR Robin's Almanack for 1745. Philadelphia: William Bradford. 12 ll. DLC (ntp) 9662

POOR Will's Almanack for 1745. By William Birkett. Philadelphia: I. Warner and C. Bradford. [Sabin 64094] 9663

The AMERICAN Almanack for 1746. By John Jerman. Philadelphia: Cornelia Bradford. PHi (10 ll.) 9664

The AMERICAN Country Almanack for 1746. By Thomas More. Philadelphia: B. Franklin. DLC (10 ll.) 9665

The GENUINE Leeds Almanack. The American Almanack for 1746. By Titan Leeds. Philadelphia: Cornelia Bradford. 12 ll. DLC; PHi (7 ll.) 9666

Der HOCH-DEUTSCH Americanische Calender auf 1746. Germantown: Christoph Saur. 16 ll. MWA (5 ll.); PDoBHi; PHi. 9667

The NEW-JERSEY Almanack for 1746. By William Ball. Philadelphia: William Bradford. [Morrison] 9668

PENSILVANIA. 1746. An Almanack, and Ephemeris for 1746. By Jacob Taylor. Philadelphia: William Bradford. 16 ll. MWA; DLC; InU; NjMoW; PPL. 9669

A POCKET Almanack for 1746. By R. Saunders. Philadelphia: B. Franklin. 12 ll. DLC; NN; CtY; PHi; PPL. 9670

POOR Richard, 1746. An Almanack for 1746. By Richard Saunders. Philadelphia: B. Franklin. 12 ll. MWA; NN (impf); MB; MH; CtY; CSmH; PHi; PPAmP; PPL (impf); PPRF; PU. 9671

POOR Robin's Almanack for 1746. Philadelphia: William Bradford. [Morrison] 9672

POOR Will's Almanack for 1746. By William Birkett. Philadelphia: Cornelia Bradford. 12 ll. DLC;

PPAmP.   9673

POOR Will's Almanack for 1746. By William Birkitt [sic]. Philadelphia: W. Bradford. 12 ll. MWA; InU (5 ll.); PHi.   9674

An ALMANACK for 1747. By William Birkett. Philadelphia: Cornelia Bradford. [Morrison]   9675

An ALMANACK for 1747. By Thomas More. Philadelphia: B. Franklin. [Morrison]   9676

AMERICAN Almanack for 1747. By John Jerman. Germantown: Christopher Sower. 12 ll. NjMoW. 9677

Der HOCH-DEUTSCH Americanische Calender auf 1747. Germantown: Christoph Saur. 16 ll. MWA; DLC; PHi; PPG.   9678

NEU-EINGERICHTETER Americanischer Geschichts-Kalender auf 1747. Philadelphia: B. Franklin. [Morrison]   9679

The NEW-JERSEY Almanack for 1747. By William Ball. Philadelphia: W. Bradford. 18 ll. DLC (17 ll.)
                                                                                      9680

A POCKET Almanack for 1747. By R. Saunders. Philadelphia: B. Franklin. 12 ll. DLC; CtY; PHi; PU.
                                                                                      9681

POOR Richard, 1747. An Almanack for 1747. By Richard Saunders. Philadelphia: B. Franklin. 12 ll. MWA (impf); NN; CtY; MB; InU (fragment); MoU (impf); PHi; PPAmP (impf); PPL; PPRF; PU. 9682

POOR Robin's Spare Hours, Employ'd in calculating, A Diary, or Almanack for 1747. Philadelphia: W. Bradford. 18 ll. PHi.   9683

POOR Will's Almanack for 1747. By William Birkett. Philadelphia: Cornelia Bradford. 12 ll. MWA (impf); PHi (ntp)   9684

TAYLOR'S Successor: a new Almanack and Ephemeris

for 1747. By Zach. Butcher. Philadelphia: Printed
for the Author. PHi (13 ll.)   9685

The AMERICAN Almanack for 1748. By John Jerman.
Philadelphia: B. Franklin. 12 ll. PU (10 ll.)   9686

The AMERICAN Country Almanack for 1748. By
Thomas More. Philadelphia: B. Franklin. 12 ll. PHi
(11 ll.)   9687

Der HOCH-DEUTSCH Americanische Calender auf 1748.
Germantown: Christoph Saur; Philadelphia: David
Tascher. 16 ll. MWA; DLC (impf); PHi; PPG. 9688

NEU-EINGERICHTETER Americanischer Geschichts-
Kalender auf 1748. Philadelphia: Gotthard Armbruster.
[Seidenstricker]   9689

NEU-EINGERICHTETER Americanischer Geschichts-
Kalender auf 1748. Philadelphia: B. Franklin und J.
Boehm. [Morrison]   9690

The NEW-JERSEY Almanack for 1748. By William
Ball. Philadelphia: William Bradford. [Morrison]
                                                                 9691
A POCKET Almanack for 1748. By R. Saunders.
Philadelphia: B. Franklin. 12 ll. DLC; CtY; MHi;
PHi.   9692

POOR Richard improved: being an Almanack and
Ephemeris for 1748. By Richard Saunders. Philadelphia: B. Franklin. 18 ll. (Verso F-1: List of gover-
nors of Pennsylvania...) NN (impf); MB (ntp);
PPAmP (impf); PU; DLC; PPL; PPRF (impf); Woodward (impf); CSmH.   9693

(Verso F-1: Court Calendar for New-England...) 18 ll.
MWA; RPJCB; MH; InU (impf); CtY.   9694

(Verso F-1: Court Calendar for Virginia, North-Carolina and South-Carolina...) 18 ll. DLC; CSmH; PHi.
                                                               9695
POOR Robin's Spare Hours, Employ'd in Calculating,

A Diary, or Almanack for 1748. Philadelphia: W.
Bradford. 18 ll. PHi. 9696

POOR Will's Almanack for 1748. By William Birkett.
Philadelphia: Cornelia Bradford. 12 ll. PHi. 9697

An ALMANACK for 1749. By John Jerman. Philadelphia: B. Franklin and D. Hall. [Morrison] 9698

An ALMANACK for 1749. By Thomas More. Philadelphia: B. Franklin and D. Hall. [Morrison] 9699

The AMERICAN Almanack for 1749. Philadelphia: A.
Bradford. [Sabin 36058] 9700

Der HOCH-DEUTSCH Americanische Kalender auf 1749.
Germantown: Christoph Saur; Philadelphia: David
Tascher. 18 ll. MWA (17 ll.); DLC; PHi; PPL. 9701

Der NEU-EINGERICHTETER Americanischer Geschichts
Calender auf 1749. Philadelphia: A. Armbruster. 18
ll. MWA (16 ll.) 9702

The NEW-JERSEY Almanack for 1749. By William
Ball. Philadelphia: William Bradford. [Morrison]
9703

A POCKET Almanack for 1749. By R. Saunders.
Philadelphia: B. Franklin, and D. Hall. 12 ll. DLC;
PHi. 9704

POOR Richard improved: being an Almanack and
Ephemeris for 1749. By Richard Saunders. Philadelphia: B. Franklin and D. Hall. 18 ll. MWA; PPAmP
(impf); MB (impf); RPJCB; DLC; CSmH; InU (fragment); PPL (impf); NN; PHi; PU; NjP; PPRF (impf);
Woodward. 9705

-- "Errors corrected" 18 ll. MWA (impf); CtY;
PPRF (impf) 9706

POOR Robin's Spare Hours, Employ'd in Calculating,
A Diary, or Almanack for 1749. Philadelphia: W.
Bradford. 16 ll. MB. 9707

POOR Will's Almanack for 1749. Philadelphia. 12 ll.
MWA (10 ll., ntp) 9708

An AMERICAN Almanack for 1750. By John Jerman.
Philadelphia: B. Franklin and D. Hall. [Morrison]
9709

No entry. 9710

The AMERICAN Country Almanack for 1750. By
Thomas More. Philadelphia: B. Franklin, and D.
Hall. 12 ll. PHi. 9711

Der HOCH-DEUTSCH Americanische Calender auf 1750.
Germantown: Christoph Saur; Philadelphia: David
Tascher. 18 ll. MWA (16 ll.); DLC; NBLiHi; InU
(impf); PDoBHi; PHi. 9712

NEU-EINGERICHTETER Americanischer Geschichts-
Kalender auf 1750. Philadelphia: Benjam. Fraencklin,
und Joh. Boehm. 19 ll. CtY; PHi (17 ll.) 9713

The NEW-JERSEY, Almanack for 1750. By William
Ball. Philadelphia: W. Bradford. 16 ll. PHi. 9714

A POCKET Almanack for 1750. By R. Saunders.
Philadelphia: B. Franklin, and D. Hall. 12 ll. DLC;
CtY; PHi; PU; RNHi. 9715

POOR Richard improved: being an Almanack and Ephem-
eris for 1750. By Richard Saunders. Philadelphia: B.
Franklin, and D. Hall. 18 ll. MWA (impf); PPAmP;
MB; DLC; CSmH; PPL; InU (fragment); PHi; PU;
PPRF; CtY; Woodward (impf) 9716

POOR Robin's Almanack for 1750. Philadelphia: William
Bradford. [Morrison] 9717

POOR Will's Almanack for 1750. By William Birkett.
Philadelphia: Cornelia Bradford. [Morrison] 9718

POOR Will's Almanack for 1750. By William Birkett.
Philadelphia: William Bradford. 12 ll. PHi. 9719

The AMERICAN Almanack for 1751. By John Jerman. Philadelphia: B. Franklin and D. Hall. 12 ll. PHi (tp impf); PPAmP. 9720

The AMERICAN Country Almanack for 1751. By Thomas More. Philadelphia: B. Franklin, and D. Hall. 12 ll. DLC; NN; CSmH. 9721

Der HOCH-DEUTSCH Americanische Calender auf 1751. Germantown: Christoph Saur. 18 ll. MWA (16 ll.); PHi. 9722

NEU-EINGERICHTETER Americanische Geschichts-Kalender auf 1751. Philadelphia: B. Franklin und G. Armbruster. [Morrison] 9723

NEU-EINGERICHTETER Americanischer Geschichts-Calender auf 1751. Philadelphia: Benjam. Fräncklin, und Joh. Böhm. 20 ll. CtY (19 ll.) 9724

The NEW-JERSEY Almanack for 1751. By William Ball. Philadelphia: William Bradford. 16 ll. MWA (11 ll., ntp) 9725

A POCKET Almanack for 1751. By R. Saunders. Philadelphia: B. Franklin, and D. Hall. 12 ll. MWA; DLC; CtY; ICN; CSmH; PHi; PU. 9726

POOR Richard improved: being an Almanack and Ephemeris for 1751. By Richard Saunders. Philadelphia: B. Franklin, and D. Hall. 18 ll. MWA; DLC; MB; NN (impf); CtY; CSmH; PPL; PPAmP (impf); P; PHi; PU (14 ll.); PPRF; Woodward (impf) 9727

POOR Robin's Spare Hours, Employ'd in calculating, A Diary or Almanack for 1751. Philadelphia: W. Bradford. 16 ll. MWA; PHi (5 ll.) 9728

POOR Will's Almanack for 1751. By William Birkett. Philadelphia: Cornelia Bradford. [Morrison] 9729

An ALMANACK for 1752. By G. G. Lancaster: James Chattin. 8 ll. PPL; PPL-R. 9730

The **AMERICAN** Almanack for 1752. By John Jerman.
Philadelphia: B. Franklin and D. Hall. 12 ll. DLC;
PHi.   9731

The **AMERICAN** Country Almanack for 1752. By
Thomas More. Philadelphia: B. Franklin and D. Hall.
12 ll. DLC; PU (11 ll.)   9732

The **BARBADOES** Almanac for 1752. By Theophilus
Grew. Philadelphia: B. Franklin and D. Hall. Broadside. PPL.   9733

Der **HOCH-DEUTSCH** Americanische Calender auf 1752.
Germantown: Christoph Saur. 18 ll. MWA; InU;
PDoBHi; PHi.   9734

NEU-EINGERICHTETER Americanischer Geschichts-
Calender auf 1752. Philadelphia: Benj. Fränklin. 20 ll.
PPG.   9735

The **NEW-JERSEY** Almanack for 1752. By William
Ball. Philadelphia: W. Bradford. 14 ll. MWA (7 ll.);
PHi.   9736

A **POCKET** Almanack for 1752. By R. Saunders.
Philadelphia: B. Franklin, and D. Hall. 12 ll. MWA;
DLC; NN; MB; CtY; PHi; PPF; PU.   9737

POOR Richard improved: being an Almanack and Ephemeris for 1752. Philadelphia: B. Franklin, and D. Hall.
18 ll. MWA; MB; RPJCB; DLC; MH; CSmH; InU
(ntp); NN; NjP; CtY; RPA; NjR (17 ll.); PPAmP
(impf); P (impf); PPL; PHi; PU; PPRF; Gimbel (impf);
Woodward (impf)   9738

POOR Robin's Spare Hours. An Almanack for 1752.
Philadelphia: W. Bradford. 16 ll. MWA; NN (11 ll.,
ntp)   9739

POOR Will's Almanack for 1752. By William Birkett.
Philadelphia: Cornelia Bradford. [Morrison]   9740

The **AMERICAN** Almanack for 1753. By John Jerman.

Philadelphia: B. Franklin and D. Hall. 12 ll. DLC (impf); P (impf); PPF. 9741

The AMERICAN Country Almanack for 1753. By Thomas More. Philadelphia: B. Franklin, and D. Hall. 12 ll. MWA (impf); CtY; GHi. 9742

Der HOCH-DEUTSCH Americanische Calender auf 1753. Germantown: Christoph Saur. 22 ll. MWA; DLC (20 ll.); InU; WHi; PHi; PPcSchw. 9743

NEU-EINGERICHTETER Americanische Geschichts-Calender auf 1753. Philadelphia: B. Franklin und G. Armbruster. [Morrison] 9744

The NEW-JERSEY Almanack for 1753. By William Ball. Philadelphia: W. Bradford. 16 ll. MWA. 9745

A POCKET Almanack for 1753. By R. Saunders. Philadelphia: B. Franklin, and D. Hall. 12 ll. MWA; DLC; NN; CtY; TxU (fragment); PU; PHi. 9746

POOR Richard improved: being an Almanack and Ephemeris for 1753. By Richard Saunders. Philadelphia: B. Franklin and D. Hall. 18 ll. MWA; DLC; NN; MB; NHi; ScC; MiU-C; NjP; CSmH; CtY; ViU; RPA; PPL (ntp); P; PU; PHi; PPF; PPAmP; PPRF; Woodward. 9747

POOR Robin's Almanack for 1753. Philadelphia: William Bradford. [Morrison] 9748

The AMERICAN Almanack for 1754. By John Jerman. Philadelphia: B. Franklin and D. Hall. 12 ll. DLC; PU. 9749

The AMERICAN Country Almanack for 1754. By Thomas More. Philadelphia: B. Franklin, and D. Hall. 12 ll. PHi; PU. 9750

Der HOCH-DEUTSCH Americanische Calender auf 1754. Germantown: Christoph Saur. 24 ll. MWA; NBLiHi; NjR; PPG; P; PHi (23 ll.) 9751

Pennsylvania - 1754   937

NEU-EINGERICHTETER Americanischer Geschichts-
Kalender auf 1754. Philadelphia: Antony Armbrüester.
18 ll. PHi; PPG. 9752

The NEW-JERSEY Almanack for 1754. By William
Ball: Philadelphia: William Bradford. [Morrison]
9753

The PENNSYLVANIA Town and Country-man's Alman-
ack for 1754. By John Tobler. Germantown: C.
Sower, jr. 20 ll. MWA (14 ll., ntp); InU (fragment);
PNortHi. 9754

A POCKET Almanack for 1754. By R. Saunders.
Philadelphia: B. Franklin, and D. Hall. 12 ll. DLC;
CtY; PHi; PU. 9755

POOR Richard improved: being an Almanack and Ephem-
eris for 1754. By Richard Saunders. Philadelphia: B.
Franklin and D. Hall. 18 ll. MWA; DLC; MB; MFran;
MH; CSmH; NN; CtY; RPA; NjMoW; PPAmP; PPF;
P; PPL (impf); PHi; PU; PPRF; Woodward. 9756

POOR Robin's Spare Hours. Almanack for 1754. Philadelphia: W. Bradford. 16 ll. MWA (13 ll., ntp) 9757

The AMERICAN Almanack for 1755. By John Jerman.
Philadelphia: B. Franklin and D. Hall. 12 ll. DLC
(impf); CtY (9 ll.); NHi; PHi. 9758

The AMERICAN Country Almanack for 1755. By
Thomas More. Philadelphia: B. Franklin and D. Hall.
12 ll. PHi; PPL; PU (11 ll.) 9759

Der HOCH-DEUTSCH Americanische Calender auf 1755.
Germantown: Christoph Saur; Philadelphia: David Tasch-
ler; Lancaster: Heinrich Walter. 24 ll. MWA (impf);
DLC (impf); N; WHi; PHi; PPeSchw. 9760

NEU-EINGERICHTETER Americanischer Geschichts-
Calender auf 1755. Philadelphia: Anton Armbrüester.
20 ll. MWA; PLF (17 ll.) 9761

The NEW-JERSEY Almanack for 1755. By William Ball.

Philadelphia: William Bradford. 16 ll. PPL. 9762

The **PENNSYLVANIA** Town and Country-Man's Almanack for 1755. By John Tobler. Germantown: C. Sower, jun.; Philadelphia: C. Marshall & T. Maule. 20 ll. MWA; DLC; NHi; P. 9763

-- Later issue. Cf recto leaf 20. 20 ll. PHi. 9764

A **POCKET** Almanack for 1755. By R. Saunders. Philadelphia: B. Franklin, and D. Hall. 12 ll. DLC; MB; CtY; PHi; PPL. 9765

POOR Richard improved: being an Almanack and Ephemeris for 1755. By Richard Saunders. Philadelphia: B. Franklin, and D. Hall. 18 ll. MWA; DLC; MB; MH; CSmH; InU (ntp); P; NN; CtY; RPA; NjMoW; PPAmP; PPF; PHi; PPL (impf); PU; PPRF; Woodward, Drake (16 ll.) 9766

POOR Robin's Spare Hours. Almanack for 1755. Philadelphia: William Bradford. 16 ll. DLC; PHi (3 ll., ntp) 9767

The **SOUTH-CAROLINA** Almanack for 1755. By John Tobler. Germantown: Christopher Sower; Charles-Town: Jacob Viart. 12 ll. NHi. 9768

An **ALMANACK** for 1756. By Thomas Moore. Philadelphia: B. Franklin and D. Hall. [Morrison] 9769

The **AMERICAN** Almanack for 1756. By John Jerman. Philadelphia: The Author. 12 ll. PHi. 9770

Der **HOCH-DEUTSCH** Americanische Calender auf 1756. Germantown: Christoph Saur. 24 ll. MWA (impf); DLC (18 ll.); N; PHi; PPeSchw. 9771

NEU-EINGERICHTETER Americanischer Geschichts-Calender auf 1756. Philadelphia: Anthon Armbrüester. 24 ll. MWA (22 ll.) 9772

The **NEW-JERSEY** Almanack for 1756. By William Ball.

Philadelphia: William Bradford. [Morrison]   9773

The PENNSYLVANIA Town and Country-Man's Almanack for 1756. By John Tobler. Germantown: C. Sower jun.; Philadelphia: Thomas Maule. 20 ll. MWA (ntp); DLC; NHi; P; PHi; PNortHi.   9774

A POCKET Almanack for 1756. By R. Saunders. Philadelphia: B. Franklin, and D. Hall. 12 ll. DLC; CtY; CSmH; PHi; PPAmP; PU.   9775

POOR Richard improved: being an Almanack and Ephemeris for 1756. By Richard Saunders. Philadelphia: B. Franklin, and D. Hall. 18 ll. MWA; PPAmP (impf); MB; MWiW-C; DLC; PPL; CSmH; InU (ntp); NN; PHi; P; PU; PPRF; CtY; NjR (12 ll.); Woodward (impf)   9776

POOR Robin's Almanack for 1756. Philadelphia: William Bradford. [Morrison]   9777

POOR Roger, 1756. The American Country Almanack for 1756. By Roger More. Philadelphia: B. Franklin, and D. Hall. 12 ll. NjR (photocopy of original owned by Norman C. Wittwer)   9778

The SOUTH-CAROLINA Almanack for 1756. By John Tobler. Germantown: Christopher Sower; Charles-Town: Jacob Viart. 12 ll. NN (11 ll.); ScHi.   9779

An ALMANACK for 1757. By John Jerman. Philadelphia: B. Franklin and D. Hall. [Morrison]   9780

Der HOCH-DEUTSCH Americanische Calender auf 1757. Germantown: Christoph Saur; Philadelphia: David Taschler; Lancaster: Ludwig Laumann. 24 ll. MWA (23 ll.); DLC; InU; PHi; PPG; PLF; PAtM; PPeSchw.   9781

NEU-EINGERICHTETER Americanischer Geschichts-Calender auf 1757. Philadelphia: B. Fräncklin und A. Armbrüester. [Morrison]   9782

The NEW-JERSEY Almanack for 1757. By William

Pennsylvania - 1757

Ball. Philadelphia: W. Bradford. 16 ll. Drake (impf) 9783

The PENNSYLVANIA Town and Country-Man's Almanack for 1757. By John Tobler. Germantown: C. Sower jun.; Philadelphia: Solomon Fussel; Christopher Marshall; Thomas Say. 20 ll. MWA; DLC; InU; DeWint; PHi; NjR (18 ll.) 9784

A POCKET Almanack for 1757. By R. Saunders. Philadelphia: B. Franklin, and D. Hall. 12 ll. MWA; DLC; CtY; PHi; PPL; PU. 9785

POOR Richard improved: being an Almanack and Ephemeris for 1757. By Richard Saunders. Philadelphia: B. Franklin, and D. Hall. 18 ll. MWA; PPAmP; MB; DLC (impf); CSmH; PPRF; PHi; P; InU (ntp); PPL (15 ll.); PU; CtY; ICN (impf); NN (impf); NjR (13 ll.); Woodward. 9786

POOR Robin's Almanack for 1757. Philadelphia: William Bradford. [Morrison] 9787

POOR Roger, 1757. The American Country Almanack for 1757. By Roger Moore. Philadelphia: B. Franklin and D. Hall. 12 ll. RPJCB; PU (11 ll.) 9788

The SOUTH-CAROLINA Almanack for 1757. By John Tobler. Germantown: Christopher Sower; Charles-Town: Jacob Viart. 12 ll. ScHi. 9789

The AMERICAN Almanack for 1758. By John Jerman. Philadelphia: [Franklin & Hall]. 12 ll. PU (9 ll.) 9790

Der HOCH-DEUTSCH Americanische Calender auf 1758. Germantown: Christoph Saur; Philadelphia: David Taschler; Lancaster: Ludwig Laumann. 24 ll. MWA (impf); DLC; NN (23 ll.); PHi; PLF; MB; N; RPJCB; DeWint. 9791

NEU-EINGERICHTETER Americanischer Geschichts-Calender auf 1758. Philadelphia: B. Fränklin und A. Armbrüster. [Morrison] 9792

Pennsylvania - 1758   941

NEW-JERSEY Almanack for 1758. By William Ball.
Philadelphia: William Bradford. [Morrison]   9793

The PENNSYLVANIA Town and Country-Man's Almanack for 1758. By John Tobler. Germantown: C. Sower jun.; Philadelphia: Solomon Fussel; Christopher Marshall; Thomas Say. 20 ll. DLC; DeWint; PHi; PPL; MWA (17 ll.)   9794

A POCKET Almanack for 1758. By R. Saunders. Philadelphia: B. Franklin, and D. Hall. 12 ll. DLC; PHi; RNHi; CtY.   9795

POOR Richard improved: being an Almanack and Ephemeris for 1758. By Richard Saunders. Philadelphia: B. Franklin and D. Hall. 18 ll. MWA; PPAmP; MB; RPJCB; DLC; PPF; PU; P; CSmH; InU (impf); PPL; PHi; PPRF; CtY; NBLiHi; NN (two varieties); MH; Gimbel; Woodward.   9796

POOR Robin's Spare Hours. Almanack for 1758. Philadelphia: W. Bradford. 16 ll. MWA (13 ll., ntp)   9797

The SOUTH-CAROLINA Almanack for 1758. By John Tobler. Germantown: Christopher Sower; Charles-Town: Jacob Viart. 16 ll. NHi; ScHi.   9798

An ALMANACK for 1759. By John Jerman. Philadelphia: W. Dunlap. [Morrison]   9799

FATHER Abraham's Almanack for 1759. By Abraham Weatherwise. Philadelphia: W. Dunlap. 21 ll. MWA (two varieties); DLC; NHi (impf); CSmH; P (20 ll.); PHi; MH (ntp); NjR (16 ll.)   9800

FATHER Abraham's Almanack for 1759. By Abraham Weatherwise. Philadelphia: W. Dunlap, for Daniel Henchman. 21 ll. MHi.   9801

FATHER Abraham's Almanack for 1759. By Abraham Weatherwise. Philadelphia: W. Dunlap; New-York: G. Noel. 21 ll. [Morrison]   9802

Der HOCH-DEUTSCH Americanische Calender auf 1759.
Germantown: Christoph Saur. 24 ll. MWA (impf);
InU (impf); P; PHi; PDoBHi (impf)   9803

NEU-EINGERICHTETER Americanischer Geschichts-
Kalender auf 1759. Philadelphia: Anton Armbrüester.
20 ll. PHi (19 ll.); PLF.   9804

The NEW-JERSEY Almanack for 1759. By William
Ball. Philadelphia: William Bradford. [Morrison]
9805

The PENNSYLVANIA Town and Country-Man's Almanack for 1759. By John Tobler. Germantown: C.
Sower jun.; Philadelphia: Solomon Fussel; Christopher
Marshall; Jonathan Zane. 20 ll. MWA; DLC; InU (18
ll.); N; DeWint; PPL; PHi (ntp)   9806

A POCKET Almanack for 1759. By R. Saunders.
Philadelphia: B. Franklin, and D. Hall. 12 ll. MWA
(ntp); DLC; CtY; PHi; PPL; PU.   9807

POOR Richard improved: being an Almanack and Ephemeris for 1759. By Richard Saunders. Philadelphia: B.
Franklin and D. Hall. 18 ll. MWA (impf); PPAmP
(impf); MB; MH; CtY; DLC (impf); InU (impf); PPL
(impf); NN; PHi; PU (17 ll.); PPRF; CSmH; NjR
(15 ll.); Drake; Woodward.   9808

The AMERICAN Almanac for 1760. By John Jerman.
Philadelphia: W. Dunlap. 14 ll. DLC; PHi.   9809

FATHER Abraham's Almanac for 1760. By Abraham
Weatherwise. Philadelphia: W. Dunlap. 21 ll. with
plate: MWA; PHi; ICU; MB; MH; CtY; PPL (20 ll.)
9810
lack plate: DLC; NN (19 ll.)   9811

FATHER Abraham's Almanac for 1760. By Abraham
Weatherwise. Philadelphia: William Dunlap, for the
Author. private collection (17 ll.)   9812

Der HOCH-DEUTSCH Americanische Calender auf 1760.
Germantown: Christoph Saur. 24 ll. MWA (impf); InU

Pennsylvania - 1760 943

(fragment); PPG; PHi; PLF; PPL; PPeSchw.   9813

MR. WEATHERWISE'S Pocket-Almanac for 1760. By
A. Weatherwise. Philadelphia: W. Dunlap. 15 ll.
MWA; NN; NHi; PHi.   9814

NEU-EINGERICHTETER Americanischer Calender auf
1760. Philadelphia: Anton Armbrüester. 18 ll. MWA;
PHi (16 ll., ntp)   9815

NEU-EINGERICHTETER Americanischer Geschichts-
und Haus-Calender auf 1760. Philadelphia: Peter Müller. 22 ll. MWA (18 ll.); PPeSchw.   9816

The PENNSYLVANIA Almanac, or Ephemeris for 1760.
By Thomas Thomas. Philadelphia: W. Dunlap, for the
Author. 19 ll. MWA; CLU; PHi (impf)   9817

The PENNSYLVANIA Pocket Almanac for 1760. Philadelphia: William Bradford. [Morrison]   9818

The PENNSYLVANIA Town and Country-Man's Almanack for 1760. By John Tobler. Germantown: C.
Sower; Philadelphia: Solomon Fussel; Christopher Marshall; Jonathan Zane. 20 ll. MWA; DLC; DeWint;
NHi; PHi.   9819

A POCKET Almanack for 1760. By R. Saunders.
Philadelphia: B. Franklin, and D. Hall. 12 ll. MWA
(ntp); CtY; PHi; PU.   9820

POOR Richard improved: being an Almanack and Ephemeris for 1760. Philadelphia: B. Franklin, and D. Hall.
18 ll. MWA; DLC; PHi; NN (15 ll.); PU; CSmH;
MWiW-C; PPL; CtY (impf); MB; PPAmP.   9821

The UNIVERSAL American Almanack: Or, Yearly
Astronomical Magazine for 1760. By Andrew Ague-
cheek. Philadelphia: William Bradford; Andrew Steu-
art. 20 ll. MWA (impf); DLC (15 ll.); NN (19 ll.);
NHi (impf); MiD-B; RNHi; PHi; PPL-R (19 ll.);
Drake (19 ll.)   9822

FATHER Abraham's Almanac for 1761. By Abraham Weatherwise. Philadelphia: W. Dunlap. 28 ll. MWA (impf); DLC; MH; RNHi; CSmH; PHi. 9823

FATHER Abraham's Almanac for 1761. By Abr. Weatherwise. Philadelphia: W. Dunlap, for the Author. 12 ll. NHi. 9824

Der HOCH-DEUTSCH Americanische Calender auf 1761. Germantown: Christoph Saur. 24 ll. MWA; DLC (impf); InU (fragment); PPG; PHi (impf); PLF; PPeSchw.
9825

MR. WEATHERWISE'S Pocket-Almanac for 1761. By A. Weatherwise. Philadelphia: W. Dunlap. 12 ll. MWA; DLC; PHi. 9826

NEU-EINGERICHTETER Americanischer Calender auf 1761. Philadelphia: Anton Armbrüster. [Morrison]
9827

The PENNSYLVANIA Almanac, or Ephemeris for 1761. By Thomas Thomas. Philadelphia: William Dunlap. 16 ll. DeWint; P. 9828

The PENNSYLVANIA Pocket Almanack for 1761. Philadelphia: W. Bradford. 12 ll. MWA; DLC. 9829

The PENNSYLVANIA Town and Country-Man's Almanack for 1761. By John Tobler. Germantown: C. Sower; Philadelphia: Solomon Fussel; Christopher Marshall; Jonathan Zane. 20 ll. MWA (impf); DLC (18 ll.); DeWint; InU; PHi; NjR (17 ll.) 9830

A POCKET Almanack for 1761. By R. Saunders. Philadelphia: B. Franklin, and D. Hall. 12 ll. CtY; PHi; PU. 9831

POOR Richard improved: being an Almanack and Ephemeris for 1761. By Richard Saunders. Philadelphia: B. Franklin, and D. Hall. 18 ll. MWA; DLC; NN; CtY; MB; NCH; InU; PHi; PU; PPAmP; NjR (15 ll.) 9832

The UNIVERSAL American Almanack; or Yearly Astro-

nomical Magazine for 1761. By Andrew Aguecheek.
Philadelphia: W. Bradford; A. Steuart. 20 ll. MWA
(16 ll., ntp); DeWint; PHi. 9833

The AMERICAN Almanac for 1762. By John Jerman.
Philadelphia: W. Dunlap. 12 ll. DLC. 9834

FATHER Abraham's Almanac for 1762. By Abraham
Weatherwise. Philadelphia: W. Dunlap. (Fitted for
the Latitude of New-York) 20 ll. PHi. 9835

FATHER Abraham's Almanac for 1762. By Abraham
Weatherwise. Philadelphia: W. Dunlap. (Fitted for
the Latitude of Philadelphia) 20 ll. MWA; DLC (15 ll.);
NN (16 ll.); MH; RPJCB; WHi; MBAt; InU; N; PHi.
9836

The GENTLEMAN and Citizen's Pocket-Almanack for
1762. By Andrew Steuart. Philadelphia: Andrew Steuart. 24 ll. PHi (23 ll.) 9837

Der HOCH-DEUTSCH Americanische Calender auf 1762.
Germantown: Christoph Saur. 24 ll. MWA; DLC; N;
PHi; PLF; PPG. 9838

MERRY Andrew's Almanack, or, the Entertaining and
Comical City and Country Register for 1762. Philadelphia: Andrew Stewart. 12 ll. MWA (11 ll.); DLC.
9839

MR. WEATHERWISE'S Pocket-Almanac for 1762. By
A. Weatherwise. Philadelphia: W. Dunlap. 12 ll.
MWA; DLC; PHi (11 ll.) 9840

Der NEU-EINGERICHTETER Americanischer Geschichts-
und Haus-Calender auf 1762. Philadelphia: P. Müller.
22 ll. MWA; N; PLF (20 ll.) 9841

The PENNSYLVANIA Pocket Almanack for 1762. Philadelphia: W. Bradford. 12 ll. DLC; PHi (badly foxed)
9842

The PENNSYLVANIA Town and Country-Man's Almanack
for 1762. By John Tobler. Germantown: C. Sower;
Philadelphia: Solomon Fussel; Jonathan Zane. 20 ll.
MWA; DLC; InU; PNortHi; NjR (17 ll.) 9843

A POCKET Almanack for 1762. By R. Saunders.
Philadelphia: B. Franklin, and D. Hall. 12 ll. DLC;
CtY; PHi. 9844

POOR Richard improved: being an Almanack and
Ephemeris for 1762. By Richard Saunders. Philadelphia: B. Franklin, and D. Hall. 18 ll. MWA; DLC
(impf); NN; CSmH; MH; MWiW-C; CtY; MB; PHi;
PPAmP; PU. 9845

THOMAS, 1762: being an Almanac, and Ephemeris for
1762. By Thomas Thomas. Philadelphia: W. Dunlap.
16 ll. DLC. 9846

The UNIVERSAL American Almanack, or, Yearly Astronomical, Historical and Geographical Magazine for
1762. By Andrew Aguecheek. Philadelphia: W. Bradford; A. Steuart. 20 ll. MWA; DLC; MnU; InU (fragment); PHi. 9847

FATHER Abraham's Almanac for 1763. By Abraham
Weatherwise. Philadelphia: W. Dunlap. 20 ll. DLC;
NN (16 ll.); CtY; MHi (19 ll.) 9848

The GENTLEMAN and Citizen's Pocket-Almanack for
1763. By Andrew Steuart. Philadelphia: Andrew Steuart. 24 ll. PHi. 9849

Der HOCH-DEUTSCH Americanische Calender auf 1763.
Germantown: Christoph Saur. 24 ll. MWA; DLC (impf);
NN (19 ll.); RPJCB; WHi; PHi; PLF; PPG. 9850

MR. WEATHERWISE'S Pocket Almanac for 1763. By A.
Weatherwise. Philadelphia: W. Dunlap. 12 ll. MWA.
9851

NEU-EINGERICHTETER Americanischer Stadt und Land
Calender auf 1763. Philadelphia: A. Armbrüester und
N. Hasselbach. 22 ll. MWA (13 ll.); N (impf); PPL.
9852

Der NEUESTE, Verbessert-und Zuverlässige Americanische Calender auf 1763. Philadelphia: Henrich Miller.
20 ll. PHi. 9853

The PENNSYLVANIA Pocket Almanack for 1763. Philadelphia: W. Bradford. 20 ll. PHi. 9854

The PENNSYLVANIA Town and Country-man's Almanack for 1763. By John Tobler. Germantown: C. Sower; Philadelphia: Solomon Fussel; Jonothan Zane. 18 ll. MWA; DLC; InU; NHi; NjR (19 ll.) 9855

A POCKET Almanack for 1763. By R. Saunders. Philadelphia: B. Franklin, and D. Hall. 12 ll. MWA; CtY; MB; PHi; PU. 9856

POOR Richard improved: being an Almanack and Ephemeris for 1763. By Richard Saunders. Philadelphia: B. Franklin, and D. Hall. 18 ll. MWA; DLC; NN; CtY; MB (impf); KyHi; PU; PHi; PPL; PPAmP.
9857
The UNIVERSAL American Almanack, or, Yearly Astronomical, Historical, and Geographical Magazine for 1763. By Andrew Aguecheek. Philadelphia: Andrew Steuart. 20 ll. MWA; DLC; N; PHi. 9858

Der EHRLICHE Kurzweiliche Deutsche; Americanische Geschichts und Haus, Calender auf 1764. T-Schesnut-Hull [sic]: N. Hasselbach; Philadelphia: G. Christoph Reinhold; A. Armbrüster. 20 ll. PHi. 9859

FATHER Abraham's Almanack for 1764. By Abraham Weatherwise. Philadelphia: W. Dunlap. 20 ll. MWA (17 ll.); DLC (17 ll.); MHi; PPL; PHi (impf) 9860

The GENTLEMAN and Citizen's Pocket-Almanack for 1764. By Andrew Steuart. Philadelphia: Andrew Steuart. 24 ll. DLC; PHi. 9861

Der HOCH-DEUTSCH Americanische Calender auf 1764. Germantown: Christoph Saur. 24 ll. MWA; DLC (impf); InU; N; DeWint; WHi; PHi; PLF; PPG. 9862

NEU-EINGERICHTETER Americanische Stadt und Land Calender auf 1764. Philadelphia: Anton Armbrüester. 20 ll. MWA (18 ll.) 9863

Der NEUESTE, Verbessert und Zuverlässige Americanische Calender auf 1764. Philadelphia: Heinrich Miller. 24 ll. DLC; PHi. 9864

PENNSYLVANIA Pocket Almanac for 1764. Philadelphia: William Bradford. [Morrison] 9865

The PENNSYLVANIA Town and Country-man's Almanack for 1764. Germantown: C. Sower; Philadelphia: William Wilson; Jonathan Zane. 20 ll. MWA; DLC (18 ll.); NN; InU (17 ll., ntp); PNortHi; PPL (17 ll.)
9866

A POCKET Almanack for 1764. By R. Saunders. Philadelphia: B. Franklin, and D. Hall. 12 ll. DLC; CtY; PHi; PU. 9867

POOR Richard improved: being an Almanack and Ephemeris for 1764. By Richard Saunders. Philadelphia: B. Franklin, and D. Hall. 18 ll. MWA; DLC (impf); NN; CSmH; MWiW-C; CtY; MiU-C; PHi; PU (impf); PPL; PPAmP; Drake (15 ll.) 9868

The UNIVERSAL American Almanack, or Yearly Magazine for 1764. By Andrew Aguecheek. Philadelphia: Andrew Steuart. 18 ll. MWA; DLC; MHi; InU; NjMoW; PHi; PPFM; PU. 9869

-- Issue with 20 ll. PPL. 9870

FATHER Abraham's Almanack for 1765. By Abraham Weatherwise. Philadelphia: W. Dunlap. 20 ll. MWA (impf); DLC; InU; NjMoW; RNHi; PHi (19 ll.); PPAmP; PPL-R. 9871

The GENTLEMAN and Citizen's Pocket-Almanack for 1765. By Andrew Steuart. Philadelphia: Andrew Steuart. 24 ll. MWA. 9872

Der HOCH-DEUTSCH Americanische Calender auf 1765. Germantown: Christoph Saur. 24 ll. MWA; DLC (20 ll.); InU; PHi; PLF; PPG. 9873

MR. WEATHERWISE'S Pocket-Almanack for 1765. By

A. Weatherwise. Philadelphia: W. Dunlap. 14 ll.
Drake. 9874

NEU-EINGERICHTETER Americanischer Calender auf
1765. Philadelphia: Anton Armbrüster. [Morrison]
9875
Der NEUESTE, Verbessert und Zuverlässige Americanische Calender auf 1765. Philadelphia: Henrich
Miller. 18 ll. DLC (impf); PHi. 9876

The PENNSYLVANIA Pocket Almanack for 1765. Philadelphia: W. Bradford. 12 ll. DLC; PHi. 9877

The PENNSYLVANIA Town and Country-man's Almanack for 1765. By John Tobler. Germantown: C.
Sower; Philadelphia: William Wilson; Jonathan Zane.
20 ll. DLC; PPL; NjR (18 ll.) 9878

A POCKET Almanack for 1765. By R. Saunders.
Philadelphia: B. Franklin, and D. Hall. 12 ll. MWA;
DLC; CtY; PHi; PPL; PU. 9879

POOR Richard improved: being an Almanack and
Ephemeris for 1765. By Richard Saunders. Philadelphia: B. Franklin, and D. Hall. 18 ll. MWA; DLC;
NN; NjR (impf); CSmH; MdBJ; CtY; MB; InU; PHi;
PPF (impf); PPAmP; PPL; PU. 9880

The UNIVERSAL American Almanack, or Yearly Magazine for 1765. By Andrew Aguecheek. Philadelphia:
Andrew Steuart. 20 ll. MWA; DLC. 9881

FATHER Abraham's Almanack for 1766. By Abraham
Weatherwise. Philadelphia: W. Dunlap. 20 ll. MWA;
DLC; ICN; CtY; InU; PHi (19 ll.); PPL. 9882

The GENTLEMAN and Citizen's Pocket-Almanack for
1766. By Andrew Steuart. Philadelphia: Andrew Steuart. 24 ll. DLC; PHi. 9883

Der HOCH-DEUTSCHE Americanische Calender auf 1766.
Germantown: Christoph Saur. 24 ll. MWA; DLC; NjR
(23 ll.); DeWint; InU; WHi; PHi; PP; PPG; PPL (16

Pennsylvania - 1766

11.) Drake (14 11.)   9884

NEU-EINGERICHTETER Amerikanischer Geschichts-und Haus- Calender auf 1766. Philadelphia: Anton Armbrüester. [Evans]   9885

Der NEUESTE, Verbessert-und Zuverlässige Americanische Calender auf 1766. Philadelphia: Henrich Miller. 21 11. PHi.   9886

The PENNSYLVANIA Pocket Almanack for 1766. Philadelphia: W. Bradford. 18 11. MWA; DLC.   9887

The PENNSYLVANIA Town and Country-Man's Almanack for 1766. By John Tobler. Germantown: C. Sower; Philadelphia: William Wilson; Jonathan Zane. 20 11. MWA; PHi.   9888

A POCKET Almanack for 1766. By R. Saunders. Philadelphia: B. Franklin, and D. Hall. 12 11. MWA; DLC; CtY; PHi; PU.   9889

POOR Richard improved: being an Almanack and Ephemeris for 1766. By Richard Saunders. Philadelphia: B. Franklin, and D. Hall. 18 11. MWA; DLC; WaSp; CtY; MB; PHi; PPL; PU; P; PPF; PDoBHi (impf); PPAmP.   9890

The UNIVERSAL American Almanack, or Yearly Magazine for 1766. By Andrew Aguecheek. Philadelphia: Andrew Steuart. 20 11. MWA; DLC; InU; PHi; PPL.   9891

The AMERICAN Calendar; or, An Almanack for 1767. By Philo Copernicus. Philadelphia: William and Thomas Bradford. DLC (20 11.); MHi (16 11.)   9892

FATHER Abraham's Almanack for 1767. By Abraham Weatherwise. Philadelphia: W. Dunlap. 20 11. MWA (impf); DLC; NjP (18 11., ntp); PHi.   9893

The GENTLEMAN and Citizen's Pocket-Almanack for 1767. By Andrew Steuart. Philadelphia: Andrew Steuart. 24 11. MWA.   9894

Der HOCH-DEUTSCHE Americanische Calender auf
1767. Germantown: Christoph Saur. 24 ll. MWA;
DLC; NjP (impf); InU; PHi; PP; PPG. 9895

NEU-EINGERICHTETER Americanischer Stadt und Land
Calender auf 1767. [Philadelphia: Anton Armbrüester.]
19 ll. DeWint (tp impf) 9896

Der NEUESTE, Verbessert-und Zuverlässige Americanische Calender auf 1767. Philadelphia: Henrich
Miller. 20 ll. DLC; PHi. 9897

Der NEUESTE, Verbessert-und Zuverlässige Americanische Calender auf 1767. Philadelphia: Henrich Miller.
(Zweyte Auflage) 20 ll. N. 9898

Der NEUESTE, Verbessert-und Zuverlässige Americanische Calender auf 1767. Philadelphia: Henrich Miller.
(Dritte Auflage) 20 ll. [Evans] 9899

The PENNSYLVANIA Pocket Almanack for 1767. Philadelphia: W. and T. Bradford. 12 ll. DLC; PHi. 9900

A POCKET Almanack for 1767. By R. Saunders.
Philadelphia: D. Hall, and W. Sellers. 12 ll. MWA;
NN (10 ll., ntp); PHi. 9901

POOR Richard improved: being an Almanack and
Ephemeris for 1767. By Richard Saunders. Philadel-
phia: D. Hall, and W. Sellers. 18 ll. MWA; DLC; NN;
MHi; CSmH; CtY (16 ll.); N; MB; PHi; PPAmP;
PPL; PU; MdHi. 9902

The UNIVERSAL American Almanack, or Yearly Magazine for 1767. By Andrew Aguecheek. Philadelphia:
Andrew Steuart. 20 ll. N; PHi; PPL. 9903

The AMERICAN Calendar; or, An Almanack for 1768.
By Philo Copernicus. Philadelphia: William and Thomas
Bradford. 20 ll. MWA (impf); DLC; MHi (impf); InU;
PHi. 9904

The AMERICAN Pocket Almanac for 1768. Philadelphia:

W. and T. Bradford. [Morrison] 9905

FATHER Abraham's Almanack for 1768. By Abraham
Weatherwise. Philadelphia: W. Dunlap. 20 ll. MWA
(impf); DLC; N; PHi; PPL. 9906

The GENTLEMAN and Citizen's Pocket-Almanack for
1768. By Andrew Steuart. Philadelphia: Andrew Steuart. 12 ll. MWA; CtY; PHi. 9907

Der HOCH-DEUTSCHE Americanische Calender auf 1768.
Germantown: Christopher Saur. 24 ll. MWA; DLC (20
ll.); NN (20 ll.); NBLiHi; InU; N; TxU; PHi; PP;
PPG; PPeSchw. 9908

NEU-EINGERICHTETER Americanischer Stadt und Land
Calender auf 1768. Philadelphia: Anton Armbrüester.
20 ll. PHi (19 ll.) 9909

Der NEUESTE, Verbessert-und Zuverlässige Americanische Calender auf 1768. Philadelphia: Henrich Miller.
20 ll. DLC; PHi. 9910

The PENNSYLVANIA Pocket Almanac for 1768. Philadelphia: W. and T. Bradford. [Morrison] 9911

A POCKET Almanack for 1768. By R. Saunders.
Philadelphia: D. Hall, and W. Sellers. 12 ll. MWA;
MWiW-C; CtY; PHi. 9912

POOR Richard improved: being an Almanack and
Ephemeris for 1768. By Richard Saunders. Philadelphia: D. Hall, and W. Sellers. 18 ll. MWA; DLC;
NN; CSmH; MWiW-C; CtY; PPAmP; MiU-C; PHi; PU;
PPL; MB (17 ll.) 9913

The UNIVERSAL American Almanack, or Yearly Magazine for 1768. By Andrew Aguecheek. Philadelphia:
Andrew Steuart. 20 ll. MWA (two varieties, one a
fragment); DLC; PHi. 9914

The AMERICAN Calendar; or an Almanack for 1769.
By Philo Copernicus. Philadelphia: William and Thomas

Bradford. 18 ll. PHi (17 ll.) 9915

The AMERICAN Pocket Almanac for 1769. Philadelphia: W. & T. Bradford. [Morrison] 9916

FATHER Abraham's Almanack for 1769. By Abraham Weatherwise. Philadelphia: John Dunlap. 21 ll. MWA; DLC; NN (18 ll.); NB; MdHi; PHi. 9917

The GENTLEMAN and Citizen's Pocket Almanack for 1769. By Andrew Steuart. Philadelphia: Andrew Steuart. 24 ll. MWA; PHi; PPL. 9918

Der HOCH-DEUTSCHE Americanische Calender auf 1769. Germantown: Christoph Saur. 24 ll. MWA; DLC (18 ll.); InU; DeWint; ViU; PHi; PPAmP; PPG; PPeSchw. 9919

Der NEUESTE, Verbessert-und Zuverlässige Americanische Calender auf 1769. Philadelphia: Henrich Miller. 18 ll. PP. 9920

The PENNSYLVANIA Pocket Almanack for 1769. Philadelphia: W. and T. Bradford. 14 ll. MWA; PHi. 9921

The PENNSYLVANIA Town and Country-Man's Almanack for 1769. By John Tobler. Philadelphia: W. & T. Bradford. [Morrison] 9922

A POCKET Almanack for 1769. By R. Saunders. Philadelphia: D. Hall, and W. Sellers. 12 ll. DLC; CtY; MB; PHi. 9923

POOR Richard improved: being an Almanack and Ephemeris for 1769. By Richard Saunders. Philadelphia: D. Hall, and W. Sellers. 18 ll. MWA; DLC; NN; CSmH; CtY; InU (ntp); MB; RPA (15 ll.); ViU; PHi; PPAmP; PPL; PU. 9924

The UNIVERSAL American Almanack, or Yearly Magazine for 1769. By Andrew Aguecheek. Philadelphia: Andrew Steuart. 20 ll. DLC; NHi; ICHi; PHi. 9925

The AMERICAN Calendar; or an Almanack for 1770.

By Philo Copernicus. Philadelphia: William and Thomas Bradford. 20 ll. MWA (19 ll.); ICHi; MHi. 9926

The AMERICAN Pocket Almanac for 1770. Philadelphia: W. & T. Bradford. [Morrison] 9927

FATHER Abraham's Almanack for 1770. By Abraham Weatherwise. Philadelphia: John Dunlap. 18 ll. MWA (17 ll.); DLC; InU; CSmH; PHi; PPL. 9928

The GENTLEMAN and Citizen's Pocket Almanack for 1770. By Andrew Steuart. [Philadelphia:] William Evitt. 24 ll. MWA; DLC. 9929

The GENTLEMAN and Citizen's Pocket Almanack for 1770. By Andrew Steuart. Philadelphia: Thomas Magee. 24 ll. MWA; NHi. 9930

The GENTLEMAN and Citizen's Pocket Almanack for 1770. By Andrew Steuart. Philadelphia: Thomas Magee. (Second Edition) 24 ll. [Sabin 91386] 9931

Der HOCH-DEUTSCHE Americanische Calender auf 1770. Germantown: Christoph Saur. 24 ll. MWA; DLC; NN; N; InU; PHi; PPG; Drake (impf) 9932

Der NEUESTE, Verbessert-und Zuverlässige Americanische Calender auf 1770. Philadelphia: Heinrich Miller. 22 ll. DLC; PHi; PP. 9933

The PENNSYLVANIA Pocket Almanack for 1770. Philadelphia: W. and T. Bradford. 14 ll. MWA; PHi. 9934

A POCKET Almanack for 1770. Philadelphia: John Dunlap. 16 ll. MWA; DLC; MB. 9935

A POCKET Almanack for 1770. By R. Saunders. Philadelphia: D. Hall, and W. Sellers. 12 ll. DLC. 9936

POOR Richard improved: being an Almanack and Ephemeris for 1770. By Richard Saunders. Philadelphia: D. Hall, and W. Sellers. 18 ll. MWA; DLC; NN; MH; CtY; MB; PHi; PPAmP; PPL; PU (16 ll.) 9937

POOR Will's Almanack for 1770. By William Andrews.
Philadelphia: Joseph Crukshank. 18 ll. NHi. 9938

POOR Will's Pocket Almanack for 1770. Philadelphia:
Joseph Crukshank. 16 ll. MWA; DLC (ntp); InU; PHi.
9939

The UNIVERSAL American Almanack, or Yearly Magazine for 1770. By Andrew Aguecheek. Philadelphia:
Thomas Magee. 20 ll. PHi. 9940

The AMERICAN Calendar; or, an Almanack for 1771.
By Philo Copernicus. Philadelphia: William and Thomas Bradford. 24 ll. MHi; PPL. 9941

FATHER Abraham's Almanack for 1771. By Abraham
Weatherwise. Philadelphia: John Dunlap. 18 ll.
MWA; DLC; NjR (nfp); N; MiU-C; MnU; NRMA; PHi;
PPL. 9942

FATHER Abraham's Pocket Almanack for 1771. Philadelphia: John Dunlap. 18 ll. MWA; NN; PHi. 9943

The GENTLEMAN and Citizen's Pocket Almanack for
1771. By William Evitt. Philadelphia: William Evitt.
24 ll. DLC; PPL. 9944

Der HOCH-DEUTSCHE Americanische Calender auf 1771.
Germantown: Christoph Saur. 24 ll. MWA; DLC; NN
(23 ll.); NjR (23 ll.); InU; PHi; PPG; PYHi; Drake
(impf) 9945

Der NEUESTE, Verbessert-und Zuverlässige Americanische Calender auf 1771. Philadelphia: Heinrich Miller.
22 ll. MWA; N; InU (20 ll.); PHi; PP; PPG; PPL;
PPeSchw. 9946

The PENNSYLVANIA Pocket Almanack for 1771. Philadelphia: W. and T. Bradford. 16 ll. MWA; DLC; PPL.
9947

A POCKET Almanack for 1771. By R. Saunders.
Philadelphia: D. Hall, and W. Sellers. 12 ll. MWA;
DLC; PHi. 9948

POOR Richard improved: being an Almanack and Ephemeris for 1771. By Richard Saunders. Philadelphia: D. Hall, and W. Sellers. 18 ll. MWA; DLC; NN; ICHi; CSmH; CtY; MB; InU; ViU; PHi; PPAmP; PPL; PU. 9949

POOR Robin's Almanac for 1771. Philadelphia: William Evitt. [Morrison] 9950

POOR Will's Almanack for 1771. By William Andrews. Philadelphia: Joseph Crukshank. 16 ll. MWA; DLC; InU; MB; NHi; PHi; PPFM. 9951

POOR Will's Pocket Almanack for 1771. Philadelphia: Joseph Crukshank. 18 ll. MWA (two varieties; one 8 ll.); DLC; PHi. 9952

The UNIVERSAL American Almanack, or Yearly Magazine for 1771. By Andrew Aguecheek. Philadelphia: William Evitt. 20 ll. MWA; PHi. 9953

The AMERICAN Calendar; or, An Almanack for 1772. By Philo Copernicus. Philadelphia: William & Thomas Bradford. 18 ll. DLC (17 ll.) 9954

Der AMERICANISCHE Calender auf 1772. Ephrata: Albert Conrad Reben. 20 ll. DLC. 9955

FATHER Abraham's Almanack for 1772. By Abraham Weatherwise. Philadelphia: John Dunlap. 18 ll. MWA; DLC; NN; NjR (16 ll.); NT; MnU; WHi; NBuG (impf); MB; MoU; PHi; PPL; PPL-R; Drake. 9956

FATHER Abraham's Pocket Almanack for 1772. Philadelphia: John Dunlap. 18 ll. MWA; DLC (17 ll.); CSmH. 9957

The GENTLEMAN and Citizen's Pocket-Almanack for 1772. By William Evitt. 24 ll. MWA; PHi. 9958

Der HOCH-DEUTSCHE Americanische Calender auf 1772. Germantown: Christoph Saur. 24 ll. MWA; DLC; NN; NBLiHi; NjR; InU; RPJCB; NBuG (20 ll.);

Pennsylvania - 1772

DeWint; P; PHi; PPG; PPL (18 ll.); PYHi. 9959

The LANCASTER Almanac for 1772. Lancaster:
Francis Bailey. [Morrison] 9960

Der NEUESTE, Verbessert-und Zuverlässige Americanische Calender auf 1772. Philadelphia: Heinrich Miller.
28 ll. MWA; DLC (impf); PHi (25 ll.); PP. 9961

The PENNSYLVANIA Pocket Almanac for 1772. Philadelphia: W. & T. Bradford. [Morrison] 9962

A POCKET Almanack for 1772. By R. Saunders.
Philadelphia: D. Hall, and W. Sellers. no copy found.
9963

POOR Richard improved: being an Almanack and Ephem-
eris for 1772. By Richard Saunders. Philadelphia: D.
Hall, and W. Sellers. 18 ll. MWA; DLC; NN; ICHi;
CtY; MB;CSmH; InU; MiU-C; ViU; PHi; PPAmP; PU;
Drake (17 ll.) 9964

POOR Robin's Almanack for 1772. By Robert More.
Philadelphia: William Evitt. 20 ll. MWA (impf) 9965

POOR Will's Almanack for 1772. By William Andrews.
Philadelphia: Joseph Crukshank. 18 ll. MWA; DLC;
ICHi; MB; CSmH; PHi. 9966

POOR Will's Pocket Almanack for 1772. Philadelphia:
Joseph Crukshank. [Morrison] 9967

The UNIVERSAL American Almanack, or Yearly Magazine for 1772. By Andrew Aguecheek. Philadelphia:
William Evitt. 20 ll. MWA; DLC; NjR (19 ll.); PHi
(impf); Drake (14 ll.) 9968

The UNIVERSAL American Almanack, or Yearly Magazine for 1772. By Andrew Aguecheek. Philadelphia:
William Evitt. ["Strawberry-Alley" not in imprint.]
20 ll. NN (16 ll.) 9969

AITKEN'S General American Register, and the Gentleman's and Tradesman's Complete Annual Account Book,

and Calendar for the Pocket or Desk for 1773. Philadelphia: Joseph Crukshank, for R. Aitken. 85 ll.
DLC; NHi (impf); NN (62 ll.); MB; ICN; CtY.   9970

-- Issue with 88 ll. PHi.   9971

The AMERICAN Calendar; or, an Almanack for 1773. By Philo Copernicus. Philadelphia: William and Thomas Bradford. 18 ll. PPL (17 ll.)   9972

Der CHRISTLICHE Kalender auf 1773. Ephrata. [Bausman]   9973

FATHER Abraham's Almanack for 1773. By Abraham Weatherwise. Philadelphia: John Dunlap. 18 ll.
MWA (impf); DLC (impf); NjR (14 ll.); MB (impf); MoU; MnU; InU; NjT (15 ll.); PHi.   9974

FATHER Abraham's Pocket Almanack for 1773. Philadelphia: John Dunlap. 18 ll. MWA; NN; NHi.   9975

Der HOCH-DEUTSCH-AMERICANISCHE Calender auf 1773. Germantown: Christoph Saur. 24 ll. MWA; DLC (impf); N; NN; PHi; PP; PPG; PPL.   9976

The LANCASTER Almanac for 1773. Lancaster: Francis Bailey. [Morrison]   9977

Der NEUESTE, Verbessert-und Zuverlässige Americanische Calender auf 1773. Philadelphia: Heinrich Miller. 21 ll. DLC; N; PP; PYHi.   9978

The PENNSYLVANIA Pocket Almanack for 1773. Philadelphia: Wm. and Thomas Bradford. 18 ll. PHi.   9979

A POCKET Almanack for 1773. By R. Saunders. Philadelphia: D. Hall, and W. Sellers. 12 ll. DLC.
  9980
POOR Richard improved: being an Almanack and Ephemeris for 1773. By Richard Saunders. Philadelphia: D. Hall, and W. Sellers. 18 ll. MWA (impf); DLC; NN (16 ll.); NjR (impf); RNHi; CSmH; CtY; MB; CLU; InU; TxDN; PHi; PPAmP; PPL; PU.   9981

POOR Will's Almanack for 1773. By William Andrews.
Philadelphia: Joseph Crukshank. 16 ll. DLC (impf);
PHi.   9982

POOR Will's Pocket Almanack for 1773. Philadelphia:
J. Crukshank. 18 ll. DLC; CtY; CSmH; PHi.   9983

The UNIVERSAL Almanack for 1773. Philadelphia:
James Humphreys, Junr. 18 ll. DLC (14 ll.); NHi;
PHi.   9984

The UNIVERSAL Almanack for 1773. Philadelphia:
James Humphreys, jun'r. (Second Edition) 18 ll.
[Evans]   9985

AITKEN'S General American Register, and Calendar for
1774. Philadelphia: R. Aitken. 107 ll. DLC; NN; NHi;
MB; InU; PHi; PYHi.   9986

The AMERICAN Calendar; or, an Almanack for 1774.
By Philo Copernicus. Philadelphia: William & Thomas
Bradford. 18 ll. MWA; NHi.   9987

FATHER Abraham's Almanack for 1774. By Abraham
Weatherwise. Philadelphia: John Dunlap. 18 ll. MWA;
DLC (16 ll.); NHi; WHi; NjP (16 ll.); MB; CtY;
MnU; InU; NjMoW; PHi; Drake.   9988

FATHER Abraham's Pocket Almanac for 1774. Philadelphia: John Dunlap. [Morrison]   9989

Der HOCH-DEUTSCH-AMERICANISCHE Calender auf
1774. Germantown: Christoph Saur. 24 ll. MWA;
DLC (impf); NN; NBLiHi; MiU-C; PP; PHi; PPG; InU;
DeWint; Drake (impf)   9990

The LANCASTER Almanack for 1774. By Anthony Sharp.
Lancaster: Francis Bailey. 20 ll. MWA; NHi; WHi.
                                                    9991
Der NEUESTE, Verbessert-und Zuverlässige Americanische Calender auf 1774. Philadelphia: Heinrich Miller.
20 ll. MWA (impf); PHi; InU (18 ll.); PP.   9992

The PENNSYLVANIA Pocket Almanack for 1774. Philadelphia: Wm. and Thomas Bradford. 18 ll. DLC. 9993

A POCKET Almanack for 1774. By R. Saunders. Philadelphia: Hall and Sellers. 12 ll. PHi; PPL. 9994

POOR Richard improved: being an Almanack and Ephemeris for 1774. By Richard Saunders. Philadelphia: Hall and Sellers. 18 ll. MWA; DLC; NN (13 ll.); NHi; CSmH; TxDN; CtY; MB; PHi; PPL (17 ll.); PPAmP; Drake (17 ll.) 9995

POOR Will's Almanack for 1774. Philadelphia: Joseph Crukshank. 18 ll. MWA; NHi; PHi. 9996

POOR Will's Pocket Almanack for 1774. Philadelphia: J. Crukshank. 16 ll. MWA; InU; CSmH; PHi. 9997

The UNIVERSAL Almanack for 1774. Philadelphia: James Humphreys, jun. 18 ll. MWA; DLC (16 ll.); PHi; PPL; Drake. 9998

The AMERICAN Calendar; or, an Almanack for 1775. By Philo Copernicus. Philadelphia: W. & T. Bradford. [Evans] 9999

COUNTING-HOUSE Almanac for 1775. Philadelphia: Robert Aitken. Broadside. [Morrison] 10000

The COUNTRYMAN'S Almanac for 1775. Lancaster: Stewart Herbert, junior. [Morrison] 10001

FATHER Abraham's Almanack for 1775. By Abraham Weatherwise [and] David Rittenhouse. Philadelphia: John Dunlap. 18 ll. MWA; DLC (16 ll.); InU; MB; NjR (13 ll.); N; PHi; PPL-R; Drake. 10002

FATHER Abraham's Pocket Almanack for 1775. Philadelphia: John Dunlap. 24 ll. MWA; DLC; NN; PHi; PPL. 10003

Der HOCH-DEUTSCH-AMERICANISCHE Calender auf 1775. Germantown: Christopher Saur. 24 ll. MWA;

Pennsylvania - 1775

NN (23 ll.); InU; P; PAtM; PHi; PPG; PPeSchw; PYHi. 10004

The LANCASTER Almanack for 1775. By Anthony Sharp. Lancaster: Francis Bailey. 20 ll. MWA (19 ll.); PHi. 10005

The LANCASTER Almanack, (Improved) for 1775. Lancaster: Stewart Herbert, junior. 18 ll. PHi (9 ll.) 10006

Der NEUESTE, Verbessert-und Zuverlässige Americanische Calender auf 1775. Philadelphia: Heinrich Miller. 24 ll. MWA; DLC; PHi; PPL. 10007

The PENNSYLVANIA Pocket Almanac for 1775. Philadelphia: W. & T. Bradford. [Morrison] 10008

The PHILADELPHIA Newest Almanack for 1775. By Timothy Telescope. Philadelphia: R. Aitken. 24 ll. DLC; PHi. 10009

A POCKET Almanack for 1775. By R. Saunders. Philadelphia: Hall and Sellers. 12 ll. MWA; PHi; PPL. 10010

POOR Richard improved: being an Almanack and Ephemeris for 1775. By Richard Saunders. Philadelphia: Hall and Sellers. 18 ll. MWA; DLC; NN (16 ll.); CtY; MB (impf); CLU; MiU-C; InU; PHi; PPAmP; PU. 10011

POOR Will's Almanack for 1775. Philadelphia: Joseph Crukshank. 16 ll. MWA; DLC; WHi; PHi. 10012

POOR Will's Pocket Almanack for 1775. Philadelphia: J. Crukshank. 24 ll. DLC. 10013

The UNIVERSAL Almanack for 1775. [By] D. Rittenhouse. Philadelphia: James Humphreys, jun. 18 ll. MWA; DLC; NN; PHi; PPL-R. 10014

The AMERICAN Calendar; or, an Almanack for 1776. By Philo Copernicus. Philadelphia: W. & T. Bradford. [Morrison] 10015

FATHER Abraham's Almanack for 1776. By Abraham Weatherwise. Philadelphia: John Dunlap. 18 ll. MWA; DLC; NN (13 ll.); InU; N; PHi (nfp); Drake (two varieties)
10016

FATHER Abraham's Pocket Almanack for 1776. Philadelphia: J. Dunlap. 24 ll. MWA; NN; PHi. 10017

Der GANTZ Neue Verbesserte Nord-Americanische Calender auf 1776. Von Anthony Sharp. Lancaster: Franz Bailey. 18 ll. P (23 ll.); PPG. 10018

Der HOCH-DEUTSCH-AMERICANISCHE Calender auf 1776. Germantown: Christoph Saur. 24 ll. MWA; DLC; NN (23 ll.); PHi; PPG; PPL; PPeSchw; PYHi. 10019

Der HOCH Deutsche Americanische Calender auf 1776. Philadelphia: Henrich Miller. DLC. 10020

The LANCASTER Almanack for 1776. By Anthony Sharp. Lancaster: Francis Bailey. 16 ll. MWA (14 ll.); DLC (12 ll.); WHi. 10021

-- Issue with 20 ll. RPA. 10022

Der NEUESTE, Verbessert-und Zuverlässige Americanische Calender auf 1776. Philadelphia: Heinrich Miller. 24 ll. MWA; DLC; PHi; PPG; PPL. 10023

NORD-AMERICANISCHE Calender des 1776. Von Gottlieb Zimmels-Bewunderer. Lancaster: Franz Bailey. 22 ll. NHi.
10024

The PENNSYLVANIA Pocket Almanac for 1776. Philadelphia: W. & T. Bradford. [Morrison] 10025

The PHILADELPHIA Newest Almanack for 1776. By Timothy Telescope. Philadelphia: R. Aitken. 24 ll. MWA; DLC; MHi; NcU; CSmH; PHi. 10026

A POCKET Almanack for 1776. By R. Saunders. Philadelphia: Hall and Sellers. 12 ll. MWA; DLC; PP. 10027

POOR Richard improved: being an Almanack and Ephemeris for 1776. By Richard Saunders. Philadelphia: Hall and Sellers. 18 ll. MWA (impf); DLC; CSmH; CtY; MB; PHi; PPL (ntp); PU. 10028

POOR Will's Almanack for 1776. Philadelphia: Joseph Crukshank. 18 ll. MWA (17 ll.); DLC; CSmH; MBAt; PHi.
10029

POOR Will's Pocket Almanack for 1776. Philadelphia: J. Crukshank. 24 ll. MWA; DLC; MiU-C; CSmH; PHi; Drake.
10030

The UNIVERSAL Almanack for 1776. [By] David Rittenhouse. Philadelphia: James Humphreys, Jun. 18 ll. MWA; CtHi; CtY; PHi; PPL-R.
10031

The AMERICAN Calendar; or an Almanack for 1777. By Philo Copernicus. Philadelphia: W. & T. Bradford. [Morrison]
10032

CALENDRIER de Philadelphia, ou le Moraliste Americain [pour 1777]. A Philadelphia. [Sabin 61510]
10033

FATHER Abraham's Almanack for 1777. By Abraham Weatherwise. Philadelphia: John Dunlap. 18 ll. MWA; DLC; NN (14 ll.); MB; MBAt; InU; MnU; PHi (17 ll.); PPL (16 ll.); Drake.
10034

FATHER Abraham's Pocket Almanack for 1777. Philadelphia: John Dunlap. 12 ll. MWA; DLC; N; PPAmP.
10035

Der GANTZ Neue Verbesserte Nord-Americanisch Calender auf 1777. Von Anthony Sharp. Lancaster: Franz Bailey. 18 ll. PPG.
10036

Der HINCKEND-UND Stolpernd-doch eilfertig-fliegend-und laufende Americanische Reichs-Bott, Das ist der Allerneueste Verbesserte und Zuverlässigste Americanische Reichs-Staats-Kriegs-Siegs-und Geschichts-Calender Auf 1777. Lancaster: Matthias Bartgis und Daniel Waldenberger. NjR (16 ll.)
10037

Der HOCH-DEUTSCH-AMERICANISCHE Calender auf 1777. Germantown: Christoph Saur. 24 ll. MWA; DLC; NN (23 ll.); NjR (20 ll.); InU; RPJCB; WHi; PAtM; PHi; PPG; PPeSchw.
10037a

The LANCASTER Almanack for 1777. By Anthony Sharp. Lancaster: Francis Bailey. 18 ll. WHi.
10037b

Der NEUE, Verbessert-und Zuverlässige Americanische Calender auf 1777. Philadelphia: Heinrich Miller. 24 ll. MWA; PHi (22 ll., impf); PPG. 10038

The PENNSYLVANIA Pocket Almanac for 1777. Philadelphia: W. & T. Bradford. [Morrison] 10039

A POCKET Almanac for 1777. By R. Saunders. Philadelphia: Hall and Sellers. [Morrison] 10040

POOR Richard improved: being an Almanack and Ephemeris for 1777. By Richard Saunders. Philadelphia: Hall and Sellers. 18 ll. MWA; DLC; MB (17 ll.) 10041

POOR Will's Almanack for 1777. Philadelphia: Joseph Crukshank. 18 ll. MWA (impf); DLC; NN (16 ll.); NHi; NjR (17 ll.); WHi; MiD-B; MB; RPA; PHi. 10042

POOR Will's Pocket Almanack for 1777. Philadelphia: J. Crukshank... opposite the Butcher's Shambles. 12 ll. MWA; NN. 10043

POOR Will's Pocket Almanack for 1777. Philadelphia: J. Crukshank... opposite the Presbyterian Meetinghouse. 12 ll. MWA; DLC; DeWint; InU; MdBP; PHi; PP. 10044

The UNIVERSAL Almanack for 1777. By D. Rittenhouse. Philadelphia: James Humphreys, Jun. 18 ll. MWA. 10045

An ALMANACK for 1778. By John Tobler. Doyle's-Town: James Adams. [M'Culloch] 10046

The AMERICAN Calendar; or an Almanack for 1778. By Philo Copernicus. Philadelphia: William and Thomas Bradford. [Evans] 10047

CALENDRIER de Philadelphie; ou, Constitutions de Sancho-Panca et du Bonne Homme Richard en Pennsylvanie. 1778. [np, np] 74 ll. DLC; MB; PU. 10048

FATHER Abraham's Almanack for 1778. By Abraham
Weatherwise [and] David Rittenhouse. Lancaster:
John Dunlap. 18 ll. MWA; DLC; NjR; RPA (12 ll.);
MiD-B; PHi; CSmH; P (14 ll.); BritMus. 10049

FATHER Abraham's Pocket Almanack for 1778. Lancaster: John Dunlap. 16 ll. DLC; NBLiHi; ICN; MB;
PHi; Drake. 10050

Der GANTZ Neue Verbesserte Nord-Americanische Calender auf 1778. Lancaster: Franz Bailey. 22 ll. MWA;
PHi; PLF. 10051

Der GANTZ Neue Verbesserte Nord-Americanische Calender auf 1778. Von Anthony Sharp. Lancaster:
Franz Bailey. (Second Edition) 22 ll. Advertised in
"Das Pennsylvanische Zeitungs-Blatt," February 11,
1778. 10052

Der HINCKEND-UND Stolpernd-doch Eilfertig-Fliegend-
und Laufende Americanische Reichs-Bott, das ist der
Allerneueste, Verbesserte und Zuverlassigste Americanische Reichs-Staats-Kriegs-Siegs-und Geschichts-
Calender auf 1778. Lancaster: Matthias Bartgis. 19 ll.
MWA; DLC; PHi (15 ll.) 10053

Der HOCH-DEUTSCH-AMERICANISCHE Calender auf
1778. Germantown: Christoph Saur, jun. and Peter
Saur. 24 ll. MWA; DLC (impf); InU; MiU-C; WHi;
PPG; PHi; PLF (20 ll.); P; PAtM; PYHi; PPCS (tp
impf); PPeSchw. 10054

Der HOCH Deutsche Americanische Calender auf 1778.
Philadelphia: Johann Dunlap. 16 ll. MWA; PHi; PPG.
10055

The LANCASTER Almanack for 1778. By Athony Sharp.
Lancaster: Francis Bailey. 18 ll. MWA; DLC; NHi;
MdBP; WHi. 10056

The LANCASTER Pocket Almanack for 1778. By Anthony
Sharp. Lancaster: Francis Bailey. 12 ll. MWA; DLC;
PHi; PPL. 10057

Der NEUE, Verbessert-und Zuverlässige Americanische Calender auf 1778. Philadelphia: Heinrich Miller. 20 ll. MWA (19 ll.); PHi; PPG. 10058

The PHILADELPHIA Almanack for 1778. [np, np] 10 ll. DLC; PHi; PP (ntp) 10059

A POCKET Almanac for 1778. By R. Saunders. York-Town: Hall and Sellers. [Morrison] 10060

POOR Richard improved: being an Almanack and Ephemeris for 1778. By Richard Saunders. York-Town: Hall and Sellers. 18 ll. MWA. 10061

POOR Will's Almanack for 1778. Philadelphia: Joseph Crukshank. 18 ll. MWA; DLC; NN (16 ll., ntp); NHi (impf); NjR; MiU-C; CtY; InU; WHi; TxDN; PHi; PDoBHi (ntp) 10062

POOR Will's Pocket Almanack for 1778. Philadelphia: J. Crukshank. 12 ll. MWA; DLC (impf); NN (impf); MB; PHi; DeWint. 10063

The WILMINGTON Almanack, or Ephemeris for 1778. By Thomas Fox. New-Briton: James Adams. 16 ll. NjP. 10064

Der ALLERNEUESTE Nord-Americanische Calender auf 1779. Lancaster: Matthias Bartgis. [Bausman] 10065

The AMERICAN Calendar; or an Almanack for 1779. By Philo Copernicus. Philadelphia: Thomas Bradford. [Morrison] 10066

CALENDRIER de Philadelphie, en Pensylvanie [pour 1779]. A Philadelphie: [np] 59 ll. DLC; MB. 10067

FATHER Abraham's Almanack for 1779. By Abraham Weatherwise. Philadelphia: John Dunlap. 16 ll. MWA; DLC; MB; NjP; InU; CSmH; PHi. 10068

FATHER Abraham's Pocket Almanack for 1779. Philadelphia: J. Dunlap. 12 ll. MWA (10 ll.); DeWint; PHi;

PP.   10069

Der GANTZ Neue Verbesserte Nord-Americanische-
Calender auf 1779. Von David Rittenhouse. Lancaster:
Francis Bailey. 20 ll. MWA (18 ll., ntp); DLC; N;
DeWint; NN (two varieties); P (impf); PHi; PLF;
PLHi; PPG; PPeSchw.   10070

The GENTLEMAN and Lady's Pocket Memorandum Book
for 1779. Philadelphia: James Humphreys, jun. [Morrison]
                                                      10071

Der HOCH-DEUTSCH-AMERICANISCHE Calender auf
1779. Philadelphia: Johann Dunlap. 16 ll. MWA
(impf); PHi; PPG.   10072

The LANCASTER Almanack for 1779. By Anthony
Sharp. Lancaster: Francis Bailey. 16 ll. MWA; WHi.
                                                      10073
The LANCASTER Pocket Almanac for 1779. By Anthony
Sharp. Lancaster: Francis Bailey. [Morrison] 10074

Der NEUGESTELLTE, Verbessert-und Zuverlässige
Americanische Staats-Calender auf 1779. Philadelphia:
Henrich Miller. 20 ll. MWA; DLC (impf); N; InU;
PAtM; PHi; PPG.   10075

The PENNSYLVANIA Pocket Almanac for 1779. Philadelphia: Thomas Bradford. [Morrison]   10076

The PHILADELPHIA Almanack for 1779. [np, np] 11 ll.
DLC; MHi; PHi.   10077

A POCKET Almanack for 1779. By R. Saunders.
Philadelphia: Hall and Sellers. [Morrison]   10078

POOR Richard improved: being an Almanack and Ephemeris for 1779. By Richard Saunders. Philadelphia:
Hall and Sellers. 18 ll. MWA; DLC (impf); InU; MB;
CSmH; PHi; P (17 ll.); PPAmP; PU (16 ll.)   10079

POOR Will's Almanack for 1779. Philadelphia: Joseph
Crukshank. 18 ll. MWA; DLC; WHi; MBAt; N; NBLiHi;

TxDN; PHi; PPL (16 ll.); Drake (impf)   10080

POOR Will's Pocket Almanac for 1779. Philadelphia: J. Crukshank. 12 ll. MWA; DLC (impf); NjR; MB; CSmH; PU; MiU-C; PHi (ntp); Drake.   10081

Der REPUBLIKANISCHE Kalender auf 1779. Lancaster: Theophilus Cossart und Companie. 20 ll. DLC; NN; PLHi.   10082

An ALMANACK for 1780. Philadelphia: John Norman. Broadside. [Evans]   10083

The AMERICAN Calendar; or an Almanack for 1780. By Philo Copernicus. Philadelphia: Thomas Bradford. [Morrison]   10084

AMERICANISCHER Haus-und Wirthschafts-calender auf 1780. Philadelphia: Steiner und Cist. 18 ll. MWA (16 ll.); DLC; PHi; PPGi; PPeSchw.   10085

The CONTINENTAL Almanac for 1780. Philadelphia: Francis Bailey. 18 ll. MWA (16 ll.); DLC; NjP.
    10086
The CONTINENTAL Pocket Almanac for 1780. By Anthony Sharp. Philadelphia: Francis Bailey. 12 ll. NN; NHi.   10087

FATHER Abraham's Almanack for 1780. By Abraham Weatherwise. Philadelphia: John Dunlap. 16 ll. DLC (15 ll.); PHi; NjR (14 ll.)   10088

FATHER Abraham's Pocket Almanack for 1780. Philadelphia: John Dunlap. 12 ll. NjGlaN; PHi.   10089

Der GANTZ Neue Verbesserte Nord-Americanische Calender auf 1780. Lancaster: Francis Bailey. MWA (fragment, 6 ll.)   10090

Der HOCH-DEUTSCH-AMERICANISCHE Calender auf 1780. Germantown. MWA (12 ll., ntp)   10091

Der HOCH-DEUTSCH-AMERICANISCHE Calender auf

1780. Philadelphia: Johann Dunlap. 16 ll. MWA; DLC;
N; NN (15 ll.); P; PAtM; PHi; PPG.   10092

The LANCASTER Almanac for 1780. By Anthony
Sharp. Lancaster: Francis Bailey. [Morrison] 10093

The LANCASTER Pocket Almanac for 1780. By Anthony Sharp. Lancaster: Francis Bailey. [Morrison]
10094

Der NEUGESTELLTE und Verbesserte Americanische
Staats-Calender auf 1780. Philadelphia: Henrich Miller. 18 ll. MWA (impf); DLC; N; InU; P; PHi (16
ll.); PPG.   10095

The PENNSYLVANIA Pocket Almanac for 1780. Philadelphia: Thomas Bradford. [Morrison]   10096

The PHILADELPHIA Almanack for 1780. [Philadelphia:
engraved by J. Norman] 18 ll. NjR.   10097

PHILADELPHIA Almanack for 1780. [Philadelphia:]
"Engraved Printed and Sold by Norman and Bedwell."
Broadside. NjR.   10098

A POCKET Almanack for 1780. By R. Saunders. Philadelphia: Hall and Sellers. 12 ll. MWA; DLC. 10099

POOR Richard improved: being an Almanack and
Ephemeris for 1780. By Richard Saunders. Philadelphia: Hall and Sellers. 18 ll. MWA; DLC; CtY; CSmH;
PHi; PPAmP.   10100

POOR Will's Almanack for 1780. Philadelphia: Joseph
Crukshank. 18 ll. MWA; DLC; InU; MB; WHi; PHi;
PPL.   10101

POOR Will's Pocket Almanack for 1780. Philadelphia:
Joseph Crukshank. 12 ll. MWA; DLC; MB; NN;
Dewint; PP (ntp); PHi.   10102

Der REPUBLIKANISCHE Kalender auf 1780. Lancaster:
Theophilus Cossart und Companie. 18 ll. P (16 ll.);
PLHi.   10103

The AMERICAN Almanac for 1781. By Father Jacobus Bumbo. Philadelphia: Thomas Bradford. 18 ll. MWA; DLC (impf); N; NHi; NjR. 10104

AMERICANISCHER Haus-und Wirthschafts-Calender auf 1781. Philadelphia: Steiner und Cist. 20 ll. MWA (impf); DLC; DeWint; InU; P; PHi; PPG; PPeSchw. 10105

The CONTINENTAL Almanac for 1781. By Anthony Sharp. Philadelphia: Francis Bailey. 18 ll. MWA; DLC; NjR (16 ll., ntp); MB; CLU; CtY (impf); CtHi; PHi (impf) 10106

The CONTINENTAL Pocket Almanac for 1781. By Anthony Sharp. Philadelphia: Francis Bailey. 12 ll. NN; NHi; PHi. 10107

FATHER Abraham's Almanack for 1781. By Abraham Weatherwise. Philadelphia: John Dunlap. 16 ll. MWA; DLC (14 ll.); CLU; PHi; Drake. 10108

FATHER Abraham's Pocket Almanac for 1781. Philadelphia: John Dunlap. [Morrison] 10109

Der GANTZ Neue Verbesserte Nord-Americanische Calender auf 1781. Von David Rittenhaus. Lancaster: Francis Bailey. 18 ll. MWA (16 ll.); DLC (impf); InU (ntp) 10110

The GENTLEMAN and Lady's Pocket Memorandum Book and Almanac for 1781. Philadelphia: William Mentz. [Morrison] 10111

Der HOCH-DEUTSCH-AMERICANISCHE Calender auf 1781. Philadelphia: Johann Dunlap. 16 ll. MWA; DLC; NN (15 ll.); InU (fragment); PHi; PPG. 10112

LANCASTER Almanac for 1781. WHi (16 ll., ntp) 10113

The PENNSYLVANIA Pocket Almanac for 1781. Philadelphia: Thomas Bradford. 12 ll. DLC; PHi; PPL. 10114

A POCKET Almanack for 1781. By R. Saunders. Phila-

Pennsylvania - 1781

delphia: Hall and Sellers. 18 ll. DLC.   10115

POOR Richard improved: being an Almanack and Ephemeris for 1781. By Richard Saunders. Philadelphia: Hall and Sellers. 18 ll. MWA (impf); DLC; NjR; CtY; VtU; PHi; PU.   10116

POOR Will's Almanack for 1781. Philadelphia: Joseph Crukshank. 18 ll. MWA; DLC; InU; MiD-B; NHi; NN (17 ll.); NjR (impf); PHi.   10117

POOR Will's Pocket Almanack for 1781. Philadelphia: Joseph Crukshank. 12 ll. MWA; DLC; InU (ntp); DeWint; PHi.   10118

Der REPUBLIKANISCHE Calender auf 1781. Lancaster: Theophilus Cossart und Companie. MWA (fragment of 13 ll.)   10119

The AMERICAN Almanac for 1782. By Father Jacobus Bumbo. Philadelphia: T. Bradford and P. Hall. 18 ll. DLC; NHi (impf); PHi.   10120

AMERICANISCHER Haus-und Wirthschafts-Calender auf 1782. Philadelphia: Carl Cist. 20 ll. N; DeWint; PHi (19 ll.)   10121

AMERICANISCHER Haus-und Wirthschafts-Calender auf 1782. Philadelphia: Melchior Steiner. 20 ll. DLC; PHi (19 ll.)   10122

The CONTINENTAL Almanac for 1782. By Anthony Sharp. Philadelphia: Francis Bailey. 18 ll. MWA; DLC; NjR; MHi; CLU; NBuG; MiD-B; InU (ntp); PHi.   10123

The CONTINENTAL Pocket Almanac for 1782. By Anthony Sharp. Philadelphia: Francis Bailey. [Morrison]   10124

FATHER Abraham's Almanack for 1782. By Abraham Weatherwise. Philadelphia: John Dunlap. [Evans]   10125

FATHER Abraham's Almanack for 1782. By Abraham

Pennsylvania - 1782

Weatherwise. Philadelphia: George Kline. 16 ll. MWA; PHi; PU.
10126

FATHER Abraham's Pocket Almanack for 1782. Philadelphia: John Dunlap. [Evans]
10127

Der GANTZ Neue Verbesserte Nord-Americanische Calender auf 1782. Von David Rittenhaus. Lancaster: Francis Bailey. 18 ll. MWA (16 ll.); PLHi (14 ll.)
10128

Der HOCH-DEUTSCH-AMERICANISCHE Calender auf 1782. Philadelphia: Johann Dunlap. 16 ll. MWA (15 ll.); DLC; PHi; PPG; PYHi.
10129

The PENNSYLVANIA Pocket Almanack for 1782. Philadelphia: T. Bradford and P. Hall. [Evans]
10130

A PLAIN Almanack for 1782. Philadelphia: Joseph Crukshank. 18 ll. MWA; DLC; NN; PHi; PPAmP.
10131

A POCKET Almanack for 1782. By R. Saunders. Philadelphia: Hall and Sellers. [Morrison]
10132

POOR Richard improved: being an Almanack and Ephemeris for 1782. By Richard Saunders. Philadelphia: Hall and Sellers. 18 ll. MWA; DLC; NN; NjR; CtY; MB (17 ll.); VtU; PHi; PPL; PU.
10133

POOR Will's Almanack for 1782. Philadelphia: Joseph Crukshank. 18 ll. MWA; DLC; NjP; InU; WHi; P; PHi.
10134

POOR Will's Pocket Almanack for 1782. Philadelphia: Joseph Crukshank. 12 ll. MWA; DLC; NHi; MB; NjGlaN; DeWint; PHi.
10135

Der REPUBLIKANISCHE Calender auf 1782. Lancaster: Theophilus Cossart und Companie. 18 ll. MWA (15 ll.); PHi.
10136

WEATHERWISE'S Town and Country Almanack for 1782. By Abraham Weatherwise. Philadelphia: DLC (15 ll., tp impf)
10137

Pennsylvania - 1783

The AMERICAN Almanac for 1783. By Father Jacobus Bumbo. Philadelphia: T. Bradford. 18 ll. MWA (impf); DLC; InU (fragment); PHi; CSmH (impf); N (impf)   10138

AMERICANISCHER Haus-und Wirthschafts-Calender auf 1783. Philadelphia: Carl Cist. 20 ll. DLC; DeWint; PHi.   10139

AMERICANISCHER Haus-und Wirthschafts-Calender auf 1783. Philadelphia: Melchior Steiner. 20 ll. N; PHi; PPG.   10140

The CONTINENTAL Almanac for 1783. By Anthony Sharp. Philadelphia: Francis Bailey. 18 ll. MWA (two varieties); NjR (ntp); WHi; MiU-C; RPJCB.   10141

FATHER Abraham's Almanack for 1783. By Abraham Weatherwise. Philadelphia: John Dunlap. 16 ll. MWA; DLC; PHi.   10142

FATHER Abraham's Pocket Almanac for 1783. Philadelphia: John Dunlap. [Morrison]   10143

Der GANTZ Neue Verbesserte Nord-Americanische Calender auf 1783. Von Isaac Briggs. Lancaster: Francis Bailey. 18 ll. MWA (fragment); DLC; DeWint; PPG.   10144

Der HOCH-DEUTSCH-AMERICANISCHE Calender auf 1783. Philadelphia: Johann Dunlap. [Morrison] 10145

Der NEUE, Verbessert und Zuverlässige Americanische Calender auf 1783. Philadelphia: Theophilus Cossart. 20 ll. PPeSchw.   10146

Der NEUE, Verbessert-und Zuverlässige Americanische Calender auf 1783. Philadelphia: Joseph Crukshank. 20 ll. MWA (19 ll.); DLC; PHi.   10147

The PENNSYLVANIA Pocket Almanac for 1783. Philadelphia: Thomas Bradford. 12 ll. MWA (11 ll.); MWiW-C.   10148

A PLAIN Almanack for 1783. Philadelphia: Joseph
Crukshank. 18 ll. MWA; PHi. 10149

A POCKET Almanack for 1783. By R. Saunders.
Philadelphia: Hall and Sellers. 12 ll. MWA; DLC;
PP. 10150

POOR Richard improved: being an Almanack and
Ephemeris for 1783. By Richard Saunders. Philadelphia: Hall and Sellers. 18 ll. MWA; DLC; CtY; MB
(16 ll.); MdBJ (15 ll.); VtU; ViU (16 ll.); PDoBHi
(15 ll.); PHi; PU (17 ll.); CSmH. 10151

POOR Will's Almanack for 1783. Philadelphia: Joseph
Crukshank. 18 ll. MWA; DLC; NjR (15 ll.); TxU;
NjP (ntp); MB; InU; WHi; P; PHi; PP; PPL; PPM.
10152

POOR Will's Pocket Almanack for 1783. Philadelphia:
Joseph Crukshank. 12 ll. MWA; DLC (ntp); NN;
DeWint; PHi. 10153

Der REPUBLIKANISCHE Calender auf 1783. Philadelphia: Theophilus Cossart. [Morrison] 10154

The AMERICAN Almanac for 1784. By Father Jacobus
Bumbo. Philadelphia: T. Bradford. 18 ll. MWA;
DLC; MHi; MoU; PHi; Drake (impf) 10155

AMERICANISCHER Haus-und Wirthschafts-Calender auf
1784. Philadelphia: Carl Cist. 20 ll. DeWint. 10156

AMERICANISCHER Haus-und Wirthschafts-Calender auf
1784. Philadelphia: Melchior Steiner. 20 ll. MWA;
DLC (18 ll.); N; CLU; InU; P (impf); PHi; PDoBHi
(18 ll.); PYHi; PPeSchw; PPG; PPL. 10157

AMERICANISCHER Stadt und Land Calender auf 1784.
Philadelphia: Carl Cist. 20 ll. MWA; DLC; InU (impf);
N; PAtM; PHi; PLF; PPG; PPeSchw. 10158

BAILEY'S Pocket Almanac, being an American Annual
Register for 1784. Philadelphia: Francis Bailey. 40 ll.
NHi; NjR; PHC. 10159

Pennsylvania - 1784

The CONTINENTAL Almanac for 1784. By Anthony
Sharp. Philadelphia: Francis Bailey. 18 ll. MWA;
DLC; NN; RPJCB; NCH; WHi; MiU-C; N; CSmH;
PHi (impf)   10160

FATHER Abraham's Almanack for 1784. By Abraham
Weatherwise. Philadelphia: John Dunlap. 20 ll. MWA;
DLC.   10161

FATHER Abraham's Pocket Almanac for 1784. Philadelphia: John Dunlap. [Morrison]   10162

Der GANTZ Neue Verbesserte Nord-Americanische
Calender auf 1784. Von Anthony Sharp. Lancaster:
Francis Bailey. 18 ll. MWA; DLC; PPG.   10163

Der HOCH-DEUTSCH Americanische Calender auf 1784.
Philadelphia: Johann Dunlap. [Morrison]   10164

The PENNSYLVANIA Pocket Almanac for 1784. Philadelphia: Thomas Bradford. 12 ll. DLC.   10165

A PLAIN Almanack for 1784. Philadelphia: Joseph
Crukshank. 18 ll. MWA; DLC; PHi.   10166

A POCKET Almanack for 1784. By R. Saunders.
Philadelphia: Hall and Sellers. [Morrison]   10167

POOR Richard improved: being an Almanack and
Ephemeris for 1784. By Richard Saunders. Philadelphia: Hall and Sellers. 18 ll. MWA; DLC; NjR
(impf); CtY; CLU; VtU; MdBJ (14 ll.); PHi; PDoBHi.
    10168

POOR Will's Almanack for 1784. Philadelphia: Joseph
Crukshank. 18 ll. MWA; DLC; NN (16 ll.); NjP;
NjR; MB; P; MiU-C; CtY; InU; WHi; PHi; PDoBHi
(ntp)   10169

POOR Will's Pocket Almanack for 1784. Philadelphia:
Joseph Crukshank. 12 ll. MWA; DLC; MB (impf);
CtY; InU; DeWint; PHi; PP.   10170

The AMERICAN Almanac for 1785. By Father Jacobus
Bumbo. Philadelphia: T. Bradford. 20 ll. MWA (19
ll.); DLC; NN (15 ll.); CLU; PHi; PP.   10171

AMERICANISCHER Haus-und Wirthschafts-Calender auf
1785. Philadelphia: Melchior Steiner. 20 ll. MWA;
DLC; InU; PHi; PPeSchw; PYHi.   10172

AMERICANISCHER Stadt und Land Calender auf 1785.
Philadelphia: Carl Cist. 20 ll. MWA; N; PAtM; PHi;
PPG; PYHi.   10173

BAILEY'S Pocket Almanac for 1785. Philadelphia:
Francis Bailey. 40 ll. DLC; NHi (no map, no plate);
MH; PHC; PHi; PP.   10174

The CONTINENTAL Almanac for 1785. By Anthony
Sharp. Philadelphia: Francis Bailey. 18 ll. MWA
(16 ll.); DLC; NN; CSmH; PHi.   10175

The CONTINENTAL Almanac for 1785. By Anthony
Sharp. Philadelphia: Kline and Reynolds. [Evans]
                                                 10176

FATHER Abraham's Almanac for 1785. By Abraham
Weatherwise. Philadelphia: John Dunlap. [Morrison]
                                                 10177

FATHER Abraham's Pocket Almanac for 1785. Philadelphia: John Dunlap. [Morrison]   10178

Der GANTZ Neue Verbesserte Nord-Americanische Calender auf 1785. Von Anthony Sharp. Lancaster:
Francis Bailey. 18 ll. MWA; DLC; PPG.   10179

Der HOCH-DEUTSCHE Americanische Calender auf
1785. Germantown: Leibert und Billmeyer. 20 ll.
MWA (17 ll.); DLC (18 ll.); InU (15 ll.); N; PHi;
PPG; PPL (18 ll.); PYHi.   10180

Der NEUE, Verbessert-und Zuverlässige Americanische
Calender auf 1785. Philadelphia: Joseph Crukshank.
20 ll. MWA (18 ll.); DLC.   10181

The PENNSYLVANIA Pocket Almanac for 1785. Philadelphia: Thomas Bradford. [Morrison] 10182

A PLAIN Almanac for 1785. Philadelphia: Joseph Crukshank. [Morrison] 10183

A POCKET Almanack for 1785. By R. Saunders. Philadelphia: Hall and Sellers. [Morrison] 10184

A POCKET Memorandum Book, or Daily Journal for 1785. Philadelphia: Joseph Crukshank. 38 ll. DLC. 10185

POOR Richard improved: being an Almanack and Ephemeris for 1785. By Richard Saunders. Philadelphia: Hall and Sellers. 18 ll. MWA; DLC; CtY; MB; VtU; ViU; PDoBHi; PHi; PU (17 ll.) 10186

POOR Will's Almanack for 1785. Philadelphia: Joseph Crukshank. 22 ll. MWA; DLC; NN; NjP (impf); MB; CtY; P; N; WHi; PHi (19 ll.); PPL (18 ll.); InU; PDoBHi; NjR (19 ll.) 10187

POOR Will's Pocket Almanack for 1785. Philadelphia: Joseph Crukshank. 16 ll. MWA; DLC; CtY; DeWint. 10188

AMERICANISCHER Haus-und Wirthschafts-Calender auf 1786. Philadelphia: Melchior Steiner. 20 ll. PHi (19 ll.); PPeSchw; PYHi. 10189

AMERICANISCHER Stadt und Land Calender auf 1786. Philadelphia: Carl Cist. 15 ll. MWA (ntp); N; PPeSchw; PYHi. 10190

BAILEY'S Counting-House Almanac for 1786. Philadelphia: Francis Bailey. Broadside. [Evans] 10191

BAILEY'S Miniature Almanac for 1786. Philadelphia: Francis Bailey. 12 ll. MWA. 10192

BAILEY'S Pocket Almanac for 1786. Philadelphia: Francis Bailey. 40 ll. DLC; NHi; NjR; PPRF. 10193

The BALLOON Almanac for 1786. Philadelphia: John Steele. 20 ll. MWA; DLC (19 ll.); PHi (14 ll.) 10194

FATHER Tammany's Almanac for 1786. By a son of Tammany. Philadelphia: Young and McCulloch. 18 ll. KyLoF. 10195

FATHER Tammany's Almanac for 1786. By a son of Tammany. Philadelphia: Young, Stewart, and M'Culloch. 20 ll. MWA (18 ll.); DLC; MHi; PHi (16 ll.) 10196

FATHER Tammany's Pocket Almanac for 1786. By a son of Tammany. Philadelphia: Young, Stewart, and M'Culloch. 34 ll. NN (20 ll.); PPiU. 10197

Der GANTZ Neue Verbesserte Nord-Americanische Calender auf 1786. Lancaster: Jacob Bailey. [Morrison] 10198

Der HOCH-DEUTSCHE Americanische Calender auf 1786. Germantaun: Leibert und Billmeyer. 20 ll. MWA; DLC (impf); NN (19 ll.); CtY; N; NjR (19 ll.); NBuG (19 ll.); DeWint; InU (impf); PHi; PPG; PLF; PPeSchw; PYHi. 10199

Der NEUE, Verbesserte-und Zuverlässige Americanische Calender auf 1786. Philadelphia: Joseph Crukshank. 20 ll. MWA (19 ll.) 10200

The PENNSYLVANIA Pocket Almanac for 1786. Philadelphia: Thomas Bradford. [Evans] 10201

POOR Richard improved: being an Almanack and Ephemeris for 1786. By Richard Saunders. Philadelphia: Hall and Sellers. 18 ll. MWA; DLC; CtY (16 ll.); MB; VtU; MdBJ (16 ll.); PDoBHi; PHi; PU. 10202

POOR Will's Almanack for 1786. Philadelphia: Joseph Crukshank. 20 ll. MWA; DLC; NHi; NjR; MB; MHi; N; CtY; NjJ; InU; P; PHi; PDoBHi; Drake. 10203

POOR Will's Pocket Almanack for 1786. Philadelphia: Joseph Crukshank. 16 ll. MWA; DLC; DeWint; PHi; WHi; NN. 10204

AMERICANISCHER Haus-und Wirthschafts-Calender auf 1787. Philadelphia: Melchior Steiner. 20 ll. MWA;

Pennsylvania - 1787

DLC; PHi; PLF; PPL (14 ll.)   10205

AMERICANISCHER Stadt und Land Calender auf 1787. Philadelphia: Carl Cist. 20 ll. MWA (ntp); DLC; DeWint; NjR; N; PHi; PPG; PYHi.   10206

BAILEY'S Pocket Almanac for 1787. Philadelphia: Francis Bailey. 40 ll. DLC; NN; PHi.   10207

The BALLOON Almanac for 1787. [Philadelphia:] F. Bailey; J. Steele; J. Bailey; [etc]. 20 ll. MWA (impf); MB.   10208

CALENDRIER de Philadelphie, ou Le Moraliste Americain [pour 1787]. Philadelphie. 65 ll. NHi.   10209

FATHER Tammany's Almanac for 1787. By a son of Tammany. Philadelphia: Young and M'Culloch. 16 ll. DLC; WHi; PHi (has tipped-in cut)   10210

-- Issue with 18 ll. MWA; Drake.   10211

FATHER Tammany's Pocket Almanac for 1787. Philadelphia: Young and M'Culloch. [Evans]   10212

Der GANTZ Neue Verbesserte Nord-Americanische Calender auf 1787. Lancaster: Jacob Bailey. 18 ll. MWA.   10213

Der HOCH-DEUTSCHE Americanische Calender auf 1787. Germantaun: Leibert und Billmeyer. 20 ll. MWA; DLC; NN; InU (impf); N; PHi; PPG; P; PAtM; PPeSchw.   10214

MARK Time's Almanack, and Ephemeris for 1787. Philadelphia: Eleazer Oswald. 20 ll. [Evans]   10215

The NEW Pennsylvania Almanac for 1787. Philadelphia: F. Bailey; J. Steele; J. Bailey. 20 ll. MWA (19 ll.); P.   10216

The PENNSYLVANIA Pocket Almanac for 1787. Philadelphia: Thomas Bradford. [Evans]   10217

POOR Richard improved: being an Almanack and Ephemeris for 1787. By Richard Saunders. Philadelphia: Hall and Sellers. 18 ll. MWA; DLC; NN (impf); CtY; MB; InU; VtU; PHi; PDoBHi; PPAmP; PU; Wittwer. 10218

POOR Will's Almanack for 1787. Philadelphia: Joseph Crukshank. 22 ll. MWA; DLC; NjR; InU; PP; PHi (ntp); PPT; PPL (20 ll.); PDoBHi; PU; Drake. 10219

POOR Will's Pocket Almanack for 1787. Philadelphia: [Joseph] Crukshank. 19 ll. Private collection. 10220

POOR Will's Pocket Almanack for 1787. Philadelphia: Joseph Crukshank. 16 ll. MWA; DLC; NN; NHi; MB; CoCC; DeWint; PP; PHi. 10221

AMERICANISCHER Haus-und Wirthschafts-Calender auf 1788. Philadelphia: Melchior Steiner. 20 ll. PHi.
10222
AMERICANISCHER Stadt und Land Calender auf 1788. Philadelphia: Carl Cist. 20 ll. MWA; DLC; NjR; PHi (impf); PPG; PYHi. 10223

BAILEY'S Pocket Almanac for 1788. Philadelphia: Francis Bailey. 16 ll. MWA; DLC; DeWint; PHi.
10224
The BALLOON Almanac for 1788. [Philadelphia:] F. Bailey; J. Steele; J. Bailey; [etc]. 20 ll. PHi. 10225

FATHER Tammany's Almanac for 1788. By B. Workman [and] a Son of Tammany. Philadelphia: Young and M'Culloch. 18 ll. MWA; DLC (9 ll.); NN (impf); NjP; MB; MdBJ; PHi. 10226

FATHER Tammany's Pocket Almanac for 1788. Philadelphia: W. Young; J. M'Culloch. 18 ll. PHi. 10227

Der HOCH-DEUTSCHE Americanische Calender auf 1788. Germantaun: Michael Billmeyer. 20 ll. MWA; DLC; NBLiHi; DeWint; PHi; PPAmP; PPG; PPL; PYHi; PPeSchw. 10228

Der NEUE, Gemeinnützige Landwirthschafts Calender
auf 1788. Lancaster: Steimer [sic], Albrecht und
Lahn. 21 ll. MWA (18 ll.); DLC; InU (fragment);
PLF; P (20 ll.) 10229

Der NEUE Gemeinnutzige Landwirthschafts Calender auf
1788. Lancaster: Steiner, Albrecht und Lahn. (Zweyte
Auflage) [Evans] 10230

The PENNSYLVANIA Almanac for 1788. [Philadelphia:]
F. Bailey; J. Steele; J. Bailey; [etc]. 18 ll. PHi;
WHi. 10231

The PENNSYLVANIA Almanac for 1788. By Mark
Time. Philadelphia: Eleazer Oswald. 20 ll. MWA.
10232

The PITTSBURG [sic] Almanac, or Western Ephemeris
for 1788. Pittsburg: Scull and Boyd. 20 ll. MWA;
PPL (impf); Drake (16 ll.) 10233

POOR Richard improved: being an Almanack and Ephemeris for 1788. By Richard Saunders. Philadelphia:
Hall and Sellers. 18 ll. DLC; CtY; PHi. 10234

POOR Will's Almanack for 1788. By Wm. Waring.
Philadelphia: Joseph Crukshank. 20 ll. MWA; DLC
(18 ll.) NN (19 ll.); ICN; InU; NjR (18 ll.); MiU-C;
CtY; PDoBHi; PHi. 10235

POOR Will's Pocket Almanack for 1788. Philadelphia:
Joseph Crukshank. 16 ll. MWA; DLC; DeWint; NN;
NjR; PHC; PHi. 10236

The TOWN and Countryman's Almanack for 1788. Philadelphia: Joseph Crukshank. 22 ll. MWA; DLC;
PPAmP; PPiU. 10237

AMERICANISCHER Haus-und Wirthschafts-Calender auf
1789. Philadelphia: Melchior Steiner. 20 ll. PHi.
10238

AMERICANISCHER Stadt und Land Calender auf 1789.
Philadelphia: Carl Cist. 24 ll. DLC (19 ll.); PHi;
PPG; PPeSchw; PYHi. 10239

BAILEY'S Pocket Almanac for 1789. Philadelphia:
Francis Bailey. 16 ll. MWA; PHi. 10240

The BALLOON Almanac for 1789. [Philadelphia:] F.
Bailey; J. Steele; J. Bailey; [etc]. 20 ll. MWA; NN;
PHi; PPL (19 ll.) 10241

FATHER Tammany's Almanac for 1789. By a Son of
Tammany. Philadelphia: W. Young. 18 ll. MWA
(impf); DLC; PHi (15 ll.); BritMus. 10242

FATHER Tammany's Pocket Almanac for 1789. Philadelphia: W. Young. 18 ll. PHi. 10243

The FEDERAL Almanack for 1789. Philadelphia: W.
Young. 16 ll. N (ntp); MB. 10244

Der GANTZ Neue Verbesserte Nord-Americanische
Calender auf 1789. Von Anthony Sharp. Lancaster:
Jacob Bailey. 17 ll. MWA; DLC (16 ll.); DeWint; P
(impf) 10245

Der HOCH-DEUTSCHE Americanische Calender auf
1789. Germantaun: Michael Billmeyer. 20 ll. MWA;
DLC (18 ll.); InU (impf); WHi; DeWint; PHi; PPAmP;
PPG; PPL (15 ll.); PPeSchw. 10246

MARK Time's Almanack for 1789. Philadelphia:
Eleazer Oswald. Broadside. [Evans] 10247

Der NEUE, Gemeinnützige Landwirthschafts Calender auf
1789. Lancaster: Albrecht und Lahn. 22 ll. MWA (20
ll.); DLC; PHi; PLF. 10248

The PENNSYLVANIA Almanac for 1789. [Philadelphia:]
F. Bailey; J. Steele; J. Bailey; [etc]. 20 ll. MWA;
DLC. 10249

The PENNSYLVANIA Almanack for 1789. By Mark
Time. Philadelphia: Eleazer Oswald. NHi (15 ll.);
Drake (6 ll.) 10250

The PENNSYLVANIA Almanack for 1789. By Mark

Time. Philadelphia: John H. Simon. PDoBHi (17
ll.) 10251

The PENNSYLVANIA Sheet Almanack for 1789. Philadelphia: B. Towne. Broadside. PHi. 10252

POOR Richard improved: being an Almanack and Ephemeris for 1789. By Richard Saunders. Philadelphia: Hall and Sellers. 18 ll. MWA (16 ll.); DLC; CtY; PDoBHi; PHi; PPAmP; PPL. 10253

POOR Tom's Almanack for 1789. Philadelphia: John Clark. 16 ll. MWA. 10254

POOR Will's Almanack for 1789. By William Waring. Philadelphia: Joseph Crukshank. 22 ll. MWA; MB; WHi; PHi (impf) 10255

POOR Will's Pocket Almanack for 1789. Philadelphia: Joseph Crukshank. 16 ll. MWA; DLC; DeWint; NHi; PHi. 10256

POULSON'S Town and Country Almanac for 1789. By William Waring. Philadelphia: Zachariah Poulson, junior. 20 ll. MWA; DLC (18 ll.); MB; CtY (impf); P; PHi; PPAmP; PPL; PPPrHi; PPiU; PU. 10257

AMERICANISCHER Haus-und Wirthschafts-Calender auf 1790. Philadelphia: Melchior Steiner. [Morrison]
10258
AMERICANISCHER Stadt und Land Calender auf 1790. Philadelphia: Carl Cist. 22 ll. MWA (19 ll.); DLC; CtY; InU (impf); NjR (21 ll.); PHi (two varieties); PLF; PPG; PYHi. 10259

BAILEY'S Pocket Almanac for 1790. Philadelphia: Francis Bailey. 16 ll. MWA; DLC. 10260

The BALLOON Almanac for 1790. Philadelphia: F. Bailey; J. Steele; J. Bailey. 20 ll. MWA; N. 10261

The COLUMBIAN Almanack for 1790. By B. Workman. Philadelphia: Peter Stewart. 20 ll. MWA; PHi;

PPPrHi. 10262

FATHER Tammany's Almanack for 1790. Philadelphia: John M'Culloch. [Evans] 10263

The FEDERAL Almanac for 1790. Philadelphia: W. Young. 18 ll. MWA; DLC. 10264

Der HOCH-DEUTSCHE Americanische Calender auf 1790. Germantaun: Michael Billmeyer. 20 ll. MWA; DLC (18 ll.); N; DeWint; P (impf); PDoBHi; PHi; PPAmP; PPG; PPL (15 ll.); PPeSchw. 10265

MARK Time's Pennsylvania Almanack for 1790. Philadelphia: Eleazer Oswald. [Evans] 10266

Der NEUE, Gemeinnützige Landwirthschafts Calender auf 1790. Lancaster: Albrecht und Lahn. 22 ll. MWA; P (21 ll.); PHi (21 ll.); PPeSchw; PPL (21 ll.) 10267

The PENNSYLVANIA Almanac for 1790. [Philadelphia:] F. Bailey; J. Steele; J. Bailey; [etc]. 20 ll. MWA; DLC; MHi; RPJCB; PDoBHi. 10268

POOR Richard improved: being an Almanack and Ephemeris for 1790. By Richard Saunders. Philadelphia: Hall and Sellers. 20 ll. MWA; DLC; NN (19 ll.); CSmH; MB; CtY; PDoBHi; PHi; PPAmP. 10269

POOR Robin's House Almanac for 1790. Philadelphia: John M'Culloch. [Evans] 10270

POOR Will's Almanack for 1790. By Wm. Waring. Philadelphia: Joseph Crukshank. 20 ll. MWA; DLC (18 ll.); CtY; MHi; PDoBHi; PHi; PPL; PPiU. 10271

POOR Will's Pocket Almanack for 1790. Philadelphia: Joseph Crukshank. 20 ll. MWA; DLC; DeWint; NN (19 ll.); PHi; PP. 10272

POULSON'S Town and Country Almanac for 1790. By William Waring. Philadelphia: Zachariah Poulson, Junior. 18 ll. MWA; DLC; NHi; MB; MnU; MdBJ;

OCHP; P (17 ll.); PHi (impf); PPAmP; PPL;
PPPrHi; PPiU; PU. 10273

AMERICANISCHER Haus-und Wirthschafts-Calender.
[Seidensticker advises none issued this year.] 10274

AMERICANISCHER Stadt und Land Calender auf 1791.
Philadelphia: Carl Cist. 22 ll. MWA; DLC (20 ll.);
CLU; PHi; PLF; PPCS (18 ll.); PPeSchw; PYHi.
10275

BAILEY'S Pocket Almanac for 1791. Philadelphia:
Francis Bailey. 16 ll. PHi; Drake. 10276

The BALLOON Almanac for 1791. Lancaster: Jacob
Bailey. 20 ll. NHi. 10277

The COLUMBIAN Almanack for 1791. Philadelphia:
Peter Stewart. 24 ll. MWA; DLC; PHi. 10278

FATHER Tammany's Almanac for 1791. By B. Workman. Philadelphia: William Young. 20 ll. MWA;
CLU; CtY. 10279

The GERMAN Almanac, or the North American Calendar for 1791. Philadelphia: Francis Bailey. [Evans]
10280

Der HOCH-DEUTSCHE Americanische Calender auf
1791. Germantaun: Michael Billmeyer. 22 ll. MWA
(two varieties); DLC; NN; CtY; InU; DeWint; N; PHi;
PPG; PPL; PPeSchw. 10281

Der HOCH-DEUTSCHE Americanische Calender auf
1791. Lancaster: M. Bartgis; [etc]. 18 ll. DLC.
10282

Der NEUE, Gemeinnutzige Landwirthschafts Calender
auf 1791. Lancaster: Johann Albrecht und Comp. 20
ll. MWA (19 ll.); PLHi; PHi; PPG; PPeSchw (19
ll.); PYHi. 10283

-- Sheet Almanac issue. Broadside. MWA. 10284

Der NEUE Hoch Deutsche Americanische Calender auf
1791. Chesnut-Hill [sic]: Samuel Saur. 20 ll. PHi;

PPL.   10285

Der NEUESTE und Verbesserte Nord-Americanische
Calender auf 1791. Lancaster: Jacob Bailey. PHi (14
ll.)   10286

The PENNSYLVANIA Almanac for 1791. Lancaster:
Jacob Bailey. CtY.   10287

The PENNSYLVANIA Pocket Almanac for 1791. Phila-
delphia: Francis Bailey. [Evans]   10288

The PENNSYLVANIA Pocket Almanac for 1791. Phila-
delphia: Thomas Lang; Robert Campbell. 14 ll. PHi.
                                                                  10289
A POCKET Almanac for 1791. Philadelphia: John
M'Culloch. [Evans]   10290

POOR Richard improved: being an Almanack and
Ephemeris for 1791. By Richard Saunders. Philadel-
phia: Hall & Sellers. 22 ll. MWA (impf); DLC; NjR
(impf); CtY; RPA; MB; PDoBHi; PHi (impf); PPL.
                                                                  10291
POOR Robin's Almanac for 1791. By B. Workman.
Philadelphia: John M'Culloch. 20 ll. PHi (12 ll.)
                                                                  10292
POOR Will's Almanack for 1791. By Wm. Waring.
Philadelphia: Joseph Crukshank. 22 ll. MWA; DLC;
CLU; NBuG; InU; PDoBHi; PHC; PHi; PPAmP; PU.
                                                                  10293
POOR Will's Pocket Almanack for 1791. Philadelphia:
Joseph Crukshank. 20 ll. MWA; NN; MB; DeWint;
PP.   10294

POULSON'S Town and Country Almanac for 1791. By
William Waring. Philadelphia: Zachariah Poulson,
Junior; [etc]. 18 ll. MWA; DLC; InU; MdBJ; P;
PHi; PPL; PPiU; PPPrHi; PU.   10295

The AMERICAN Almanac for 1792. Philadelphia:
Thomas Bradford. 18 ll. DLC; MB; PHi.   10296

AMERICANISCHER Haus-und Wirthschafts-Calender.

Pennsylvania - 1792   987

[Seidensticker advises none issued this year.]   10297

AMERICANISCHER Stadt und Land Calender auf 1792.
Philadelphia: Carl Cist. 22 ll. MWA; DLC (20 ll.);
NN (impf); ICU; InU (impf); PHi; PPG; PRHi; PYHi.
10298

BANNEKER'S Almanac for 1792. By Benjamin Banneker. Philadelphia: William Young. 18 ll. OCHP (ntp)
10299

The COLUMBIAN Almanac for 1792. Philadelphia:
Peter Stewart. 20 ll. MWA (18 ll.); PHi.   10300

FATHER Abraham's Almanac for 1792. Philadelphia:
Peter Stewart. 20 ll. MWA; DLC (18 ll.); InU; NHi;
NN; ViWC (impf)   10301

FATHER Tammany's Almanac for 1792. Philadelphia:
John M'Culloch. 18 ll. PHi (15 ll.); Vi.   10302

The FEDERAL Almanac for 1792. Philadelphia: William Young. 18 ll. MWA; PHC (16 ll.)   10303

Der HOCH-DEUTSCHE Americanische Calender auf
1792. Germantaun: Michael Billmeyer. 22 ll. MWA;
DLC; NN; PHi; PPG.   10304

M'Culloch's Pocket Almanac for 1792. Philadelphia:
John M'Culloch. 16 ll. MWA (two varieties); DLC.
10305

Der NEUE, Gemeinnützige Landwirthschafts Calender auf
1792. Lancaster: Johann Albrecht und Comp. 22 ll.
MWA; DLC; N; WHi; NjP; InU; DeWint; P; PHi (21
ll.); PLHi; PPG.   10306

Der NEUE Hoch Deutsche Americanische Calender auf
1792. Chesnut-Hill [sic]: Samuel Saur. 20 ll. MWA
(impf); NNC-Typ; MiD; MiU-C; PAtM; P (21 ll.);
PHi; PPG.   10307

Der NEUESTE und Verbesserte Nord-Americanische
Calender auf 1792. Lancaster: Jacob Bailey. 18 ll.
PLHi (15 ll.); PPL (two varieties)   10308

The NEW Pennsylvania Almanac for 1792. Philadelphia: Robert Campbell. 16 ll. NN (impf) 10309

The PENNSYLVANIA Pocket Almanac for 1792. Philadelphia: Francis Bailey. [Evans] 10310

POOR Richard improved: being an Almanack and Ephemeris for 1792. By Richard Saunders. Philadelphia: Hall & Sellers. 22 ll. MWA; DLC; CtY; MdBJ; RPA (20 ll.); PHi; PDoBHi (impf); PPL; PPAmP; Drake. 10311

POOR Robin's Almanac for 1792. By Joshua Sharp. Philadelphia: John M'Culloch. 18 ll. MWA; InU (impf) 10312

POOR Will's Almanack for 1792. By Wm. Waring. Philadelphia: Joseph Crukshank. 24 ll. MWA; DLC; CtY; WHi; P (21 ll.); PDoBHi (18 ll.); PHi; PPL (22 ll.); PPiU. 10313

POOR Will's Almanack for 1792. By William Waring. Philadelphia: Joseph Crukshank. 24 ll. NjR. 10314

POOR Will's Pocket Almanack for 1792. Philadelphia: Joseph Crukshank. 22 ll. MWA; DLC; MH; MB; MHi; NBuG; DeWint; P (ntp); PHi; PP. 10315

POULSON'S Town and Country Almanac for 1792. By William Waring. Philadelphia: Zachariah Poulson, Junior. 18 ll. MWA; DLC; NN; MiU-C; MdBJ; N; Nj; ICHi; Ct; MB; P; PHi; PPL; PPPrHi; PPiU; PU. 10316

The WESTERN Almanac for 1792. By James M'Cormick. Carlisle: George Kline. Advertised in the "Carlisle Gazette," October 12, 1791. 10317

The AMERICAN Pocket Almanac for 1793. Philadelphia: Thomas Lang. 24 ll. MWA; DLC; PP. 10318

AMERICANISCHER Haus-und Wirthschafts-Calender auf 1793. Philadelphia: Steiner und Kämmerer. 20 ll. DLC; PHi; PPG. 10319

Pennsylvania - 1793

AMERICANISCHER Stadt und Land Calender auf 1793.
Philadelphia: Carl Cist. 22 ll. MWA; DLC (21 ll.);
MH; InU (impf); PHi; DeWint; PPG; PYHi.   10320

BAILEY'S Pocket Almanac for 1793. Philadelphia:
Francis Bailey. 21 ll. MWA; PHi.   10321

BAILEY'S Pocket Almanac for 1793. Philadelphia:
Thomas Lang. 16 ll. DLC.   10322

The BALLOON Almanac for 1793. Lancaster: J.
Bailey and W. Dickson. 18 ll. NjP.   10323

BANNEKER'S Almanack, and Ephemeris for 1793.
Philadelphia: Joseph Crukshank. 24 ll. MWA; DLC
(21 ll.); NN; MHi (impf); PPL; OCHP (14 ll., ntp);
P (22 ll.); NjMoW; PHC; PHi (21 ll.)   10324

The COLUMBIAN Almanac for 1793. Philadelphia:
Stewart & Cochran. 20 ll. MWA; DLC; NN (18 ll.);
PHi; NjR (18 ll.)   10325

The COLUMBIAN Almanac for 1793. By James Login.
Philadelphia: Robert Campbell. NcD (17 ll.)   10326

FATHER Abraham's Almanac for 1793. Philadelphia:
Stewart & Cochran. 20 ll. MWA; DLC; CtY; PDoBHi
(17 ll.); PHC.   10327

FATHER TAMMANY'S Almanac for 1793. Philadelphia:
John M'Culloch. 18 ll. DLC; CtY; PHi (16 ll.) 10328

FATHER Tammany's Almanac for 1793. Philadelphia:
William Young. 18 ll. MWA.   10329

Der HOCH-DEUTSCHE Americanische Calender auf
1793. Germantaun: Michael Billmeyer. 24 ll. MWA;
DLC (impf); NN (23 ll.); NBuG; PHi; PPAmP; PPL
(21 ll.); PPeSchw.   10330

M'CULLOCH'S Pocket Almanac for 1793. Philadelphia:
John M'Culloch. 16 ll. MWA; NN; NHi; MH; PHi.
10331

Der NEUE, Gemeinnützige Landwirthschafts Calender auf 1793. Lancaster: Johann Albrecht und Comp. 22 ll. MWA; DLC; NN (11 ll.); InU; WHi; PHi; PLHi; PPG; PPeSchw.　　　　　　　　　　　　　　　　　　　　10332

Der NEUE Hoch Deutsche Americanische Calender auf 1793. Chesnut-Hill: Samuel Saur. 23 ll. MiU-C; P; PHi.　　　　　　　　　　　　　　　　　　　　10333

The NEW Pennsylvania Almanac for 1793. By James Login. Philadelphia: Robert Campbell. 18 ll. MWA.
10334

POOR Richard improved: being an Almanack and Ephemeris for 1793. By Richard Saunders. Philadelphia: Hall & Sellers. 22 ll. MWA; DLC; MB; RPA (21 ll.); PHi; PPAmP.　　　　　　　　　　　　10335

POOR Robin's Almanack for 1793. Philadelphia. [Evans]　　　　　　　　　　　　　　　　　　　10336

POOR Will's Almanack for 1793. By William Waring. Philadelphia: Joseph Crukshank. 24 ll. MWA; DLC; NjR (21 ll., ntp); MB; NBuG; MdBJ (20 ll.); N; PDoBHi (ntp); PHi; Drake.　　　　　　　　　10337

POOR Will's Pocket Almanack for 1793. Philadelphia: Joseph Crukshank. 21 ll. MWA; DLC; NHi; DeWint; MB; PHi.　　　　　　　　　　　　　　　　　　10338

POULSON'S Town and Country Almanac for 1793. Philadelphia: Zachariah Poulson, Junior. 20 ll. MWA; DLC; NN (impf); NHi; N; MiU-C; MB; MdBJ (19 ll.); PDoBHi (16 ll.); PHi; PPAmP; PPPrHi; PPiU; NjR.
10339

POULSON'S Town and Country Almanac for 1793. Philadelphia: Zachariah Poulson, Junior. (Second Edition) 20 ll. MWA; P; PPL; PU.　　　　　　　　10340

The WESTERN Almanac for 1793. By James M'Cormick. Carlisle: George Kline. 18 ll. DeWint. 10341

AMERICAN Calendar, or United States Register for

1794. Philadelphia. [National Union Catalog] 10342

AMERICANISCHER Haus-und Wirthschafts-Calender auf 1794. Philadelphia: Steiner und Kämmerer. 22 ll. DLC; NN; PHi. 10343

AMERICANISCHER Stadt und Land Calender auf 1794. Philadelphia: Carl Cist. 22 ll. MWA (20 ll.); DLC; N; PDoBHi (impf); PHi (ntp); PPG; PYHi. 10344

BAILEY'S Pocket Almanac for 1794. Philadelphia: Francis Bailey. 16 ll. DLC; MB; PHi. 10345

BAILEY'S Pocket Almanac for 1794. Philadelphia: Thomas Lang. 16 ll. DLC. 10346

BANNEKER'S Almanack and Ephemeris for 1794. Philadelphia: Joseph Crukshank. 22 ll. MWA; MHi. 10347

BENJAMIN Banneker's Almanac for 1794. Philadelphia: William Young. 18 ll. NjP (17 ll.); OCHP. 10348

The COLUMBIAN Almanac for 1794. By David Hale. Philadelphia: Stewart & Cochran. 20 ll. DLC (19 ll.); CtY; MdBJ. 10349

FATHER Abraham's Almanac for 1794. By David Hale. Philadelphia: Stewart & Cochran. 20 ll. MWA; DLC (18 ll.); NjR (17 ll.); Drake. 10350

FATHER Tammany's Almanac for 1794. Philadelphia: John M'Culloch. [Evans] 10351

Der HOCH-DEUTSCHE Americanische Calender auf 1794. Germantaun: Michael Billmeyer. 24 ll. MWA (23 ll.); DLC; DeWint; P (23 ll.); PHi; PPG; PYHi. 10352

M'CULLOCH'S Pocket Almanac for 1794. Philadelphia: John M'Culloch. 16 ll. MWA; DLC; InU; NHi; PDoBHi (19 ll.); PHi. 10353

Der NEUE, Gemeinnützige Landwirthschafts Calender auf 1794. Lancaster: Johann Albrecht und Comp. 22 ll.

MWA; DLC; N; NjP; CtY; InU; DeWint; OC; P; PHi
(17 ll., ntp); PLHi; PPCS; PPG; PPL.   10354

Der NEUE Hoch Deutsche Americanische Calender auf
1794. Chesnut-Hill: Samuel Saur. 22 ll. MWA; DLC;
InU (fragment); DeWint; PHi; PYHi (18 ll.)   10355

POOR Richard improved: being an Almanack and
Ephemeris for 1794. By Richard Saunders. Philadelphia: Hall & Sellers. 22 ll. MWA; DLC; NN; InU; PHi;
PPAmP; PPL (19 ll.); BritMus.   10356

POOR Robin's Almanac for 1794. By Robin Goodfellow.
Philadelphia: John M'Culloch. 18 ll. NN (16 ll.);
PPPrHi; PPiU.   10357

POOR Will's Almanack for 1794. By William Waring.
Philadelphia: Joseph Crukshank. 24 ll. MWA; DLC;
MB; CLU; MiU-C; CtY; OCl; N; InU; PDoBHi; PHi;
MHi.   10358

POOR Will's Pocket Almanack for 1794. Philadelphia:
Joseph Crukshank. 24 ll. MWA; DLC; CtY; DeWint;
MHi; PHi; PP.   10359

POULSON'S Town and Country Almanac for 1794.
Philadelphia: Zachariah Poulson, Junior. 24 ll. MWA;
DLC (22 ll.); NN; NHi; Nj; CLU; Nh; CtY (impf);
InU; MdBJ (22 ll.); N; MiD-B; PU; PPiU; PHi; PPL;
P; PPPrHi; PDoBHi.   10360

The UNITED States Register for 1794. Philadelphia:
Stewart & Cochran, and John M'Culloch. 101 ll. NN;
NjR; MB; RPB; CLU; CtY; PHi; PPAmP; N.   10361

The WESTERN Almanac for 1794. By James M'Cormick. Carlisle: George Kline. Advertised in the
"Carlisle Gazette," November 6, 1793.   10362

The AMERICAN Repository of Useful Information [for
1795]. Philadelphia: B. Davies. 24 ll. DLC (23 ll.);
NN; NjR; MH; MHi.   10363

AMERICANISCHER Haus-und Wirthschafts-Calender auf 1795. Philadelphia: Steiner und Kämmerer. 22 ll. P (21 ll.); PHi. 10364

AMERICANISCHER Stadt und Land Calender auf 1795. Philadelphia: Carl Cist. 22 ll. MWA (fragment); DLC; PHi; PYHi. 10365

BAILEY'S Pocket Almanac for 1795. Philadelphia: Francis Bailey. 16 ll. MWA; ICU; PHi. 10366

The BALLOON Almanac for 1795. Lancaster: J. Bailey and W. Dickson. 20 ll. DLC; PHi. 10367

BANNEKER'S Almanac for 1795. Philadelphia: William Young. 18 ll. DLC; NN; NcD. 10368

BENJAMIN Banneker's Pennsylvania, Delaware, Maryland and Virginia Almanac for 1795. Philadelphia: William Gibbons. 18 ll. MWA. 10369

BENJAMIN Banneker's Pennsylvania, Delaware, Maryland and Virginia Almanac for 1795. Philadelphia: Jacob Johnson & Co. 18 ll. NHi. 10370

The COLUMBIAN Almanac for 1795. By D. Hale. Philadelphia: Stewart & Cochran. 20 ll. MWA; DLC; N; ICHi; MiU-C (impf); RPJCB; InU; PHi. 10371

The COLUMBIAN Almanac for 1795. By James Logan. Philadelphia: Robert Campbell. 19 ll. MWA. 10372

FATHER Abraham's Almanac for 1795. By D. Hale. Philadelphia: Printed and sold by Stewart & Cochran, No. 34, South Second Street. 20 ll. MWA (18 ll.); P; PHi; PPL (ntp) 10373

FATHER Abraham's Almanac for 1795. By D. Hale. Philadelphia: Printed and Sold by Stewart & Cochran, No. 34, South Second-street. 20 ll. PHi. 10374

FATHER Tammany's Almanac for 1795. [Philadelphia: John M'Culloch.] 18 ll. Drake (lower half of title leaf lacking.) 10375

Der HOCH-DEUTSCHE Americanische Calender auf 1795. Germantaun: Michael Billmeyer. 24 ll. MWA; DLC (impf); InU (impf); NN (23 ll.); N; NjR; PHi; PPG; PPL; PPeSchw. 10376

M'CULLOCH'S Pocket Almanac for 1795. Philadelphia: J. M'Culloch. 16 ll. MWA; DLC; MoU. 10377

Der NEUE, Gemeinnützige Landwirthschafts Calender auf 1795. Lancaster: Johann Albrecht und Comp. 22 ll. MWA (impf); DLC (impf); N; CtY; DeWint; NjP (20 ll.); P; PLHi. 10378

Der NEUE Hoch Deutsche Americanische Calender auf 1795. Philadelphia: Samuel Saur. 19 ll. MWA; DLC; PHi (18 ll.); PPG; PPL. 10379

Der NEUE Hoch Deutsche Americani-Sche [sic] Calender auf 1795. Philadelphia: Samuel Saur. 18 ll. PPL. 10380

The NEW Pennsylvania Almanac for 1795. By James Login. Philadelphia: Robert Campbell. 18 ll. NjP. 10381

POOR Richard improved: being an Almanack and Ephemeris for 1795. By Richard Saunders. Philadelphia: Hall & Sellers. 22 ll. MWA; DLC; MB; NBuG (21 ll.); CSmH; PHi; BritMus. 10382

POOR Robin's Almanac for 1795. Philadelphia: John M'Culloch. 18 ll. MWA; Drake (impf) 10383

POOR Will's Almanack for 1795. Philadelphia: Joseph Crukshank. 22 ll. MWA; DLC; NN (20 ll.); NCH; WHi; MiD-B; MB; NBuG; InU; InRE (20 ll.); PDoBHi; PHi; PPL; PPiU. 10384

POOR Will's Pocket Almanack for 1795. Philadelphia: Joseph Crukshank. 24 ll. MWA; DLC; NN (22 ll.); NjR; MB; CtY; InU; PHi; NHi; NjGlaN. 10385

POULSON'S Town and Country Almanac for 1795. Phila-

delphia: Zachariah Poulson, Junior. 22 ll. MWA;
DLC; NjHi; OClWHi; MdBJ; PU; PHi; PPiU; PPL; P;
PPPrHi. 10386

The UNITED States Register for 1795. Philadelphia:
Mathew Carey. 98 ll. NN; MB; NPV; MHi; MiU-C;
PHi; CSt; CtY; InU; PPAmP. 10387

The WESTERN Almanac for 1795. Carlisle: George
Kline. [Thompson] 10388

An ALMANACK for 1796. Washington: Colerick,
Hunter & Beaumont. 18 ll. DLC; PU (impf) 10389

The AMERICAN Repository of Useful Information [for
1796]. Philadelphia: B. Davies. 52 ll. MWA; DLC;
MH; PHi; PPL; Drake. 10390

AMERICANISCHER Haus-und Wirthschafts-Calender auf
1796. Philadelphia: Steiner und Kämmerer. 22 ll.
DLC; NN (21 ll.); PHi. 10391

AMERICANISCHER Stadt und Land Calender auf 1796.
Philadelphia: Carl Cist. 22 ll. MWA; DLC; PHi (17
ll., ntp); PPG; PPL; PPi (ntp); PYHi. 10392

BAILEY'S Pocket Almanac for 1796. Philadelphia:
Francis & Robert Bailey. 16 ll. MWA; PHi; Drake.
10393

The BALLOON Almanac for 1796. Lancaster: J. Bailey
and W. Dickson. [Evans] 10394

The BALLOON Almanac for 1796. Lancaster: William &
Robert Dickson for John Wyeth, Harrisburg. 20 ll. N.
10395

CALENDRIER Republicain pour [1796]. Philadelphie:
Benj. Franklin Bache. 20 ll. NHi. 10396

The COLUMBIAN Almanac for 1796. Lancaster: William & Robert Dickson. 24 ll. MWA (impf); DLC (20
ll.) 10397

The COLUMBIAN Almanac for 1796. By D. Hale.

Philadelphia: Stewart & Cochran. 20 ll. MWA; DLC
(18 ll.); NN (impf); NBuG; InU. 10398

FATHER Abraham's Almanac for 1796. By D. Hale.
Philadelphia: Stewart & Cochran. 20 ll. MWA; DLC;
MB; PHi; PPiU. 10399

FATHER Tammany's Almanac for 1796. Philadelphia:
William Young. 18 ll. MWA (16 ll.); NjHi (16 ll.);
MoSHi; BritMus. 10400

Der HOCH-DEUTSCHE Americanische Calender auf
1796. Germantaun: Michael Billmeyer. 22 ll. MWA;
DLC; NN; InU; DeWint; PAtM; PHi; PPG; PYHi;
PPeSchw. 10401

M'CULLOCH'S Pocket Almanac for 1796. Philadelphia:
J. M'Culloch. 16 ll. MWA; DLC; NBuG (11 ll.); MHi;
PHi. 10402

Der NEUE, Gemeinnützige Landwirthschafts Calender auf
1796. Lancaster: Johann Albrecht und Cimp. 22 ll.
MWA; DLC (impf); MoHi; WHi; N; InU; P; PHi; PPG;
PPL; PYHi; PLHi. 10403

The NEW-JERSEY, Pennsylvania and Maryland Almanac
for 1796. Philadelphia: Jacob Johnson & Co. 18 ll.
MWA. 10404

The PENNSYLVANIA Almanac for 1796. By Joshua
Sharp. Philadelphia: Mathew Carey. 18 ll. PHi. 10405

The PENNSYLVANIA Almanac for 1796. By Joshua
Sharp. Philadelphia: Jacob Johnson & Co. 18 ll.
MWA; NN; PHi. 10406

The PENNSYLVANIA, New-Jersey, Delaware, Maryland and Virginia Almanac for 1796. By D. Hale.
Philadelphia: Stewart & Cochran. 20 ll. MWA; DLC;
CtY; InU; PHi. 10407

PENNSYLVANISCHE Calender auf 1796. Ephrata:
Salomon Mayer. 22 ll. DLC; PLHi; PPG; PYHi. 10408

Pennsylvania - 1796

POOR Robin's Almanac for 1796. By Robin Goodfellow. Philadelphia: John M'Culloch. 12 ll. PHi (11 ll.) 10409

POOR Will's Almanack for 1796. Philadelphia: Joseph Crukshank. 22 ll. MWA; DLC; MB; OClWHi; CLU; MoU; CtY; N; NBuG; InU; WHi; TxDN; MiD-B; PHi; PPiU; PDoBHi; PPAmP. 10410

POOR Will's Almanack for 1796. By William Waring. Philadelphia: Joseph Crukshank. 22 ll. CLU; PPiU (21 ll.) 10411

POOR Will's Pocket Almanack for 1796. Philadelphia: Joseph Crukshank. 24 ll. MWA; DLC; DeWint; NN; InU; PHi; NjR (23 ll.) 10412

POULSON'S Town and Country Almanac for 1796. Philadelphia: Zachariah Poulson, Junior. 24 ll. MWA; DLC; N; NBuG; MdBJ; P; PHi; PP; PPL; PPPrHi; PPiU; PU; NjR. 10413

The WESTERN Almanac for 1796. Carlisle: George Kline. [Thompson] 10414

The WESTERN Ephemeris for 1796. Pittsburgh: John Scull. 22 ll. MWA. 10415

An ALMANACK for 1797. Washington: Colerick, Hunter and Beaumont. 18 ll. NjP; MiU-C (15 ll.); OCHP. 10416

AMERICAN Ladies Pocket Book for 1797. Philadelphia: W. Y. Birch. 78 ll. MWA; InU; PHi; PPAmP. 10417

The AMERICAN Repository of Useful Information [for 1797]. Philadelphia: B. Davies. 43 ll. DLC; MB (40 ll.); MH; MiU-C; PHi. 10418

AMERICANISCHER Haus-und Wirthschafts-Calender auf 1797. Philadelphia: Steiner und Kämmerer. 20 ll. DLC; DeWint. 10419

AMERICANISCHER Stadt und Land Calender auf 1797. Philadelphia: Carl Cist. 22 ll. MWA (two varieties); DLC; InU; MH; PHi; PPG; PPL (21 ll.); PPeSchw; PPi; PYHi; PPL (21 ll.)   10420

BAILEY'S Pocket Almanac for 1797. Philadelphia: Francis & Robert Bailey. 16 ll. MWA; DLC; PHi.   10421

CALENDRIER Republicain pour [1797]. Philadelphie: Benj. Franklin Bache. 20 ll. MWA; NN; NHi.   10422

The COLUMBIAN Almanac for 1797. Lancaster: William & Robert Dickson. 20 ll. MWA; DLC.   10423

The COLUMBIAN Almanac for 1797. Lancaster: William & Robert Dickson for John Wyeth, Harrisburg. 20 ll. MWA.   10424

The COLUMBIAN Almanac for 1797. Philadelphia: R. Campbell. 18 ll. MWA (17 ll.); PDoBHi.   10425

The COLUMBIAN Almanack for 1797. Philadelphia: B. & J. Johnson. 20 ll. MWA.   10426

The COLUMBIAN Almanac for 1797. Philadelphia: H. & P. Rice. 20 ll. MWA; PHi.   10427

The COLUMBIAN Almanac for 1797. By Samuel Ivins. Philadelphia: Stewart & Cochran. 20 ll. NN; InU; NbHi (impf)   10428

DICKSON'S Balloon Almanac for 1797. Lancaster: William and Robert Dickson. [Bausman]   10429

FATHER Abraham's Almanac for 1797. Philadelphia: H. & P. Rice. 20 ll. MWA (impf); NjR.   10430

FATHER Abraham's Almanac for 1797. Philadelphia: Stewart & Cochran. 18 ll. MWA; DLC; Nj; PDoBHi.   10431

FATHER Tamany's [sic] Almanac for 1797. Philadelphia: W. Young, Mills & Son. PPiU (15 ll.)   10432

Der HOCH-DEUTSCHE Americanische Calender auf
1797. Germantaun: Michael Billmeyer. 22 ll. MWA;
DLC; MdBSHG; P (13 ll.); PHi (17 ll.); PPG. 10433

M'CULLOCH'S Pocket Almanac for 1797. Philadelphia:
J. M'Culloch. 16 ll. MWA; CLU; DeWint. 10434

Der NEUE, Gemeinnützige Landwirthschafts Calender auf
1797. Lancaster: Johann Albrecht und Comp. 22 ll.
MWA; DLC (impf); NN (21 ll.); MdHi; InU; WHi; N;
DeWint; P; PHi; PLHi; PPG; PPL (17 ll.); PPeSchw.
10435

The PENNSYLVANIA, New-Jersey, Delaware, Maryland, and Virginia Almanac for 1797. By Samuel Ivins.
Philadelphia: James Rice & Co. 20 ll. MWA; BritMus.
10436

The PENNSYLVANIA, New-Jersey, Delaware, Maryland, and Virginia Almanac for 1797. By Samuel
Ivins. Philadelphia: Stewart & Cochran. 20 ll. MWA;
DLC; NjR (16 ll., ntp); PP; PPM. 10437

PENNSYLVANISCHER Calender auf 1797. Ephrata:
Benjamin Mayer. [Morrison] 10438

PENNSYLVANISCHER Calender auf 1797. York: Salomon Mayer. 22 ll. PHi. 10439

POOR Robin's Almanac for 1797. By Robin Goodfellow. Philadelphia: John M'Culloch. 20 ll. MWA (impf);
DLC; NN; NcU. 10440

POOR Will's Almanack for 1797. Philadelphia: Joseph
Crukshank. 18 ll. MWA; DLC; NN (16 ll.); RHi;
MB; MH; CLU; MoU; MiU-C; MoSHi; NBuG; InU;
WHi; PHi; N; MiD-B; PPiU; PDoBHi (ntp) 10441

POOR Will's Pocket Almanack for 1797. Philadelphia:
Joseph Crukshank. 19 ll. MWA; PHi. 10442

POULSON'S Town and Country Almanac for 1797.
Philadelphia: Zachariah Poulson, Junior. 24 ll. MWA;
DLC; NN; MB; InU; MdBJ; InRE (19 ll.); N; PU;
PPiU; PPPrHi; PHi; PPL; P; PPAmP; Drake. 10443

The WESTERN Almanac for 1797. Carlisle: George Kline. Advertised in the "Carlisle Gazette," October 19, 1796.   10444

An ALMANACK for 1798. Washington: Colerick, Hunter and Beaumont. 12 ll. NjP (impf)   10445

The AMERICAN Ladies Pocket Book, with an Almanac for 1798. Philadelphia: William Y. Birch. [Evans]   10446

The AMERICAN Repository, and Annual Register of the United States for 1798. Philadelphia: B. Davies; H. Sweitzer, printer. 50 ll. DLC; RNHi; WHi; PHi.   10447

AMERICANISCHER Calender auf 1798. Ephrata: Benjamin Mayer. 22 ll. MWA (ntp); PLHi.   10448

AMERICANISCHER Stadt und Land Calender auf 1798. Philadelphia: Carl Cist. 21 ll. MWA; DLC (20 ll.); NN; PHi; PRHi; PYHi.   10449

BAILEY'S Pocket Almanac for 1798. Philadelphia: Francis Bailey. 16 ll. NN; MiD-B; MiU-C; PHi; PPL.   10450

The BALLOON Almanac for 1798. Philadelphia: Mathew Carey; Lancaster: William and Robert Dickson, printers. MWA (17 ll.)   10451

CALENDRIER Republicain pour [1797-98]. Philadelphie: Benj. Franklin Bache. 24 ll. MWA; DLC; PPL.   10452

The COLUMBIAN Almanac for 1798. Philadelphia: Mathew Carey; Lancaster: William & Robert Dickson, printers. 20 ll. DLC; N; PPiU.   10453

The COLUMBIAN Almanac for 1798. Philadelphia: Stewart & Cochran. 20 ll. NjR.   10454

The COLUMBIAN Almanac for 1798. By Samuel Ivins. Philadelphia: H. & P. Rice. 19 ll. DLC.   10455

The COLUMBIAN Almanac for 1798. By Samuel Ivins.

Philadelphia: Stewart & Cochran. 20 ll. MWA; DLC;
NN; NHi; InU; PHi. 10456

The COLUMBIAN Almanac for 1798. By Joshua Sharp.
Philadelphia: Robert Campbell. PPiU (17 ll.) 10457

DICKSON'S Balloon Almanac for 1798. Lancaster: W.
& R. Dickson. 20 ll. DLC (19 ll.); PHi. 10458

FATHER Abraham's Almanac for 1798. Philadelphia:
H. & P. Rice. 20 ll. DLC. 10459

FATHER Abraham's Almanac for 1798. Philadelphia:
Stewart and Cochran. 20 ll. DLC; NjR (16 ll.) 10460

FATHER Tammany's Almanac for 1798. By Joshua
Sharp. Philadelphia: William Young. 18 ll. MWA;
InU (ntp); BritMus. 10461

Der GEMEINNÜTZIGE Landwirthschafts Calender auf
1798. Lancaster: Johann Albrecht und Comp. PDoBHi.
10462

Der HOCH-DEUTSCHE Americanische Calender auf
1798. Germantaun: Michael Billmeyer. 20 ll. MWA;
DLC; NN (16 ll.); NjR; InU; PHi; DeWint; PHershM;
PPG; PPL. 10463

M'CULLOCH'S Pocket Almanac for 1798. Philadelphia:
J. M'Culloch. 16 ll. MWA; NN (15 ll.); PHi. 10464

Der NEUE, Gemeinnützige Landwirthschafts Calender
auf 1798. Lancaster: Johann Albrecht und Comp. 22 ll.
MWA; DLC; NN (20 ll.); DeWint; InU; P; PHi (impf);
PLHi; PPi. 10465

NEUER Hauswirthschafts Calender auf 1798. Reading:
Gottlob Jungmann und Comp. 22 ll. MWA; DLC;
DeWint; InU; P (21 ll.); PR; PHi (19 ll.); PPL.
10466

The PENNSYLVANIA Almanack for 1798. By Joshua
Sharp. Philadelphia: Robert Campbell. 16 ll. PDoBHi.
10467

The PENNSYLVANIA, New-Jersey, Delaware, Maryland

and Virginia Almanac for 1798. By Samuel Ivins.
Philadelphia: Stewart & Cochran. 18 ll. MWA; DLC.
10468

PENNSYLVANISCHER Kalender auf 1798. Ephrata: Salomon Mayer. 21 ll. PPG. 10469

PENNSYLVANISCHER Calender auf 1798. York: Salomon Mayer. 22 ll. MWA; PAtM (20 ll.); PHi; PPG.
10470

POOR Richard improved: being an Almanack and Ephemeris for 1798. By Richard Saunders. Philadelphia: Hall & Sellers. 22 ll. MB; PDoBHi; PHi (21 ll.) 10471

POOR Robin's Almanac for 1798. By Joshua Sharp.
Philadelphia: John M'Culloch. 18 ll. MWA; NN; InU (ntp) 10472

POOR Will's Almanack for 1798. Philadelphia: Joseph and James Crukshank. 18 ll. MWA; DLC; NN; MB; MH; MiU-C; NBuG; InU; PDoBHi; PHi; NjR. 10473

POOR Will's Pocket Almanack for 1798. Philadelphia: Joseph & James Crukshank. 24 ll. MWA; DLC; NHi; DeWint; PHi; PP; PPL (22 ll.); NjR. 10474

POULSON'S Town and Country Almanac for 1798.
Philadelphia: Zachariah Poulson, Junior. 24 ll. MWA; DLC; NN; Nj; PU; OClWHi; CLU; P; PPPrHi; PPM; PPiU; PHi; InU; MdBJ; N; PP; PPAmP; PPL. 10475

Der VEREINIGTEN Staaten Calender auf 1798. Philadelphia: H. Kämmerer, Jun. und Comp. 20 ll. MWA (19 ll.); PHi (19 ll.); PPG. 10476

The WESTERN Almanac for 1798. Carlisle: Archibald Loudon; George Kline, printer. 18 ll. MWA (17 ll.)
10477

The WESTERN Calendar or an Almanack for 1798.
Washington: John Colerick. OCHP. 10478

An ALMANACK for 1799. Washington: John Colerick.
[Evans] 10479

Pennsylvania - 1799

The AMERICAN Ladies Pocket Book for 1799: containing an Almanack. Philadelphia: William Y. Birch. 72 ll. MWA; NN. 10480

The AMERICAN Repository [for 1799]. Philadelphia: Benjamin Davies. BritMus. 10481

AMERICANISCHER Calender auf 1799. Ephrata: Benjamin Mayer. 20 ll. MWA (19 ll.); PP; PPL. 10482

AMERICANISCHER Stadt und Land Calender auf 1799. Philadelphia: Carl Cist. 24 ll. MWA; DLC; N; PHi (23 ll.); PPG; PPL. 10483

BAILEY'S Pocket Almanac for 1799. Philadelphia: Francis Bailey. 16 ll. MWA; PHi. 10484

CALENDER Für 1799. Philadelphia: Henrich Schweitzer. 20 ll. MWA (ntp); N; PHi; PPG. 10485

The CITIZEN and Farmer's Almanac for 1799. Philadelphia: John M'Culloch. 18 ll. ViLxV (17 ll.) 10486

The CITIZEN and Farmer's Almanac for 1799. By Farmer Washington. Philadelphia: [np] 18 ll. MB. 10487

DICKSON'S Balloon Almanac for 1799. Lancaster: W. & R. Dickson. 20 ll. MWA; PHi. 10488

DICKSON'S Columbian Almanac for 1799. Lancaster: W. & R. Dickson. 20 ll. MWA. 10489

FATHER Abraham's Almanac for 1799. By Tom Tattle. Philadelphia: Peter Stewart. 20 ll. MWA (two varieties, both impf); DLC (19 ll.); NN; NCH; InU; P; PHi (impf); Drake. 10490

FATHER Tammany's Almanac for 1799. By Joshua Sharp. Philadelphia: John M'Culloch. 12 ll. MWA; PPiU (9 ll.); BritMus. 10491

Der HOCH-DEUTSCHE Americanische Calender auf 1799. Germantaun: Michael Billmeyer. 20 ll. MWA;

Pennsylvania - 1799

DLC (impf); NHi (impf); InU; CtY; N; PHi (19 ll.)
10492

M'CULLOCH'S Pocket Almanac for 1799. Philadelphia: J. M'Culloch. 16 ll. MWA; PHi.
10493

Der NEUE, Gemeinnützige Landwirthschafts Calender auf 1799. Lancaster: Johann Albrecht und Comp. 22 ll. MWA (impf); DLC (21 ll.); InU (impf); P; WHi; NjP (nfp); DeWint; PHi; PLHi; PYHi.
10494

NEUER Hauswirthschafts Calender auf 1799. Philadelphia: Henrich Schweitzer. 20 ll. DeWint.
10495

NEUER Hauswirthschafts Calender auf 1799. Reading: Gottlob Jungmann und Comp. 22 ll. MWA; DLC; P; PHi; PPG; PRHi.
10496

The PENNSYLVANIA, New-Jersey, Delaware, Maryland and Virginia Almanac for 1799. By Tom Tattle. Philadelphia: H. & P. Rice. 20 ll. PHi (12 ll.); NjR.
10497

The PENNSYLVANIA, New-Jersey, Delaware, Maryland and Virginia Almanac for 1799. By Tom Tattle. Philadelphia: Peter Stewart. 20 ll. MWA; NN (ntp); NBuG; NjR; PHi.
10498

PENNSYLVANISCHER Calender auf 1799. York: Salomon Mayer. 22 ll. DLC; PPG.
10499

POOR Robin's Almanac for 1799. By Robin Goodfellow. Philadelphia: John M'Culloch. [Evans]
10500

POOR Robin's Almanac for 1799. By Joshua Sharp. Philadelphia: John M'Culloch. 15 ll. MWA (13 ll.); DLC.
10501

POOR Will's Almanack for 1799. Philadelphia: Joseph and James Crukshank. 18 ll. MWA; DLC (impf); WHi; N; MH; CtY; InU; MiU-C; PHi; PPiU.
10502

POOR Will's Pocket Almanack for 1799. Philadelphia: Joseph & James Crukshank. 24 ll. MWA; DLC; NN; PHi; PP.
10503

Pennsylvania - 1799

POULSON'S Town and Country Almanac for 1799.
Philadelphia: Zachariah Poulson, Junior. 24 ll. MWA;
DLC (impf); NN; N; MHi; CSmH; ICU; Nj; MB; CLU;
MoU; InU; MdBJ (22 ll.); P; NBuG; PU; PPiU; PHi;
PPL; PPPrHi; PPAmP. 10504

The STARRY Calculator; being an Almanac for 1799.
Chambersburg: Robert Harper. 20 ll. MWA. 10505

The TOWN and Country Almanac for 1799. Philadelphia: Isaac Pearson. 20 ll. PHi (19 ll.) 10506

The TOWN and Country Almanac for 1799. Philadelphia: Zachariah Poulson, Junior. 20 ll. PHi (4 ll.)
10507
VERBESSERT Hoch-Deutsch-Americanischer Land und Staats Calender auf 1799. York: Salomon Mayer. 20 ll. PHi. 10508

Der VEREINIGTEN Staaten Calender auf 1799. Philadelphia: J. R. Kämmerer, und Comp. 19 ll. PHi.
10509
WESTERN Almanac for 1799. Carlisle: George Kline.
Advertised in the "Carlisle Gazette," October 24, 1798.
10510
The WESTERN Calendar: or, an Almanack for 1799.
Washington: John Colerick. 18 ll. OCHP; PPiU.
10511
AMERICAN Repository, and Annual Register of the United States for 1800. Philadelphia: B. Davies.
[Sabin] 10512

AMERICANISCHER Calender auf 1800. Harrisburg:
Benjamin Mayer. 16 ll. DeWint; P. 10513

AMERICANISCHER Stadt und Land Calender auf 1800.
Philadelphia: Carl Cist. 24 ll. MWA; DLC (20 ll.);
DeWint; NN; PHi. 10514

BAILEY'S Pocket Almanac for 1800. Philadelphia:
Francis & Robert Bailey. 16 ll. MWA; DLC; PHi.
10515
CITIZENS and Farmer's Almanac for 1800. By Joshua

Sharp. Philadelphia: John M'Culloch. 18 ll. MWA;
DLC; NN; NjHi (16 ll.)   10516

DICKSON'S Balloon Almanac for 1800. Lancaster: W.
& R. Dickson. [Evans]   10517

The FARMERS Almanac for 1800. Greensburg: Snowden & M'Corkle. 18 ll. MWA; DLC; MoSHi; PPiU.
    10518

FATHER Abraham's Almanac for 1800. Philadelphia:
Peter Stewart. 20 ll. DLC (19 ll.); NCH.   10519

FATHER Tammany's Almanac for 1800. Philadelphia:
John M'Culloch. PDoBHi (14 ll.)   10520

FATHER Tammany's Almanac for 1800. By Joshua
Sharp. Philadelphia: David Hogan. 18 ll. DLC.   10521

FATHER Tammany's Almanac for 1800. By Joshua
Sharp. Philadelphia: William Young. 18 ll. MWA (16
ll.); PDoBHi (impf)   10522

The GENTLEMAN'S Annual Pocket Remembrancer for
1800. Philadelphia: John Bioren. 80 ll. MWA. 10523

Der HOCH-DEUTSCHE Americanische Calender auf
1800. Germantaun: Michael Billmeyer. 20 ll. DLC (16
ll.); N; PHi; PPCS (12 ll.); PPeSchw.   10524

M'CULLOCH'S Pocket Almanac for 1800. Philadelphia:
J. M'Culloch. 16 ll. MWA; CSmH.   10525

Der NEUE, Gemeinnützige Landwirthschafts Calender auf
1800. Lancaster: Johann Albrecht und Comp. 22 ll.
MWA; DLC (21 ll.); WHi; DeWint; PHi; P; PLHi;
PPG; PYHi.   10526

NEUER Hauswirthschafts Calender auf 1800. Philadelphia: Henrich Schweitzer. 20 ll. MWA; PHi; PPeSchw.
    10527

NEUER Hauswirthschafts Calender auf 1800. Reading:
Gottlob Jungmann und Comp. 22 ll. MWA; DLC; N;
DeWint; P (21 ll.); PHi.   10528

The PENNSYLVANIA, New-Jersey, Delaware, Maryland and Virginia Almanac for 1800. By Tom Tattle. Philadelphia: Peter Stewart. 20 ll. MWA; NN; NjR (impf); InU (16 ll.); PPPrHi; Drake.   10529

PENNSYLVANISCHER Calender auf 1800. York: Salomon Mayer. 20 ll. MWA.   10530

PHILADELPHIA Almanac for 1800. By Enoch Lewis. Philadelphia: B. & J. Johnson. 24 ll. MWA; DLC; NN (5 ll.); NHi; N; P; PHC; PHi.   10531

POOR Richard improved: being an Almanack and Ephemeris for 1800. By Richard Saunders. Philadelphia: Hall & Sellers. 22 ll. MWA; CLU; CSmH; PHi; NjR (18 ll.)   10532

POOR Will's Almanack for 1800. Philadelphia: Joseph and James Crukshank. 18 ll. MWA; DLC; NN; OClWHi; MB; MH; PDoBHi; PHC; PPiU.   10533

POOR Will's Pocket Almanack for 1800. Philadelphia: Joseph & James Crukshank. 24 ll. MWA; DLC; NHi; DeWint; PHi; PP (ntp); NjR (22 ll.)   10534

POULSON'S Town and Country Almanac for 1800. Philadelphia: Zachariah Poulson, Junior. 24 ll. MWA; DLC; NN; NHi; ICHi; OClWHi; MB; N; Ct; InU; MdBJ (23 ll.); P; PU; PPL; PPPrHi; PPiU; PHi; PP; PHC; PDoBHi; NjR (21 ll.); Drake.   10535

The REPUBLICAN Calendar for 1800. Washington: John Israel. 18 ll. MWA; OCHP.   10536

The STARRY Calculator; being an Almanac for 1800. Lancaster: Henry and Benjamin Grimber. 18 ll. MWA.
   10537

Der VEREINIGTEN Staaten Calender auf 1800. Philadelphia: Joseph R. Kämmerer und G. Helmhold, jun. 21 ll. N; InU (19 ll., ntp); PHi.   10538

The WESTERN Almanack for 1800. Pittsburgh: John Scull. Advertised in the "Pittsburgh Gazette," November 16, 1799. 10539

The WESTERN Calendar, or, an Almanack for 1800. Washington: John Colerick. OHi (17 ll.) 10540

AMERICAN Repository, and Annual Register of the United States for 1801. Philadelphia: B. Davies. [Sabin] 10541

AMERICANISCHER Stadt und Land Calender auf 1801. Philadelphia: Carl Cist. 24 ll. MWA; DLC; N; PHi; PPG. 10542

CALENDAR for the Nineteenth Century. D. Mandeville invenit. Philada. 1801. [printed on silk] 1 ll. MWA; NN. 10543

CAREY'S Franklin Almanac for 1801. Mathew Carey; John Bioren, printer. 24 ll. MWA; DLC (22 ll.); NN (23 ll.); CtY; InU; Vi (22 ll.); PHi; PPL; BritMus. 10544

CITIZEN'S and Farmer's Almanac for 1801. By Joshua Sharp. Philadelphia: John M'Culloch. 20 ll. DLC; PPiU; Drake. 10545

DICKSON'S Balloon Almanac for 1801. Lancaster: W. & R. Dickson. 20 ll. DeWint. 10546

FATHER Abraham's Almanac for 1801. By Joshua Sharp. Philadelphia: Peter Stewart. 20 ll. MWA; NHi (impf); NjR; InU (2 ll.); PHi; OClWHi; PP. 10547

FATHER Tammany's Almanac for 1801. By Joshua Sharp. Philadelphia: John M'Culloch. 18 ll. PDoBHi (ntp; imprint assumed from advertisements at end) 10548

FATHER Tammany's Almanac for 1801. By Joshua Sharp. Philadelphia: Wm. Young. 18 ll. MB. 10549

Der GEMEINNÜTZIGE Americanische Kalender auf 1801. Reading: Jacob Schneider. 20 ll. MWA (19 ll.); DeWint. 10550

HARPER'S Almanac for 1801. Chambersburg: R. &
G. K. Harper. CSmH (11 ll.)   10551

Der HOCH-DEUTSCHE Americanische Calender auf
1801. Germantaun: Michael Billmeyer. 20 ll. DLC;
N; NN; CtY; DeWint; PAtM; PHi.   10552

The MASONIC Almanac and Pocket Companion for [July
through December] 1801. Philadelphia: John Bioren,
for John Rain. 24 ll. PPFM.   10553

M'CULLOCH'S Pocket Almanac for 1801. Philadelphia:
J. M'Culloch. 16 ll. MWA; DLC; PHi.   10554

Der NEUE Allgemein Nützliche Volks-Calender auf
1801. Lancaster: Christian Jacob Hutter. 20 ll.
MWA (impf); DLC; NBuG.   10555

Der NEUE, Gemeinnützige Landwirthschafts Calender
auf 1801. Lancaster: Johann Albrecht und Comp. 22 ll.
MWA; DLC; CLU; InU; WHi; P; PHi; PPCS; PPG;
PAnL (10 ll.); PLHi; PYHi.   10556

NEUER Hauswirthschafts Calender auf 1801. Philadelphia: Henrich Schweitzer. 22 ll. MWA (21 ll.); DLC;
PHi (20 ll.); PPL (20 ll.)   10557

NEUER Hauswirthschafts Calender auf 1801. Reading:
Jungmann und Bruckmann. 23 ll. P (18 ll.); PHi (22
ll.); PPeSchw (impf); PRHi.   10558

The PENNSYLVANIA Almanac for 1801. Philadelphia:
Francis and Robert Bailey. 18 ll. MWA (impf); DLC;
PHi.   10559

The PENNSYLVANIA, New-Jersey, Delaware, Maryland and Virginia Almanac for 1801. By Joshua Sharp.
Philadelphia: Peter Stewart. 20 ll. MWA; DLC; NjR;
InU; OHi; PP; PPPrHi.   10560

PENNSYLVANISCHER Calender auf 1801. York: Salomon Mayer. 20 ll. PPi.   10561

Pennsylvania - 1801

The PITTSBURH [sic] Almanack for 1801. By John
Israel. Pittsburgh: 18 ll. MWA (imprint lacking) 10562

POOR Richard improved: being an Almanack and Ephem-
eris for 1801. By Richard Saunders. Philadelphia:
Hall & Sellers. 18 ll. MWA; MH; CSmH; PDoBHi;
PHi.   10563

POOR Will's Almanack for 1801. Philadelphia: Joseph
and James Crukshank. 18 ll. MWA; DLC (16 ll.);
NN (impf); MB; MiD-B; CtY; WHi; PDoBHi.   10564

POOR Will's Pocket Almanack for 1801. Philadelphia:
Joseph & James Crukshank. 24 ll. MWA; DLC; NHi;
PHi; PP; NjR (22 ll.)   10565

POULSON'S Town and Country Almanac for 1801.
Philadelphia: Zachariah Poulson, Junior. 24 ll. MWA;
DLC; N (impf); CLU; InU; NBuG; P; PHi; PPL;
PPPrHi; PPiU; PU.   10566

The UNITED States Almanac for 1801. Harrisburgh:
John Wyeth. 18 ll. PHi (17 ll.)   10567

UNITED States Almanac for 1801. Reading: Jungmann
und Bruckmann. 20 ll. MWA; P.   10568

Der VEREINIGTEN Staaten Calender auf 1801. Philadel-
phia: G. Helmhold und J. Geyer. 21 ll. NHi; PHi.
                                                  10569
The WESTERN Calendar: or, An Almanack for 1801.
Pittsburgh: John Scull. 18 ll. MWA.   10570

The ALMANACK for 1802. Greensburgh: Snowden and
McCorkle. PPiU (17 ll.)   10571

ALMANAC American pour 1802. A Philadelphia. [np]
112 ll. MWA; DLC; ViU; PHi; PPL; PU.   10572

AMERICAN Repository, and Annual Register of the U-
nited States for 1802. Philadelphia: B. Davies. [Sabin]
                                                  10573
AMERICANISCHER Calender auf 1802. Harrisburg:

Pennsylvania - 1802

Benjamin Mayer. 20 ll. DLC; NBuG; PPCS.   10574

AMERICANISCHER Stadt und Land Calender auf 1802. Philadelphia: Carl Cist. 22 ll. MWA; DLC; PAtM; PHi (ntp)   10575

CAREY'S Franklin Almanack for 1802. By Abraham Shoemaker. Philadelphia: Mathew Carey. 24 ll. MWA; DLC; N (impf); NjR (23 ll.); NBuG; MB; MH; CtY; CLU (impf); PDoBHi (20 ll.); PHi; PPL; InU.   10576

CITIZEN'S and Farmer's Almanac for 1802. Philadelphia: John M'Culloch. 18 ll. MWA (17 ll.); PHi; PPiU (12 ll.)   10577

DICKSON'S Balloon Almanac for 1802. Lancaster: W. & R. Dickson. 20 ll. Hostetter.   10578

FATHER Abraham's Almanac for 1802. Philadelphia: John Conrad & Co.; Baltimore: M. & U. Conrad & Co.; Washington City: Rapin, Conrad & Co. 20 ll. DLC (19 ll.); OHi.   10579

FATHER Abraham's Almanac for 1802. Philadelphia: H. & P. Rice. 20 ll. MWA (impf); DeWint; NbHi.
10580

FATHER Abraham's Almanac for 1802. Philadelphia: Peter Stewart. 20 ll. MWA; NN (16 ll.); NjR (14 ll., ntp); InU (ntp); NCH; PHi (impf); PDoBHi.   10581

FATHER Tammany's Almanac for 1802. By Joshua Sharp. Philadelphia: William Young. 18 ll. MWA; DLC; InU (ntp); MiU-C; PHi.   10582

Der GEMEINÜZIGE Americanische Calender auf 1802. Reading: Jacob Schneider und Comp. 20 ll. MWA; DLC (17 ll.); N; DeWint; InU; PHi; PPG.   10583

Der HOCH-DEUTSCHE Americanische Calender auf 1802. Germantaun: Michael Billmeyer. 20 ll. MWA; DLC; PHi; PPG; PPL (18 ll.); PPeSchw.   10584

M'CULLOCH'S Pocket Almanac for 1802. Philadelphia:

J. M'Culloch. 16 ll. MWA; PHi; PU. 10585

Der NEUE Allgemein Nützliche Volks-Calender auf
1802. Lancaster: Christian Jacob Hutter. 19 ll. MWA;
PPi. 10586

Der NEUE, Gemeinnützige Landwirthschafts Calender
auf 1802. Lancaster: Johann Albrecht. 22 ll. MWA
(impf); DLC; DeWint; P; PHi; PPG; PPeSchw; PYHi.
10587
NEUER Hauswirthschafts Calender auf 1802. Philadelphia: Henrich Schweitzer. 24 ll. MWA; DLC (22 ll.);
PHi; WHi. 10588

NEUER Hauswirthschafts Calender auf 1802. Reading:
Jungmann und Bruckmann. 23 ll. PPeSchw. 10589

The PENNSYLVANIA, New-Jersey, Delaware, Maryland and Virginia Almanac for 1802. Philadelphia:
John Conrad & Co.; Baltimore: M. & J. Conrad & Co.;
Washington-City: Rapin, Conrad & Co. 20 ll. MWA;
DLC. 10590

The PENNSYLVANIA, New-Jersey, Delaware, Maryland
and Virginia Almanac for 1802. Philadelphia: H. & P.
Rice. 20 ll. DLC; NbHi. 10591

The PENNSYLVANIA, New-Jersey, Delaware, Maryland
and Virginia Almanac for 1802. Philadelphia: Peter
Stewart. 20 ll. MWA; NjR (12 ll., ntp) 10592

The PITTSBURGH Almanack for 1802. By John Israel.
Pittsburgh: Zadock Cramer. 24 ll. MWA; ODa (11 ll.,
ntp) 10593

POOR Robin's Almanac for 1802. By Joshua Sharp.
Philadelphia: D. Hogan. 18 ll. DLC. 10594

POOR Will's Almanack for 1802. Philadelphia: Joseph
and James Crukshank. 18 ll. MWA; DLC; NN (15 ll.);
MB; MH; CtY; InU; OCHP; MiD-B; PDoBHi; PHi; NjR.
10595
POOR Will's Pocket Almanack for 1802. Philadelphia:

Pennsylvania - 1802

Joseph & James Crukshank. 24 ll. MWA; NHi (23 ll.);
DeWint; PDoBHi; PP; PHi; PPL; NjR. 10596

POULSON'S Town and Country Almanac for 1802.
Philadelphia: John Bioren. 24 ll. MWA; DLC; NN;
NHi; Ct (22 ll.); OMC; InU; NBuG; MdBJ (23 ll.); N;
WHi; PHi; PDoBHi (impf); PP; PPL; Drake (two varieties) 10597

The UNITED States Almanac for 1802. Harrisburgh:
John Wyeth. MWA (19 ll.) 10598

Der VEREINIGTEN Staaten Calender auf 1802. Philadelphia: J. Geyer. 21 ll. PHi (impf) 10599

The WESTERN Calendar: or, An Almanack for 1802.
Pittsburgh: John Scull. 16 ll. MWA. 10600

The AMERICAN Ladies Pocket Book for 1803. Philadelphia: John Bioren, for William Birch. 77 ll. MnU.
10601

AMERICAN Ladies' Pocket-Book; or, Useful Register
for 1803. Philadelphia: Samuel F. Bradford, and John
Conrad and Co.; R. Carr, printer. 36 ll. PPL. 10602

The AMERICAN Repository, and Annual Register of the
United States for 1803. Philadelphia: B. Davies; J.
W. Scott, printer. 52 ll. MH; PHi. 10603

AMERICANISCHER Stadt und Land Calender auf 1803.
Philadelphia: Carl Cist. 24 ll. MWA; DLC; NN; PHi;
PPG; PYHi. 10604

CAREY'S Franklin Almanack for 1803. By Abraham
Shoemaker. Philadelphia: John Adams. 24 ll. PHi;
PPL; NjR. 10605

CAREY'S Franklin Almanack for 1803. By Abraham
Shoemaker. Philadelphia: John Adams, for M. Carey.
24 ll. MWA; DLC; N; Ct; InU; WHi; PHi. 10606

CITIZEN'S and Farmer's Almanac for 1803. Philadelphia: John M'Culloch. 18 ll. PHi. 10607

DICKSON'S Balloon Almanac for 1803. Lancaster: W.
& R. Dickson. 20 ll. MWA; DLC; InU; PHi. 10608

FATHER Abraham's Almanac for 1803. Philadelphia:
Peter Stewart. 20 ll. MWA; DLC; MiU-C; PHi. 10609

FATHER Tammany's Almanac for 1803. Philadelphia:
William Young. 18 ll. DLC. 10610

Der GEMEINÜZIGE Americanische Calender auf 1803.
Reading: Schneider und Ritter. 20 ll. MWA; DLC;
DeWint; WHi; P; PHi; PPeSchw; PR. 10611

Der HOCH-DEUTSCHE Americanische Calender auf
1803. Germantaun: Michael Billmeyer. 20 ll. MWA;
DLC; CLU; CtY; DeWint; PPCS (6 ll.); PHi. 10612

M'CULLOCH'S Pocket Almanac for 1803. Philadelphia:
John M'Culloch. [Spieseke] 10613

Der NEUE Allgemein Nützliche Volks-Calender auf
1803. Lancaster: Christian Jacob Hutter. 19 ll. MWA;
PPi. 10614

Der NEUE, Gemeinnützige Landwirthschafts Calender
auf 1803. Lancaster: Johann Albrecht. 22 ll. MWA;
DLC; OClWHi; NjP (19 ll.); DeWint; WHi; P; PPG;
PHi; PPL; PPeSchw; PYHi. 10615

NEUER Hauswirthschafts Calender auf 1803. Philadelphia: Henrich Schweitzer. 24 ll. MWA; DeWint; PHi
(22 ll.); PPL (ntp) 10616

NEUER Hauswirthschafts Calender auf 1803. Reading:
Jungmann und Bruckmann. 21 ll. MWA. 10617

The PENNSYLVANIA Almanac for 1803. By Abraham
Shoemaker. Philadelphia: John Adams, for J. Johnson.
24 ll. MWA; PHi. 10618

The PENNSYLVANIA, New-Jersey, Delaware, Maryland
and Virginia Almanac for 1803. Philadelphia: Peter
Stewart. 20 ll. MWA; N; CLU; PPiU. 10619

The PITTSBURGH Almanack for 1803. Pittsburgh: Zadok Cramer; John Israel, printer. 24 ll. MWA (18 ll.); InHi (tp only); PPi; PPiU. 10620

A POCKET Almanac for 1803. Philadelphia: J. M'Culloch. 16 ll. MWA; DLC; PHi. 10621

POOR Robin's Almanac for 1803. By Joshua Sharp. Philadelphia: David Hogan. 24 ll. MWA; DLC; PHi (25 ll.) 10622

POOR Will's Almanack for 1803. Philadelphia: Joseph and James Crukshank. 24 ll. MWA; DLC; NN; MH; InU; MnU; PDoBHi; PHi (27 ll.); NjR; Drake. 10623

POOR Will's Pocket Almanack for 1803. Philadelphia: Joseph & James Crukshank. 24 ll. MWA; DLC; NHi; DeWint; InU; PHi; PP. 10624

POULSON'S Town and Country Almanac for 1803. By Abraham Shoemaker. Philadelphia: John Bioren. 24 ll. MWA (two varieties); DLC; NHi (impf); NBuG; CLU; KyLo; PHi; PPL (20 ll.) 10625

POULSON'S Town and Country Almanac for 1803. By Abraham Shoemaker. Philadelphia: John Bioren for John Conrad & Co.; M. and J. Conrad and Co. 24 ll. CtLHi; NjHi; OHi. 10626

POULSON'S Town and Country Almanac for 1803. By Abraham Shoemaker. Philadelphia: John Bioren, for Benjamin Johnson and Jacob Johnson. 24 ll. MWA; NN (19 ll.); NHi; N; MB; CtY; PHi; PDoBHi (impf); PHC; PPL; NjR (20 ll.); Drake. 10627

Der VEREINIGTEN Staaten Calender auf 1803. Philadelphia: Johann Geyer. [Seidensticker] 10628

The WESTERN Calendar; or, An Almanack for 1803. Washington: John Colerick. 18 ll. PPi. 10629

AMERICANISCHER Stadt und Land Calender auf 1804. Philadelphia: Carl Cist. 24 ll. DLC; P (21 ll.);

PHi. 10630

CAREY'S Franklin Almanac for 1804. By Abraham Shoemaker. Philadelphia: M. Carey. 24 ll. DLC; CLU; CtY. 10631

CITIZEN'S and Farmer's Almanac for 1804. By Joshua Sharp. Philadelphia: John M'Culloch. 18 ll. MWA; Drake (20 ll.) 10632

DICKSON'S Balloon Almanac for 1804. Lancaster: William Dickson. 20 ll. MWA; DLC; PHi. 10633

FATHER Abraham's Almanac for 1804. Philadelphia: H. & P. Rice. 16 ll. DLC. 10634

FATHER Abraham's Almanac for 1804. Philadelphia: Peter Stewart. 18 ll. MWA; NN; NjR (10 ll., ntp); Drake. 10635

FATHER Abraham's Almanac for 1804. Philadelphia: William W. Woodward. 18 ll. P. 10636

FATHER Tammany's Almanack for 1804. Philadelphia. [Sabin 23911] 10637

Der HOCH-DEUTSCHE Americanische Calender auf 1804. Germantaun: Michael Billmeyer. 20 ll. MWA; DLC; CtY; DeWint; PHi; PPL (19 ll.); PPeSchw; PYHi.
10638

JOHNSON'S Pennsylvania and New-Jersey Almanac for 1804. By Joshua Sharp. Philadelphia: B. Johnson; J. Johnson; R. Johnson. 18 ll. MWA; DLC; NN; NHi; N; NjR; InU; MiU-C; Ct; P; Drake. 10639

JOHNSON'S Pennsylvania and New-Jersey Almanac for 1804. By Joshua Sharp. Philadelphia: Jacob Johnson. 16 ll. PDoBHi. 10640

The MAGAZINE Almanack for 1804. Pittsburgh: John Israel for Zadock Cramer. MWA (17 ll.) 10641

M'CULLOCH'S Pocket Almanac for 1804. Philadelphia:

Pennsylvania - 1804

J. MᶜCulloch. 16 ll. MWA; DLC; DeWint; NBuG; PHi.
10642

Der NEUE, Gemeinnütziger Landwirthschafts Calender auf 1804. Lancaster: Johann Albrecht. 22 ll. MWA; DLC; NN; NjP (impf); CtY; DeWint; InU (impf); P; PHi; PLHi; PPCS; PPG; PPeSchw; PYHi. 10643

NEUER Hauswirthschafts Calender auf 1804. Philadelphia: Jacob Meyer. 24 ll. CLU (23 ll.) 10644

NEUER Hauswirthschafts Calender auf 1804. Philadelphia: Henrich Schweitzer. 24 ll. MWA; N; PHi. 10645

NEUER Hauswirthschafts Calender auf 1804. Reading: Jungmann und Bruckmann. 21 ll. P (20 ll.); PPL (20 ll.); PPi. 10646

PENNSYLVANIA, New-Jersey, Delaware, Maryland and Virginia Almanac for 1804. Philadelphia: H. & P. Rice. 18 ll. DeWint. 10647

PENNSYLVANIA, New-Jersey, Delaware, Maryland and Virginia Almanac for 1804. Philadelphia: Peter Stewart. 18 ll. MWA; DLC; ViHi; Drake. 10648

PENNSYLVANIA, New-Jersey, Delaware, Maryland and Virginia Almanac for 1804. Philadelphia: William W. Woodward. 18 ll. PHi. 10649

The PITTSBURGH Almanack for 1804. By John Israel. Pittsburgh: Zadock Cramer. 20 ll. MWA (18 ll.)
10650

The PITTSBURGH Magazine Almanack for 1804. Pittsburgh: Zadock Cramer; John Israel, printer. 30 ll. MWA; InU (26 ll., ntp); PPi. 10651

POOR Robin's Almanac for 1804. By Joshua Sharp. Philadelphia: D. Hogan. 20 ll. PHi. 10652

POOR Will's Almanack for 1804. Philadelphia: Joseph and James Crukshank. 24 ll. MWA; DLC; NjHi (20 ll.); MH; NBuG; InU (ntp); PDoBHi (ntp); PHC; PHi; Drake. 10653

POOR Will's Pocket Almanack for 1804. Philadelphia:
Joseph & James Crukshank. 24 ll. MWA; DLC; PHi;
PP; NjR. 10654

POULSON'S Town and Country Almanac for 1804. By
Abraham Shoemaker. Philadelphia: John Bioren. 24 ll.
MWA (21 ll.); DLC; N; NHi; CLU; InU; PHi; PP;
PPL (23 ll.); PPiU; Drake. 10655

SHEET Almanac for 1804. Philadelphia: John M'Culloch. Broadside. MWA. 10656

Der VEREINIGTEN Staaten Calender auf 1804. Philadelphia: Johann Geyer. 20 ll. DeWint. 10657

WEEMS'S Washington Almanack for 1804. By Abraham
Shoemaker. Philadelphia: John Adams. 24 ll. MWA
(two varieties, both impf); NNC; Vi; MB; OHi (22 ll.);
InU (impf); ViRVal; Drake. 10658

The WESTERN Calendar: or, an Almanack for 1804.
Washington: John Colerick. 18 ll. NN (8 ll.) 10659

The AMERICAN Ladies Pocket Book for 1805. Philadelphia: John Bioren. 72 ll. MWA. 10660

AMERICANISCHER Stadt und Land Calender auf 1805.
Philadelphia: Carl Cist. 24 ll. MWA; DLC; NN (23
ll.); N; PAtM; PHi; PPG; PPL; PYHi. 10661

ANNUAL Counting-House Sheet Almanac for 1805. Philadelphia: John Bioren. Broadside. Private collection.
10662

CAREY'S Franklin Almanack for 1805. By Abraham
Shoemaker. Philadelphia: Mathew Carey; Trenton: J.
J. Wilson, printer. 24 ll. MWA; DLC; InU (ntp);
WHi; PHi; PPL (28 ll.); Drake. 10663

CITIZEN'S and Farmer's Almanac for 1805. By Joshua
Sharp. Philadelphia: John M'Culloch. 18 ll. MWA;
DLC; NN; NjR; N; PHi; Drake (20 ll.) 10664

DICKSON'S Balloon Almanac for 1805. Lancaster:

William Dickson. 18 ll. MWA; DLC; NN (16 ll.);
DeWint; MoSHi; PDoBHi (14 ll.); PHC.   10665

FATHER Abraham's Almanac for 1805. Philadelphia:
Benjamin Johnson. 20 ll. MWA.   10666

FATHER Abraham's Almanac for 1805. Philadelphia:
Benjamin Johnson; Jacob Johnson; Robert Johnson; P.
Stewart, printer. 18 ll. PPL.   10667

FATHER Abraham's Almanac for 1805. Philadelphia:
Peter Stewart. 18 ll. MWA (16 ll.); DLC; PHi (impf);
PP; NjR (10 ll., ntp); Drake.   10668

FATHER Tammany's Almanac for 1805. By Joshua
Sharp. Philadelphia: W. W. Woodward. 18 ll. DLC;
PHC (imprint lacking)   10669

Der GEMEINÜZIGE Americanische Calender auf 1805.
Reading: Johann Ritter und Comp. 20 ll. MWA; CtY;
P; PHi; PR; PRHi.   10670

Der HOCH-DEUTSCHE Americanische Calender auf 1805.
Germantaun: Michael Billmeyer. 20 ll. MWA; DLC;
NN; CLU; CtY; NBuG; WHi; PHi; PPAmP; PPG;
PYHi.   10671

JOHNSON'S Pennsylvania and New-Jersey Almanack for
1805. By Abraham Shoemaker. Philadelphia: John
Bioren for B. Johnson, J. Johnson, R. Johnson. 24 ll.
MWA; DLC; NN (19 ll.); N; PHi; PPL.   10672

KIMBER'S Almanac for 1805. By Enoch Lewis. Philadelphia: Emmor Kimber; Solomon W. Conrad, printer.
24 ll. MWA; DLC; NN; NBLiHi; CLU; InU; N; PP;
PPAmP.   10673

M'CULLOCH'S Pocket Almanac for 1805. Philadelphia:
J. M'Culloch. 16 ll. MWA; DLC; DeWint; PHi. 10674

Der NEUE, Americanische Landwirthschafts Calender
auf 1805. Reading: Johann Ritter. 18 ll. PPG. 10675

Pennsylvania - 1805

Der NEUE, Gemeinnütziger Landwirthschafts Calender auf 1805. Lancaster: Johann Albrecht. 22 ll. MWA; N; NHi; CLU; InU; DeWint; WHi; PHi; P; PLHi; PPL; PPCS; PPeSchw; PYHi. 10676

NEUER Hauswirthschafts Calender auf 1805. Philadelphia: Henrich Schweitzer. 24 ll. DLC (22 ll.); DeWint; PDoBHi (23 ll.); PHi; PPG; PPL (ntp) 10677

NEUER Hauswirthschafts-Calender auf 1805. Reading: Jungmann und Bruckmann. 20 ll. DLC; MH; WHi. 10678

The PENNSYLVANIA, New-Jersey, Delaware, Maryland and Virginia Almanac for 1805. Philadelphia: Benjamin Johnson; Jacob Johnson; Robert Johnson; P. Stewart, printer. 18 ll. NN (20 ll.); Ct; NbHi; PHi. 10679

The PENNSYLVANIA, New-Jersey, Delaware, Maryland and Virginia Almanac for 1805. Philadelphia: Peter Stewart. 18 ll. MWA; DLC; InU; PHi; PPL (6 ll.); Drake. 10680

The PENNSYLVANIA Pocket Almanac for 1805. Philadelphia: John Bioren. 18 ll. DLC. 10681

-- With added leaf: "New Table of High Water." 19 ll. PHi. 10682

The PITTSBURGH Almanack for 1805. By John Taylor. Pittsburgh: Zadok Cramer. 18 ll. OMC (17 ll.); PPiU. 10683

-- Issue with 30 ll. PPi (29 ll.) 10684

The PITTSBURGH Magazine Almanack for 1805. By John Taylor. Pittsburgh: Zadok Cramer. 18 ll. MWA (impf); NN; OClWHi. 10685

The PITTSBURGH Pocket Almanac for 1805. By John Taylor. Pittsburgh: Zadock Cramer. 12 ll. PPi. 10686

The PITTSBURGH Republican Calendar for 1805. Pittsburgh: John Israel. 18 ll. PPi. 10687

POOR Robin's Almanac for 1805. By Joshua Sharp.
Philadelphia: D. Hogan. 24 ll. MWA. 10688

-- Issue with 26 ll. Drake. 10689

POOR Will's Almanack for 1805. Philadelphia: James
Crukshank. 24 ll. MWA; DLC; N; NBuG; InU; CtY;
Drake. 10690

-- Issue with 26 ll. PHi. 10691

POOR Will's Pocket Almanack for 1805. Philadelphia:
James Crukshank. 24 ll. MWA; NHi; InU; PHi; PP.
10692

POULSON'S Town and Country Almanac for 1805. By
Abraham Shoemaker. Philadelphia: John Bioren. 24 ll.
MWA (two varieties); DLC; NN; NHi; CLU; MB; OHi;
InU; N; OCHP; PDoBHi (impf); PHC; PHi; PPL; NjR
(21 ll.); Drake. 10693

Der VEREINIGTEN Staaten Calender auf 1805. Philadelphia: Johann Geyer. 21 ll. DLC; NN (20 ll.); PHi;
PPG. 10694

The WESTERN Calendar: or, An Almanack for 1805.
Washington: Printed for the benefit of the family of the
late John Colerick. MWA (15 ll.) 10695

AMERICANISCHER Stadt und Land Calender auf 1806.
Philadelphia: Carl Cist. 22 ll. MWA; DLC; NN; PHi;
PPi. 10696

ANNUAL Counting-House Sheet Almanac for 1806. Philadelphia: John Bioren. Advertised in "Poulson's Town
and Country Almanac," for 1806. 10697

CAREY'S Franklin Almanack for 1806. By Abraham
Shoemaker. Philadelphia: Mathew Carey; John Bioren,
printer. 24 ll. MWA; DLC; NN; WHi; P; PHi (impf);
PPAmP. 10698

CITIZEN'S and Farmer's Almanac for 1806. By Joshua
Sharp. Philadelphia: John M'Culloch. 18 ll. MWA;

DLC; NjP (16 ll.); PHi (impf)　　　　　　　　10699

CRAMER'S Pittsburgh Almanack for 1806. Pittsburgh: Zadock Cramer. 18 ll. MWA; OClWHi; OHi; NjP; PPiU (15 ll., ntp)　　　　　　　　10700

CRAMER'S Pittsburgh Magazine Almanack for 1806. Pittsburgh: Zadock Cramer. 30 ll. MWA; OClWHi; OMC (8 ll.); PPi.　　　　　　　　10701

DICKSON'S Balloon Almanac for 1806. Lancaster: William Dickson. 20 ll. MWA (19 ll.); P (impf); PHi.　　　　　　　　10702

FATHER Abraham's Almanac for 1806. By Joshua Sharp. Philadelphia: Peter Stewart. 18 ll. MWA (16 ll.); CtY; MHi; MoSHi; PHi; NjR.　　　　　　　　10703

FATHER Abraham's Almanac for 1806. By Joshua Sharp. Philadelphia: William W. Woodward. 18 ll. MWA (16 ll.); MoSHi.　　　　　　　　10704

FATHER Tammany's Almanack for 1806. Philadelphia. [Sabin 23911]　　　　　　　　10705

Der GEMEINNÜTZIGE Americanische Calender auf 1806. Reading: Johann Ritter und Comp. 20 ll. PHi; PRHi.　　　　　　　　10706

Der HOCH-DEUTSCHE Americanische Calender auf 1806. Germantaun: Michael Billmeyer. 20 ll. MWA; DLC; NBuG; P (impf); PAtM; PHi; PPG; PPeSchw.　　　　　　　　10707

KIMBER, Conrad, & Co.'s Almanac for 1806. By Enoch Lewis. Philadelphia: Kimber, Conrad, & Co. 24 ll. MWA; DLC; InU; P; PDoBHi (16 ll.); PHi; PPL; PHC.　　　　　　　　10708

M'CULLOCH'S Pocket Almanac for 1806. Philadelphia: J. M'Culloch. 16 ll. MWA.　　　　　　　　10709

Der NEUE Americanische Landwirthschafts Calender auf 1806. Reading: Johann Ritter & Comp. PRHi.　10710

Der NEUE, Gemeinnützige Landwirthschafts Calender

Pennsylvania - 1806

auf 1806. Lancaster: Johann Albrecht. 22 ll. MWA; NHi (21 ll.); NjR (21 ll.); DeWint; InU; WHi; P; PHi; PLHi; PPeSchw; PYHi.   10711

NEUER Hauswirthschafts-Calender auf 1806. Reading: Jungmann und Bruckmann. 16 ll. MWA; DLC; MH; InU (ntp)   10712

The PENNSYLVANIA, New-Jersey, Delaware, Maryland and Virginia Almanac for 1806. By Joshua Sharp. Philadelphia: Peter Stewart. 18 ll. MWA (two varieties); DLC; NjR (two varieties); InU (16 ll.)   10713

The PENNSYLVANIA Pocket Almanack for 1806. Philadelphia: John Bioren. 18 ll. MWA; DLC; InU.   10714

POOR Robin's Almanac for 1806. By Joshua Sharp. Philadelphia: David Hogan. 20 ll. MWA; DLC (impf)   10715

POOR Will's Almanack for 1806. Philadelphia: James Crukshank. 18 ll. MWA; NHi; Ct; MnU; NBuG; WHi; PHi.   10716

POOR Will's Pocket Almanac for 1806. Philadelphia: J. Crukshank. 24 ll. MWA (23 ll.); NN; PHi; PP; NjR.   10717

POULSON'S Town and Country Almanac for 1806. By Abraham Shoemaker. Philadelphia: John Bioren. 24 ll. MWA; NHi; CLU; MdBJ; PHi; PP; PPAmP; PDoBHi (impf); PHC; PPL; NjR (12 ll.); Drake.   10718

POULSON'S Town and Country Almanac for 1806. By Abraham Shoemaker. Philadelphia: John Bioren, for Conrad & Co. 24 ll. MWA (two varieties); DLC; NN (impf); N; InU; PPL.   10719

Der VEREINIGTEN Staaten Calender auf 1806. Philadelphia: Johann Geyer. 21 ll. MWA (20 ll.); PHi.   10720

The WASHINGTON Almanac for 1806. By Andrew Beers. Philadelphia: Robert Stewart. 18 ll. MWA.   10721

The WESTERN Calendar: or, An Almanack for 1806. Washington: Printed for the benefit of the family of the late John Colerick. 12 ll. MWA. 10722

AMERICANISCHER Stadt und Land Calender auf 1807. Philadelphia: Carl Cist's Witwe. 21 ll. MWA; N; NN; DeWint; PHi; PPCS. 10723

AMERICANISCHER Stadt und Land Calender auf 1807. Philadelphia: Conrad Zentler. 22 ll. DLC; CLU; PPG; PPL (21 ll.) 10724

ANNUAL Counting-House Sheet Almanac for 1807. Philadelphia: John Bioren. Broadside. Advertised in "Poulson's Town and Country Almanac" for 1807. 10725

BAILEY'S Rittenhouse Almanac for 1807. Philadelphia: Pryor; R. Bailey, printer. 24 ll. MWA; PHi; NjR; Drake. 10726

BAILEY'S Rittenhouse Almanac for 1807. By Abraham Shoemaker. Philadelphia: R. Bailey. 24 ll. NjR. 10727

BIOREN'S Pennsylvania Pocket Remembrancer for 1807. Philadelphia: John Bioren. 16 ll. MWA (ntp) 10728

CAREY'S Franklin Almanac for 1807. By Abraham Shoemaker. Philadelphia: M. Carey. 24 ll. MWA; OClWHi; PHi; WHi; NjR (23 ll.) 10729

CITIZEN'S and Farmer's Almanac for 1807. Philadelphia: 18 ll. PPiU. 10730

CRAMER'S Pittsburgh Almanack for 1807. [Pittsburgh:] Zadok Cramer. 18 ll. DLC; ICHi; InU (tp only); OClWHi; OHi; MiU-C; PHi; PPi. 10731

-- Issue with 28 ll. PPiU. 10732

CRAMER'S Pittsburgh Magazine Almanack for 1807. Pittsburgh: Zadock Cramer. 30 ll. MWA; InU (28 ll.); OCHP. 10733

Pennsylvania - 1807

-- Issue with 31 ll. MWA. 10734

The CUMBERLAND Almanac for 1807. Carlisle: A. Loudon. Advertised in the "Cumberland Register," September 23, 1806. 10735

DICKINSON College Almanac for 1807. Carlisle: George Kline for Archibald Loudon. [Thompson] 10736

DICKINSON College Almanac for 1807. By D. P. Carlisle: A. Loudon. 20 ll. CtY; PHi. 10737

DICKSON'S Balloon Almanac for 1807. Lancaster: William Dickson. 20 ll. MWA; DeWint; PHi. 10738

FATHER Abraham's Almanac for 1807. By Joshua Sharp. Philadelphia: Peter Stewart. 18 ll. MWA (two varieties); DLC; CtY; NN; NjR (14 ll., ntp); PHi. 10739

FATHER Abraham's Almanac for 1807. By Joshua Sharp. Philadelphia: William W. Woodward. 18 ll. MWA. 10740

FATHER Tammany's Almanack for 1807. Philadelphia. [Sabin 23911] 10741

The GENTLEMAN'S Annual Pocket Remembrancer for 1807. Philadelphia: John Bioren. 88 ll. MWA. 10742

Der HOCH-DEUTSCHE Americanische Calender auf 1807. Germantaun: Michael Billmeyer. 21 ll. MWA; DLC (16 ll.); N; NN; DeWint; InU; P (19 ll.); PHi; PPeSchw; PPi. 10743

JOHNSON'S Almanac for 1807. By Joshua Sharp. Philadelphia: Benj. Johnson; Jacob Johnson; Robert Johnson; Bennett & Walton. 24 ll. MWA; N (impf); InU; Ct (23 ll.); PHi; PPL (22 ll.); Drake. 10744

JOHNSON'S Pennsylvania and New-Jersey Almanac for 1807. By Joshua Sharp. Philadelphia: Benj. Johnson; Jacob Johnson; Robert Johnson; Bennett & Walton. 24 ll. MWA; DLC; NjR; N; InU; CtY; PHi; PP;

Drake.   10745

MᶜCULLOCH'S Pocket Almanac for 1807.   Philadelphia:
J. MᶜCulloch. 16 ll. MWA; DLC; PHi.   10746

MINER'S Pennsylvania & New-Jersey Almanac for 1807.
By Joshua Sharp.   Doylestown: Asher Miner. 18 ll.
MWA (16 ll.); PDoBHi (impf); PPAmP.   10747

Der NEUE Americanische Landwirthschafts Calender
auf 1807. Reading: Johann Ritter und Comp. [Seiden-
sticker]   10748

Der NEUE Gemeinnützige Landwirthschafts Calender auf
1807. Lancaster: Johann Albrecht. 22 ll. MWA; NN;
N; NjR (two varieties, one 20 ll., one 5 ll.); CLU;
InU; DeWint; MiD-B; P; PLHi; PHi; PPCS; PPG;
PPeSchw; PYHi; WHi.   10749

Der NEUE, Gemeinnützige Landwirhtschafts [sic] Calender auf 1807. Lancaster: Johann Albrecht. 22 ll.
PPL.   10750

NEUER Hauswirthschafts-Calender auf 1807. Reading:
Gottlob Jungmann.   20 ll. MWA; DLC; PHi; PPL; PR.
                                                 10751
The NEW-JERSEY Town and Country-man's Almanac for
1807. By Joshua Sharp. Philadelphia: Joseph Lippincott. 18 ll. PHi (impf); PPL (12 ll.)   10752

The PENNSYLVANIA, New-Jersey, Delaware, Maryland
and Virginia Almanac for 1807. By Joshua Sharp.
Philadelphia: Jacob Johnson. 18 ll. MWA; DLC; N.
                                                 10753
The PENNSYLVANIA, New-Jersey, Delaware, Maryland
and Virginia Almanac for 1807. By Joshua Sharp.
Philadelphia: Peter Stewart. 18 ll. MWA; NjR; P;
PHi; PP.   10754

The PENNSYLVANIA Pocket Almanack for 1807. Philadelphia: John Bioren. 18 ll. DLC; NHi; PHi (15 ll.)
                                                 10755
The PITTSBURGH Magazine Almanack for 1807. Pitts-

Pennsylvania - 1807

burgh: MWA (wrappers only) 10756

POOR Robin's Almanac for 1807. By Joshua Sharp.
Philadelphia: D. Hogan. 21 ll. MWA; DLC. 10757

POOR Will's Almanack for 1807. Philadelphia: James
Crukshank. 24 ll. MWA; DLC; NN; InU; MH; MnU;
PHi; PPL. 10758

POOR Will's Pocket Almanack for 1807. Philadelphia:
J. Crukshank. 24 ll. MWA; DLC; PHi; PP; PPL;
NjR. 10759

POULSON'S Town and Country Almanack for 1807. By
Abraham Shoemaker. Philadelphia: John Bioren. 24 ll.
MWA; DLC (impf); NN (two varieties); NHi; PHC;
PHi; PPL; Drake. 10760

POULSON'S Town and Country Almanack for 1807. By
Abraham Shoemaker. Philadelphia: John Bioren, for
Kimber, Conrad, & Co. 24 ll. MWA; Drake. 10761

POULSON'S Town and Country Almanack for 1807. By
Abraham Shoemaker. Philadelphia: John Conrad, &
Co.; Baltimore: M. & J. Conrad & Co. 24 ll. NNA.
10762

Der VEREINIGTEN Staaten Calender auf 1807. Philadelphia: Johann Geyer. 20 ll. DLC; PHi (19 ll.)
10763

AMERICANISCHER Stadt und Land Calender auf 1808.
Philadelphia: Conrad Zentler. 21 ll. MWA (18 ll.);
DLC; PHi (ntp); PPCS (impf); PPL (19 ll.) 10764

The ANNUAL Compting House Sheet Almanac for 1808.
By Abraham Shoemaker. Philadelphia: John Bioren.
Broadside. Advertised in "Bioren's Town and Country
Almanack" for 1808. 10765

BAILEY'S Rittenhouse Almanac for 1808. By Abraham
Shoemaker. Philadelphia: R. Bailey. 22 ll. MWA;
PHi. 10766

BIOREN'S Town and Country Almanack for 1808. By

Abraham Shoemaker. Philadelphia: John Bioren. 24 ll.
MWA; DLC; NN (23 ll.); InU; MH; NRMA; PDoBHi
(impf); PHC; PHi; PPAmP. 10767

CAREY'S Franklin Almanac for 1808. By Abraham
Shoemaker. Philadelphia: Mathew Carey; Robert
Bailey, printer. 24 ll. MWA (impf); DLC (19 ll.);
MB; CtY; WHi; PHi (22 ll.); PP; PPL; PPiU. 10768

COCHRAN'S Philadelphia Almanac for 1808. By Abraham Shoemaker. Philadelphia: R. Cochran. 24 ll.
MWA; P (22 ll.) 10769

CRAMER'S Pittsburgh Almanack for 1808. [Pittsburgh:]
Zadok Cramer. 18 ll. KyU (16 ll., ntp); OHi; PPiU.
10770

CRAMER'S Pittsburgh Magazine Almanack for 1808.
[Pittsburgh:] Zadok Cramer. 30 ll. MWA; InU (28 ll.,
ntp); NjP (29 ll.); OClWHi; PHi (29 ll.); PPi. 10771

FATHER Abraham's Almanac for 1808. Philadelphia:
Peter Stewart. 18 ll. MWA; CtY. 10772

FATHER Abraham's Almanac for 1808. By Joshua
Sharp. Philadelphia: W. W. Woodward. 18 ll. DLC.
10773

FATHER Tammany's Almanack for 1808. Philadelphia.
[Sabin 23911] 10774

Der HOCH-DEUTSCHE Americanische Calender auf 1808.
Germantaun: Michael Billmeyer. 20 ll. MWA; DLC;
NN (19 ll.); CLU; CtY; NBuG; InU; WHi; DeWint; P
(16 ll.); PAtM; PDoBHi; PHi; PPCS; PPeSchw; PYHi.
10775

JOHNSON'S Almanac for 1808. By Joshua Sharp.
Philadelphia: Bennett & Walton. 24 ll. DLC. 10776

JOHNSON'S Almanac for 1808. By Joshua Sharp. Philadelphia: Benjamin Johnson; Jacob Johnson; Robert
Johnson; Bennett & Walton; Benjamin C. Buzby; Benjamin & Thomas Kite. 24 ll. MWA; DLC; N; InU;
MdBP; PHi; NjR (22 ll.) 10777

JOHNSON'S Pennsylvania & New-Jersey Almanac for 1808. By Joshua Sharp. Philadelphia: Benjamin Johnson; Jacob Johnson; Robert Johnson; Bennett & Walton; Benjamin C. Buzby; Benjamin & Thomas Kite. 24 ll. MWA; DLC; N; NjR; CtY; InU; MB; PHi; PPL; Drake (23 ll.) 10778

NEUE Americanische Landwirthschafts Calender auf 1808. Reading: Gottlob Jungmann. 15 ll. MWA (fragment) 10779

Der NEUE Americanische Landwirthschafts Calender auf 1808. Reading: Ritter und Retzler. [Seidensticker] 10780

Der NEUE, Gemeinnützige Landwirthschafts Calender auf 1808. Lancaster: Georg und Peter Albrecht. 20 ll. MWA (impf); NN; NjR (13 ll.); DeWint; P; PHi; PLHi; PPCS; PPG; PPL (18 ll.); PPeSchw; PYHi; PPi. 10781

NEUER Hauswirthschafts Calender auf 1808. Libanon: J. Schnee. 20 ll. PAnL. 10782

NEUER Hauswirthschafts Calender auf 1808. Philadelphia: Heinrich Schweitzer; Libanon: J. Schnee. 22 ll. MWA; DLC; DeWint (20 ll.); InU (20 ll.) 10783

NEUER Hauswirthschafts Calender auf 1808. Reading: Gottlob Jungmann. 20 ll. PPG; PRHi. 10784

The NEW Jersey Town & Country Almanac for 1808. By Joshua Sharp. Philadelphia: Printed for the Purchasers. 12 ll. MWA; NjR (28 ll.) CtY. 10785

The PENNSYLVANIA, New-Jersey, Delaware, Maryland and Virginia Almanac for 1808. By Joshua Sharp. Philadelphia: Peter Stewart. 18 ll. MWA; DLC; NHi; InU; PHi (impf) 10786

The PENNSYLVANIA, New-Jersey, Delaware, Maryland, and Virginia Almanac for 1808. By Joshua Sharp. Philadelphia: William W. Woodward. MWA (10 ll.) 10787

The PENNSYLVANIA Pocket Almanack for 1808. Philadelphia: John Bioren. 24 ll. MWA; MH; NBuG; P; PHi. 10788

POOR Richard Improved: An Almanack for 1808. By Richard Saunders. Philadelphia: Hall & Pierie. 24 ll. PDoBHi (17 ll.) 10789

POOR Robin's Almanac for 1808. By Joshua Sharp. Philadelphia: D. Hogan. 20 ll. MWA. 10790

POOR Will's Almanack for 1808. Philadelphia: J. Crukshank. 18 ll. MWA; CLU; InU; WHi; PHi; PDoBHi (ntp) 10791

POOR Will's Almanack for 1808. Philadelphia: James Crukshank. 18 ll. CtY; PPL; NjR (17 ll.) 10792

POOR Will's Almanack for 1808. Philadelphia: Kimber, Conrad, & Co. 18 ll. DLC; NjR. 10793

POOR Will's Pocket Almanack for 1808. Philadelphia: J. Crukshank. 24 ll. MWA; DLC; DeWint; PHi; PP; NjR; Drake. 10794

STEWART'S Washington Almanac for 1808. By Andrew Beers. Philadelphia: Robert Stewart. 18 ll. MWA; NN; InU (impf); NjHi; NjMoW; NjR. 10795

Der VEREINIGTEN Staaten Calender auf 1808. Philadelphia: Johann Geyer. 21 ll. MWA; DLC (20 ll.); PHi.
 10796

WASHINGTON Citizen and Farmer's Almanac for 1808. By Joshua Sharp. Philadelphia: Ebenezer M'Culloch. 24 ll. MWA; CtY; PHi; PPFM; Drake. 10797

The AMERICAN Ladies Pocket Book for 1809. Philadelphia: Wm. Y. Birch; John Bioren, printer. 72 ll. PHi (folded fashion-plate lacking) 10798

Der AMERICANISCHE Calender auf 1809. Harrisburg: Benjamin Mayer und Johann Hirschberger. 18 ll. PPL (impf) 10799

Pennsylvania - 1809

AMERICANISCHER Stadt und Land Calender auf 1809.
Philadelphia: Conrad Zentler. 21 ll. MWA; DLC (20
ll.); InU; PHi; PPeSchw. 10800

The ANNUAL Compting House Sheet Almanac for 1809.
Philadelphia: John Bioren. Broadside. Advertised in
"Bioren's Town and Country Almanac" for 1809. 10801

BAILEY'S Rittenhouse Almanac for 1809. By Abraham
Shoemaker. Philadelphia: Lydia R. Bailey. 24 ll.
MWA (two varieties); DLC; P; PHi; PP. 10802

BIOREN'S Town and Country Almanack for 1809. By
Abraham Shoemaker. Philadelphia: John Bioren. 24 ll.
MWA; DLC (23 ll.); N; NN; NjR; InU; PP; PHC;
PHi; PDoBHi (impf); PPL; Drake. 10803

CAREY'S Franklin Almanac for 1809. By Abraham
Shoemaker. Philadelphia: Mathew Carey; Lydia R.
Bailey, printer. 24 ll. MWA; DLC; N; NN; NjR; MH;
CtY; MiU-C; OHi (22 ll.); InU; WHi; P; PDoBHi;
PHi; Drake. 10804

COCHRAN'S Philadelphia Almanac for 1809. By Abraham Shoemaker. Philadelphia: Robert Cochran. 18 ll.
PHi; PPiU. 10805

CRAMER'S Pittsburgh Almanack for 1809. [Pittsburgh:]
Zadok Cramer; Cramer and Spear. 18 ll. MWA; DLC;
ICHi; NbHi; PPiU. 10806

CRAMER'S Pittsburgh Magazine Almanack for 1809.
Pittsburgh: Zadock Cramer; Cramer & Spear. 30 ll.
MWA; InU (29 ll.); NjP (29 ll.); InHi; PPi. 10807

The FARMERS Almanac for 1809. By John Taylor.
Pittsburgh: John Scull and William Foster. 18 ll. MWA.
10808
FATHER Abraham's Almanac for 1809. By Joshua
Sharp. Philadelphia: Peter Stewart. 18 ll. MWA; N;
NN; NjR (17 ll.); InU; PHi; Drake. 10809

FATHER Tammany's Almanac for 1809. By Joshua

Sharp. [Philadelphia:] W. M'Culloch. 18 ll. MWA; DLC.   10810

The GENTLEMAN'S Annual Pocket Remembrancer for 1809. Philadelphia: Wm. Y. Birch; John Bioren, printer. Advertised in "The American Ladies Pocket Book" for 1809.   10811

GRIMLER'S Town and Country Almanac for 1809. Lancaster: Benjamin Grimler. 18 ll. MWA; MoSHi.
  10812
Der HOCH-DEUTSCHE Americanische Calender auf 1809. Germantaun: Michael Billmeyer. 20 ll. MWA; DLC; CLU; CtY; NBuG; DeWint; PHi; PPAmP; PPCS; PPeSchw; PYHi.   10813

JOHNSON and Warner's Almanac for 1809. By Joshua Sharp. Philadelphia: Johnson and Warner. 18 ll. DLC.
  10814
JOHNSON'S Almanac for 1809. By Joshua Sharp. Philadelphia: Bennett and Walton; John Bouvier, printer. 24 ll. MWA; CLU; PHi; PP.   10815

JOHNSON'S Almanac for 1809. By Joshua Sharp. Philadelphia: Jacob Johnson. 24 ll. CtY.   10816

JOHNSON'S Almanac for 1809. By Joshua Sharp. Philadelphia: Johnson and Warner; John Bouvier, printer. 24 ll. MWA; MdBP; PHi.   10817

JOHNSON'S Almanac for 1809. By Joshua Sharp. Philadelphia: Benjamin and Thomas Kite. 24 ll. MWA; CtY.
  17118
JOHNSON'S Pennsylvania and New Jersey Almanac for 1809. By Joshua Sharp. Philadelphia: Johnson and Warner. 24 ll. MWA (impf)   10819

M'CULLOCH'S for 1809. Philadelphia: J. M'Culloch. 16 ll. MWA; DLC; PHi.   10820

Der NEUE Americanische Landwirthschafts Calender auf 1809. Reading: Johann Ritter und Comp. [Seidensticker]   10821

Der NEUE, Gemeinnützige Landwirthschafts Calender auf 1809. Lancaster: Georg und Peter Albrecht. 22 ll. MWA; DLC (18 ll.); NjR (4 ll.); DeWint; WHi; P; PHi; PYHi. 10822

NEUER Hauswirthschafts-Calender auf 1809. Carlisle: Frdr. Sanno. 20 ll. DeWint (19 ll.); PPG. 10823

NEUER Hauswirthschafts-Calender auf 1809. Libanon: Jacob Schnee. 20 ll. MWA; DLC (impf); CtY; DeWint; P (18 ll.); PAnL; PHi (17 ll.) 10824

The NEW Jersey Town & Country Almanac for 1809. By Joshua Sharp. Philadelphia: Joseph Lippincott. 16 ll. MWA; PHi (impf) 10825

PENNSYLVANIA, Jersey, Delaware, and Maryland Almanac for 1809. By Joshua Sharp. Philadelphia: Bennett and Walton; John Bouvier, printer. 24 ll. PHi (14 ll.); PPAmP; NjR. 10826

The PENNSYLVANIA, New-Jersey, Delaware, Maryland and Virginia Almanac for 1809. By Joshua Sharp. Philadelphia: Peter Stewart. 18 ll. MWA (two varieties); PHi; NjR. 10827

PENNSYLVANIA Pocket Almanac for 1809. Philadelphia: John Bioren. Advertised in "Bioren's Town and Country Almanack" for 1809. 10828

The PITTSBURGH Magazine Almanack for 1809. Pittsburgh: MWA (wrappers only) 10829

POOR Richard Improved. An Almanack for 1809. By Richard Saunders. Philadelphia: Hall & Pierie. 24 ll. PHC. 10830

POOR Robin's Almanac for 1809. By Joshua Sharp. Philadelphia: David Hogan. 20 ll. PHi. 10831

POOR Will's Almanack for 1809. Philadelphia: J. Crukshank. 18 ll. DLC; NN; CtY; MnU; OCl; TxDN; PHi; PPL. 10832

POOR Will's Almanack for 1809. Philadelphia: Kimber
& Conrad. 18 ll. MWA. 10833

POOR Will's Pocket Almanack for 1809. Philadelphia:
J. Crukshank. 24 ll. MWA; DLC; MB; InU; PHi;
PP; PPL; NjR. 10834

STEWART'S Washington Almanac for 1809. Philadelphia: Robert Stewart. MWA (15 ll.) 10835

Der VEREINIGTEN Staaten Calender auf 1809. Philadelphia: Johann Geyer. 21 ll. PHi. 10836

WASHINGTON'S Citizen's and Farmer's Almanac for
1809. By Joshua Sharp. Philadelphia: Ebenezer
M'Culloch. 18 ll. PHi. 10837

The AMERICAN Ladies' Pocket-Book for 1810. Philadelphia: W. Y. Birch, Bradford & Inskeep; New-York:
Inskeep & Bradford; J. Bioren, printer. 70 ll. PHi.
10838

AMERICANISCHER Stadt und Land Calender auf 1810.
Philadelphia: Conrad Zentler. 21 ll. MWA; DLC (20
ll.); InU; PAtM; PHi. 10839

BAILEY'S Rittenhouse Almanac for 1810. By Abraham
Shoemaker. Philadelphia: Lydia R. Bailey. 24 ll.
MWA; N; PHi (22 ll.); PPL (23 ll.); PPiHi (23 ll.);
NjR (23 ll.) 10840

BIOREN'S Annual Compting-House Sheet Almanack for
1810. Philadelphia: John Bioren. Broadside. Advertised in "Bioren's Town and Country Almanack" for 1810.
10841

BIOREN'S Pennsylvania Pocket Remembrancer for 1810.
Philadelphia: John Bioren. 30 ll. MWA; P; PHi.
10842

BIOREN'S Town and Country Almanack for 1810. By
Abraham Shoemaker. Philadelphia: John Bioren. 24 ll.
MWA; DLC; N; NN; NjR (impf); MBC; CLU; MdBP;
OCl; InU; PDoBHi; PHi; PHC; PP; PPL (16 ll., ntp);
Drake. 10843

CAREY'S Franklin Almanac for 1810. By Abraham Shoemaker. Philadelphia: Mathew Carey; Lydia R. Bailey, printer. 24 ll. MWA; DLC; N; MB; CtY (impf); ICHi; WHi; PPiU. 10844

-- Issue with 30 ll. MWA; PHi (26 ll.); OHi (29 ll.); PPL. 10845

COCHRAN'S Philadelphia Almanac for 1810. Philadelphia: R. Cochran. 18 ll. MWA; PPL. 10846

CRAMER'S Pittsburgh Almanack for 1810. Pittsburgh: Zadok Cramer; Cramer & Spear, printers. 18 ll. MWA; NHi; NjP; KyU (16 ll., ntp); PPiU (ntp) 10847

CRAMER'S Pittsburgh Magazine Almanack for 1810. Pittsburgh: Zadok Cramer; Cramer & Spear, printers. 36 ll. MWA; DLC (34 ll.); OMC (30 ll.); PPi. 10848

CRAMER'S Pittsburgh Magazine Almanack for 1810. Pittsburgh: Zadock Cramer; Cramer & Spear, printers. (Second Edition) 30 ll. MWA; InU (fragment) 10849

The FARMER'S Almanac for 1810. By Joshua Sharp. Philadelphia: R. Cochran. 18 ll. NjR; PPiU (17 ll.) 10850

FATHER Abraham's Almanac for 1810. By Joshua Sharp. Philadelphia: Peter Stewart. 18 ll. NjR (impf); PHi. 10851

FATHER Tammany's Almanack for 1810. Philadelphia. [Sabin 23911] 10852

Der GEMEINNÜTZIGE Landwirthschafts Calender auf 1810. Lancaster: Anton Albrecht. 18 ll. MWA; DLC; NN; NHi (impf); WHi; PHi; PPG; PPeSchw. 10853

The GENTLEMAN'S Annual Pocket Remembrancer for 1810. Philadelphia: Wm. Y. Birch; John Bioren, printer. 96 ll. MWA (ntp) 10854

Der HOCH-DEUTSCHE Americanische Calender auf 1810. Germantaun: Michael Billmeyer. 20 ll. MWA;

DLC; NN (16 ll.); CLU; InU; NBuG; DeWint; P (13 ll.); PHi; PLF; PPG; PYHi. 10855

JOHNSON'S Almanac for 1810. By Joshua Sharp. Philadelphia: Bennett & Walton. 24 ll. MWA; DLC; NjR. 10856

JOHNSON'S Almanac for 1810. By Joshua Sharp. Philadelphia: Benjamin Johnson. 24 ll. InRE. 10857

JOHNSON'S Almanac for 1810. By Joshua Sharp. Philadelphia: Johnson and Warner. 24 ll. MWA; N; InU (impf); CLU; CtY; P; PPL (23 ll.); PHi. 10858

KITE'S Town & Country Almanac for 1810. By Joshua Sharp. Philadelphia: Benjamin and Thomas Kite. 24 ll. MWA; DLC; InU (impf); P; PHC; PHi. 10859

No entry 10860

M'CULLOCH'S Pocket Almanac for 1810. Philadelphia: J. M'Culloch. 16 ll. PHi. 10861

Der NEUE Americanische Landwirthschafts Calender auf 1810. Reading: Johann Ritter und Comp. [Seidensticker] 10862

Der NEUE Chambersburger Stadt und Land Calender auf 1810. Chambersburg: Johann Herschberger. 20 ll. MWA. 10863

Der NEUE Gemeinnützige Landwirthschafts Calender für 1810. Lancaster: Johann Albrecht. 18 ll. CLU; DeWint; InU; OClWHi; PYHi. 10864

-- Issue with 20 ll. PPCS. 10865

NEUER Hauswirthschafts-Calender auf 1810. Carlisle: Friedrich Sanno. 21 ll. PHi (impf) 10866

NEUER Hauswirthschafts-Calender auf 1810. Libanon:

Pennsylvania - 1810

Jacob Schnee. 21 ll. MWA; DLC (18 ll.); InU; NjR;
P; PAnL; PHi; PPG.   10867

NEUER Hauswirthschafts Calender auf 1810. Philadelphia: Johnson und Warner. 21 ll. MWA; DLC (20 ll.);
MH; MiU-C (20 ll.); PHi (impf)   10868

The PENNSYLVANIA Almanac for 1810. By Joshua
Sharp. Philadelphia: R. Cochran. NjR (15 ll.);
PDoBHi (17 ll.)   10869

The PENNSYLVANIA, New-Jersey, Delaware, Maryland & Virginia Almanac for 1810. By Joshua Sharp.
Northern-Liberties, Philadelphia: Peter Stewart. MWA;
PHi (6 ll.)   10870

The PITTSBURGH Magazine Almanack for 1810. Pittsburgh: Zadock Cramer. MWA (34 ll.)   10871

POOR Richard Improved. An Almanack for 1810. By
Richard Saunders. Philadelphia: Hall & Pierie. 24 ll.
MWA; NN; InU; NjR.   10872

POOR Will's Almanack for 1810. Philadelphia: Benjamin C. Buzby. 24 ll. DLC; N; PHi.   10873

POOR Will's Almanack for 1810. Philadelphia: Joseph
Crukshank, No. 87, High-street. 24 ll. Drake (22 ll.)
   10874

POOR Will's Almanack for 1810. Philadelphia: Joseph
Crukshank, No. 87, Market Street. 24 ll. MWA (22
ll.); InU; MB; OCl; OClWHi; PHi.   10875

POOR Will's Pocket Almanack for 1810. Philadelphia:
J. Crukshank. 24 ll. MWA; DLC; NN (23 ll.); InU;
PHi; PP; NjR.   10876

Der VEREINIGTEN Staaten Calender auf 1810. Philadelphia: Johann Geyer. 21 ll. DLC (18 ll.); PHi.
   10877

WASHINGTON'S Citizen and Farmer's Almanac for 1810.
Philadelphia: John M'Culloch. 18 ll. PPL.   10878

ALMANACK for 1811. [Philadelphia:] United States Gazette. Broadside. PHi. 10879

AMERICANISCHER Stadt und Land Calender auf 1811. Philadelphia: Conrad Zentler. 21 ll. MWA; DLC (impf); NN (20 ll.); InU; PAtM; PHi. 10880

BAILEY'S Rittenhouse Almanac for 1811. By Abraham Shoemaker. Philadelphia: Lydia R. Bailey. 24 ll. MWA (two varieties, one impf); DLC; MiD-B; P. 10881

BENNET & Walton's Almanac for 1811. By Joshua Sharp. Philadelphia: Bennett [sic] and Walton. 24 ll. MWA; DLC; PHi. 17182

BENNETT & Walton's Almanac for 1811. By Joshua Sharp. Philadelphia: Bennett and Walton. 24 ll. PHi; NjR (impf) 10883

BIOREN'S Annual Compting-House Sheet Almanack for 1811. Philadelphia: John Bioren. Broadside. Advertised in "Bioren's Town and Country Almanack" for 1811. 10884

BIOREN'S Pennsylvania Pocket Remembrancer for 1811. Philadelphia: John Bioren. 24 ll. DeWint; Phi. 10885

BIOREN'S Town and Country Almanack for 1811. By Abraham Shoemaker. Philadelphia: John Bioren. 24 ll. MWA; NN (21 ll.); NHi (23 ll.); CLU; InU; MnU; NjR; P; PDoBHi; PHi. 10886

CAREY'S Franklin Almanac for 1811. By Joshua Sharp. Philadelphia: Mathew Carey; Lydia R. Bailey, printer. 24 ll. MWA; P. 10887

CAREY'S Franklin Almanac for 1811. By Abraham Shoemaker. Philadelphia: Mathew Carey. 24 ll. N; NBuG; CtY; PDoBHi; PHi (22 ll.); PPL. 10888

COCHRAN'S Philadelphia Almanac for 1811. By Joshua Sharp. Philadelphia: R. Cochran. 18 ll. MWA; NjR. 10889

CRAMER'S Pittsburgh Almanack for 1811. By Rev.

John Taylor. Pittsburgh: Cramer, Spear & Eichbaum.
18 ll. MWA; ICHi; MoSHi; OC; OHi; PPiU (13 ll.)
10890

CRAMER'S Pittsburgh Magazine Almanack for 1811.
Pittsburgh: Cramer, Spear & Eichbaum. 30 ll. MWA
(28 ll.); DLC (24 ll.); InU (11 ll.); OCHP; OClWHi;
PPi. 10891

CRAMER'S Pittsburgh Magazine Almanack Extra for
1811. Pittsburgh: Cramer, Spear & Eichbaum. 42 ll.
MWA; InHi; InU; PHi; PPi. 10892

FATHER Tammany's Almanac for 1811. Philadelphia:
W. M'Culloch. 18 ll. MWA (16 ll.) 10893

Der GEMEINNÜTZIGE Landwirthschafts Calender auf
1811. Lancaster: Anton Albrecht. 20 ll. MWA; DLC;
N; CLU; NjP (impf); DeWint; InU (18 ll.); P; PDoBHi;
PHi; PPG; PYHi; PPeSchw. 10894

Der GEMEINNÜTZIGE Landwirth sachfts [sic] Calender
auf 1811. Lancaster: Anton Albrecht. 20 ll. PPL (19
ll.) 10895

Der HOCH-DEUTSCHE Americanische Calender auf 1811.
Germantaun: Michael Billmeyer. 21 ll. MWA; DLC
(impf); NjR; CLU; CtY; InU; MnU; DeWint; WHi; P
(20 ll.); PHi; PPG; PAnL; PPCS; PPT; PDoBHi;
PPeSchw. 10896

Der HUNDERTJAHRIGE Calender auf 1799-1899. Harrisburg: Cleim und Wiestling. [1811]. 80 ll. MWA.
10897

JOHNSON & Warner's Almanac for 1811. By Joshua
Sharp. Philadelphia: Johnson & Warner. 24 ll. MWA;
DLC (23 ll.); N; InU; P; PHC; PHi; PPL. 10898

KITE'S Town & Country Almanac for 1811. By Abraham Shoemaker. Philadelphia: Benjamin and Thomas
Kite; Lydia R. Bailey, printer. 24 ll. MWA (22 ll.);
P. 10899

Der NEUE, Americanische Landwirthschafts-Calender

auf 1811. Reading: Johann Ritter und Comp. 21 ll.
P (20 ll.); PHi; PPG (18 ll.); PR; PRHi; Drake (20
ll.) 10900

Der NEUE Chambersburger Stadt und Land Calender auf
1811. Chambersburg: Johann Herschberger. 18 ll.
MWA; DLC. 10901

NEUER Hauswirthschafts-Calender auf 1811. Carlisle:
F. Sanno. [Thompson] 10902

NEUER Hauswirthschafts Calender auf 1811. Libanon:
Jacob Schnee. 21 ll. MWA; DLC (20 ll.); NN; NHi
(impf); CtY; OHi; P; PAnL (18 ll.); PHi (19 ll.);
PPL (16 ll.); PYHi; Drake (impf) 10903

NEUER Hauswirthschafts Calender auf 1811. Philadelphia: Jacob Meyer. 20 ll. MWA; DLC; NBuG. 10904

The PITTSBURGH Magazine Almanack for 1811. Pittsburgh: Cramer, Spear & Eichbaum. 30 ll. MWA
(wrappers only); PPiU (28 ll.) 10905

POOR Richard Improved. An Almanack for 1811. By
Joshua Sharp. Philadelphia: Hall & Pierie. 24 ll.
MWA; PHi. 10906

POOR Robin's Almanac for 1811. By Joshua Sharp.
Philadelphia: David Hogan. 20 ll. MWA. 10907

POOR Will's Almanack for 1811. Philadelphia: Joseph
Crukshank. 24 ll. MWA; DLC; N; InU; NjR (23 ll.);
MH; OClWHi; P; PHi; PPL; PPT. 10908

POOR Will's Pocket Almanack for 1811. Philadelphia:
J. Crukshank. 24 ll. MWA; DLC; PHi; PP; PPL;
NjR. 10909

Der VEREINIGTEN Staaten Calender auf 1811. Philadelphia: Johann Geyer. 20 ll. PPeSchw. 10910

WASHINGTON'S Citizen and Farmer's Almanac for 1811.
Philadelphia: John M'Culloch. 18 ll. Drake. 10911

The AMERICAN Lady's Pocket-Book for 1812. Philadelphia: W. Y. Birch. 72 ll. PPAmP. 10912

AMERICANISCHER Stadt und Land Calender auf 1812. Philadelphia: Conrad Zentler. 21 ll. MWA; DLC (19 ll.); N; PDoBHi (nfp, ntp); PHi (20 ll.); PPeSchw; Drake (18 ll.) 10913

BAILEY'S Rittenhouse Almanac for 1812. By William Collom. Philadelphia: Lydia R. Bailey. 24 ll. MWA; N; InU. 10914

BAILEY'S Rittenhouse Almanac for 1812. By William Collom. Philadelphia: R. C. Buzby. 24 ll. DLC (22 ll.); MWA (19 ll.) 10915

BENNET & Walton's Almanac for 1812. By Joshua Sharp. Philadelphia: Bennett [sic] & Walton. 24 ll. MWA; DLC. 10916

BENNETT & Walton's Almanac for 1812. By Joshua Sharp. Philadelphia: Bennett & Walton. 24 ll. InU; PHi; PPAmP; PPL. 10917

BIOREN'S Annual Compting-House Sheet Almanack for 1812. Philadelphia: John Bioren. Broadside. Advertised in "Bioren's Town and Country Almanack" for 1812. 10918

BIOREN'S Pennsylvania Pocket Remembrancer for 1812. Philadelphia: John Bioren. 24 ll. PHi. 10919

BIOREN'S Town and Country Almanack for 1812. By William Collom. Philadelphia: John Bioren. 24 ll. MWA; NN; NHi; NjR; InU; PDoBHi (impf); PHi (21 ll.); PPiU; Drake. 10920

CAREY'S Franklin Almanac for 1812. By William Collom. Philadelphia: Mathew Carey; Lydia R. Bailey, printer. 24 ll. MWA; MB; PHi. 10921

COCHRAN'S Philadelphia Almanac for 1812. Philadelphia: No. 108 Race-street. 19 ll. MWA; DLC. 10922

CRAMER'S Magazine Almanack for 1812. Pittsburgh:
MWA (wrappers only)   10923

CRAMER'S Pittsburgh Almanack for 1812. By Rev.
John Taylor. Pittsburgh: Cramer, Spear & Eichbaum.
18 ll. MWA (impf); InU; MoSHi; ICHi; OMC; WvU;
PPiU (impf)   10924

CRAMER'S Pittsburgh Almanack for 1812. By Rev.
John Taylor. Pittsburgh: Cramer, Spear & Eichbaum.
(Second Edition) 20 ll. MWA.   10925

CRAMER'S Pittsburgh Magazine Almanack for 1812. By
Rev. John Taylor. Pittsburgh: Cramer, Spear &
Eichbaum. 30 ll. MWA; DLC; NN; InHi; InU;
OClWHi; PPi.   10926

E. M'CULLOCH'S Washington Almanac for 1812. Philadelphia: E. M'Culloch. 14 ll. PHi.   10927

FATHER Tammany's Almanac for 1812. Philadelphia:
W. M'Culloch. 14 ll. MWA; CtY; PHi.   10928

Der GEMEINNÜTZIGE Landwirthschafts Calender auf
1812. Lancaster: Anton Albrecht. 20 ll. MWA; DLC;
InU; WHi; DeWint; P; PHi; PLHi; PPCS; PPL;
PPeSchw; PYHi.   10929

The GENTLEMAN'S Annual Pocket Remembrancer for
1812. Philadelphia: W. Y. Birch. 96 ll. NN (44 ll.);
NHi; ViHi.   10930

Der HOCH-DEUTSCHE Americanische Calender auf 1812.
Germantaun: Michael Billmeyer. 21 ll. MWA; DLC
(impf); NN; CLU; CtY; DeWint; P; PHi; PPCS; PPG;
PPT; PYHi.   10931

The HONEST Man's Almanac, for the City of Pittsburgh
[for 1812]. By Rev. John Taylor, and R. Patterson.
Pittsburgh: Patterson & Hopkins; S. Engles & Co.,
printers. 18 ll. OClWHi.   10932

JOHNSON and Warner's Almanac for 1812. By Joshua

Pennsylvania - 1812   1043

Sharp. Philadelphia: Johnson & Warner. 24 ll. MWA; DLC (impf); N; InU; PDoBHi (23 ll.); PPL; NjR; Drake.   10933

KITE'S Town and Country Almanac for 1812. By William Collom. Philadelphia: Benjamin and Thomas Kite. 24 ll. MWA.   10934

Des LANDMANNS Freund; oder, Ganz Neuer Westliche Calender auf 1812. Somerset: Friedrich Goeb. 21 ll. MWA; PPi.   10935

MASONIC and Citizens Annual Almanac for 1812. Philadelphia: Thomas DeSilver; Robert DeSilver; John Bioren, printer. 95 ll. PPFM.   10936

M'CULLOCH'S Pocket Almanac for 1812. Philadelphia: Wm. M'Culloch. 16 ll. MWA; DLC; PHi.   10937

Der NEUE, Americanische Landwirthschafts-Calender auf 1812. Reading: Johann Ritter und Comp. 20 ll. MWA; DLC (18 ll.); N; NHi (impf); P; PHi; PPL (16 ll.); PRHi.   10938

Der NEUE Chambersburger Stadt und Land Calender auf 1812. Chambersburg: Johann Herschberger. [Seidensticker]   10939

NEUER Hauswirthschafts-Calender auf 1812. Carlisle: Frdr. Sanno. 20 ll. PPG.   10940

NEUER Hauswirthschafts-Calender auf 1812. Libanon: Jacob Schnee. 21 ll. MWA; DLC (20 ll.); NN; PAnL (20 ll.); PHi; PYHi.   10941

NEUER Hauswirthschafts-Calender auf 1812. Philadelphia: Jacob Meyer. 20 ll. MWA; CLU; PPeSchw.   10942

The PENNSYLVANIA Pocket Almanac for 1812. Philadelphia: Griggs & Dickinson. [Phillips]   10943

POOR Richard Improved. An Almanack for 1812. By Joshua Sharp. Philadelphia: Hall & Pierie. 24 ll.

MWA; CLU; InU; MB; P; PHC; PHi. 10944

POOR Robin's Almanac for 1812. By Joshua Sharp.
Philadelphia: David Hogan. 18 ll. MWA; DLC; InU.
  10945
POOR Will's Almanack for 1812. Philadelphia: Joseph
Crukshank. 24 ll. MWA; DLC; MB; NjR; InU; MnU;
OCl; WHi; PDoBHi; PHi. 10946

POOR Will's Pocket Almanack for 1812. Philadelphia:
J. Crukshank. 24 ll. MWA; DLC; DeWint; PHi; PP;
NjR. 10947

STEWART'S Washington Almanac for 1812. By Joshua
Sharp. Philadelphia: Robert Stewart. 18 ll. MWA;
DLC (impf); NN; NjMoW; NjR (17 ll.) 10948

The UNITED States Calendar for 1812. By Joshua
Sharp. Bellavista: John Bouvier. 24 ll. MWA (two varieties); DLC (8 ll.); CtY; NN (22 ll.); NjR (22 ll.);
ViU; Drake (22 ll.) 10949

Der VEREINIGTEN Staaten Calender auf 1812. Philadelphia: Johann Geyer. 21 ll. DLC (20 ll.); PHi.
  10950
WASHINGTON'S Citizens & Farmer's Almanac for 1812.
Philadelphia: W. M'Culloch. 18 ll. MWA (impf) 10951

The AMERICAN Lady's Pocket-Book for 1813. Philadelphia: W. Y. Birch. 72 ll. PPAmP. 10952

AMERICANISCHER Stadt und Land Calender auf 1813.
Philadelphia: Conrad Zentler. 21 ll. MWA; DLC; MH;
InU; DeWint; N; PAtM; PHi; PPG; PPeSchw; PYHi.
  10953
BAILEY'S Rittenhouse Almanac for 1813. By William
Collom. Philadelphia: Lydia R. Bailey. 24 ll. MWA
(23 ll.); MB; NjP (19 ll.); PHi; PPAmP. 10954

BAILEY'S Rittenhouse Almanac for 1813. By William
Collom. Philadelphia: B. C. Buzby. 24 ll. MWA;
DLC; InU. 10955

BENNET and Walton's Almanac for 1813. By Joshua
Sharp. Philadelphia: Bennett [sic] & Walton. 24 ll.
MH; P. 10956

BENNETT and Walton's Almanac for 1813. By Joshua
Sharp. Philadelphia: Bennett & Walton. 24 ll. MWA;
DLC (impf); NjR (23 ll.); PHi. 10957

BIOREN'S Annual Compting-House Sheet Almanack for
1813. Philadelphia: John Bioren. Broadside. Advertised in "Bioren's Town and Country Almanack" for
1813. 10958

BIOREN'S Pennsylvania Pocket Remembrancer for 1813.
Philadelphia: John Bioren. 24 ll. MWA (22 ll.);
DeWint; PHi. 10959

BIOREN'S Town and Country Almanack for 1813. By
William Collom. Philadelphia: John Bioren. 24 ll.
MWA; DLC; N (impf); NjR (23 ll.); RPB; P; PHi
(impf); PP; PPL; PPiU; Drake (19 ll.) 10960

CAREY'S Franklin Almanac for 1813. By William Collom. Philadelphia: Mathew Carey; Lydia R. Bailey,
printer. 24 ll. MWA; ICHi; InU; P; PHi. 10961

COCHRAN'S Pennsylvania Almanac for 1813. By Joshua
Sharp. Philadelphia: Ann Cochran. 24 ll. NBuG.10962

CRAMER'S Pittsburgh Almanack for 1813. By Rev.
John Taylor. Pittsburgh: Cramer, Spear and Eichbaum. 18 ll. MWA; DLC; OClWHi; MiU-C; MoSHi;
OHi; ICHi; InU; OC; PPi; PPiU. 10963

CRAMER'S Pittsburgh Almanack for 1813. By Rev.
John Taylor. Pittsburgh: Cramer, Spear and Eichbaum.
36 ll. CtY; NjP; OMC; InHi; InU; OC; OCHP; PPi.
10964
FATHER Tammany's Almanack for 1813. Philadelphia.
[Sabin 23911] 10965

Der GEMEINNÜTZIGE Landwirthschafts Calender auf
1813. Lancaster: Anton Albrecht. 20 ll. MWA; DLC

(impf); NN; NBuG; InU; WHi; DeWint; P; PHi; PLHi; PPG; PPeSchw; PDoBHi; PYHi. 10966

The GENTLEMAN'S Annual Pocket Remembrancer for 1813. [Philadelphia:] W. Y. Birch; New York: Bradford and Inskeep. 102 ll. MH; MHi; PHi. 10967

Der HOCH-DEUTSCHE Americanische Calender auf 1813. Germantaun: Michael Billmeyer. 21 ll. MWA; DLC; NN (20 ll.); DeWint; CtY; MH; WHi; P; PHi; PPAmP; PPG; PPeSchw; PYHi. 10968

The HONEST Man's Almanac, for the city of Pittsburgh [for 1813]. By Rev. John Taylor and R. Patterson. [np, np] 18 ll. MWA; NN; OClWHi. 10969

The HONEST Man's Extra Almanac for the city of Pittsburgh [for 1813]. Pittsburgh: Patterson & Hopkins; S. Engles & Co., printers. 24 ll. MWA; InU (title leaf only); PPi. 10970

JOHNSON and Warner's Almanac for 1813. By Joshua Sharp. Philadelphia: Johnson & Warner. 24 ll. MWA; DLC; N; InU; NjR; CtY; P; PHi (impf); Drake (two varieties) 10971

KITE'S Town and Country Almanac for 1813. By William Collom. Philadelphia: Benjamin and Thomas Kite. 24 ll. MWA (22 ll.); PDoBHi (16 ll.) 10972

Des LANDMANNS Freund, oder, Ganz neuer Westlicher Calender auf 1813. Somerset: Friedrich Goeb. 24 ll. MWA; CLU; PPi. 10973

Des LANDMANNS Freund, oder, Ganz neuer Westlicher Calender auf 1813. Somerset: Friedrich Goeb, Für Cramer, Spear u. Eichbaum in Pittsburg. 24 ll. Drake (impf) 10974

MAGAZINE Almanac for 1813. Pittsburgh: Cramer, Spear & Eichbaum. MWA (front wrapper only) 10975

MASONIC and Citizens' Annual Almanac for 1813. Philadelphia: Thomas DeSilver.   74 ll. MWA.   10976

M'CULLOCH'S Pocket Almanac for 1813.   Philadelphia:
W. M'Culloch.   16 ll. MWA; InU; PHi.   10977

Der NEUE, Americanische Landwirthschafts-Calender
auf 1813.   Reading: Johann Ritter und Comp.   21 ll.
MWA (19 ll.); DLC (20 ll.); NN (impf); P (20 ll.);
PHi; PPG; PPCS (20 ll.); PR; PRHi.   10978

Der NEUE Chambersburger Stadt und Land Calender auf
1813.   Chambersburg: Johann Herschberger. [Seiden-
sticker]   10979

NEUER Hauswirthschafts Calender auf 1813.   Libanon:
Jacob Schnee.   21 ll. MWA (two varieties); DLC (18
ll.); NHi; DeWint; P (20 ll.); PHi (20 ll.); PPL (19
ll.)   10930

NEUER Hauswirthschafts-Calender auf 1813.   Philadelphia: Jacob Meyer.   20 ll. PPeSchw.   10981

NEW Jersey and Pennsylvania Almanack for 1813.   By
William Collom.   Philadelphia: John Bioren, for John
C. Moore, Trenton.   19 ll. DLC; NjR.   10982

PENNSYLVANIA Annual Almanac, and Reference for
1813.   By Josiah S. Kay.   Philadelphia: Griggs &
Dickinson.   36 ll. MWA; N; PHi.   10983

The PENNSYLVANIA & New-Jersey Almanac for 1813.
By Joshua Sharp.   Philadelphia: Isaac Peirce.   24 ll.
P; PHi.   10984

PENNSYLVANIA Masonic and Civil Almanac for 1813.
Philadelphia.   [Sabin 60347]   10985

POOR Richard Improved.   An Almanack for 1813.   By
Richard Saunders.   Philadelphia: Hall & Pierie.   24 ll.
MWA; DLC (22 ll.); CtY; MB; P; PHi.   10986

POOR Robin's Almanac for 1813.   By Joshua Sharp.
Philadelphia: D. Hogan.   24 ll. DeU (23 ll.);

Drake. 10987

POOR Will's Almanack for 1813. Philadelphia: Joseph
Crukshank. 24 ll. MWA; DLC; MB; InU (ntp); P;
PHi; PPT; PPiU. 10988

POOR Will's Pocket Almanack for 1813. Philadelphia:
J. Crukshank. 24 ll. MWA; PHi; PP; NjR. 10989

ROBINSON Crusoe's Almanac for 1813. Philadelphia:
W. M'Culloch. 18 ll. MWA; CtY; P; PHi. 10990

The UNITED States' Almanac for 1813. By Joshua
Sharp. Philadelphia: Thomas M. Longstreth. 24 ll.
MWA; DLC; N; NN; CtY; MiD-B; P; PHC; PHi.
10991

An ALMANAC for Pennsylvania and New Jersey for
1814. By Joshua Sharp. Doylestown: Asher Miner.
16 ll. PDoBHi. 10992

The AMERICAN Lady's Pocket Book for 1814. Philadelphia: W. Y. Birch. 72 ll. PPAmP. 10993

AMERICANISCHER Stadt und Land Calender auf 1814.
Philadelphia: Conrad Zentler. 21 ll. MWA; DLC; NN
(20 ll.); CLU; InU; MnU; PHi; PLF; PP; PPCS (20
ll.); PPG; PPeSchw. 10994

BAILEY'S Rittenhouse Almanac for 1814. By William
Collom. Philadelphia: Lydia R. Bailey. 24 ll. MWA;
InU (19 ll.); P (23 ll.) 10995

BAILEY'S Rittenhouse Almanac for 1814. By William
Collom. Philadelphia: B. C. Buzby. 24 ll. MWA;
PHC; NjR. 10996

BENNETT & Walton's Almanac for 1814. By Joshua
Sharp. Philadelphia: Bennett & Walton. 24 ll. MWA;
NjHi (20 ll.); MiD-B; P; PHi; Drake (22 ll.) 10997

BIOREN'S Annual Compting-House Sheet Almanack for
1814. Philadelphia: John Bioren. Broadside. Advertised in "Bioren's Town and Country Almanack" for

1814.   10998

BIOREN'S Pennsylvania Pocket Remembrancer for 1814.
Philadelphia: John Bioren.   24 ll.   MWA; DLC; PHi;
PPAmP.   10999

BIOREN'S Town and Country Almanack for 1814. By
William Collom.   Philadelphia: John Bioren. 24 ll.
MWA; DLC; N; NN; NHi; NBuG; InU; MiD-B; P;
PHi; PP; MH.   11000

CAREY'S American Pocket Atlas [Almanac] for 1814.
Philadelphia: Mathew Carey.   24 ll.   NjR (23 ll.)11001

CAREY'S Franklin Almanac for 1814. By William Collom.   Philadelphia: Mathew Carey; Lydia R. Bailey,
printer.   24 ll. MWA; DLC; InU; P; PHi; Drake.
                                                                         11002
CRAMER'S Pittsburgh Almanack for 1814. By Rev.
John Taylor.   Pittsburgh: Cramer, Spear and Eichbaum.   18 ll.   DLC; InU; MoSHi; OC; OHi; PHi (16
ll.); PPi; PPiU (ntp)   11003

-- Issue with 36 ll. NjP; PPiU.   11004

CRAMER'S Pittsburgh Magazine Almanack for 1814.
By Rev. John Taylor.   Pittsburgh: Cramer, Spear and
Eichbaum.   36 ll. MWA (32 ll.); NN; CtY; OC; OMC;
PPi.   11005

DESILVER'S Naval Almanac for 1814. By Joshua Sharp.
Philadelphia: Robert DeSilver [sic].   24 ll. DeU (21 ll.);
P (21 ll.)   11006

DESILVER'S Naval Almanac for 1814. By Joshua Sharp.
Philadelphia: Thomas DeSilver [sic].   24 ll. MWA;
PHi.   11007

FAGAN'S Almanac for 1814. By Joshua Sharp. Philadelphia: A. Fagan. 24 ll. MWA; InU (ntp); MiD-B;
NjR (22 ll.); ViHi (23 ll.)   11008

FATHER Tammany's Almanack for 1814. Philadelphia:

[Sabin 23911]   11009

Der GEMEINNÜTZIGE Landwirthschafts Calender auf
1814. Lancaster: Anton Albrecht. 20 ll. MWA; DLC
(impf); N; NBuG; NHi; InU; DeWint; WHi; P; PDoBHi;
PHi; PLHi; PPCS; PPL; PPeSchw; PYHi.   11010

The GENTLEMAN'S Annual Pocket Remembrancer for
1814. Philadelphia: William Y. Birch. 102 ll. MWA
(fragment); PHi.   11011

Der HOCH-DEUTSCHE Americanische Calender auf
1814. Germantaun: Michael Billmeyer. 22 ll. MWA;
DLC (20 ll.); NN; InU; MH; CLU; CtY; DeWint; PPG;
PHi (21 ll.); PPL; PPeSchw; P (21 ll.); PYHi;
PPAmP; PDoBHi.   11012

JOHNSON & Warner's Almanac for 1814. By Joshua
Sharp. Philadelphia: Johnson & Warner. 24 ll. MWA;
NHi; CtY; InU; MiD-B; OCHP; PHC; PHi.   11013

JOHNSON'S Almanac for 1814. By Joshua Sharp.
Philadelphia: Benjamin Johnson. 24 ll. MWA; P.
                                                  11014
KITE'S Town and Country Almanac for 1814. By William Collom. Philadelphia: Benjamin and Thomas Kite;
Lydia R. Bailey, printer. 24 ll. MWA (21 ll.); DLC
(impf); InU; MB; MiD-B; PHi.   11015

MASONIC and Citizens' Annual Almanac for 1814.
Philadelphia: Thomas DeSilver; Robert DeSilver. 107
ll. PPFM.   11016

MINER'S Pennsylvania & New-Jersey Almanac for 1814.
By Theophilus. Doylestown: Asher Miner. MWA (17
ll.)   11017

Der NEUE, Americanische Landwirthschafts-Calender
auf 1814. Reading: Johann Ritter und Comp. 21 ll.
MWA (18 ll.); DLC (20 ll.); NHi (17 ll.); InU; P;
PHi; PPG; PRHi; PR; PDoBHi (15 ll.); PPCS (20 ll.);
PPL (14 ll.)   11018

Der NEUE Chambersburger Stadt und Land Calender auf 1814. Chambersburg: Johann Herschberger. 18 ll. MWA; DLC; N; PPi. 11019

NEUER Hauswirthschafts Calender auf 1814. Libanon: Joseph Schnee. 21 ll. MWA (19 ll.); DLC (20 ll.); P; PPL. 11020

The PENNSYLVANIA Almanac for 1814. By Joshua Sharp. Philadelphia: Ann Coles. 24 ll. MWA (impf); CtY; P; PHi (23 ll.) 11021

PENNSYLVANIA Almanac for 1814. By Joshua Sharp. Philadelphia: Jordon Downing. 22 ll. MWA. 11022

PENNSYLVANIA Calendar for 1814. By Joshua Sharp. Philadelphia: Jordon Downing. 24 ll. MWA (impf) 11023

The PITTSBURGH Town & Country Almanac, for Rogues and Honest Folks for 1814. By John Armstrong. Pittsburgh: R. & J. Patterson; S. Engles & Co., printers. 18 ll. DLC; ICU; OClWHi. 11024

POOR Richard Improved. An Almanack for 1814. By Joshua Sharp. Philadelphia: Hall & Pierie. 24 ll. MiD-B; PHi. 11025

POOR Robin's Almanac for 1814. By Joshua Sharp. Philadelphia: D. Hogan. 24 ll. MWA; DLC; MiD-B. 11026

POOR Will's Almanack for 1814. Philadelphia: Joseph Crukshank. 24 ll. MWA; DLC; NN; MB; MiD-B; TxU; P; PHC; PHi; PDoBHi (ntp) 11027

POOR Will's Pocket Almanack for 1814. Philadelphia: J. Crukshank. 24 ll. MWA; PHi; PP; NjR. 11028

STEWART'S East and West Jersey Almanac for 1814. By Joshua Sharp. Philadelphia: Robert Stewart. 21 ll. MWA; CtY. 11029

The UNITED States' Almanac for 1814. By Joshua Sharp. Philadelphia: Thomas M. Longstreth. 24 ll.

MWA; DLC; N; NjR; CtY; InU; MiD-B; PHi. 11030

The UNITED States Kalendar, and Annual Register for 1814. Philadelphia: M. M'Connell, jun.; G. Palmer, printer. 16 ll. NN. 11031

The WASHINGTON Almanac for 1814. By Joshua Sharp. Philadelphia: Thos. Hirst; Ann Coles, printer. 24 ll. PHi (23 ll.) 11032

WASHINGTON'S Citizens' & Farmers' Almanac for 1814. Philadelphia: W. M'Culloch. 18 ll. MWA; MiD-B. 11033

An ALMANAC for Pennsylvania and New Jersey for 1815. By Joshua Sharp. Doylestown: Asher Miner. 16 ll. PDoBHi. 11034

The AMERICAN Lady's Pocket Book for 1815. Philadelphia: A. Small. 78 ll. PHi. 11035

AMERICAN Naval Almanac for 1815. By Joshua Sharp. Philadelphia: R. & T. Desilver. 30 ll. MWA; NN (two varieties); P (impf); PHi; PPT; PPiU (8 ll.) 11036

AMERICANISCHER Stadt und Land Calender auf 1815. Philadelphia: Conrad Zentler. 21 ll. MWA; DLC; NHi (18 ll.); NjP; MH; MHi; CtY; InU; NBuG; PPG; PHi; PPL; PDoBHi. 11037

BAILEY'S Rittenhouse Almanac for 1815. By William Collom. Philadelphia: Lydia R. Bailey. 24 ll. MWA; DLC; N; InU; NBuG; P; PHi; PPL; PU. 11038

BENNETT & Walton's Almanac for 1815. By Joshua Sharp. Philadelphia: Bennett & Walton. 24 ll. MWA; P; PHi. 11039

BIOREN'S Annual Compting-House Sheet Almanack for 1815. Philadelphia: John Bioren. Broadside. Advertised in "Bioren's Town and Country Almanack" for 1815. 11040

BIOREN'S Pennsylvania Pocket Remembrancer for 1815. Philadelphia: John Bioren. 30 ll. PHi. 11041

BIOREN'S Town and Country Almanack for 1815. By William Collom. Philadelphia: John Bioren. 24 ll. MWA; DLC; NN; NHi; NjR (22 ll.); InU; P; PHi; PP.
11042

CRAMER'S Magazine Almanack for 1815. Pittsburgh: Cramer, Spear and Eichbaum. MWA (wrappers only)
11043

CRAMER'S Pittsburgh Almanack for 1815. By Rev. John Taylor. Pittsburgh: Cramer, Spear and Eichbaum. 18 ll. MWA; NN; CLU; MiU-C; OHi; ICHi; WvU; PPi; PPiU.
11044

CRAMER'S Pittsburgh Magazine Almanack for 1815. By Rev. John Taylor. Pittsburgh: Cramer, Spear and Eichbaum; Robert Ferguson and Co., printers. 36 ll. MWA; DLC; NHi; OClWHi; NjP (impf); OC; O; CtY; OMC (35 ll.); InHi; InU; OCHP; PPi; PPiU (35 ll.); OHi.
11045

FATHER Tammany's Almanack for 1815. Philadelphia. [Sabin 23911]
11046

Der GEMEINNÜTZIGE Landwirthschafts Calender auf 1815. Lancaster: Anton Albrecht. 20 ll. MWA; DLC (impf); N; NN; NHi (19 ll.); NjP (impf); CLU; CtY; InU; DeWint; WHi; P; PHi; PPeSchw; PYHi; Drake (impf)
11047

The GENTLEMAN'S Annual Pocket Remembrancer for 1815. Philadelphia: Abraham Small. 114 ll. N; NcD; ViHi; PHi.
11048

Der HOCH-DEUTSCHE Americanische Calender auf 1815. Philadelphia: G. und D. Billmeyer. 22 ll. MWA; DLC; N; NN; NjR; RPB; CLU; CtY; MnU; InU; WHi; DeWint; P (16 ll.); PHi; PYHi; Drake (impf)
11049

JOHNSON & Warner's Almanac for 1815. By Joshua Sharp. Philadelphia: Johnson & Warner; Griggs & Dickinson, printers. 24 ll. MWA (two varieties); InU; Drake.
11050

KITE'S Town and Country Almanac for 1815. By Willi-

am Collom. Philadelphia: Benjamin and Thomas Kite;
Lydia R. Bailey, printer. 24 ll. MWA; DLC (20 ll.);
MB; P; PDoBHi. 11051

MASONIC and Citizens' Annual Almanac for 1815.
Philadelphia: Robert De Silver. 98 ll. PPFM. 11052

M'CULLOCH'S Pocket Almanac for 1815. Philadelphia:
W. M'Culloch. 16 ll. PHi. 11053

MINER'S Pennsylvania and New-Jersey Almanac for
1815. Doylestown: Asher Miner. 24 ll. MWA; NjR;
NBuHi (22 ll.); P; PDoBHi (16 ll.) 11054

Der NEUE, Americanische Landwirthschafts-Calender
auf 1815. Reading: Johann Ritter und Comp. 21 ll.
MWA (impf); DLC (20 ll.); NN; InU; MHi (20 ll.);
PPG; PHi (20 ll.); P; PR; PRHi; PPCS; Drake (18
ll.) 11055

Der NEUE Pittsburger Calender auf 1815. Pittsburgh:
Cramer, Spear und Eichbaum. 24 ll. MWA; CLU; OHi.
11056

Der NEUE Pittsburger Calender auf 1815. Pittsburgh:
Robert Ferguson. 24 ll. PPi. 11057

NEUER Hauswirthschafts-Calender auf 1815. Philadelphia: Johnson und Warner. 21 ll. MWA; DLC (16 ll.);
MiU-C (20 ll.); PHi. 11058

NEUER Hauswirthschafts-Calender auf 1815. Philadelphia: James Stackhause. 21 ll. MWA. 11059

The PENNSYLVANIA Almanac for 1815. By Joshua
Sharp. Philadelphia: Ann Coles. 24 ll. MWA; DLC;
NN; Drake. 11060

The PITTSBURGH Town & Country Almanac, for
Rogues and Honest Folks for 1815. By John Armstrong.
Pittsburgh: R. & J. Patterson; S. Engles, printer. 18
ll. MWA; DLC; InHi; OClWHi; PPi. 11061

-- Issue with 30 ll. O. 11062

Der PITTSBURGHER Calender auf 1815. Den John Taylor. Pittsburgh: Cramer, Spear und Eichbaum; Robert Ferguson und Comp., [printers]. 24 ll. PPi.
11063

POOR Robin's Almanac for 1815. Philadelphia: D. Hogan. 24 ll. MWA; DLC; CtY; InU; WHi; P; Drake (impf)
11064

POOR Will's Almanack for 1815. Philadelphia: Joseph Crukshank. 24 ll. MWA; DLC; CtY; InU; OCl; PDoBHi (ntp); PHi; PPL (22 ll.)
11065

POOR Will's Pocket Almanack for 1815. Philadelphia: J. Crukshank. 12 ll. MWA; PHC; PHi; PP (ntp); Nj; NjR (24 ll.)
11066

-- Printed on one side of leaves, pasted on folded cardboard. 16 ll. Drake.
11067

POUNDER'S Wesleyan Almanac for 1815. Philadelphia: Jonathan Pounder. 22 ll. MWA; InU; P; PHi. 11068

SOMERSETER Calender auf 1815. Schellsburg: Friedrich Goeb. [Seidensticker]
11069

STEWART'S East and West Jersey Almanac for 1815. By Joshua Sharp. Philadelphia: Robert Stewart; Ann Coles, printer. 24 ll. MWA; NjR (23 ll.); ViHi; PHi.
11070

The UNITED States Almanac for 1815. By William Collom. Philadelphia: Thomas W. Longstreth. 24 ll. MWA (20 ll.); P.
11071

WASHINGTON'S Citizens' & Farmers' Almanac for 1815. Philadelphia: W. M'Culloch. 18 ll. ICHi.
11072

The AMERICAN Calendar, or Naval and Military Almanac for 1816. By William Collom. Philadelphia: Thomas DeSilver; Robert DeSilver. 24 ll. PHi (impf); PPL (8 ll., impf)
11073

-- Imprint error: "Market steeet." 24 ll. NHi. 11074

Pennsylvania - 1816

The **AMERICAN** Lady's Pocket Book for 1816. Philadelphia: A. Small. 78 ll. PHi. 11075

AMERICANISCHER Stadt und Land Calender auf 1816. Philadelphia: Conrad Zentler. 21 ll. MWA; DLC (20 ll.); NN; NjP (15 ll.); CLU; MH; CtY; InU; P (19 ll.); PAnL (18 ll.); PHi; PLF; PPG; PYHi. 11076

BAILEY'S Rittenhouse Almanac for 1816. By William Collom. Philadelphia: Lydia R. Bailey. 24 ll. MWA; DLC; InU; PHi. 11077

BENNETT & Walton's Almanac for 1816. By William Collom. Philadelphia: Bennett and Walton; Lydia R. Bailey, printer. 18 ll. MWA; DLC; N; PHi; Drake. 11078

BIOREN'S Annual Compting-House Sheet Almanack for 1816. Philadelphia: John Bioren. Broadside. Advertised in "Bioren's Town and Country Almanack" for 1816. 11079

BIOREN'S Pennsylvania Pocket Remembrancer for 1816. Philadelphia: John Bioren. 24 ll. P; PHi. 11080

BIOREN'S Town and Country Almanack for 1816. By William Collom. Philadelphia: John Bioren. 18 ll. CLU; InU; NjP; PHi; PPL; PPiU; NjR (17 ll.) 17381

-- Issue with 24 ll. PDoBHi; PPL. 11082

BIOREN'S Town and Country Almanack for 1816. By Abraham Shoemaker. Philadelphia: John Bioren. 18 ll. MWA; DLC; NN; NHi (17 ll.); PHi. 11083

COLUMBIAN Almanac for 1816. Philadelphia: David Dickinson. 18 ll. MWA; Drake. 11084

COLUMBIAN Almanac for 1816. Philadelphia: David Dickinson; D. Dickinson, printer. 18 ll. MWA; DLC; InU (ntp); NjR; PHi (17 ll.); CU; Drake (10 ll.) 11085

CRAMER'S Pittsburgh Almanack for 1816. By Rev. John Taylor. Pittsburgh: Cramer, Spear and Eichbaum;

Robert Ferguson & Co., printers. 18 ll.　MWA; NN;
IChi; InU (titleleaf only); WvU.　　　　　　11086

CRAMER'S Pittsburgh Magazine Almanack for 1816. By
Rev. John Taylor. Pittsburgh: Cramer, Spear and
Eichbaum; Robert Ferguson & Co., printers. 36 ll.
MWA; DLC (34 ll.); NN; OHi; OClWHi; NjP; CtY;
OMC; InHi; InU; PHi; PPi; PPiU.　　　　　11087

FARMERS' and Citizens' Almanac for 1816. Philadelphia: David Dickinson. 18 ll. MWA (two varieties);
DLC (16 ll.); PPL.　　　　　　　　　　　　11088

FATHER Tammany's Almanac for 1816. Philadelphia:
18 ll. MWA (imprint torn off)　　　　　　　11089

Der GEMEINNÜTZIGE Landwirthschafts Calender auf
1816. Lancaster: Anton Albrecht. 20 ll. MWA; N;
DeWint; InU (19 ll.); WHi; P; PHi; PPG; PPL. 11090

The GENTLEMAN'S Annual Pocket Remembrancer for
1816. Philadelphia: A. Small. 102 ll. MWA; MHi;
MiU-C; PHi.　　　　　　　　　　　　　　　11091

Der HOCH-DEUTSCHE Americanische Calender auf 1816.
Philadelphia: G. und D. Billmeyer. 21 ll. MWA; DLC;
NN; NHi (impf); NjR (20 ll.); RPB; CLU; CtY; InU;
WHi; PHi; PPG; PDoBHi; PPCS; PPeSchw; PYHi.
　　　　　　　　　　　　　　　　　　　　11092
JOHNSON & Warner's Almanac for 1816. By Joshua
Sharp. Philadelphia: Johnson & Warner; Lydia R.
Bailey, printer. 24 ll. MWA; DLC; InU; PP.　11093

KITE'S Town and Country Almanac for 1816. By William Collom. Philadelphia: Benjamin and Thomas Kite;
Lydia R. Bailey, printer. 18 ll. MWA; DLC; NN
(impf); N; CtY; PDoBHi; PHC; PHi (impf)　　11094

M'CULLOCH'S Pocket Almanac for 1816. Philadelphia:
W. M'Culloch. 16 ll. MWA; DLC (12 ll., ntp); DeWint;
PHi.　　　　　　　　　　　　　　　　　　　11095

MINER'S Pennsylvania & New-Jersey Almanac for 1816.

Doylestown: Asher Miner. 19 ll. MWA; PDoBHi.
11096

Der NEUE, Americanische Landwirthschafts-Calender auf 1816. Reading: Johann Ritter und Comp. 21 ll. MWA; DLC; N; InU (20 ll.); DeWint; P; PHi; PPeSchw; PRHi; PR.
11097

Der NEUE Pittsburger, für die Westliche Gegend eingerichteter Calender auf 1816. Pittsburgh: J. Schnee und Companie. 20 ll. MWA; PPi.
11098

PENNSYLVANIA Almanac for 1816. Philadelphia: Porter. DLC.
11099

The PENNSYLVANIA & New-Jersey Almanac for 1816. Doylestown: Asher Miner. 20 ll. MWA; P.
11100

The PITTSBURGH Town & Country Almanac, for Rogues and Honest Folks for 1816. By John Armstrong. Pittsburgh: R. Patterson; S. Engles, printer. 30 ll. MWA (two varieties, one 24 ll.); DLC (29 ll.); MBAt; OMC (25 ll., ntp); PPiU (16 ll.)
11101

POOR Will's Almanack for 1816. Philadelphia: Joseph Crukshank; Solomon W. Conrad. 24 ll. MWA; DLC; N; MH; CtY; OCl; InU; PHC; PHi.
11102

POUNDER'S Wesleyan Almanac for 1816. Philadelphia: Jonathan Pounder; D. Dickinson, printer. 18 ll. MWA; DLC; InU; PHi; PP; PPL; Drake.
11103

SOMERSETER Calender auf 1816. Schellsburg: Friedrich Goeb. [Seidensticker]
11104

The AGRICULTURAL Almanack for 1817. Philadelphia: Solomon W. Conrad. 20 ll. MWA; DLC (impf); NHi; NjR; CtY; PDoBHi (ntp); PHC; PHi; PPAmP; PPL; Drake.
11105

AMERICAN Calendar, or Naval & Military Almanac for 1817. By Joshua Sharp. Philadelphia: Thomas DeSilver; Robert DeSilver. 20 ll. NjR.
11106

Pennsylvania - 1817

The AMERICAN Lady's Pocket Book for 1817. Philadelphia: A. Small. 84 ll. ViU. 11107

AMERICANISCHER Stadt und Land Calender auf 1817. Philadelphia: Conrad Zentler. 18 ll. MWA; DLC; N; CLU; InU; PHi; Drake (17 ll.) 11108

BAILEY'S Rittenhouse Almanac for 1817. By Joshua Sharp. Philadelphia: Lydia R. Bailey. 18 ll. MWA; DLC; InU; MB; PHi. 11109

BENNETT & Walton's Almanac for 1817. By Joshua Sharp. Philadelphia: Bennet [sic] & Walton. 18 ll. N; PHi; NjR. 11110

BENNETT & Walton's Almanac for 1817. By Joshua Sharp. Philadelphia: Bennett & Walton. 18 ll. MWA; DLC; NjR; PHi. 11111

BIOREN'S Annual Compting-House Sheet Almanack for 1817. Philadelphia: John Bioren. Broadside. Advertised in "Bioren's Town and Country Almanack" for 1817. 11112

BIOREN'S Pennsylvania Pocket Remembrancer for 1817. Philadelphia: John Bioren. 32 ll. MWA; DLC (31 ll.); PHi. 11113

BIOREN'S Town and Country Almanack for 1817. By William Collom. Philadelphia: John Bioren. 24 ll. MWA; DLC; NN; NHi (impf); NjR; CLU; InU; MiD-B; PHi; PP; PPL (23 ll.); PPiU; Drake. 11114

BIOREN'S Town and Country Almanack for 1817. By Abraham Shoemaker. Philadelphia: John Bioren. 24 ll. PDoBHi. 11115

The COUNTING-HOUSE Almanac for 1817. Carlisle: Carlisle Herald. Broadside. MWA. 11116

CRAMER'S Magazine Almanack for 1817. By Rev. John Taylor. Pittsburgh: Cramer, Spear and Eichbaum; Robert Ferguson & Co., printers. 36 ll. MWA; DLC; NN (impf); NjR; OClWHi; MBAt; NjP; CtY; InHi; InU;

OHi; PPi; PPiHi (34 ll.); PPiU. 11117

CRAMER'S Pittsburgh Almanack for 1817. By Rev. John Taylor. Pittsburgh: Cramer, Spear and Eichbaum; Robert Ferguson and Co., printers. 18 ll. MWA; ICHi; InU; OClWHi; PPiU. 11118

CRAMER'S Pittsburgh Magazine Almanack for 1817. By Rev. John Taylor. Pittsburgh: Cramer, Spear and Eichbaum; Robert Ferguson and Co., printers. 36 ll. OC; OCHP; WHi. 11119

The FARMER'S Almanac for 1817. Philadelphia: McCarthy. [Phillips] 11120

The FARMERS & Mechanics' Almanac for 1817. Philadelphia: Joseph Rakestraw, for David Dickinson. 18 ll. MWA; DLC; NjP; PU. 11121

Der GEMEINNÜTZIGE Landwirthschafts Calender auf 1817. Lancaster: Anton Albrecht. 20 ll. MWA; DLC; DeWint; InU; P; PAnL; PHi; PPG; PYHi. 11122

The GENTLEMAN'S Annual Pocket Remembrancer for 1817. Philadelphia: A. Small. 102 ll. NHi; NcD; MiU-C. 11123

Der HOCH-DEUTSCHE Americanische Calender auf 1817. Philadelphia: G. und D. Billmeyer. 21 ll. MWA; DLC (20 ll.); NN (19 ll.); NjR; InU; CtY; WHi; P (20 ll.); RPB; PHi; PPCS; PYHi. 11124

KITE'S Town and Country Almanac for 1817. By Joshua Sharp. Philadelphia: Benjamin and Thomas Kite; Lydia R. Bailey, printer. 18 ll. MWA; CtY; NjR; PHi. 11125

MINER'S Agricultural and Miscellaneous Almanac, for Pennsylvania & New-Jersey for 1817. By William Collom. Doylestown: Asher Miner. 18 ll. MWA (two varieties); DLC (16 ll.); NN (2 ll.); PDoBHi (16 ll.); PHi. 11126

Der NEUE, Americanische Landwirthschafts-Calender
auf 1817. Reading: Johann Ritter und Comp. 18 ll.
MWA; DLC; NN (15 ll.); P; PHi; PPG; PPeSchw;
PRHi; PPL (17 ll., ntp)   11126

Der NEUE Pittsburger, für die Westliche Gegend Eingerichteter Calender auf 1817. Greensburgh: J. Schnee
und Co. 21 ll. MWA.   11127

Der NEUE Pittsburger, für die Westliche Gegend eingerichteter Calender auf 1817. Greensburgh: J. Schnee
und Co. und Cramer, Spear und Eichbaum, Pittsburgh.
21 ll. PHi (18 ll.)   11128

The NEW-JERSEY Almanac for 1817. Philadelphia:
Joseph Rakestraw. 18 ll. MWA (16 ll.)   11129

The NEW JERSEY Almanac for 1817. Philadelphia:
Joseph Rakestraw, for David Dickinson. 18 ll. MWA;
DLC; NjR; NbHi.   11130

The NEW St. Tammany Almanac for 1817. Philadelphia: George W. Mentz. 18 ll. MWA (two varieties);
PHi.   11131

The PENNSYLVANIA and New-Jersey Almanac for 1817.
By William Collom. Doylestown: Asher Miner. 18 ll.
DLC; PDoBHi (14 ll.); NjR.   11132

The PITTSBURGH Town & Country Almanac, for Rogues
and Honest Folks for 1817. By John Armstrong. Pittsburgh: R. Patterson; S. Engles, printer. 18 ll. OClWHi;
OHi.   11133

The PITTSBURGH Town & Country Magazine Almanac,
for Rogues and Honest Folks for 1817. By John Armstrong. Pittsburgh: R. Patterson; S. Engles, printer.
30 ll. MWA; DLC (26 ll.); InU; OClWHi; OMC; PHi
(28 ll.); PPi.   11134

POOR Will's Almanac for 1817. Philadelphia: Joseph
Rakestraw. 18 ll. MWA; MH; OCl; OClWHi; WHi;
PHi; Drake (17 ll.)   11135

POOR Will's Pocket Almanack for 1817. Philadelphia: Solomon W. Conrad. 24 ll. MWA; PHi; NjR. 11136

POUNDER'S Wesleyan Almanac for 1817. Philadelphia: Jonathan Pounder. 18 ll. MWA; DLC; NN; De-Ar; PPL (15 ll.) 11137

SOMERSETER Calender auf 1817. Schellsburg: Friedrich Goeb. [Seidensticker] 11138

WARNER'S Almanac for 1817. By Joshua Sharp. Philadelphia: Benjamin Warner. 18 ll. MWA; DLC; NN; N; CtY; InU; DeHi; PHi. 11139

The AGRICULTURAL Almanack for 1818. Philadelphia: Solomon W. Conrad. 24 ll. MWA; DLC; NHi; IU; PHC; PHi; PPL. 11140

AMERICAN Almanac for 1818. By William Collom. Philadelphia: T. Desilver; R. Desilver. 27 ll. MWA; DLC; NN (14 ll.); PHi. 11141

The AMERICAN Lady's Pocket Book for 1818. Philadelphia: A. Small. PHi. 11142

AMERICANISCHER Stadt und Land Calender auf 1818. Philadelphia: Conrad Zentler. 18 ll. MWA; DLC; N; NN; CLU; InU (ntp); PDoBHi (nfp, ntp); PHi; PPG. 11143

BAILEY'S Rittenhouse Almanac for 1818. By Joshua Sharp. Philadelphia: Lydia R. Bailey. 18 ll. MWA; DLC; NHi; InU; PHi; PPL. 11144

BENNETT & Walton's Almanac for 1818. By Joshua Sharp. Philadelphia: Bennett & Walton. 18 ll. MWA; DLC; InU; NjR (17 ll.); PHC; PHi; PPL. 11145

BIOREN'S Annual Compting-House Sheet Almanack for 1818. Philadelphia: John Bioren. Broadside. Advertised in "Bioren's Town and Country Almanack" for 1818. 11146

BIOREN'S Pennsylvania Pocket Remembrancer for 1818.

Philadelphia: John Bioren. 24 ll. MWA; MH; NBuG;
PHi (23 ll.); NjR. 11147

BIOREN'S Town and Country Almanack for 1818. By
William Collom. Philadelphia: John Bioren. 24 ll.
MWA; DLC; N; NN; NjR (23 ll.); NjGlaN; DeU (19
ll.); MnU; InU; MiD-B; ViW; PU; PHi; PYHi; NHi
(impf); Drake (20 ll.) 11148

COLUMBIAN Almanac for 1818. Philadelphia: David
Dickinson. 18 ll. MWA; InU (ntp); PDoBHi. 11149

The COUNTING-HOUSE Almanac for 1818. Carlisle:
Carlisle Herald. Broadside. MWA. 11150

CRAMER'S Magazine Almanack for 1818. By Rev.
John Taylor. Pittsburgh: Cramer & Spear; Cramer &
Spear, printers. 36 ll. MWA (wrappers only); InHi;
PPi; PPiHi. 11151

CRAMER'S Pittsburgh Almanack for 1818. By Rev.
John Taylor. Pittsburgh: Cramer and Spear. 18 ll.
MWA; ICHi; InHi; OO. 11152

CRAMER'S Pittsburgh Magazine Almanack for 1818. By
Rev. John Taylor. Pittsburgh: Cramer and Spear. 36
ll. MWA; InU; NjP (impf); CtY; OC; OHi; OMC;
WHi; PPi; PPiU; OClWHi. 11153

The FARMER'S Almanac for 1818. By David Young.
Philadelphia: Printed for every purchaser. 18 ll. NN;
NHi; NjR; Drake. 11154

Der GEMEINNÜTZIGE Landwirthschafts Calender auf
1818. Lancaster: Anton Albrecht. 20 ll. MWA; DLC;
DeWint; InU; P; PDoBHi; PHi; PPL; PPeSchw; PYHi.
11155

The GENTLEMAN'S Annual Pocket Remembrancer for
1818. Philadelphia: A. Small. 104 ll. MH; PHi.
11156

Der HOCH-DEUTSCHE Americanische Calender auf 1818.
Philadelphia: G. und D. Billmeyer. 21 ll. MWA; DLC
(16 ll.); CLU; CtY; InU; PPCS; P (20 ll.); PHi; PLF;

PPG; PPL (19 ll.); PYHi.   11157

KITE'S Town and Country Almanac for 1818. By Joshua Sharp. Philadelphia: Benjamin and Thomas Kite; Lydia R. Bailey, printer. 18 ll. MWA; DLC (impf); N; PHi; PP.   11158

MINER'S Agricultural Almanac for 1818. By William Collom. Doylestown: Asher Miner. 18 ll. MWA; DLC; PHi.   11159

Der NEUE, Americanische Landwirthschafts-Calender auf 1818. Reading: Johann Ritter und Comp. 18 ll. MWA; DLC; N; NN; NHi (16 ll.); CLU; InU; P; PHi; PPAmP; PPCS; PPeSchw; PPL; PR; PRHi.   11160

Der NEUE für die Westliche Gegend Eingerichteter Calender auf 1818. Grünsburg: J. Armbrust und Co. 20 ll. MWA.   11161

The NEW St. Tammany Almanac for 1818. Philadelphia: George W. Mentz. 18 ll. MWA (impf); InU (16 ll., ntp); PHi.   11162

PATTERSON'S Ohio Magazine Almanac for 1818. By John Armstrong. Pittsburgh: R. Patterson; S. Engles, printer. 36 ll. MWA (18 ll., impf); MBAt; OMC (30 ll.)   11163

PATTERSON'S Pittsburgh, Town and Country Almanac for 1818. By John Armstrong. Pittsburgh: R. Patterson; S. Engles, printer. 18 ll. MWA; PPi.   11164

PATTERSON'S Pittsburgh Town and Country Magazine Almanac for 1818. By John Armstrong. Pittsburgh: R. Patterson; S. Engles, printer. 30 ll. PHi (impf); PPiHi (26 ll.)   11165

The PITTSBURGH Town and Country Magazine Almanac for Rogues and Honest Folk for 1818. By John Armstrong. Pittsburgh: R. Patterson. 18 ll. OMC. 11166

POOR Robin's Almanac for 1818. Philadelphia: David

Pennsylvania - 1818

Hogan. 18 ll. MWA; DLC (impf); InU. 11167

POOR Will's Almanac for 1818. Philadelphia: Joseph Rakestraw. 18 ll. MWA; DLC; WHi; PHi; PPL; PPiU; NjR; Drake. 11168

POUNDER'S Wesleyan Almanac for 1818. Philadelphia: Jonathan Pounder. 18 ll. MWA; CtY; PDoBHi (15 ll.); PHi; PPL. 11169

SOMERSETER Calender auf 1818. Schellsburg: Friedrich Goeb. [Seidensticker] 11170

The UNITED States' Almanac for 1818. By Joshua Sharp. Philadelphia: Thomas M. Longstreth. 18 ll. PHi. 11171

WARNER'S Almanac for 1818. By Joshua Sharp. Philadelphia: Benjamin Warner. 24 ll. MWA; DLC; N; CtY; InU; PHC. 11172

-- Issue with 30 ll. PDoBHi (28 ll.); PHi; PPL (26 ll.) 11173

The WESTERN Reserve Almanac for 1818. By Samuel Roberts. Pittsburgh: Butler & Lambdin. 8 ll. OClWHi; OHi. 11174

The AGRICULTURAL Almanack for 1819. Philadelphia: Solomon W. Conrad. 24 ll. MWA (two varieties); DLC (19 ll.); N; NHi; NjR; NcD; CtY; Ms-Ar (22 ll.); MnU; CtHi; PHi; PP; PPAmP; PPL; PHC; Drake. 11175

The AMERICAN Ladies Pocket Book for 1819. Phila.: A. Small. 90 ll. PHi. 11176

AMERICANISCHER Stadt und Land Calender auf 1819. Philadelphia: Conrad Zentler. 18 ll. MWA (impf); DLC; N; NN (17 ll.); NjR (16 ll.); P; PHi; PLF; PPG. 11177

ANNUAL Compting House Sheet Almanack for 1819. Philadelphia: John Bioren. Broadside. Advertised in

1066   Pennsylvania - 1819

"Bioren's Town and Country Almanack" for 1819. 11178

BAILEY'S Rittenhouse Almanac for 1819. By Joshua Sharp. Philadelphia: Lydia R. Bailey. 18 ll. MWA; DLC; InU; PHi; PPL.   11179

BENNETT & Walton's Almanac for 1819. By Joshua Sharp. Philadelphia: Bennett & Walton. 18 ll. MWA; DLC; N (impf); InU; PHC; PHi.   11180

BIOREN'S Pennsylvania Pocket Remembrancer for 1819. Philadelphia: John Bioren. 24 ll. MWA (22 ll.); DLC (23 ll.); NBuG; PHi.   11181

BIOREN'S Town and Country Almanack for 1819. By William Collom. Philadelphia: John Bioren. 24 ll. MWA; DLC; N (impf); NN (22 ll.); KyHi; NjR; CLU; InU (23 ll.); WHi (23 ll.); PHi; PPL; PHC; PP; PPiU.   11182

BIOREN'S Town and Country Almanack for 1819. By Abraham Shoemaker. Philadelphia: John Bioren. 24 ll. PDoBHi.   11183

CENTURY Almanac for 1799 to 1899. Harrisburg: Westling. 1819. 16 ll. [Stapleton]   11184

CRAMER'S Deutscher Pittsburger für die Westliche Gegund Eingerichteter Calender auf 1819. Von dem Ehrw. Johan Taylor. Pittsburgh: Cramer und Spear; Grünsburg: J. Armbrust und Co. 22 ll. MWA (20 ll.); PPiU (18 ll.)   11185

CRAMER'S Magazine Almanack for 1819. By Rev. John Taylor. Pittsburgh: Cramer and Spear. 36 ll. MWA; MBAt; CtY; InHi; InU; NBuG; ICU; OC; P; PPPrHi; PPi; PPiHi (17 ll.)   11186

CRAMER'S Pittsburgh Almanack for 1819. By Rev. John Taylor. Pittsburgh: Cramer & Spear. 18 ll. OClWHi (15 ll.); PPiU (ntp)   11187

The FARMER'S Almanac for 1819. By Andrew Beers.

Philadelphia: S. Potter & Co. 18 ll. MWA; PHi.
11188

The FRANKLIN Almanac for 1819. By John Armstrong. Pittsburgh: Eichbaum & Johnston. 18 ll. MWA; PPiU (ntp)
11189

The FRANKLIN Magazine Almanac for 1819. By John Armstrong. Pittsburgh: Eichbaum and Johnston. 36 ll. PPi.
11190

Der GEMEINNÜTZIGE Landwirthschafts Calender auf 1819. Lancaster: Anton Albrecht. 20 ll. PHi. 11191

The GENTLEMAN'S Annual Pocket Remembrancer for 1819. Philadelphia: A. Small. 102 ll. CU 11192

Der HOCH-DEUTSCHE Americanische Calender auf 1819. Philadelphia: G. und D. Billmeyer. 21 ll. MWA; DLC (18 ll.); NN; NjR; InU; RPB; CLU; MH; CtY; WHi; DeWint; PHi; PLF; PPL (20 ll.); PYHi; PAnL (18 ll.); PPCS; PPeSchw.
11193

KITE'S Town and Country Almanac for 1819. By Joshua Sharp. Philadelphia: Benjamin and Thomas Kite; Lydia R. Bailey, printer. 18 ll. MWA (impf); DLC; N; InU; MB; PHi.
11194

The MAGAZINE Almanack for 1819. Pittsburgh: The Pittsburgh Bible Society. 24 ll. PPiHi (23 ll.) 11195

MINER'S Agricultural Almanac for 1819. By William Collom. Doylestown: Asher Miner. 18 ll. MWA; DLC; NHi (17 ll.); NjR; WHi.
11196

MINIATURE Almanack for 1819. Philadelphia: Sold by the Booksellers and most traders in city and country. 12 ll. PHi.
11197

Der NEUE, Americanische Landwirthschafts-Calender auf 1819. Reading: Johann Ritter und Comp. 18 ll. MWA; DLC; NN (16 ll.); InU; P; PHi (impf); PPCS; PPeSchw; PPL; PRHi.
11198

1068 Pennsylvania - 1819

NEW Jersey Almanac for 1819. Philadelphia: D. Dickinson. MWA (17 ll.) 11199

The NEW St. Tammany Almanac for 1819. Philadelphia: George W. Mentz. 18 ll. MWA; DLC (17 ll.); CtY; ICHi; InU; NcD; P; PP; PHi; PDoBHi (16 ll.); NjR. 11200

-- Issue with added signature. PPL (21 ll.) 11201

Der NORTHAMPTON Bauern Calender auf 1819. Easton: Christian J. Huetter und Sohn. 19 ll. PBL.
11202

PATTERSON'S Pittsburgh, Town & Country Almanac for 1819. By John Armstrong. Pittsburgh: R. Patterson. 18 ll. MWA; InHi; OClWHi; PPi. 11203

PATTERSON'S Pittsburgh, Town and Country Magazine Almanac for 1819. By John Armstrong. Pittsburgh: R. Patterson & Lambdin; Butler & Lambdin, printers. 30 ll. MWA; NjP; OClWHi; PHi (28 ll.); PPi; PPiHi.
11204

The PENNSYLVANIA and New-Jersey Almanac for 1819. By William Collom. Doylestown: Asher Miner. 18 ll. MWA; DLC; NjR; PDoBHi; PHi. 11205

PENNSYLVANIA & New Jersey Almanac for 1819. By Joshua Sharp. Philadelphia: D. Dickinson. 16 ll. PDoBHi.
11206

The PITTSBURGH Town and Country Magazine Almanac for Rogues and Honest Folk for 1819. By John Armstrong. Pittsburgh: R. Patterson & Lambdin. OMC (25 ll.) 11207

POOR Robin's Almanac for 1819. Philadelphia: D. Dickinson. 18 ll. MWA; PPL (12 ll.) 11208

POOR Will's Almanack for 1819. Philadelphia: Joseph Rakestraw. 18 ll. MWA; DLC; NjR (14 ll.); WHi; PHi; PU. 11209

POOR Will's Pocket Almanack for 1819. Philadelphia:

Solomon W. Conrad. 24 ll. MWA; PHC; PHi; NjR.
11210

POUNDER'S Wesleyan Almanac for 1819. Philadelphia: Jonathan Pounder. 18 ll. MWA; DLC; N; InU; PHi; NcD. 11211

SOMERSETER Calender auf 1819. Schellsburg: Friedrich Goeb. [Seidensticker] 11212

The UNION Almanac for 1819. By Joshua Sharp. Philadelphia: Isaac Peirce. 18 ll. PHi (17 ll.) 11213

WARNER'S Almanac for 1819. By Joshua Sharp. Philadelphia: Benjamin Warner. 18 ll. MWA; DLC; PHi. 11214

WASHINGTON Almanac for 1819. Philadelphia: D. Dickinson. 18 ll. MWA (two varieties); DLC; N; NN; CLU; CtY; NjR; NjT (17 ll.); ViU; PHi; PPL. 11215

The WESTERN Reserve Almanac for 1819. By Samuel Roberts. Pittsburgh: Butler & Lambdin. 8 ll. DLC.
11216

The AGRICULTURAL Almanack for 1820. Philadelphia: Solomon W. Conrad. 24 ll. MWA; DLC (19 ll.); N; NN (14 ll.); PPAmP; NjR; CLU; CtY; PDoBHi; PHC; PHi; PPL. 11217

The AMERICAN Ladies Pocket Book for 1820. Phila.: A. Small. 90 ll. MWA; NHi. 11218

AMERICANISCHER Stadt und Land Calender auf 1820. Philadelphia: Conrad Zentler. 18 ll. MWA; DLC; N; NN; PDoBHi; PHi; PPAmP; PPL (16 ll.); PYHi.
11219

BAILEY'S Rittenhouse Almanac for 1820. By Joshua Sharp. Philadelphia: Lydia R. Bailey. 18 ll. MWA (16 ll.); DLC; PU; Drake. 11220

BAILEY'S Rittenhouse Almanac for 1820. By Joshua Sharp. Philadelphia: Robert Desilver. 18 ll. PHi.
11221

BAILEY'S Rittenhouse Almanac for 1820. By Joshua

Sharp. Philadelphia: Thomas Desilver. 18 ll. MWA;
InU; PHi. 11222

The BAPTIST Almanac, for the Middle States for 1820.
By Wm. Collom. Philadelphia: Anderson and Meehan.
16 ll. MWA; DeU; PHi. 11223

BENNETT & Walton's Almanac for 1820. By Joshua
Sharp. Philadelphia: Bennett & Walton. 18 ll. MWA;
DLC; InU; PHC; PHi. 11224

BIOREN'S Annual Compting-House Sheet Almanack for
1820. Philadelphia: John Bioren. Broadside. Advertised in "Bioren's Town and Country Almanack" for
1820. 11225

BIOREN'S Pennsylvania Pocket Remembrancer for 1820.
Philadelphia: John Bioren. 24 ll. MWA; DLC; MH;
NBuG; PHi; PPL; NjR. 11226

BIOREN'S Town and Country Almanack for 1820. By
William Collom. Philadelphia: John Bioren. 18 ll.
MWA; DLC; NN; NHi; NBuHi; NjR; NjGlaN; InU; PHi;
PPAmP; PPL. 11227

BIOREN'S Town and Country Almanack for 1820. By
Abraham Shoemaker. Philadelphia: John Bioren. 24 ll.
PDoBHi. 11228

CITIZENS & Farmers' Almanack for 1820. Philadelphia: Published for the booksellers. 14 ll. PHi. 11229

CITIZENS & Farmers' Almanack for 1820. By Joshua
Sharp. Philadelphia: Griggs & Dickinson. [Phillips]
11230

CRAMER'S Deutscher Pittsburger für die Westliche
Gegend Eingerichteter Calender auf 1820. Pittsburg:
Cramer und Spear. 18 ll. MWA (impf) 11231

CRAMER'S Magazine Almanack for 1820. By Rev.
John Taylor. Pittsburgh: Cramer and Spear. 36 ll.
MWA; CtY; InU; OC; OClWHi; KyU (34 ll., ntp);
Wv-Ar; PHi; PPi; PPiU. 11232

CRAMER'S Pittsburgh Almanack for 1820. By Rev.
John Taylor. Pittsburgh: Cramer and Spear. 18 ll.
MWA; OHi. 11233

CRAMER'S Pittsburgh Magazine Almanack for 1820. By
Rev. John Taylor. Pittsburgh: Cramer & Spear. 36
ll. OMC. 11234

DEUTSCHER Pittsburger für die Westliche Gegend Eingerichteter Calender auf 1820. Von Johann Armstrong.
Pittsburg: Eichbaum und Johnston; Grünsberg: Jacob S.
Steck. 18 ll. DLC (17 ll.) 11235

The FRANKLIN Almanac for 1820. By John Armstrong.
Pittsburgh: Eichbaum & Johnston. 18 ll. OHi. 11236

The FRANKLIN Magazine Almanac for 1820. By John
Armstrong. Pittsburgh: Eichbaum & Johnston; Eichbaum & Johnston, printers. 36 ll. MWA; DLC (35 ll.);
InU; PPi (impf); PPiHi. 11237

Der GEMEINNÜTZIGE Landwirthschafts Calender auf
1820. Lancaster: Anton Albrecht. 20 ll. PHi. 11238

Der HOCH-DEUTSCHE Americanische Calender auf
1820. Germantaun: M. Billmeyer. 21 ll. MWA; DLC;
NjR; CLU; CtY; NBuG; InU; WHi; DeWint; PPG; PHi;
PLF; PPeSchw; PPL (18 ll.); PYHi; PPCS; PDoBHi;
PPAmP. 11239

KITE'S Town and Country Almanac for 1820. By William and Thomas Kite. 18 ll. MWA (two varieties);
DLC; CtY; PHi. 11240

M'CARTY & Davis' Pennsylvania Almanac for 1820. By
William Collom. Philadelphia: M'Carty & Davis. 24 ll.
MWA; DLC; DeWint; InU; MBC; NjR (18 ll.) 11241

-- Issue with 30 ll. MWA; N; PHi. 11242

MINER'S Agricultural Almanac for 1820. By William
Collom. Doylestown: Asher Miner. 18 ll. DLC; PHi;
PDoBHi. 11243

Der Neue Allentauner Calender auf 1820. Allentaun:
Carl Ludwig Hutter. 21 ll. MWA (19 ll.); DLC (20
ll.); InU; PRHi; PHi. 11244

Der NEUE, Americanische Landwirthschafts-Calender
auf 1820. Reading: Johann Ritter und Comp. 18 ll.
MWA; DLC; NN; CLU; InU; P; PHi; PPL (17 ll.);
PPeSchw; PR; PRHi. 11245

The NEW St. Tammany Almanac for 1820. By William
Collom. Philadelphia: George W. Mentz. 18 ll. MWA
(impf); DLC; NN; PHi; NjR. 11246

Der NORTHAMPTON Bauern Calender auf 1820. Easton:
Christian J. Hutter und Sohn. 21 ll. MWA; DLC (20
ll.); PPL. 11247

PATTERSON'S Magazine Almanac for 1820. By John
Armstrong. Pittsburgh: R. Patterson & Lambdin. 30
ll. OClWHi; OMC (18 ll.); PPi. 11248

PATTERSON'S Pittsburgh, Town & Country Almanac for
1820. By John Armstrong. Pittsburgh: R. Patterson
& Lambdin. 18 ll. MWA; OClWHi; ViW; WHi; PPiHi.
11249

PATTERSON'S Pittsburgh, Town & Country Magazine
Almanac for 1820. By John Armstrong. Pittsburgh:
R. Patterson & Lambdin; Butler & Lambdin, printers.
PPiHi (31 ll.) 11250

The PENNSYLVANIA Almanac for 1820. Philadelphia:
McCarty & Davis. CtY. 11251

PENNSYLVANIA and New Jersey Almanack for 1820.
Philadelphia: Griggs & Co. 18 ll. CtY; NjR; NjT (15
ll.) 11252

The PENNSYLVANIA and New-Jersey Almanac for 1820.
By William Collom. Doylestown: Asher Miner. 22 ll.
MWA; NjR (20 ll.) 11253

PENNSYLVANIA & New Jersey Almanack for 1820. By
Joshua Sharpe [sic]. Philadelphia: Published for the

Pennsylvania - 1820

Booksellers. 18 ll. MWA; CtY; PHi (17 ll.) 11254

POOR Robin's Almanac for 1820. By Joshua Sharp. Philadelphia: David Hogan. 18 ll. MWA; PHi (14 ll.); PPL (17 ll.) 11255

POOR Will's Almanac for 1820. By William Collom. Philadelphia: Joseph Rakestraw. 18 ll. MWA; N; NN; NjR; WHi; P (17 ll.); PHi; PPL. 11256

POUNDER'S Wesleyan Almanack for 1820. Philadelphia: Jonathan Pounder. 18 ll. MWA; NHi (17 ll.); PHi; PP. 11257

SOMERSETER Calender auf 1820. Schellsburg: Friedrich Goeb. [Seidensticker] 11258

WARNER'S Almanack for 1820. By Joshua Sharpe [sic]. Philadelphia: Benjamin Warner. 24 ll. MWA; DLC; N (impf); CtY; InU; PHi. 11259

WASHINGTON Almanac for 1820. By Joshua Sharp. Philadelphia: D. Dickinson. 18 ll. MWA (two varieties); DLC; NN; ViHi; NjR; CtY (14 ll.); ViU; PHC; PHi; Drake. 11260

The AGRICULTURAL Almanack for 1821. Philadelphia: Solomon W. Conrad. 26 ll. MWA; DLC (impf); N; NN; NjR; CLU; CtY; NBuG; PDoBHi; PHi; PPAmP; PPL; Drake (impf) 11261

The AMERICAN Agricultural Almanack for 1821. Philadelphia: Robert DeSilver. 19 ll. MWA; DLC; CtY. 11262

The AMERICAN Ladies Pocket Book for 1821. Philadelphia: A. Small. 90 ll. PHi. 11263

AMERICANISCHER Stadt und Land Calender auf 1821. Philadelphia: Conrad Zentler. 18 ll. MWA; DLC; NHi; CLU; InU; DeWint; PHi; PPCS (12 ll.); PDoBHi; PPG; PYHi; Drake (17 ll.) 11264

BAILEY'S Rittenhouse Almanac for 1821. By Joshua

Sharp. Philadelphia: Lydia R. Bailey. 18 ll. MWA; NjR; PHi. 11265

BENNETT and Walton's Almanack for 1821. By Joshua Sharp. Philadelphia: Bennett and Walton. 18 ll. MWA; Nj (17 ll.); PHC; PHi. 11266

BIOREN'S Pennsylvania Pocket Remembrancer for 1821. Philadelphia: John Bioren. 24 ll. MWA; DLC (23 ll.); PHi. 11267

BIOREN'S Town and Country Almanack for 1821. Philadelphia: John Bioren. 18 ll. MWA. 11268

The CITIZEN and Farmers Almanac for 1821. By Joshua Sharp. Philadelphia. 18 ll. DLC (impf) 11269

CITIZENS & Farmers' Almanack for 1821. By Joshua Sharp. Philadelphia: Griggs & Dickinson. 18 ll. MWA (two varieties); N; PHi; NjR; Drake (14 ll.) 11270

CITIZENS and Farmers' Almanack for 1821. Philadelphia: Griggs & Dickinson: New Brunswick: Joseph C. Griggs. 18 ll. MWA (impf); CtY. 11271

CRAMER'S Magazine Almanack for 1821. By Rev. John Taylor. Pittsburgh: Cramer and Spear. 36 ll. MWA (35 ll.); NBuG; InHi; InU; PHi; CtY; OClWHi; OHi; OMC; OC; Wv-Ar; WvU; PPiU (30 ll.); PPi (ntp); PPiHi. 11272

CRAMER'S Pittsburgh Almanack for 1821. By Rev. John Taylor. Pittsburgh: Cramer & Spear. 18 ll. OClWHi (17 ll.) 11273

DEUTSCHER Pittsburger, für die Westliche Gegund Eingerichteter Calender auf 1821. Von Johann Armstrong. Pittsburg: Eichbaum und Johnston; Grünsburg: Jacob S. Steck. 18 ll. OHi; PPCS (impf) 11274

DEUTSCHER Pittsburger, für die Westliche Gegend Eingerichteter Calender auf 1821. Pittsburg: R. Patterson und Lambdin. 18 ll. MWA (17 ll.) 11275

The FARMERS' Almanac for 1821. By John Ward.
Philadelphia: M°Carty & Davis. 18 ll. MWA (impf);
CtY; InU; PHi. 11276

The FARMERS & Mechanics' Almanack for 1821.
Philadelphia: Thomas DeSilver. 18 ll. MWA; CtY;
NjR. 11277

The FRANKLIN Almanac for 1821. By John Armstrong.
Pittsburgh: Eichbaum & Johnston. 18 ll. MWA; PHi;
PPi. 11278

The FRANKLIN Magazine Almanac for 1821. By John
Armstrong. Pittsburgh: Eichbaum & Johnston. 36 ll.
MWA (17 ll.); PPi. 11279

Der GEMEINNÜTZIGE Landwirthschafts Calender auf
1821. Lancaster: William Albrecht. 18 ll. MWA; DLC;
NjP; CLU; CtY; InU; PAnL; PDoBHi; PHi; PPL.
11280
Der HOCH-DEUTSCHE Americanische Calender auf 1821.
Germantaun: M. Billmeyer. 21 ll. MWA; DLC; NN;
MBAt; CLU; MH; InU; PHi; DeWint; PLF; PPL (19
ll.); PPCS; PYHi; PPeSchw. 11281

KITE'S Town and Country Almanac for 1821. By William
Collom. Philadelphia: Benjamin and Thomas Kite.
18 ll. MWA (two varieties); DLC; NN (8 ll.); NHi;
CLU; CtY; NjR; PHi; PP; PPL (17 ll.) 11282

M°CARTY & Davis' Franklin Almanac for 1821. By
John Ward. Philadelphia: M°Carty & Davis. 18 ll.
MWA; DLC; NN (15 ll.); MB; NjR; PHi; PPL (17 ll.);
PPiHi. 11283

M°CARTY & Davis' Pennsylvania Almanac for 1821. By
John Ward. Philadelphia: M°Carty & Davis. 18 ll.
MWA; DLC; InU; PHi; PPL. 11284

MINER'S Agricultural Almanac for 1821. By William
Collom. Doylestown: Asher Miner. 18 ll. MWA; DLC;
PHi; PPL. 11285

Der NEUE Allentauner Calender auf 1821. Allentaun:
Georg Hanke. [Shoemaker] 11286

Der NEUE, Americanische Landwirthschafts-Calender
auf 1821. Reading: Johann Ritter und Comp. 18 ll.
MWA; NN; NHi (17 ll.); CLU; InU; N; PR; P; PHi
(17 ll.); PDoBHi; PPAmP; PRHi; PPL. 11287

NEW Brunswick, (N. J.) Almanac for 1821. By Joshua
Sharp. Philadelphia: Griggs & Dickinson; for Joseph
C. Griggs, New Brunswick. 18 ll. NjR (17 ll.) 11288

The NEW St. Tammany Almanac for 1821. By William
Collom. Philadelphia: George W. Mentz. 18 ll. MWA;
DLC; NHi; InU; WHi; PHi; Drake (17 ll.) 11289

Der NORTHAMPTON Bauern Calender auf 1821. Easton:
Christian J. Hutter. 20 ll. DLC; PAtM. 11290

PATTERSON'S Magazine Almanac for 1821. By John
Armstrong. Pittsburgh: R. Patterson & Lambdin. 30
ll. OClWHi; OMC (29 ll.) 11291

PATTERSON'S Pittsburgh, Town & Country Almanac for
1821. By John Armstrong. [Pittsburgh:] R. Patterson & Lambdin; Pittsburgh: Butler & Lambdin, printers.
20 ll. MWA; NHi; CLU; ICHi; InHi; T (17 ll.) 11292

The PENNSYLVANIA Almanac for 1821. By John Ward.
Philadelphia: M'Carty & Davis. 18 ll. CtY; PDoBHi.
11293
The PENNSYLVANIA & New-Jersey Almanac for 1821.
By William Collom. Doylestown: Asher Miner. 18 ll.
DLC. 11294

The PENNSYLVANIA Farmer's Almanac for 1821. By
Andrew Beers. Philadelphia: S. Potter & Co. 18 ll.
PHC; PHi. 11295

POOR Robin's Almanac for 1821. By Joshua Sharp.
Philadelphia: D. Dickinson. 18 ll. MWA; DLC; CtY;
InU; PHi; PP; PPL. 11296

POOR Will's Almanac for 1821. By William Collom.
Philadelphia: Joseph Rakestraw. 18 ll. NHi (16 ll.);
WHi; PHi; Drake. 11297

POOR Will's Almanac for 1821. By Joshua Sharp.
Philadelphia: D. Dickinson. 18 ll. MWA. 11298

POOR Will's Pocket Almanack for 1821. Philadelphia:
Solomon W. Conrad. 24 ll. MWA; DLC; OClWHi;
PHC; PHi. 11299

POUNDER'S Wesleyan Almanack for 1821. Philadelphia:
Jonathan Pounder. 18 ll. MWA; PHi; NjR. 11300

SOMERSETER Calender auf 1821. Schellsburg: Friedrich Goeb. [Seidensticker] 11301

WARNER'S Almanack for 1821. By Joshua Sharp.
Philadelphia: Benjamin Warner. 18 ll. MWA; DLC; N;
InU; NjR; PHi; PPiU. 11302

WASHINGTON Almanac for 1821. By Joshua Sharp.
Philadelphia: D. Dickinson. 18 ll. NN (12 ll.); P;
PDoBHi; PHi. 11303

The AGRICULTURAL Almanack for 1822. Philadelphia:
Solomon W. Conrad. 24 ll. MWA; DLC; N; NHi (23
ll.); NNA; CtY; ViU; PHi; PPAmP; PPL (23 ll.)
11304
The AGRICULTURAL Almanack for 1822. Philadelphia:
Griggs & Dickinson. 20 ll. MWA; DLC. 11305

The AMERICAN Farmers' Agricultural Almanack for
1822. Philadelphia: Griggs & Dickinson. 24 ll. MWA
(23 ll.) 11306

The AMERICAN Ladies Pocket Book for 1822. Philadelphia: A. Small. 90 ll. PHi. 11307

AMERICANISCHER Stadt und Land Calender auf 1822.
Philadelphia: Conrad Zentler. 18 ll. MWA; DLC; N;
NBuG; DeWint; CLU; CtY; InU; NjP; OC (17 ll.);
PDoBHi; PHi; PLF; PPG; PYHi; Drake (17 ll.) 11308

BENNETT and Walton's Almanack for 1822. By William Collom. Philadelphia: Bennett & Walton. 18 ll.
MWA; DLC; N; NjR; InU; PHi; PP.   11309

BIOREN'S Annual Compting-House Sheet Almanack for 1822. Philadelphia: John Bioren. Broadside. Advertised in "Bioren's Town and Country Almanack" for 1822.   11310

BIOREN'S Pennsylvania Pocket Remembrancer for 1822. Philadelphia: John Bioren. Advertised in "Bioren's Town and Country Almanack" for 1822.   11311

BIOREN'S Town and Country Almanack for 1822. Philadelphia: John Bioren. 18 ll. MWA; DLC; NN (17 ll.); NjGlaN; NjR; P; PHi.   11312

CITIZENS & Farmers' Almanack for 1822. By Joshua Sharp. Philadelphia: Griggs & Dickinson. 18 ll. MWA; DLC; NjR; CtY; InU; NjT; PHi.   11313

The COUNTING-HOUSE Almanac for 1822. [Carlisle: Carlisle Herald] Broadside. MWA.   11314

CRAMER'S Magazine Almanack for 1822. By Rev. John Taylor. Pittsburgh: Cramer and Spear. 36 ll.
MWA; CLU; CtY; InU; PHi; PPi; PPiHi.   11315

CRAMER'S Pittsburgh Almanack for 1822. By Rev. John Taylor. Pittsburgh: Cramer and Spear. 18 ll.
MWA; DLC; InHi; OC; Wv-Ar.   11316

The FARMERS' Almanac for 1822. By John Ward. Philadelphia: M'Carty & Davis. 18 ll. MWA; DLC; NN; CtY; InU; PHi.   11317

The FRANKLIN Magazine Almanac for 1822. Pittsburgh. PPi (22 ll., ntp)   11318

Der GEMEINNÜTZIGE Landwirthschafts Calender auf 1822. Lancaster: William Albrecht. 18 ll. MWA; DLC; N; NN (15 ll.); NjP (ntp); CLU; CtY; InHi; InU; WHi; P; PHi; PLHi; PYHi.   11319

The GENTLEMAN'S Annual Pocket Remembrancer for 1822. Philadelphia: A. Small. 90 ll. PPL. 11320

Der HOCH-DEUTSCHE Americanische Calender auf 1822. Germantaun: M. Billmeyer. 18 ll. MWA; DLC; NN (17 ll.); NHi (impf); PPAmP; NjR; PHi; PPL; CLU; MH; CtY; InU; PAtM; WHi; DeWint; PYHi; PPeSchw; PDoBHi. 11321

KITE'S Town and Country Almanac for 1822. By William Collom. Philadelphia: Benjamin and Thomas Kite. 18 ll. MWA; DLC; N; NN; NjR; CtY; InU; PHi.
11322

M'CARTY & Davis' Franklin Almanac for 1822. By John Ward. Philadelphia: M'Carty & Davis. 18 ll. MWA; NHi; PHi. 11323

M'CARTY & Davis Pennsylvania Almanac for 1822. By John Ward. Philadelphia: M'Carty & Davis. 18 ll. MWA; DLC; InU. 11324

MINER'S Pennsylvania & New-Jersey Almanac for 1822. By William Collom. Doylestown: Asher Miner. 18 ll. MWA; DLC. 11325

Der NEUE Allentauner Calender auf 1822. Allentaun: Georg Hanke. 18 ll. DLC. 11326

Der NEUE, Americanische Landwirthschafts-Calender auf 1822. Reading: Johann Ritter und Comp. 18 ll. MWA; DLC; InU; NjP; P; PHi; PPL; PR; PRHi.
11327

NEW Brunswick, (N. J.) Almanac for 1822. By Joshua Sharp. [Philadelphia:] Griggs & Dickinson for Joseph C. Griggs, New Brunswick, (N. J.) 18 ll. MWA; NjHi; Honeyman. 11328

The NEW St. Tammany Almanac for 1822. By John Ward. Philadelphia: George W. Mentz. 18 ll. MWA; NjR. 11329

Der NORTHAMPTON Bauern Calender auf 1822. Easton: Christian Jac. Hutter. 18 ll. DLC; PBL; PHi (16 ll.);

PPCS. 11330

The PENNSYLVANIA Almanac for 1822. By John Ward.
Philadelphia. 18 ll. MWA (15 ll., ntp) 11331

The PENNSYLVANIA Farmer's Almanac for 1822. By
Andrew Beers. Philadelphia: S. Potter, & Co. 16 ll.
PHi. 11332

PITTSBURGH Almanac for 1822. By John Armstrong.
Pittsburgh: R. Patterson & Lambdin; Butler & Lambdin, printers. 18 ll. MWA; DLC; InHi; PPiHi (17 ll.); OClWHi. 11333

The PITTSBURGH Magazine Almanac for 1822. Pittsburgh: R. Patterson & Lambdin; Butler & Lambdin, printers. 30 ll. OClWHi (18 ll.); OHi (21 ll.); OMC (29 ll.); PPi; WHi. 11334

POOR Robin's Almanac for 1822. By Joshua Sharp.
Philadelphia: D. Dickinson. 18 ll. MWA; DLC; N; NjR; InU (2 ll.); MB; MBC; NBuG; PHi. 11335

POOR Will's Almanac for 1822. By William Collom.
Philadelphia: Joseph Rakestraw. 18 ll. MWA; DLC; NHi; PPL (impf) 11336

POOR Will's Pocket Almanack for 1822. Philadelphia: Solomon W. Conrad. 24 ll. MWA; DLC; PHC; PHi.
11337

POUNDER'S Wesleyan Almanack for 1822. Philadelphia: Jonathan Pounder. 18 ll. MWA; DLC; NHi; InU (impf); Nj; PHi; NjR. 11338

The UNIVERSAL Almanack for 1822. By Joshua Sharp.
Philadelphia: Robert Desilver. 18 ll. MWA (17 ll.)
11339

The UNIVERSAL Almanack for 1822. By Joshua Sharp.
Philadelphia: Thomas Desilver. 18 ll. MWA (15 ll.)
11340

WARNER'S Almanack for 1822. By Joshua Sharp.
Philadelphia: Benjamin Warner. 18 ll. MWA (two varieties); DLC; CtY; PDoBHi; PHi; NjR (ntp) 11341

Der WESTLICHE Menschenfreund u. Schellsburger Calender auf 1822. Von John Armstrong. Schellsburg: Friedrich Goeb. 21 ll. MWA; PPL. 11342

The AGRICULTURAL Almanack for 1823. Philadelphia: Solomon W. Conrad. 24 ll. MWA; DLC; N (impf); NN; CtY; PDoBHi; PHi; PPL. 11343

AMERICAN Ladies Pocket Book for 1823. Philadelphia: A. Small. 90 ll. PHi. 11344

AMERICANISCHER Stadt und Land Calender auf 1823. Philadelphia: Conrad Zentler. 18 ll. MWA; DLC; N; NN; NjP; CLU; CtY; P (17 ll.); PDoBHi; PHi; PPCS; PPeSchw; PYHi; Drake. 11345

BAILEY'S Washington Almanac for 1823. Philadelphia: Lydia R. Bailey. 18 ll. MBAt; PHi. 11346

BAILEY'S Washington Almanac for 1823. Philadelphia: Robert Desilver. 18 ll. PP; PPAmP; PPL. 11347

BAILEY'S Washington Almanac for 1823. Philadelphia: Thomas Desilver. 18 ll. MWA; NN; ICHi. 11348

BENNETT & Walton's Almanack for 1823. By Joshua Sharp. Philadelphia: Bennett & Walton. 18 ll. MWA; NHi (12 ll.); InU; WHi; PHi. 11349

CITIZENS & Farmers' Almanack for 1823. By Joshua Sharp. Philadelphia: Griggs & Dickinson. 18 ll. MWA; N; InU. PHi; Drake. 11350

CRAMER'S Magazine Almanack for 1823. By Rev. John Taylor. Pittsburgh: Cramer and Spear. 36 ll. MWA; CtY; InU; OC; OClWHi; OMC. 11351

CRAMER'S Pittsburgh Almanack for 1823. By Rev. John Taylor. Pittsburgh: Cramer and Spear. 18 ll. MWA; DLC; ICHi; InU; TKL; Wv-Ar; WvU; PPi.
11352

The FARMERS' Almanac for 1823. By John Ward. Philadelphia: M'Carty & Davis. 18 ll. MWA; NN; CLU;

CtY; InU; PHi. 11353

The FRANKLIN Almanack for 1823. By Dr. John Armstrong. Pittsburgh: Eichbaum & Johnston. 18 ll. DLC; PPi; PPiU (16 ll.) 11354

Der GEMEINNÜTZIGE Landwirthschafts Calender auf 1823. Von Carl F. Egelmann. Lancaster: William Albrecht. 18 ll. MWA; DLC; CLU; PHi (16 ll.); PLF (17 ll.); PLHi; PPL; PPeSchw; PYHi. 11355

Der HOCH-DEUTSCHE Americanische Calender auf 1823. Von Carl Friederich Egelmann. Germantaun: M. Billmeyer. 18 ll. MWA; DLC; NN; NHi (16 ll.); CLU; CtY; InU; MH; DeWint; WHi; PAtM; PHi; PYHi; PLF; PPL; PDoBHi; PPAmP; PPeSchw. 11356

JOHNSON'S Almanac for 1823. By Joshua Sharp. Philadelphia: Richards Johnson. 18 ll. MWA. 11357

JOHNSON'S Pennsylvania and New Jersey Almanack for 1823. By Joshua Sharp. Philadelphia: Richards Johnson. 20 ll. MWA; DLC; CtY; NBuHi; PHi. 11358

KITE'S Town and Country Almanac for 1823. By William Collom. Philadelphia: Benjamin and Thomas Kite. 18 ll. MWA; N; InU; MB; NbHi; PHi (13 ll.) 11359

M'CARTY & Davis Pennsylvania Almanac for 1823. By John Ward. Philadelphia: M'Carty & Davis. 18 ll. MWA. 11360

Der NEUE Allentauner Calender auf 1823. Allentaun: George Hanke. 18 ll. DLC. 11361

Der NEUE, Americanische Landwirthschafts-Calender auf 1823. Von Carl Friedrich Egelmann. Reading: Johann Ritter und Comp. 18 ll. MWA; DLC; N; CLU; MBAt; P (17 ll.); PAnL (16 ll.); PDoBHi; PHi; PPL; PR; PRHi. 11362

Der NEUE Pennsylvanische Stadt- und Land-Calender auf 1823. Allentown: Heinrich Ebner und Comp. 18 ll.

MWA; DLC; DeWint; CLU; CtY; MnU; NjR; P; PAtM;
PDoBHi (17 ll.); PHi; PPG; PPL; PPeSchw; PRHi.
11363

NEW Brunswick, (N. J.) Almanack for 1823. By
Joshua Sharp. [Philadelphia:] Griggs & Dickinson for
Joseph C. Griggs, New Brunswick, (New Jersey.) 18
ll. MWA; CtY; NjHi; NjR; PHi; Honeyman. 11364

The NEW St. Tammany Almanac for 1823. By Wm.
Collom. Philadelphia: George W. Mentz. 18 ll. MWA;
DLC; InU; NjR; CtY; PHi; PPL. 11365

Der NORTHAMPTON Bauern Calender auf 1823. Easton:
Christian Jac. Huetter. 18 ll. [Shoemaker] 11366

The NORTHAMPTON Farmer's Almanac for 1823.
Easton: Henry & William Hutter. 18 ll. MWA. 11367

The PENNSYLVANIA Agricultural Almanack for 1823.
Lancaster: William Albright. 18 ll. MWA (impf); PHi.
11368
The PENNSYLVANIA Almanack for 1823. Philadelphia:
Richards Johnson. [Phillips] 11369

The PENNSYLVANIA Almanac for 1823. By John Ward.
Philadelphia: M'Carty & Davis. 18 ll. MWA; PHi;
NjR. 11370

The PENNSYLVANIA Almanac for 1823. By John Ward.
Philadelphia: Isaac Pugh. 18 ll. MWA; NjT; PPL
(impf) 11371

The PENNSYLVANIA Almanac, and Rural Economist's
Assistant for 1823. By Charles F. Egelman [sic].
Harrisburg: John Wyeth, J. S. Wiestling and C. Gleim.
18 ll. MWA; InU; PHi; PLF (16 ll.) 11372

PENNSYLVANIA & New Jersey Almanac for 1823. By
Joshua Sharp. Philadelphia: D. Dickinson. 18 ll.
MWA; DLC; InU; NjR; PDoBHi; PHi (15 ll.); Drake.
11373
PITTSBURGH Almanac for 1823. By John Armstrong.
Pittsburgh: R. Patterson & Lambdin; J. B. Butler,

printer. 18 ll. MWA; DLC; InHi. 11374

The PITTSBURGH Magazine Almanac for 1823. By John Armstrong. Pittsburgh: R. Patterson. 30 ll. OMC. 11375

The PITTSBURGH Magazine Almanac for 1823. Pittsburgh: R. Patterson & Lambdin; J. B. Butler, printer. 30 ll. OClWHi; OHi; PPi; WHi. 11376

POOR Robin's Almanac for 1823. By Joshua Sharp. Philadelphia: D. Dickinson. 18 ll. MWA; DLC; N; NHi; CtY; InU (8 ll.); P; PHi; PPL; NjR. 11377

POOR Will's Almanac for 1823. By William Collom. Philadelphia: Kimber and Sharpless. 18 ll. MWA; DLC; NHi; NjR; NjGlaN; IU; CtY; WHi; PHi; PP. 11378

POOR Will's Pocket Almanack for 1823. Philadelphia: Kimber & Sharpless. 24 ll. MWA; DLC; PHC; PHi. 11379

POUNDER'S Wesleyan Almanack for 1823. Philadelphia: Jonathan Pounder. 16 ll. MWA; PHi. 11380

WARNER'S Almanack for 1823. By Joshua Sharp. Philadelphia: Benjamin Warner. 18 ll. MWA. 11381

WARNER'S Almanack for 1823. By Joshua Sharp. Philadelphia: Benjamin Warner's Executors. 18 ll. MWA; InU (16 ll.); PHi; NjR. 11382

Der WESTLICHE Menschenfreund u. Schellsburger Calender auf 1823. Schellsburg: Friedrich Goeb. 18 ll. N. 11383

The AGRICULTURAL Almanack for 1824. Philadelphia: Solomon W. Conrad. 24 ll. MWA; NjHi (20 ll.); PPL; PPiHi (23 ll.); NjR. 11384

-- Issue with 32 ll. N; CtY (ntp); PHi; PPAmP. 11385

ALMANAC for 1824. By William Collom. Philadelphia: Benjamin and Thomas Kite. 18 ll. DLC. 11386

Pennsylvania - 1824   1085

AMERICANISCHER Stadt und Land Calender auf 1824.
Philadelphia: Conrad Zentler. 18 ll. MWA; DLC; InU;
NjP; DeWint; P; PPG; PHi (ntp); PYHi; PPL (16 ll.)
11387

BAILEY'S Washington Almanac for 1824. By Joshua
Sharp. Philadelphia: Lydia R. Bailey. 18 ll. MWA;
DLC; N; NN; CtY; PP; PPL; Drake.   11388

BAILEY'S Washington Almanac for 1824. By Joshua
Sharp. Philadelphia: Robert Desilver. 18 ll. MWA.
11389

BAILEY'S Washington Almanac for 1824. By Joshua
Sharp. Philadelphia: Thomas Desilver. 18 ll. MWA;
InU (impf)   11390

BENNETT & Walton's Almanac for 1824. By Joshua
Sharp. Philadelphia: Bennett & Walton. 18 ll. MWA;
DLC; N; CtY; InU; PHC; PHi; NjR (17 ll.); Drake.
11391

BIOREN'S Annual Compting-House Sheet Almanack for
1824. Philadelphia: John Bioren. Broadside. Advertised in "Bioren's Town and Country Almanack" for
1824.   11392

BIOREN'S Pennsylvania Pocket Remembrancer for 1824.
Philadelphia: John Bioren. Advertised in "Bioren's
Town and Country Almanack" for 1824.   11393

BIOREN'S Town and Country Almanack for 1824. By
William Collom. Philadelphia: John Bioren. 18 ll.
MWA; DLC; NN; MnU; PHi; PPL.   11394

The CHRISTIAN Almanack for 1824. Boston: Lincoln
& Edmands; Pittsburgh: Re-printed by John Andrews.
24 ll. PPiU.   11395

The CHRISTIAN Almanack for 1824. Philadelphia:
American Tract Society; Philadelphia Sunday and Adult
School Union. 24 ll. MWA; DLC; CtY; NjR.   11396

CITIZENS & Farmers' Almanack for 1824. By Joshua
Sharp. Philadelphia: Griggs & Dickinson. 18 ll. MWA;
DLC; IU; InU; NjGlaN; PHi; NjR.   11397

Pennsylvania - 1824

The COLUMBIAN Almanack for 1824. By Joshua Sharp. Philadelphia: Isaac Pugh. 18 ll. MWA; DLC; CLU; PHi; PPL (17 ll.); NjR. 11398

CRAMER'S Magazine Almanack for 1824. By Rev. John Taylor. Pittsburgh: Cramer & Spear; Steubenville: James Trumbull. 36 ll. MWA; DLC; InHi; InU; PPi. 11399

CRAMER'S Pittsburgh Almanack for 1824. By Rev. John Taylor. Pittsburgh: Cramer & Spear. 18 ll. ICHi; OClWHi (16 ll.) 11400

The FARMER'S Almanac for 1824. By John Armstrong. Philadelphia: Davis & M'Carty. 18 ll. MWA. 11401

The FARMER'S Almanac for 1824. By John Armstrong. Pittsburgh: Davis & M'Carty. Wv-Ar (14 ll.) 11402

The FARMERS' Almanac for 1824. By John Ward. Philadelphia: M'Carty & Davis. 18 ll. MWA; DLC; NN; NjR; PHi; ULA. 11403

The FARMERS & Mechanics' Almanac for 1824. By William Collom. Philadelphia: Robert Desilver. 18 ll. DLC; PHi. 11404

The FRANKLIN Almanac for 1824. By John Armstrong. Pittsburgh: Eichbaum & Johnston. 30 ll. MWA; CLU; PHi; PPi; PPiHi (26 ll.) 11405

Der GEMEINNÜTZIGE Landwirthschafts Calender auf 1824. Lancaster: William Albrecht. 18 ll. MWA; DLC; N; NN; CtY; InU; NjP; WHi; P (17 ll.); PHi; PLHi; PPG; PYHi; CLU. 11406

Der HOCH-DEUTSCHE Americanische Calender auf 1824. Von Carl Friederich Egelmann. Germantaun: M. Billmeyer. 18 ll. MWA; DLC; NN (16 ll.); CtY; InU; MH; WHi; PDoBHi; PHi; PLF; PPAmP; PYHi. 11407

HUNT'S Almanac for 1824. By Joshua Sharp. Philadelphia: Uriah Hunt. 16 ll. MWA; DLC; CLU; NjR

(18 ll.)   11408

JOHNSON'S Pennsylvania, New Jersey, Delaware, Maryland, and Virginia Almanack for 1824. By Joshua Sharp. Philadelphia: Richards Johnson. 18 ll. MWA; DLC; InU; PHi; ViU.   11409

KITE'S Town and Country Almanac for 1824. By William Collom. Philadelphia: Benjamin & Thomas Kite. 24 ll. MWA; DLC; NN; CtY; DeU; InU; NjR; NjT (20 ll.); P (23 ll.); PHi (impf); PP; Drake.   11410

MINER'S Agricultural Almanac for 1824. By Wm. Collom. Doylestown: Asher Miner. 18 ll. MWA; DLC; PDoBHi; PHi.   11411

Der NEUE Allentauner Calender auf 1824. Allentaun: Georg Hanke. 18 ll. DLC; PHi (17 ll.); PPCS; PPeSchw.   11412

Der NEUE, Americanische Landwirthschafts-Calender auf 1824. Von Carl Friedrich Egelmann. Reading: Johann Ritter und Comp. 18 ll. MWA; DLC (17 ll.); NN; InU; P; PHi; PPG; PPeSchw; PPL; PRHi.   11413

Der NEUE Pennsylvanische Stadt-und Land-Calender auf 1824. Allentown: Heinrich Ebner und Comp. 18 ll. MWA; DLC; NN; CLU; CtY; DeWint; InU; P; PDoBHi; PHi (17 ll.); PPG; PPeSchw; PPL; Drake (impf)   11414

NEW Brunswick (N. J.) Almanack for 1824. By Joshua Sharp. Philadelphia: Griggs & Dickinson for Joseph C. Griggs, New Brunswick, (New Jersey.) 18 ll. NjR.   11415

The NEW Brunswick, (N. J.), Almanack for 1824. By Joshua Sharp. [Philadelphia:] Griggs & Dickinson for Joseph C. Griggs, New Brunswick, (New Jersey). 18 ll. MWA; NjMo.   11416

The NEW St. Tammany Almanac for 1824. By John Ward. Philadelphia: George W. Mentz. 18 ll. MWA; DLC; NN (4 ll.); InU; PHi.   11417

Der NORTHAMPTON Bauern Calender auf 1824.
Easton: Heinrich und Wilhelm Hutter. 18 ll. MWA
(impf); DLC; PBL (17 ll.); PPL (17 ll.); PPeSchw.
11418

The NORTHAMPTON Farmer's Almanac for 1824.
Easton: Henry & William Hutter. 18 ll. MWA; MBAt
(ntp); PHi (17 ll.); PPL. 11419

The PENNSYLVANIA Agricultural Almanac for 1824.
Lancaster: William Albright. 18 ll. MWA; PLHi (17 ll.) 11420

PENNSYLVANIA Almanac for 1824. By John Ward.
Philadelphia: G. W. Mentz. 19 ll. PHi. 11421

PENNSYLVANIA Almanac for 1824. By John Ward.
Philadelphia: G. W. Mentz and M'Carty & Davis. 19 ll.
MWA; FSaHi (17 ll.) 11422

The PENNSYLVANIA Almanac, and Rural Economist's Assistant for 1824. By Charles F. Egelman. Harrisburg: John Wyeth, J. S. Wiestling and C. Gleim. 18 ll.
MWA (17 ll.); DLC; P (17 ll.); PHi. 11423

PITTSBURGH Almanac for 1824. By John Armstrong.
Pittsburgh: Assignees of R. Patterson & Lambdin; J. B. Butler, printer. 18 ll. DLC; InHi; OClWHi; PHi (16 ll.); PPi; PPiHi. 11424

The PITTSBURGH Magazine Almanac for 1824. By John Armstrong. Pittsburgh: R. Patterson & Lambdin. 30 ll. Wv-Ar (29 ll.) 11425

POOR Robin's Almanack for 1824. By Joshua Sharp.
Philadelphia: D. Dickinson. 18 ll. MWA; DLC; CtY; InU (impf); NjR; PHi. 11426

POOR Will's Almanac for 1824. By William Collom.
Philadelphia: Kimber and Sharpless. 18 ll. MWA; DLC; N; NHi; NjR; OClWHi; WHi; PDoBHi; PHi; PPL.
11427
POOR Will's Almanac for 1824. By William Collom.
Philadelphia: Joseph Rakestraw. 18 ll. PHi; PPL. 11428

POOR Will's Pocket Almanack for 1824. Philadelphia: Kimber & Sharpless. 24 ll. MWA; DLC; NjR; PHC; PHi. 11429

POUNDER'S Wesleyan Almanack for 1824. Philadelphia: Jonothan Pounder. 18 ll. MWA; PHi. 11430

Der WESTLICHE Menschenfreund u. Schellsburger Calender auf 1824. Von Carl F. Egelmann. Schellsburg: Friedrich Goeb. 21 ll. MWA; PPL (20 ll.) 11431

AGRICULTURAL Almanac for 1825. Lancaster: John Baer. Hostetter. 11432

The AGRICULTURAL Almanack for 1825. Philadelphia: S. W. Conrad. 24 ll. MWA; DLC; N; CLU; CtY; PDoBHi (ntp) 11433

The AGRICULTURAL Almanack for 1825. Philadelphia: S. W. Conrad; Marot & Walter; Bennett & Walton; Kimber & Sharpless. 24 ll. NHi; NjR (22 ll.); PHi. 11434

The AMERICAN Ladies Pocket Book for 1825. Philadelphia: A. Small. 84 ll. MHi; MdBP (ntp) 11435

AMERICANISCHER Stadt und Land Calender auf 1825. Allentown: Heinrich Ebner und Co. 18 ll. PPeSchw. 11436

AMERICANISCHER Stadt und Land Calender auf 1825. Philadelphia: Conrad Zentler. 18 ll. MWA; DLC; NN; CLU; CtY; InU; NjP; PDoBHi; PHi; PPG; PPL (15 ll.); PPAmP; PYHi. 11437

BAILEY'S Washington Almanac for 1825. By Joshua Sharp. Philadelphia: Lydia R. Bailey. 18 ll. MWA; DLC (impf); NN; NHi; CtY; InU (impf); PHi; PP; Drake. 11438

BAILEY'S Washington Almanac for 1825. By Joshua Sharp. Philadelphia: Robert Desilver. 18 ll. MWA. 11439

BAILEY'S Washington Almanac for 1825. By Joshua Sharp. Philadelphia: Thomas Desilver. 18 ll.

MWA. 11440

BENNETT & Walton's Almanac for 1825. By Joshua Sharp. Philadelphia: Bennett & Walton. 18 ll. MWA; DLC (impf); NN (impf); CtY; InU; PDoBHi; PHi (20 ll.); PPL (16 ll.) 11441

The CHRISTIAN Almanack for 1825. Philadelphia: American Tract Society; American Sunday School Union. 18 ll. MWA; DLC; N; CtY; NjR. 11442

The CHRISTIAN Almanac for 1825. [Pittsburgh:] John Andrews. 24 ll. MWA; CLU; OClWHi; OMC; Drake. 11443

The CITIZEN'S & Farmer's Almanack for 1825. By Joshua Sharp. Philadelphia: Griggs & Dickinson. 18 ll. MWA; PHi (17 ll.) 11444

CRAMER'S Magazine Almanack for 1825. By Rev. John Taylor. Pittsburgh: Cramer & Spear; [etc.] 36 ll. MWA; DLC; InHi; InU; OC; OClWHi; PHi; PP; PPi; PPiU (28 ll., ntp) 11445

CRAMER'S Pittsburgh Almanack for 1825. By Rev. John Taylor. Pittsburgh: Cramer and Spear. 18 ll. MWA; OClWHi; OMC (12 ll.); PPiU; Wv-Ar; WvU. 11446

The FRANKLIN Almanac for 1825. By John Armstrong. Pittsburgh: Eichbaum & Johnston. 18 ll. MWA. 11447

-- With added "Magazine." 30 ll. MWA; OMC; PPi (ntp) 11448

Der GEMEINNÜTZIGE Landwirthschafts Calender auf 1825. Lancaster: William Albrecht. 18 ll. MWA; DLC; NN (16 ll.); InU; P; PHi; PLHi; PPG; PPeSchw; PYHi. 11449

GRIGG'S Almanack for 1825. By Joshua Sharp. Philadelphia: Griggs & Dickinson. 18 ll. MWA; CtY. 11450

Der HOCH-DEUTSCHE Americanische Calender auf 1825. Von Carl Friederich Egelmann. Germantaun:

Pennsylvania - 1825

M. Billmeyer. 18 ll. MWA; NN; CLU; CtY; InU (16 ll.); PDoBHi; PHi; PPCS; PPG; PPL; PPeSchw; PYHi; NjR.　　　　　　　　　　　　　　11451

Der HOCHDEUTSCHE Nordamericanische Calender auf 1825. Von Carl F. Egelman. Easton: Heinrich Held. 18 ll. MWA (two varieties); DLC; CtY; DeWint; InU; PPL (14 ll.)　　　　　　　　　　　　　11452

HUNT'S Almanack for 1825. By Joshua Sharp. Philadelphia: Uriah Hunt. 16 ll. MWA; DLC; N; CtY; P (19 ll.)　　　　　　　　　　　　　　　11453

KITE'S Town and Country Almanac for 1825. By William Collom. Philadelphia: Benjamin & Thomas Kite. 18 ll. MWA; DLC; NN (17 ll.); CLU; InU; PHi; PP.
　　　　　　　　　　　　　　　　　　11454

The LA FAYETTE Almanac for 1825. Philadelphia: M'Carty & Davis; G. W. Mentz. 19 ll. MWA (two varieties); DLC; N; NjR (14 ll.); InU; MnU; P (ntp); PHi; PPL.　　　　　　　　　　　　　　11455

LANGSTROTH & M'Dowell's Almanack for 1825. By Joshua Sharp. Philadelphia: Griggs & Dickinson, for Langstroth & M'Dowell. 16 ll. MWA; DLC.　　11456

-- Issue with added signature. PPiHi (19 ll.)　11457

MAROT & Walter's Almanack for 1825. Philadelphia: Marot & Walter. 18 ll. MWA; DLC (15 ll.); DeU (11 ll.); InU; NPV; NjR; P (17 ll.); PHi; Drake.　11458

Der NEUE Allentauner Calender auf 1825. Allentaun: Carl L. Hutter. 18 ll. MWA; PDoBHi (16 ll.); PPL; PRHi.　　　　　　　　　　　　　　　　11459

Der NEUE, Americanische Landwirthschafts-Calender auf 1825. Von Carl Friedrich Egelmann. Reading: Johann Ritter. 18 ll. MWA; DLC; P; PHi; PPL (17 ll.); PRHi.　　　　　　　　　　　　　　　11460

Der NEUE Pennsylvanische Stadt-und Land-Calender auf 1825. Allentown: Heinrich Ebner und Comp. 18 ll.

MWA (impf); DLC; NN (15 ll.); PHi (17 ll.);
PPeSchw. 11461

NEW Brunswick, (N. J.) Almanack for 1825. By
Joshua Sharp. Philadelphia: Griggs & Dickinson, for
Joseph C. Griggs, New Brunswick, (N. J.) 18 ll.
MWA; DLC; NjHi; NjR (17 ll.); ViHi; Honeyman (16
ll.) 11462

Der NORTHAMPTON Bauern Calender auf 1825. Easton:
Heinrich und Wilhelm Hutter. 18 ll. MWA; DLC; PPL.
11463

The NORTHAMPTON Farmer's Almanac for 1825.
Easton: Henry and William Hutter. 18 ll. MWA; DLC
(16 ll.); NN; PHi; PPL. 11464

PENNSYLVANIA Almanac for 1825. By John Ward.
Lancaster: William Albright. 18 ll. DLC. 11465

PENNSYLVANIA Almanac for 1825. By John Ward.
Philadelphia: G. W. Mentz, and M'Carty & Davis. 18
ll. MWA; CtY; NBuG; NjR; FSaHi (17 ll.); PHi;
PYHi. 11466

PENNSYLVANIA and New Jersey Almanac for 1825. By
William Collom. Philadelphia: Isaac Pugh. 18 ll.
MWA; DLC; InU; OMC (15 ll.); PHi; NjR. 11467

POOR Robin's Almanack for 1825. By Joshua Sharp.
[Philadelphia:] D. Dickinson; Marot & Walter. 18 ll.
MWA; DLC; CtY; InU; PHi. 11468

POOR Will's Almanac for 1825. By William Collom.
Philadelphia: Kimber and Sharpless. 18 ll. MWA; CtY;
MB; WHi; PHi (impf); PP. 11469

POOR Will's Almanac for 1825. By William Collom.
Philadelphia: J. Rakestraw. 18 ll. MWA; DLC; N;
NHi (17 ll.); NjGlaN; NjR; CLU; WHi; PHi; PPL (17
ll.); PDoBHi. 11470

POOR Will's Pocket Almanack for 1825. Philadelphia:
Kimber & Sharpless. 24 ll. MWA; DLC; NN; CLU;

Pennsylvania - 1825

InU (ntp); MnU; NjR; PHC; PHi; Drake. 11471

Le SOUVENIR, or, Picturesque Pocket Diary for 1825. Philadelphia: A. R. Poole. 67 ll. MWA; CtY. 11472

The UNITED States National Almanac [for 1825]. By David M'Clure. Philadelphia: R. Desilver. [On page 26: "Navy Department."] 30 ll. PPL (impf) 11473

-- On page 26: "War Department." 28 ll. MWA; DLC; NHi; InU; MB; MBAt; PHi; PPL. 11474

Der WESTLICHE Menschenfreund u. Schellsburger Calender auf 1825. Von Carl F. Egelmann. Schellsburg: Friedrich Goeb. 18 ll. MWA; PPiHi; NjR. 11475

AGRICULTURAL Almanac for 1826. Lancaster: John Baer. [Bausman] 11476

The AGRICULTURAL Almanack for 1826. Philadelphia: S. W. Conrad. 24 ll. MWA; DLC; N; NN; CtY; NBuG; PHi; PPL. 11477

The AMERICAN Ladies Pocket Book for 1826. Philadelphia: R. H. Small. 80 ll. PHi. 11478

AMERICANISCHER Stadt und Land Calender auf 1826. Philadelphia: Conrad Zentler. 18 ll. MWA; DLC; NN; CtY; InU; NjR; P (17 ll.); PDoBHi; PHi; PLF; PPG; PYHi; Drake. 11479

BAILEY'S Washington Almanac for 1826. By Joshua Sharp. Philadelphia: Lydia R. Bailey. 18 ll. MWA; NN; CtY; InU (impf); PP; PPL; Drake. 11480

BAILEY'S Washington Almanac for 1826. By Joshua Sharp. Philadelphia: Thomas Desilver. 18 ll. DLC; MB; NjGlaN; PHi. 11481

BENNETT & Walton's Almanac for 1826. By Joshua Sharp. Philadelphia: Bennett & Walton. 18 ll. MWA; DLC; N; NN; CLU; CtY; InU; MiU-C; NjR; OCl; WHi; P (16 ll.); PDoBHi; PHC; PHi. 11482

The **CHRISTIAN** Almanack for 1826. Pittsburgh: Office of the Statesman, Diamond; H. Holdship; J.C. & P.C.M. Andrews, printers. 24 ll. MWA; OMC; PPi; Drake.
 11483

CITIZENS & Farmers' Almanack for 1826. By Joshua Sharp. Philadelphia: Griggs & Dickinson. 18 ll. MWA; DLC; CtY; InU; NjR (17 ll.)
 11484

CITIZENS & Farmers' Almanac for 1826. By Joshua Sharp. Philadelphia: Griggs & Dickinson for Towar & Hogan. 18 ll. PHi.
 11484a

CRAMER'S Magazine Almanack for 1826. By Rev. John Taylor. Pittsburgh: Cramer & Spear. 18 ll. DLC; Wv-Ar.
 11485
-- Issue with 26 ll. MWA; InU; OC; OMC; PHi (35 ll.); PPi; PPiU.
 11486

CRAMER'S Pittsburgh Almanack for 1826. By Rev. John Taylor. Pittsburgh: Cramer & Spear; [etc]. 18 ll. NN; OClWHi; PPiHi (17 ll.); PPiU.
 11487

DESILVER'S United States Almanac [for 1826]. Philadelphia: [np] 34 ll. MWA; NjR.
 11488

The **FARMERS'** Almanac for 1826. By John Ward. Philadelphia: M'Carty & Davis. 18 ll. MWA; PDoBHi; PHi (17 ll.)
 11489

FARMERS' & Mechanicks' Almanack for 1826. By Joshua Sharp. Philadelphia: Marot & Walter. 18 ll. MWA; DLC; N; NjR; PHi; PPL; PPiU; Drake.
 11490

The **FRANKLIN** Almanac for 1826. Philadelphia: Uriah Hunt. 18 ll. MWA; DLC (15 ll.); NHi; InU; PHi. 11491

The **FRANKLIN** Almanac for 1826. By John Armstrong. Pittsburgh: Eichbaum & Johnston. 30 ll. OClWHi; Drake.
 11492

Der **GEMEINNUTZIGE** Landwirthschafts Calender auf 1826. Lancaster: William Albrecht. 18 ll. MWA; DLC; NHi; CLU; CtY; InU; NjP; P; WHi; PHi; PPG; PPL; PPeSchw; PYHi.
 11493

Der HOCH-DEUTSCHE Americanische Calender auf
1826. Von Carl Friederich Egelmann. Germantaun:
M. Billmeyer. 18 ll. MWA; DLC; NN; CLU; CtY;
InU; PAnL; PDoBHi; PHi; PPCS. 11494

Der HOCH Deutscher Nord Americanischer Kalender
auf 1826. Easton: Heinrich Held. [Stapleton] 11495

HUNT'S Almanack for 1826. By Joshua Sharp. Philadelphia: Griggs & Dickinson. 18 ll. MWA. 11496

HUNT'S Almanack for 1826. By Joshua Sharp. Philadelphia: Griggs & Dickinson, for Uriah Hunt. 18 ll.
PHi. 11497

KITE'S Town and Country Almanac for 1826. By William Collom. Philadelphia: Benjamin & Thomas Kite.
18 ll. MWA; DLC; InU (2 ll.); CtY; PHi; PP; NjR.
11498

The LA FAYETTE Almanac for 1826. Philadelphia:
G. W. Mentz. 18 ll. MWA; DLC; N; InU; NN;
PDoBHi (17 ll.); PHi. 11499

MAROT & Walter's Almanack for 1826. By Joshua
Sharp. Philadelphia: Marot & Walter. 18 ll. MWA;
DLC (17 ll.); N; InU; PHi. 11500

Der NEUE Allentauner Calender auf 1826. Allentaun:
Carl L. Hutter. 18 ll. DLC; PPL. 11501

Der NEUE, Americanische Landwirthschafts-Calender
auf 1826. Von Carl Friedrich Egelmann. Reading:
Johann Ritter. 18 ll. MWA; DLC; InU; NjP; PDoBHi;
PHi; PPCS; PPL (17 ll.); PPeSchw; PR; PRHi;
Drake. 11502

Der NEUE Pennsylvanische Stadt-und Land-Calender auf
1826. Allentown: Heinrich Ebner und Comp. 18 ll.
MWA; DLC; N; NN; CLU; CtY; InU; PBMC; NjR
(impf); P; PHi; PPT; PPeSchw; PRHi; Drake. 11503

NEW Brunswick, (N. J.) Almanack for 1826. By Joshua
Sharp. Philadelphia: Griggs & Dickinson, for Joseph C.

Griggs, New Brunswick, (N. J.). 18 ll. MWA; NjHi; NjR; Honeyman. 11504

Der NORTHAMPTON Bauern Calender auf 1826.
Easton: Heinrich und Wilhelm Hutter. 18 ll. DLC. 11505

The NORTHAMPTON Farmer's Almanac for 1826.
Easton: Henry and William Hutter. No copy found. 11506

The NORTHAMPTON Farmer's Almanac for 1826.
Easton: Henry and William Hutter. (Second Edition)
18 ll. MWA; NN; FSaHi (17 ll.) 11507

-- Issue with 24 ll. PPL. 11508

PENNSYLVANIA Almanac for 1826. By John Ward.
Lancaster: William Albright. 18 ll. MWA (15 ll.) 11509

PENNSYLVANIA Almanac for 1826. By John Ward.
Philadelphia: G. W. Mentz. 18 ll. NjR; PHC. 11510

PENNSYLVANIA Almanac for 1826. By John Ward.
Philadelphia: G. W. Mentz; M'Carty & Davis. 18 ll.
MWA; DLC; NN; NBuG; InU; CtY; PHi; PLF; PYHi;
NjR. 11511

PENNSYLVANIA & New-Jersey Almanac for 1826. By
William Collom. Philadelphia: Isaac Pugh. 18 ll.
MWA; DLC; N; NHi (16 ll.); InU; NjR (two varieties);
PDoBHi; PHi. 11512

POOR Robin's Almanack for 1826. By Joshua Sharp.
Philadelphia: D. Dickinson. 18 ll. MWA; DLC; InU;
MBC; PHi; PPL. 11513

POOR Wills Almanac for 1826. By William Collom.
Philadelphia: Kimber and Sharpless. 18 ll. PHi. 11514

POOR Will's Almanac for 1826. By William Collom.
Philadelphia: Kimber and Sharpless. 18 ll. MWA;
DLC; NHi; MB; NjR; WHi; PHi; PPL; PU. 11515

POOR Will's Almanac for 1826. By William Collom.

Philadelphia: J. Rakestraw. 16 ll. NHi. 11516

POOR Will's Pocket Almanack for 1826. Philadelphia: Kimber & Sharpless. 24 ll. MWA; DLC; InU; MnU; NjR; PHC; PHi; Drake. 11517

Le SOUVENIR, or, Picturesque Pocket Diary for 1826. Philadelphia: A. R. Poole. 70 ll. MWA; NN; CtY. 11518

The UNITED States' Almanac [for 1826]. By Seth Smith. Philadelphia: R. Desilver. 32 ll. MWA; DLC (30 ll.); N; NHi; NNS; CtY; MH; MnU; MBAt; PPL (31 ll.); PPiU (30 ll.); NjR. 11519

WESLEYAN Almanack for 1826. By Joshua Sharp. Philadelphia: Griggs & Dickinson. 16 ll. MWA; PHi (15 ll.) 11520

Der WESTLICHE Menschenfreund u. Schellsburger Calender auf 1826. Schellsburg: Friedrich Goeb. 18 ll. MWA (ntp) 11521

AGRICULTURAL Almanac for 1827. Lancaster: John Baer. [Bausman] 11522

The AGRICULTURAL Almanack for 1827. Philadelphia: S. W. Conrad. 24 ll. MWA; DLC; N; NN; NPV; CtY; OClWHi; PHi; PPAmP; PPL. 11523

The AMERICAN Ladies Pocket Book for 1827. Philadelphia: R. H. Small. 80 ll. PHi. 11524

AMERICANISCHER Stadt und Land Calender auf 1827. Philadelphia: Conrad Zentler. 18 ll. MWA; DLC; N; NN; CLU; CtY; InU; NjP; DeWint; PHi; PLF; PPCS (17 ll.); PPG; PPeSchw; PPL; PYHi. 11525

BAILEY'S Franklin Almanac for 1827. By Joshua Sharp. Philadelphia: Lydia R. Bailey. 18 ll. PPL (12 ll., ntp) 11526

BAILEY'S Washington Almanac for 1827. By Joshua Sharp. Philadelphia: Lydia R. Bailey. 18 ll. MWA; CtY; NBuG; PPL; Drake (16 ll.) 11527

BAILEY'S Washington Almanac for 1827. By Joshua Sharp. Philadelphia: Thomas Desilver. 18 ll. NjGlaN; PHi. 11528

BENNET & Walton's Almanac for 1827. Philadelphia: Bennet & Walton; D. & S. Neale, printers. 18 ll. NjR (17 ll.) 11529

BENNET & Walton's Almanac for 1827. Philadelphia: Bennett [sic] & Walton; D. & S. Neall, printers. 18 ll. MWA; PHi. 11530

BENNET & Walton's Almanac for 1827. Philadelphia: D. & S. Neall. 18 ll. Drake. 11531

BENNETT & Walton's Almanac for 1827. Philadelphia: Bennett & Walton; D. & S. Neall, printers. 18 ll. MWA; DLC; CtY; PDoBHi. 11532

CITIZENS & Farmers' Almanack for 1827. By Joseph Cramer. Philadelphia: Griggs & Dickinson. 18 ll. MWA; DLC; N; CtY; InU; PHi; NjR. 11533

COLUMBIAN Almanac for 1827. By William Collom. Philadelphia: Joseph M'Dowell. 18 ll. MWA; DLC; N; NBuG; PHi; NjR. 11534

CRAMER'S Magazine Almanack for 1827. By Rev. John Taylor. Pittsburgh: Cramer & Spear; [etc]. 36 ll. MWA; CLU; InHi; InU; Wv-Ar; PPi; Drake.
11535
CRAMER'S Pittsburgh Almanack for 1827. By Rev. John Taylor. Pittsburgh: Cramer and Spear. 20 ll. MWA; ICHi; OFH. 11536

The FARMER'S Almanac for 1827. By John Armstrong. Pittsburgh: John F. M'Carty. 18 ll. DLC. 11537

FARMERS Almanac for 1827. By Joseph Crammer [sic]. Philadelphia: Isaac Pugh; D. & S. Neall, printers. 18 ll. MWA; CtY; InU; PHi; PPiU; NjR; Drake. 11538

Pennsylvania - 1827   1099

The **FARMERS'** Almanac for 1827. By John Ward.
Philadelphia: M'Carty & Davis. 18 ll. MWA; NN (15
ll.); InU; PHi; Drake (14 ll.)   11539

The **FARMERS'** & Mechanics' Almanac for 1827. By
Patrick Leonard. Pittsburgh: H. Holdship; R. Patterson; D. & M. Maclean, printers. 18 ll. NN; NBuHi;
CLU; OClWHi; OHi; OMC; PHi; PPi; Drake.   11540

-- Issue with added "Magazine." 36 ll. PPiHi; PPiU
(35 ll.)   11541

FARMERS & Mechanics Almanack for 1827. By Joshua
Sharp. Philadelphia: Marot & Walter. 18 ll. MWA;
DLC; InU; NjR; PHi.   11542

The **FRANKLIN** Almanac for 1827. By John Armstrong.
Pittsburgh: Johnston and Stockton. 18 ll. DLC; OClWHi;
WvU.   11543

-- Issue with added "Magazine." 30 ll. MWA; NBuHi
(29 ll.); OMC (25 ll.); Drake.   11544

Der **GEMEINNÜTZIGE** Landwirthschafts Calender auf
1827. Lancaster: William Albrecht. 18 ll. MWA;
DLC; NN; InU; NjP; OC; P; PDoBHi; PPL; Drake
(impf)   11545

Der **HOCH-DEUTSCH** Americanische Calender auf 1827.
Von Carl Friederich Egelmann. Germantaun: M. Billmeyer. 18 ll. MWA; NN (17 ll.); CtY; InU; WHi; P;
PHi; PDoBHi; PLF; PPL (17 ll.); PPeSchw; PYHi. 11546

KITE'S Town and Country Almanac for 1827. By William Collom. Philadelphia: Benjamin & Thomas Kite.
18 ll. MWA; DLC; NN; InU; P (17 ll.); PDoBHi;
PHi; PPL.   11547

LADIES' Diary for 1827. Philadelphia: A. R. Poole;
Washington: P. Thompson. 60 ll. MdBP (impf) 11548

MAROT & Walter's Almanack for 1827. By Joshua
Sharp. Philadelphia: Marot & Walter. 18 ll. MWA;

DLC; InU; MiU-C; NjGlaN; PHi; PP. 11549

NEALL'S Almanac for 1827. By Joseph Cramer.
Philadelphia: D. & S. Neall; D. & S. Neall, printers.
18 ll. MWA; PHi. 11550

Der NEUE Allentauner Calender auf 1827. Allentaun:
Carl Ludwig Hutter. 18 ll. N; PHi; PPL; PRHi.
11551
Der NEUE, Americanische Landwirthschafts-Calender
auf 1827. Von Carl Friedrich Egelmann. Reading:
Johann Ritter. 18 ll. MWA; DLC; InU; NjP; P;
PDoBHi; PHi; PPCS; PR; PRHi. 11552

Der NEUE Pennsylvanische Stadt- und Land-Calender
auf 1827. Allentaun: Heinrich Ebner und Comp. 18 ll.
MWA; DLC; NHi (impf); N (impf); CLU; CtY; InU;
NjR; PHi (17 ll.); PRHi; PDoBHi; PPeSchw. 11553

NEW Brunswick, (N. J.) Almanack for 1827. By Joseph
Cramer. Philadelphia: Griggs & Dickinson. 18 ll. MB.
11554
NEW Brunswick, (N. J.) Almanack for 1827. By Joseph
Cramer. Philadelphia: Griggs & Dickinson, for Joseph
C. Griggs, New Brunswick, (New Jersey.) 18 ll.
MWA; N; InU; NjHi; NjR (16 ll.); Drake (15 ll.)
11555
Der NORTHAMPTON Bauern Calender auf 1827. Easton:
Heinrich und Wilhelm Hutter. 18 ll. MWA (17 ll.);
DLC; PPL (17 ll.) 11556

The NORTHAMPTON Farmers' Almanac for 1827.
Easton: Henry and William Hutter. 18 ll. MWA; NNU-
H (ntp); PHi (15 ll.); NjR (17 ll.) 11557

The PENNSYLVANIA Almanac for 1827. By John Ward.
Philadelphia: M'Carty & Davis. 18 ll. CtY; PDoBHi
(16 ll.) 11558

PENNSYLVANIA Almanac for 1827. By John Ward.
Philadelphia: G. W. Mentz; M'Carty & Davis; Lancaster:
Wm. Albright. 18 ll. MWA; DLC (17 ll.); NN; NHi;
InU; CLU; NjR; P (17 ll.); PHi (17 ll.); PP (13 ll.);

PPeSchw; PPiHi; PPL (15 ll.); PYHi.   11559

The PENNSYLVANIA Medical Almanac and Repository of Useful Science for 1827. By David Young. Philadelphia: Printed for the Proprietor. 18 ll. MWA.
11560
POOR Will's Almanac for 1827. By William Collom. Philadelphia: Kimber and Sharpless. 18 ll. MWA; DLC; NHi; InU; NBuG; WHi; CLU.   11561

POOR Wills Almanac for 1827. By William Collom. Philadelphia: J. Rakestraw. 18 ll. PHi; NjR.   11562

POOR Will's Pocket Almanack for 1827. Philadelphia: Kimber & Sharpless. 24 ll. MWA; DLC; MB; MnU; NjR; PHC; PHi.   11563

Le SOUVENIR, or, Picturesque Pocket Diary for 1827. Philadelphia: A. R. Poole. 76 ll. MWA; MHi.   11564

-- With added "and P. Thompson, Washington" on half-title. 36 ll. NBLiHi.   11565

The UNITED States' Almanac [for 1827]. By Seth Smith. Philadelphia: R. Desilver. 36 ll. MWA; NHi; NBuG; CtY; IaCrM; MH; NjR; PHi; PP; PPL.   11566

-- with folding "Constitution." 35 ll. DLC; N; MBAt; CLU; IHi; MHi; PPL.   11567

Der WESTLICHE Menschenfreund u. Schellsburger Calender auf 1827. Schellsburg: Friedrich Goeb. 18 ll. MWA.
11568
The AGRICULTURAL Almanack for 1828. By John Armstrong. Blairsville: James F. M'Carty; Zanesville: William Davis. 18 ll. PHi.   11569

AMERICANISCHER Stadt und Land Calender auf 1828. Philadelphia: Conrad Zentler. 18 ll. MWA; DLC; N; CLU; CtY; InU; DeWint; RPB; NjR (17 ll.); O (17 ll.); PAnL; PDoBHi; PHi; PPeSchw; NjP; PPL.   11570

BAILEY'S Franklin Almanac for 1828. By Joshua Sharp.

Philadelphia: Lydia R. Bailey. 18 ll. MWA; DLC (17 ll.); CLU; NjR; PHi; PPL. 11570a

BAILEY'S Franklin Almanac for 1828. By Joshua Sharp. Philadelphia: Thomas Desilver; Lydia R. Bailey, printer. 18 ll. Ct (17 ll.); CtY. 11571

BAILEY'S Washington Almanac for 1828. By Joshua Sharp. Philadelphia: Lydia R. Bailey. 18 ll. MWA; DLC; NN (15 ll.); CtY; PHi. 11572

BENNET & Walton's Almanack for 1828. By Joseph Cramer. Philadelphia: D. & S. Neall. 18 ll. MWA; DLC; NjR; PHi; Drake. 11573

BENNETT & Walton's Almanack for 1828. By Joseph Cramer. Philadelphia: D. & S. Neall. 18 ll. N; CtY; InU; WHi; PDoBHi; PHi; PPL (14 ll.) 11574

The CHRISTIAN Almanac, for Pennsylvania for 1828. Philadelphia: Philadelphia branch of the American Tract Society; Nicholas Murray. 18 ll. MWA; DLC; NjR; PHi; PP; PPL. 11575

The CHRISTIAN Almanac, for Pennsylvania, and Ohio for 1828. Pittsburgh: American Tract Society; R. Patterson. 18 ll. MWA. 11576

CITIZENS & Farmers' Almanack for 1828. By Joseph Cramer. Philadelphia: Griggs & Dickinson. 18 ll. MWA; DLC; MBC; PDoBHi; PHi; PP; PPL; NjR. 11577

COLUMBIAN Almanac for 1828. By William Collom. Philadelphia: Joseph M'Dowell. 18 ll. MWA; DLC; InU; N; PDoBHi; PHi. 11578

CRAMER's Magazine Almanack for 1828. Pittsburgh: Cramer & Spear; [etc]. 36 ll. MWA; InU (ntp); OC; Wv-Ar (17 ll.); PPi. 11579

CRAMER'S Pittsburgh Almanack for 1828. Pittsburgh: Cramer & Spear. 18 ll. MWA; CLU; ICHi; OClWHi; PPiU. 11580

The FARMER'S Almanac for 1828. By John Armstrong.

Pennsylvania - 1828 1103

Blairsville: James F. M'Carty. 18 ll. PPiU. 11581

The FARMERS' Almanac for 1828. By John Ward.
Philadelphia: M'Carty & Davis. 18 ll. MWA; CLU;
CtY; ICU; PHi; PPL. 11582

The FRANKLIN Almanac for 1828. By John Armstrong. Pittsburgh: Johnson and Stockton. 18 ll.
OClWHi; PPi; WvU. 11583

-- Issue with added "Magazine." 30 ll. MWA; InU;
OClWHi; OMC; Wv-Ar; PHi (29 ll.) 11584

Der GEMEINNÜTZIGE Landwirthschafts Calender auf
1828. Lancaster: William Albrecht. 18 ll. MWA;
DLC; NN (impf); CLU; InU; WHi; P (19 ll.); PLHi;
PPL (16 ll.); Drake. 11585

Der HOCH-DEUTSCHE Americanische Calender auf
1828. Von Carl Friederich Egelmann. Germantaun:
M. Billmeyer. 18 ll. MWA; DLC; N; NN; CLU; CtY;
InU; MH; WHi; NNU-H (20 ll.); PDoBHi; PHi; PLF;
PPL (17 ll.); PPAmP; PPeSchw. 11586

JACKSON Almanac for 1828. Philadelphia. 13 ll.
DLC. 11587

KITE'S Town and Country Almanac for 1828. By William Collom. Philadelphia: Benjamin and Thomas Kite.
18 ll. MWA; DLC; N; CLU; InU; PHC; PHi; PPiHi.
11588

LANCASTER Agricultural Almanac for 1828. By
Charles F. Egelman. Lancaster: John Bear. 18 ll.
MWA; DLC; PHi (15 ll.); PYHi. 11589

MAROT & Walter's Almanack for 1828. By Joshua Sharp.
Philadelphia: Marot & Walter. 16 ll. MiU-C (impf) 11590

Der NEUE Allentauner Calender auf 1828. Von Carl
Friedrich Egelmann. Allentaun: Carl Ludwig Hutter.
18 ll. PPeSchw. 11591

Der NEUE, Americanische Landwirthschafts-Calender
auf 1828. Von Carl Friedrich Egelmann. Reading:

Johann Ritter u. Comp. 18 ll. MWA; DLC (16 ll.);
InU (impf); WHi; PPG; P; PHi (17 ll.); PPL (17 ll.);
PPeSchw; PPL; PR; PRHi.   11592

Der NEUE Pennsylvanische Stadt- und Land-Calender
auf 1828. Allentaun: Heinrich Ebner und Comp. 18 ll.
MWA; DLC; NN (16 ll.); NjR; CLU; CtY; P; OC;
PAtHi; PAtM; PDoBHi; PHi; PPCS; PPL; PPT;
PPeSchw; PRHi; InU.   11593

NEW Brunswick, (N. J.) Almanack for 1828. By
Joseph Cramer. Philadelphia: Griggs & Dickinson, for
Joseph C. Griggs, New Brunswick, (New Jersey.) 18 ll.
NjR; Honeyman (16 ll.)   11594

NEW Brunswick, (N. J.), Almanack for 1828. By
Joshua Sharp. Philadelphia: Griggs & Dickinson, for
Joseph C. Griggs, New Brunswick, (N. J.) 18 ll.
MWA; NjHi; Honeyman (16 ll.)   11595

Der NORTHAMPTON Bauern Calender auf 1828.
Easton: Heinrich und Wilhelm Hutter. 18 ll. DLC.
                                                11596
The NORTHAMPTON Farmer's Almanac for 1828.
Easton: Henry & William Hutter. 18 ll. MWA; MBAt.
                                                11597
PENNSYLVANIA Almanac for 1828. By John Ward.
Philadelphia: M'Carty & Davis. 18 ll. PDoBHi; PP;
PPiHi (17 ll.)   11598

PENNSYLVANIA Almanac for 1828. By John Ward.
Philadelphia: G. W. Mentz, and M'Carty & Davis. 18
ll. MWA; DLC; NN; InU; CtY; NBuG; PHi (14 ll.);
PLF; PYHi; NjR; Drake (15 ll.)   11599

PENNSYLVANIA and New Jersey Almanack for 1828.
Philadelphia: Griggs & Co. CtY.   11600

PENNSYLVANIA and New Jersey Almanack for 1828.
By Joseph Cramer. Philadelphia: Isaac Pugh. 18 ll.
MWA; FSaHi; InU; NjR; PHi; PP.   11601

POOR Wills Almanac for 1828. By William Collom.

Philadelphia: Kimber and Sharpless. 18 ll. MWA;
DLC; N; InU (impf); CtY; MB; NjR (7 ll.); WHi;
PHi; PPL.   11602

POOR Wills Almanac for 1828. By William Collom.
Philadelphia: J. Rakestraw. 18 ll. MWA; NHi;
NjGlaN.   11603

POOR Will's Pocket Almanack for 1828. Philadelphia:
Kimber & Sharpless. 24 ll. MWA; NjR; PHi.   11604

TOWN & Country Almanac for 1828. By Joseph
Cramer. Philadelphia: D. & S. Neall. 18 ll. MWA;
PP.   11605

TOWN and Country Almanack for 1828. By Joseph
Cramer. Philadelphia: D. & S. Neall. 18 ll. MWA;
CtY; PDoBHi; PHi; Drake (9 ll.)   11606

UNCLE Sam's Almanack for 1828. By Joseph Cramer.
Philadelphia: Griggs & Dickinson. 18 ll. MWA. 11607

UNCLE Sam's Almanack for 1828. By Joseph Cramer.
Philadelphia: Griggs & Dickinson, for Denny & Walker.
18 ll. DLC; WHi; PHi.   11608

The UNITED States' Almanac [for 1828]. By Seth
Smith. Philadelphia: R. Desilver. 28 ll. MWA (three
varieties); CLU; CtY; InU; MB; P; Drake.   11609

The UNITED States' Almanac [for 1828]. By Seth
Smith. Philadelphia: R. Desilver; T. Desilver; John
Grigg. 28 ll. DLC; N; IaU; MH; NBuHi; PPAmP;
PPL.   11610

The WESTERN Farmer's Almanac for 1828. By Rev.
John Taylor. Pittsburgh: H. Holdship & Son; D. and
M. Maclean, printers. 18 ll. CLU; OHi (16 ll.);
PPiHi (16 ll.)   11611

-- Issue with added "Magazine." 36 ll. MWA; NN;
OMC; PHi; PPPrHi (35 ll.); PPi.   11612

Pennsylvania - 1828

Der WESTLICHE Menschenfreund u. Schellsburger Calender auf 1828. Von Carl F. Egelmann. Schellsburg: Friedrich Goeb. 18 ll. DLC; WHi (impf); PPL (17 ll.); NjR. 11613

AGRICULTURAL Almanac for 1829. Lancaster: John Baer. 18 ll. MWA; DLC; NN; NNU-H; CLU; CtHT-W; PPL; PHi (11 ll., ntp) 11614

The AGRICULTURAL Almanack for 1829. Philadelphia: Thomas Desilver. 18 ll. MWA; DLC; NN; NHi (impf); CtY; NBuHi; PHi. 11615

AMERICANISCHER Stadt und Land Calender auf 1829. Philadelphia: Conrad Zentler. 18 ll. MWA; DLC; N; NN; CtY; NjP; NjR; CLU; P; PDoBHi; PHi; PPG; PPL (9 ll.) 11616

BAILEY'S Franklin Almanac for 1829. By Joshua Sharp. Philadelphia: Lydia R. Bailey. 18 ll. MWA; InU; PHi. 11617

BAILEY'S Franklin Almanac for 1829. By Joshua Sharp. Philadelphia: Thomas Desilver; Lydia R. Bailey, printer. 18 ll. CtY. 11618

BAILEY'S Washington Almanac for 1829. By Joshua Sharp. Philadelphia: Lydia R. Bailey. 18 ll. MWA; DLC; CtY; NjGlaN; PPL. 11619

BENNETT & Walton's Almanack for 1829. By Joseph Cramer. Philadelphia: D. & S. Neall. 18 ll. MWA; DLC; N; NBuG; InU; NjR; PHi; PP (ntp); PPL; Drake. 11620

Der CALENDER Eines Christen auf 1829. Philadelphia: Pennsylvanischen Zweig der Amerikanischen Traktat-Gesellschaft; Conrad Zentler. 18 ll. MWA; N; P; PAnL; PPL (16 ll.) 11621

The CHRISTIAN Almanac for 1829. Pittsburgh: American Tract Society; R. Patterson. 18 ll. OClWHi. 11622

Pennsylvania - 1829   1107

The CHRISTIAN Almanac, for Pennsylvania and Delaware for 1829. Philadelphia: Pennsylvania branch of the American Tract Society; Nicholas Murray. 18 ll. MWA; DLC; N; InU; KHi; PHi; PP.   11623

The CHRISTIAN Almanac, for Pennsylvania & Ohio for 1829. Pittsburgh: American Tract Society. 18 ll. OHi.   11624

CITIZEN & Farmers' Almanack for 1829. By Joseph Cramer. Philadelphia: Griggs & Dickinson. 18 ll. NjR (17 ll.)   11625

COLUMBIAN Almanac for 1829. By William Collom. Philadelphia: Joseph M'Dowell. 18 ll. MWA (impf); DLC (14 ll.); NHi; NBuHi; CtY; InU; NjR (16 ll.); DeU (16 ll.); PHi; Drake (17 ll.)   11626

CRAMER'S Magazine Almanack for 1829. Pittsburgh: Cramer & Spear; [etc]. 36 ll. DLC; OC; PPi. 11627

CRAMER'S Pittsburgh Almanack for 1829. Pittsburgh: Cramer & Spear; [etc]. 18 ll. MWA; OClWHi; OFH; OHi (17 ll.); Drake.   11628

DESILVER'S United States' Almanac for 1829. Philadelphia: R. Desilver; T. Desilver; J. Grigg. By Seth Smith. 28 ll. MWA; DLC; NHi; CLU; InU; MB; PHi; PP; PPAmP; NjR.   11629

-- Issue with 36 ll. N; CtY; PPL.   11630

The FARMERS' Almanac for 1829. By John Ward. Philadelphia: M'Carty & Davis. 18 ll. PHi; PPL (15 ll.); NjR.   11631

The FRANKLIN Almanac for 1829. By John Armstrong. Pittsburgh: Johnston and Stockton. 18 ll. MWA; CLU; OMC; TxF.   11632

-- Issue with 30 ll. MWA.   11633

FRANKLIN Almanac for 1829. By Charles Hoffman.

Philadelphia: M'Carty & Davis. MWA (17 ll.) 11634

Der GEMEINNÜTZIGE Landwirthschafts Calender auf 1829. Lancaster: William Albrecht. 18 ll. MWA; DLC; CLU; CtY; InU; NjP; OC; WHi; PDoBHi; PHi; PPeSchw; PYHi; PPL. 11635

Der HOCH-DEUTSCHE Americanische Calender auf 1829. Von Carl Friederich Egelmann. Germantaun: M. Billmeyer. 18 ll. MWA; DLC; NN; InU; MH; WHi; PHi; PLF; PPG; PPL; PPeSchw. 11636

JOHN Grigg's Almanack for 1829. By Joseph Cramer. Philadelphia: D. & S. Neall. 18 ll. MWA; DLC; InU; NBuHi (17 ll.); PHi; PPL; NjR (14 ll.) 11637

KITE'S Town and Country Almanac for 1829. By William Collom. Philadelphia: Thomas Kite. 18 ll. MWA; MiU-C; NBuHi; PHi. 11638

The MECHANIC'S and Working Man's Almanac for 1829. Philadelphia: Mechanic's Free Press. 18 ll. MWA. 11639

Der NEUE Americanische Landwirthschafts-Calender auf 1829. Von Carl Friedrich Egelmann. Reading: Johann Ritter u. Comp. 18 ll. MWA; DLC (16 ll.); NHi (impf); InU; NjP; P; PHi; PPCS; PPL; PR; PRHi; Drake. 11640

Der NEUE Hochdeutsche Orwigsburger Calender auf 1829. Orwigsburg: Thoma und May. 18 ll. MWA; NN (17 ll.); PHi; PPL. 11641

Der NEUE Pennsylvanische Stadt-und Land-Calender auf 1829. Allentaun: Heinrich Ebner und Comp. 18 ll. MWA; DLC; N; CLU; CtY; PAtHi; PAtM; PDoBHi; PPL; PRHi. 11642

The NEW Brunswick, (N. J.) Almanack for 1829. By Joseph Cramer. Philadelphia: Griggs & Dickinson, for Joseph C. Griggs, New Brunswick, (New Jersey.) 18 ll. MWA; CtY; MBC; NjR; PHi. 11643

PENNSYLVANIA Almanac for 1829. By John Ward.
Lancaster: William Allbright. 18 ll. MWA (17 ll.);
InU; PYHi. 11644

PENNSYLVANIA Almanac for 1829. By John Ward.
Philadelphia: M'Carty & Davis. 18 ll. CtY; PDoBHi;
PP; PPL (17 ll.) 11645

PENNSYLVANIA Almanac for 1829. By John Ward.
Philadelphia: M'Carty & Davis, and George W. Mentz.
18 ll. MWA; DLC; InU; PHi; PPL. 11646

PHILADELPHIA Almanack for 1829. By Joseph
Cramer. Philadelphia: Uriah Hunt; D. & S. Neall,
printers. 18 ll. MWA (two varieties); DLC; NN;
CtY; InU; DeWint; MBC; Nj; WHi. 11647

PHILADELPHIA Almanack for 1829. By Joseph ramer
[sic]. Philadelphia: Uriah Hunt; D. & S. Neall,
printers. 18 ll. PHi. 11648

PHILADELPHIA Almanack for 1829. By Joseph
Cramer. Philadelphia: D. & S. Neall. 18 ll. PDoBHi
(16 ll.) 11649

POOR Will's Almanac for 1829. By William Collom.
Philadelphia: Kimber & Sharpless. 18 ll. DLC;
NBuHi; PPL. 11650

POOR Will's Almanac for 1829. By William Collom.
Philadelphia: J. Rakestraw. 18 ll. MWA; N (impf);
NHi; InU; MB; NjR; WHi; PHi; PPL; Drake (15 ll.)
11651
POOR Will's Pocket Almanack for 1829. Philadelphia:
Kimber & Sharpless. 24 ll. MWA; DLC; NN; NjR;
PHi; PP. 11652

UNCLE Sam's Almanack for 1829. By Joseph Cramer.
Philadelphia: Denny & Walker. 18 ll. MWA; DLC; MB;
Drake. 11653

The WESTERN Farmers' Almanac for 1829. By Rev.
John Taylor. Pittsburgh: H. Holdship & Son; D. & M.

Maclean, printers. 18 ll. N; OHi (17 ll.); WvU.
11654
-- Issue with added "Magazine." 36 ll. MWA; DLC; InU; NBuHi (34 ll.); OMC (35 ll.); OClWHi; WHi; Wv-Ar (35 ll.); P; PHi; PPi (35 ll.); PPiU.   11655

Der WESTLICHE Menschenfreund u. Schellsburger Calender auf 1829. Von Carl Friedrich Egelmann. Schellsburg: Friedrich Goeb. 18 ll. Drake.   11656

AGRICULTURAL Almanac for 1830. Lancaster: John Bear. 18 ll. MWA; NNU-H (17 ll.); NBuG; PDoBHi; PHi (impf)   11657

AMERICANISCHER Stadt und Land Calender auf 1830. Philadelphia: Conrad Zentler. 18 ll. MWA; DLC; CtY; InU; NjP; PDoBHi; PHi; PPG; PPL (16 ll., ntp)
11658
BENNETT & Walton's Almanack for 1830. By Joseph Cramer. Philadelphia: Garden & Thompson. 18 ll. MWA; DLC; CLU; CtY; InU (ntp); NjR; PHi.   11659

Der CALENDER Eines Christen auf 1830. Philadelphia: Pennsylvanischen Zweig, der Amerikanischen Traktat-Gesellschaft; Gedruckt bey Conrad Zentler. 18 ll. MWA; InU; P; PHi; PPL; PPeSchw.   11660

CALENDER für den Westlichen Bürger und Landmann auf 1830. Von dem ehrw. Johann Taylor. Pittsburgh: H. Holdship u. Sohn; Gedruckt bey D. und M. Maclean. 18 ll. MWA; DLC (17 ll.); InU; PPiHi. 11661

The CHRISTIAN Almanack for 1830. By Charles Frederick Egelmann. Philadelphia: Pennsylvania Branch of the American Tract Society; Clark & Raser, printers. 18 ll. NjP; P; PHi (17 ll.)   11662

The CHRISTIAN Almanac, for Pennsylvania and Delaware for 1830. Philadelphia: Pennsylvania Branch of the American Tract Society. 18 ll. PP.   11663

The CHRISTIAN Almanac, for Pennsylvania, Delaware, and West New-Jersey for 1830. Philadelphia: Pennsyl-

vania Branch of the American Tract Society. 20 ll.
MWA; InU.   11664

The **CHRISTIAN** Almanac, for Pennsylvania, Delaware, and West New-Jersey for 1830. Philadelphia: Pennsylvania Branch of the American Tract Society; Rev. Joel T. Benedict. 18 ll. MWA; DLC (impf); PHi (impf); PP; PPL.   11665

CITIZENS & Farmers' Almanack for 1830. Philadelphia: Griggs & Dickinson. 18 ll. MWA; DLC; InU.
   11666

COLUMBIAN Almanac for 1830. By William Collom. Philadelphia: Joseph M'Dowell. 18 ll. MWA; DLC; NN; InU; FSaHi (17 ll.); WHi; NjR; PDoBHi; PPL; PU.
   11667

CRAMER'S Magazine Almanack for 1830. By Sanford C. Hill. Pittsburgh: Cramer & Spear. 36 ll. OClWHi; PPiU (32 ll., ntp)   11668

CRAMER'S Pittsburgh Almanack for 1830. By Sanford C. Hill. Pittsburgh: Cramer & Spear. 18 ll. MWA; N; OHi; PPiU.   11669

DESILVER'S United States' Register and Almanac for 1830. By Seth Smith. Philadelphia: R. Desilver; T. Desilver; J. Grigg; William Sharpless, printer. 32 ll. MWA; DLC; CLU; MB; MH; ODa; PHi; PLF; PPAmP; PPL.   11670

-- Issue with 36 ll. PPL.   11671

The **FARMER'S** Almanac for 1830. By John Ward. Philadelphia: M'Carty & Davis. 18 ll. MWA; NHi (17 ll.); InU; PHi; NjR (16 ll.)   11672

The **FARMERS** and Mechanics Almanack for 1830. By Charles Frederick Egelmann. Philadelphia: George W. Mentz. 18 ll. MWA; DLC; MH; NcD; NjR; ViU; PHi; PLF; PP; PPFM; PPL.   11673

The **FRANKLIN** Almanac for 1830. By John Armstrong. Pittsburgh: Johnson and Stockton. 18 ll. OClWHi. 11674

-- Issue with added "Magazine." 30 ll. MWA; DLC (28 ll.); OClWHi; WvU.   11675

The FRANKLIN Almanac for 1830. By John Ward. Philadelphia: M'Carty & Davis. 18 ll. MWA; NjR; PHi.   11676

Der GEMEINNÜTZIGE Landwirthschafts Calender auf 1830. Lancaster: William Albrecht. 18 ll. MWA; DLC; N; NN (15 ll.); CLU; CtY; InU; NjP; WHi; P; PHi; PLF; PLHi; PPL (17 ll.); PPeSchw; PYHi; Drake (17 ll.)   11677

GRIGG'S City and Country Almanack for 1830. By Joseph Cramer. Philadelphia: John Grigg; W. Pilkington & Co., printers. 18 ll. MWA; DLC; CtY; InU; P (17 ll.); PHi; PPL.   11678

Der HOCH-DEUTSCHE Americanische Calender auf 1830. Von Carl Friederich Egelmann. Germantaun: M. Billmeyer. 18 ll. MWA; DLC; NN (17 ll.); NHi (17 ll.); InU (impf); CtY; DeWint; WHi; P; PHi; PPeSchw; PPL.   11679

KITE'S Town and Country Almanac for 1830. By William Collom. Philadelphia: Thomas Kite. 18 ll. MWA; DLC; NjR; PHi; PP.   11680

Der NEUE, Americanische Landwirthschafts-Calender auf 1830. Von Carl Friedrich Egelmann. Reading: Johann Ritter u. Comp. 18 ll. MWA; PDoBHi; PHi; PPCS; PPeSchw; PR; PRHi; PPL.   11681

Der NEUE Hochdeutsche Orwigsburger Calender auf 1830. Orwigsburg: Thoma und May. 18 ll. MWA; CLU; CtY; InU (ntp); NjR.   11682

Der NEUE Pennsylvanische Stadt-und Land-Calender auf 1830. Allentown: Heinrich Ebner und Comp. [Seidensticker]   11683

NEUER Gemeinüzige Pennsylvanischer Calender auf 1830. Lancaster: Johann Baer. [Bausman]   11684

NEW Brunswick, (N. J.) Almanack for 1830. Philadelphia: Griggs & Dickinson, for Joseph C. Griggs, New Brunswick, (New Jersey.) 18 ll. MWA; NjHi; NjR; Honeyman.   11685

NEW Brunswick, (N. J.), Almanack for 1830. By Joshua Sharp. Philadelphia: Griggs & Dickinson, for Joseph C. Griggs, New Brunswick, (N. J.) 18 ll. OClWHi; Honeyman.   11686

ORWIGSBURG Almanac for 1830. By Charles Fred'k. Egelman. Orwigsburg: Thoma & May. 18 ll. MWA; NN; MiU-C; PDoBHi (16 ll.)   11687

The PENNSYLVANIA Almanac for 1830. By John Ward. Philadelphia: M'Carty & Davis. 18 ll. MWA; DLC (impf); InU; PLF (15 ll.)   11688

The PENNSYLVANIA Anti-Masonic Almanac for 1830. Reading: J. R. Christian. [Phillips]   11689

The PENNSYLVANIA Anti-Masonic Almanac for 1830. By Edward Giddins. Lancaster: Anti-Masonic Herald. 24 ll. MWA; N; NHi; NNFM; CLU; ICHi; NjR; WHi; PHi; PPFM.   11690

Der PENNSYLVANISCHE Anti-Freimaurer Calender auf 1830. Lancaster: Samuel Wagner. [Bausman] 11691

Der PENNSYLVANISCHE Anti-Freymaurer Calender auf 1830. Von Carl Friedrich Egelman. Reading: Johann R. Christian. 24 ll. MWA (ntp); DLC; NNFM; DeWint; P; PPG; PPFM; PPL; PPeSchw; PRHi.
 11692

PHILADELPHIA Almanack for 1830. By Joseph Cramer. Philadelphia: Uriah Hunt; W. Pilkington & Co., printers. 18 ll. MWA; CtY; InU; NjGlaN; PHi; PPL; NjR; Drake.
 11693

POOR Will's Almanac for 1830. By William Collom. Philadelphia: Kimber & Sharpless. 18 ll. MWA; DLC; MB; NjR; WHi; PHi; PPL.   11694

POOR Will's Pocket Almanack for 1830. Philadelphia:

Kimber & Sharpless. 24 ll. MWA; DLC; MnU; PHi;
PP. 11695

The TABLET of Memory; or, Ladies' Entertaining and
Useful Diary for 1830. Philadelphia: A. R. Poole.
73 ll. ICN. 11696

TOWAR & Hogan's Farmer's and Citizen's Almanack
for 1830. By Joseph Cramer. Philadelphia: Towar &
Hogan; W. Pilkington & Co., printers. 18 ll. MWA;
PHi; Drake. 11697

UNCLE Sam's Almanack for 1830. Philadelphia: Denny
& Walker. 18 ll. MWA; DLC; NHi; CtY; DeU (17
ll.); PPiU. 11698

The VILLAGE Almanack for 1830. Philadelphia:
Griggs & Dickinson. 18 ll. MWA; PHi. 11699

The WESTERN Farmer's Almanac for 1830. By Rev.
John Taylor. Pittsburgh: H. Holdship & Son; D. and
M. Maclean, printers. 18 ll. CLU; InU; MiU-C;
PPiHi. 11700

The WESTERN Farmer's Magazine Almanac for 1830.
By Rev. John Taylor. Pittsburgh: H. Holdship & Son;
D. and M. Maclean, printers. 36 ll. MWA; DLC (20
ll.); OC; OMC; PHi; PPi; WvU. 11701

AGRICULTURAL Almanac for 1831. Lancaster: John
Bear. 18 ll. MiU-C; NjR (17 ll.); PPeSchw. 11702

AMERICANISCHER Stadt und Land Calender auf 1831.
Philadelphia: Conrad Zentler. 18 ll. MWA; DLC; N;
NN; NHi; CLU; CtY; InU (impf); NjP; Njr (17 ll.);
RPB; PDoBHi; PHi; PPeSchw; PYHi. 11703

BENNETT & Walton's Almanack for 1831. By Joseph
Cramer. Philadelphia: Bennett & Walton; W. Pilkington & Co., printers. 18 ll. MWA (two varieties); DLC;
NN; InU; PHC; PHi; PPL; Drake. 11704

Der CALENDER Eines Christen für 1831. Philadelphia:

Conrad Zentler. [Seidensticker] 11705

CALENDER, Für den Westliche Büerger und Landmann auf 1831. Von dem ehrw. Johann Taylor. Pittsburgh: H. Holdschip und Sohn; Gedruckt bey D. und M. Maclean. 18 ll. PHi. 11706

The CHRISTIAN Almanack for 1831. By Charles Frederick Egelmann. Philadelphia: Pennsylvania branch of the American Tract Society. 18 ll. NjP. 11707

The CHRISTIAN Almanac, for Pennsylvania, Delaware, and West New-Jersey for 1831. Philadelphia: Pennsylvania branch of the American Tract Society. 20 ll. MWA; InU; NjJ; PPi (impf) 11708

The CHRISTIAN Almanac, for Pennsylvania, Delaware, and West New-Jersey for 1831. Philadelphia: Pennsylvania branch of the American Tract Society; Rev. Joel T. Benedict. 18 ll. MWA; DLC (impf); NHi. 11709

CITIZENS' Almanack for 1831. Philadelphia: Griggs & Dickinson for L. B. Clarke. 18 ll. MWA; PPL. 11710

CITIZENS' Almanack for 1831. Philadelphia: Griggs & Dickinson, for John Grigg. 18 ll. MWA; PHi; PP (impf) 11711

CITIZENS and Farmers' Almanack for 1831. Philadelphia: L. B. Clarke. 18 ll. MWA (impf) 11712

CITIZENS & Farmers' Almanack for 1831. Philadelphia: Griggs & Dickinson. 18 ll. PDoBHi. 11713

CITIZENS & Farmers Almanack for 1831. Philadelphia: Griggs & Dickinson, for John Grigg. 18 ll. PHi (16 ll.) 11714

COLUMBIAN Almanac for 1831. By William Collom. Philadelphia: Joseph McDowell. 18 ll. MWA; NN; NHi; InU; MiU-C; PHi; NjR. 11715

CRAMER'S Magazine Almanack for 1831. By Sanford C. Hill. Pittsburgh: Cramer & Spear. 36 ll. OClWHi;

PPi.   11716

CRAMER'S Pittsburgh Almanack for 1831. By Sanford
C. Hill.   Pittsburgh: Cramer & Spear. 18 ll. CLU;
OFH; PPi.   11717

DESILVER'S United States Register and Almanac for
1831.   Philadelphia: R. Desilver; T. Desilver; J.
Grigg; William Sharpless, printer. (By Seth Smith).
28 ll. MWA; DLC; CtY; PPAmP.   11718

-- Issue with 32 ll. NHi; PPL.   11719

The FARMERS' Almanac for 1831. By John Ward.
Philadelphia: M'Carty & Davis. 18 ll. MWA; DeU
(17 ll.); InU; PHi; PPL; NjR [Drake (Ward's manuscript of this almanac)]   11720

The FARMERS & Mechanics Almanack for 1831.
Easton: Henry Hamman. 18 ll. MWA.   11721

The FARMERS and Mechanics Almanack for 1831. By
Charles Frederick Egelmann. Philadelphia: George W.
Mentz & Son. 18 ll. MWA; N; NN; NHi; P; PYHi;
ViU; PLF.   11722

-- Issue with 19 ll. PHi; NNU-H; PPL; NjR.   11723

The FRANKLIN Almanac for 1831. By John Armstrong. Pittsburgh: Johnson and Stockton; [etc]. 18 ll.
OClWHi; OHi (17 ll.); OMC.   11724

-- Issue with added "Magazine." 30 ll. MWA; DLC;
OC; OClWHi; Wv-Ar; WvU.   11725

-- Issue with added "Magazine," no "Hogan & Co." in
imprint. 30 ll. PPiU (29 ll.)   11726

The FRANKLIN Almanac for 1831. By John Ward.
Philadelphia: M'Carty & Davis. 18 ll. DLC; InU; PHi
(16 ll., ntp); PPL [Drake (Ward's manuscript of this
almanac)]   11727

The FRANKLIN Almanac for 1831. By John Ward.
Philadelphia: Joseph M'Dowell. 18 ll. MWA; NBuG;
PDoBHi.   11728

FRIENDS' Almanac for 1831. Philadelphia: M. T. C.
Gould. 18 ll. MWA (two varieties); CtY; ICN. 11729

Der GEMEINNÜTZIGE Landwirthschafts Calender auf
1831. Lancaster: William Albrecht. 18 ll. MWA;
DLC (impf); CLU; CtY; InU; NjP; WHi; MH; OC; P;
PDoBHi; PHi; PLHi; PPL; PPeSchw.   11730

GRIGG'S City and Country Almanack for 1831. By
Joseph Cramer. Philadelphia: John Grigg; W. Pilkington & Co., printers. 18 ll. MWA; DLC; N; CLU;
InU; PHi; PPL.   11731

Der HOCH-DEUTSCHE Americanische Calender auf
1831. Von Carl Friederich Egelmann. Germantaun:
M. Billmeyer. 18 ll. MWA; DLC (16 ll.); CLU; CtY;
InU; MH; WHi; P; PHi; PPG; PPL; PPeSchw; PYHi.
                                                     11732

KITE'S Town and Country Almanac for 1831. By William Collom. Philadelphia: Thomas Kite. 18 ll. MWA;
N; CLU; CtY; NjGlaN; NjR; PHi; PP.   11733

Der NEUE, Americanische Landwirthschafts-Calender
auf 1831. Von Carl Friedrich Egelmann. Reading:
Johann Ritter u. Comp. 18 ll. MWA; InU; P (17 ll.);
PPAmP; PPeSchw; PPL; PR; PRHi.   11734

Der NEUE Pennsylvanische Stadt-und Land-Calender auf
1831. Allentown: Heinrich Ebner. [Seidensticker]
                                                     11735

NEUER Gemeinnüzige Pennsylvanischer Calender auf
1831. Lancaster: Johann Baer. [Bausman] 11736

NEW Brunswick, (N. J.), Almanack for 1831. Philadelphia: Griggs & Dickinson, for Joseph C. Griggs,
New Brunswick, (N. J.) 18 ll. NjHi; Honeyman.
                                                     11737
NEW Brunswick, (N. J.) Almanack for 1831. Philadel-

Pennsylvania - 1831

phia: Griggs & Dickinson, for Joseph C. Griggs, New Brunswick, (New Jersey.) 18 ll. NBLiHi; NjR. 11738

NEW Brunswick, (N. J.), Almanac for 1831. By Joshua Sharp. Philadelphia: Griggs & Dickinson, for Joseph C. Griggs, New Brunswick, (N. J.) 18 ll. Honeyman. 11739

PENNSYLVANIA Almanac for 1831. By John Ward. Philadelphia: M'Carty & Davis. 18 ll. MWA; N (ntp); CtY; InU; NjR; PDoBHi (ntp); PHi (13 ll.); PLF; [Drake (Ward's manuscript of this almanac)] 11740

Der PENNSYLVANISCHE Anti-Freimaurer Calender auf 1831. Lancaster: Samuel Wagner. [Bausman] 11741

PHILADELPHIA Almanack for 1831. By Joseph Cramer. Philadelphia: Uriah Hunt; W. Pilkington & Co., printers. 18 ll. DLC; NBLiHi (17 ll.); PHi (17 ll.); PPL. 11742

POOR Will's Almanac for 1831. By William Collom. Philadelphia: Joseph Rakestraw. 18 ll. CtY; PDoBHi. 11743

POOR Will's Pocket Almanack for 1831. Philadelphia: Kimber & Sharpless. 24 ll. MWA; InU; MnU; NjR; PHi. 11744

The SUN Anti-Masonic Almanac for 1831. By Wm. Collom. Philadelphia: J. Clarke. 18 ll. MWA; N; InU (impf); NIC; NNFM; NjR; PP; PPFM; PPeSchw. 11745

UNCLE Sam's Almanack for 1831. Philadelphia: Denny & Walker. 18 ll. MWA; CLU; CtY; NjR (16 ll.); PHi. 11746

The WESTERN Farmer's Almanac for 1831. By Rev. John Taylor. Pittsburgh: H. Holdship & Son; D. and M. Maclean, printers. 18 ll. MWA; DLC (15 ll.); NN (13 ll.); ICHi; InU; OClWHi; OMC; PHi; PPi. 11747

-- Issue with added "Magazine." 36 ll. Private collection. 11748

AGRICULTURAL Almanac for 1832. Lancaster: John Bear. 18 ll. MWA; CtY; InU; NBuG; WHi; PHi (17 ll.) 11749

ALLYN'S Anti-Masonic Almanac for 1832. By Avery Allyn. Philadelphia: John Clarke. 12 ll. MWA; MB; NNFM. 11750

The AMERICAN Comic Almanac for 1832. Philadelphia: John Grigg. 24 ll. MWA (two varieties); DLC; NN; NBuHi. 11751

AMERICANISCHER Stadt und Land Calender auf 1832. Philadelphia: Conrad Zentler. 18 ll. MWA; DLC; N; NN; CLU; CtY; InU; NjP; PDoBHi; PHi; PLF; PPG; Drake. 11752

The ANTI-MASONIC Sun Almanac for 1832. By Avery Allyn [and] William Collom. Philadelphia: J. Clarke. 18 ll. MWA (17 ll.); N; NIC; InU; OClWHi; PP; PPFM; PPL. 11753

BENNETT & Walton's Almanack for 1832. Philadelphia: Bennett & Walton. 18 ll. MWA; NN; NjR. 11754

The CHRISTIAN Almanack for 1832. By Charles Frederick Egelmann. Philadelphia: Pennsylvania branch of the American Tract Society. 18 ll. MWA; DLC; CLU; InU; NjP; PHi. 11755

The CHRISTIAN Almanac, for Pennsylvania, and West New-Jersey for 1832. Philadelphia: Pennsylvania branch of the American Tract Society; Rev. Joel T. Benedict. 18 ll. MWA; PHi. 11756

The CHRISTIAN Almanac, for Pennsylvania, Delaware, and West New-Jersey for 1832. Philadelphia: Pennsylvania branch of the American Tract Society. 20 ll. MWA. 11757

CITIZENS' Almanack for 1832. Philadelphia: Griggs & Dickinson, for L. B. Clarke. 18 ll. MWA. 11758

CITIZENS' Almanack for 1832. Philadelphia: Griggs & Dickinson, for John Grigg. 18 ll. MWA. 11759

CITIZENS' Almanack for 1832. Philadelphia: Griggs & Dickinson, for Grigg & Elliot. 18 ll. PPL. 11760

The CITIZENS and Farmers Annual Magazine, or New Philadelphia Almanac for 1832. By Charles F. Egelmann. Philadelphia: John T. Hanzsche. 18 ll. MWA; N; PLF. 11761

COLUMBIAN Almanac for 1832. By William Collom. Philadelphia: Joseph M'Dowell. 18 ll. MWA; DeU; InU (ntp); NjGlaN; PHi; Drake (17 ll.) 11762

CRAMER'S Magazine Almanack for 1832. By Sanford C. Hill. Pittsburgh: Cramer & Spear; [etc]. 36 ll. OCHP; OClWHi; PHi; PPi. 11763

CRAMER'S Pittsburgh Almanack for 1832. By Sanford C. Hill. Pittsburgh: Cramer & Spear. 18 ll. OFH. 11764

DESILVER'S United States Register and Almanac [for 1832]. By Seth Smith. Philadelphia: R. Desilver; T. Desilver; J. Grigg; T. Town, printer. 28 ll. MWA; NN; NHi; WHi; PDoBHi; PHi. 11765

-- Issue with 32 ll. PPiU. 11766

The FARMERS' Almanac for 1832. By John Ward. Philadelphia: M'Carty & Davis. 18 ll. MWA; CtY; InU; PHi (two copies, one is the printer's proof - 31 ll., printed on one side only); PPL; PPiHi; Drake (also has Ward's manuscript for this almanac) 11767

The FARMERS and Mechanics Almanack for 1832. By Charles Frederick Egelmann. Philadelphia: George W. Mentz & Son. 18 ll. InU (16 ll.); CtY; KHi; NjR; MB; ViU; P; PLF; PPeSchw; PYHi. 11768

-- Issue with 21 ll. MWA; NN; PHi. 11769

The FARMERS and Mechanics Almanack for 1832. By

Charles Frederick Egelmann. Philadelphia: George W. Mentz & Son; Easton: Henry Hamman. 18 ll. PPL.   11770

FOULKE'S Almanac for 1832. By Joseph Foulke. Philadelphia: John Richards. 24 ll. MWA; NN; NHi; InU; NjR; PDoBHi; PPL; Drake.   11771

The FRANKLIN Almanac for 1832. By John Armstrong. Pittsburgh: Johnson and Stockton. 18 ll. CLU; WHi; OClWHi; Wv-Ar; WvU (17 ll.); PPiHi (11 ll.); PPiU.   11772

-- Issue with added "Magazine." 30 ll. MWA; OClWHi; OMC (29 ll.)   11773

The FRANKLIN Almanac for 1832. By John Ward. Philadelphia: M'Carty & Davis. 18 ll. DLC; MiD-B; PHi; [Drake (Ward's manuscript for this almanac)]   11774

FRIENDS' United States Almanac for 1832. Philadelphia: Marcus T. C. Gould; J. Harding, printer. 29 ll. MWA; N; NBuG; ICN; PDoBHi.   11775

Der GEMEINNÜTZIGE Landwirthschafts Calender auf 1832. Lancaster: William Albrecht. 18 ll. MWA; DLC (impf); CtY; DeWint; NjP; PHi; PPCS; PPL; PPeSchw; PYHi.   11776

The GIRARD Almanac for 1832. By William Collom. Philadelphia: W. Johnson. 14 ll. MWA.   11777

Der HOCH-DEUTSCHE Americanische Calender auf 1832. Von Carl Friederich Egelmann. Germantaun: M. Billmeyer. 18 ll. MWA; NN; InU; CLU; CtY; MH; MnU; WHi; NjR; P; PDoBHi; PHi; PPCS (17 ll.); PPG; PPL; PPT; PPeSchw; PYHi.   11778

HUNT'S Philadelphia Almanack for 1832. By Joseph Cramer. Philadelphia: Uriah Hunt. 18 ll. MWA; DLC; InU; NBuG; PHi; PPL.   11779

JOHNSON'S Almanac for 1832. By William Collom. Philadelphia: W. Johnson. 14 ll. PU (13 ll.); NjR (13 ll.)   11780

Der NEUE, Americanische Landwirthschafts-Calender auf 1832. Von Carl Friedrich Egelmann. Reading: Johann Ritter u. Comp. 16 ll. MWA; NN; PPCS; PPeSchw; PPL; PR; PRHi. 11781

NEUER Gemeinnüzige Pennsylvanischer Calender auf 1832. Lancaster: Johann Baer. [Bausman] 11782

NEW Brunswick, (N. J.) Almanack for 1832. New Brunswick: Printed for Joseph C. Griggs; Philadelphia: Griggs & Dickinson, printers. 20 ll. MWA; NjHi; NjR; PHi; Honeyman; Pickersgill. 11783

The NEW St. Tammany Almanac for 1832. By John Ward. Philadelphia: George W. Mentz. 18 ll. NjR. 11784

PENNSYLVANIA Almanac for 1832. By John Ward. Philadelphia: M'Carty & Davis. 18 ll. MWA (17 ll.); PDoBHi (impf); [Drake (has Ward's manuscript for this almanac)] 11785

PENNSYLVANIA & New Jersey Almanack for 1832. By Joseph Cramer. Philadelphia: Thomas L. Bonsal. 18 ll. MWA (two varieties); NN. 11786

PENNSYLVANIA Anti-Masonic Almanac for 1832. Philadelphia: S. W. Tobey; Pittsburgh: John Willock; [etc]. 24 ll. N; ICHi; PPL. 11787

Der PENNSYLVANISCHE Anti-Freimaurer Calender auf 1832. Von Carl Friedrich Egelman. Lancaster: Samuel Wagner. 24 ll. MWA (two varieties); DLC; MBAt; WHi; PLF; PPFM. 11788

A POCKET Almanac for 1832. Philadelphia: Willard Johnson. 10 ll. NjR. 11789

POOR Robin's Almanack for 1832. Philadelphia: Griggs & Dickinson. PDoBHi (7 ll.) 11790

POOR Wills Almanac for 1832. By William Collom. Philadelphia: Kimber & Sharpless. 18 ll. MWA; MB; P; PHi; PPeSchw. 11791

POOR Will's Pocket Almanack for 1832. Philadelphia: Kimber & Sharpless; A. Waldie, printer. 24 ll. MWA; DLC; InU; MnU; NjR; PHi; PP. 11792

PORTER'S Health Almanac for 1832. Calculated generally for... By William Collom. Philadelphia: Henry H. Porter. 40 ll. MWA; N; NHi; NBuG; NR; Ct; MiU-C; NcD; WHi; PHi; NjR; Drake. 11793

PORTER'S Health Almanac for 1832. Calculated more particularly for... By William Collom. Philadelphia: Henry H. Porter. 40 ll. MWA; DLC; NN; NHi; NjP; PPL; MHi; OClWHi; NSyOHi (ntp); F; MB; NjHi; MH; CLU; IU; MnU; CtY; CoCC (39 ll.); NjMo; OMC; InU; OC; MAtt; MiD-B; MDedHi; PP; PHC; O; PPAmP. 11794

UNCLE Sam's Almanack for 1832. Philadelphia: S. C. Atkinson. 18 ll. PPeSchw. 11795

UNCLE Sam's Almanack for 1832. Philadelphia: Denny & Walker. 18 ll. MWA; MnU; NjR; PHi. 11796

UNCLE Sam's Almanack for 1832. Philadelphia: Griggs & Dickinson. 18 ll. MWA. 11797

UNCLE Sam's Almanack for 1832. Philadelphia: Griggs & Dickinson for Grigg & Elliot. 18 ll. InU. 11798

UNCLE Sam's Large Almanack for 1832. Philadelphia: Denny & Walker. 18 ll. MWA (impf); NHi (impf); F (14 ll.); PHi; PLF; PPL. 11799

UNCLE Sam's Large Almanack for 1832. Philadelphia: Wm. W. Walker. 18 ll. PP. 11800

WASHINGTON Almanack for 1832. Philadelphia: Joseph M'Dowell. 18 ll. MWA; PHi (impf) 11801

The WESTERN Farmer's Almanac for 1832. By Rev. John Taylor. Pittsburgh: H. Holdship & Son; D. and M. Maclean, printers. 18 ll. MWA; NN; OMC. 11802

-- Issue with added "Magazine." 36 ll. MWA; OHi (35

ll.); PPi.   11803

AGRICULTURAL Almanac for 1833. Lancaster: John Bear. 18 ll. MWA (impf); CtY (impf); PHi (17 ll.); PLHi.   11804

The AMERICAN Comic Almanac for 1833. Philadelphia: Grigg & Elliot; Boston: Charles Ellms. 24 ll. MWA; NN; PHi (23 ll.)   11805

AMERICANISCHER Stadt und Land Calender auf 1833. Philadelphia: Conrad Zentler. 18 ll. MWA; DLC; CLU; CtY; InU; NjR; NjP; RPB; PPG; PDoBHi; PPeSchw; PYHi.   11806

The ANTIMASONIC Sun Almanac for 1833. By William Collom. Philadelphia: J. Clarke. 18 ll. MWA; InU; MnU; OClWHi; PP; PPFM.   11807

BAILEY'S Franklin Almanac for 1833. By William Collom. Philadelphia: Lydia R. Bailey. 18 ll. MWA (17 ll.)   11808

BENNETT & Walton's Almanac for 1833. Philadelphia: Bennett & Walton. 18 ll. MWA; CtY; InU; PHi; PPL; NjR.   11809

Der CALENDER Eines Christen auf 1833. Philadelphia: Conrad Zentler. 18 ll. MWA (impf)   11810

CHESTER County Almanac for 1833. By Hannum and Rutter. West Chester: Denny & Whitehead. 16 ll. MWA; DLC; InU.   11811

The CHRISTIAN Almanack for 1833. By Charles Frederick Egelmann. Philadelphia: Pennsylvania branch of the American Tract Society. 18 ll. P.   11812

The CHRISTIAN Almanac, for Pennsylvania, Delaware, and West New-Jersey for 1833. Philadelphia: Pennsylvania branch of the American Tract Society; Rev. Joel T. Benedict. 18 ll. MWA; DLC; PHi.   11813

CITIZENS' Almanack for 1833. Philadelphia: Griggs &

Dickinson, for L. B. Clarke. 18 ll. MWA; NjR (17 ll.); PHi. 11814

CITIZENS' Almanack for 1833. Philadelphia: Griggs & Dickinson for Key, Mielke & Biddle. 18 ll. MWA. 11815

The CITIZENS & Farmers' Almanack for 1833. Philadelphia: Griggs & Dickinson. 18 ll. ICHi. 11816

COLUMBIAN Almanac for 1833. Philadelphia: Jos. M'Dowell. 18 ll. MWA; DLC; PDoBHi; PHi; PPL; WHi. 11817

CRAMER'S Magazine Almanack for 1833. By Sanford C. Hill. Pittsburgh: Cramer & Spear; [etc.] 30 ll. MWA; OClWHi; PPi. 11818

CRAMER'S Pittsburgh Almanack for 1833. By Sanford C. Hill. Pittsburgh: Cramer & Spear. 18 ll. MWA; OClWHi; OHi; PPiU. 11819

DESILVER'S United States Register and Almanac [for 1833]. By Seth Smith. Philadelphia: R. Desilver; T. Desilver; J. Grigg. 28 ll. MWA; DLC; NN; NHi (24 ll.); CtY; MB; PPL; MdBJ; PPAmP. 11820

-- Issue with 40 ll. MWA; NSyOHi; PHi. 11821

ERIE Almanac for 1833. Erie: O. Spafford. NHi (11 ll.) 11822

The FARMERS' Almanac for 1833. By John Ward. Philadelphia: M'Carty & Davis. 18 ll. MWA; DLC; NjR; PHi; Drake (16 ll.; also has Ward's manuscript for this almanac) 11823

The FARMERS and Mechanics Almanack for 1833. By Charles Frederick Egelmann. Philadelphia: George W. Mentz & Son. 18 ll. MWA; N; NN; InU; CLU; CtY; MiU-C; NBuG; NjR; KHi; ViW (16 ll.); PHi; PYHi; Drake (impf) 11824

The FARMERS and Mechanics Almanack for 1833. By

Charles Frederick Egelmann. Philadelphia: George W. Mentz & Son; Easton: Henry Hammann. 18 ll. PPL.
11825

FOULKE'S Almanac for 1833. By Joseph Foulke. Philadelphia: John Richards. 24 ll. MWA; N; InU; NjR; PDoBHi; PP.
11826

The FRANKLIN Almanac for 1833. By John Armstrong. Pittsburgh: Johnston and Stockton; [etc]. 18 ll. OClWHi; OMC (17 ll.); PPiU.
11827

-- Issue with added "Magazine." 30 ll. MWA; DLC; InU; OClWHi; PPiHi; PPiU (27 ll., ntp)
11828

The FRANKLIN Almanac for 1833. By John Ward. Philadelphia: M'Carty & Davis. 18 ll. PHi; PPL; PPeSchw; [Drake (has Ward's manuscript for this almanac)]
11829

Der GEMEINNÜTZIGE Landwirthschafts Calender auf 1833. Lancaster: William Albrecht. 18 ll. MWA; PDoBHi; PHi; PPL (17 ll.)
11830

The GENTLEMAN'S Almanac and Pocket Companion for 1833. Philadelphia: Thomas T. Ash. 64 ll. MWA.
11831

GIRARD Almanack for 1833. By Joseph Cramer. Philadelphia: Thomas L. Bonsal. 18 ll. MWA; InU; PHi; PPL; NjR (ntp)
11832

The HEALTH Almanac for 1833. Philadelphia: Key, Mielke & Biddle. 42 ll. MWA; N; MHi; MnU; InU; O; PP; WHi; NjR (39 ll.)
11833

Der HOCH-DEUTSCHE Americanische Calender auf 1833. Von Carl Friedrich Egelmann. Germantaun: M. Billmeyer. 18 ll. MWA; InU; NjR (17 ll.); PHi (15 ll.); PPL; PPeSchw; PYHi.
11834

HUNT'S Philadelphia Almanack for 1833. By Joseph Cramer. Philadelphia: Uriah Hunt. 24 ll. MWA; DLC; N; InU; CtY; DeU; NjR; PHi; Drake (impf)
11835

JOHNSON'S Almanac for 1833. By William Collom.
Philadelphia: Willard Johnson. 14 ll. MWA; NN. 11836

Der NEUE, Americanische Landwirthschafts-Calender
auf 1833. Von Carl Friedrich Egelmann. Reading:
Johann Ritter u. Comp. 16 ll. MWA; N; NN (12 ll.);
InU (impf); P; PHi; PPeSchw; PPL; PR; PRHi. 11837

NEUER Calender für die Bauern und Handwerker auf
1833. Von Carl Egelmann. Philadelphia: Georg W.
Mentz und Sohn. 18 ll. MWA; CLU; CtY; InU; NjP;
P; PLF; PHi; PPL (14 ll.); PDoBHi; PPeSchw;
Drake. 11838

-- Issue with 21 ll. MWA. 11839

NEUER Gemeinnütziger Pennsylvanischer Calender auf
1833. Lancaster: Johann Baer. 18 ll. CtY; P; PHi;
PLF; PLHi; PPG. 11840

NEW Brunswick, (N. J.), Almanack for 1833. New
Brunswick: Joseph C. Griggs; Philadelphia: Griggs &
Dickinson, printers. 18 ll. MWA; N; NjHi; NjP;
Honeyman. 11841

PENNSYLVANIA Almanac for 1833. Philadelphia:
M'Carty & Davis. 18 ll. MWA (17 ll.); CtY; PHi.
11842

Der PENNSYLVANISCHE Anti-Freimaurer Calender auf
1833. Von Carl Friedrich Egelmann. Lancaster:
Samuel Wagner. 18 ll. MWA; CtY; DeWint; PP;
PYHi. 11843

POOR Robin's Almanack for 1833. Philadelphia:
Griggs & Dickinson, for Hogan & Thompson. 18 ll.
MWA; DLC; PDoBHi; PHi. 11844

POOR Wills Almanac for 1833. By William Collom.
Philadelphia: Joseph M'Dowell. 18 ll. MWA; NHi (14
ll.); CLU; CtY; InU; NBuG; NjR (17 ll.); MB; DeU
(17 ll.); NjGlaN; PHi; PP; PPL; PPeSchw. 11845

POOR Will's Pocket Almanac for 1833. Philadelphia:

Uriah Hunt. 32 ll. MWA; DLC; InU; MnU; PHi; PP.
11846
PORTER'S Health Almanac for 1833. Philadelphia:
Henry H. Porter. 40 ll. MWA; N; InU; OClWHi.
11847
UNCLE Sam's Almanack for 1833. Philadelphia:
Denny & Walker. 18 ll. FSaHi; MiU-C; PHi. 11848

UNCLE Sam's Almanack for 1833. By Joseph Cramer.
Philadelphia: Griggs & Dickinson. 18 ll. MWA. 11849

UNCLE Sam's Almanack for 1833. Philadelphia:
Griggs & Dickinson, for Denny & Walker. 18 ll. NjR.
11850
UNCLE Sam's Almanack for 1833. By Joseph Cramer.
Philadelphia: Griggs & Dickinson, for Denny & Walker.
18 ll. InU. 11851

UNCLE Sam's Large Almanack for 1833. Philadelphia:
Denny & Walker. 18 ll. MWA; N; NNU-H; CtY;
DeWint; InU; WHi; PHi; PP; PYHi. 11852

The UNITED States Baptist Annual Register and Almanac for 1833. By I. M. Allen. Philadelphia: T. W.
Ustick. 120 ll. InU; MB; ViW (114 ll.) 11853

The WESTERN Farmer's Almanac for 1833. By Rev.
John Taylor. Pittsburgh: H. Holdship & Son; D. and
M. Maclean, printers. 18 ll. DLC; MoSHi; WHi;
Wv-Ar; WvU. 11854

-- Issue with added "Magazine." 36 ll. MWA; KyHi
(ntp); OClWHi; PHi (35 ll.); PPi; PPiHi; PPiU (25
ll.) 11855

AGRICULTURAL Almanac for 1834. Lancaster: John
Bear. 18 ll. MWA; InU; PDoBHi; PHi. 11856

ALMANAC for 1834. By John Ward. Philadelphia:
M'Carty & Davis. 18 ll. DLC. 11857

The AMERICAN Comic Almanac for 1834. Philadelphia:
Grigg & Elliot; Boston: Charles Ellms 24 ll.

FSaHi. 11858

AMERICANISCHER Stadt und Land Calender auf 1834.
Philadelphia: Conrad Zentler. 15 ll. MWA; DLC; N;
DeWint; NjP; ViU; PHi; PPG; PPeSchw. 11859

The ANTI-MASONIC Almanack for 1834. Pittsburgh:
S. J. Sylvester; A. Jaynes, printer. 12 ll. PPiHi.
11860

BENNETT & Walton's Almanack for 1834. By Joseph
Cramer. Philadelphia: Thomas L. Bonsal. 18 ll.
MWA (15 ll.); InU; MiU-C; PHi; WHi; NjR; Drake
(17 ll.) 11861

The CHRISTIAN Almanac for Pennsylvania and Ohio for
1834. Pittsburgh: American Tract Society; Robert
Patterson. 24 ll. PPi. 11862

The CHRISTIAN Almanac for Pennsylvania, Delaware,
and West New-Jersey for 1834. Philadelphia: Pennsylvania branch of the American Tract Society. 24 ll.
MWA; InU; OMC; PP. 11863

CITIZENS' Almanack for 1834. Philadelphia: Griggs &
Dickinson. 18 ll. MWA; N; PHi. 11864

CITIZENS' Almanack for 1834. Philadelphia: Griggs &
Dickinson for Grigg & Elliott. 18 ll. MWA. 11865

The CITIZEN'S and Farmer's Annual Magazine, or New
Philadelphia Almanac for 1834. By Charles F. Egelmann. Philadelphia: [np] 16 ll. GU. 11866

The CITIZENS' and Farmers' Annual Magazine, or New
Philadelphia Almanac for 1834. By Charles Frederick
Egelmann. Philadelphia: J. G. Ritter; Baltimore: J.
T. Hanzsche. 16 ll. CLU; MdBE; PYHi. 11867

COLUMBIAN Almanac for 1834. Philadelphia: Jos.
M'Dowel [sic]. 18 ll. DLC; NNU-H; PPL (16 ll.,
ntp) 11868

CRAMER'S Magazine Almanac for 1834. By Sanford C.

Pennsylvania - 1834

Hill. Pittsburgh: M. P. O'Hern. 30 ll. MWA; PPi; PPiU; NjR. 11869

CRAMER'S Pittsburgh Almanack for 1834. By Sanford C. Hill. Pittsburgh: M. P. O'Hern. 18 ll. CLU; OClWHi (17 ll.); PPiU. 11870

DESILVER'S United States Register and Almanac [for 1834]. By Seth Smith. Philadelphia: Robert Desilver [etc.]. 28 ll. MWA; DLC; N; NN; NHi; NNU-H; CLU; CtY; InU; MB; WHi; P; PHi; PPL; Drake. 11871

The FARMERS' Almanac for 1834. By John Ward. Philadelphia: M'Carty & Davis. 18 ll. MWA; InU (ntp); NjR; PHi; PU; [Drake (Ward's manuscript for this almanac)] 11872

The FARMERS and Mechanics Almanack for 1834. By Charles Frederick Egelmann. Philadelphia: George W. Mentz & Son. 18 ll. MWA; N; NN; CLU; CtY; InU; KHi; NBuG; WHi; PDoBHi (17 ll.); PHi; PLF; PPL; Drake. 11873

The FRANKLIN Almanac for 1834. By John Armstrong. Pittsburgh: Johnston and Stockton. 18 ll. MWA; CLU; InU; OClWHi; OHi (17 ll.); PPiU; Wv-Ar. 11874

-- Issue with added "Magazine." 30 ll. MWA; OClWHi; PHi (29 ll.); Wv-Ar (28 ll.) 11875

The FRANKLIN Almanac for 1834. By John Ward. Philadelphia: M'Carty & Davis. 18 ll. MWA; CtY; DeWint; NjR; PHi; [Drake (has Ward's manuscript for this almanac)] 11876

FRIENDS' Almanac for 1834. By Joseph Foulke. Philadelphia: Evan Lewis; John Richards, printer. 24 ll. MWA; N; InU; PHC. 11877

GIRARD Almanack for 1834. Philadelphia: Thomas L. Bonsal. 18 ll. MWA; Nj (impf); PHi. 11878

The HEALTH and Temperance Almanac for 1834. Phila-

delphia: Edward C. Mielke; J. Johnson, printer. 40
ll. MWA; N; InU; MB; MH; MnU; OClWHi; OMC
(39 ll.)   11879

JOHNSON'S Almanac for 1834. Philadelphia: Willard
Johnson. 14 ll. PHi; NjR.   11880

JOHNSON'S Pocket Almanac for 1834. Philadelphia:
Willard Johnson. 12 ll. MWA; PHi; PP.   11881

MAROT & Walter's Almanac for 1834. Philadelphia:
Marot & Walter. [Phillips]   11882

MERCHANT'S Pocket Almanac for 1834. Philadelphia:
Uriah Hunt. 24 ll. MWA; InU; NjR; PHi; PP.   11883

Der NEUE, Americanische Landwirthschafts-Calender
auf 1834. Von Carl Friedrich Egelmann. Reading:
Johann Ritter u. Comp. 16 ll. MWA; InU; NjP; P;
PHi; PPG; PPL; PPeSchw; PR; PRHi; PYHi.   11884

NEUER Calender für die Bauern und Handwerker auf
1834. Von Carl Egelmann. Philadelphia: Georg W.
Mentz und Sohn. 18 ll. MWA; NN (impf); CLU; CtY;
InU; NjP; NjR; PDoBHi; PHi; PPCS (17 ll.); PPT;
PPeSchw; PYHi; Drake.   11885

NEUER Gemeinnütziger Pennsylvanischer Calender auf
1834. Lancaster: Johann Baer. 18 ll. MWA; NN;
CtY; InU; NjP; NjR; OC; PLF; PLHi; PYHi.   11886

PENNSYLVANIA Almanac for 1834. Philadelphia:
M'Carty & Davis. 18 ll. MWA (2 ll.); CLU; CtY;
PHi; PP; [Drake (has John Ward's manuscript for this
almanac)]   11887

The PEOPLE'S Almanac for 1834. Philadelphia: Grigg
& Elliot. 24 ll. MWA; ICHi; MB; MBAt (22 ll.) OMC.
  11888
PHILADELPHIA Almanack for 1834. By Joseph Cramer.
Philadelphia: Uriah Hunt. 18 ll. MWA; CtY; InU;
NjGlaN; PDoBHi; PHi.   11889

Philadelphia - 1834

POOR Wills Almanac for 1834. By William Collom.
Philadelphia: Joseph M'Dowell. 18 ll. MWA; DLC;
CtY; InU; MB; MH; NjR (16 ll.); WHi; PHi; PPL.
11890

The TEMPERANCE Almanac for 1834. Philadelphia:
I. S. Lloyd; Albany: N. Y. State Temperance Society;
Hoffman & White, printers. 24 ll. MWA; InU; PHi.
11891

TEMPERANCE Almanack for 1834. By Joseph Cramer.
Philadelphia: Uriah Hunt. 18 ll. MWA; CtY; NjR;
Drake.
11892

UNCLE Sam's Almanack for 1834. Philadelphia:
Griggs & Dickinson for Denny & Walker. 18 ll. MWA
(two varieties); DLC; InU; MB; PHi; PPL. 11893

UNCLE Sam's Large Almanack for 1834. Philadelphia:
Denny & Walker. 18 ll. MWA; InU; NjR; WHi; PHi;
PP; PPL; PPeSchw; PYHi.
11894

The WESTERN Farmer's Almanac for 1834. By Rev.
John Taylor. Pittsburgh: H. Holdship & Son; D. and
M. Maclean, printers. 18 ll. MWA (15 ll.); OClWHi;
OHi (17 ll.)
11895

-- Issue with added "Magazine." 36 ll. PPi; PPiHi.
11896

AGRICULTURAL Almanac for 1835. Lancaster: John
Bear. 18 ll. MWA (impf); NHi (17 ll.); NBuG; PHi
(16 ll.); PLF.
11897

The AMERICAN Comic Almanac for 1835. Philadelphia:
Grigg & Elliot; Boston: Charles Ellms. 24 ll. NPV.
11898

AMERICANISCHER Stadt und Land Calender auf 1835.
Philadelphia: Conrad Zentler. 15 ll. MWA; DLC; N;
CLU; CtY; DeWint; InU; NjP; PDoBHi; PHi; PPCS;
PPG; PPeSchw; PPL (18 ll.); PYHi.
11899

BAILEY'S Franklin Almanac for 1835. Philadelphia:
Lydia R. Bailey. 18 ll. MWA; PHi.
11900

BAILEY'S Washington Almanac for 1835. Philadelphia:

Pennsylvania - 1835

Lydia R. Bailey. 18 ll. MWA; PHi.   11901

BENNETT & Walton's Almanac for 1835. Philadelphia: Thomas L. Bonsal. 18 ll. PHi; PP; PPL (17 ll.)
11902
BENNETT & Walton's Almanac for 1835. By Joseph Cramer. Philadelphia: Thomas L. Bonsal. 18 ll. MWA.   11903

CHRISTIAN Almanac for Pennsylvania and Delaware for 1835. Philadelphia: Pennsylvania branch of the American Tract Society. [Phillips]   11904

CITIZENS' Almanack for 1835. Philadelphia: Griggs & Co. 18 ll. MWA; PHi.   11905

COLUMBIAN Almanac for 1835. Philadelphia: Jos. M'Dowell. 18 ll. MWA; DLC; MBC; MBAt (ntp); PHi.
11906
COLUMBIAN Almanac for 1835. Philadelphia: Jos. McDowell. 18 ll. NjR.   11907

DESILVER'S United States Register and Almanac for 1835. By Seth Smith. Philadelphia: Robert Desilver. 32 ll. MWA; DLC (30 ll.); NN; CtY; InU; P; PHi; PPL; PPAmP.   11908

-- Issue with 34 ll. PPL.   11909

Der DEUTSCHE Mässigkeits-Calender auf 1835. Philadelphia: M'Carty und Davis. 18 ll. MWA (17 ll.); CLU; DeWint.   11910

The FARMERS' Almanac for 1835. By John Ward. Philadelphia: M'Carty & Davis. 18 ll. MWA; NjR.
11911
The FARMERS and Mechanics Almanack for 1835. By Charles Frederick Egelmann. Easton: G. W. Mentz & Son, for Henry Hamman. 18 ll. PPL.   11912

The FARMERS and Mechanics Almanack for 1835. By Charles Frederick Egelmann. Philadelphia: George W. Mentz & Son. 18 ll. MWA; DLC; N; NN (impf);

NNU-H; CtY; MH; InU; MiU-C; PHi (17 ll.); PPL.
11913

The FARMERS and Mechanics Almanack for 1835.
Philadelphia: Isaac M. Moss. [Phillips] 11914

The FARMERS and Mechanics Almanack for 1835.
Pittsburgh: R. Patterson. 18 ll. MWA; InU; OClWHi.
11915

The FARMER'S Calendar for 1835. By Charles F.
Egelmann. Philadelphia: Grigg & Elliot. 16 ll. NjR;
PHi. 11916

The FARMER'S Calendar for 1835. By Charles F.
Egelmann. Philadelphia: George W. Mentz & Son. 16
ll. MWA; PYHi. 11917

The FRANKLIN Almanac for 1835. By John Armstrong. Pittsburgh: Johnston & Stockton. 18 ll. PPi;
PPiU (17 ll.); WvU (17 ll.); Drake. 11918

-- Issue with added "Magazine." 30 ll. MWA; CLU;
InU; OCHP; OClWHi; OHi; OMC; PPiHi (27 ll.) 11919

The FRANKLIN Almanac for 1835. By John Ward.
Philadelphia: M'Carty & Davis. 18 ll. MWA; InU (17
ll.); KHi; PHi (15 ll.) 11920

FRIENDS' Almanac for 1835. By Joseph Foulke.
Philadelphia: Elijah Weaver; John Richards, printer.
24 ll. MWA; N; ICN; InU; NjR; OClWHi; PDoBHi;
PHC. 11921

GIRARD Almanac for 1835. Philadelphia: Thomas L.
Bonsal. 18 ll. MWA; DLC; InU; NjR; PPT. 11922

HAT Almanac for 1835. Philadelphia: A. Walde.
Broadside. DLC; CtY. 11923

JACKSON Almanack [for] 1835. Philadelphia: F.
Turner; Marsh & Harrison, printers. 18 ll. NjR.
11924
JOHNSON'S Almanac for 1835. Philadelphia: Willard
Johnson. 14 ll. PHi (impf) 11925

Pennsylvania - 1835

LOOMIS'S Magazine Almanac for 1835. By Sanford C. Hill. Pittsburgh: Luke Loomis; A. Jaynes, printer. 36 ll. MWA (impf); OC; PHi; PPi; PPiHi; PPiU.
11926

LOOMIS'S Pittsburgh Almanac for 1835. By Sanford C. Hill. Pittsburgh: Luke Loomis; A. Jaynes, printer. 18 ll. MWA; CLU; ICHi.
11927

MERCHANT'S Pocket Remembrancer for 1835. Philadelphia: Uriah Hunt. 24 ll. MWA; NjR; PHi; PP.
11928

Der NEUE, Americanische Landwirthschafts-Calender auf 1835. Von Carl Friedrich Egelmann. Reading: Johann Ritter u. Comp. 16 ll. MWA; InU (impf); P; PDoBHi; PHi; PPL; PPeSchw; PR; PRHi.
11929

NEUER Calender für Bauern und Handwerker auf 1835. Von Carl F. Egelmann. Philadelphia: Georg W. Mentz und Sohn. 18 ll. MWA (17 ll.); CtY; InU (17 ll.); CLU; NjR; NjP; PDoBHi; PHi; PLF; PPiHi; PPL; PYHi; PPCS (17 ll.); PPeSchw.
11930

NEUER Gemeinnütziger Pennsylvanischer Calender auf 1835. Lancaster: Johann Baer. 18 ll. MWA; N; NN (16 ll., ntp); CtY; MH; OC; PPG; PHi; PLF; PLHi; PPL (16 ll.); P; PDoBHi (16 ll.); PPeSchw; Drake.
11931

PENNSYLVANIA and New-Jersey Temperance Almanac for 1835. Philadelphia: Temperance Depository. 18 ll. MWA; FSaHi; MH.
11932

PHILADELPHIA Almanack for 1835. Philadelphia: Uriah Hunt. 18 ll. MWA; CLU; InU.
11933

PHILADELPHIA Comic Almanac for 1835. Philadelphia: Thomas L. Bonsal. 18 ll. NN; NjR.
11934

The PHILADELPHIA Comic Almanac for 1835. Philadelphia: G. Strong. 18 ll. MWA (two varieties); DLC; OMC; PHi; PPL.
11935

POOR Wills Almanac for 1835. By William Collom.

Philadelphia: Joseph M'Dowell. 18 ll. MWA; DLC; CtY; InU; MB; NjGlaN; NjR; OClWHi; PDoBHi; PPL; PU; PHi.   11936

TEMPERANCE Almanack for 1835. Philadelphia: Uriah Hunt. 18 ll. MWA; N; OClWHi.   11937

UNCLE Sam's Almanack for 1835. By Joseph Cramer. Philadelphia: Denny & Walker. 18 ll. MWA.   11938

UNCLE Sam's Large Almanac for 1835. Philadelphia: Denny & Walker. 18 ll. MWA; InU; MBAt; ViU; PHi; PP; PYHi; NjR (ntp)   11939

The WESTERN Farmer's Almanac for 1835. By Rev. John Taylor. Pittsburgh: George W. Holdship. 36 ll. MWA.   11940

The WESTERN Farmer's Almanac for 1835. By Rev. John Taylor. Pittsburgh: H. Holdship & Son; D. and M. Maclean, printers. 36 ll. OClWHi; PPiHi.   11941

AGRICULTURAL Almanac for 1836. Lancaster: John Bear. 18 ll. CtY; NBuG; PHi.   11942

AMERICAN Comic Almanack for 1836. Philadelphia: Grigg & Elliot; Boston: Chas. Ellms. 24 ll. MWiW.
11943

AMERICANISCHER Stadt und Land Calender auf 1836. Philadelphia: Conrad Zentler. 15 ll. MWA; DLC; N; NHi; CLU; CtY; InU; NjP; NjR; OC (14 ll.); PHi; PPG; PDoBHi; PPeSchw.   11944

The CHRISTIAN Almanac, for Pennsylvania and the Middle States for 1836. [Philadelphia:] Philadelphia Tract Society. 24 ll. NjR.   11945

The CHRISTIAN Almanac for Pennsylvania and the Middle States for 1836. Philadelphia: Philadelphia Tract Society. 24 ll. MWA; PHi.   11946

The COLUMBIAN Almanac for 1836. Philadelphia: Jos. McDowell. 18 ll. MWA; NjR; PDoBHi.   11947

DESILVER'S United States Register and Almanac [for 1836]. By Seth Smith. Philadelphia: Robert Desilver; [etc]. 32 ll. InU; PPL; NjR. 11948

DEUTSCHER Mässigkeits-Calender auf 1836. Von Carl F. Egelmann. Philadelphia: Georg W. Mentz und Sohn. 18 ll. MWA; DeWint; InU (17 ll.); PHi (17 ll.); PLF (16 ll.); PPL; PYHi. 11949

The ENTERTAINING Almanac for 1836. Philadelphia: M. Fithian. 16 ll. PDoBHi. 11950

The FARMERS' Almanac for 1836. By John Ward. Philadelphia: M'Carty & Davis. 18 ll. MWA (also has Ward's manuscript for this almanac), N; InU; CLU; NjR; PHi; PPL. 11951

The FARMERS and Mechanics Almanack for 1836. By Charles Frederick Egelmann. Philadelphia: George W. Mentz & Son. 18 ll. MWA; CtY; InU; NBLiHi (impf); PPL; PPeSchw; ViU. 11952

The FARMERS and Mechanics Almanack for 1836. By Charles Frederick Egelmann. Pittsburgh: R. Patterson. 18 ll. MWA; PPiU; TxDaHi (17 ll.) 11953

The FARMER'S Calendar for 1836. By Charles F. Egelmann. Philadelphia: Grigg & Elliott. 16 ll. MWA; KHi. 11954

The FRANKLIN Almanac for 1836. By John Armstrong. Pittsburgh: Johnston & Stockton. 18 ll. OHi (17 ll.) 11955

-- Issue with added "Magazine." 30 ll. MWA; InU; OC; PHi. 11956

The FRANKLIN Almanac for 1836. By William Collom. Philadelphia: Thomas L. Bonsal. 16 ll. MWA; DLC; InU; PDoBHi; NjR (18 ll.) 11957

The FRANKLIN Almanac for 1836. By John Ward. Philadelphia: M'Carty & Davis. 18 ll. MWA (also has

Ward's manuscript for this almanac); NjR; PHi. 11958

FRIENDS' Almanac for 1836. By Joseph Foulke. Philadelphia: Elijah Weaver; John Richards, printer. 24 ll. MWA; N; ICN; InU; OClWHi; PHC; PPiU; Drake.
11959

The GIRARD Almanac for 1836. By W. Collom. Philadelphia: Thomas L. Bonsal. 18 ll. DLC; PHi; PPL. 11960

JOHNSON'S Almanac for 1836. Philadelphia: Willard Johnson. 14 ll. MWA (impf); PDoBHi (13 ll.); PHi (impf) 11961

Der LANDWIRTHSCHAFTLICHER Calender auf 1836. Von Benjamin Hofinger. Lancaster: [np] 16 ll. OClWHi. 11962

LOOMIS'S Magazine Almanac for 1836. By Sanford C. Hill. Pittsburgh: Luke Loomis; A. Jaynes, printer. 36 ll. MWA; InU (33 ll., ntp); OClWHi; PPiHi; PPiU; WvU. 11963

LOOMIS'S Pittsburgh Almanac for 1836. By Sanford C. Hill. Pittsburgh: Luke Loomis; A. Jaynes, printer. 18 ll. OClWHi; PPi; PPiU. 11964

MERCHANT'S Pocket Remembrancer for 1836. Philadelphia: Uriah Hunt. 18 ll. MWA; InU; NBuG; NjR; PHi; PP. 11965

Der NEUE, Americanische Landwirthschafts-Calender auf 1836. Von Carl Friedrich Egelmann. Reading: Johann Ritter u. Comp. 16 ll. MWA; N; InU; NjP; P; PDoBHi; PHi; PPL; PR; PRHi. 11966

NEUER Calender für Bauern und Handwerker auf 1836. Von Carl F. Egelmann. Philadelphia: Georg W. Mentz und Sohn. 18 ll. MWA; N; NN; CLU; InU; NjP; NjR; P; PHi; PPCS (15 ll.); PPL; PDoBHi; PPeSchw; PYHi. 11967

NEUER Calender für Nord-Amerika auf 1836. Von

Carl F. Egelmann. Philadelphia: Georg W. Mentz und Sohn. 18 ll. MWA; N; CtY; InU; P; PDoBHi; PHi; PPL; PPeSchw. 11968

NEUER Gemeinnütziger Pennsylvanischer Calender auf 1836. Lancaster: Johann Baer. 18 ll. MWA; CtY; CLU; InU (15 ll., ntp); OClWHi; P; PDoBHi; PLF; PLHi; PHi; PPL; PPeSchw. 11969

PENNSYLVANIA Almanac for 1836. By John Ward. Philadelphia: M'Carty & Davis. 18 ll. MWA (also has Ward's manuscript for this almanac); CLU; InU; WHi. 11970

PENNSYLVANIA and New Jersey Almanac for 1836. By William Collom. Philadelphia: T. L. Bonsal; M. Fithian, printer. 18 ll. MWA; DLC; InU; Drake (14 ll.) 11971

The PEOPLE'S Almanac of Useful and Entertaining Knowledge for 1836. Philadelphia: Grigg & Elliot; Boston: Charles Ellms. 24 ll. MWA; MB. 11972

PETER Parley's Almanac for old and young for 1836. Philadelphia: Desilver, Thomas, & Company; [etc]. 48 ll. MWA; DLC; N; InU; NjP; TxDaHi; NjR. 11973

The PHILADELPHIA Almanac for 1836. By William Collom. Philadelphia: Uriah Hunt. 18 ll. MWA; CtY; InU; NjGlaN; PHi (impf); PP; PU; NjR. 11974

POOR Wills Almanac for 1836. By William Collom. Philadelphia: Joseph M'Dowell. 18 ll. MWA; N; CtY; InU; CLU; NjR; PHi; Drake. 11975

TEMPERANCE Almanac for 1836. Philadelphia: Sold at the Depository; I. Ashmead and Co., printers. 12 ll. PHi; PPL. 11976

TEMPERANCE Almanac for 1836. Philadelphia: Sold at the Depository, 1-1/2 South Fifth Street; I. Ashmead and Co., printers. 12 ll. MWA; N; InU; NjR. 11977

The TEMPERANCE Almanac for 1836. Philadelphia:

1140　　　　　Pennsylvania - 1836

Sold at the Depository; William Brown, printer. 13 ll.
MWA; PPL (12 ll.); PPeSchw.　　　　　　　　11978

TEMPERANCE Almanac for 1836. Philadelphia: Pennsylvania State Temperance Society. 12 ll. MB.　11979

The TEMPERANCE Almanack for 1836. By William Collom.　Philadelphia: Uriah Hunt. 18 ll. CtY; OClWHi.　　　　　　　　　　　　　　　　　　11980

TOWN and Country Almanack of Useful and Entertaining Knowledge for 1836. Philadelphia: John Royer. 16 ll.　MB; PHi; PPL (9 ll.)　　　　　　　　　11981

UNCLE Sam's Comic Almanac for 1836. Philadelphia: Turner & Fisher. 16 ll. MWA.　　　　　　　　11982

UNCLE Sam's Comic Almanac for 1836. Philadelphia: Turner & Fisher; New-York: Elton. 16 ll. PPL. 11983

UNCLE Sam's Large Almanac for 1836. Philadelphia: Denny & Walker. 18 ll.　MWA; N; FSaHi; InU; NNU-H; PDoBHi (16 ll.); PHi; PPL; PYHi; NjR (17 ll.)　　　　　　　　　　　　　　　　　　　　11984

The UNITED States Almanack for 1836. By Charles Frederick Egelmann.　Philadelphia: George W. Mentz & Son.　18 ll.　MWA; ICHi; PHi; ViU; ViW (13 ll.); NjR.　　　　　　　　　　　　　　　　　　　　11985

The UNITED States Register and Almanac [for 1836]. By Seth Smith.　Philadelphia: Robert Desilver. 30 ll. MWA; NjR (28 ll.); PHi.　　　　　　　　　　　11986

The WESTERN Comic Almanac for 1836. Pittsburgh: Johnston & Stockton. Wv-Ar (17 ll.)　　　　　　11987

The WESTERN Farmer's Almanac for 1836. By Rev. John Taylor.　Pittsburgh: George W. Holdship. 18 ll. CLU; PPi.　　　　　　　　　　　　　　　　　　11988

-- Issue with added "Magazine." 36 ll. PPiHi.　11989

Pennsylvania - 1837

AGRICULTURAL Almanac for 1837. Lancaster: John Bear. 18 ll. MWA; N; InU; NNU-H; NBuG; PHi; PLHi; PYHi; NjR; Drake (17 ll.) 11990

The AMERICAN Comic Almanac for 1837. Philadelphia: Grigg & Elliot; Boston: Charles Ellms. 18 ll. NHi. 11991

AMERICANISCHER Stadt und Land Calender auf 1837. Philadelphia: Conrad Zentler. 15 ll. MWA; DLC; N; NN; CLU; CtY; InU; NjP; NjR; RPB; PDoBHi; PHi; PPCS (13 ll.); PPeSchw; PPL; Drake. 11992

The CHRISTIAN Almanac, for Pennsylvania and the Middle States for 1837. [Philadelphia:] Philadelphia Tract Society. 24 ll. MWA; NjR; PHi. 11993

COLUMBIAN Almanac for 1837. Philadelphia: Jos. McDowell. 18 ll. MWA; DLC; N; InU; NjR; MBC; PHi; PPL. 11994

DESILVER'S United States Register and Almanac for 1837. By Seth Smith. Philadelphia: Robert Desilver. 24 ll. DLC; NN; InU; PPAmP. 11995

-- Issue with 32 ll. MWA; PHi (31 ll.); PPL (25 ll.) 11996

Der DEUTSCHE Mässigkeits-Calender auf 1837. Von Carl F. Egelmann. Philadelphia: Georg W. Mentz und Sohn. 18 ll. MWA; CLU; CtY; DeWint. 11997

The FARMERS' Almanac for 1837. By John Ward. Philadelphia: M'Carty & Davis. 18 ll. MWA; InU; PHi. 11998

The FARMERS and Mechanics Almanack for 1837. By Charles Frederick Egelmann. Philadelphia: George W. Mentz & Son. 18 ll. MWA; NN; IHi; InU; OClWHi; PHi (17 ll.); PPL; PPiU; PPeSchw; ViU. 11999

FARMER'S Calendar for 1837. Philadelphia: Grigg, Elliot & Co. 16 ll. KyBgW. 12000

Pennsylvania - 1837

The **FARMER'S** Calendar for 1837. By Charles F. Egelmann. Philadelphia: U. Hunt. 16 ll. MWA. 12001

The **FRANKLIN** Almanac for 1837. By John Armstrong. Pittsburgh: Johnston and Stockton. 18 ll. MWA; CLU; InU; PPiHi (15 ll.) 12002

-- Issue with added "Magazine." 30 ll. MWA; OC; PHi. 12003

The **FRANKLIN** Almanac for 1837. By William Collom. Philadelphia: Thomas L. Bonsal. 18 ll. MWA; DLC; NHi; MB; NjR (16 ll.); PHi. 12004

-- '[Publis]hed by Thomas L. Bonsal" [i.e., first six letters of "Published" are lacking] 18 ll. NjR. 12005

The **FRANKLIN** Almanac for 1837. By John Ward. Philadelphia: M'Carty & Davis. 18 ll. MWA; InU; NBuG; MiU-C; PHi; PPL. 12006

FRIENDS' Almanac for 1837. By Joseph Foulke. Philadelphia: Elijah Weaver. 24 ll. MWA; ICN; OClWHi; PDoBHi. 12007

FRIENDS' Pocket Almanac for 1837. By Joseph Foulke. Philadelphia: T. E. Chapman. 32 ll. MWA; InU. 12008

GEST'S Anti-Masonic Almanac for 1837. By Joseph E. Howard. Philadelphia: William K. Boden. 24 ll. MWA; MB. 12009

The **GIRARD** Almanac for 1837. Philadelphia: Thomas L. Bonsal. 18 ll. MWA (two varieties); DLC; DeU (12 ll.); NjR. 12010

Der **HOCH-DEUTSCHE** Germantaun Calender auf 1837. Von Carl F. Egelmann. Philadelphia: Wm. W. Walker. 18 ll. MWA; InU; PHi; PPeSchw; Drake. 12011

JOHNSON'S Almanac for 1837. Philadelphia: Willard Johnson. 14 ll. NN. 12012

JOHNSON'S Pocket Almanac for 1837. Philadelphia: Printed for the Publisher. 24 ll. MWA. 12013

LADIES' Almanac and Calculator for 1837. Philadelphia: William Marshall & Co. 26 ll. PCDHi. 12014

LANDWIRTHSCHAFTLICHER Calender auf 1837. Lancaster: Benjamin Hofinger. 16 ll. MWA. 12015

LOOMIS' Pittsburgh Almanac for 1837. By Sanford C. Hill. Pittsburgh: Luke Loomis, printer & bookseller. 18 ll. PPiHi. 12016

LOOMIS' Pittsburgh Almanac for 1837. By Sanford C. Hill. Pittsburgh: Luke Loomis; A. Jaynes, printer. 18 ll. OClWHi; PPi; PPiHi; PPiU (17 ll.) 12017

LOOMIS'S Magazine Almanac for 1837. By Sanford C. Hill. Pittsburgh: Luke Loomis; A. Jaynes, printer. 30 ll. MWA; OC; OClWHi; PPiU (28 ll.) 12018

Der NEUE Allentauner Calender auf 1837. Allentaun: A. und W. Blumer. 16 ll. CLU; NjR; PDoBHi; PPeSchw. 12019

Der NEUE, Americanische Landwirthschafts-Calender auf 1837. Von Carl Friedrich Egelmann. Reading: Johann Ritter u. Comp. 16 ll. MWA; DLC (impf); N; InU; P; PDoBHi; PHi; PPG; PR; PRHi. 12020

NEUER Calender für Bauern und Handwerker auf 1837. Von Carl F. Egelmann. Philadelphia: Georg W. Mentz und Sohn. 18 ll. MWA (17 ll.); NjP; PHi. 12021

NEUER Calender für Nord-Amerika auf 1837. Von Carl F. Egelmann. Philadelphia: Georg W. Mentz und Sohn. 18 ll. MWA; NN (17 ll.); P; PHi; PPCS (16 ll.); PPL (17 ll.); PPeSchw. 12022

NEUER Gemeinnütziger Pennsylvanischer Calender auf 1837. Lancaster: Johann Baer. 18 ll. MWA; NN; NHi (16 ll.); CtY; DeWint; InU; PDoBHi; PHi; PLF; PLHi; PPG; PYHi. 12023

PENNSYLVANIA Almanac for 1837. Philadelphia:
M'Carty & Davis. 18 ll. MWA (2 ll.); NjR (15 ll.);
PHi. 12024

PENNSYLVANIA Temperance Almanac for 1837. Philadelphia: State Temperance Society. 18 ll. MB. 12025

PENNSYLVANISCHER Mässigkeits-Calender auf 1837.
Von Carl F. Egelmann. Philadelphia: G. W. Mentz
und Sohn. 18 ll. InU; PDoBHi. 12026

PEOPLE'S Almanac for 1837. Philadelphia: Grigg &
Elliott; Boston: Charles Ellms. 24 ll. N. 12027

The PHILADELPHIA Almanac for 1837. By William
Collom. Philadelphia: Uriah Hunt. 18 ll. MWA; InU;
PHi; PPL. 12028

POOR Wills Almanac for 1837. By William Collom.
Philadelphia: Joseph M'Dowell. 18 ll. MWA; DLC;
NjR; OClWHi; MB; MH; CLU; CtY; OCl; InU; WHi;
PHi; PP; PHC; PPL; PPiHi; Drake. 12029

The TEMPERANCE Almanac for 1837. Philadelphia:
State Temperance Society; I. Ashmead & Co., printers.
18 ll. MWA (17 ll.); MB; NjR. 12030

TOWN and Country Almanack for 1837. By C. F.
Egelmann. Philadelphia: John Royer. 12 ll. MWA;
InU. 12031

UNCLE Sam's Large Almanac for 1837. Philadelphia:
Wm. W. Walker. 18 ll. MWA; CtY; InU; PHi; PPL;
WHi; NjR (17 ll.) 12032

The UNITED States Almanack for 1837. By Charles
Frederick Egelmann. Philadelphia: George W. Mentz
& Son. 18 ll. MWA; DLC; CLU; ICHi; InU; MH; OC
(impf); PHi (impf); PLF. 12033

The WESTERN Farmer's Almanac for 1837. By Rev.
John Taylor. Pittsburgh: George W. Holdship. 18 ll.
MWA (two varieties); OClWHi. 12034

-- Issue with added "Magazine." 30 ll. OHi.   12035

AGRICULTURAL Almanac for 1838. Lancaster: John Bear. 18 ll. MWA; InU; NBuG; NjR; P; PHi; PLHi; PYHi.   12036

The AMERICAN Comic Almanac for 1838. Philadelphia: Grigg & Elliott. 18 ll. MWA; CtY.   12037

AMERICANISCHER Stadt und Land Calender auf 1838. Philadelphia: Conrad Zentler. 15 ll. MWA; DLC; N; PPL; DeWint; InU; CtY; NjP; NjR; CLU; PPG; PHi; PYHi; PDoBHi; Drake.   12038

BROTHER Jonathan's Almanac for 1838. Philadelphia: Thomas L. Bonsal. 18 ll. MWA; DLC; NjR; PHi.   12039

CALENDER für den Stadt-und Landmann auf 1838. Allentaun: U. und W. Blumer. 20 ll. P.   12040

The CHRISTIAN Almanac for Pennsylvania and Delaware for 1838. Philadelphia: Pennsylvania branch of the American Tract Society. [MWA card catalog. Missing from shelf.]   12041

The CHRISTIAN Almanac for Pennsylvania and the Middle States for 1838. Philadelphia: Philadelphia Tract Society. 24 ll. MWA; InU; OMC.   12042

CITIZENS' Almanack for 1838. Philadelphia: Griggs & Co., for Grigg & Elliot. 18 ll. MWA; PPL (impf)   12043

CITIZENS and Farmers' Almanack for 1838. Philadelphia: Griggs & Co. 18 ll. MWA (impf)   12044

The COLUMBIAN Almanac for 1838. Philadelphia: Jos. McDowell. 18 ll. MWA; KHi (16 ll.); NjR (17 ll.); PDoBHi; PPL; PPT; WHi.   12045

The FARMERS' Almanac for 1838. By John Ward. Philadelphia: M'Carty & Davis. 18 ll. MWA; DLC; PHi; PPL; [NN has Ward's manuscript for this almanac)]   12046

Pennsylvania - 1838

The **FARMERS** and Mechanics Almanack for 1838. By Charles Frederick Egelmann. Philadelphia: George W. Mentz & Son. 18 ll. MWA; N; InU; OHi (17 ll.); PDoBHi; PHi (16 ll.)   12047

-- On wrapper: Pittsburgh: Patterson, Ingraham & Co. 18 ll. MWA.   12048

The **FARMER'S** Calendar for 1838. By Charles F. Egelmann. Philadelphia: Grigg & Elliot. 16 ll. MWA; PLF; ViU.   12049

The **FRANKLIN** Almanac for 1838. By John Armstrong. Pittsburgh: Johnston and Stockton. 18 ll. MWA; CLU; OMC (17 ll.)   12050

-- Issue with added "Magazine." 30 ll. MWA; OC.   12051

The **FRANKLIN** Almanac for 1838. By John Ward. Philadelphia: M'Carty & Davis. 18 ll. MWA; DLC; PHi; [NN (has Ward's manuscript for this almanac)]   12052

FRIENDS' Almanac for 1838. By Joseph Foulke. Philadelphia: Elijah Weaver. 24 ll. MWA; ICN; InU; OClWHi; PHC.   12053

FRIENDS' Pocket Almanac for 1838. By Joseph Foulke. Philadelphia: T. E. Chapman; John Richards, printer. 32 ll. NN.   12054

The **GIRARD** Almanac for 1838. Philadelphia: Thomas L. Bonsal. 18 ll. MWA; DLC; CtY; InU; NjR; PHi (15 ll.)   12055

Der **HOCH-DEUTSCHE** Germantaun Calender auf 1838. Von Carl F. Egelmann. Philadelphia: Wm. W. Walker. 18 ll. MWA; InU (17 ll.); NjR (17 ll.); PHi; PPL (14 ll.); PPCS.   12056

JOHNSON'S Almanac for 1838. Philadelphia: Published at No 141 Sourh [sic] st. and Sold Wholesale. 14 ll. MWA; DLC; PHi.   12057

LOOMIS' Magazine Almanac for 1838. By Sanford C. Hill. Pittsburgh: Luke Loomis; Anderson & Loomis, printers. 18 ll. NN; Drake.   12058

-- Issue with 30 ll. PPi; PPiHi; PPiU (22 ll., ntp)
                                                12059
LOOMIS' Pittsburgh Almanac for 1838. By Sanford C. Hill. Pittsburgh: Luke Loomis. 18 ll. MWA; InU; CLU; OC; OClWHi; OMC.   12060

The MORAL Almanac for 1838. By William Collom. Philadelphia: Tract Association of Friends; J. Rakestraw, printer. 18 ll. MWA; DLC; InRE; InU; MH; NjR; OClWHi; OHi; PDoBHi; PP; PU.   12061

The NATIONAL Comic Almanac for 1838. [np] Published by an Association of Gentlemen. [Although DLC lists this as a Philadelphia publication it is more probably a product of Boston.] 18 ll. MWA; DLC; Drake.
                                                12062
Der NEUE Allentauner Calender auf 1838. Allentaun: A. und W. Blumer. Advertised in the "Friedens-Bote," December 13, 1837.   12063

Der NEUE, Americanische Landwirthschafts-Calender auf 1838. Von Carl Friedrich Egelmann. Reading: Johann Ritter u. Comp. 16 ll. MWA; InU; NjP; P; PHi; PR; PRHi; PPL (15 ll.)   12064

NEUER Calender für Bauern und Handwerker auf 1838. Von Carl F. Egelmann. Philadelphia: Georg W. Mentz und Sohn. 18 ll. MWA; PHi; PPG; PYHi.   12065

NEUER Calender für Nord-Amerika auf 1838. Von Carl F. Egelmann. Philadelphia: Georg W. Mentz und Sohn. 18 ll. MWA; NjR; PDoBHi; PLF; PPCS; PYHi; Drake.   12066

NEUER Gemeinnütziger Pennsylvanischer Calender auf 1838. Lancaster: Johann Baer. 18 ll. MWA; CtY; InU; MH; P; PDoBHi; PHi; PLF; PLHi; PPL; PPeSchw.   12067

1148   Pennsylvania - 1838

The NORTH American Almanac for 1838. Philadelphia: Printed by the Publisher, and Sold Wholesale. 14 ll. Drake.   12068

PENNSYLVANIA Almanac for 1838. Philadelphia: M'Carty & Davis. 18 ll. PHi; PU.   12069

PENNSYLVANIA & New Jersey Almanac for 1838. Philadelphia: Thomas L. Bonsal. 18 ll. MWA; DLC; InU; NjT; PHi.   12070

PENNSYLVANIA Temperance Almanac for 1838. Philadelphia: Pennsylvania State Temperance Society. 18 ll. MWA; NHi; InU (16 ll.); PHi.   12071

Der PENNSYLVANISCH Anti-Freimaurer Calender für 1838. Von Carl Friederich Egelman. Lancaster: Samuel Wagner. 18 ll. PPL (17 ll.)   12072

The PEOPLE'S Almanac for 1838. Philadelphia: Grigg & Elliott. 24 ll. MWA; ICHi; NjR.   12073

The PHILADELPHIA Almanac for 1838. By William Collom. Philadelphia: Uriah Hunt. 18 ll. MWA; InU; MBC; ViW (16 ll.)   12074

POOR Wills Almanac for 1838. By William Collom. Philadelphia: Joseph M'Dowell. 18 ll. MWA; DLC; N; CLU; CtY; InU; MB; PHi; OClWHi; PCDHi (15 ll.); PP; Drake.   12075

The THOMSONIAN Almanac for 1838. By William Collom. Philadelphia: No. 295 Market Street. 20 ll. MWA; InU.   12076

TURNER'S Comick Almanack for 1838. Philadelphia: Turner & Fisher; New York: Turner & Fisher. 18 ll. MWA; DLC; NN; ICU; InU; MBAt; OClWHi; TMC.
    12077
UNCLE Sam's Almanack for 1838. Philadelphia: Griggs & Co., For J. R. Walker. 18 ll. PHi.   12078

UNCLE Sam's Almanack for 1838. By Joseph Cramer.

Philadelphia: Griggs & Co. 18 ll. MWA; IaDaM (ntp)
12079

UNCLE Sam's Large Almanac for 1838. Philadelphia: Wm. W. Walker. 18 ll. MWA; N; NNU-H; InU (16 ll.); MnU (17 ll.); NjR (12 ll.); PHi.
12080

The UNITED States Almanack for 1838. By Charles Frederick Egelmann. Philadelphia: George W. Mentz & Son. 18 ll. MWA; DLC; CLU; CtY; InU (17 ll.); NjR; PDoBHi; PHi.
12081

AGRICULTURAL Almanac for 1839. Lancaster: John Bear. 18 ll. MWA; InU; PHi.
12082

AMERICANISCHER Stadt und Land Calender auf 1839. Philadelphia: Conrad Zentler. 15 ll. MWA; DLC; N; NN; CLU; CtY; DeWint; InU; NjP; NjR; RPB; PDoBHi; PHi; PPCS (14 ll.); PPL (15 ll.); PPeSchw; Drake.
12083

BROTHER Jonathan's Almanac for 1839. Philadelphia: Thomas L. Bonsal. 18 ll. MWA; PHi; PPL.
12084

The CHRISTIAN Almanac for Pennsylvania and Delaware for 1839. Philadelphia: Pennsylvania branch of the American Tract Society. MWA (missing from shelf)
12085

The CHRISTIAN Almanac, for Pennsylvania and the Middle States for 1839. [Philadelphia:] Philadelphia Tract Society. 24 ll. MWA; NjR; OMC.
12086

COLUMBIAN Almanac for 1839. Philadelphia: Jos. McDowell. 18 ll. MWA; InU; NjR; PHi; PYHi.
12087

CROCKETT Awl-man-axe for 1839. Philadelphia: Turner & Fisher. 12 ll. MWA; CtY; MoSM.
12088

The ECLECTIC Almanac for 1839. By John Armstrong. Pittsburgh: J. N. Patterson; Fisher's Power Press. 22 ll. MWA; OClWHi; PPi.
12089

The ECLECTIC Magazine Almanac for 1839. By John Armstrong. Pittsburgh: J. N. Patterson. PPiHi (27 ll.); PPiU (21 ll.)   12090

The ERIE Almanac for 1839. Erie: Oliver Spafford. 12 ll. OClWHi.   12091

The FARMER'S Almanac for 1839. Philadelphia: Turner & Fisher. 18 ll. MWA; PHi.   12092

The FARMER'S Almanac for 1839. By Elisha Dwelle. Pittsburgh: G. W. Holdship; Luke Loomis; Patterson Ingraham & Co. 15 ll. MtU.   12093

The FARMERS' Almanac for 1839. By John Ward. Philadelphia: M'Carty & Davis. 18 ll. MWA; DLC; InU; PHi (16 ll.); [PP (has Ward's manuscript for this almanac)]   12094

The FARMERS and Mechanics Almanack for 1839. By Charles Frederick Egelmann. Philadelphia: George W. Mentz & Son. 18 ll. MWA; N; InU; ViU; WHi; PDoBHi; PHi (impf); PPL (17 ll.); NjR (15 ll.) 12095

-- On wrapper: Pittsburgh: Patterson & Ingraham. 18 ll. MWA.   12096

The FRANKLIN Almanac for 1839. By John Armstrong. Pittsburgh: Johnston & Stockton. 20 ll. CLU; PPiU (18 ll.)   12097

-- Issue with added "Magazine." 30 ll. MWA; OC; OClWHi (13 ll., ntp); WvU.   12098

The FRANKLIN Almanac for 1839. By John Ward. Philadelphia: M'Carty & Davis. 18 ll. MWA; DLC; CLU; PHi; PPL; [PP (has Ward's manuscript for this almanac)]   12099

FRIENDS' Almanac for 1839. By Joseph Foulke. Philadelphia: Elijah Weaver; John Richards, printer. 24 ll. MWA; DLC; NN; ICN; InU; OClWHi; WHi; PDoBHi; PHC; PPAmP.   12100

The GIRARD Almanac for 1839. Philadelphia: Thomas

Pennsylvania - 1839

L. Bonsal. 18 ll. MWA; DLC; NPV. 12101

The GREAT Western Almanac for 1839. Philadelphia:
Jos. McDowell. 18 ll. MWA; NN; IaDaM (17 ll.);
PHi; PPL; Drake. 12102

Der HOCH-DEUTSCHE Germantaun Calender auf 1839.
Von Carl F. Egelmann. Philadelphia: Wm. W.
Walker. 18 ll. MWA; InU; NjR; P; PHi; PPG; PPL.
12103

JOHNSON'S Almanac for 1839. Philadelphia: No 141
South street. 14 ll. MWA (impf); DLC; PHi. 12104

JOHNSON'S Pocket Almanac for 1839. [Philadelphia:]
141 South street. 24 ll. MWA; Drake. 12105

KEYSTONE Agricultural Almanac for 1839. Philadelphia: William W. Walker. 18 ll. MWA; InU; NNU-H;
NjR; PDoBHi (17 ll.); PHi; PPL. 12106

LOOMIS' Magazine Almanac for 1839. By Sanford C.
Hill. Pittsburgh: Luke Loomis. 30 ll. MWA; OMC;
PPi. 12107

LOOMIS' Pittsburgh Almanac for 1839. By Sanford C.
Hill. Pittsburgh: Luke Loomis. 20 ll. MWA; CLU;
InU; OC; OClWHi. 12108

The MECHANICS and Tradesmen's Almanac for 1839.
Philadelphia: Turner & Fisher. 18 ll. DLC. 12109

The MORAL Almanac for 1839. By William Collom.
Philadelphia: Tract Association of Friends; J. Rake-
straw, printer. 18 ll. MWA; InRE; InU; MH; NjR;
OClWHi; OHi; PHi (impf); PP. 12110

Der NEUE, Americanische Landwirthschafts-Calender
auf 1839. Von Carl Friedrich Egelmann. Reading:
Johann Ritter und Comp. 16 ll. MWA; InU; NjP; P;
PHi; PPG; PPL; PR; PRHi. 12111

NEUER Calender für Bauern und Handwerker auf 1839.
Von Carl F. Egelmann. Philadelphia: Georg W.

Mentz und Sohn. 18 ll. MWA; InU; NjP (17 ll.);
PHi; PPCS; PPL; PPeSchw.   12112

NEUER Calender für Nord-Amerika auf 1839. Von
Carl F. Egelmann. Philadelphia: Georg W. Mentz und
Sohn. 18 ll. MWA; CLU; InU; PDoBHi; PPG.   12113

NEUER Gemeinnütziger Pennsylvanischer Calender auf
1839. Lancaster: Johann Baer. 18 ll. MWA; PDoBHi;
PHi (17 ll.); PLF; PLHi; PPeSchw.   12114

NEUER Verbesserter Calender auf 1839. Nahe bei
Reading: Carl F. Egelmann und Sohn. 16 ll. MWA;
CLU; CtY; PHi; PPL; PPT; PR; PRHi.   12115

NEUER Volks-Calender auf 1839. Philadelphia: J.
Botticher. 18 ll. MWA.   12116

PENNSYLVANIA Almanac for 1839. By John Ward.
Philadelphia: M'Carty & Davis. 18 ll. MWA (17 ll.);
PYHi; [PP (has Ward's manuscript for this almanac)]
   12117
PENNSYLVANIA Almanac for 1839. By John Ward.
Philadelphia: G. W. Mentz. 18 ll. PPeSchw.   12118

The PENNSYLVANIA and New Jersey Almanac for 1839.
Philadelphia: Thomas L. Bonsal. 18 ll. MWA; DLC;
InU; PHi.   12119

The PHILADELPHIA Almanac for 1839. By William
Collom. Philadelphia: Uriah Hunt. 18 ll. MWA; CtY;
DeU (17 ll.); PHi.   12120

POOR Wills Almanac for 1839. By William Collom.
Philadelphia: Joseph M'Dowell. 18 ll. MWA; DLC;
NN; NHi; CLU; CtY; MB; MiD-B; NjR (17 ll.); PHi;
PPL.   12121

The THOMSONIAN Almanac for 1839. By William Collom. Philadelphia: A. & J. W. Comfort. 18 ll. MWA;
InU; OClWHi; NjR (17 ll., ntp)   12122

The TOWN and Country Almanac for 1839. Philadelphia:

Turner & Fisher. 18 ll. MWA; DLC.   12123

TURNER'S Comick Almanack for 1839. Philadelphia: Turner & Fisher; New York: Turner & Fisher. 18 ll. MWA (impf); NN (impf)   12124

UNCLE Sam's Large Almanac for 1839. Philadelphia: Wm. W. Walker. 18 ll. MWA; NHi; NNU-H; CtY; F; FSaHi; WHi; PHi; PPL (17 ll.)   12125

The UNITED States Almanack for 1839. By Charles Frederick Egelmann. Philadelphia: George W. Mentz & Son. 18 ll. MWA; DLC; InU; MBAt(17 ll.); PP; PYHi.   12126

The WATCHMAN'S Calendar for 1839. [In "The City Watchman's Address on the return of Christmas, 1838."] Broadside. NHi; PHi.
   12127

AGRICULTURAL Almanac for 1840. Lancaster: John Bear. 18 ll. MWA; N; CtY; InU; NjR; WHi; PDoBHi; PHi; PLHi; PYHi.   12128

AGRICULTURAL Almanac for 1840. Philadelphia: Prouty, Libby & Prouty; J. Van Court, printer. 36 ll. MWA; DLC; CtY; NjR.   12129

AMERICANISCHER Stadt und Land Calender auf 1840. Philadelphia: Conrad Zentler. 15 ll. MWA; DLC; N; CLU; CtY; DeWint; InU; NjP; PDoBHi; PHi; PPCS (impf); PPG; PYHi.   12130

AMERIKANISCHER Unabhangigkeits-Kalender für 1840. Philadelphia: C. F. Stollmeyer. 16 ll. MWA; NN; NHi (impf); PDoBHi (14 ll.)   12131

The CHRISTIAN Almanac for Pennsylvania and Delaware for 1840. Philadelphia: Pennsylvania branch of the American Tract Society. MWA (missing from shelf)
   12132

The CHRISTIAN Almanac for Pennsylvania and the Middle States for 1840. Philadelphia: Philadelphia Tract Society. 24 ll. MWA; InU.   12133

The CHRISTIAN Almanac for Western Pennsylvania for 1840. Pittsburgh: Patterson & Ingraham. 24 ll. OClWHi.   12134

COLUMBIAN Almanac for 1840. Philadelphia: Jos. McDowell. 18 ll. MWA; DeU (17 ll.); MBC; PHi.   12135

The FARMER'S Almanac for 1840. By Elisha Dwelle. Pittsburgh: G. W. Holdship; Luke Loomis; Patterson, Ingraham & Co. 16 ll. IaDaM; InLP.   12136

The FARMERS' Almanac for 1840. By John Ward. Philadelphia: M'Carty & Davis. 18 ll. MWA; PHi; NjR (15 ll.); [Drake (has Ward's manuscript for this almanac)]   12137

The FARMERS and Mechanics Almanack for 1840. By Charles Frederick Egelmann. Philadelphia: George W. Mentz & Son. 18 ll. MWA; N; NN (17 ll.); CLU; CtY; InU; MB; NBuG; NjP; OHi (17 ll.); OMC (17 ll.); WHi; PDoBHi; PPL (16 ll.); NjR (11 ll.); Drake.   12138

-- On wrapper: Pittsburgh: Alexander Ingram, Jr. 18 ll. MWA.   12139

FITHIAN'S Silk Growers Almanac for 1840. Philadelphia: M. Fithian. 16 ll. MWA (impf); DLC; PHi; PYHi.   12140

The FRANKLIN Almanac for 1840. By John Armstrong. Pittsburgh: Johnston and Stockton. 18 ll. MWA.   12141

-- Issue with added "Magazine." 30 ll. MWA; CLU; OC; Wv-Ar.   12142

The FRANKLIN Almanac for 1840. By John Ward. Philadelphia: M'Carty & Davis. 18 ll. MWA; NHi (16 ll.); NjR; PHi; [Drake (has Ward's manuscript for this almanac)]   12143

FRIENDS' Almanac for 1840. By Joseph Foulke. Philadelphia: Elijah Weaver; John Richards, printer. 24 ll. MWA; DLC; CtY; ICN; InU; OClWHi; PDoBHi

Pennsylvania - 1840

(impf); PHC.   12144

FRIENDS' Pocket Almanac for 1840. By Joseph Foulke. Philadelphia: T. E. Chapman. 24 ll. PHi.   12145

The GIRARD Almanac for 1840. Philadelphia: Thomas L. Bonsal. 18 ll. MWA; PHi.   12146

The GREAT Western Almanac for 1840. Philadelphia: Jos. McDowell. 18 ll. MWA; NN; CLU; NjR; PHi.   12147

Der HOCH-DEUTSCHE Germantaun Calender auf 1840. Von Carl F. Egelmann. Philadelphia: Wm. W. Walker. 18 ll. MWA; P; PHi; PPCS; PPL (17 ll.)   12148

JOHNSON'S Almanac for 1840. Philadelphia: No 141 South street. 14 ll. NjR (9 ll.); PHi.   12149

JOHNSON'S Pocket Almanac for 1840. [Philadelphia:] No. 141 South street. 24 ll. MWA; Drake.   12150

KEYSTONE Agricultural Almanac for 1840. Philadelphia: William W. Walker. 18 ll. MWA; InU; NNU-H (17 ll.); PHi; PPL; PYHi; NjR (13 ll.)]   12151

Des LANDWIRTHS und Seidenbauers Calender auf 1840. Lancaster: Johann Baer. 16 ll. MWA; PLF; Hostetter.   12152

LOOMIS' Magazine Almanac for 1840. By Sanford C. Hill. Pittsburgh: Luke Loomis. 30 ll. MWA (ntp); DLC; WvU.   12153

LOOMIS' Pittsburgh Almanac for 1840. By Sanford C. Hill. Pittsburgh: Luke Loomis; A. A. Anderson, printer. 18 ll. DLC; OC; OMC; OClWHi; WHi; PPi; PPiHi.   12154

The METEOROLOGICAL Almanac and Horoscope for July, 1840. Philadelphia: J. H. Gihon & Co. [This is not an almanac.]   12155

The MORAL Almanac for 1840. Philadelphia: Tract

Association of Friends; J. & W. Kite, printers. 18 ll.
MWA; InRE; InU; MH; NBuG; OHi; NjR.   12156

Der NEUE, Amerikanische Landwirthschafts-Calender
auf 1840. Von Carl Friederich Egelmann. Reading:
John Ritter und Comp. 18 ll. MWA; DLC (15 ll.); N;
InU; NjP; P; PHi; PDoBHi; PPL; PR; PRHi; Drake.
                                             12157
NEUER Calender für Bauern und Handwerker auf 1840.
Von Carl F. Egelmann. Philadelphia: Georg W. Mentz
und Sohn. 18 ll. MWA; NN; InU; NjR; PDoBHi;
NjP; PPG; PHi (impf); PPeSchw.   12158

NEUER Calender für Nord-Amerika auf 1840. Von
Carl F. Egelmann. Philadelphia: Georg W. Mentz und
Sohn. 18 ll. MWA; NN; PHi; PLF; PPG; PPL;
PPeSchw; Drake.   12159

NEUER Gemeinnütziger Pennsylvanischer Calender auf
1840. Lancaster: Johann Baer. 18 ll. MWA; PHi;
PLF; PLHi; PAtM; Drake.   12160

PENNSYLVANIA Almanac for 1840. Philadelphia:
M'Carty & Davis. 18 ll. MWA; CtY; NjR; KHi (17 ll.);
PHi.   12161

The PENNSYLVANIA and New Jersey Almanac for
1840. Philadelphia: Thomas L. Bonsal. 18 ll. MWA;
NjR.   12162

The PENNSYLVANIA Democratic Almanac for 1840.
Harrisburg: A. F. Cox. 32 ll. WHi.   12163

PHILADELPHIA Pocket Almanac for 1840. By Joseph
Foulke. Philadelphia: T. E. Chapman. 24 ll. PP.
                                             12164
POOR Wills Almanac for 1840. Philadelphia: Joseph
M'Dowell. 18 ll. MWA; DLC; N; CtY; DeU; InU; MB;
NjR; PHi; PDoBHi; PPL; PPAmP; WHi.   12165

Der SCHLUSSSTEIN Landwirthschafts Calender auf 1840.
Von Carl F. Egelmann. Philadelphia: Wm. W. Walker.
18 ll. MWA; InU.   12166

TURNER'S Comick Almanack for 1840. New York [and] Philadelphia: Turner & Fisher. 18 ll. DLC; MB; NjR. 12167

UNCLE Sam's Large Almanac for 1840. Philadelphia: Wm. W. Walker. 18 ll. MWA; N; InU; MB; MnU; MiU-C; WHi; PHi (17 ll.); PLF; PPL. 12168

The UNITED States Almanack for 1840. By Charles Frederick Egelmann. Philadelphia: George W. Mentz & Son. 18 ll. MWA; DLC; NjR; PHi; PPiU. 12169

The WATCHMAN'S Calendar for 1840. Phila.: Massey & Boate. [In: The City Watchman's Address on the return of Christmas, 1839.] Broadside. NHi. 12170

WESTLICHER Staats Kalender auf 1840. Elisha Dwelle, editor. Philadelphia: [Hogan und Thompson]. 15 ll. OC. 12171

AGRICULTURAL Almanac for 1841. Lancaster: John Bear. 18 ll. MWA; N; NN; InU; NjR; PDoBHi; PHi; PYHi. 12172

ALMANAC for 1841. Philadelphia: Chronicle Print. [In: Carrier's Address to the patrons of the Daily Chronicle.] Broadside. PHi. 12173

ALMANAC and Baptist Register for 1841. [Philadelphia:] American Baptist Publication and S. School Society; King & Baird, printers. 18 ll. MWA; N; NHi; Ct; InU; MB; MeHi; MnU; OClWHi; NjR; PP. 12174

AMERICANISCHER Stadt und Land Calender auf 1841. Philadelphia: Conrad Zentler. 15 ll. MWA; DLC; CLU (impf); CtY; DeWint; InU; NjP; NjR; PDoBHi; PHi; PPG. 12175

AMERIKANISCHER Unabhängigkeits-Kalender für 1841. Philadelphia: C. F. Stollmeyer. 16 ll. MWA; NN; PHi; PPAmP; PPG. 12176

The COMIC Almanack for 1841. Philadelphia: Turner

& Fisher. 22 ll. OMC.   12177

The FARMERS' Almanac for 1841. By John Ward.
Philadelphia: M'Carty & Davis. 18 ll. MWA; PHi;
NjR (16 ll., ntp)   12178

The FARMERS and Mechanics Almanack for 1841. By
Charles Frederick Egelmann. Philadelphia: George W.
Mentz & Son. 18 ll. MWA; NN (16 ll.); CLU; InU;
MiU-C; PHi; WHi.   12179

The FARMERS and Mechanics' Almanac for 1841. By
Jacob Keister, Jr. Pittsburgh: A. Ingram, Jr. 18 ll.
MWA; PPi.   12180

FISHERS Comic Almanac for 1841. New York [and]
Philadelphia: Turner & Fisher. 12 ll. DLC; PHi.
                                                      12181
The FRANKLIN Almanac for 1841. By John Armstrong. Pittsburgh: Johnston & Stockton. 18 ll.
NRMA; OMC.   12182

-- Issue with added "Magazine." 30 ll. MWA; CLU
(29 ll.); InU (ntp); OClWHi; PPi.   12183

The FRANKLIN Almanac for 1841. By Joseph Foulke.
Philadelphia: Thomas L. Bonsal. 18 ll. MWA; DLC;
CtY; NjR; PHi; PPAmP; PPL.   12184

The FRANKLIN Almanac for 1841. By John Ward.
Philadelphia: M'Carty & Davis. 18 ll. MWA (impf);
PHi; PYHi.   12185

FRIENDS' Almanac for 1841. By Joseph Foulke. Philadelphia: Elijah Weaver; John Richards, printer. 24 ll.
MWA; DLC; ICN; InU; OClWHi; PDoBHi (impf); PHC.
                                                      12186
The GIRARD Almanac for 1841. Philadelphia: Thomas
L. Bonsal. 18 ll. MWA (impf); DLC; PHi (16 ll.)
                                                      12187
The GREAT Western Almanac for 1841. Philadelphia:
Jos. McDowell. 18 ll. MWA; DLC; NN; NjR (17 ll.);
PHi; PLF; PPL.   12188

HARRISON Calender auf 1841. Philadelphia: George
W. Mentz und Sohn. 18 ll. MWA; DLC; N; NHi
(impf); CLU; CtY; IHi; InU; NjR (16 ll.); P; PPG;
PPL; Drake. 12189

Der HOCH-DEUTSCHE Germantaun Calender auf 1841.
Von Carl F. Egelmann. Philadelphia: Wm. W. Walker. 18 ll. NHi (17 ll.); P; PDoBHi; PHi; PPCS;
PPL (17 ll.) 12190

JOHNSON'S Almanac for 1841. Philadelphia: W. A.
Leary. 14 ll. IaDaM. 12191

JOHNSON'S Pocket Almanac for 1841. [Philadelphia:]
Printed by the publisher & sold wholesale. 24 ll.
MWA; Drake (26 ll.) 12192

KEYSTONE Agricultural Almanac for 1841. Philadelphia: William W. Walker. 18 ll. MWA; NjR; PHi (17
ll.) 12193

The LAKE Country Almanac for 1841. Erie: Oliver
Spafford. 12 ll. NHi. 12194

LOOMIS' Magazine Almanac for 1841. By Sanford C.
Hill. Pittsburgh: Luke Loomis; A. A. Anderson,
printer. 30 ll. MWA; OC; OClWHi; PPiHi; PPiU;
WHi; WvU. 12195

LOOMIS' Pittsburgh Almanac for 1841. By Sanford C.
Hill. Pittsburgh: Luke Loomis. 19 ll. MWA; InU;
PPi. 12196

MONTGOMERY'S Tippecanoe Almanac for 1841. Philadelphia: M'Carty & Davis; [etc]. 40 ll. MWA; ICHi;
InU; O; OC; OCHP (ntp); PP; ViW. 12197

MONTGOMERY'S Tippecanoe Almanac for 1841. Philadelphia: M'Carty & Davis; [etc]. Stereotyped by L.
Johnson. (Fourth Edition) 40 ll. N; NN (impf); CU;
InHi; MB; MBAt (impf); NBLiHi; OClWHi; OMC; P;
PHi; Drake. 12198

The **MORAL** Almanac for 1841. Philadelphia: Tract Association of Friends; J. Rakestraw, printer. 18 ll. MWA; N; NN; CLU; CtHi; CtY; InRE; InU; MH; NBuG; OClWHi; OHi; PP; PPT; WHi; NjR; Drake.
 12199

Der **NEUE**, Amerikanische Landwirthschafts-Calender auf 1841. Von Carl Friedrich Egelmann. Reading: Johann Ritter und Comp. 18 ll. MWA; N; InU; P; PDoBHi; PPeSchw; PPL; PR; PRHi. 12200

NEUER Calender für Bauern und Handwerker auf 1841. Von Carl F. Egelmann. Philadelphia: George W. Mentz und Sohn. 18 ll. MWA; NHi (17 ll.); NjR (17 ll.); NjP; CLU; CtY; InU (17 ll.); PDoBHi; PHi; PYHi. 12201

NEUER Gemeinnüzige Pennsylvanischer Calender auf 1841. Lancaster: Johann Baer. 18 ll. MWA; InU; DeWint; PLF; PLHi; Drake. 12202

PENNSYLVANIA Almanac for 1841. Philadelphia: M'Carty & Davis. 18 ll. PHi. 12203

The **PENNSYLVANIA** and New Jersey Almanac for 1841. By Joseph Foulke. Philadelphia: Thomas L. Bonsal. 18 ll. MWA; DLC; NjR. 12204

PHILADELPHIA Pocket Almanac for 1841. By Joseph Foulke. Philadelphia: T. E. Chapman. 24 ll. PHi.
 12205

POOR Wills Almanac for 1841. Philadelphia: Joseph M'Dowell. 18 ll. MWA; DLC; CtY; InU; MBAt; N; PHi; PP; WHi; NjR. 12206

Der **SCHLUSSSTEIN** Landwirthschafts Calender auf 1841. Von Carl F. Egelmann. Philadelphia: Wm. W. Walker. 18 ll. MWA; NN; PDoBHi; PHi; PPL (17 ll.) 12207

The **TIPPECANOE** Almanac for 1841. Philadelphia: M'Carty & Davis; [etc]; Stereotyped by L. Johnson. 36 ll. MWA; N; NHi; IHi; InHi; InU; MB; NjR; MiD-B; OClWHi; P (34 ll., ntp); MiU-C; WHi. 12208

TURNER'S Comic Almanack for 1841. Philadelphia
[and] New York: Turner & Fisher. 18 ll. MWA; DLC;
InU (17 ll.); MB; PHi. 12209

UNCLE Sam's Large Almanac for 1841. Philadelphia:
Wm. W. Walker. 18 ll. MWA; N; CtY; F (17 ll.);
InU (16 ll.); KHi; MH; PHi; PYHi. 12210

The UNITED States Almanack for 1841. By Charles
Frederick Egelmann. Philadelphia: George W. Mentz
& Son. 18 ll. MWA; DLC (impf); CtY; InU; PHi.
12211
The WATCHMAN'S Calendar for 1841. Philadelphia:
N. B. Manning. [In: The City Watchman's Address on
the return of Christmas, 1840.] Broadside. NHi.
12212
Der WESTLICHE Calender für 1841. Pittsburgh.
[Phillips] 12213

AGRICULTURAL Almanac for 1842. Lancaster: John
Bear. 18 ll. MWA; N; NN; NjR; PHi; PLHi; PPL;
PPeSchw. 12214

AGRICULTURAL Almanac for 1842. Philadelphia: D.
O. Prouty; Gihon, Fairchild & Co., printers. 36 ll.
PPL. 12215

ALMANAC and Baptist Register for 1842. Philadelphia:
American Baptist Publication and S. School Society;
King & Baird, printers. 18 ll. MWA; N; Ct; InU; MB;
OClWHi; PPL; WHi. 12216

The AMERICAN Pocket Book for 1842. Philadelphia:
J. B. Lippincott & Co.; Jesper Harding, printer. 127
ll. PHi. 12217

AMERICANISCHER Stadt und Land Calender auf 1842.
Philadelphia: Conrad Zentler. 15 ll. MWA; DLC; N;
NN (14 ll.); CLU; CtY; InU; DeWint; NjP; OC;
PDoBHi; PHi; PPL; PPeSchw; PYHi; Drake (14 ll.)
12218
The CITIZEN'S and Farmer's Almanac for 1842. By
Charles F. Egelmann. Philadelphia: Turner & Fisher.

18 ll. MWA; InU; ViW (13 ll.) 12219

COLUMBIAN Almanac for 1842. Philadelphia: Joseph McDowell. 18 ll. MWA (17 ll.); InU; PYHi; NjR (ntp) 12220

The DELAWARE & Maryland Farmers' Almanac for 1842. Philadelphia: J. M'Dowell. 18 ll. MWA; NN; NHi (17 ll.); InU; NjGlaN (impf) 12221

EVERYBODY'S Almanac for 1842. Philadelphia: G. B. Zieber. 8 ll. MWA. 12222

The FARMERS' Almanac for 1842. By John Ward. Philadelphia: M'Carty & Davis. 18 ll. MWA; PHi; PPL (17 ll.); NjR (16 ll., ntp); [Drake (has Ward's manuscript for this almanac)] 1223

The FARMERS and Mechanics Almanack for 1842. By Charles Frederick Egelmann. Philadelphia: George W. Mentz & Son. 18 ll. MWA; NN (16 ll.); InU (16 ll.); PHi; PLF; PPeSchw. 12224

The FRANKLIN Almanac for 1842. By John Armstrong. Pittsburgh: Johnston and Stockton. 18 ll. MWA; InU. 12225

-- Issue with added "Magazine." 30 ll. MWA. 12226

FRANKLIN Almanac for 1842. By Joseph Foulke. Philadelphia: Thomas L. Bonsal. 18 ll. MWA; DLC; NjR. 12227

The FRANKLIN Almanac for 1842. By John Ward. Philadelphia: M'Carty & Davis. 18 ll. PLF (15 ll.); [Drake (has Ward's manuscript for this almanac)] 12228

FRIENDS' Almanac for 1842. By Joseph Foulke. Philadelphia: Elijah Weaver; John Richards, printer. 24 ll. MWA; ICN; InU; MnU; NjR (22 ll.); PHC; OClWHi. 12229

FRIENDS' Pocket Almanac for 1842. By Joseph Foulke. Philadelphia: T. E. Chapman. 22 ll. MWA; PHi. 12230

The GIRARD Almanac for 1842. Philadelphia: Thomas
L. Bonsal. 18 ll. MWA; InU; PHi; PPL.   12231

The GREAT National Almanack for 1842. Philadelphia:
Turner & Fisher. 18 ll. PHi; PPL.   12232

The GREAT Western Almanac for 1842. Philadelphia:
Jos. McDowell. 18 ll. MWA; DLC; NjR; PHi.   12233

Der HOCH-DEUTSCHE Germantaun Calender auf 1842.
Von Carl F. Egelmann. Philadelphia: Wm. W. Walker. 18 ll. MWA; InU; P; PHi; PPCS; PPG; PPL
(17 ll.)   12234

The HOUSEKEEPER'S Almanac and Good Wife's Receipt
Book for 1842. Philadelphia: Turner & Fisher. 18 ll.
InU; PHi (12 ll.); PPL (17 ll.)   12235

The HOUSEKEEPER'S Almanac and Good Wife's Receipt
Book for 1842. Philadelphia: Turner & Fisher; Baltimore: H. A. Turner. 18 ll. MWA (two varieties);
DLC; NNU-H; WHi.   12236

JOHNSON'S Pocket Almanac for 1842. Philadelphia:
Printed by the publisher & sold wholesale. 28 ll. MWA;
Drake.   12237

KEYSTONE Agricultural Almanac for 1842. Philadelphia: William W. Walker. 18 ll. MWA; DeWint; InU;
MnU.   12238

LOOMIS' Magazine Almanac for 1842. By Sanford C.
Hill. Pittsburgh: Luke Loomis. 30 ll. MWA; DLC;
NBuHi; OMC; PPi.   12239

LOOMIS' Pittsburgh Almanac for 1842. By Sanford C.
Hill. Pittsburgh: Luke Loomis; A. A. Anderson,
printer. 18 ll. MWA (two varieties); DLC; CLU; InU;
OClWHi; PPiHi.   12240

The MORAL Almanac for 1842. Philadelphia: Tract
Association of Friends; J. Rakestraw, printer. 18 ll.
MWA; N; NN; NHi; InU; MH; NBuG; OHi; OClWHi;

InRE; WHi; PP; NjR. 12241

Der NEUE, Amerikanische Landwirthschafts-Calender auf 1842. Von Carl Friederich Egelmann. Reading: Johann Ritter und Comp. 18 ll. MWA; NN; InU; P; PDoBHi; PHi; PPL; PR; PRHi; PYHi. 12242

NEUER Calender für Bauern und Handwerker auf 1842. Von Carl F. Egelmann. Philadelphia: Georg W. Mentz und Sohn. 18 ll. MWA (impf); CLU; CtY; DeWint; InU; NjP; NjR; PHi; PDoBHi; PPeSchw; PYHi. 12243

NEUER Gemeinnütziger Pennsylvanischer Calender auf 1842. Lancaster: Johann Baer. 18 ll. MWA; MH; PAtM; PHi; PLF; PLHi; PDoBHi; PPeSchw. 12244

The NORTH American Almanac for 1842. Philadelphia: W. A. Leary. 14 ll. MWA; PPL. 12245

PENNSYLVANIA Almanac for 1842. Philadelphia: M'Carty & Davis. 18 ll. CtY; NjR; [Drake (has Ward's manuscript for this almanac)] 12246

The PENNSYLVANIA and New Jersey Almanac for 1842. Easton: John R. McMullin. 18 ll. MWA. 12247

The PENNSYLVANIA and New Jersey Almanac for 1842. By Joseph Foulke. Philadelphia: Thomas L. Bonsal. 18 ll. MWA; InU; NjR. 12248

The PHILADELPHIA Almanac for 1842. Philadelphia: Uriah Hunt. 18 ll. MWA; PHi. 12249

PHILADELPHIA Pocket Almanac for 1842. By Joseph Foulke. Philadelphia: T. E. Chapman; J. Chapman, printer. 24 ll. DLC; ViHi. 12250

POOR Wills Almanac for 1842. Philadelphia: Joseph M'Dowell. 18 ll. MWA (impf); DLC; CLU; MB; PHi; NjR. 12251

RAPP'S Business Almanac for 1842. Philadelphia: Wm. D. Rapp. 18 ll. DLC; PHi; PPL. 12252

Der SCHLUSSSTEIN Landwirthschafts Calender auf
1842. Von Carl F. Egelmann. Philadelphia: Wm. W.
Walker. 18 ll. MWA; NN (15 ll.); CtY; InU (17 ll.);
PDoBHi; PHi; PPL. 12253

TURNER'S Comic Almanac for 1842. Philadelphia:
Turner & Fisher; [and New York]. 18 ll. MWA;
DLC (16 ll.); CtY; InU; MWiW; NBuG; NR; Drake
(17 ll.) 12254

UNCLE Sam's Almanac for 1842. By Henry Frost.
Philadelphia: Hogan & Thompson. ViU (14 ll.) 12255

UNCLE Sam's Large Almanac for 1842. Philadelphia:
Wm. W. Walker. 18 ll. MWA; N; CLU; F; FSaHi;
IaDaM; InU; MB; NjR; PDoBHi; PHi; PP; PPL; PPG.
12256

The UNITED States Almanac for 1842. By Charles F.
Egelmann. Philadelphia: Turner & Fisher. 18 ll.
MWA. 12257

VERBESSERTER Calender auf 1842. Reading: Carl F.
Egelmann. 16 ll. PR. 12258

VERBESSERTER Calender auf 1842. Von Carl F.
Egelmann. Reading: Geo. Bergner. 16 ll. MWA.
12259

VOLKS Calender auf 1842. Easton: Heinrich Held.
18 ll. PHi (17 ll.); PP; PPeSchw. 12260

AGRICULTURAL Almanac for 1843. Lancaster: John
Bear. 18 ll. MWA; N; CtY; InU; NjR; PHi; PLHi;
PPeSchw; WHi. 12261

The ALMANAC and Baptist Register for 1843. [Phila-
delphia:] American Baptist Publication and S. School
Society; King & Baird, printers. 20 ll. MWA; NHi; Ct
(18 ll.); CtY; InU; MB; OClWHi; WHi. 12262

AMERICANISCHER Stadt und Land Calender auf 1843.
Philadelphia: Conrad Zentler. 15 ll. MWA; DLC; N;
CLU; CtY; DeWint; NjP; NjR; PDoBHi; PHi; PPG;
PPeSchw; PYHi; RPB; InU; Drake. 12263

The CITIZEN'S Almanac for 1843. By Charles F.
Egelmann. Philadelphia: Turner & Fisher. 16 ll.
PHi; PP; PPL; Drake. 12264

The CITIZENS' and Farmers' Almanac for 1843. By
Henry Frost. Philadelphia: Hogan & Thompson. 16 ll.
MWA. 12265

The COLD Water Almanac for 1843. Philadelphia:
Drew & Scammell. 16 ll. MWA; DLC; OClWHi. 12266

COLUMBIAN Almanac for 1843. Philadelphia: Jos.
M'Dowell. 18 ll. MWA; DLC; NN; InU; MBC; NjR;
PHi; WHi. 12267

COUNTING-HOUSE Almanac for 1843. Philadelphia:
North American Press. [In: The Annual Address of
the Carriers of the North American.] Broadside. PHi.
12268

The DELAWARE & Maryland Farmers' Almanac for
1843. Philadelphia: J. M'Dowell. 18 ll. MWA; FSaHi;
PPAmP. 12269

The FARMERS' Almanac for 1843. By Joseph Ray.
Philadelphia: Desilver & Muir. PPi (17 ll.) 12270

The FARMERS' Almanac for 1843. By John Ward.
Philadelphia: M'Carty & Davis. 18 ll. MWA; DLC;
PDoBHi; PHi; PP; PPL; [Drake (has Ward's manuscript for this almanac)] 12271

The FARMERS and Mechanics Almanack for 1843. By
Charles Frederick Egelmann. Philadelphia: Mentz &
Rovoudt. 18 ll. MWA; CtY (14 ll.); InU (2 ll.); MB;
NNU-H (17 ll.); PDoBHi; PHi; PPL; PLF; ViW (16
ll.) 12272

FARMER'S Calendar for 1843. By Henry Frost. Philadelphia: Grigg & Elliott. KyHi. 12273

The FRANKLIN Almanac for 1843. By John Armstrong.
Pittsburgh: Johnston and Stockton. 18 ll. OHi. 12274

Pennsylvania - 1843

-- Issue with added "Magazine." 30 ll. MWA. 12275

The FRANKLIN Almanac for 1843. By John Ward. Philadelphia: M'Carty & Davis. 18 ll. DLC (impf); PYHi; Drake (17 ll., also, has Ward's manuscript for this almanac) 12276

FRIENDS' Almanac for 1843. By Joseph Foulke. Philadelphia: Elijah Weaver. 24 ll. MWA; InU; MnU; OClWHi; PHC. 12277

FRIENDS' Pocket Almanac for 1843. By Joseph Foulke. Philadelphia: T. E. Chapman. 24 ll. MWA. 12278

The GIRARD Almanac for 1843. Philadelphia: Thomas L. Bonsal. 18 ll. MWA; NjR. 12279

The GREAT National Almanack for 1843. Philadelphia: Turner & Fisher. 16 ll. MWA; InU; PHi. 12280

The GREAT Western Almanac for 1843. Philadelphia: Jos. McDowell. 18 ll. MWA; InU; MiU-C; OClWHi; PHi. 12281

The HENRY Clay Almanac for 1843. Philadelphia: Grigg & Elliott; Thomas Cowperthwait & Co.; Hogan and Thompson; T. K. & P. G. Collins. 16 ll. KyU; PPL; ViU (10 ll.) 12282

The HENRY Clay Almanac for 1843. Philadelphia: Grigg & Elliott; Thomas Cowperthwait & Co.; Hogan and Thompson; G. W. Mentz & Son; Kay & Brother; M'Carty & Davis; Carey & Hart; T. K. & P. G. Collins. 16 ll. PHi. 12283

Der HOCH-DEUTSCHE Germantaun Calender auf 1843. Von Carl F. Egelmann. Philadelphia: Wm. W. Walker. 18 ll. MWA; PDoBHi; PHi; PPeSchw. 12284

HOUSEKEEPER'S Almanac for 1843. Philadelphia: King & Baird. [Phillips] 12285

JOHNSON'S Pocket Almanac for 1843. Philadelphia:

Printed by the publisher & sold wholesale. 28 ll.
MWA; NN (11 ll.); Drake. 12286

LOOMIS' Magazine Almanac for 1843. By Sanford C.
Hill. Pittsburgh: Luke Loomis. 36 ll. MWA; OClWHi;
PPi; Wv-Ar (30 ll.) 12287

LOOMIS' Pittsburgh Almanac for 1843. By Sanford C.
Hill. Pittsburgh: Luke Loomis; A. A. Anderson,
printer. 18 ll. MWA; InU; OMC; PHi; PPiHi. 12288

-- Issue with 30 ll. PPiHi. 12289

The MORAL Almanac for 1843. Philadelphia: Tract
Association of Friends; Joseph Rakestraw, printer. 18
ll. MWA; NHi (17 ll.); CLU; CtY; InRE; InU; MH;
NBuG; OHi; PP; WHi; NjR (8 ll.) 12290

Der NEUE, Amerikanische Landwirthschafts-Calender
auf 1843. Von Carl Friederich Egelmann. Reading:
Johann Ritter und Comp. 16 ll. MWA; NN; CLU;
InU; NjP; P; PDoBHi; PHi; PPCS; PPG; PPeSchw;
PR; PRHi. 12291

-- Issue with 32 ll. PAnL. 12292

NEUER Calender für Bauern und Handwerker auf 1843.
Von Carl F. Egelmann. Philadelphia: Mentz und Rovoudt. 18 ll. MWA; CLU; CtY; InU; PDoBHi; PHi;
PLF; PPCS; PPeSchw; PYHi. 12293

NEUER Gemeinnütziger Pennsylvanischer Calender auf
1843. Lancaster: Johann Baer. 18 ll. MWA; N; CtY;
InU (impf); P; PDoBHi; PHi; PLF; PLHi; PP;
PPeSchw; PYHi. 12294

OLD Humphrey's Almanac for 1843. By Joseph Foulke.
Philadelphia: Thomas L. Bonsal. 18 ll. MWA; InU;
Drake. 12295

PENNSYLVANIA Almanac for 1843. Philadelphia:
M'Carty & Davis. 18 ll. MWA; PHi (17 ll.) 12296

The PENNSYLVANIA and New Jersey Almanac for
1843. By Joseph Foulke. Philadelphia: Thomas L.
Bonsal. 18 ll. MWA; InU; PHi. 12297

POOR Wills Almanac for 1843. Philadelphia: Joseph
M'Dowell. 18 ll. MWA; DLC; InU; MB; PHi; NjR.
12298

The PRESBYTERIAN Almanac for 1843. Philadelphia:
Presbyterian Board of Publication; Paul T. Jones. 18
ll. GDC; NcMHi; NjR; PPAmP; PPL; PPPrHi; PPiU.
12299

RAPP'S Penna. Almanack for 1843. Philadelphia: W.
D. Rapp. 24 ll. MWA (two varieties); InU; PHi.
12300

Der SCHLUSSSTEIN Landwirthschafts Calender auf
1843. Von Carl F. Egelmann. Philadelphia: Wm. W.
Walker. 18 ll. NjR (17 ll.); PHi (15 ll.); PPeSchw.
12301

STEELE'S Almanack for 1843. By Geo. R. Perkins.
Erie: O. D. Spofford. MWA (missing from shelf)
12302

TURNER'S Comic Almanac for 1843. Philadelphia:
Turner & Fisher [and New York] 18 ll. MWA (two
varieties); DLC; AU; CtY. 12303

TURNER'S Improved House-Keeper's Almanac: and
Good Wife's Recipe Book for 1843. Philadelphia:
Turner & Fisher. 16 ll. MWA; DLC; PHi; PP. 12304

UNCLE Sam's Large Almanac for 1843. Philadelphia:
Wm. W. Walker. 18 ll. MWA; PHi; PLF; PP;
PPeSchw; PYHi; NjR (16 ll.) 12305

UNCLE Sam's Large Almanac for 1843. Philadelphia:
William W. Walker for Isaac M. Moss. 18 ll. IaDaM
(17 ll.) 12306

The UNITED States' Almanac; or Complete Ephemeris
for 1843. By John Downes. Philadelphia: E. H. Butler. 176 ll. MWA; N; NN; NHi; PU; NNA; PHi;
OClWHi; MB; O; IU; CtNlC; NjJ; NBLiHi; PPL; AU;
NjP (169 ll.); MHi; DeU (162 ll.); PPAmP; NBuHi
(166 ll.); NIC; CtY; OFH (169 ll.) OMC (162 ll.);

OCl; Nh; ICHi (162 ll.); M; InU; WHi; TxGR; ViU;
MWiU; OU; MNF; ICU; P; PP.   12307

VERBESSERTER Calender auf 1843. Von Carl Friedrich Egelmann. Reading: J. C. F. Egelmann. 16 ll.
MWA; CtY; InU (15 ll.); OC; P; PPeSchw; PRHi.
                                               12308
AGRICULTURAL Almanac for 1844. Lancaster: John Bear. 18 ll. MWA; NBuG; NNU-H; NjR (17 ll.);
PDoBHi; PLHi.   12309

The ALMANAC and Baptist Register for 1844. Philadelphia: American Baptist Publication and S. School Society; King & Baird, printers. 18 ll. MWA; InU; MB; NjR; OClWHi; PDoBHi; WHi.   12310

ALMANAC and Baptist Register for 1844. Philadelphia: American Baptist Publication and S. School Society; King & Baird, printers. (Second Edition) 20 ll. MWA; Ct (18 ll.); ICU.   12311

AMERICANISCHER Stadt und Land Calender auf 1844. Philadelphia: Conrad Zentler. 15 ll. MWA; DLC; N; NjR; PPG; PHi; PLF; NjP; CLU; RPB; CtY; PPL; InU; DeWint; PAtM; P; PYHi; PPT; PPeSchw; PDoBHi; Drake.   12312

Der AMERIKANISCH-DEUTSCHE Hausfreund und Baltimore Calender auf 1844. Philadelphia: Desilver & Muir. 16 ll. MWA; CtY; PHi; PPG; Drake. 12313

The CITIZENS' and Farmers' Almanac for 1844. By Henry Frost. Philadelphia: Desilver & Muir. 16 ll. MWA (two varieties, one impf); InU; NjR (15 ll.); PPL; ViW (14 ll.); WHi.   12314

COLUMBIAN Almanac for 1844. Philadelphia: Jos. McDowell. 18 ll. MWA; DLC; InU; IaDaM; NBuG; PHi; PLF.   12315

DAILY Pocket Remembrancer for 1844. Harrisburg: Hickok & Cantine. 64 ll. PPL.   12316

DAVY Crockett's Almanac for 1844. Philadelphia:
Turner & Fisher. MWA (4 ll.); CtY. 12317

The DELAWARE & Maryland Farmers' Almanac for
1844. Philadelphia: J. M'Dowell. 18 ll. MWA; DeU
(15 ll.) 12318

DEMOCRATIC Almanac for 1844. Philadelphia: Mifflin & Parry. 18 ll. MWA; NHi; PHi. 12319

-- Issue with added signature. ArU (20 ll.); PPL (22 ll.) 12320

The FARMERS' Almanac for 1844. By John Ward.
Philadelphia: M'Carty & Davis. 18 ll. MWA; IU; PHi;
[Drake (has Ward's manuscript for this almanac)]
12321

The FARMERS and Mechanics Almanack for 1844.
Philadelphia: Isaac M. Moss. [Phillips] 12322

The FARMERS and Mechanics Almanack for 1844. By
Charles Frederick Egelmann. Philadelphia: Mentz &
Rovoudt. 18 ll. MWA; N; CLU; InU; MBAt (16 ll.);
PHi; PLF; PPL; WHi; Drake (16 ll.) 12323

FISHER'S Comic Almanac for 1844. Philadelphia:
Turner & Fisher. 18 ll. MWA; CtY; MBAt. 12324

FISHER'S Economical Housekeeper's Almanac for 1844.
Philadelphia and New York: Turner & Fisher. 12 ll.
MWA (impf) 12325

FLEISSIGE Amerikaner. Ein Calender für Stadt und
Land auf 1844. Philadelphia: W. L. J. Riderlen. 16 ll.
MWA; PHi; PPL; PPeSchw. 12326

The FRANKLIN Almanac for 1844. By John Armstrong.
Pittsburgh: Johnston & Stockton. 18 ll. OMC (17 ll.)
12327
The FRANKLIN Almanac for 1844. By John Ward.
Philadelphia: M'Carty & Davis. 18 ll. DLC; N; NjR
(17 ll.); Drake (also has Ward's manuscript for this
almanac) 12328

FRIENDS' Almanac for 1844. By Joseph Foulke.
Philadelphia: Elijah Weaver. 24 ll. MWA; InU; OClWHi;
PDoBHi (impf); PHC. 12329

FRIENDS' Pocket Almanac for 1844. By Joseph
Foulke. Philadelphia: T. E. Chapman. 23 ll. MWA;
PHi. 12330

GIRARD Almanac for 1844. Philadelphia: Thomas L.
Bonsal. 18 ll. MWA. 12331

The GREAT Western Almanac for 1844. Philadelphia:
Jos. McDowell. 18 ll. MWA; DLC; NN; InU; MnU;
NjR; PHi. 12332

The HENRY Clay Almanac for 1844. Philadelphia:
Grigg & Elliot; [etc]; T. K. & P. G. Collins, printers.
16 ll. MWA; N; NHi; CLU; InU; MBC; OClWHi; PHi;
PPL. 12333

The HENRY Clay Almanac for 1844. Philadelphia:
Thomas, Cowperthwait & Co. 16 ll. MB (impf) 12334

Der HOCH-DEUTSCHE Germantaun Calender auf 1844.
Von Carl F. Egelmann. Philadelphia: Wm. W. Walker.
18 ll. PPL. 12335

HUNT'S Almanac, and Catalogue for 1844. Philadelphia:
Uriah Hunt. 36 ll. MWA; PHi; PPL (23 ll.) 12336

JOHNSON'S Pocket Almanac for 1844. Philadelphia:
Printed by the publisher & sold wholesale. 28 ll. MWA;
Drake. 12337

KEYSTONE Agricultural Almanac for 1844. Philadelphia: William W. Walker. 18 ll. PHi; PPL. 12338

LOOMIS' Magazine Almanac for 1844. By Sanford C.
Hill. Pittsburgh: Luke Loomis; A. Jaynes, printer.
30 ll. OClWHi; OMC; PPi. 12339

LOOMIS' Pittsburgh Almanac for 1844. By Sanford C.
Hill. Pittsburgh: Luke Loomis. 18 ll. MWA; OMC. 12340

The MORAL Almanac for 1844. Philadelphia: Tract Association of Friends; Joseph Rakestraw, printer. 18 ll. MWA; CtY; InRE; InU; MH; NBuG; NjR; OHi; PDoBHi; PP; PPL. 12341

Der NEUE, Amerikanische Landwirthschafts-Calender auf 1844. Von Carl Friederich Egelmann. Reading: Johann Ritter und Comp. 16 ll. MWA; NHi (impf); CLU; InU; NjP; NjR; P; PAtM; PDoBHi; PHi; PPG; PPL; PPeSchw; PR; PRHi; Drake (ntp) 12342

NEUER Calender für Bauern und Handwerker auf 1844. Von Carl F. Egelmann. Philadelphia: Mentz und Rovoudt. 18 ll. MWA; InU; NjR; PDoBHi; PHi; PPCS; PPeSchw. 12343

NEUER Gemeinnütziger Pennsylvanischer Calender auf 1844. Lancaster: Johann Baer. 18 ll. MWA; NN (impf); CtY; NjP; P; PDoBHi; PLF; PLHi; PPeSchw; PYHi. 12344

PENNSYLVANIA Almanac for 1844. Philadelphia: M'Carty & Davis. 18 ll. MWA (4 ll.); PHi. 12345

The PENNSYLVANIA & New Jersey Almanac for 1844. Philadelphia: Thomas L. Bonsal. 18 ll. MWA; InU; NjR. 12346

PHILADELPHIA Pocket Almanac for 1844. By Joseph Foulke. Philadelphia: T. E. Chapman. 24 ll. MWA. 12347

The PIRATE'S Almanac for 1844. Philadelphia: Turner & Fisher. [Sabin 63014] 12348

POOR Wills Almanac for 1844. Philadelphia: Joseph M'Dowell. 18 ll. MiU-C; OClWHi; PHC; PHi. 12349

The PRESBYTERIAN Almanac for 1844. Philadelphia: Presbyterian Board of Publication; Paul T. Jones. 18 ll. MWA; NjR; PPPrHi. 12350

RAPP'S Comic Almanack for 1844. [np, np] 18 ll. PHi; PPL. 12351

Pennsylvania - 1844

RAPP'S House-keepers' and Farmers' Temperance Almanack for 1844. [Philadelphia:] Thomas T. Mahan. 18 ll. PP.   12352

Der SCHLUSSSTEIN Landwirthschafts Calender auf 1844. Von Carl F. Egelmann. Philadelphia: Wm. W. Walker. 18 ll. MWA; CtY.   12353

SPAFFORD'S Almanack for 1844. By G. R. Perkins. Erie: O. D. Spafford; Cochran & Riblet, printers. NSyOHi (10 ll.)   12354

TEMPERANCE Cooking Almanac for 1844. Philadelphia: Turner & Fisher. 12 ll. MWA.   12355

TURNER'S Comic Almanac for 1844. Philadelphia: Turner & Fisher. 18 ll. MDedHi.   12356

TURNER'S Improved House-Keeper's Almanac: and Family Recipe Book for 1844. Philadelphia and New York: Turner & Fisher. 18 ll. MWA (16 ll.); DLC; InU (impf); PHi; PPL; PPT.   12357

UNCLE Sam's Large Almanac for 1844. Philadelphia: Wm. W. Walker. 18 ll. MWA; CLU; CtY; InU; N; PDoBHi; PHi; PP; PPL; PPT; PPeSchw; ViU; WHi.   12358

The UNITED States' Almanac; or Complete Ephemeris for 1844. By John Downes [and] Freeman Hunt. Philadelphia: E. H. Butler. 158 ll. CoCC; NBuHi; NjP; OClW; OMC; MdBJ; PHC; PPL.   12359

-- Issue with 161 ll. Ct; MeP; NHi; O; OFH.   12360

-- Issue with 164 ll. MWA; NN; PU; NNA; NjR; PHi; M; OClWHi; P; MBAt; NBLiHi; MB; MHi; NIC; CtNlC; CtY; OO; NBuG; InU; WHi; ViU; MWiW; N; MNF; PPAmP.   12361

VERBESSERTER Calender auf 1844. Von Carl Friedrich Egelmann. Reading: I.C.F. Egelman. 16 ll. MWA (two varieties); CLU; CtY; PPeSchw; PHi (15 ll.); PPG; PP; PR; PRHi.   12362

Pennsylvania - 1844

The WATCHMAN'S Calendar for 1844. [Philadelphia:] Manning's Locomotive Card & Job Printing Press. [In: The City Watchman's Address on the return of Christmas, 1843.] Broadside. NHi. 12363

AGRICULTURAL Almanac for 1845. Lancaster: John Bear. 18 ll. MWA; N; IaDaM; InU; NjR; PHi; PYHi. 12364

ALMANAC and Baptist Register for 1845. Philadelphia: American Baptist Publication Society; King & Baird, printers. 20 ll. MWA; Ct (18 ll.); ICU; InU; MB; OClWHi; PP; WHi. 12365

ALMANAC and Baptist Register for 1845. Philadelphia: American Baptist Publication Society; King & Baird, printers. (Second Edition) 20 ll. WHi. 12366

The AMERICAN Almanac for 1845. Philadelphia: Griffith & Simon. 18 ll. NNC; PPL. 12367

The AMERICAN Farmer's Almanac for 1845. Philadelphia: Turner & Fisher. 18 ll. InU. 12368

AMERICANISCHER Stadt und Land Calender auf 1845. Philadelphia: Conrad Zentler. 15 ll. MWA; DLC; N; CLU; CtY; DeWint; NjP; NjR; P; PAnL (16 ll.); PDoBHi; PHi; PLF; PPG; PPeSchw; PYHi; RPB; InU; PPL. 12369

Der BAUERN und Handwerker Calender auf 1845. Philadelphia: 16 ll. MWA (imprint torn off) 12370

CALENDER des Bauern und Handwerkesmannes auf 1845. Philadelphia: Desilver und Muir. 18 ll. MWA. 12371

CALENDER des Bauern und Handwerkesmannes auf 1845. Philadelphia: Edmund Y. Schelly. 18 ll. PPeSchw. 12372

The CITIZENS' and Farmers' Almanac for 1845. By Edward Hagerty. Philadelphia: Desilver & Muir. 16 ll. MWA; InU. 12373

COLUMBIAN Almanac for 1845. Philadelphia: Joseph McDowell. 18 ll. MWA; DLC; FSaHi; InU; NNU-H; PHi (17 ll.); PPeSchw. 12374

DAVY Crockett's Almanac for 1845. Philadelphia: Turner & Fisher. 18 ll. DLC; CtY; MoSM; Tx. 12375

The DELAWARE & Maryland Farmers' Almanac for 1845. Philadelphia: J. M'Dowell. 18 ll. MWA; PHi. 12376

The FARMER'S Almanac for 1845. Philadelphia [and] New York: Turner & Fisher. 16 ll. MWA. 12377

The FARMER'S Almanac for 1845. Philadelphia [and] New York: Turner & Fisher; Baltimore: J. B. Keller. 16 ll. PHi. 12378

The FARMERS' Almanac for 1845. By John Ward. Philadelphia: Thomas Davis. 18 ll. MWA; PHi; [Drake (has Ward's manuscript for this almanac)] 12379

The FARMERS and Mechanics Almanack for 1845. By Charles Frederick Egelmann. Philadelphia: Mentz & Rovoudt. 18 ll. MWA; NN; CtY; InU; MB (impf); MnU; PHi; WHi. 12380

The FARMER'S Calendar for 1845. By Edward Hagerty. Philadelphia: Grigg & Elliot; S. Sands, printer. 16 ll. NjR. 12381

FISHER'S Comic Almanac for 1845. Philadelphia: Turner & Fisher. [Phillips] 12382

FLEISSIGE Amerikaner. Ein Calender fur Stadt und Land auf 1845. Philadelphia: W. L. J. Riderlen. 18 ll. MWA; CtY; InU; OClWHi; PHi. 12383

The FRANKLIN Almanac for 1845. Philadelphia: Wm. A. Leary. [Phillips] 12384

The FRANKLIN Almanac for 1845. By John Armstrong. Pittsburgh: Johnston and Stockton. 18 ll. MWA; CLU; InU; OCl; PPi. 12385

-- Issue with 24 ll. NR. 12386

The FRANKLIN Almanac for 1845. By John Ward.
Philadelphia: Thomas Davis. 18 ll. PHi; PPL (impf);
[Drake (has Ward's manuscript for this almanac)]
12387
FRIENDS' Almanac for 1845. By Joseph Foulke.
Philadelphia: Elijah Weaver; John Richards, printer.
24 ll. MWA; ICN; InU; MnU; Nj; OClWHi; PDoBHi;
PHC. 12388

FRIENDS' Pocket Almanac for 1845. By Joseph
Foulke. Philadelphia: T. E. Chapman. 24 ll. MWA.
12389
The GIRARD Almanac for 1845. By Joseph Foulke.
Philadelphia: Thomas L. Bonsal. 18 ll. MWA; PDoBHi
(16 ll.); PHi. 12390

The GREAT Western Almanac for 1845. Philadelphia:
Jos. McDowell. 18 ll. MWA; NN; NHi; InU; PLF.
12391
HUNT'S Almanac for 1845. Philadelphia: Uriah Hunt &
Son. 18 ll. MWA (17 ll.) 12392

JOHNSON'S Pocket Almanac for 1845. Philadelphia:
Printed by the publisher and sold wholesale. 17 ll.
MWA; NN. 12393

LOOMIS' Magazine Almanac for 1845. By Sanford C.
Hill. Pittsburgh: Luke Loomis. 30 ll. MWA (ntp);
DLC; PPi. 12394

LOOMIS' Pittsburgh Almanac for 1845. By Sanford C.
Hill. Pittsburgh: Luke Loomis. 18 ll. MWA; PPiHi.
12395
-- Issue with 24 ll. OMC. 12396

The MORAL Almanac for 1845. Philadelphia: Tract
Association of Friends; Joseph Rakestraw, printer. 18
ll. MWA; N; CLU; CtHT-W; CtHi; FSaHi; In; InRE;
InU; MH; MHi; MoS; NBuG; NjR; OClWHi; NHi;
PDoBHi; PP; PPL; PU; CtY; WHi. 12397

The NATIONAL Clay Almanack for 1845. By Seth
Smith. Philadelphia: Henry F. Anners; King & Baird,
printers. 18 ll. PHi.   12398

The NATIONAL Clay Almanack for 1845. By Seth
Smith. Philadelphia: Desilver & Muir; King & Baird,
printers. 18 ll. MWA (two varieties); DLC; InU;
NcD; NjR; PPL; ViW (impf)   12399

The NATIONAL Clay Almanack for 1845. By Seth
Smith. Philadelphia: Hogan & Thompson; King &
Baird, printers. 18 ll. InU.   12400

The NATIONAL Clay Almanack for 1845. By Seth
Smith. Philadelphia: Kay & Brother; King & Baird,
printers. 18 ll. PPiU (17 ll.)   12401

The NATIONAL Clay Almanack for 1845. By Seth
Smith. Philadelphia: W. A. Leary; King & Baird,
printers. 18 ll. CtY.   12402

The NATIONAL Clay Almanack for 1845. By Seth
Smith. Philadelphia: Isaac M. Moss; King & Baird,
printers. 18 ll. Mi.   12403

The NATIONAL Clay Almanack for 1845. By Seth
Smith. Philadelphia: Thomas, Cowperthwait & Co.;
King & Baird, printers. 18 ll. PP; PPeSchw.   12404

Der NEUE, Amerikanische Landwirthschafts-Calender
auf 1845. Von Carl Friederich Egelmann. Reading:
Johann Ritter und Comp. 16 ll. MWA; NHi (impf);
InU; NjP; P; PAnL; PAtM; PDoBHi; PHi; PR; PRHi.
                                                                12405
NEUER Calender fur Bauern und Handwerker auf 1845.
Von Carl F. Egelmann. Philadelphia: Mentz und Ro-
voudt. 18 ll. MWA; CLU; CtY; InU; NjP; OC (17
ll.); OClWHi; P; PAnL; PDoBHi; PHi; PPCS;
PPeSchw; Drake.   12406

NEUER Calender fur Nord-Amerika auf 1845. Von Carl
F. Egelmann. Philadelphia: Mentz und Rovoudt. 18 ll.
MWA; InU (16 ll.); PDoBHi; PPCS; PPG;

PPeSchw. 12407

NEUER Gemeinnutziger Pennsylvanischer Calender auf 1845. Lancaster: Johann Baer. 18 ll. MWA; N; CLU; CtY; MH; NjP; PDoBHi; PHi; PLF; PLHi; PPL; Drake. 12408

The NORTH American Almanac for 1845. By S. S. Steele. Philadelphia: Turner & Fisher; [and New York]. 18 ll. MWA; NHi (impf); InU; WHi (17 ll.) 12409

PENNSYLVANIA Almanac for 1845. Philadelphia: Thomas Davis. 18 ll. PHi; PPL; NjR; [Drake (has Ward's manuscript for this almanac)] 12410

The PENNSYLVANIA and New Jersey Almanac for 1845. By Joseph Foulke. Philadelphia: Thomas L. Bonsal. 18 ll. MWA. 12411

PERKINS & Purves' Almanac for 1845. Philadelphia: Perkins & Purves. 12 ll. MWA. 12412

PIRATICAL and Tragical Almanac for 1845. Philadelphia: John B. Perry. 18 ll. MWA; PP; NjR (ntp) 12413

PIRATICAL and Tragical Almanac for 1845. Philadelphia: John B. Perry; New York: Nafis & Cornish. 18 ll. PHi. 12414

POOR Wills Almanac for 1845. Philadelphia: Joseph M'Dowell. 18 ll. MWA; NN (17 ll.); DeU (16 ll.); MB; PHi; PU; WHi; NjR. 12415

The PRESBYTERIAN Almanac for 1845. Philadelphia: Presbyterian Board of Publication. 24 ll. MWA; GDC; NBLiHi; NcMHi; NjR; OMC; PPPrHi. 12416

SPAFFORD'S Almanack for 1845. By Geo. R. Perkins. Erie: O. D. Spafford; Cochran & Riblet, printers. 12 ll. NSyOHi (impf) 12417

TURNER'S Comic Almanac for 1845. New York [and] Philadelphia: Turner & Fisher. 18 ll. PHi. 12418

TURNER'S Improved House-Keeper's Almanac; and Family Recipe Book for 1845. Philadelphia [and] New York: Turner & Fisher. 16 ll. MWA; PHi.   12419

UNCLE Sam's Large Almanac for 1845. Philadelphia: Wm. W. Walker. 18 ll. MWA; InU; MiU-C; NjR (17 ll., ntp); PHi; PPL; PPeSchw; WHi.   12420

The UNITED States Almanac for 1845. Philadelphia: E. H. Butler. [Phillips]   12421

The UNITED States Almanack for 1845. By Charles Frederick Egelmann. Philadelphia: Mentz & Rovoudt. 18 ll. MWA; InU; OClWHi; PDoBHi; PHi (17 ll.)
12422

The UNITED States Almanac; or Complete Ephemeris for 1845. By John Downes [and] John Philips Montgomery. Philadelphia: B. Walker; New York: C. J. Gillis; Cincinnati: H. C. Gillis. 101 ll. MWA; N; NN; NHi; PU; NNA; NjR; PHi; MB; MBAt; NBLiHi; PPL; DeU; NRU; NcD; CtY; CtNlC; OFH; WHi; ViU; VtU; PHC; PPAmP; Drake.   12423

VERBESSERTER Calender auf 1845. Von Carl Friederich Egelman. Reading: J. C. F. Egelman. 15 ll. MWA (two varieties); N; InU (16 ll.); P; NjR; PPG; PPL; CtY; PP; PPeSchw; PR; PRHi.   12424

Der VEREINIGTEN Staaten Calender auf 1845. Philadelphia: Edmund J. Schelly. 15 ll. MWA; PPeSchw.
12425

The WASHINGTON Almanack for 1845. By Seth Smith. Philadelphia: Thomas Cowperthwait & Co.; King & Baird, printers. 18 ll. PHi; PPL (13 ll.)   12426

The WASHINGTON Almanack for 1845. By Seth Smith. Philadelphia: Uriah Hunt; King & Baird, printers. 18 ll. MWA (16 ll.); PPeSchw; Drake (impf)   12427

The WASHINGTON Almanack for 1845. By Seth Smith. Philadelphia: W. A. Leary; King & Baird, printers. 18 ll. NjR.   12428

Pennsylvania - 1845   1181

The WASHINGTON Almanack for 1845. By Seth Smith.
Philadelphia: Isaac Moss; King & Baird, printers. 18
ll. Drake.   12429

WATCHMAN'S Calendar for 1845. Philadelphia: [np]
[In: The City Watchman's Address on the return of
Christmas, 1844.] Broadside. PHi.   12430

AGRICULTURAL Almanac for 1846. Lancaster: John
Bear. 18 ll. MWA; InU; NjR; P; PHi; PYHi.   12431

The ALMANAC and Baptist Register for 1846. Philadelphia: American Baptist Publication Society; King & Baird, printers. 20 ll. MWA; N; Ct; ICU; InU; MB; MeHi; NcD; P; OClWHi; ViRVal; WHi.   12432

The AMERICAN Farmer's Almanac for 1846. Lancaster: S. & C. Beates. [Bausman]   12433

The AMERICAN Farmer's Almanac for 1846. By Edward Hagerty. Lancaster: J. Gish. PLHi (17 ll.)
                                                     12434

AMERICANISCHER Stadt und Land Calender auf 1846.
Philadelphia: Conrad Zentler. 15 ll. MWA; N; CLU;
CtY; InU; DeWint; MnU; NjP; NjR; PDoBHi; PHi;
PPG; PPeSchw; PPL.   12435

BRISTOL'S Free Almanac for 1846. By George R.
Perkins. Philadelphia: J. Harding. 16 ll. Ct; WHi.
                                                     12436

COLUMBIAN Almanac for 1846. Philadelphia: Joseph
McDowell. 18 ll. DLC; KHi (16 ll.); MBAt; NjR.
                                                     12437

CROCKETT'S Almanac for 1846. Philadelphia: Turner
& Fisher. 18 ll. MWA; DLC; CtY; MB; MoSM; NjR
(17 ll.)   12438

De DARKIE'S Comic All-Me-Nig for 1846. By David
Young. [Philadelphia:] Colon & Adriance. 18 ll. MWA.
                                                     12439

De DARKIE'S Comic All-Me-Nig for 1846. By David
Young. Philadelphia [and] New York: Turner & Fisher.
18 ll. MB; MoSHi (12 ll.); WHi.   12440

The DELAWARE & Maryland Farmers' Almanac for 1846. Philadelphia: J. M'Dowell. 18 ll. MWA; NN.
12441

DESILVER'S Pocket Diary and Almanac for 1846. Philadelphia: R. Wilson Desilver. 9 ll. MWA. 12442

The FARMERS' Almanac for 1846. By John Ward. Philadelphia: Thomas Davis. 18 ll. MWA; PHi; [Drake (has Ward's manuscript for this almanac)] 12443

The FARMER'S and Farrier's Almanac for 1846. Philadelphia: John B. Perry. 18 ll. CLU; PPeSchw.
12444

The FARMER'S and Farrier's Almanac for 1846. Philadelphia: John B. Perry; New-York: Nafis & Cornish. 18 ll. MWA; NHi; InU; PHi; PPL; NjR. 12445

The FARMERS and Mechanics Almanack for 1846. By Charles Frederick Egelmann. Philadelphia: Mentz & Rovoudt. 18 ll. MWA; N; NN; NHi (impf); InU; MB; PHi; PP; PPeSchw; NjR; Drake. 12446

FISHER'S Comic Almanac for 1846. Philadelphia [and] New York: Turner & Fisher. 18 ll. MWA; DLC; MB; NBuG. 12447

The FRANKLIN Almanac for 1846. By John Armstrong. Pittsburgh: Johnston and Stockton. 30 ll. MWA; CLU (26 ll.); InU; OClWHi (25 ll.) 12448

The FRANKLIN Almanac for 1846. By John Ward. Philadelphia: Thomas Davis. 18 ll. MWA; DLC; MnU; NjHi (17 ll.); NjR; PHi; PPAmP; PPL; [Drake (has Ward's manuscript for this almanac)] 12449

FRIENDS' Almanac for 1846. By Joseph Foulke. Philadelphia: Elijah Weaver; John Richards, printer. 24 ll. MWA; ICN; InU; Nj; OClWHi; P; PHC. 12450

FRIENDS' Pocket Almanac for 1846. By Joseph Foulke. Philadelphia: T. E. Chapman. 24 ll. MWA; MB. 12451

The GIRARD Almanac for 1846. Philadelphia: Thomas

L. Bonsal. 18 ll. MWA; NjR; PHi. 12452

The GREAT Western Almanac for 1846. Philadelphia: Jos. McDowell. 18 ll. MWA (two varieties); DLC; NN; CLU; CtY; InU; NNC; PHi. 12453

HAGUE'S Christian Almanac for 1846. By Thomas Hague. Philadelphia: Printed for the Author. 26 ll. MWA; InU; PHi; PPL. 12454

JAYNE'S Medical Almanac for 1846. Philadelphia: Dr. D. Jayne; Owen & Fithian, printers. 12 ll. MHi. 12455

JOHNSON'S Pocket Almanac for 1846. Philadelphia: [np] 28 ll. MB; Drake (impf) 12456

LOOMIS' Magazine Almanac for 1846. By Sanford C. Hill. Pittsburgh: Luke Loomis. 26 ll. PPi. 12457

LOOMIS' Pittsburgh Almanac for 1846. By Sanford C. Hill. Pittsburgh: Luke Loomis. 20 ll. MWA (two varieties); OClWHi; OMC. 12458

The MORAL Almanac for 1846. Philadelphia: Tract Association of Friends; Joseph Rakestraw, printer. 18 ll. MWA (two varieties); CtY; InRE; InU; MH; MHi; MoS; NBuG; NjR; OClWHi; PP. 12459

NATIVE Almanac for 1846. Philadelphia: For sale at No. 45 Chestnut Street. 12 ll. MWA; NHi; WHi. 12460

Der NEUE, Amerikanische Landwirthschafts-Calender auf 1846. Von Carl Friederich Egelmann. Reading: Johann Ritter und Comp. 16 ll. MWA; PAtM; PDoBHi; PHi; PR; PRHi; PPL (15 ll.) 12461

NEUER Calender für Bauern und Handwerker auf 1846. Von Carl F. Egelmann. Philadelphia: Mentz und Rovoudt. 18 ll. MWA; N; CLU; CtY; InU; NjP; P; PDoBHi; PHi; PLF; PPeSchw; PYHi; PPL. 12462

NEUER Calender für Nord-Amerika auf 1846. Von Carl F. Egelmann. Philadelphia: Mentz und Rovoudt.

18 ll. OClWHi; PDoBHi; PHi; PPL; PPeSchw. 12463

NEUER Calender für die Vereinigten Staaten auf 1846. Philadelphia: R. Wilson Desilver. 18 ll. MWA; InU; PHi; PDoBHi (16 ll.); PPG; PP; PPCS (15 ll.); PPeSchw; Drake. 12464

NEUER Gemeinnütziger Pennsylvanischer Calender auf 1846. Lancaster: Johann Baer. 18 ll. MWA; N; CtY; InU; PDoBHi; PHi; PLF; PLHi; PPeSchw; Drake.
12465
PENNSYLVANIA Almanac for 1846. Philadelphia: Thomas Davis. 18 ll. MWA; InU; MHi (14 ll.); NjR; PHi. 12466

The PENNSYLVANIA, New Jersey & Delaware Almanac for 1846. Philadelphia: Thomas L. Bonsal. 18 ll. MWA. 12467

PHILADELPHIA Pocket Diary and Almanac for 1846. Philadelphia: R. Wilson Desilver. 9 ll. MWA; CtY.
12468
PHILADELPHIA Pocket Diary and Almanac for 1846. Philadelphia: Henry Longstreth. 8 ll. NN. 12469

PIRATICAL & Tragical Almanac for 1846. Philadelphia: John B. Perry; Z. Eber & Co. 18 ll. PHi.
12470
PIRATICAL & Tragical Almanac for 1846. Philadelphia: John B. Perry; New-York: Nafis & Cornish. 18 ll. MWA; NN; IU; InU; PDoBHi. 12471

POOR Wills Almanac for 1846. Philadelphia: Joseph M'Dowell. 18 ll. MWA; DLC; NHi; CLU; CtY; InU; Nj; NjR; OClWHi; PHi. 12472

POOR Wills Almanac for 1846. Philadelphia: William D. Parrish. 18 ll. PPL. 12473

The PRESBYTERIAN Almanac for 1846. Philadelphia: The Presbyterian Board of Publication. 24 ll. GDC; MB; PPPrHi; PPiU. 12474

TURNER'S Improved Housekeeper's Almanac, and Family Receipt Book for 1846. Lancaster: J. Gish.
PDoBHi (17 ll.) 12475

The UNITED States Almanack for 1846. By Charles Frederick Egelmann. Philadelphia: Mentz & Rovoudt. 18 ll. MWA; CtY; InU; MH; OClWHi; PHi (impf); PYHi (17 ll.); NjR. 12476

The UNITED States Almanac for 1846. By Seth Smith. Philadelphia: Philip Borbeck; King & Baird, printers. 18 ll. IaDaM; PYHi (17 ll.) 12477

The UNITED States Almanac for 1846. By Seth Smith. Philadelphia: R. Wilson Desilver. 18 ll. MWA (impf) 12478

The UNITED States Almanac for 1846. By Seth Smith. Philadelphia: Hogan & Thompson. 18 ll. NjR. 12479

The UNITED States Almanac for 1846. By Seth Smith. Philadelphia: Uriah Hunt & Son. 18 ll. MWA (impf); InU (17 ll.) 12480

The UNITED States Almanac for 1846. By Seth Smith. Philadelphia: Kay & Brother. 18 ll. OClWHi (17 ll.); PPL (17 ll.) 12481

VERBESSERTER Calender auf 1846. Von Carl Friderich Egelman. Reading: J. C. F. Egelman. 15 ll. MWA; CLU; CtY; DeWint; NjR; PDoBHi; PPeSchw; PR. 12482

The WASHINGTON Almanac for 1846. By Seth Smith. Philadelphia: Philip Borbeck. 18 ll. DLC. 12483

The WASHINGTON Almanac for 1846. By Seth Smith. Philadelphia: Thomas Cowperthwait & Co.; King & Baird, printers. 18 ll. CSmH. 12484

The WASHINGTON Almanac for 1846. By Seth Smith. Philadelphia: R. Wilson Desilver. 18 ll. MWA; InU; NRMA. 12485

The WASHINGTON Almanac for 1846. By Seth Smith.
Philadelphia: Hogan & Thompson. 18 ll. MWA; InU;
NcD.   12486

The WASHINGTON Almanac for 1846. By Seth Smith.
Philadelphia: Uriah Hunt & Son; King & Baird,
printers. 18 ll. MWA; PPL (17 ll.); PYHi.   12487

The WASHINGTON Almanac for 1846. By Seth Smith.
Philadelphia: Kay & Brother; King & Baird, printers.
18 ll. MWA; OClWHi; PLF (17 ll.)   12488

The WASHINGTON Almanac for 1846. By Seth Smith.
Philadelphia: Wm. A. Leary. 18 ll. PDoBHi; PHi.
    12489

AGRICULTURAL Almanac for 1847. Lancaster: John
Bear. 18 ll. MWA; InU; MiU-C; NBuG; NjR; P; PHi;
PYHi.   12490

ALLGEMEINER Welt-Calender auf 1847. Philadelphia:
J. B. Lippincott & Co. 18 ll. PPeSchw.   12491

The AMERICAN Farmer's Almanac for 1847. Lancaster: S. & C. Beates. 19 ll. NN.   12492

The AMERICAN Farmer's Almanac for 1847. Philadelphia: Fisher & Brother. 18 ll. InU.   12493

AMERICANISCHER Stadt und Land Calender auf 1847.
Philadelphia: Conrad Zentler. 15 ll. MWA; N; NHi
(impf); CLU; CtY; NjP; NjR; P; PDoBHi; PHi; PPG;
PPeSchw; PYHi; InU.   12494

The BAPTIST Almanac and Annual Register for 1847.
Thomas S. Malcom, editor. Philadelphia: American
Baptist Publication Society. 20 ll. MWA; Ct (18 ll.);
ICU; InU; MB; MoSM; OClWHi; P; WHi.   12495

BROTHER Jonathan's Almanac for 1847. By Seth
Smith. Philadelphia: C. G. Sower. 18 ll. MWA; DLC;
CtY; DeWint; InU (impf); PDoBHi (17 ll.); PHi (16
ll.); TxU.   12496

COLUMBIAN Almanac for 1847. Philadelphia: Joseph McDowell. 18 ll. MWA; DLC; NHi; CtY; InU; OClWHi; PHi; PPeSchw; NjR.   12497

DAVY Crockett's Almanac for 1847. Philadelphia: R. Magee. 18 ll. MWA (17 ll.); PDoBHi (14 ll.)   12498

DAVY Crockett's Almanac for 1847. Philadelphia: Turner & Fisher. 18 ll. DLC; MoSM.   12499

The FARMERS' Almanac for 1847. By John Ward. Philadelphia: Thomas Davis. 18 ll. MWA; PHi; TKL; [Drake (has Ward's manuscript for this almanac)]
   12500

The FARMER'S and Farrier's Almanac for 1847. Philadelphia: John B. Perry. 18 ll. MWA; CLU; InU; MnU; PDoBHi.   12501

The FARMER'S and Farrier's Almanac for 1847. Philadelphia: John B. Perry; New-York: Nafis & Cornish. 18 ll. PHi; PPL; NjR; Drake.   12502

The FARMERS and Mechanics Almanack for 1847. By Charles Frederick Egelmann. Philadelphia: Mentz & Rovoudt. 18 ll. MWA; N; NN; InU; KHi (17 ll.); PHi; PPG; PPL (17 ll.); WHi; NjR.   12503

FISHER'S Comic Almanac for 1847. Philadelphia: R. Magee. 18 ll. MWA; DLC.   12504

FISHER'S Comic Almanac for 1847. Philadelphia [and] New York: Turner & Fisher. 18 ll. InU; MBAt; MWiW; NSyOHi; PHi; WHi.   12505

The FRANKLIN Almanac for 1847. By John Armstrong. Pittsburgh: Johnston & Stockton. 30 ll. OMC; PPi.
   12506

The FRANKLIN Almanac for 1847. By John Ward. Philadelphia: Thomas Davis. 18 ll. MWA; DLC; PHi; PYHi; [Drake (has Ward's manuscript for this almanac)]   12507

FRIENDS' Almanac for 1847. By Joseph Foulke, Jun'r.

Philadelphia: Elijah Weaver; John Richards, printer.
24 ll. MWA; ICN; InU; Nj; OClWHi; PHC; PP; WHi.
12508

FRIENDS' Pocket Almanac for 1847. By Joseph Foulke.
Philadelphia: T. E. Chapman. 24 ll. MWA. 12509

The GENERAL Taylor Almanac for 1847. By Seth
Smith. Philadelphia: Griffith & Simon. 18 ll. MnU
(17 ll.); WHi. 12510

The GENERAL Taylor, or "Rough and Ready!" Almanac for 1847. By Seth Smith. Philadelphia: Griffith
and Simon; King & Baird, printers. 18 ll. MWA; NjR.
12511

GENERAL Taylor's Old Rough and Ready Almanac for
1847. By Seth Smith. Lancaster: S. & C. Beates.
18 ll. PLHi (16 ll.) 12512

GENERAL Taylor's Old Rough and Ready Almanac for
1847. Philadelphia [and] New York: Turner & Fisher.
18 ll. InU; PHi. 12513

GENERAL Taylor's Rough and Ready Almanac for 1847.
Philadelphia: Turner & Fisher. 18 ll. CU-B; InU.
12514

GIRARD Amanac [sic] for 1847. Philadelphia: Thomas
L. Bonsal. 18 ll. MWA; PHi; WHi. 12515

The GREAT Western Almanac for 1847. Philadelphia:
Jos. McDowell. 18 ll. MWA (two varieties); DLC; NN;
NHi; NNU-H; InU; PDoBHi; PHi; PPT; PYHi. 12516

HUNT'S Family Almanac for 1847. Philadelphia: Uriah
Hunt & Son. 18 ll. MWA; InU; PHi; PPL; PYHi;
NjR. 12517

HUNT'S North American Almanac for 1847. Philadelphia: Uriah Hunt & Son. 18 ll. MWA; CtY; InU;
MiU-C; OC; ViW. 12518

JAYNE'S Medical Almanac, and Guide to Health for
1847. Philadelphia: Dr. D. Jayne; Owen & Fithian,
printers. 18 ll. NcD; NjR. 12519

JAYNE'S Medical Almanac, and Guide to Health for 1847. By Dr. D. Jayne. Philadelphia: Owen & Fithian. 16 ll. De-Ar. 12520

JOHNSON'S Pocket Almanac for 1847. Philadelphia: Published at 14 Vaux court 10th below Pine St. 28 ll. MWA; PHi; Drake. 12521

The KEYSTONE Almanac for 1847. By Seth Smith. Philadelphia: Griffith & Simon; King & Baird, printers. 18 ll. MWA; NjR; PLF. 12522

LANDRETH'S Rural Register and Almanac for 1847. By D. Landreth. [Philadelphia: M'Calla & Stavely.] 74 ll. NjR. 12523

LOOMIS' Pittsburgh Almanac for 1847. By Sanford C. Hill. Pittsburgh: Luke Loomis. 18 ll. MWA; CLU; NjR; OC; PPi. 12524

-- Issue with 24 ll. OMC. 12525

The MORAL Almanac for 1847. Philadelphia: Tract Association of Friends; Joseph Rakestraw, printer. 18 ll. MWA; N; NHi; CLU; CtY; InRE; InU; MH; MHi; MoS; NBuG; NjR; PP; WHi. 12526

Der NEUE, AMERIKANISCHE Landwirthschafts-Calender auf 1847. Von Carl Friederich Egelmann. Reading: Johann Ritter und Comp. 16 ll. MWA (15 ll.); InU; NjP; PDoBHi; PHi; PPCS; PPeSchw; PR; PRHi; Drake (14 ll.) 12527

NEUER Calender für Bauern und Handwerker auf 1847. Von Carl F. Egelmann. Philadelphia: Mentz und Rovoudt. 18 ll. MWA; N; NN; CtY; InU; NjP; NjR; P; PDoBHi; PHi; PP; PPG; PPeSchw; Drake. 12528

NEUER Calender für Nord-Amerika auf 1847. Von Carl F. Egelmann. Philadelphia: Mentz und Rovoudt. 18 ll. MWA; InU; P; PDoBHi; PHi; PPL. 12529

NEUER Calender für die Vereinigten Staaten auf 1847.

Philadelphia: R. Wilson Desilver. 18 ll. MWA; InU
(16 ll.); OC; OClWHi; PDoBHi.   12530

NEUER Calender für die Vereinigten Staaten auf 1847.
Philadelphia: Grigg und Elliot. 18 ll. MWA.   12531

NEUER Gemeinnütziger Pennsylvanischer Calender auf
1847. Lancaster: Johann Baer. 18 ll. MWA; N; CtY;
DeWint; InU; NjP; P; PDoBHi; PHi; PLF; PLHi.
12532

The NORTH American Almanac for 1847. Philadelphia:
Robinson, Collins, & Co. 18 ll. NHi; OMC; PHi.
12533

PENNSYLVANIA Almanac for 1847.   Philadelphia:
Thomas Davis. 18 ll. NNC; PHi; PPL (17 ll.) 12534

PENNSYLVANIA Almanac for 1847. By John Ward.
Philadelphia: G. W. Mentz. 18 ll. PPeSchw.   12535

The PENNSYLVANIA & New-Jersey Almanac for 1847.
Philadelphia: Thomas L. Bonsal. 18 ll. PHi.   12536

PHILADELPHIA Pocket Diary and Almanac for 1847.
Philadelphia: R. Wilson Desilver. 68 ll. DLC. 12537

PHILADELPHIA Pocket Diary and Almanac for 1847.
Philadelphia: Henry Longstreth. 8 ll. MWA; NN; InU.
12538
PIRATICAL & Tragical Almanac for 1847. Philadelphia: John B. Perry. 18 ll. MWA; NjR (14 ll.) 12539

PIRATICAL & Tragical Almanac for 1847. Philadelphia: John B. Perry; New-York: Nafis & Cornish. 18
ll. PHi.   12540

POOR Wills Almanac for 1847. Philadelphia: Joseph
M'Dowell. 18 ll. MWA; DLC; N; NN; CLU; CtY; InU;
MB; NjR; OClWHi; PHi; WHi.   12541

POOR Wills Almanac for 1847. Philadelphia: William
D. Parrish. 18 ll. MWA; PP; Drake.   12542

The PRESBYTERIAN Almanac for 1847. Philadelphia:

Presbyterian Board of Publication. 27 ll. MB; NcMHi; PPPrHi. 12543

The RURAL Register and Almanac for 1847. Philadelphia: Lea & Blanchard; Stavely & McCalla, printers. 71 ll. NN. 12544

The TEACHER'S Almanac for 1847. Philadelphia: E. C. & J. Biddle. 18 ll. MWA; N; CtY; InU. 12545

TURNER'S Comic Almanac for 1847. Philadelphia [and] New York: Turner & Fisher. 18 ll. DLC; N; NN; MB; MWiW; WHi. 12546

TURNER'S Improved House-Keeper's Almanac and Family Receipt Book for 1847. Philadelphia: Richard Magee. 18 ll. MWA; DLC; PHi (impf) 12547

TURNER'S Improved House-Keeper's Almanac, and Family Receipt Book for 1847. New York and Philadelphia: Turner & Fisher. 18 ll. PDoBHi; PHi. 12548

UNCLE Sam's Almanac for 1847. By Seth Smith. Philadelphia: Griffith & Simon; King & Baird, printers. 18 ll. CtY; PPL (16 ll.) 12549

UNCLE Sam's Large Almanac for 1847. Philadelphia: Wm. W. Walker. 18 ll. MWA; MiU-C; NNU-H; PHi; PP; PPL. 12550

The UNITED States Almanack for 1847. By Charles Frederick Egelmann. Philadelphia: Mentz & Rovoudt. 18 ll. MWA; CtY; InU; OClWHi; PHi. 12551

The UNITED States Almanac for 1847. By Seth Smith. Philadelphia: Philip Borbeck. 18 ll. IaDaM. 12552

The UNITED States Almanac for 1847. By Seth Smith. Philadelphia: R. Wilson Desilver; King & Baird, printers. 18 ll. DLC; PHi; PLF. 12553

UNIVERSALIST Companion, with an Almanac and Register for 1847. A. B. Grosh, editor. Philadelphia:

Pennsylvania - 1847

John H. Gihon. 36 ll. CLU; InU; N.   12554

VERBESSERTER Calender auf 1847. Von Carl Friderich Egelmann. Reading: J. C. F. Egelmann. 16 ll. MWA; PPL; PPeSchw; PRHi.   12555

The WASHINGTON Almanac for 1847. By Seth Smith. Philadelphia: Philip Borbeck. 18 ll. MWA; DLC; CLU.   12556

The WASHINGTON Almanac for 1847. By Seth Smith. Philadelphia: R. Wilson Desilver; King & Baird, printers. 18 ll. MiU-C; NRMA; NjR; PHi; PPL; ViU.   12557

The WASHINGTON Almanac for 1847. By Seth Smith. Philadelphia: Uriah Hunt. [Phillips]   12558

WATCHMAN'S Calendar for 1847. [np, np] [In: The City Watchman's Address on the return of Christmas, 1846.] Broadside. PHi.   12559

AGRICULTURAL Almanac for 1848. Lancaster: John Bear. 18 ll. MWA; InU; NjR; P; PHi; PLHi.   12560

ALMANAC for 1848. Philadelphia: King & Baird. [In: Watchman's Address, on the return of Christmas Day, December 25, 1847.] Broadside. PHi.   12561

AMERICAN Farmers' Almanac for 1848. Philadelphia: Grigg, Elliot & Co. 18 ll. LNHT.   12562

The AMERICAN Farmer's Almanac for 1848. New York and Philadelphia: Turner & Fisher. 18 ll. MWA; OClWHi; PHi; PYHi.   12563

The AMERICAN Medical Almanac for 1848. Philadelphia: Lindsay & Blakiston. 112 ll. NHi; OClWHi.   12564

AMERICANISCHER Stadt und Land Calender auf 1848. Philadelphia: Conrad Zentler. 15 ll. MWA; N; NN; NHi (impf); CLU; CtY; InU; NjP; NjR; P; PDoBHi; PHi; PPG; PPeSchw; PYHi; RPB; PPL.   12565

B. A. FAHNSTOCK & Co.'s Free Almanac for 1848.

Pittsburgh: B. A. Fahnstock & Co.; M'Millen & Shryock, printers. 18 ll. OClWHi. 12566

The BAPTIST Almanac and Annual Register for 1848. Philadelphia: American Baptist Publication Society. 20 ll. MWA (impf); N; ABH; Ct (18 ll.); ICU; InU; MB; OClWHi; WHi. 12567

BROTHER Jonathan's Almanac for 1848. Philadelphia: C. G. Sower. 18 ll. MWA; DLC; InU (impf); PHi; PPL; PPeSchw; NjR (16 ll.) 12568

COLUMBIAN Almanac for 1848. Philadelphia: Joseph McDowell. 18 ll. MWA; CLU; InU; MnU; PDoBHi; PHi; NjR (16 ll.) 12569

CROCKETT'S Almanac for 1848. Philadelphia: Philip Borbeck. 18 ll. MoSM. 12570

CROCKETT'S Almanac for 1848. Philadelphia: R. Magee. 18 ll. P; PDoBHi (impf) 12571

CROCKETT'S Almanac for 1848. Philadelphia: Turner & Fisher. 18 ll. MWA. 12572

DAILY Pocket Remembrancer for 1848. Philadelphia: Isaac M. Moss. 17 ll. MWA (has additional blank leaves) 12573

The FARMER'S and Farrier's Almanac for 1848. Philadelphia: John B. Perry; New-York: Nafis & Cornish. 18 ll. MWA; N; CLU; CtY; InU; NjR (17 ll.); OC; OClWHi; PHi; ScU-S; PPL. 12574

The FARMERS and Mechanics Almanack for 1848. By Charles Frederick Egelmann. Philadelphia: Mentz & Rovoudt. 18 ll. MWA; N; CtY; IaDaM; InU; KHi; P; PHi; PP; PPeSchw; PYHi. 12575

-- Cover imprint: Loomis & Peck. 18 ll. MWA; NjR. 12576

-- Cover imprint: Isaac M. Moss. 18 ll. PPL. 12577

FISHER'S Comic Almanac for 1848. Philadelphia: Turner & Fisher. 20 ll. MWA; InU. 12578

The FRANKLIN Almanac for 1848. By John Armstrong. Pittsburgh: Johnston and Stockton. 18 ll. MWA; CLU; OClWHi. 12579

-- Issue with added "Magazine." 30 ll. MWA; OClWHi; OMC. 12580

The FRANKLIN Almanac for 1848. By John Ward. Philadelphia: Thomas Davis. 18 ll. DLC; PHi; PPL (17 ll.); [NjR (has Ward's manuscript for this almanac)] 12581

FRIENDS' Almanac for 1848. By Joseph Foulke. Philadelphia: Elijah Weaver; J. Richard, printer. 24 ll. MWA; ICN; InU; OClWHi; PHC; PPL. 12582

FRIENDS' Pocket Almanac for 1848. By Joseph Foulke. Philadelphia: T. E. Chapman. 24 ll. MWA. 12583

The GENERAL Scott Almanac for 1848. By Charles F. Egelmann. Philadelphia: Griffith & Simon; King & Baird, printers. 16 ll. Drake. 12584

The GENERAL Taylor Almanac for 1848. By Charles F. Egelmann. Philadelphia: Griffith & Simon; King & Baird, printers. 18 ll. MWA; DeU (17 ll.) 12585

The GENERAL Taylor or, "Rough and Ready" Almanac for 1848. Philadelphia: Griffith & Simon; King & Baird, printers. 18 ll. PLF (16 ll.); PPL. 12586

GENERAL Taylor's Rough and Ready Almanac for 1848. Lancaster: S. Beates. 18 ll. PLHi. 12587

GEN. TAYLOR'S Rough and Ready Almanac for 1848. Philadelphia: Grigg, Elliot & Co. 18 ll. MWA. 12588

GEN. TAYLOR'S Rough and Ready Almanac for 1848. Philadelphia: R. Magee. 18 ll. PHi. 12589

GEN. TAYLOR'S Rough and Ready Almanac for 1848.
Philadelphia: Turner & Fisher. 18 ll. MWA; OClWHi;
TxSa. 12590

GEN. TAYLOR'S Rough and Ready Almanac for 1848.
Philadelphia [and] New York: Turner & Fisher. 18 ll.
PHi. 12591

GEN. TAYLOR'S Rough and Ready Almanac for 1848.
[Philadelphia: Turner & Fisher?] [12 mo; same text
and cuts as in issues of ''Gen. Zachary Taylor's Old
Rough & Ready'' almanac which are small 4to] 18 ll.
NN (17 ll., imprint torn off) 12592

GENERAL Taylor's Rough and Ready Almanac for 1848.
Pittsburgh: C. Yeager. 18 ll. PPiHi (17 ll.) 12593

GEN. ZACHARY Taylor's Old Rough & Ready Almanac
for 1848. Philadelphia: Grigg, Elliot, & Co. 18 ll.
NN. 12594

GEN. ZACHARY Taylor's Old Rough & Ready Almanac
for 1848. Philadelphia: R. Magee. 18 ll. MWA; MnU.
12595

GEN. ZACHARY Taylor's Old Rough & Ready Almanac
for 1848. Philadelphia: Turner & Fisher. 18 ll. CLU;
NjR (16 ll.) 12596

GIRARD Almanac for 1848. Philadelphia: Thomas L.
Bonsal. 18 ll. PHi. 12597

The GREAT Western Almanac for 1848. Philadelphia:
Jos. McDowell. 18 ll. MWA; DLC; InU; NjP (15 ll.,
ntp); NjR; PHi; PLF; PPL (17 ll.) 12598

HUNT'S Family Almanac for 1848. Philadelphia: Uriah
Hunt & Son. 18 ll. MWA; CtY; InU; Nj; PHi; PLF.
12599

JAYNE'S Medical Almanac, and Guide to Health for
1848. Philadelphia: Dr. D. Jayne; Stavely & McCalla,
printers. 18 ll. MWA; N; NHi (16 ll.); MHi; MiD-B;
NjR; OC (16 ll.); VtHi. 12600

JOHNSON'S Pocket Almanac for 1848. Philadelphia: Published at 14 Vaux Court below Pine St. 18 ll. MWA (two varieties); PHi. 12601

LANDRETH'S Rural Register and Almanac for 1848. Philadelphia: Grigg, Elliot & Co. 60 ll. MWA; MBAt (48 ll., ntp) 12602

LANDRETH'S Rural Register and Almanac for 1848. Philadelphia: Lea & Blanchard, and Grigg, Elliot & Co.; Stavely & McCalla, printers. 75 ll. MWA; ICU; InU; NcD (54 ll.); OClWHi; WHi. 12603

LANDRETH'S Rural Register and Almanac for 1848. By David Landreth. Philadelphia: David Landreth & Son. 46 ll. OMC. 12604

LOOMIS' Pittsburgh Almanac for 1848. By Sanford C. Hill. Pittsburgh: Luke Loomis. 24 ll. MWA; CLU; InU; OClWHi; OHi (18 ll.); PPi. 12605

-- Issue with 30 ll. OMC. 12606

The MORAL Almanac for 1848. Philadelphia: Tract Association of Friends; Joseph Rakestraw, printer. 18 ll. MWA; N; NHi (16 ll.); CtY; InU; InRE; MoS; NBuG; NjR; OClWHi; PP; Wv-Ar (17 ll.) 12607

The NATIONAL Medical Almanac for 1848. By L. Thompson. Philadelphia: Lindsay & Blakiston. 16 ll. IU; MH. 12608

Der NEUE, Amerikanische Landwirthschafts-Calender auf 1848. Von Carl Friederich Egelmann. Reading: Johann Ritter und Comp. 16 ll. MWA; N; CLU; InU; NjP; P; PDoBHi; PHi; PPeSchw; PR; PRHi; WHi; NN; PPL; Drake. 12609

NEUER Calender für Bauern und Handwerker auf 1848. Von Carl F. Egelmann. Philadelphia: Mentz und Rovoudt. 18 ll. MWA (two varieties); NN (impf); CLU; P; CtY; InU; NjR; OClWHi; PDoBHi; PPeSchw; PPT; NjP. 12610

NEUER Calender für Nord-Amerika auf 1848. Von
Carl F. Egelmann. Philadelphia: Mentz und Rovoudt.
18 ll. MWA; DLC; InU; NHi; PAtM; PHi; PLF; PPG;
PPeSchw; PPL (16 ll.); Drake. 12611

NEUER Calender für die Vereinigten Staaten auf 1848.
Philadelphia: R. Wilson Desilver. 18 ll. MWA; DLC
(17 ll.); PHi; PPCS (17 ll.) 12612

NEUER Calender für die Vereinigten Staaten auf 1848.
Philadelphia: Grigg und Elliot. MWA (missing from
shelf) 12613

NEUER Gemeinnütziger Pennsylvanischer Calender auf
1848. Lancaster: Johann Baer. 18 ll. MWA; N;
CtY; InU (16 ll.); MH; NjP; P; PDoBHi; PLF; PLHi;
PPeSchw. 12614

PENNSYLVANIA Almanac for 1848. By John Ward.
Philadelphia: Thomas Davis. 18 ll. PDoBHi; PPL;
[NjR (has Ward's manuscript for this almanac)] 12615

The PENNSYLVANIA & New Jersey Almanac for 1848.
Philadelphia: Thomas L. Bonsal. 18 ll. MWA; InU;
NjR; PHi. 12616

The PENNSYLVANIA, New Jersey & Delaware Almanac
for 1848. Philadelphia: John B. Perry. 18 ll. MWA;
CtY; MiU-C; NjR. 12617

The PEOPLE'S Almanac for 1848. Philadelphia: Dyott.
[Phillips] 12618

The PHILADELPHIA Almanac and General Business Directory for 1848. By John Downes. Philadelphia:
Charles J. Gillis; H. L. Lipman; Stereotyped by L.
Johnson & Co. 95 ll. N; NHi; CtY; MB; PHi; PPL;
PU. 12619

PHILADELPHIA Comic Almanac for 1848. Philadelphia:
John Downes. [Phillips] 12620

PHILADELPHIA Pocket Diary and Almanac for 1848.

Philadelphia: Henry Longstreth. 8 ll. NN. 12621

PIRATICAL & Tragical Almanac for 1848. Philadelphia: John B. Perry. 18 ll. MWA; MiU-C. 12622

POOR Wills Almanac for 1848. Philadelphia: Joseph M'Dowell. 18 ll. MWA; DLC; CtY; InU; MB; PHi; PP; WHi; NjR. 12623

POOR Wills Almanac for 1848. Philadelphia: Joseph Rakestraw. 18 ll. PPL. 12624

The PRESBYTERIAN Almanac for 1848. Philadelphia: Presbyterian Board of Publication. 24 ll. MB; NcMHi; O (25 ll.); KyU; PPL; PPPrHi; ViU. 12625

ROUGH and Ready Almanac for 1848. Philadelphia: R. Wilson Desilver. 18 ll. ICHi; InU (17 ll.); MBAt; PHi. 12626

The SUNDAY-SCHOOL Teachers' Pocket Almanack for 1848. Philadelphia: The American Sunday-School Union. 8 ll. MWA; PP. 12627

TURNER und Fischer's Deutscher Bilder Kalender auf 1848. Philadelphia: Turner und Fischer. 18 ll. MWA; PPG. 12628

TURNER und Fischer's Deutscher Bilder Kalender auf 1848. Philadelphia und New-York: Turner und Fischer. 18 ll. NjR; PPL. 12629

TURNER und Fischer's Deutscher Bilder Kalender auf 1848. Philadelphia: Turner und Fischer; Cincinnati: John G. Hanzsche. 18 ll. OC; Drake (17 ll.) 12630

TURNER'S Comic Almanac for 1848. Philadelphia [and] New York: Turner & Fisher. 18 ll. MWA; MB; MWiW. 12631

TURNER'S Improved House-Keeper's Almanac, and Family Receipt Book for 1848. Philadelphia: Philip Borbeck. 18 ll. PHi. 12632

Pennsylvania - 1848

TURNER'S Improved House-Keeper's Almanac, and Family Receipt Book for 1848. Philadelphia: Grigg, Elliot, & Co. 18 ll. NHi. 12633

TURNER'S Improved House-Keeper's Almanac, and Family Receipt Book for 1848. Philadelphia: R. Magee. 18 ll. NN (impf) 12634

TURNER'S Improved House-Keeper's Almanac, and Family Receipt Book for 1848. Pittsburgh: G. W. Kuhn. 18 ll. PPi. 12635

The UNITED States Almanac for 1848. Philadelphia: R. Wilson Desilver. 18 ll. MWA; DLC; CLU; InU; MBAt; PDoBHi; PPT. 12636

The UNITED States Almanack for 1848. By Charles Frederick Egelmann. Philadelphia: Mentz & Rovoudt. 18 ll. MWA; InU; KHi (17 ll.); PHi; PPG; T; NjR.
12637

The UNIVERSALIST Companion for 1848. A. B. Grosh, editor. Philadelphia: John H. Gihon. 38 ll. N; InU; MiD-B; OClWHi; WHi. 12638

WASHINGTON Almanac for 1848. Philadelphia: R. Wilson Desilver. 18 ll. MWA (two varieties); N; NN; CtY; InU; MBAt; PHi; PPG; PYHi. 12639

The WASHINGTON Almanack for 1848. Philadelphia: Uriah Hunt. [Phillips] 12640

AGRICULTURAL Almanac for 1849. Lancaster: John Bear. 18 ll. MWA; NHi; InU; NjR; PHi; PLHi. 12641

The AMERICAN Farmer's Almanac for 1849. Lancaster: Judd & Murray. 18 ll. MWA; Drake. 12642

The AMERICAN Farmer's Almanac for 1849. Philadelphia: Grigg, Elliot & Co. 18 ll. MWA (impf) 12643

The AMERICAN Farmer's Almanac for 1849. Whitehall: A. J. Warfield. 18 ll. PYHi. 12644

AMERICANISCHER Stadt und Land Calender auf 1849.
Philadelphia: Conrad Zentler. 15 ll. MWA; N; CLU;
CtY; InU; NjP; NjR; P; PDoBHi; PHi; PPCS (14 ll.);
PPG; PPL; PPeSchw; PYHi; Drake.   12645

B. A. FAHNESTOCK & Co.'s Free Almanac for 1849.
Pittsburgh: B. A. Fahnestock & Co.; M'Millin and
Shryock, printers. 18 ll. MWA; KHi (13 ll.); MiD-B.
    12646

The BAPTIST Almanac and Annual Register for 1849.
Thomas S. Malcom, editor. Philadelphia: American
Baptist Publication Society. 20 ll. Ct (18 ll.); ICU;
InU; MB; MnU; OClWHi; WHi.   12647

The BAPTIST Almanac and Annual Register for 1849.
Thomas S. Malcom, editor. Philadelphia: American
Baptist Publication Society. (Second Edition) 20 ll.
MWA; WHi.   12648

BROTHER Jonathan's Almanac for 1849. Philadelphia:
C. G. Sower. 18 ll. MWA; MBAt; PHi (16 ll.); PPL;
PYHi.   12649

The CASS and Butler Almanac for 1849. Philadelphia:
John B. Perry. 18 ll. MWA; DLC; N; InU; PHi.
    12650

COLUMBIAN Almanac for 1849. Philadelphia: Joseph
McDowell. 18 ll. MWA; DLC; InU; NjR; PHi; PPL.
    12651

CROCKETT Almanac for 1849. Philadelphia: Turner
and Fisher. 18 ll. DLC; CtY; PDoBHi (impf); WHi.
    12652

DESILVER'S Pocket Diary and Almanac for 1849.
Philadelphia: R. Wilson Desilver. 9 ll. MWA (also
has blank diary leaves)   12653

DR. JAYNE'S Arzenei-Kalender und Gesundheits-Wegweiser für 1849. Philadelphia: Dr. D. Jayne. 24 ll.
PPeSchw.   12654

DR. SWAYNE'S Guide to Health [for 1849]. Philadelphia: Dr. Swayne's Principal Office. 16 ll. PPeSchw.
    12655

Pennsylvania - 1849

The FARMERS Almanac for 1849. Philadelphia: R.
Wilson Desilver. 18 ll. MWA. 12656

The FARMER'S and Farrier's Almanac for 1849.
Philadelphia: John B. Perry; New-York: Nafis & Cornish. 18 ll. MWA; CLU; InU; NjR. 12657

FARMERS & Mechanics Almanack for 1849. By Charles
F. Eagelmann [sic]. Philadelphia: William G. Mentz.
18 ll. IaDaM (17 ll.) 12658

The FARMERS and Mechanics Almanack for 1849. By
Charles Frederick Egelmann. Philadelphia: Mentz &
Rovoudt. 18 ll. MWA; N; NHi; InU; PLF; PPG;
PPL; PYHi. 12659

-- Cover imprint: Philadelphia: Isaac M. Moss and
Brother. 18 ll. PHi. 12660

FISHER'S Comic Almanac for 1849. Philadelphia:
Moss & Brother. 18 ll. PHi. 12661

FISHER'S Comic Almanac for 1849. Philadelphia:
Turner & Fisher. 18 ll. MWA (impf) 12662

The FRANKLIN Almanac for 1849. By John Ward.
Philadelphia: Thomas Davis. 18 ll. DLC; PHi (also, has Ward's manuscript for this almanac); PLF. 12663

The FRANKLIN Family Almanac for 1849. By Sanford
C. Hill. Pittsburgh: Johnston & Stockton. 24 ll. OC;
OMC. 12664

FRIENDS' Almanac for 1849. By Joseph Foulke, Jun'r.
Philadelphia: Elijah Weaver. 24 ll. MWA; ICN; InU;
OClWHi; PHC; WHi. 12665

FRIENDS' Pocket Almanac for 1849. By Joseph Foulke,
Jr. Philadelphia: T. E. Chapman. 24 ll. MWA. 12666

The GEN. TAYLOR Almanac or Rough and Ready Text
Book for 1849. Philadelphia: King and Baird. 16 ll.
MWA; NN; PHi; Drake. 12667

GENERAL Taylor's Calender für 1849. Philadelphia: King und Baird. 16 ll. CtY. 12668

GIRARD Almanac for 1849. Philadelphia: Thos. L. Bonsal. 18 ll. MWA; CtY. 12669

The GREAT Western Almanac for 1849. Philadelphia: Jos. McDowell. 18 ll. MWA; NHi; CLU; InU; FSaHi; NjP; PHi. 12670

HOUSEKEEPERS' Almanac and Family Receipt Book for 1849. Philadelphia: Turner & Fisher. 18 ll. LNHT. 12671

Der HUNDERTJAHRIGE Calender für 1800-1899. Harrisburg: Jonath. Heilman. 1849. 53 ll. MWA. 12672

HUNTS' Family Almanac for 1849. Philadelphia: Uriah Hunt & Son. 18 ll. MWA; N; MnU; PPL. 12673

-- Issue with 36 ll. PDoBHi. 12674

JAYNE'S Medical Almanac, and Guide to Health for 1849. Philadelphia: Dr. D. Jayne; Stavely & McCalla, printers. 22 ll. MWA (two varieties); N; Ct (20 ll.); F; MnU; NBLiHi; NSyOHi; OClWHi; PHi; PPL. 12675

JOHNSON'S Pocket Almanac for 1849. Philadelphia: 14 Vaux Court. 18 ll. MWA. 12676

LONGSTRETH'S Pocket Diary and Almanac for 1849. Philadelphia: Henry Longstreth. 9 ll. MWA. 12677

LOOMIS' Magazine Almanac for 1849. By Sanford C. Hill. Pittsburgh: Luke Loomis. 30 ll. InU; OClWHi; PPiHi. 12678

LOOMIS' Pittsburgh Almanac for 1849. By Sanford C. Hill. Pittsburgh: Luke Loomis. 18 ll. MWA; InU; OC; OMC; PPi. 12679

The MORAL Almanac for 1849. Philadelphia: Tract Association of Friends; Joseph Rakestraw, printer. 18 ll. MWA; N; CtY; InRE; InU; MoS; NBuG; NjR;

OClWHi; PP; WHi; Wv-Ar. 12680

Der NEUE, Amerikanische Landwirthschafts-Calender auf 1849. Von Carl Friederich Egelmann. Reading: Johann Ritter und Comp. 16 ll. MWA; NN; CLU; InU; NjP; P; PDoBHi; PHi; PPG; PPeSchw; PPL; PR; PRHi. 12681

NEUER Calender für Nord-Amerika auf 1849. Von Carl F. Egelmann. Philadelphia: Mentz und Rovoudt. 18 ll. MWA; DLC; NHi; DeWint; InU; NjR; OClWHi; PDoBHi; PHi; PP; PPCS; PPAmP; PPG. 12682

NEUER Calender für die Vereinigten Staaten auf 1849. Philadelphia: R. Wilson Desilver. 16 ll. PPeSchw.
12683

NEUER Gemeinnütziger Pennsylvanischer Calender auf 1849. Lancaster: Johann Baer. 18 ll. MWA; N; NN (17 ll.); CtY; P; PLF; PLHi; Drake. 12684

NEUER Kalender für Bauern und Handwerker auf 1849. Von Carl F. Egelmann. Philadelphia: Mentz and Rovoudt. 18 ll. MWA; CLU; CtY; InU; MnU; NjP; NjR; P; PAnL; PDoBHi; PPCS (14 ll.); PPT; PPeSchw. 12685

The OLD Rough and Ready Almanac for 1849. Philadelphia: Philip Borbeck. 16 ll. Drake. 12686

The OLD Rough and Ready Almanac for 1849. Philadelphia: R. Magee. 18 ll. MWA 12687

The OLD Rough and Ready Almanac for 1849. Philadelphia [and] New York: Turner & Fisher. [12x19 cm] 18 ll. MWA; NHi (17 ll.); AzTP (17 ll.); CLU; Ct (13 ll.); CtY; InU; NjHi; OClWHi; PHi; NjR.
12687a
-- Varying contents. [16x20 cm] 18 ll. PHi. 12688

The OLD Rough & Ready Almanac for 1849. Pittsburgh: George W. Kuhn. 18 ll. PPiHi. 12689

The OLD Rough and Ready Almanac for 1849. Whitehall: A. J. Warfield. 18 ll. PYHi. 12690

PENNSYLVANIA Almanac for 1849. Philadelphia:

Thomas Davis. 18 ll. PHi.   12691

PENNSYLVANIA and New Jersey Almanac for 1849.
Philadelphia: Thos. L. Bonsal. 18 ll. PPL; NjR.
12692

The PENNSYLVANIA, New-Jersey & Delaware Almanac for 1849. Philadelphia: John B. Perry. 18 ll. MWA; CtY; InU; Nj; NjR; PHi; Drake.   12693

The PENNSYLVANIAN Almanac for 1849. Philadelphia: John H. Simon. 18 ll. MWA; PDoBHi; NjR (15 ll.)
12694

Der PHILADELPHIA Kalender auf 1849. Philadelphia: Martin Kuhns. OC (17 ll.)   12695

POOR Wills Almanac for 1849. Philadelphia: Joseph M'Dowell. 18 ll. MWA; DLC; InU; MB; MnU; PHi; WHi; NjR.   12696

The PRESBYTERIAN Almanac for 1849. By David Young. Philadelphia: Presbyterian Board of Publication. 26 ll. N; KyU; MB; O; OC; PPL; PPPrHi; WHi.   12697

The ROUGH and Ready Almanac for 1849. Philadelphia: R. Wilson Desilver; King & Baird, printers. 18 ll. NN.   12698

SELLER'S United States Almanac for 1849. Pittsburgh: R. E. Sellers. 12 ll. OClWHi.   12699

The SUNDAY School Pocket Almanac for 1849. Philadelphia: American Sunday-School Union. 16 ll. MWA; DLC; CLU.   12700

TURNER und Fischer's Deutscher Bilder Kalender auf 1849. Philadelphia [and] Neu-York: Turner und Fischer. 18 ll. MWA; NHi.   12701

TURNER und Fischer's Deutscher Bilder Kalender auf 1849. Philadelphia: A. J. Warfield. 18 ll. MWA.
12702

TURNER'S Comic Almanac for 1849. Philadelphia:

Turner & Fisher. 18 ll. MWA. 12703

TURNER'S Comic Almanack for 1849. Philadelphia and New York: Turner & Fisher. 18 ll. MBAt (17 ll.); NBuG. 12704

TURNER'S Improved House-Keeper's Almanac, and Family Receipt Book for 1849. Lancaster: Judd and Murray. 18 ll. PLHi. 12705

TURNER'S Improved House-Keeper's Almanac, and Family Receipt Book for 1849. Philadelphia: R. Magee. 18 ll. PP. 12706

TURNER'S Improved House-Keeper's Almanac, and Family Receipt Book for 1849. Philadelphia [and] New York: Turner & Fisher. 18 ll. MWA; PHi. 12707

UNCLE Sam's Almanac for 1849. Philadelphia: R. Wilson Desilver. 18 ll. PP. 12708

UNCLE Sam's Almanac for 1849. Philadelphia: Richard Magee; King & Baird, printers. 18 ll. NN. 12709

UNCLE Sam's Almanac for 1849. By Joseph Cramer. Philadelphia: Denny & Walker. 18 ll. MB. 12710

UNCLE Sam's Almanac for 1849. By Joseph Cramer. Philadelphia: John H. Simon. 18 ll. MWA. 12711

The UNITED States Almanack for 1849. By Charles Frederick Egelmann. Philadelphia: Mentz & Rovoudt. 18 ll. MWA; DLC; InU; MnU; OClWHi; PDoBHi; PHi (17 ll.); PU; PYHi; NjR; Drake. 12712

AGRICULTURAL Almanac for 1850. Lancaster: John Bear. 18 ll. MWA; NHi (17 ll.); InU; PHi (16 ll.); PLHi. 12713

Der ALTE Germantown Calender auf 1850. Philadelphia: Ch. G. Sauer. 18 ll. MWA; CLU; P; PAnL; PHi; PP; PPG; PPL; PPeSchw. 12714

Pennsylvania - 1850

The AMERICAN Farmer's Almanac for 1850. Philadelphia: Fisher & Brothers. 16 ll. MWA (impf) 12715

The AMERICAN Farmer's Almanac for 1850. Philadelphia: R. Magee. 18 ll. PPeSchw. 12716

Der AMERIKANISCHE Stadt-und Land-Calender auf 1850. Philadelphia: Ch. G. Sauer. 18 ll. MWA; NN; CLU; CtY; InU; NjP; P; PAtM; PDoBHi; PHi; PP; PPG; PPL (17 ll.); PPeSchw; PYHi; Drake. 12717

APPLETON'S Pocket Almanac for 1850. Philadelphia: George S. Appleton. 16 ll. PPL. 12718

ASTROLOGICAL Almanack for 1850. By C. W. Roback. Philadelphia. [Phillips] 12719

B. A. FAHNESTOCK & Co.'s Free Almanac for 1850. Pittsburgh: B. A. Fahnestock & Co. 18 ll. ICU.
12720

The BAPTIST Almanac and Annual Register for 1850. Thomas S. Malcom, editor. Philadelphia: American Baptist Publication Society. 20 ll. MWA; Ct (18 ll.); ICU; InU; MB; MeHi; OClWHi; WHi. 12721

BROTHER Jonathan's Almanac for 1850. Philadelphia: C. G. Sower. 18 ll. MWA; DLC (17 ll.); CtY; PHi; PPeSchw; PYHi; NjR. 12722

COLUMBIAN Almanac for 1850. Philadelphia: Joseph McDowell. 18 ll. MWA; DLC; FSaHi; InU; MnU; PHi; PPL; NjR (16 ll.) 12723

The COMIC Almanac for 1850. Philadelphia: King & Baird; King & Baird, printers. 18 ll. PHi. 12724

The COMIC Almanac for 1850. Pottsville: B. Bannan. 18 ll. ICHi. 12725

The COMIC Almanac for 1850. York: A. J. Warfield; King & Baird, printers. 16 ll. PYHi. 12726

CROCKETT'S Almanac for 1850. Philadelphia: Fisher

& Brothers. 18 ll. MoSM.   12727

CROCKETT'S Almanac for 1850. Philadelphia: R. Magee. 18 ll. MWA.   12728

Der DEUTSCHE Bilder Kalender auf 1850. Philadelphia: Fischer und Bruder. 18 ll. MWA.   12729

DEUTSCHER Volks Kalender für 1850. Philadelphia: Walz und Ketterlinus. PPG.   12730

DR. JAYNE'S Arzenei-Kelender, und Gesundheits-Wegweiser auf 1850. Philadelphia: Dr. D. Jayne. CLU (23 ll.)   12731

The FARMERS Almanac for 1850. Philadelphia: George W. Childs & Co. 18 ll. MWA; PAnL.   12732

The FARMERS Almanac for 1850. Philadelphia: King & Baird. 18 ll. MWA.   12733

The FARMERS Almanac for 1850. York: A. J. Warfield. 18 ll. MWA.   12734

The FARMERS and Mechanics Almanack for 1850. By Charles F. Eagelmann [sic]. Philadelphia: William G. Mentz. 18 ll. MWA; ICHi; IaDaM (17 ll.); MnU; PDoBHi; PHi; PYHi; ViU.   12735

FISHERS Comic Almanac for 1850. [Philadelphia, New York and Boston:] Fisher & Brothers. 18 ll. MWA; N; InU; MBAt; MWiW; PHi.   12736

FISHER'S Improved House-Keeper's Almanac, and Family Receipt Book for 1850. Philadelphia: Fisher & Brothers. 18 ll. MWA; MoSHi; PPi; NjR.   12737

FISHER'S Improved House-Keeper's Almanac, and Family Receipt Book for 1850. Philadelphia: R. Magee. 18 ll. MWA; MiU-C.   12738

FRIENDS' Almanac for 1850. By Joseph Foulke, Jun'r. Philadelphia: W. D. Parrish & Co. 24 ll. MWA; ICN;

Pennsylvania - 1850

InU; MnU; NjR; PDoBHi; PHC. 12739

FRIENDS' Pocket Almanac for 1850. Philadelphia: T. E. Chapman; New York: George C. Baker; Baltimore: I. J. Grahame. 22 ll. MWA; PHi. 12740

FRIENDS' Pocket Almanac for 1850. Philadelphia: King & Baird. 25 ll. MWA; InRE; InU. 12741

The GREAT Western Almanac for 1850. Philadelphia: Jos. McDowell. 18 ll. MWA; DLC; InU; NjP; PHi (17 ll.); PPL; NjR; Drake. 12742

HUNTS' Family Almanac for 1850. Philadelphia: Uriah Hunt & Son. 18 ll. MWA; CtY; InU; LNHT; PDoBHi; PHi; PPL; NjR. 12743

JAYNE'S Medical Almanac, and Guide to Health for 1850. Philadelphia: Dr. D. Jayne; Stavely & McCalla, printers. 26 ll. MWA; N; NHi; InU; MiD-B; NIC; NRMA; NSyOHi; NR; NRU; IU; VtHi; WHi; PHi; OClWHi; NjR. 12744

JOHNSON'S Pocket Almanac for 1850. Philadelphia: South 7th Street. 18 ll. MWA (two varieties); DLC. 12745

KING & Baird's Deutsche Illustrirte Calender auf 1850. Philadelphia: King & Baird. 18 ll. MWA. 12746

LOOMIS' Magazine Almanac for 1850. By Sanford C. Hill. Pittsburgh: Luke Loomis. 30 ll. MWA; InU; PPiHi. 12747

LOOMIS' Pittsburgh Almanac for 1850. By Sanford C. Hill. Pittsburgh: Luke Loomis. 18 ll. MWA (wrappers only); OHi; OMC; PPi. 12748

M. EGOLF'S Deutscher Illustrirter Calender auf 1850. Philadelphia: M. Egolf. MWA (17 ll.) 12749

The MORAL Almanac for 1850. Philadelphia: Tract Association of Friends; Joseph Rakestraw, printer. 18 ll. MWA; CtY; InRE; InU; MoS; NBuG; PPL; Wv-Ar;

NjR. 12750

Der NEUE, Amerikanische Landwirthschafts-Calender
auf 1850. Von Carl Friederich Egelmann. Reading:
Johann Ritter und Comp. 16 ll. MWA; InU (impf); P;
PDoBHi; PHi; PPCS; PR; PRHi; PPL (15 ll.) 12751

NEUER Kalender für Bauern und Handwerker auf 1850.
Von Carl F. Egelmann. Philadelphia: Wilhelm G.
Mentz. 18 ll. MWA; NN; NHi; CtY; InU (impf);
OClWHi; P; PHi (17 ll.); NjP; PPCS (17 ll.); PPT;
PPeSchw; NjR; Drake. 12752

NEUER Calender für Nord-Amerika auf 1850. Von
Carl F. Egelmann. Philadelphia: Wilhelm G. Mentz.
18 ll. MWA; DLC; N; InU; P; PAtM; PDoBHi; PHi;
PPeSchw; PPL (17 ll.); Drake. 12753

NEUER Gemeinnütziger Pennsylvanischer Calender auf
1850. Lancaster: Johann Baer. 18 ll. MWA; CtY;
PDoBHi; PLF; PPeSchw; Drake. 12754

The NORTH American Almanac for 1850. Philadelphia:
C. G. Sower. 18 ll. MWA; InU; PHi; PPAmP; NjR.
 12755

The PENNSYLVANIA Almanac for 1850. Philadelphia:
John H. Simon. 18 ll. MWA. 12756

PENNSYLVANIA and New Jersey Almanac for 1850.
Philadelphia: Thomas L. Bonsal. 18 ll. PHi. 12757

The PENNSYLVANIA, New-Jersey & Delaware Almanac
for 1850. Philadelphia: John B. Perry. 18 ll. NNU-H
(17 ll.) 12758

The PEOPLE'S Almanac for 1850. Philadelphia: R.
Wilson Desilver. 18 ll. MWA. 12759

The PEOPLE'S Almanac for 1850. York: A. J. Warfield. 18 ll. PHi (17 ll.); PLF; PYHi. 12760

PERRY'S Pictorial Almanac for 1850. Philadelphia:
John B. Perry. 16 ll. NR; PDoBHi; PPG. 12761

Pennsylvania - 1850

PHILADELPHIA Comic Almanac for 1850. Philadelphia: John Downes. [Phillips] 12762

POOR Wills Almanac for 1850. Philadelphia: Joseph M'Dowell. 18 ll. MWA; DLC; InU; MB; PHi; PPL; WHi; NjR. 12763

The PRESBYTERIAN Almanac for 1850. By David Young. Philadelphia: The Presbyterian Board of Publication. 36 ll. MWA; InU; KyU; MB; O; PPL; PPPrHi. 12764

R. WILSON Desilver's Deutscher Illustrirter Calender auf 1850. Philadelphia: R. Wilson Desilver. 18 ll. PHi. 12765

STADT- und Land- Calender auf 1850. Philadelphia: John H. Simon. 16 ll. MWA; CtY; PHi; PLF; PPeSchw. 12766

STADT- und Land- Calender auf 1850. Philadelphia: John Weik. 16 ll. PPeSchw. 12767

STADT- und Land- Calender auf 1850. York: A. J. Warfield. 16 ll. PYHi. 12768

The SUNDAY-SCHOOL Pocket Almanac for 1850. Philadelphia: The American Sunday-School Union. 16 ll. MWA; MB; NjP. 12769

TURNER'S Comic Almanac for 1850. Philadelphia and New York: Fisher & Brothers. 18 ll. MBAt. 12770

UNCLE Sam's Almanac for 1850. Philadelphia: John H. Simon. 18 ll. MWA; NN; N; PHi; Drake. 12771

UNCLE Sam's Almanac for 1850. Pottsville: B. Bannan. 18 ll. MWA (impf) 12772

UNCLE Sam's Almanac for 1850. By Joseph Cramer. Philadelphia: King & Baird. 18 ll. MWA. 12773

The UNITED States Almanack for 1850. By Charles

F. Eagelmann [sic]. Philadelphia: William G. Mentz.
18 ll. MWA; InU; MnU; OClWHi; PCDHi; PDoBHi;
PHi; ViW (16 ll.); NjR. 12774

UNSER Kalender auf 1850. Philadelphia: M. Brummer
u. Co. 18 ll. MWA; PPeSchw; PYHi; NjR. 12775

WATCHMAN'S Calendar for 1850. [np, np] [In: The
City Watchman's Address on the return of Christmas,
1849.] Broadside. PHi. 12776

RHODE ISLAND

LEEDS, 1713. The American Almanack for 1713. Sold by Elkana Pembrook in Newport. [New York: William Bradford] 12 ll. NHi; RHi; Drake.   12777

The RHODE-ISLAND Almanack for 1728. By Poor Robin. Newport: J. Franklin. 8 ll. DLC.   12778

The RHODE-ISLAND Almanack for 1729. By Poor Robin. Newport: J. Franklin. 8 ll. MWA (6 ll.); DLC; RHi.   12779

The RHODE-ISLAND Almanack for 1729. By Poor Robin. Newport: J. Franklin; Boston: T. Fleet. 8 ll. Terry.   12780

LEEDS, 1730. The American Almanack for 1730. By Titan Leeds. Philadelphia: Printed; Newport: Edward Nearegreas, and Daniel Arnot. 16 ll. MWA; PPL (4 ll.)   12781

A PERPETUAL Almanack. Newport: James Franklin. 1730. Broadside. RHi.   12782

The RHODE-ISLAND Almanack for 1730. By Poor Robin. Newport: J. Franklin. 8 ll. PPL; RHi (6 ll.)   12783

LEEDS 1731. The American Almanack for 1731. By Titan Leeds. Newport: Daniel Ayrault and Edward Nearegreas. [New York: William Bradford] 12 ll. MWA; NHi (10 ll.)   12784

NEWPORT 1731. An Almanack for 1731. By Samuel Maxwell. Newport: J. Franklin. 8 ll. MWA; MBC; RHi (7 ll.); RPB.   12785

The RHODE-ISLAND Almanack for 1731. By Poor Robin. Newport: James Franklin. [Sabin 62743] 12786

The RHODE-ISLAND Almanack for 1732. By Poor Robin. Newport: James Franklin. 8 ll. MWA; DLC; MBC; MHi; NBuG; RHi. 12787

The RHODE-ISLAND Almanack for 1733. By Poor Robin. Newport: J. Franklin, ... Frinting [sic] House. 8 ll. MBC; MHi; RHi. 12788

The RHODE-ISLAND Almanack for 1733. By Poor Robin. Newport: J. Franklin, ... Printing House. 8 ll. MWA; DLC; MBC; MHi; RHi. 12789

The RHODE-ISLAND Almanack for 1734. By Poor Robin. Newport: J. Franklin. 8 ll. MWA; MBC; MSaE; RNHi (ntp); RHi. 12790

The RHODE-ISLAND Almanack for 1735. By Poor Robin. Newport: J. Franklin. 8 ll. MWA; DLC; MB; MH; RHi; RP. 12791

The RHODE-ISLAND Almanack for 1735. By Poor Robin. Newport: J. Franklin; Boston: T. Fleet. 8 ll. MB. 12792

The RHODE-ISLAND Almanack for 1737. By Joseph Stafford. Newport: Widow Franklin. 8 ll. MWA (impf); RHi (impf) 12793

The RHODE-ISLAND Almanack for 1738. By Joseph Stafford. Newport: Widow Franklin. 8 ll. MWA (impf); DLC; RHi. 12794

The RHODE-ISLAND Almanack for 1739. By Poor Robin. Newport: Widow Franklin. 8 ll. CtY; RHi.
12795

The RHODE-ISLAND Almanack for 1740. By Poor Robin. Newport: Widow Franklin. 8 ll. MWA; DLC. 12796

The RHODE-ISLAND Almanack for 1741. By Poor Robin. Newport: Widow Franklin. 8 ll. MWA; DLC;

PPL; RHi.   12797

POOR Job, 1750. An Almanack for 1750. By Job
Shepherd. Newport: James Franklin. 12 ll. MWA (10
ll., ntp); DLC (9 ll., ntp); MH; PHi (11 ll.); RHi
(6 ll.)   12798

POOR Job, 1750 [sic, 1751]. An Almanack for 1750
[sic]. By Job Shepherd. Newport: James Franklin.
12 ll. MWA.   12799

POOR Job, 1751. An Almanack for 1751. By Job
Shepherd. Newport: James Franklin. 12 ll. MWA;
MB (impf); RHi; RNHi (ntp); RPB; Drake (11 ll.)
                                                       12800
POOR Job, 1752. An Almanack for 1752. By Job
Shepherd. Newport: James Franklin. 12 ll. MWA;
DLC; N (impf); ICN; MoU; MB; MSaE; MH; MHi;
RHi (6 ll.); NN; NT; RNHi; RP; RPB; NhAu (6 ll.);
Drake (two varieties; one, 10 ll.)   12801

POOR Job, 1753. An Almanack for 1753. By Job
Shepherd. Newport: James Franklin. 12 ll. MWA;
DLC; RP; InU (10 ll., ntp); RNHi; RPB; MB;
MDedHi; RHi; NHi; NN.   12802

POOR Job, 1754. An Almanack for 1754. By Job
Shepherd. Newport: James Franklin. 12 ll. MWA;
DLC; MB (impf); RNHi; RHi; RPB.   12803

POOR Job, 1755. An Almanack for 1755. By Job Shepherd. Newport: James Franklin. 12 ll. MWA; DLC;
RP; MB; MSaE; N; RPB; RHi; NHi; NN (impf) 12804

POOR Job's Country and Townsman's Almanack for
1758. By Job Shedherd [sic]. Newport: J. Franklin.
8 ll. PHi; RPJCB; BritMus.   12805

POOR Job's Country and Townsman's Almanack for
1758. By Job Shepherd. Newport: J. Franklin. 8 ll.
MWA (6 ll.); PPAmP; RHi.   12806

WHITEFIELD'S Almanack for 1760. By Nathaniel White-

field. Newport: James Franklin. 12 ll. MWA; DLC;
N; RHi; RNHi; RPB. 12807

An ALMANACK for 1763. By Benjamin West. Providence: William Goddard. 12 ll. MWA; DLC; PHi;
MB; RPB; RHi; NHi; RP. 12808

An ASTRONOMICAL Diary: Or Almanack for 1764. By
Nathaniel Ames. Newport: Samuel Hall. 12 ll. MWA;
DLC; NN; RHi; RNHi; RNR; RPB; RPJCB. 12809

The NEW-ENGLAND Almanack, Or Lady's and Gentleman's Diary for 1764. By Benjamin West. Providence:
William Goddard. 12 ll. MWA; DLC; NHi; PHi; RHi;
RP; RPB; RPJCB; BritMus. 12810

An ASTRONOMICAL Diary: Or, Almanack for 1765. By
Nathaniel Ames. Boston: R. & S. Draper; [etc]; Newport: S. Hall. 12 ll. RHi. 12811

An ASTRONOMICAL Diary: or, Almanack for 1765.
By Nathaniel Ames. Newport: Re-Printed by Samuel
Hall. 12 ll. RHi. 12812

The NEW-ENGLAND Almanack, or Lady's and Gentleman's Diary for 1765. By Benjamin West. Providence:
William Goddard. 12 ll. MWA; DLC; N; NN (7 ll.);
NHi; CSmH; PHi; MH; RNHi; RHi; RPB; MB; RP;
RPJCB; InU; NBuHi. 12813

AMES'S Almanack revived and improved: Or, An Astronomical Diary for 1766. Boston: R. & S. Draper;
[etc]; S. Hall in Rhode Island. 12 ll. MWA; RHi.
12814

An ASTRONOMICAL Diary: Or Almanac for 1766. By
Nathaniel Ames. Newport: Re-printed and sold by
Samuel Hall. 12 ll. MWA; DLC; N; RHi (11 ll.);
RNR (6 ll., ntp) 12815

The NEW-ENGLAND Almanack, or Lady's and Gentleman's Diary for 1766. By Benjamin West. Providence: Sarah and William Goddard. 12 ll. MWA; DLC;
N; NN; NHi; MoU; RP; MHi; MB; PHi; MBAt; NBuHi;

MH; RHi; RNHi; RPB; RPJCB; BritMus. 12816

An ASTRONOMICAL Diary; or, an Almanack for 1767. By Nathaniel Ames. Newport: Samuel Hall. Advertised in the "Newport Mercury," December 22, 1766.
12817

The NEW-ENGLAND Almanack, or Lady's and Gentleman's Diary for 1767. By Benjamin West. Providence: Sarah Goddard and Company. 12 ll. MWA; AU; CSmH (two varieties); DLC; ICN; InU (fragment); MB; MH; MHi; MiU-C; N (impf); NBuHi; NHi (two varieties); NN; NjMoW; PHi (two varieties); RHi; RNHi; RPB; RPJCB; WHi. 12818

An ASTRONOMICAL Diary: Or, Almanack for 1768. By Nathaniel Ames. Newport: Re-printed and sold by Samuel Hall. 12 ll. MWA; DLC; NN; RHi; RNHi; RPB. 12819

The NEW-ENGLAND Almanack, Or Lady's and Gentleman's Diary for 1768. By Benjamin West. Providence: Sarah Goddard and John Carter. 12 ll. MWA; DLC; N; NjMoW; AU; InU (ntp); CtY; RPJCB; RPB; WHi (8 ll.); RP; MB; PHi; CSmH; MiU-C; RNHi; RHi; NN; NHi; CLU; Drake. 12820

The NEW-ENGLAND Almanack, Or Lady's and Gentleman's Diary for 1769. By Benjamin West. Boston: Mein and Fleeming; Providence: Benjamin West. 12 ll. MWA; NjMoW; PHi; RHi; WHi. 12821

The NEW-ENGLAND Almanack; or Lady's and Gentleman's Diary for 1769. By Benjamin West. Providence: John Carter. 16 ll. CLU. 12822

The NEW-ENGLAND Town and Country Almanack for 1769. By Abraham Weatherwise. Providence: John Carter. 16 ll. PHi (12 ll.) 12823

The NEW-ENGLAND Town and Country Almanack for 1769. By Abraham Weatherwise. Providence: Sarah Goddard and John Carter. 16 ll. MWA; RHi; RNHi; MDedHi; RPA; NHi; RPB; NN (impf); MB; NT; RP;

BritMus. 12824

The NEW-ENGLAND Town and Country Almanack for 1769. By Abraham Weatherwise. Providence: Sarah Goddard and John Carter. (Second Edition) Advertised in the "Providence Gazette." 12825

The NEW-ENGLAND Town and Country Almanack for 1769. By Abraham Weatherwise. Providence: Sarah Goddard and John Carter. (Third Edition) Advertised in the "Providence Gazette." 12826

The NEW-ENGLAND Almanack, Or Lady's and Gentleman's Diary for 1770. By Benjamin West. Providence: John Carter. 16 ll. MWA; DLC; RHi; N; RPA; ViU; CLU; RNHi; AU; OCl; InU; PHi; CSmH; OCHP; MB; RP; CtY; MH; NN; NHi; RPB; WHi (9 ll.); MReh; Drake. 12827

An ASTRONOMICAL Diary: Or, Almanack for 1771. By Nathaniel Ames. Newport: Re-printed. 12 ll. MWA; DLC (11 ll.); N; Drake (11 ll.) 12828

The NEW-ENGLAND Almanack, Or Lady's and Gentleman's Diary for 1771. By Benjamin West. Providence: John Carter. 12 ll. MWA; DLC; N; NN; NHi; RHi; RWe; MB; RP; RPJCB; RNHi; RNR; RPB; InU; CLU; PHi; CSmH (11 ll.); MSaE; AU; MiD-B; NjMoW; RPA; WHi; Drake. 12829

WEST'S Sheet Almanack for 1771. Providence: John Carter. Broadside. Advertised in the "Providence Gazette." 12830

The NEW-ENGLAND Almanack, Or Lady's and Gentleman's Diary for 1772. By Benjamin West. Newport: Ebenezer Campbell. 12 ll. MWA; DLC; NHi; RHi.
12831
The NEW-ENGLAND Almanack, Or Lady's and Gentleman's Diary for 1772. By Benjamin West. Providence: John Carter. 12 ll. MWA; DLC; N; NjMoW; WHi; MB; RPJCB; RPA; MiU-C; PHi; CSmH; CtY; RNHi; CtHi (impf); RHi; NN; RPB; RWe (impf); ICN; RP;

Drake (11 ll.) 12832

The RHODE-ISLAND Almanack, or Astronomical Diary for 1772. By John Anderson. Newport: Solomon Southwick. 12 ll. MWA; DLC; RHi; InU (7 ll.); RPB; AU; PHi; CSmH; MB; RNHi; Ct (11 ll.); NHi; NN (impf); RPJCB (11 ll.); Drake (ntp) 12833

WEST'S Sheet Almanack for 1772. Providence: John Carter. Broadside. Advertised in the "Providence Gazette." 12834

ANDERSON improved: being an Almanack, and Ephemeris for 1773. By John Anderson. Newport: Solomon Southwick. 16 ll. MWA; DLC; RHi; N; NRMA; MSaE; NBuG; RNHi; RP; RPB; RPJCB; RU; CLU; MoU; InU; CtHT-W (14 ll.); CtY; ICN; MB; NHi; NjR; NN (impf) 12835

The NEW-ENGLAND Almanack, or Lady's and Gentleman's Diary for 1773. By Benjamin West. Providence: John Carter. 16 ll. MWA; DLC; N; NN; NHi; RHi; RP; RPA; RPB; RPJCB; MH; CtY; PHi; CSmH; RNHi; COT; NBuHi; MoU; InU; Aldrich; Drake (15 ll.) 12836

ANDERSON improved: being an Almanack and Ephemeris for 1774. By John Anderson. Newport: Solomon Southwick. 16 ll. MWA (two varieties); N (two varieties); RHi (two varieties); DLC; CtY; RPJCB; NN (impf); NHi; RNHi; RP; RPB; InU; MB; MH; MHi (14 ll.); NBuG; ICN; NjMoW (15 ll.); NjR; DeWint; Drake (11 ll., ntp) 12837

ANDERSON improved: being an Almanack and Ephemeris for 1774. By John Anderson. Newport: Solomon Southwick. (Second Edition) 16 ll. MWA; RHi (10 ll.); RNHi. 12838

ANDERSON Improved: Being a new Almanack, and Ephemeris for 1774. By John Anderson. Newport: Solomon Southwick. 16 ll. NRMA. 12839

The NEW-ENGLAND Almanack, or Lady's and Gentleman's Diary for 1774. By Benjamin West. Providence: John Carter. 12 ll. MWA; DLC; N; NN; NHi; RHi; MiU-C; RPB; RNHi; WHi (11 ll.); RPJCB; NBuHi; MBAt; RP; PHi; MB; CtY; InU; RPA; NjMoW; Aldrich. 12840

ANDERSON improved: being an Almanack and Ephemeris for 1775. By John Anderson. Newport: Solomon Southwick. 16 ll. MWA; DLC; N; RHi; MoU; NRMA; CtW; CtY; MB; MBC; RP; RPB; RPJCB; NGos; NjMoW; PHi; CSmH; NBuG; RNHi; CLU; NHi; MiU-C (15 ll.); NN (impf); Drake. 12841

The NEW-ENGLAND Almanack, or Lady's and Gentleman's Diary for 1775. By Benjamin West. Providence: John Carter. 12 ll. MWA; DLC; N; RHi; NN; NHi; NjMoW; MB; RPA; RPJCB; NBuHi; PHi; ICN (11 ll.); MBAt; MiU-C; WHi (10 ll.); RNHi; RP; Aldrich. 12842

An ALMANACK, and Ephemeris for 1776. By John Anderson. Newport: Solomon Southwick. 12 ll. MWA (two varieties); DLC; N; NHi; MH; RNHi (two varieties); MB; RHi; NjMoW; CtY; RPA; RPB; MBC; NjR (11 ll.); RPJCB; OCHP. 12843

An ALMANACK, and Ephemeris for 1776. By John Anderson. Newport: Solomon Southwick. (Second Edition) 12 ll. MWA; NN; NHi; NRMA; RHi. 12844

The NEW-ENGLAND Almanack, or Lady's and Gentleman's Diary for 1776. By Benjamin West. Providence: John Carter. 16 ll. [Recto D1, 7th line from bottom: "Beginning of June..."] N; InU; DeWint; NjMoW; PP; MiU-C; AU; MnU; RP; PHi (ntp); CSmH; NBuHi; RHi; MB; NN; ICHi; Drake. 12845

-- Recto D1, 7th line from bottom "May, or beginning ..."[sic]. 16 ll. MWA; DLC; CSmH; ICHi; MHi; NHi; RNHi; NjR. 12846

WEST'S Almanack for 1776. Providence: John Carter. Broadside. MWA; NN; Drake. 12847

An ALMANACK, and Ephemeris for 1777. By John Anderson. Newport: Solomon Southwick. 12 ll. [Hammett] 12848

The NEW-ENGLAND Almanack, or Lady's and Gentleman's Diary for 1777. By Benjamin West. Providence: John Carter. 12 ll. MWA; DLC; N; NN; NHi; NjMoW; MB; RPJCB; AU; CtY; InU; PHi (impf); CSmH; PP; RP; OCHP; RNHi; Ct (10 ll.); WHi; RPB; RPE; RPA (8 ll.); RHi; Aldrich; Drake. 12849

The NEW-ENGLAND Almanack, or Lady's and Gentleman's Diary for 1778. By Benjamin West. Providence: John Carter. 12 ll. MWA; DLC; N; NN; NHi; RHi; NjMoW; NBuG; InU; RPA; CtY; AU; MiU-C; NBuHi; RPJCB; NT; MB; RPB; RPE; NBLiHi (11 ll.); CSmH; RP; PHi; RNHi (ntp); WHi; CLU; Aldrich; Drake. 12850

The NEW-ENGLAND Almanack, or Lady's and Gentleman's Diary for 1779. By Benjamin West. Providence: John Carter. 12 ll. MWA; DLC; N; NN; NHi (10 ll.); RHi; PHi; MB; CSmH; MiU-C; WHi; OCHP; RPB; RNHi; OClWHi; RP; RPA; CLU; AU; RPJCB; MBAt; Ct (9 ll.); Aldrich; Drake. 12851

ANDERSON revived: The North-American Calendar; or, an Almanack for 1780. By John Anderson. Providence: Bennett Wheeler. 12 ll. MWA; DLC; N; NN; NHi; RHi; InU; RPJCB; CLU; MoU; OMC; MB; RNHi; RPB. 12852

ANDERSON revived: The North-American Calendar; or, an Almanack for 1780. By John Anderson. Providence: Bennett Wheeler. (Second Edition) Advertised in the "American Journal," December 10, 1779. 12853

The NEW-ENGLAND Almanack, or Lady's and Gentleman's Diary for 1780. By Benjamin West. Providence: John Carter. 18 ll. MWA; DLC; N; NN (17 ll.); NHi; RHi; InU; NBuG; RPA (17 ll.); MoU; MiU-C; CLU; MB; NNMus; RP; OClWHi; RPJCB; RNHi; MiGr; PHi; CSmH; OCHP; WHi; Ct (17 ll.); RPB; RWe; Aldrich;

Drake. 12854

ALMANACK for 1781. By John Anderson. Newport: Southwick and Barber. RNHi (ntp; title from Chapin)
12855

BICKERSTAFF'S New-England Almanack, Or, Lady's and Gentleman's Diary for 1781. By Isaac Bickerstaff. Providence: John Carter. 16 ll. MWA; DLC; N; NN; RHi; PHi; MiU-C; WHi; Ct; RP; RPB; RPJCB; RNHi; CLU; InU; RPA. 12856

BICKERSTAFF'S New-England Almanack, or, Lady's and Gentleman's Diary for 1781. By Isaac Bickerstaff. Providence: John Carter. (Second Edition) 16 ll. RHi. 12857

BICKERSTAFF'S New-England Almanack, or, Lady's and Gentleman's Diary for 1781. By Isaac Bickerstaff. Providence: John Carter. (Third Edition) Advertised in the "Providence Gazette." 12858

BICKERSTAFF'S New-England Almanack, or, Lady's and Gentleman's Diary for 1781. By Isaac Bickerstaff. Providence: John Carter. (Fourth Edition) Advertised in the "Providence Gazette." 12859

CALENDRIER Français Pour 1781. Newport: De l'Imprimerie de l'Escadre. RHi (21 ll.); RPJCB (14 ll.)
12860

The NEW-ENGLAND Almanack, or Lady's and Gentleman's Diary for 1781. By Isaac Bickerstaff. Providence: John Carter. 16 ll. NHi; RNHi. 12861

The NEW-ENGLAND Almanack, or Lady's and Gentleman's Diary for 1781. By Benjamin West. Providence: John Carter. 16 ll. MWA; NN; RHi; RP; RPE; CLU; NjMoW; MiU-C; DLC; RPJCB; Aldrich. 12862

-- Issue with 18 ll. MiGr. 12863

The NORTH AMERICAN Calendar; or, an Almanack for 1781. By Benjamin West. Providence: Bennett Wheeler; Newport: Henry Barber. 12 ll. MWA; DLC;

N; NN; NHi; RHi; CLU; MiU-C; InU; CtHi; NjR; CSmH; RNHi; RPJCB; RPB; NRMA (11 ll.); MB.
12864

The NEW-ENGLAND Almanack, or Lady's and Gentleman's Diary for 1782. By Isaac Bickerstaff. Providence: John Carter. 12 ll. MWA; DLC; N; NN; NHi; RHi; CtY; ICN; MiU-C; RNHi (two varieties); InU; RPB; RWe; MHi; NjR; PHi; MiGr; WHi; MB; RP; Drake.
12865

The NORTH-AMERICAN Calendar, and Rhode-Island Register for 1782. By Benjamin West. Providence: Bennett Wheeler. 20 ll. MWA; DLC; N; NN; NHi; RHi; ICU; InU; OCHP; MDedHi; NjMoW; AU; CLU; PHi; RPB; CSmH; RNHi; MAtt (16 ll.); MiU-C; RPJCB; MB; MHi; CRedl; Drake (19 ll.)
12866

The NORTH-AMERICAN Calendar, and Rhode-Island Register for 1782. By Benjamin West. Providence: Bennett Wheeler; Newport: Henry Barber. 20 ll. [Evans]
12867

The NEW-ENGLAND Almanack, or Lady's and Gentleman's Diary for 1783. By Isaac Bickerstaff. Providence: John Carter. 12 ll. MWA; DLC; N (ntp); RP; NHi; RHi; MiU-C; NN (ntp); ICHi; InRE; InU; CLU; NjMoW; RNHi; RPA; MiGr; Ct; PHi; MBAt; RPB; MoU; Aldrich.
12868

The NORTH-AMERICAN Calendar: or the Rhode-Island Almanack for 1783. By Benjamin West. Providence: Bennett Wheeler. 16 ll. MWA; DLC; N; NN; RHi; ICU; CLU; MoU; InU (8 ll.); NjMoW; Ct; MHi; RPE; RPJCB; MB; RNHi; RPA.
12869

The NORTH-AMERICAN Calendar: or the Rhode-Island Almanack for 1783. By Benjamin West. Providence: Bennett Wheeler; Newport: Henry Barber. 16 ll. MWA; N; NHi; RHi; NBuHi (impf); AU; MB; NBuG; RNHi; MH; RPB; RPJCB; InU (impf); TxF.
12870

The NEW-ENGLAND Almanack; or Lady's and Gentleman's Diary for 1784. By Isaac Bickerstaff. Provi-

dence: John Carter. 12 ll. MWA; DLC; N; NHi;
PHi; CSmH; RNHi; RPB; RP; RHi; MoU; InU; RPA;
MiD-B.   12871

The NEW-ENGLAND Almanack; or Lady's and Gentleman's Diary for 1784. By Isaac Bickerstaff. Providence: Carter and Wilkinson. 12 ll. CLU.   12872

NORTH American Calendar; or an Almanack for 1784.
By Benjamin West. Providence: Solomon Southwick.
12 ll. [National Union Catalog]   12873

The NORTH-AMERICAN Calendar; or, the Rhode-Island Almanack for 1784. By Benjamin West. Newport: Solomon Southwick. 12 ll. MWA; N; NN; NHi;
RHi; CtY; InU; RNHi; RPE.   12874

The NORTH-AMERICAN Calendar; or, the Rhode-Island Almanack for 1784. By Benjamin West. Newport:
Bennett Wheeler. 12 ll. MWA; DLC; N; RHi; RNHi;
RPB; RPJCB; Aldrich.   12875

The NORTH-AMERICAN Calendar: or, the Rhode Island Almanack for 1784. By Benjamin West. Providence:
Bennett Wheeler, at his Office, on the Parade. 12 ll.
MWA; DLC; N; NHi; RHi; AU; MHi; MiU-C; RNHi;
MB; RPJCB.   12876

The NORTH-AMERICAN Calendar: or, the Rhode Island Almanack for 1784. By Benjamin West. Providence:
Bennett Wheeler, at his Office, on the west side the
Bridge. 12 ll. NN.   12877

The NORTH-AMERICAN Calendar: or, the Rhode Island Almanack for 1784. By Benjamin West. Providence:
Bennett Wheeler. (Second Edition) Advertised in the
"U.S. Chronicle," January 1, 1784.   12878

The NORTH-AMERICAN Calendar; or the Rhode-Island Almanack for 1784. By Benjamin West. Providence:
Bennett Wheeler; Terrence Reilly; [etc] 12 ll. MWA;
DLC; N; NN; RHi; NBuHi (11 ll.)   12879

Rhode Island - 1785

The NEW-ENGLAND Almanack, or Lady's and Gentleman's Diary for 1785. By Isaac Bickerstaff. Providence: John Carter. 12 ll. MWA; DLC; N; NHi; RHi; MB; RP; MHi; AU; OO; PHi; RNHi; MiU-C; WHi; RPJCB; ICU; NBuG; RPB; CtY; InU; MnU.
12880

The NORTH-AMERICAN Calendar; or, the Rhode Island Almanack for 1785. By Copernicus Partridge. Providence: Bennett Wheeler. [Chapin] 12881

The NORTH-AMERICAN Calendar; or, the Rhode-Island Almanack for 1785. By Benjamin West. Providence: Bennett Wheeler. 18 ll. AU; MoU; RPA; RNHi; MB; NBuG; MiU-C; InU (16 ll., ntp); CLU; MTaHi; RPB; MHi; RPJCB; NHi; RHi; Aldrich; Drake (17 ll.) [Two varieties each:] MWA; DLC; NN; NjR. 12882

The NEW-ENGLAND Almanack, or Lady's and Gentleman's Diary for 1786. By Isaac Bickerstaff. Providence: John Carter. 12 ll. MWA; DLC; N; NN; NHi; RHi; RPA; MiD-B; AU; MoU; CU; InU; CtY; PHi; CSmH; RPB; MiU-C; RNHi (10 ll.); NjR; RP; RPJCB; MB; Drake (11 ll.) 12883

The NORTH-AMERICAN Calendar; or, the Rhode-Island Almanack for 1786. By Copernicus Partridge. Providence: Bennett Wheeler. 12 ll. MWA; N; NN; RHi; NBuG; RU; DLC; MH; ICN; MiU-C; RPB; CLU; RNHi (10 ll.); CtY; RPE; RPJCB; MHi; Drake. 12884

-- On back page the printer's "request" is omitted. 12 ll. MWA; RHi; RNHi. 12885

The NORTH-AMERICAN Calendar; or, the Rhode-Island Almanack for 1786. By Copernicus Partridge. Providence: Bennett Wheeler. (Second Edition) 12 ll. MWA; DLC; NN; RHi; RNHi (10 ll.); MHi; MB; Aldrich.
12886

The NORTH-AMERICAN Calendar: or, the Rhode Island Almanack for 1786. By Benjamin West. Providence: Bennett Wheeler. 12 ll. MWA; DLC; RHi; RNHi; AU; MoU; MH. 12887

The NEW-ENGLAND Almanack, or Lady's and Gentleman's Diary for 1787. By Isaac Bickerstaff. Providence: John Carter. 12 ll. MWA; N; DLC; NN; NHi; RHi; WHi; RNHi; MB; AU; MBC; PHi; MiU-C; RPJCB; MoU; RP; MiD-B; NjMoW; CLU; CtY; RPB; MnU; InU; Drake. 12888

The NORTH-AMERICAN Calendar: or, the Rhode-Island Almanack for 1787. By Benjamin West. Providence: Bennett Wheeler. 12 ll. MWA; DLC; N; MTaHi; RPA; RPB; MB; MH; NjMoW; MoU; CLU; ICU; WHi; AU; RPJCB; PHi; ICMcHi; MHi; MSaE; Aldrich; Drake; [Two varieties each:] NHi; RHi; RNHi. 12889

-- On titlepage "Eleventh of American Independence" in Old English type. 12 ll. MWA; RHi; MH. 12890

-- Scrolls around titlepage border. 12 ll. MWA; NN; NHi; RHi; RNHi; RPJCB. 12891

-- On back page, advertisement for "Rhode Island Sheet Almanack." 12 ll. MWA; DLC; Drake. 12892

The RHODE Island Sheet Almanack for 1787. By Benjamin West. Providence: Bennett Wheeler. Broadside. RHi. 12893

An ALMANACK for 1788. By Elisha Thornton. Newport: Peter Edes. 12 ll. MWA; DLC; N; NN (10 ll.); NHi; MB; RP; MHi; RNHi; RPJCB; RHi. 12894

An ASTRONOMICAL Diary, or Almanack for 1788. By Daniel Freebetter. Newport: Peter Edes. 12 ll. MWA; DLC; N; RHi; MB; InU; RPB; RPJCB. 12895

The NEW-ENGLAND Almanack, or Lady's and Gentleman's Diary for 1788. By Isaac Bickerstaff. Providence: John Carter. 12 ll. MWA; DLC; N; NN; NHi; RHi; RP; AU; PHi; Ct; NCH; RNHi; RPB; WHi (11 ll.); MoU; CtY; RPA; NjMoW. 12896

The NORTH American Calendar: or, the Rhode-Island

Almanack for 1788. Providence: Bennett Wheeler. 12
ll. MWA; DLC; N; NN; RHi; RNHi; RPB; MoU;
OCHP; Drake. 12897

WHEELER'S North-American Calendar, and Rhode-Island Almanack for 1788. Providence: Bennett Wheeler.
12 ll. MWA; DLC; N; NN; RHi; MB; RPB; MTaHi;
RNHi; ICMcHi; InU; PHi; RPJCB; NjR; Drake. 12898

WHEELER'S Sheet Almanack for 1788. Providence:
Bennett Wheeler. Broadside. NHi. 12899

An ALMANACK for 1789. By Elisha Thornton. Newport: Peter Edes. 12 ll. MWA; DLC; NN (two varieties); RHi; RPJCB; InU; MB; MBAt; RNHi; RPB;
RPE; Aldrich. 12900

The NEW-ENGLAND Almanack, or Lady's and Gentleman's Diary for 1789. By Isaac Bickerstaff. Providence: John Carter. 12 ll. MWA; DLC; NN; NHi;
RHi; NBuG; RPA; N; RPB; RWe; WHi; RP; CtY;
MiD-B; PHi; MTaHi; MiU-C; RNHi; InU; Drake (10
ll.); Aldrich. 12901

POOR Richard's Rhode-Island Almanack for 1789. By
Poor Richard. [Newport:] Peter Edes. 12 ll. MWA;
DLC; MB; RHi; RNHi; RP; InU (impf); Drake (impf)
12902

The RHODE-ISLAND Almanack for 1789. By Benjamin
West. Providence: Bennett Wheeler. Broadside.
[Alden] 12903

WHEELER'S North-American Calendar, and Rhode-Island Almanack for 1789. Providence: Bennett Wheeler.
12 ll. MWA; DLC; N; NN; NHi (impf); RU; PPAmP;
CtY; InU; WHi; RPB; RPE; MB; RHi; OCHP; RPJCB;
Ct; ICMcHi; ICU; NBuG; RNHi. 12904

An ALMANACK for 1790. By Elisha Thornton. Newport: Peter Edes. 12 ll. MWA; DLC (11 ll.); RHi;
RPA (9 ll.); CSmH; MB; RNHi; RPB; RPJCB; InU.
12905
The NEW-ENGLAND Almanack, or Lady's and Gentle-

man's Diary for 1790. By Isaac Bickerstaff. Providence: John Carter. 12 ll. MWA; DLC; N; NN (two varieties); NHi; MTaHi; RPB; RPE; RP; NBuG; MoU; VtStjF; MiU-C; CtY; NjR; PHi; RNHi (ntp); RHi; RPJCB; WHi; MB; RWe; MHi; OCl; InU; RPA; Aldrich; Drake (10 ll., ntp)   12906

The RHODE-ISLAND Almanack for 1790. Newport: Peter Edes. 12 ll. MWA; DLC; RHi; MB; CSmH; RNHi; RP.   12907

WHEELER'S North-American Calendar, or an Almanack for 1790. Providence: Bennett Wheeler. 12 ll. MWA (11 ll.); DLC; N; NN (two varieties); NHi; RHi (ntp); PHi; MHi; CtY; ICHi; MB; RPJCB; RU; RP; RPB; MiU-C; InU (9 ll., ntp); NjMoW; RNHi (two varieties)   12908

-- Issue with 18 ll. MWA; DLC; RHi; RNHi.   12909

WHEELER'S North-American Calendar, or an Almanack for 1790. Providence: Bennett Wheeler. (Second Edition) 18 ll. MWA (17 ll.); RHi.   12910

An ALMANACK for 1791. By Elisha Thornton. Newport: Peter Edes. 12 ll. DLC.   12911

The COLUMBIAN Almanack, and Magazine of Knowledge and Fun for 1791. By William Lilly Stover. Newport: P. Edes. 12 ll. MWA; DLC; NN; NHi; RPB; PHi; MB (impf); RNHi; MHi; RPJCB; MiU-C; RP; RHi.
     12912
The NEW-ENGLAND Almanack, or Lady's and Gentleman's Diary for 1791. By Isaac Bickerstaff. Providence: John Carter. 12 ll. MWA; DLC; N; NN (impf); NHi; RHi; RNHi; RPA; MiD-B; PHi; CSmH; MiU-C; CtY; OCl; RP; MH; RPB; InU (8 ll.); NjMoW; Aldrich.   12913

The NEW-ENGLAND Almanack, or Lady's and Gentleman's Diary for 1791. By Isaac Bickerstaff. Providence: John Carter; Newport: Jacob Richardson. 12 ll. [Evans]   12914

The RHODE-ISLAND Almanack for 1791. By E. Thornton. Newport: P. Edes. 12 ll. MWA (two varieties); DLC; NN (10 ll.); NHi; RHi; RNHi; MB; RPE; MiGr (11 ll.); RP ; RPB. 12915

WHEELER'S North-American Calendar, or an Almanack for 1791. Providence: Bennett Wheeler. 12 ll. MWA; DLC; N; NN; RHi; RP; CLU; IU; CtY; PHi; RPB; RNHi (11 ll.); NBuG; InU; MB; WaSp. 12916

The NEW-ENGLAND Almanack for 1792. By Isaac Bickerstaff. Providence: John Carter. 12 ll. [Chapin] 12917

The NEW-ENGLAND Almanack, or, Lady's and Gentleman's Diary for 1792. By Isaac Bickerstaff. Providence: John Carter. 12 ll. MWA; DLC; N; NN; NHi; RHi; NjMoW; MTaHi; InU; RPB; CtY; RP; OCl; PHi; MB; MiU-C; RNHi; RNR; RPJCB; NjR; Aldrich; Drake. 12918

The NEW-ENGLAND Almanack, or Lady's and Gentleman's Diary for 1792. By Isaac Bickerstaff. Providence: John Carter; Newport: Jacob Richardson. [Evans] 12919

The RHODE-ISLAND Almanack for 1792. By E. Thornton. Newport: P. Edes. 12 ll. MWA; DLC; N; NN; NHi; RHi; RPJCB; CSmH; MB; RNHi; CtY; RP; RPB; RWe; WaSp; InU; NjMoW; Aldrich; Drake. 12920

The RHODE-ISLAND Almanack for 1792. By Elisha Thornton. Newport: Nathaniel Phillips for Jacob Richardson. 12 ll. MoU. 12921

WHEELER'S North-American Calendar, or an Almanack for 1792. Providence: Bennett Wheeler. 12 ll. MWA; DLC; N; NHi; RHi; Ct; MiU-C; ICHi; RPB; PHi; RNHi; MB; RP; NBuHi; AU; InU; NBuG; RU; RPA; NjMoW. 12922

The NEW-ENGLAND Almanack, or Lady's and Gentleman's Diary for 1793. By Isaac Bickerstaff. Providence: John Carter. 12 ll. MWA; DLC; N; NN; NHi;

RHi; NjMoW; RNHi; WHi; MTaHi; CtY; InU; CLU;
AU; RP; OCl; RPE; RWe; PHi; MiU-C; RPB.   12923

The NEW-ENGLAND Almanack, or Lady's and Gentleman's Diary for 1793. By Isaac Bickerstaff. Providence: John Carter; Newport: Jacob Richardson.
[Evans]   12924

PHILLIPS'S United States Diary, or an Almanack for 1793. Warren: Nathaniel Phillips. 12 ll. RHi (11 ll.)
                                          12925
PHILLIPS'S United States Diary, or an Almanack for 1793. Warren: Nathaniel Phillips. (Second Edition) 12 ll. MWA (11 ll.); DLC (11 ll.); NN (11 ll.); CLU; RPB; RPJCB; RU.   12926

The RHODE-ISLAND Almanack for 1793. By Elisha Thornton. Warren: Nathaniel Phillips. 12 ll. MWA; DLC; N; RHi; ICN; InU; MB; RNHi; RPB.   12927

The RHODE-ISLAND Almanack for 1793. By Elisha Thornton. Warren: Nathaniel Phillips; Newport: Jacob Richardson. 12 ll. MWA; MeP; RHi; RNHi.   12928

WHEELER'S North-American Calendar, or an Almanack for 1793. Providence: B. Wheeler. 12 ll. MWA; DLC; N; NN (ntp); NHi; MiU-C; InU; MB; ICHi; RNHi; RPJCB; RP; RPB; Drake.   12929

BENJAMIN West's Sheet Almanack for 1794. Providence: Carter & Wilkinson. Broadside. [Alden] 12930

The LADIES New Memorandum Book for 1794. Providence: Carter and Wilkinson. [Evans]   12931

The NEW-ENGLAND Almanack, or Lady's and Gentleman's Diary for 1794. By Isaac Bickerstaff. Providence: Carter and Wilkinson. 12 ll. MWA; NN; NHi; NjMoW; NBuHi; AU; MB; CLU; PHi; RPJCB; OCl; NBuG; MdBJ; PPL; MiU-C; WHi (impf); RP; RHi.
                                          12932
The NEW-ENGLAND Almanack, or, Lady's and Gentleman's Diary for 1794. By Isaac Bickerstaff. Provi-

dence: J. Carter. 12 ll. MWA; DLC; N; NHi; RHi; RNHi; RPB. 12933

PHILLIPS'S United States Diary, or an Almanack for 1794. Warren: Nathaniel Phillips. 12 ll. MWA; DLC; N; NN (impf); NHi; RHi; MoU; CtY; RU; RPA; RP; RPJCB; PHi; OCHP; RNHi; RPB; MB; CLU. 12934

The RHODE-ISLAND Almanack, with an Ephemeris for 1794. By Elisha Thornton. Warren: Nathaniel Phillips. 12 ll. RHi; RNHi. 12935

The RHODE-ISLAND Almanack, with an Ephemeris for 1794. By Elisha Thornton. Warren: Nathaniel Phillips; Newport: Jacob Richardson. 12 ll. MWA; DLC; NHi; RHi; RNHi; RPJCB; InU; MiD-B; MB; RPB; RPE; OC (9 ll.); Aldrich. 12936

WHEELER'S North-American Calendar, or an Almanack for 1794. Providence: Bennett Wheeler. 12 ll. MWA; DLC; NN; NHi; MoU (11 ll.); RPJCB; CtY; InU (ntp); CSmH; RNHi; Ct; MiU-C; N; RP; RU; MiD-B; RPB; OClWHi; MB; CLU; RHi. 12937

ANDERSON revived: Being an Almanack, and Ephemeris for 1795. By John Anderson. Newport: Henry C. Southwick and Co. 12 ll. MWA; DLC; N; NN; RHi; RNHi; RP; RPB; RPJCB; InU. 12938

COLUMBIAN Almanac for 1795. Newport: 20 ll. MoU (titlepage imperfect) 12939

NEW-ENGLAND Almanack, or Lady's and Gentleman's Diary for 1795. By Isaac Bickerstaff. Providence: Carter and Wilkinson. 12 ll. MWA (impf); NHi; RHi; RNHi; RPJCB; MB; MSaE; PHi; RP; RPB; AU; OCl; MiD-B. 12940

The NEW-ENGLAND Almanack, or Lady's and Gentleman's Diary for 1795. By Elisha Thornton. Providence: Carter and Wilkinson. 12 ll. MWA; DLC; N; NN; NHi; RHi; NjMoW; InU; MB; PHi; RNHi; RPJCB; MiU-C; ICHi; RPB; RPE; RWe; CLU; Aldrich. 12941

Rhode Island - 1795   1231

PHILLIPS'S United States Diary; or an Almanack for 1795... Year 5798. Warren: Nathaniel Phillips. 12 ll. RHi; RPJCB (impf)   12942

-- "Year 5757." 12 ll. MWA; DLC; RHi; RNHi; MoU; CtY; RP; RPB.   12943

THORNTON'S Sheet Almanack for 1795. Providence: Carter and Wilkinson. Broadside. Advertised in the "Providence Gazette," January 10, 1795.   12944

WHEELER'S North-American Calendar, or an Almanack for 1795. Providence: Bennett Wheeler. ["Roads" on leaf 12.] 12 ll. MWA; DLC (9 ll.); NN (9 ll.); NHi (8 ll.); RHi; RNHi; RPJCB; ICHi; MB; RPB; NBuG; NBuHi; NjMoW.   12945

-- "Roads" on leaf 8. 12 ll. MWA; NN (11 ll.); PHi; RHi; RNHi; RP; InU (9 ll., ntp); Drake.   12946

ANDERSON Revived; being an Almanack and Ephemeris for 1796. By John Anderson. Newport: Henry C. Southwick and Co. [Evans]   12947

The NEW-ENGLAND Almanack, or Lady's and Gentleman's Diary for 1796. By Isaac Bickerstaff. Providence: Carter and Wilkinson. 12 ll. MWA; DLC; N; RHi; OClWHi; MB; RP; PHi; MoU; OCl; RNHi; RPB; MiD-B.   12948

The NEW-ENGLAND Almanack, or Lady's and Gentleman's Diary for 1796. By Elisha Thornton. Providence: Carter and Wilkinson. 12 ll. MWA; DLC; N; NN; NHi; RHi; RPB; RNHi; MB; PHi; CSmH (9 ll.); CLU; MiU-C; NBuHi; InU; NBuG; RPA; NjMoW; Aldrich; Drake.   12949

PHILLIPS'S United States Diary; or an Almanack for 1796. Warren: Nathaniel Phillips. 12 ll. MWA; DLC; N; NN; NHi; RHi; CtY; RNHi; MB; PHi; CSmH; OCHP; InU; NjR; CLU; RP; RU; RPB.   12950

THORNTON'S Sheet Almanack for 1796. Providence:

Carter and Wilkinson. Broadside. Advertised in the
"Providence Gazette," January 2, 1796. 12951

WHEELER'S North-American Calendar, or Almanack
for 1796. Providence: B. Wheeler. 10 ll. MWA;
DLC; N; NN; NHi; RHi; RNHi; RPB; RPJCB; RP;
CLU; MB; NBuG; CtHi; Drake (8 ll.) 12952

The NEW-ENGLAND Almanack, or Lady's and Gentleman's Diary for 1797. By Isaac Bickerstaff. Providence: Carter and Wilkinson. 12 ll. MWA (11 ll.); NN
(11 ll.); RHi (11 ll.); OCl; MB; NBuHi; RP; MiU-C;
MiD-B; RPB; MoU. 12953

The NEW-ENGLAND Almanack, or Lady's and Gentleman's Diary for 1797. By Elisha Thornton and Eliab
Wilkinson. Providence: Carter and Wilkinson. 12 ll.
MWA; DLC; N; NN; NHi; RHi; RNHi; MoU; NjMoW;
ICHi; PHi; MiU-C; MB; InU; CLU; MBAt; RP; RPB;
Aldrich; Drake. 12954

PHILLIPS'S United States Diary; or an Almanack for
1797. Warren: Nathaniel Phillips. 12 ll. MWA; DLC;
N; NN (two varieties); InU; CtY; MH; PHi; OCHP;
RNHi; RPJCB; RPB; RP; RU; MB; RHi; NjR. 12955

WHEELER'S North-American Calendar, or an Almanack
for 1797. Providence: B. Wheeler. 12 ll. MWA; DLC;
N; NN; RHi; RP; RPJCB; RPB; Ct; RNHi; MB.
  12956

NEW-ENGLAND Almanack, or Lady's and Gentleman's
Diary for 1798. By Isaac Bickerstaff. Providence:
Carter and Wilkinson. 12 ll. MWA; DLC; N; NN;
NHi; RHi; RWe; MBAt; RPB; PHi; MiU-C; WHi;
RNHi; NjMoW; RPA; CLU; MiD-B; CtY; RP; RU; AU;
MoU; OCl; InU; Aldrich; Drake. 12957

PHILLIPS'S United States Diary; or an Almanack for
1798. Warren: Nathaniel Phillips. 12 ll. MWA; DLC;
N; NN; NHi; RHi; RU; InU; CtY; RP; RPB; RNHi;
NjR (11 ll.); PHi; CSmH; MB; MoU. 12958

The RHODE-ISLAND Calendar or Almanack for 1798.

Rhode Island - 1798

By Isaac Bickerstaff. Providence and Newport: Joseph J. Todd. 12 ll. MWA; N; RHi; RP; RPB (4 ll.) 12959

WHEELER'S North-American Calendar, or an Almanack for 1798. Providence: B. Wheeler. 12 ll. MWA; DLC; MB; RHi; RNHi; RP; RPB; Drake. 12960

The NEW-ENGLAND Almanack, or Lady's and Gentleman's Diary for 1799. By Isaac Bickerstaff. Providence: Carter and Wilkinson. 12 ll. MWA; DLC; N; NN; NHi; RHi; ICHi; MiD-B; RU; CLU; MoU; OCl; InU; MB; RP; RPJCB; AU; MBAt; RNHi; RPE; PHi; CSmH; MiU-C; Ct (10 ll.); Aldrich; Drake. 12961

WHEELER'S North-American Calendar, or an Almanack for 1799. Providence: B. Wheeler. [Evans] 12962

The NEW-ENGLAND Almanack, or Lady's and Gentleman's Diary for 1800. By Isaac Bickerstaff. Providence: John Carter. 12 ll. MWA; DLC; N; NN; NHi; RHi; NjMoW; MiD-B; AU; VtStjF; OCl; CLU; MHi; NjR; RP; RPB; RPE; Ct; MBAt; MoS; NIl; PHi; MiU-C; WHi; Aldrich. 12963

The NEW-ENGLAND Almanack, or Lady's and Gentleman's Diary for 1800. By Isaac Bickerstaff. Providence: Carter and Wilkinson. 12 ll. ICHi. 12964

The NEW-ENGLAND Calendar, and Ephemeris for 1800. By Eliab Wilkinson. Newport: Jacob Richardson. 12 ll. MWA; DLC; NcD; RHi; RP; RPB. 12965

The NEW-ENGLAND Calendar, and Ephemeris for 1800. By Eliab Wilkinson. Warren: Nathaniel Phillips. 12 ll. MWA; MB; NBuG; RHi; RPB. 12966

The NEWPORT Almanack for 1800. Newport: Oliver Farnsworth. 12 ll. MWA (10 ll.); DLC (10 ll.); NHi; RHi; RNHi (9 ll., ntp); RPJCB. 12967

The UNITED States Almanack for 1800. By Eliab Wilkinson. Warren: Nathaniel Phillips. RWa. 12968

Rhode Island - 1801

The NEW-ENGLAND Almanack, or Lady's and Gentleman's Diary for 1801. By Isaac Bickerstaff. Providence: John Carter. 12 ll. MWA; DLC; N; NN; NHi; RHi; CLU; RP; AU; NBuHi; NcD; WHi; MiD-B; RU; OC; MiU-C; OCl; NjR; PHi; RNHi; RPB; Aldrich; Drake. 12969

The NEW-ENGLAND Calendar and Ephemeris for 1801. Newport: Oliver Farnsworth for Jacob Richardson. [Hammett] 12970

The NEWPORT Almanac for 1801. By Oliver Farnsworth. Newport: Oliver Farnsworth. 12 ll. MWA; DLC; NHi; NcD; RHi; RNHi (8 ll.); RPB. 12971

The RHODE-ISLAND Almanac for 1801. Newport: Oliver Farnsworth. 12 ll. MWA (impf); RHi (impf); Ct (10 ll.); MB; RPB; InU; RNHi; RP; RPE; RPJCB. 12972

The RHODE-ISLAND Almanac for 1801. Newport: Oliver Farnsworth... Great Allowance to those who purchase quantities. 12 ll. MWA; DLC; NN; NHi; RHi. 12973

The RHODE-ISLAND Almanac for 1801. Newport: Jacob Richardson; O. Farnsworth, printer. 12 ll. DLC; RNHi. 12974

The RHODE-ISLAND Almanack for 1801. Newport: William R. Wilder; O. Farnsworth, printer. 12 ll. Ct; MB; RHi. 12975

The RHODE-ISLAND Almanack for 1801. By Elisha Thornton. Newport: Oliver Farnsworth. 12 ll. Aldrich. 12976

The NEW-ENGLAND Almanack, or Lady's and Gentleman's Diary for 1802. By Isaac Bickerstaff. Providence: John Carter. 12 ll. MWA; DLC; N; NN; NHi; RHi; MiD-B; MBAt; NjMoW; WHi; RU; OCl; PHi; AU; NjR. 12977

The NORTH-AMERICAN Calendar and Rhode-Island Almanack for 1802. Providence: Bennett Wheeler. 12 ll. MWA; DLC; N; NN (11 ll.); NHi; RHi; InU; NBuG;

MB; RPB; Ct; RP; Aldrich; Drake. 12978

The NORTH-AMERICAN Calendar and Rhode-Island Almanack for 1802. Providence: Bennett Wheeler. (Second Edition) 12 ll. RHi. 12979

The RHODE-ISLAND Almanack for 1802. By R. Southwick. Newport: Oliver Farnsworth. 12 ll. MWA; DLC; N; NN; NHi; RHi; MBC; RPJCB; RPB; CtY; MB; RP; InU; Aldrich. 12980

ALMANACK for 1803. By R. Thomas. Newport: Oliver Farnsworth. [Hammett] 12981

The NEW-ENGLAND Almanack, or Lady's and Gentleman's Diary for 1803. By Isaac Bickerstaff. Providence: John Carter. 12 ll. MWA; DLC; N; NHi; RHi; MiD-B; RU; NBuG; NjMoW; MiU-C; PHi; NBuHi; OCl; CLU; Ct; InU; Aldrich. 12982

The RHODE-ISLAND Almanac for 1803. By R. Southwick. Newport: Oliver Farnsworth. 12 ll. MWA; DLC; N; NN; NHi (impf); RHi; RPB; CtY; MB; RP; Aldrich; Drake (ntp) 12983

WHEELER'S North-American Calendar, and Rhode-Island Almanack for 1803. Providence: Bennett Wheeler. 12 ll. MWA; DLC; N; NN; RHi; NBuG; InU; NCH; CLU; RP; RPB. 12984

WHEELER'S North American Calendar, and Rhode-Island Almanack for 1803. Providence: Bennett Wheeler; Newport: Wm. R. Wilder. 12 ll. NjR (11 ll.) 12985

The NEW-ENGLAND Almanack, or Lady's and Gentleman's Diary for 1804. By Isaac Bickerstaff. Providence: John Carter. 12 ll. MWA; DLC; N; NHi; RHi; RU; MTaHi; InU; MiU-C; Ct; MiD-B; NjMoW; WHi; OCl; NjR; PHi; NcD; CLU; Aldrich. 12986

The RHODE-ISLAND Almanac for 1804. By Benjamin West. Newport: Oliver Farnsworth. 12 ll. MWA; DLC; N; NN; NHi; RHi; MAtt; InU; WHi; PHi; MB; RP;

RPB; CLU; NjR (17 ll.); Aldrich.   12987

The NEW-ENGLAND Almanack, or Lady's and Gentleman's Diary for 1805. By Isaac Bickerstaff. Providence: John Carter. 12 ll. MWA; DLC; N; NN; NHi; RHi; NjMoW; InU; RU; MiD-B; WHi; MiU-C; Ct; OCl; MB; AU; NjR; PHi; CLU; OMC; Aldrich.   12988

The RHODE-ISLAND Almanac for 1805. By Benjamin West. Newport: Oliver Farnsworth. 12 ll. MWA; DLC; N; NHi; RHi; MB; RP; RPB; MH; CLU; Ct; InU; WHi; RU; Aldrich.   12989

The COLUMBIAN Calendar or Almanac for 1806. By Remington Southwick. Newport: Printed for the author. 12 ll. MWA; DLC; N; NN; NHi; RHi; MDedHi; RP; RPB; CLU; Ct; NBuG; InU (impf); Aldrich.   12990

A LUNAR Calendar for A. M. 5566 [1806]. By Moses Lopez. Newport: Newport Mercury. 66 ll. MWA; InU; NHi.   12991

The NEW-ENGLAND Almanack, or Lady's and Gentleman's Diary for 1806. By Isaac Bickerstaff. Providence: John Carter. 12 ll. MWA; DLC; N; NN; NHi; RHi; WHi; OCl; InU; Ct; OO; RU; NjR; MH; IU; CLU; MB; Aldrich.   12992

The RHODE-ISLAND Almanac for 1806. By Benjamin West. Newport: Oliver Farnsworth. 12 ll. MWA; DLC; N; NN; RHi; MDedHi; WHi; RP; NBuG; PHi; MB; RPB; MBC; InU; RPA; Aldrich; Drake.   12993

The NEW-ENGLAND Almanack, or Lady's and Gentleman's Diary for 1807. By Isaac Bickerstaff. Providence: John Carter. 12 ll. MWA; DLC; N; NN; NHi; RHi; MiD-B; RPA; NjMoW; InU; RU; NjR; PHi; Ct; OCl; RP; NBuG; WHi; RPB; CLU; ICN; MiU-C; MBAt; MB; MBC; Aldrich.   12994

The NEW-ENGLAND Almanack, or Lady's and Gentleman's Diary for 1808. By Isaac Bickerstaff. Providence: John Carter. 12 ll. MWA (two varieties); DLC;

N; NN; NHi; RHi; PPL; WHi; RU; MiD-B; NjMoW;
MBAt; RP; CLU; NcD; Ct; NjR; PHi; MBC; MiU-C;
AU; ICN; InU; Aldrich. 12995

The RHODE-ISLAND Almanac for 1808. By R. Southwick. Newport: Oliver Farnsworth. 12 ll. DLC; Ct
(ntp) 12996

The NEW-ENGLAND Almanack, or Lady's and Gentleman's Diary for 1809. By Isaac Bickerstaff. Providence: John Carter. 12 ll. MWA; DLC; N; NN (11
ll.); NHi; RHi; RU; MiD-B; ViW (10 ll.); NjMoW;
InU; MiU-C; WHi; Ct; AU; ICN; CLU; NcD; RP;
MBAt; NjR; PHi; MB; Aldrich; Drake. 12997

The NEW-ENGLAND Almanack, or Lady's and Gentleman's Diary for 1810. By Isaac Bickerstaff. Providence: John Carter. 12 ll. MWA; DLC; N; NN; NHi;
RHi; RU; MB; RP; MiU-C; WHi; InU; ICN; Ct; CLU;
AU; IU; NjR (11 ll.); PHi; MBAt; NjMoW; Aldrich;
Drake. 12998

The NEW-ENGLAND Almanack, or Lady's and Gentleman's Diary for 1811. By Isaac Bickerstaff. Providence: John Carter. 12 ll. MWA; DLC; N; NN; NHi;
RHi; NjMoW; WHi; PP; MiD-B; MiU-C; InU; AU; Ct;
IU; MB; CLU; NcD; NjR (10 ll.); PHi; MBAt; RP;
Aldrich; Drake. 12999

The NEW-ENGLAND Almanack, or Lady's and Gentleman's Diary for 1812. By Isaac Bickerstaff. Providence: John Carter. 12 ll. MWA; DLC; N; NN; NHi;
RHi; NjMoW; InU; PP; WHi; AU; MiU-C; CLU; NcD;
IU; NjR; RPB; PHi; MB; MBAt; RP; Aldrich; Drake.
13000

The NEW-ENGLAND Almanack, or Lady's and Gentleman's Diary for 1813. By Isaac Bickerstaff. Providence: John Carter. 12 ll. MWA; DLC; N; NN; NHi;
RHi; NjMoW; WHi; MiD-B; MiU-C; InU; CLU; AU;
IU; MBAt; ICN; NjR; NNC; RP; MB; Aldrich; Drake.
13001

The NEW-ENGLAND Almanack, or Lady's and Gentleman's Diary for 1814. By Isaac Bickerstaff. Provi-

dence: John Carter. 12 ll. MWA; N; NN; NHi; WHi; PP; MBAt; NBuG; NjR; PHi; MB; RP; RPB; CLU; IU; MAtt; MiU-C; Ct; InU; MiD-B; NjMoW; Aldrich.
13002

The NEW-ENGLAND Almanack, or Lady's and Gentleman's Diary for 1814. By Isaac Bickerstaff. Providence: John Carter; Newport: George Wanton. 12 ll. MWA; DLC; NN; RHi; NcD; Ct (impf) 13003

The RHODE-ISLAND Almanack for 1815. By Isaac Bickerstaff. Providence: Brown & Wilson. 12 ll. MWA; DLC; N; NN; NjMoW; MAtt; RPA; InU; RU; Ct; MBC; CLU; ICN; RPB; PHi; MBAt; NBuG; WHi; RP; MHi (impf); NjR; RHi; Aldrich; Drake. 13004

The RHODE-ISLAND Almanack for 1816. By Isaac Bickerstaff. Providence: Brown & Wilson. 12 ll. MWA; DLC; N; NN; NHi; RHi; NjMoW; MH; RPA; RU; MAtt; Ct (ntp); WHi; MnU; MB; RPB; CLU; PHi; NjR; RP; Aldrich. 13005

-- Issue with 14 ll. MWA (13 ll.); NjHi. 13006

The RHODE-ISLAND Almanack for 1817. By Isaac Bickerstaff. Providence: Hugh H. Brown. 12 ll. MWA; DLC; N; NN; NHi; RHi; RU; InU; WHi; ICHi; NBuG; CLU; Ct; RPB; MB; NjR; PHi; RP; Aldrich; Drake.
13007

The RHODE-ISLAND Almanack for 1818. By Isaac Bickerstaff. Providence: Hugh H. Brown. 12 ll. MWA; DLC; N; NHi; RHi; RPA; RU; NBuG; WHi; InU; PPL; MBC (11 ll.); CLU; MnU; RPB; PHi; MB; RP; NjR; Ct; MiD-B; Aldrich; Drake (two varieties) 13008

The RHODE-ISLAND Almanack for 1819. By Isaac Bickerstaff. Providence: Hugh H. Brown. 12 ll. MWA; DLC; N; NHi; RHi; MnU; InU; RPA; RU; WHi; MBC; MAtt; NBuG; CLU; RPB; ICN; MH; MB; RP; OClWHi; NjR (10 ll.); Aldrich; Drake. 13009

-- Issue with 24 ll. MWA; Ct; PHi; RHi. 13010

The RHODE-ISLAND Almanack for 1820. By Isaac

Bickerstaff. Providence: Hugh H. Brown. 14 ll.
MWA; DLC; N; NHi; RHi; NjMoW; RU; MB; RPA;
NBuG; WHi; CLU; Ct; RPB; MnU; ICN; InU; NjR;
PHi; TxU; RP; Aldrich; Drake. 13011

The RHODE-ISLAND Register and United States Calendar for 1820. Providence: H. H. Brown. 54 ll. MWA;
N; RHi; RPB; InU; RPE; RP; In; RPA. 13012

The RHODE-ISLAND Almanack for 1821. By Isaac
Bickerstaff. Providence: Brown and Danforth. 14 ll.
MWA (three varieties); DLC; N; NHi; NjMoW; RPA;
WHi; RU; InU; PHi; RHi; RPB; NBuG; RP; MH; MHi;
MB; NjR; CLU; Ct; Aldrich. 13013

The RHODE-ISLAND Register and United States Calendar
for 1821. Providence: Brown & Danforth. 48 ll. MWA;
N; RHi; NN; MiD-B; NHi; RPB; RP; InU. 13014

The RHODE-ISLAND Almanack for 1822. By Isaac
Bickerstaff. Providence: Brown and Danforth. 14 ll.
MWA (two varieties); DLC; N; NHi; RHi; NjMoW; RU;
RPA; InU; WHi; MBC; NBuG; MH; RP; CU; MB; ICN;
PHi; NjR; RPB; CLU; Aldrich; Drake. 13015

The RHODE-ISLAND Register and United States Calendar for 1822. Providence: Brown and Danforth. 48 ll.
MWA; N; NN; RHi; In; InU; RP; RPB. 13016

RHODE-ISLAND Almanack for 1823. By Isaac Bickerstaff. Providence: Brown and Danforth. 14 ll. MWA
(two varieties); DLC; N; NHi; NBuG; RHi; NjMoW;
InU; WHi; RU; RPA; MnU; MH; PPL; RPB; CLU;
PHi; OClWHi; MB; NjR; RP; Aldrich. 13017

RHODE-ISLAND Register and United States Calendar for
1823. Providence: Brown and Danforth. 48 ll. MWA;
N; RHi; RP; RPB; MH; In; WHi. 13018

RHODE-ISLAND Almanack for 1824. By Isaac Bickerstaff. Providence: Brown and Danforth. 14 ll. MWA;
DLC; N; NHi; RHi; NjMoW; RPA; MAtt; RU; NBuG;
WHi; CU; Ct; PHi; MB; RPB; RP; NjR; CLU; MH;

ICN; InU; Aldrich. 13019

RHODE-ISLAND Register and United States Calendar for 1824. Providence: Brown and Danforth. 54 ll.
MWA; N; RHi; RPB; MH; InU; WHi. 13020

The RHODE-ISLAND Almanack for 1825. By Isaac Bickerstaff. Providence: Brown & Danforth. 12 ll.
MWA; DLC; N; NHi; RHi; RU; MnU; RPA; RP; MBC; MB; RPB; CLU; WHi; NjR; ICN; NBuG; InU; Aldrich; Drake. 13021

The RHODE-ISLAND Register and United States Calendar for 1825. Providence: Brown & Danforth. 66 ll.
MWA; NHi; RHi; Nh; In; InU; WHi; MiD-B; RP; RPB; CLU. 13022

The RHODE-ISLAND Almanack for 1826. By Isaac Bickerstaff. Providence: Carlile & Brown. 18 ll.
MWA; DLC; N; NHi; RPA; RU; NBuG; WHi; PHi; MB; RP; RPB; CLU; MH; NjR; ICN; Ct; NR; InU; Aldrich. 13023

The RHODE-ISLAND Register and United States Calendar for 1826. Providence: Carlile & Brown. 48 ll.
MWA; NN; NHi; RHi; MB; MHi; RPB; MH; InU.
13024

The RHODE-ISLAND Almanack for 1827. By Isaac Bickerstaff. Providence: Carlile & Brown. 14 ll.
MWA (three varieties); DLC; N; NHi; MB; CtHi; RPA; WHi; NBuG; InU; PHi; RPB; RP; NjR; CLU; MnU; OMC; RHi; Aldrich; Drake. 13025

The RHODE-ISLAND Register and United States Calendar for 1827. Providence: Carlile & Brown. 54 ll. MWA; RHi; OC; RPB. 13026

The RHODE-ISLAND Almanack for 1828. By Isaac Bickerstaff. Providence: H. H. Brown. 18 ll. MWA (two varieties); DLC; N; NHi; NBuG; NjMoW; ICU; ICN; MH; CLU; NjR (16 ll.); MB; RP; PHi; RPB; NR; NB; InU; WHi; RU; RPA; RHi; Aldrich; Drake (16 ll.) 13027

The RHODE-ISLAND Register and United States Calendar for 1828. Providence: H. H. Brown. 48 ll. MWA; NN; NHi; RHi; RPB; MH; InU; RU; RP. 13028

The CHRISTIAN Almanack for Rhode-Island for 1829. Providence: American Tract Society; J. Wilcox; Newport: Dr. Phails. 19 ll. MWA; DLC; N; RHi; WHi; RU; CLU; NRU; InU; RP; RPB; NBuG; Drake. 13029

The RHODE-ISLAND Almanack for 1829. By Isaac Bickerstaff. Providence: H. H. Brown. 12 ll. MWA; DLC; N; NHi; RHi; PHi; MB; RP; CU; RPB; CLU; NjR; NcD; ICN; NBuG; InU; RU; WHi; RPA; Aldrich. 13030

The RHODE-ISLAND Register and United States Calendar for 1829. Providence: H. H. Brown. 48 ll. MWA; NN; RHi; InU; RP; RPB. 13031

The RHODE-ISLAND Almanack for 1830. By Isaac Bickerstaff. Providence: H. H. Brown. 12 ll. MWA (two varieties); DLC; N; NHi; RHi; MiD-B; NcD; RPA (10 ll.); CLU; RPB; RU; NBuG; MB; RP; NjR; WHi; Aldrich; Drake. 13032

The RHODE-ISLAND Register and United States Calendar for 1830. Providence: H. H. Brown. 24 ll. MWA; NN; RHi; RPB; RP; InU; WHi. 13033

The RHODE-ISLAND Almanack for 1831. By Isaac Bickerstaff. Providence: H. H. Brown. 12 ll. MWA (two varieties); DLC; N; NHi; RHi; NjMoW; ICU; InU; RPA; MBC; OMC; CLU; CU; RPB; ICN; MB; Ct; RU; WHi; MH; RP; NjR; Aldrich. 13034

The RHODE-ISLAND Register and United States Calendar for 1831. Providence: H. H. Brown. 24 ll. MWA; NN; RHi; RPB; WHi. 13035

The RHODE-ISLAND Almanack for 1832. By Isaac Bickerstaff. Providence: H. H. Brown. 12 ll. MWA; N; NHi; RHi; NjMoW; ICU; WHi; InU; RU; ICN; NBuG; CLU; MH; MB; RP; RPB; NjR; Aldrich. 13036

The **RHODE-ISLAND** Register, and Counting-House Companion for 1832. Providence: H. H. Brown. 24 ll.
CLU; N.   13037

The **RHODE-ISLAND** Register and United States Calendar for 1832. Providence: H. H. Brown. 24 ll.
MWA; RHi; RPB; RP; WHi.   13038

The **RHODE-ISLAND** Almanack, Enlarged and Improved for 1833. By R. T. Paine. Providence: H. H. Brown. 12 ll. MWA (two varieties); N; NHi; RHi; ICU; MiD-B; NBuG; OMC; MB; RP; MH; NjR; RPB; Aldrich.
     13039

The **RHODE-ISLAND** Almanack for 1834. By Isaac Bickerstaff. Providence: H. H. Brown. 12 ll. MWA (two varieties); N; NHi; RHi; OMC; RPA (10 ll.); NjMoW; InU; CLU; ICN; MH; RP; RPB; MB; RU; NjR; WHi; Aldrich.   13040

The **RHODE-ISLAND** Almanack for 1835. By Isaac Bickerstaff. Providence: H. H. Brown. 12 ll. MWA (two varieties); N; NHi; RHi; RPA; InU; WHi; NcD; MH; CLU; RPB; RU; MB; RP; Aldrich.   13041

-- Issue with added signatures. NjR (20 ll.)   13042

The **RHODE-ISLAND** Almanac for 1836. By Isaac Bickerstaff. Providence: H. H. Brown. 12 ll. MWA; N; NHi; RHi; RU; RP; MH; MB; RPE; NjR; RPB; CLU; OMC; NBuG; InU; WHi; Aldrich.   13043

The **RHODE-ISLAND** Almanac for 1837. By Isaac Bickerstaff. Providence: H. H. Brown. 12 ll. MWA; N; NHi; RHi; NjMoW; NBuG; InU; RU; MB; RP; RPB; OMC; NjR (11 ll.); CLU; WHi; Aldrich; Drake.
     13044

The **RHODE-ISLAND** Almanac for 1838. By Isaac Bickerstaff. Providence: H. H. Brown. 12 ll. MWA; N; NHi; RHi; WHi; RU; MB; NjR; RPB; CLU; OMC; InU; NBuG; Aldrich.   13045

The **RHODE-ISLAND** Almanac for 1839. By Isaac Bickerstaff. Providence: H. H. Brown. 12 ll. MWA;

N; NHi; RHi; ICU; PHi; NjR (11 ll.); MB; RP; MH;
RPB; OMC; Aldrich. 13046

The RHODE-ISLAND Almanac for 1840. By Isaac
Bickerstaff. Providence: H. H. Brown. 12 ll. MWA
(two varieties); N; NHi; RHi; RPB; NBuG; CU; MB;
NjR; NcD; MH; Aldrich. 13047

The RHODE-ISLAND Almanac for 1841. By Isaac
Bickerstaff. Providence: H. H. Brown. 12 ll. MWA;
N; NHi; RHi; MH; RPB; RU; MB; NjR; CLU; InU;
WHi; Aldrich. 13048

The RHODE-ISLAND Almanac for 1842. By Isaac
Bickerstaff. Providence: H. H. Brown. 12 ll. MWA;
N; NHi; RHi; NcD; MH; InU; RPB; MB; CLU; WHi;
Aldrich. 13049

The PROVIDENCE Almanac and Business Directory for
1843. By Benjamin F. Moore. Providence: B. F.
Moore. 56 ll. MWA; N; RHi; MHi; RPB; CtY; InU.
13050

The RHODE-ISLAND Almanac for 1843. By Isaac Bickerstaff. Providence: H. H. Brown. 12 ll. MWA; N;
NHi; RHi; RPB; CLU; NjR; InU; WHi; RU; MB; Aldrich. 13051

The PROVIDENCE Almanac and Business Directory for
1844. By Benjamin F. Moore. Providence: B. F.
Moore. 67 ll. MWA; N; NHi; RHi; RPB; InU; RPE;
CtY; MH. 13052

The RHODE-ISLAND Almanac for 1844. By Isaac Bick-
erstaff. Providence: H. H. Brown. 12 ll. MWA; N;
NN; NHi; RHi; NjP; MB; MHi; InU; RPB; RPE; CLU;
WHi; Aldrich; Drake. 13053

The PROVIDENCE Almanac and Business Directory for
1845. By Benjamin F. Moore. Providence: John F.
Moore. 75 ll. RHi; MH; RPB; InU; CtHT-W. 13054

The RHODE-ISLAND Almanac for 1845. By Isaac Bickerstaff. Providence: H. H. Brown. 12 ll. MWA; N;

RHi; MB; RPB; InU; WHi; Aldrich; Drake.   13055

-- Issue with 30 ll. NHi.   13056

The PROVIDENCE Almanac and Business Directory for
1846. By John F. Moore. Providence: H. H. Brown.
60 ll. RHi; MH; RPB; InU.   13057

The RHODE-ISLAND Almanac for 1846. By Isaac Bickerstaff. Providence: H. H. Brown. 18 ll. MWA; N;
NHi; RHi; InU; OMC; RP; RPB; NRU; Aldrich;
Drake.   13058

The PROVIDENCE Almanac and Business Directory for
1847. By John F. Moore. Providence: H. H. Brown.
60 ll. RHi; CtHT-W; MH; RPB.   13059

The RHODE-ISLAND Almanac for 1847. By Isaac Bickerstaff. Providence: H. H. Brown. 18 ll. MWA; N;
NHi; RHi; WHi; RU; RPB; NRU; CU; PHi; InU; RP;
NR; Aldrich; Drake.   13060

The NEW Farmer's Almanac for 1848. By A. Maynard.
Newport: W. A. Barber; Stereotyped by Geo. A. Curtis.
24 ll. NN.   13061

The NEW Farmer's Almanac for 1848. By A. Maynard.
Providence: Charles Burnett, Jr. 24 ll. MWA; NN;
InU; TxDN.   13062

The PROVIDENCE Almanac and Business Directory for
1848. By John F. Moore. Providence: J. F. Moore.
60 ll. N; RHi; CtY; MH; MHi; InU; RPB.   13063

The RHODE-ISLAND Almanac for 1848. By Isaac Bickerstaff. Providence: H. H. Brown. 18 ll. MWA; N;
NHi; RHi; WHi; RU; RP; RPB; CLU; InU; Aldrich;
Drake (10 ll.)   13064

The PROVIDENCE Almanac and Business Directory for
1849. By John F. Moore. Providence: John F.
Moore. 56 ll. MWA; N; RHi; MH; RPB; InU.   13065

The RHODE-ISLAND Almanac for 1849. By Isaac
Bickerstaff. Providence: H. H. Brown. 20 ll. MWA
(two varieties); N; NHi; RHi; CU; CLU; NRU; WHi;
RP; RPB; InU; Aldrich. 13066

The PROVIDENCE Almanac and Business Directory for
1850. By John F. Moore. Providence: John F. Moore.
50 ll. RHi; RPB; InU; CtY. 13067

The RHODE-ISLAND Almanac for 1850. By Isaac Bick-
erstaff. Providence: H. H. Brown. 16 ll. MWA; N;
NHi; RHi; CU; MBC; InU; RP; RPB; NRU; Aldrich;
Drake. 13068

SOUTH CAROLINA

The SOUTH-CAROLINA Almanack for 1733. Charles-Town: Thomas Whitmarsh. Advertised in the "South Carolina Gazette," April 28, 1733.　　　　13069

SOUTH-CAROLINA Almanack for 1738. Charles-Town: Lewis Timothy. Advertised in the "South Carolina Gazette," October 29, 1737.　　　　13070

The SOUTH-CAROLINA Almanack for 1749. By John Tobler. Charles-Town: Peter Timothy. Advertised in the "South Carolina Gazette," November 14, 1748.
　　　　13071

ALMANACK for 1750. By Joseph Grover. Charles-Town: John Remington. Advertised in the "South Carolina Gazette," January 8, 1750.　　　　13072

ALMANACK for 1751. By Joseph Grover. Charles-Town: John Remington. Advertised in the "South Carolina Gazette," November 19, 1750.　　　　13073

The SOUTH-CAROLINA Almanack for 1752. By John Tobler. Charlestown: Peter Timothy. Advertised in the "South Carolina Gazette," December 6, 1751. 13074

The SOUTH-CAROLINA Almanack for 1754. By John Tobler. Charlestown: Peter Timothy. Advertised in the "South Carolina Gazette," October 22, 1753. 13075

The SOUTH-CAROLINA Almanack for 1755. By John Tobler. Germantown: Christopher Sower; Charles-Town: Jacob Viart. 12 ll. NHi.　　　　13076

The SOUTH-CAROLINA Almanack for 1756. By John Tobler. Germantown: Christopher Sower; Charles-Town: Jacob Viart. 12 ll. NN (11 ll.); ScHi. 13077

South Carolina - 1757   1247

The SOUTH-CAROLINA Almanack for 1757. By John Tobler. Germantown: Christopher Sower; Charles-Town: Jacob Viart. 12 ll. ScHi.   13078

The SOUTH-CAROLINA Almanack for 1758. By John Tobler. Germantown: Christopher Sower; Charles-Town: Jacob Viart. 16 ll. NHi; ScHi.   13079

The SOUTH-CAROLINA Almanack for 1759. By John Tobler. Charles-Town: Peter Timothy. 16 ll. DLC; ScHi.   13080

The SOUTH-CAROLINA Almanack for 1760. By John Tobler. Charles-Town: Peter Timothy. Advertised in the "South Carolina Gazette," January 5, 1760.   13081

The SOUTH-CAROLINA Almanack and Register for 1760. By George Andrews. Charles Town: Robert Wells. 25 ll. MWA (ntp); DLC (ntp); NN (20 ll., ntp); NHi; ScC; ScHi; ScU-S.   13082

An ALMANACK for 1761. By George Andrews. Charles-Town: Peter Timothy. [Morrison]   13083

The SOUTH-CAROLINA Almanack and Register for 1762. By George Andrews. Charlestown: Robert Wells. 16 ll. DLC (15 ll., ntp); ScHi (ntp)   13084

The SOUTH-CAROLINA and Georgia Almanack for 1762. By John Tobler. Charlestown: Peter Timothy. Advertised in the "South Carolina Gazette," January 16, 1762.   13085

The SOUTH-CAROLINA Almanack and Register for 1763. By George Andrews. Charles Town: Robert Wells. 24 ll. MWA (22 ll.); ScHi.   13086

The SOUTH-CAROLINA and Georgia Almanack and Register for 1763. Charlestown: Peter Timothy. Advertised in the "South Carolina Gazette," November 20, 1762.   13087

The SOUTH-CAROLINA Sheet Almanack for 1763. By

John Tobler. Charlestown: Peter Timothy. Broadside. Advertised in the "South Carolina Gazette," November 20, 1762. 13088

The SOUTH-CAROLINA Almanack and Register for 1764. By George Andrews. Charlestown: Robert Wells. DLC (15 ll.); NN (20 ll.) 13089

The SOUTH-CAROLINA Almanack for 1765. By John Tobler. Charles Town: R. Wells and D. Bruce. 16 ll. ScHi. 13090

The SOUTH-CAROLINA Almanack and Register for 1765. By George Andrews. Charlestown: Robert Wells. 26 ll. ScC (ntp) 13091

The SOUTH-CAROLINA & Georgia Almanack for 1765. By John Tobler. Charles Town: R. Wells and D. Bruce. 16 ll. DLC; ScHi. 13092

The SOUTH Carolina & Georgia Almanack for 1766. By the late John Tobler. Charles-Town: Robert Wells. 16 ll. NHi; GU-De; ScC. 13093

The SOUTH-CAROLINA & Georgia Almanack for 1767. By John Tobler. Charlestown: Robert Wells. 16 ll. Private collection. 13094

An ALMANACK for 1768. By William Ball. Charles-Town: Charles Crouch. 22 ll. DLC; NHi; GU-De.
13095

The SOUTH-CAROLINA & Georgia Almanack for 1768. By John Tobler. Charles Town: Robert Wells. 16 ll. MWA (impf); ScC. 13096

WELL'S [sic] Register of the Southern British American Provinces, together with an Almanack [for 1768]. By George Andrews. Charlestown: Robert Wells. [Sabin 87753] 13097

An ALMANACK for 1769. By William Ball. Charlestown: Charles Crouch. 18 ll. MHi. 13098

South Carolina - 1769

ANDREWS'S Almanack for 1769. Charleston: Robert Wells. Broadside. MWA. 13099

REGISTER of the Southern British American Colonies for 1769. Charleston: Robert Wells. [Sabin 87755]
13100

The SOUTH-CAROLINA and Georgia Almanack for 1769. By John Tobler. [Savannah:] Clay & Habersham; [Charleston:] Robert Wells; James Johnston, printer. 16 ll. ScC. 13101

POOR Tom Revived: being More's Almanack for 1770. By Thomas More. Charles-Town: Charles Crouch. 12 ll. DLC; MWA. 13102

The SOUTH-CAROLINA and Georgia Almanack for 1770. By John Tobler. Charles Town: Robert Wells; Savannah: James Johnston. 16 ll. NHi; GU-De (impf); ScC; ScHi. 13103

The GEORGIA Almanack for 1771. By John Tobler. Charlestown: Printed for the Editor; Savannah: James Johnston; Charlestown: Robert Wells. 16 ll. ICN; ScHi. 13104

POOR Tom Revived: being More's Almanack for 1771. By Thomas More. Charles-Town: Charles Crouch. 12 ll. DLC; MHi. 13105

The SOUTH-CAROLINA and Georgia Almanack for 1771. By John Tobler. Charlestown: Printed for the Editor; Robert Wells; Savannah: James Johnston. 16 ll. MWA; NHi; InU. 13106

POOR Tom Revived: being More's Almanack for 1772. By Thomas More. Charles-Town: Charles Crouch. 12 ll. DLC; MHi. 13107

The SOUTH-CAROLINA and Georgia Almanack for 1772. By John Tobler. Charlestown: Printed for the Editor; Robert Wells; Savannah: James Johnston. 16 ll. DLC.
13108

POOR Tom Revived: being More's Almanack for 1773.

By Thomas More. Charles-Town: Charles Crouch. 12 ll. [Sabin 87759]   13109

A SHEET Almanack for 1773. Charles-Town: T. Powell & Co. Broadside. Advertised in the "South Carolina Gazette," December 31, 1772.   13110

The SOUTH-CAROLINA Almanack for 1773. Charles-Town: Peter Timothy. Possibly not issued. An advertisement in the "South Carolina Gazette," December 31, 1772, says an "unforseen circumstance has happened ..."   13111

The SOUTH-CAROLINA and Georgia Almanack for 1773. By John Tobler. Charlestown: Printed for the Editor; Robert Wells; Savannah: James Johnston. 16 ll. ScC.   13112

WELLS'S Register, together with an Almanack for 1773. Charlestown: Robert Wells. 60 ll. PPiU.   13113

The GEORGIA and South-Carolina Almanack for 1774. By John Tobler. Charlestown: Printed for the Editor; Savannah: James Johnston; [Charleston:] Robert Wells. 16 ll. NHi; ScHi.   13114

The SOUTH-CAROLINA and Georgia Almanack for 1774. By John Tobler. Charlestown: Printed for the Editor; Robert Wells; Savannah: James Johnston. 16 ll. ScHi; ViU.   13115

WELL'S [sic] Register: together with an Almanack for 1774. By George Andrews. Charlestown: Robert Wells. 48 ll. ScHi.   13116

The SOUTH-CAROLINA Almanack for 1775. By Benjamin West. Charles-Town: Charles Crouch. 12 ll. MWA.   13117

The SOUTH-CAROLINA and Georgia Almanack for 1775. By John Tobler. Charleston: Printed for the Editor; Robert Wells; Savannah: James Johnston. 16 ll. MWA; ScC (14 ll., ntp)   13118

The SOUTH-CAROLINA and Georgia Almanack for 1776.
By John Tobler. Charleston: Printed for the Editor;
Robert Wells; Savannah: James Johnston. 16 ll. DLC;
PHi; ScC (12 ll.); ScHi. 13119

The SOUTH-CAROLINA and Georgia Almanack for 1777.
By John Tobler. Charlestown: Robert Wells & Son.
16 ll. NHi; ScC (12 ll.); ScU-S. 13120

The SOUTH-CAROLINA and Georgia Almanack for 1778.
By John Tobler. Charlestown: Robert Wells & Son.
16 ll. ScC (8 ll.); ScU-S (impf) 13121

POOR Job. An Almanack for 1779. Charles-town:
Nicholas Boden and Co. 12 ll. ScU-S. 13122

The SOUTH-CAROLINA and Georgia Almanack for 1779.
By John Tobler. Charlestown: John Wells, jun. 16 ll.
NN; ScC (ntp) 13123

The SOUTH-CAROLINA and Georgia Almanack for 1780.
By John Tobler. Charlestown: John Wells, jun. 10 ll.
GU-De; ScC (impf); ScHi (impf); ScU-S. 13124

SOUTH Carolina and Georgia Almanack for 1781. By
William Rider. Charlestown: Mills and Hicks. NcD
(11 ll.) 13125

The SOUTH-CAROLINA and Georgia Almanack for 1781.
By John Tobler. Charlestown: John Wells, jun.; Savannah: James Johnston. 18 ll. NHi; ScC; ScHi.
13126

The SOUTH-CAROLINA and Georgia Almanack for 1781.
By John Tobler. Charlestown: John Wells, jun.; Savannah: David Zubly. 18 ll. DLC; ScC (impf); ScHi;
ScU-S. 13127

The SOUTH-CAROLINA and Georgia Almanack for 1782.
By John Tobler. Charlestown: John Wells, jun. 16 ll.
ScC. 13128

The SOUTH-CAROLINA and Georgia Almanack for 1782.
By John Tobler. Charlestown: R. Wells and Son; Sa-

vannah: David Zubly. 16 ll. ScC. 13129

The CAROLINA and Georgia Almanack, or Ephemeries [sic] for 1783. Charlestown: R. Keith and J. M'Iver, jun. 12 ll. DLC; ScC. 13130

The CAROLINA and Georgia Almanack, or Ephemeris for 1783. Charlestown: R. Keith and J. M'Iver, jun. 12 ll. ScU-S. 13131

The CAROLINA and Georgia Almanack, or Astronomical Ephemeris for 1784. [Charlestown:] Printed for the author. 10 ll. MWA (impf); DLC; NT; NcD (7 ll.); ScU-S; ScC (8 ll., ntp) 13132

The SOUTH-CAROLINA and Georgia Almanack for 1784. By John Tobler. Charleston: Nathan Childs & Company. 12 ll. MWA (impf); ScC. 13133

The SOUTH-CAROLINA and Georgia Almanack for 1784. By John Tobler. Charlestown: J. Miller. 12 ll. ScC. 13134

The SOUTH-CAROLINA & Georgia Almanack, or Astronomical Ephemeris for 1784. Charles-Town: A. Timothy. [Evans] 13135

The SOUTH-CAROLINA and Georgia Almanack for 1785. By John Tobler. Charleston: N. Childs & Company. 12 ll. DLC; ScC (10 ll.) 13136

The NORTH & South Carolina and Georgia Almanack for 1786. By Isaac Bickerstaff. Charleston: A. Timothy. 12 ll. ScC (11 ll.) 13137

The SOUTH-CAROLINA and Georgia Almanack for 1786. By John Tobler. Charleston: Childs, M'Iver & Co. 18 ll. DLC; NcD. 13138

The CAROLINA and Georgia Almanack, or Astronomical Diary for 1787. [Charleston:] Printed for the editor. 10 ll. ScC. 13139

The SOUTH-CAROLINA and Georgia Almanack for 1787.

By John Tobler. Charleston: Childs, M'Iver & Co.
[Webber]   13140

The SOUTHERN States Ephemeris: or, the North and South-Carolina, and Georgia Almanac for 1787. Charleston: Bowen and Co.; Burd and Co. 22 ll. Vi.   13141

SOUTHERN States Ephemeries [sic]; or, The North and South-Carolina and Georgia Almanack for 1787. Charleston: T. B. Bowen and J. Markland. [Evans]
   13142

The PALLADIUM of Knowledge; or, The Carolinian and Georgian Almanac for 1788. Charleston: Wright and Co. 20 ll. DLC; NHi.   13143

SOUTHERN States Ephemeris: or, the North and South-Carolina and Georgia Almanack for 1788. Charleston: Bowen, Vandle and Andrews. 18 ll. MWA (14 ll.); ScCC; ScU-S.   13144

The SOUTH-CAROLINA & Georgia Almanac for 1789. Charleston: Markland & M'Iver. 14 ll. DLC (13 ll.); ScU-S; Drake.   13145

The SOUTH-CAROLINA and Georgia Almanac for 1790. By John Tobler. Charleston: Markland & M'Iver. 18 ll. MWA; DLC; InU (15 ll., ntp); ScHi; Drake (15 ll., ntp)   13146

The SOUTH-CAROLINA and Georgia Almanac for 1791. By John Tobler. Charleston: Markland & M'Iver. 22 ll. DLC; GHi; NN; ScU-S.   13147

The SOUTH Carolina and Georgia Almanac for 1792. By John Tobler. Charleston: Markland & M'Iver. 20 ll. DLC (18 ll.); NN; ScHi; ScU-S.   13148

The SOUTH-CAROLINA, North-Carolina, and Georgia Almanack for 1792. By John Tobler. Charleston: W. P. Harrison. 12 ll. MWA (11 ll.); DLC.   13149

The SOUTH-CAROLINA and Georgia Almanac for 1793. By William Waring. Charleston: Markland & M'Iver.

South Carolina - 1794

20 ll. DLC; NN; ScCC; ScU-S (impf); Drake.   13150

The SOUTH Carolina and Georgia Almanac for 1794.
Charleston: Markland & M⟨r⟩Iver. 18 ll. MWA (impf);
NN (17 ll.); MBU (16 ll.); ViU; Drake.   13151

The SOUTH-CAROLINA and Georgia Almanac for 1795.
Charleston: Markland & M⟨r⟩Iver. 18 ll. NN; MHi;
ScHi (16 ll.); ScU-S; ViU.   13152

PALLADIUM of Knowledge: or, The Carolina and
Georgia Almanac for 1796. Charleston: W. P. Young.
24 ll. DLC; NN; GHi (17 ll., ntp); GU; ViU (23 ll.)
   13153

PALLADIUM of Knowledge: or, The Carolina and
Georgia Almanac for 1796. Charleston: W. P. Young.
(Second Edition) 24 ll. ScHi; ScU-S.   13154

PALLADIUM of Knowledge: or, The Carolina and
Georgia Almanac for 1796. Charleston: W. P. Young.
(Third Edition) 24 ll. PHi (23 ll.); ScC.   13155

The SOUTH-CAROLINA and Georgia Almanac for 1796.
Charleston: Markland & M⟨r⟩Iver. 18 ll. MWA; NHi (17
ll.)   13156

PALLADIUM of Knowledge: or, The Carolina and
Georgia Almanac for 1797. Charleston: W. P. Young.
25 ll. DLC; NN; NHi; MWA (impf); GHi.   13157

The SOUTH Carolina and Georgia Almanac for 1797.
Charleston: J. M⟨r⟩Iver. 18 ll. ScHi.   13158

PALLADIUM of Knowledge: or, The Carolina and
Georgia Almanac for 1798. Charleston: W. P. Young.
24 ll. MWA; DLC; NHi; GU-De; ScC; ScHi; ScU-S.
   13159

The SOUTH-CAROLINA and Georgia Almanac for 1798.
Charleston: S. J. Elliott.   22 ll. DLC (19 ll.)   13160

PALLADIUM of Knowledge: or, The Carolina and
Georgia Almanac for 1799. By Isaac Briggs. Charleston: W. P. Young. 24 ll. N; NN; ScCC.   13161

The SOUTH-CAROLINA & Georgia Almanac for 1799.
Charleston: Freneau & Paine. 24 ll. DLC; NHi. 13162

The SOUTH-CAROLINA & Georgia Almanac for 1799.
Charleston: Freneau & Paine. (Second Edition) 24 ll.
ScC (23 ll.) 13163

PALLADIUM of Knowledge; or, the Carolina and
Georgia Almanac for 1800. By Isaac Briggs. Charleston: W. P. Young; T. C. Cox; Bailey, Waller &
Bailey. 24 ll. DLC (ntp); NN (23 ll.); GHi (21 ll.);
RPJCB; ScC. 13164

The SOUTH-CAROLINA and Georgia Almanac for 1800.
Charleston: Freneau & Paine. [Evans] 13165

The SOUTH-CAROLINA & Georgia Almanac for 1800.
Charleston: Freneau & Paine. (Second Edition) 20 ll.
MWA; DLC. 13166

PALLADIUM of Knowledge; or, the Carolina and Georgia
Almanac for 1801. By Isaac Briggs. Charleston: W.
P. Young. 24 ll. MWA; GU-De; ScC; ScU-S. 13167

PALLADIUM of Knowledge; or, the Carolina and
Georgia Almanac for 1801. By Isaac Briggs. Charleston: W. P. Young; T. C. Cox. (Second Edition)
[Evans] 13168

PALLADIUM of Knowledge: or, the Carolina and
Georgia Almanac for 1801. By Isaac Briggs. Charleston: W. P. Young; T. C. Cox. (Third Edition) 24 ll.
ScC (23 ll.); ScHi. 13169

PALLADIUM of Knowledge; or, the Carolina and
Georgia Almanac for 1802. By Isaac Briggs. Charleston: W. P. Young; Bailey & Waller. 24 ll. ScC (21
ll.) 13170

PALLADIUM of Knowledge: or, the Carolina and
Georgia Almanac for 1802. By Isaac Briggs. Charleston: W. P. Young; Bailey & Waller. (Second Edition)
24 ll. ScC (23 ll.); ScU-S. 13171

South Carolina - 1803

The **MIRROR:** or Carolina and Georgia Almanac for 1803. By William North. Charleston: Arno and Query. 24 ll. ScC.   13172

PALLADIUM of Knowledge: or, the Carolina and Georgia Almanac for 1803. By Isaac Briggs. Charleston: W. P. Young; Bailey & Waller. 18 ll. [Sabin 87780]   13173

PALLADIUM of Knowledge: or The Carolina and Georgia Almanac for 1803. By Isaac Briggs. Charleston: W. P. Young; Bailey & Waller. (Second Edition) 18 ll. DLC.   13174

PALLADIUM of Knowledge: or, The Carolina and Georgia Almanac for 1803. By Isaac Briggs. Charleston: W. P. Young; Bailey & Waller. (Third Edition) 24 ll. ScU-S (21 ll.)   13175

PALLADIUM of Knowledge: or, The Carolina and Georgia Almanac for 1804. By W. North. Charleston: W. P. Young; Bailey & Waller. 18 ll. MWA; DLC.   13176

PALLADIUM of Knowledge: or, the Carolina and Georgia Almanac for 1804. By W. North. Charleston: W. P. Young; Bailey & Waller. (Second Edition) 18 ll. ScC.   13177

The **SOCIABLE** Magazine, and Quarterly Intelligencer for 1804. Charleston: J. J. Negrin. 74 ll. ScHi [Seen. Notwithstanding title, this is an almanac.]   13178

PALLADIUM of Knowledge: or the Carolina and Georgia Almanac for 1805. Charleston: W. P. Young. 24 ll. GHi.   13179

PALLADIUM of Knowledge: or he [sic] Carolina and Georgia Almanac for 1805. Charleston: W. P. Young. 24 ll. MWA.   13180

HOFF'S Agricultural and Commercial Almanac for 1806. By Joshua Sharp. Charleston: John Hoff. 24 ll. MWA; ScU-S.   13181

PALLADIUM of Knowledge, and Charleston Pilot: or, the Carolina and Georgia Almanac for 1806. By S. A. Ruddock. Charleston: W. P. Young. 24 ll. MWA; MB.
13182

HOFF'S Agricultural and Commercial Almanac for 1807. By Joshua Sharp. Charleston: John Hoff. 24 ll. ScC.
13183

HOFF'S Agricultural and Commercial Almanac, for the States of Georgia and the Carolinas for 1807. By Joshusa Sharp. Charleston: John Hoff. 24 ll. GU-De.
13184

J. J. NEGRIN'S Directorial Register and Almanac for 1807. Charleston: J. J. Negrin. 64 ll. ScC. 13185

PALLADIUM of Knowledge: or, the Carolina and Georgia Almanac for 1807. By S. A. Ruddock. Charleston: W. P. Young. 24 ll. MWA; MB; ScC (23 ll.)
13186

HOFF'S Agricultural and Commercial Almanac for 1808. By Joshua Sharp. Charleston: John Hoff. 24 ll. MWA; ScC.
13187

HOFF'S Agricultural and Commercial Almanac for 1809. By Joshua Sharp. Charleston: John Hoff. 24 ll. MWA.
13188

MIDDLEBROOK'S Almanack calculated for the Carolinas and Georgia for 1809. [np] Printed for the Book-Sellers in Town and Country. 18 ll. GA. 13189

PALLADIUM of Knowledge: or, the Carolina and Georgia Almanac for 1809. By W. North. Charleston: W. P. Young. 24 ll. ScC. 13190

PALLADIUM of Knowledge: or, the Carolina and Georgia Almanac for 1810. By W. North. Charleston: W. P. Young. 24 ll. ScC. 13191

PALLADIUM of Knowledge: or, the Carolina and Georgia Almanac for 1810. By Isaac Briggs. Charleston: W. P. Young. (Third Edition) 24 ll. ScHi (23 ll., tp impf) 13192

HOFF'S Agricultural and Commercial Almanac for 1811.

By Joshua Sharp. Charleston: J. Hoff. 24 ll. MWA; NcD; PHi; ScC.   13193

PALLADIUM of Knowledge: or, the Carolina and Georgia Almanac for 1811. By A. Beers. Charleston: W. P. Young; J. and B. Crow. 24 ll. ScC.   13194

HOFF'S Agricultural and Commercial Almanac for 1812. By Joshua Sharp. Charleston: J. Hoff; John & B. Crow; [etc]. 24 ll. MWA; GU-De; ScC.   13195

MIDDLEBROOK'S Almanack, for Georgia and the Carolinas for 1812. By Elijah Middlebrook. Adapted to the Southern and Western States. [np, np] MWA (16 ll.)   13196

HOFF'S Agricultural and Commercial Almanac for 1813. By Joshua Sharp. Charleston: J. Hoff; W. H. Timrod; Mr. De Villers. 24 ll. GU-De; MB.   13197

PALLADIUM of Knowledge: or, the Carolina and Georgia Almanac for 1813. By W. North. Charleston: W. P. Young; [etc]. 24 ll. MWA.   13198

PALLADIUM of Knowledge: or, the Carolina and Georgia Almanac for 1813. By W. North. Charleston: W. P. Young; [etc]. (Second Edition) 24 ll. ScC; ScHi.   13199

HOFF'S Agricultural & Commercial Almanac for 1815. By Joshua Sharp. Charleston: John Hoff. 24 ll. MWA; GU-De; Sc (20 ll.); ScC.   13200

HOFF'S Agricultural and Commercial Almanac for 1816. By Joshua Sharp. Charleston: J. Hoff. 24 ll. MWA; Sc (impf); ScHi.   13201

PALLADIUM of Knowledge: or, the Carolina and Georgia Almanac for 1816. By Samuel Ruddock. Charleston: W. P. Young; Bounetheau and Bryer. 24 ll. ScC (23 ll.); ScBe (22 ll.)   13202

HOFF'S Agricultural & Commercial Almanac for 1817. By Joshua Sharp. Charleston: J. Hoff. 24 ll. MWA;

South Carolina - 1817   1259

DLC; ScHi.   13203

The PLANTERS' & Merchants' Almanac for 1817. By
Andrew Beers. Charleston: A. E. Miller. (Improved
Edition) 24 ll. MWA.   13204

The COLUMBIA Telescope Almanac for 1818. By Joshua Sharpe [sic]. Columbia: Cline & Hines. 18 ll. Sc.
13205

PALLADIUM of Knowledge: or, the Carolina and
Georgia Almanac for 1818. By Samuel Ruddock.
Charleston: W. P. Young; Bounetheau and Bryer. 24
ll. ScC.   13206

The PLANTERS' & Merchants' Almanac for 1818. By
Andrew Beers. Charleston: A. E. Miller. 24 ll.
MWA.   13207

The CAROLINA & Georgia Almanac for 1819. By Robert Grier. Abbeville: T. M. Davenport. 18 ll. NjR.
13208

HOFF'S Agricultural & Commercial Almanac for 1819.
By Joshua Sharp. Charleston: J. Hoff. 24 ll. MWA;
ScC.   13209

The PLANTERS' & Merchants' Almanac for 1819. By
Andrew Beers. Charleston: A. E. Miller; [etc]. 24
ll. MWA (22 ll.); NN (18 ll.); Sc.   13210

COUNTRY Almanack for 1820. By Joshua Sharp.
Charleston: W. P. Bason; T Omas [sic] Fleming &
Co.; [etc]. 18 ll. NBuHi (17 ll.); PHC; PHi.   13211

HOFF'S Agricultural & Commercial Almanac for 1820.
By Joshua Sharp. Charleston: J. Hoff. 18 ll. DLC;
ScC.   13212

HOFF'S Commercial or City Almanac for 1820. By
Joshua Sharp. Charleston: J. Hoff. ScC (23 ll.)
13213

The PLANTERS' & Merchants' City Almanac for 1820.
By Andrew Beers. Charleston: A. E. Miller. (Fourth
Edition) 24 ll. MWA; ScU-S (22 ll.)   13214

South Carolina - 1821

BASON'S Country Almanack for 1821. By Joshua Sharp. Charleston: W. P. Bason. 18 ll. DLC; MH; PHi (26 ll., 16 printed on one side only); Sc (12 ll.)   13215

BEERS' Carolinas and Georgia Almanac for 1821. Charleston: S. & W. R. Babcock. 18 ll. NBuHi. 13216

HOFF'S Commercial or City Almanac for 1821. By Joshua Sharp. Charleston: J. Hoff. (Second Edition) ScC (19 ll.)   13217

MILLER'S Planters' & Merchants' Almanac for 1821. By Andrew Beers. Charleston: A. E. Miller. 24 ll. Sc.   13218

MILLER'S Planters' & Merchants' Almanac for 1821. By Andrew Beers. Charleston: A. E. Miller. (Second Edition) 24 ll. ScC.   13219

MILLER'S Planters' & Merchants' Almanac for 1821. By Andrew Beers. Charleston: A. E. Miller. (Third Edition) 24 ll. MWA.   13220

BASON'S Country Almanack for 1822. By Joshua Sharp. Charleston: W. P. Bason; [etc]. 18 ll. MWA; DLC; ICU; NBuHi; PHi.   13221

BEER'S Carolinas and Georgia Almanac for 1822. Charleston: S. Babcock & Co. 24 ll. NcD; MiD-B (fragment)   13222

HOFF'S Commercial or City Almanac for 1822. By Joshua Sharp. Charleston: J. Hoff. (First Edition) 18 ll. ScC.   13223

MILLER'S Planters' & Merchants' Almanac for 1822. Charleston: A. E. Miller. 24 ll. Sc.   13224

MILLER'S Planters' & Merchants' Almanac for 1822. Charleston: A. E. Miller. (Second Edition) 24 ll. MWA; ScC.   13225

BASON'S Country Almanac for 1823. By Joshua Sharp.

South Carolina - 1823 1261

Charleston: W. P. Bason. 18 ll. CtLHi; NcA-S. 13226

-- Issue with added signature. ViU (22 ll.) 13227

BEERS' Carolinas and Georgia Almanac for 1823.
Charleston: S. Babcock & Co.; Ker Boyce and R. Missildine. 25 ll. NN (19 ll.); NBuHi (20 ll.); MiD-B; ScU-S. 13228

The CHRISTIAN Almanac for 1823. By Andrew Beers. Charleston: Charleston Religious Tract Society; S. Babcock and Co.; New Haven: Sidney's Press. 24 ll. GA (23 ll.); ScCC. 13229

MILLER'S Planters' & Merchants' Almanac for 1823. Charleston: A. E. Miller. 24 ll. Sc; ScC. 13230

MILLER'S Planters' & Merchants' Almanac for 1823. Charleston: A. E. Miller. (Second Edition) 24 ll. ScC. 13231

MILLER'S Planters' & Merchants' Almanac for 1823. Charleston: A. E. Miller. (Third Edition) 24 ll. MWA. 13232

BASON'S Country Almanack for 1824. By Joshua Sharp. Charleston: W. P. Bason. 18 ll. MWA; PHi. 13233

-- Issue with 20 ll. NBuHi. 13234

BEER'S Carolinas and Georgia Almanack for 1824. Charleston: S. Babcock and Co. 18 ll. MiD-B; NBuHi; ScU-S (16 ll.) 13235

The CHRISTIAN Almanac for 1824. By Robert Grier. Charleston: Charleston Religious Tract Society; S. Babcock & Co. 24 ll. NBuHi; ScCC. 13236

MILLER'S Planters' & Merchants' Almanac for 1824. Charleston: A. E. Miller. 24 ll. ICU; Sc; ScC. 13237

Miller's Planters' & Merchants' Almanac for 1824. Charleston: A. E. Miller. (Second Edition) 24 ll. MH. 13238

BASON'S Country Almanack for 1825. By Joshua Sharp.

Charleston: W. P. Bason. 18 ll. MWA; NBuHi (15 ll.); Drake. 13239

BEERS' Carolinas and Georgia Almanack for 1825. Charleston: S. Babcock & Co. NBuHi (23 ll.) 13240

The CHRISTIAN Almanac for 1825. Charleston: Charleston Religious Tract Society. 24 ll. ScCC. 13241

MILLER'S Planters' & Merchants' Almanac for 1825. Charleston: A. E. Miller. 24 ll. MWA (23 ll.); Sc; ScC; ScHi (impf) 13242

BASON'S Country Almanack for 1826. By Joshua Sharp. Charleston: W. P. Bason. 18 ll. DLC. 13243

BEERS' Carolinas and Georgia Almanack for 1826. Charleston: S. Babcock & Co. 24 ll. NBuHi. 13244

The CHRISTIAN Almanac for 1826. By Robert Grier. Charleston: Charleston Religious Tract Society; S. Babcock & Co. 24 ll. DLC; ScCC. 13245

The CHRISTIAN Almanac for 1826. By Joshua Sharp. Charleston: Charleston Religious Tract Society; A. E. Miller, printer. 24 ll. RPB. 13246

HOFF'S Agricultural and Commercial Almanac for 1826. By Joshua Sharp. Charleston: P. Hoff. 24 ll. ScC. 13247

MILLER'S Planters' & Merchants' Almanac for 1826. Charleston: A. E. Miller. 24 ll. MWA; CtY; Sc. 13248

MILLER'S Planters' & Merchants' Almanac for 1826. Charleston: A. E. Miller. (Second Edition) 24 ll. MWA; ScC. 13249

The CHRISTIAN Almanack for 1827. By Joshua Sharp. Charleston: Charleston Religious Tract Society; S. Babcock & Co. 24 ll. NcD; ScCC. 13250

MILLER'S Agricultural Almanac for 1827. Charleston: A. E. Miller. 20 ll. ScU-S. 13251

MILLER'S Planters' & Merchants' Almanac for 1827.
Charleston: A. E. Miller. 24 ll. MWA; ScHi.   13252

MILLER'S Planters' & Merchants' Almanac for 1827.
Charleston: A. E. Miller. (Second Edition) 24 ll. ScC.
13253

ROORBACH'S Country Almanack for 1827. By Joshua
Sharp. Charleston: Oville A. Roorbach. 18 ll. MWA.
13254

The CHRISTIAN Almanac for 1828. Charleston:
Charleston Religious Tract Society. 24 ll. ScCC. 13255

MILLER'S Agricultural Almanac for 1828. By Joshua
Sharp. Charleston: A. E. Miller. 24 ll. MWA; DLC;
ScC; ScU-S.   13256

MILLER'S Planters' & Merchants' Almanac for 1828.
Charleston: A. E. Miller. no copy found.   13257

MILLER'S Planters' & Merchants' Almanac for 1828.
Charleston: A. E. Miller. (Second Edition) 24 ll.
MWA.   13258

BEERS' Carolinas and Georgia Almanac for 1829.
Columbia. NcD (missing from shelves)   13259

The CHRISTIAN Almanac for 1829. Charleston: South
Carolina Tract Society; S. Babcock and Co. 24 ll.
ScCC.   13260

The CHRISTIAN Almanac, for South Carolina for 1829.
Charleston: South Carolina Branch of the American
Tract Society; Horace Utley. 18 ll. DLC; GA.   13261

M'CARTER'S Country Almanac for 1829. By David
Young. Charleston: J. J. M'Carter. 18 ll. DLC.
13262

MILLER'S Planters' & Merchants' Almanac for 1829.
By Joshua Sharp. Charleston: A. E. Miller. 24 ll.
AU; GEU; InU (impf); ScC.   13263

MILLER'S Planters' & Merchants' Almanac for 1829.
By Joshua Sharp. Charleston: A. E. Miller. (Second

South Carolina - 1829

Edition) 24 ll. ScC.   13264

MILLER'S Planters' & Merchants' Almanac for 1829. By Joshua Sharp. Charleston: A. E. Miller. (Third Edition) 24 ll. MWA; RPB.   13265

BEERS' Carolinas and Georgia Almanack for 1830. Charleston: S. Babcock & Co. 18 ll. NcD.   13266

BEERS' Carolinas and Georgia Almanac for 1830. Columbia: B. D. Plant. 18 ll. NcD.   13267

BEERS' Georgia and Carolinas Almanac for 1830. Charleston: S. Babcock and Co. 18 ll. GA.   13268

The CHRISTIAN Almanac, for South Carolina for 1830. Charleston: American Tract Society, South Carolina Branch. 18 ll. NcD.   13269

MAC CARTER'S [sic] Country Almanac for 1830. By David Young. Charleston: J. J. M'Carter. 18 ll. CtLHi; MB.   13270

MILLER'S Planters' & Merchants' Almanac for 1830. By Joshua Sharp. Charleston: A. E. Miller. 24 ll. Sc; ScC.   13271

MILLER'S Planters' & Merchants' Almanac for 1830. By Joshua Sharp. Charleston: A. E. Miller. (Second Edition) 24 ll. MWA (22 ll.); MHi.   13272

The SOUTH Carolina Almanac for 1830. Charleston: South Carolina Tract Society; S. Babcock & Co. 24 ll. ScCC.   13273

BEERS Carolinas and Georgia Almanack for 1831. By Elijah Middlebrook. Charleston: S. Babcock & Co. 18 ll. MWA (17 ll.)   13274

The CHRISTIAN Almanac for 1831. Charleston: South Carolina Tract Society; S. Babcock & Co. 24 ll. ScCC.
   13275

M'CARTER'S Country Almanac for 1831. By David

South Carolina - 1831   1265

Young. Charleston: J. J. M'Carter. 18 ll. MWA.
13276

MILLER'S Planters' & Merchants' Almanac for 1831.
By Joshua Sharp. Charleston: A. E. Miller. 24 ll.
ScC; ScHi.   13277

MILLER'S Planters' & Merchants' Almanac for 1831.
By Joshua Sharp. Charleston: A. E. Miller. (Second
Edition) No copy found.   13278

MILLER'S Planters' & Merchants' Almanac for 1831.
By Joshua Sharp. Charleston: A. E. Miller. (Third
Edition) 24 ll. MWA; Sc.   13279

BEERS' Carolinas and Georgia Almanac for 1832.
Charleston: S. Babcock & Co.; Root & Quill; [etc]. 18
ll. MWA; DLC; GA; GU-De.   13280

MC CARTER'S Country Almanac for 1832. By David
Young. Charleston: J. J. McCarter. 18 ll. NBuHi;
ViU.   13281

MILLER'S Almanac for 1832. Columbia: B. D. & T.
H. Plant; A. E. Miller, printer. MWA (29 ll.) 13282

MILLER'S Planters' & Merchants' Almanac for 1832.
By Joshua Sharp. Charleston: A. E. Miller. 24 ll.
MWA (23 ll.); ScC; ScHi.   13283

The STATE Rights and Free Trade Almanac for 1832.
Charleston: A. E. Miller. 42 ll. MB; MHi; NBuHi (41
ll.); PHi; ScC (41 ll.); ScU-S (impf)   13284

BEERS' Carolinas and Georgia Almanac for 1833. By
Elijah Middlebrook. Charleston: S. Babcock & Co.
18 ll. TU (17 ll.); NjR (16 ll.)   13285

The CHRISTIAN Almanac, for South Carolina for 1833.
Charleston: South Carolina branch of the American
Tract Society. 18 ll. MWA.   13286

ESTILL'S Almanac for 1833. Charleston: Wm. Estill.
18 ll. ScHi.   13287

South Carolina - 1833

M'CARTER'S Almanac for 1833. Charleston: Charleston Press. 18 ll. MWA. 13288

M'CARTER'S Country Almanac for 1833. By David Young. Charleston: J. J. M'Carter. 18 ll. CtY. 13289

MILLER'S Planters' & Merchants' Almanac for 1833. By Joshua Sharp. Charleston: A. E. Miller. No copy found. 13290

MILLER'S Planters' & Merchants' Almanac for 1833. By Joshua Sharp. Charleston: A. E. Miller. (Second Edition) 24 ll. MWA; ScC. 13291

The STATE Rights and Free Trade Almanac for 1833. Charleston: State Rights and Free Trade Association; A. E. Miller, printer. 36 ll. MWA; DLC; MHi; NBuHi; NcD (impf); ScC; WHi. 13292

The CHRISTIAN Almanac for South Carolina for 1834. Charleston: The South Carolina branch of the American Tract Society; D. W. Harrison. 24 ll. Sc; ScHi. 13293

M'CARTER'S Country Almanac for 1834. By David Young. Charleston: J. J. M'Carter. 18 ll. CtLHi; NcD. 13294

MILLER'S Planters' & Merchants' Almanac for 1834. By Joshua Sharp. Charleston: A. E. Miller. No copy found. 13295

MILLER'S Planters' & Merchants' Almanac for 1834. By Joshua Sharp. Charleston: A. E. Miller. (Second Edition) 24 ll. MWA; ScC. 13296

BEERS' Carolinas and Georgia Almanac for 1835. By J. N. Palmer. Charleston: S. Babcock & Co. 20 ll. MWA. 13297

M'CARTER'S Country Almanac for 1835. By Robert Grier. Charleston: E. J. Van Brunt. 18 ll. MWA; InU. 13298

MILLER'S Planters' & Merchants' Almanac for 1835. By Joshua Sharp. Charleston: A. E. Miller. 24 ll. ScC. 13299

MILLER'S Planters' & Merchants' Almanac for 1835. By Joshua Sharp. Charleston: A. E. Miller. (Second Edition) 24 ll. MWA; MHi; NN; Sc; ScC. 13300

BEERS' Carolinas and Georgia Almanac for 1836. By J. N. Palmer. Charleston: S. Babcock & Co. 12 ll. CtLHi; GU; NcU. 13301

-- Issue with 18 ll. OC. 13302

GEORGIA and Carolina Almanac for 1836. By Robert Grier. Charleston: E. J. Van Brunt. 18 ll. CtLHi; CtY; NcD; Sc. 13303

M'CARTER'S Country Almanac for 1836. By Robert Grier. Charleston: E. J. Van Brunt. 19 ll. KyU; NcD (15 ll.) 13304

MILLER'S Planters' & Merchants' Almanac for 1836. By Joshua Sharp. Charleston: A. E. Miller. 24 ll. ScC; ScHi. 13305

MILLER'S Planters' & Merchants' Almanac for 1836. By Joshua Sharp. Charleston: A. E. Miller. (Second Edition) 24 ll. MWA; DLC; NjP; Sc; ScHi. 13306

BEERS' Carolinas and Georgia Almanac for 1837. By Elijah Middlebrook. Charleston: S. Babcock & Co. 18 ll. MWA; GU (23 ll.) 13307

BEERS' Carolinas and Georgia Almanac for 1837. Charleston: J. J. M'Carter. 18 ll. ViU (12 ll.) 13308

GEORGIA and Carolina Almanac for 1837. By Robert Grier. Charleston: E. J. Van Brunt. 18 ll. CtY. 13309

M'CARTER'S Country Almanac for 1837. By Robert Grier. Charleston: Richard Van Brunt. 18 ll. CtLHi. 13310

MILLER'S Planters' & Merchants' Almanac for 1837 By Joshua Sharp. Charleston: A. E. Miller. 24 ll. DLC (ntp); GU-De (23 ll.); NHi (21 ll.); ScC. 13311

MILLER'S Planters' & Merchants' Almanac for 1837. By Joshua Sharp. Charleston: A. E. Miller. (Second Edition) 24 ll. MB. 13312

CAROLINA and Georgia Almanac for 1838. By Robert Grier. Charleston: J. J. M°Carter. 18 ll. GEU; GU-De (16 ll.); NcD. 13313

MILLER'S Planters' & Merchants' Almanac for 1838. By Joshua Sharp. Charleston: A. E. Miller. 24 ll. Sc. 13314

MILLER'S Planters' & Merchants' Almanac for 1838. By Joshua Sharp. Charleston: A. E. Miller. (Second Edition) 26 ll. NHi; NcD; Sc; ScC. 13315

MILLER'S Planters' & Merchants' Almanac for 1838. By Joshua Sharp. Charleston: A. E. Miller. (Third Edition) 24 ll. MWA; MB. 13316

BEERS' Carolinas and Georgia Almanac for 1839. Columbia: Elijah Middlebrook. 18 ll. NcD. 13317

BEERS' Carolinas and Georgia Almanac for 1839. By Elijah Middlebrook. Charleston: S. Babcock & Co. 18 ll. MWA; CU. 13318

M°CARTER'S Carolina & Georgia Almanac for 1839. By Robert Grier. Charleston: J. J. M°Carter & Co. 18 ll. PPL. 13319

MILLER'S Planters' & Merchants' Almanac for 1839. By David Young. Charleston: A. E. Miller. 24 ll. NHi (20 ll.); Sc. 13320

MILLER'S Planters' & Merchants' Almanac for 1839. By David Young. Charleston: A. E. Miller. (Second Edition) 24 ll. WHi. 13321

MILLER'S Planters' & Merchants' Almanac for 1839. By David Young. Charleston: A. E. Miller. (Third Edition) 24 ll. MWA; Sc; ScC; ScHi (impf); ScU-S.
13322

BARNETT'S Country Almanac for 1840. Charleston: W. N. Barnett. 16 ll. MWA. 13323

GEORGIA and Carolina Almanac for 1840. By Robert Grier. Charlestown: J. J. M'Carter & Co. 18 ll. CtY. 13324

MC CARTER'S Carolina and Georgia Almanac for 1840. By Robert Grier. Charleston: J. J. McCarter & Co. 18 ll. MWA; CtY; NcD; Sc; ScHi. 13325

MILLER'S Planters' & Merchants' Almanac for 1840. By David Young. Charleston: A. E. Miller. 24 ll. NHi; ScC. 13326

MILLER'S Planters' & Merchants' Almanac for 1840. By David Young. Charleston: A. E. Miller. (Second Edition) 24 ll. MWA; ScC; WHi. 13327

CAROLINA & Georgia Almanac for 1841. By Robert Grier. Charleston: J. J. M'Carter, & Co. CtLHi (17 ll.) 13328

MILLER'S Planters' & Merchants' Almanac for 1841. By David Young. Charleston: A. E. Miller. 24 ll. NHi; ScC; ScHi. 13329

MILLER'S Planters' & Merchants' Almanac for 1841. By David Young. Charleston: A. E. Miller. (Second Edition) 24 ll. MWA; NN; Sc; ScHi. 13330

BEERS' Caroinas [sic] and Georgia Almanac for 1842. Charleston: S. Babcock & Co. 18 ll. GU-De. 13331

CAROLINA & Georgia Almanac for 1842. By Robert Grier. Charleston: M'Carter & Allen. 18 ll. CtLHi (17 ll.); WHi. 13332

MILLER'S Planters' & Merchants' Almanac for 1842.

By David Young. Charleston: A. E. Miller. 24 ll.
DLC; NHi; GA; Sc; ScC; ScU-S.   13333

MILLER'S Planters' & Merchants' Almanac for 1842.
By David Young. Charleston: A. E. Miller. (Second Edition) 24 ll. MWA; ScC; WHi.   13334

BARNETT'S Country Almanac for 1843. Charleston: W. N. Barnett. 18 ll. GA; GEU; GU-De.   13335

CAROLINA and Georgia Almanac for 1843. By Robert Grier. Charleston: M'Carter & Allen. 18 ll. GU-De (17 ll.); NcD.   13336

CAROLINA and Georgia Almanac for 1843. By Robert Grier. Columbia: William Cunningham. 18 ll. CtLHi (17 ll.)   13337

MILLER'S Planters' & Merchants' Almanac for 1843.
By David Young. Charleston: A. E. Miller. 24 ll.
DLC; NHi; NcD; Sc; ScU-S.   13338

MILLER'S Planters' & Merchants' Almanac for 1843.
By David Young. Charleston: A. E. Miller. (Second Edition) 24 ll. DLC; ScC.   13339

MILLER'S Planters' & Merchants' Almanac for 1843.
By David Young. Charleston: A. E. Miller. (Third Edition) 24 ll. MWA; ScC; ScU-S.   13340

BEER'S Carolina and Georgia Almanac for 1844.
Charleston: Babcock & Co. [Turnbull]   13341

CAROLINA and Georgia Almanac for 1844. By Robert Grier. Charleston: M'Carter & Allen. 18 ll. MWA; KyU; ScU-S.   13342

MILLER'S Planters' & Merchants' Almanac for 1844.
By David Young. Charleston: A. E. Miller. (Second Edition) 24 ll. NHi; ScHi.   13343

MILLER'S Planters' & Merchants' Almanac for 1844.
By David Young. Charleston: A. E. Miller; Columbia:

Wm. Cunningham; Miller & Browne, printers. (Second Edition) 24 ll. MWA; NcD; ScHi. 13344

MILLER'S Planters' & Merchants' Almanac for 1844. By David Young. Charleston: A. E. Miller; Miller & Browne, printers. (Third Edition) 24 ll. NjR (23 ll.); Sc; ScC; ScU-S; WHi. 13345

BEERS' Carolinas and Georgia Almanac for 1845. By Charles Prindle. Columbia: Samuel Weir. 18 ll. MWA. 13346

CAROLINA and Georgia Almanac for 1845. By Robert Grier. Charleston: M'Carter & Allen. 18 ll. MWA (13 ll.); CtLHi; NcD. 13347

MILLER'S Planters' & Merchants' Almanac for 1845. By David Young. Charleston: A. E. Miller; Miller & Browne, printers. No copy found. 13348

MILLER'S Planters' & Merchants' Almanac for 1845. By David Young. Charleston: A. E. Miller; Miller & Browne, printers. (Second Edition) 24 ll. NHi; Sc; ScC; ScU-S. 13349

MILLER'S Planters' & Merchants' Almanac for 1845. By David Young. Charleston: A. E. Miller; Miller & Browne, printers. (Third Edition) 24 ll. MWA; InU. 13350

CAROLINA and Georgia Almanac for 1846. By Robert Grier. Charleston: M'Carter & Allen. 18 ll. NcD. 13351

CAROLINA and Georgia Almanac for 1846. By Robert Grier. Columbia: Allen, McCarter, & Co. 18 ll. Sc (17 ll.) 13352

MILLER'S Planters' & Merchants' Almanac for 1846. By David Young. Charleston: A. E. Miller; Miller & Browne, printers. 24 ll. MWA; NcD. 13353

MILLER'S Planters' & Merchants' Almanac for 1846. By David Young. Charleston: A. E. Miller; Miller & Browne, printers. (Second Edition) 24 ll. ScC. 13354

MILLER'S Planters' & Merchants' Almanac for 1846.
By David Young. Charleston: A. E. Miller; Miller &
Browne, printers. (Third Edition) 24 ll. MWA; MBAt;
MH; NHi; Sc; ScC; ScHi; ScU-S. 13355

CAROLINA and Georgia Almanac for 1847. By Robert
Grier. Charleston: M'Carter & Allen. 18 ll. NcD.
13356

MILLER'S Planters' & Merchants' Almanac for 1847.
By David Young. Charleston: A. E. Miller; Miller &
Browne, printers. 24 ll. MWA; GU; NcD (23 ll.);
ScC; NjR (22 ll., ntp) 13357

MILLER'S Planters' & Merchants' Almanac for 1847.
By David Young. Charleston: A. E. Miller; Miller &
Browne, printers. (Second Edition) 24 ll. Sc; ScC;
ScU-S; WHi. 13358

MILLER'S Planters' & Merchants' Almanac for 1847.
By David Young. Charleston: A. E. Miller; Miller &
Browne, printers. (Third Edition) 24 ll. NHi. 13359

MILLER'S Planters' & Merchants' Almanac for 1848.
By David Young. Charleston: A. E. Miller; Miller &
Browne, printers. 24 ll. NN; NcD; ScU-S (23 ll.)
13360

MILLER'S Planters' & Merchants' Almanac for 1848.
By David Young. Charleston: A. E. Miller; Miller &
Browne, printers. (Second Edition) No copy found.
13361

MILLER'S Planters' & Merchants' Almanac for 1848.
By David Young. Charleston: A. E. Miller; Miller
& Browne, printers. (Third Edition) 24 ll. MWA; InU;
NHi; Sc; ScC; WHi. 13362

CAROLINA, Georgia & Alabama Almanac for 1849. By
Robert Grier. Charleston: M'Carter & Allen. 18 ll.
ScU-S. 13363

MILLER'S Planters' & Merchants' Almanac for 1849.
By David Young. Charleston: A. E. Miller; Miller &
Browne, printers. 24 ll. NN 13364

MILLER'S Planters' & Merchants' Almanac for 1849.
By David Young. Charleston: A. E. Miller; Miller &
Browne, printers. (Second Edition) 24 ll. Sc.   13365

MILLER'S Planters' & Merchants' Almanac for 1849.
By David Young. Charleston: A. E. Miller; Miller &
Browne, printers. (Third Edition) 24 ll. MWA; GU;
InU; NHi; ScC; ScHi; ScU-S.   13366

HAYNES' American Baptist Almanac for 1850. T. W.
Haynes, Editor. Charleston: Samuel Hart, Sen. 24 ll.
Vi (17 ll.); Drake.   13367

MILLER'S Planters' & Merchants' Almanac for 1850.
By David Young. Charleston: A. E. Miller; Miller &
Browne, printers. 24 ll. NcD; Sc; ScC.   13368

MILLER'S Planters' & Merchants' Almanac for 1850.
By David Young. Charleston: A. E. Miller; Miller &
Browne, printers. (Second Edition) No copy found.
13369

MILLER'S Planters' & Merchants' Almanac for 1850.
By David Young. Charleston: A. E. Miller; Miller &
Browne, printers. (Third Edition) 24 ll. MWA; InU;
NHi; NcD; Sc; ScC; ScU-S; WHi.   13370

TENNESSEE

The **TENNESSEE** Almanac for 1801. Nashville: Benjamin J. Bradford. Advertised in the "Tennessee Gazette," February 11, 1801.   13371

The **TENNESSEE** Almanac for 1803. Nashville: Benjamin J. Bradford. Advertised in the "Tennessee Gazette," January 29, 1803.   13372

BRADFORD'S Tennessee Almanac for 1809. Nashville: B. F. & Tho. G. Bradford. T (11 ll.)   13373

BRADFORD'S Tennessee Almanac for 1810. [np, np] [Nashville: Thomas G. Bradford] 18 ll. T.   13374

BRADFORD'S Tennessee Almanac for 1811. Nashville: Thomas G. Bradford. Advertised in the "Democratic Clarion and Tennessee Gazette," October 10, 1810.
   13375

BRADFORD'S Tennessee Almanac for 1812. By Charles A. Smith. Nashville: Thomas G. Bradford. 26 ll. NcD (impf); T (25 ll.)   13376

BRADFORD'S Tennessee Almanac for 1813. By Charles A. Smith. Nashville: Thomas G. Bradford. 24 ll. NcD (23 ll.); T (23 ll.)   13377

BRADFORD'S Tennessee Almanac for 1814. Nashville: Thomas G. Bradford. Advertised in the "Democratic Clarion and Tennessee Gazette," October 15, 1813.
   13378

BRADFORD'S Tennessee Almanac for 1815. By R. Grier. Nashville: T. G. Bradford. 18 ll. T (17 ll.)
   13379

BRADFORD'S Tennessee Almanac for 1816. By Robert Grier. Nashville: T. G. Bradford. 18 ll. DLC; T (impf)   13380

BRADFORD'S Tennessee Almanac for 1817. Nashville:
T. G. Bradford. 18 ll. MWA. 13381

BRADFORD'S Tennessee Almanac for 1818. Nashville:
T. G. Bradford. 12 ll. T. 13382

BRADFORD'S Tennessee Almanac for 1819. Nashville:
T. G. Bradford. Advertised in the "Clarion and Tennessee State Gazette," September 29, 1818. 13383

BRADFORD'S Tennessee Almanac for 1820. Nashville:
Thomas G. Bradford. 18 ll. T (17 ll.) 13384

The TENNESSEE Almanac for 1821. Nashville: Wilkins & M'Keen. T (17 ll.) 13385

ALMANAC for 1822. By John Beasley. Nashville: G. Wilson. T (7 ll.) 13386

WILSON'S Tennessee Farmer's Almanac for 1823. By Wm. L. Willeford. Nashville: G. Wilson. 18 ll. MWA (12 ll.); T; ViW (15 ll.) 13387

WILSON'S Tennessee Farmer's Almanac for 1824.
Nashville: G. Wilson. MWA (17 ll.); ViW (15 ll.)
13388
WILSON'S Tennessee Farmer's Almanac for 1825.
Nashville: G. Wilson. 18 ll. MWA. 13389

HILL'S Tennessee Almanac, and State Register for 1826.
By J. B. Hill. Fayetteville: E. & J. B. Hill. 18 ll.
T (ntp) 13390

WILSON'S Tennessee Farmer's Almanac for 1826.
Nashville: G. Wilson. MWA (14 ll.) 13391

CUMBERLAND Almanac for 1827. By W. L. Willeford. Nashville: John S. Simpson. MWA (17 ll.)
13392
EAST Tennessee Almanac for 1827. By Josiah P.
Smith. Knoxville: Heiskell & Brown. 18 ll. T. 13393

HILL'S Tennessee Almanac, and State Register for 1827.

Tennessee - 1828

By J. B. Hill. Fayetteville: E. & J. B. Hill. 18 ll.
T (impf)   13394

CUMBERLAND Almanac for 1828. By W. L. Willeford. Nashville: John S. Simpson. 18 ll. MWA (ntp);
OClWHi; THi.   13395

WILSON'S Tennessee Farmer's Almanac for 1828.
Nashville: George Wilson. 18 ll. MWA (ntp)   13396

The CHRISTIAN Almanac, for Tennessee for 1829.
Nashville: American Tract Society; John Wright. 18 ll.
MWA; NN.   13397

CUMBERLAND Almanac for 1829. By W. L. Willeford.
Nashville: John S. Simpson. 18 ll. OClWHi; THi; TMC
(16 ll.)   13398

CUMBERLAND Almanac for 1830. Nashville: John S.
Simpson. 18 ll. MWA; OClWHi.   13399

CUMBERLAND Almanac for 1831. By William L.
Willeford. Nashville: Hunt, Tardiff & Co. 18 ll. DLC.
                                               13400
The CHRISTIAN Almanac for Tennessee for 1832.
Knoxville: American Tract Society; James & William
Park. 18 ll. GEU; T.   13401

CUMBERLAND Almanac for 1832. By William L.
Willeford. Nashville: Hunt, Tardiff & Co. 18 ll.
MWA; NcD.   13402

CUMBERLAND Almanac for 1833. Nashville: Hunt,
Tardiff & Co. 18 ll. MWA.   13403

CUMBERLAND Almanac for 1834. Nashville. 18 ll.
MWA (ntp)   13404

DAVY Crockett's Almanack for 1835. Nashville: Snag &
Sawyer. 24 ll. MWA; DLC; TN; MDeeP; TxDW; NHi;
MBAt; NN; MHi; MoSM; CtY; InU (impf); NT. 13405

The TENNESSEE Christian Almanac for 1835. Nashville:

Tennessee - 1835

American Tract Society; W. A. Eichbaum; Alpha Kingsley. 24 ll. NCH. 13405

The WESTERN Methodist Almanac for 1835. By C. A. Smith. Nashville: Garrett, Barnard and Bateman. 8 ll. KyLoF. 13406

CUMBERLAND Almanac for 1836. Nashville: W. Haskell Hunt and Co. 18 ll. MWA; T. 13407

DAVY Crockett's Almanack for 1836. Nashville: Published for the author. 24 ll. MWA; DLC; NHi; NB (impf); MB; MBAt; CtY; MHi (impf) 13408

HILL'S Alabama & Tennessee Almanac, and State Register for 1836. By William S. Green. Fayetteville: J. B. Hill; Winchester: E. Hill. 16 ll. T. 13409

CUMBERLAND Almanac for 1837. Nashville: W. Haskell Hunt and co. 18 ll. T. 13410

DAVY Crockett's Almanack for 1837. Nashville: Heirs of Col. Crockett. 24 ll. MWA; DLC; CSmH (21 ll.); WHi; MMedHi; NHi; MBAt; MoSM; CtY; InU (22 ll., ntp); MiU-C; TxWB (23 ll.); Drake. 13411

CUMBERLAND Almanac for 1838. Nashville: S. Nye and Co. 18 ll. MWA; T. 13412

DAVY Crockett's Almanack for 1838. Nashville: Heirs of Col. Crockett. 24 ll. MWA; DLC; MWeY; NHi; OClWHi; MB; MBAt; MH; MoSM; CtY; MeP; NjMo; InU; OC; NT; N; CSmH; Drake; Streeter. 13413

The CROCKETT Almanac for 1839. Nashville: Ben Harding. 18 ll. MWA; DLC; RJa; T; TN; WHi; NHi; MB; MH; MBAt; MoSM (two varieties); CtY; InU; N; TxWB. 13414

CUMBERLAND Almanac for 1839. Nashville: W. A. Eichbaum; S. Nye & Co., printers. 18 ll. MWA; T; THi. 13415

Tennessee - 1840

The CROCKETT Almanac for 1840. Nashville: Ben Harding. 18 ll. MWA; DLC; RJa; T; WHi; NHi; NB (10 ll.); NjP; MB; MoSM; CtY; ICHi; InU (impf); MDedHi; N; TMC (17 ll.) 13416

CUMBERLAND Almanac for 1840. Nashville: Berry & Tannehill; S. Nye & Co., printers. 18 ll. THi. 13417

CUMBERLAND Almanac for 1840. Nashville: S. Nye & Co. 18 ll. MWA. 13418

HILL'S Tennessee, Alabama, Mississippi and Arkansas Almanac, and State Register for 1840. By J. B. Hill. Fayetteville: E. Hill; Hernando, Miss.: J. B. Hill. 16 ll. MWA (15 ll.); MH (15 ll.); T; NjR (15 ll.) 13419

The CROCKETT Almanac for 1841. Nashville: Ben Harding. 18 ll. MWA; T; Ms-Ar; PHi; MB; MBAt; CtY; MiD-B; InU (fragment) 13420

CUMBERLAND Almanac for 1841. By William L. Willeford. Nashville: S. Nye & Co. 18 ll. MWA (impf); T. 13421

HILL'S Tennessee, Alabama, Mississippi and Arkansas Almanack, and State Register for 1841. By J. B. Hill. Fayetteville: E. Hill. 16 ll. MWA; T (13 ll.) 13422

CUMBERLAND Almanac for 1842. By William L. Willeford. Nashville: W. F. Bang & Co. 18 ll. MWA; T. 13423

CUMBERLAND Almanac for 1843. By William L. Willeford. Nashville: W. F. Bang & Co. 18 ll. T; THi. 13424

CUMBERLAND Almanac for 1843. By William L. Willeford. Nashville: Berry & Tannehill; W. F. Bang & Co., printers. 18 ll. DLC. 13425

The FARMER'S Almanac for 1843. By Jas. Garvin. Knoxville: Jas. C. Moses. 16 ll. TU. 13426

HILL'S Tennessee, Alabama, Mississippi and Arkansas Almanac and State Register for 1843. By J. B. Hill. Fayetteville: E. Hill. T (14 ll., ntp) 13427

CUMBERLAND Almanac for 1844. By William M. [sic] Willeford. Nashville: W. F. Bang & Co. 18 ll. MWA; N; T; TC. 13428

HILL'S Tennessee, Alabama and Mississippi Almanac and State Register for 1844. By J. B. Hill. Fayetteville: E. Hill. 20 ll. T. 13429

CUMBERLAND Almanac for 1845. By William L. Willeford. Nashville: W. F. Bang & Co. 18 ll. MWA; N; T. 13430

The FARMER'S Almanac for 1845. Knoxville: Jas. C. Moses. TKL. 13431

HILL'S Tennessee, Alabama and Mississippi Almanac and State Register for 1845. By J. B. Hill. Fayetteville: E. Hill. 16 ll. T. 13432

The FARMER'S Almanac for 1846. By James Garvin. Knoxville: Jas. C. Moses. 14 ll. MWA; TKL. 13433

HILL'S Tennessee, Alabama and Mississippi Almanac and State Register for 1846. By J. B. Hill. Fayetteville: E. Hill. 16 ll. GEU (10 ll.); T. 13434

CUMBERLAND Almanac for 1847. By William L. Willeford. Nashville: W. F. Bang & Co. 16 ll. MWA. 13435

The FARMER'S Almanac for 1847. By W. D. Carnes. Knoxville: Jas. C. Moses. 16 ll. TKL; TU. 13436

HILL'S Tennessee, Alabama and Mississippi Almanac and State Register for 1847. By J. B. Hill. Fayetteville: E. Hill. 14 ll. T. 13437

POOR Richard's Almanac for 1847. Nashville: Geo. W. House; W. F. Bang & Co., printers. 18 ll. IaDaM. 13438

CUMBERLAND Almanac for 1848. By William L. Willeford. Nashville: W. F. Bang & Co. 18 ll. MWA (ntp); T; TC; THi (impf) 13439

HILL'S Tennessee, Alabama and Mississippi Almanac and State Register for 1848. By J. B. Hill. Fayetteville: E. Hill. 20 ll. T. 13440

HILL'S Tennessee, Alabama and Mississippi Almanac and State Register for 1848. By J. B. Hill. Fayetteville: E. Hill; Huntsville: J. S. Dickson; Tuscumbia: Allan Pollack, Jr.; Florence: Josiah Pollack & Co. 18 ll. T. 13441

CUMBERLAND Almanac for 1849. By William L. Willeford. Nashville: W. F. Bang & Co. 18 ll. T; TC (17 ll.); THi (5 ll., ntp) 13442

HILL'S Tennessee, Alabama and Mississippi Almanac and State Register for 1849. By J. B. Hill. Fayetteville: E. Hill. 18 ll. T. 13443

POOR Richard's Almanac for 1849. Nashville: Geo. W. House; W. F. Bang & Co., printers. 18 ll. T (17 ll.) 13444

CUMBERLAND Almanac for 1850. By William L. Willeford. Nashville: W. F. Bang & Co. 18 ll. MWA (ntp); T; THi (17 ll.) 13445

The FARMER'S Almanac for 1850. By Richard O. Currey. Knoxville: Jno. Miller M'Kee. 16 ll. T.
13446

HILL'S Tennessee, Alabama and Mississippi Almanac and State Register for 1850. By J. B. Hill. Fayetteville: E. Hill. 16 ll. T. 13447

POOR Richard's Almanac for 1850. Nashville: Geo. W. House; W. F. Bang & Co., printers. 18 ll. T. 13448

The SOUTHERN Baptist Almanac and Annual Register for 1850. Nashville: Tennessee Publication Society; Graves & Shankland. 24 ll. MWA; DLC. 13449

The TENNESSEE Almanac, and Medical Advertiser for
1850. By Benjamin Greenleaf. Memphis: S. B. & G.
D. Johnson. 24 ll. MWA; OC; THi (14 ll.) 13450

TEXAS

MERCHANT'S and Planter's Almanac, calculated for the latitude and longitude of Texas. Galveston: J. M. Jones. Immediate predecessor of "Annexation Almanac for 1846," this title was cited as "long and favorably known in Texas" by the "Civilian and Galveston Gazette," December 17, 1845. No copy of any issue is known to exist. 13451

The METHODIST Almanac for 1843. Fitted to the horizon and meridian of Rutersville, Texas. New-York: G. Lane & P. P. Sandford, for the Methodist Episcopal Church; J. Collord, printer. 26 ll. Tx. 13452

ANNEXATION Almanac for 1846. Galveston: J. M. Jones. Advertised in the "Civilian and Galveston Gazette," December 17, 1845. 13453

UTAH

DESERET Almanac for 1851. By W. W. Phelps. G. S. L. City: W. Richards. 8 ll. USlC.   13454

DESERET Almanac for 1852. By W. W. Phelps. G. S. L. City: W. Richards. 24 ll. CtY; USlC.   13455

DESERET Almanac for 1853. By W. W. Phelps. G. S. L. City: W. Richards. 16 ll. USlC.   13456

DESERET Almanac for 1854. By W. W. Phelps. G. S. L. City: W. Richards. 16 ll. MWA; CtY; USlC. 13457

DESERET Almanac for 1855. By William W. Phelps. Great Salt Lake City: Arieh C. Brower. 16 ll. USlC.
13458

No entry.   13459

ALMANAC for 1859. By W. W. Phelps. Great Salt Lake City: J. McKnight. 8 ll. CtY (impf); USlC; Drake.   13460

ALMANAC for 1860. By W. W. Phelps. Great Salt Lake City: J. McKnight. 16 ll. NNC; CtY; USlC.
13461

ALMANAC for 1861. By W. W. Phelps. Great Salt Lake City: Deseret News. 16 ll. CtY; USlC.   13462

ALMANAC for 1862. By W. W. Phelps. Great Salt Lake City: Deseret News. 16 ll. CU-B; CtY; Drake.
13463

ALMANAC for 1863. By W. W. Phelps. Great Salt Lake City: Deseret News. 16 ll. CtY; USlC; Drake.
13464

ALMANAC for 1864. By W. W. Phelps. Great Salt

Lake City: Deseret News. 16 ll. CtY; USlC; Drake.
13465
DESERET Almanac for 1865. By W. W. Phelps.
Great Salt Lake City: Deseret News. 8 ll. MWA; USlC.
13466

VERMONT

The **VERMONT** Almanack for 1784. See the New York State list.   13467

An **ASTRONOMICAL** Diary or Almanack for 1785. By Samuel Elsworth. Bennington: Haswell & Russell. 12 ll. MWA (10 ll.); CSmH; Vt; VtU; Spargo   13468

The **VERMONT** Almanack for 1785. By Eliakim Perry, Jun. Bennington: Haswell & Russell. 12 ll. MWA; DLC (impf); InU (4 ll.); Vt; VtU; VtBennHi.   13469

An **ASTRONOMICAL** Diary, or Almanack for 1786. By Samuel Ellsworth. Bennington: Haswell & Russell. 12 ll. NHi; NRMA; Spargo (impf)   13470

The **UNIVERSAL** Calendar, and the North American Almanack for 1788. By Samuel Stearns. Bennington: Haswell & Russell. 12 ll. MWA (impf); Spargo.   13471

The **UNIVERSAL** Calendar, and the North American Almanack for 1789. By Samuel Stearns. Bennington: Haswell & Russell. 12 ll. MWA; Vt; VtU; Spargo.   13472

The **UNIVERSAL** Calendar, and Northamerican Almanack for 1790. By Samuel Stearns. Bennington: Haswell & Russell. 12 ll. MWA; DLC; NN (10 ll.); Vt; VtHi.   13473

The **UNIVERSAL** Calendar: and Northamerican Almanack for 1791. By Samuel Stearns. Bennington: Anthony Haswell. 12 ll. MWA; DLC; Spargo.   13474

HASWELL'S Vermont Almanac for 1792. By Stephen Thorn. Bennington: Anthony Haswell. 12 ll. MWA (impf); NHi; VtBennHi; VtHi; Spargo.   13475

Vermont - 1794

An ALMANACK, and Register, for the State of Vermont for 1794. See the New Hampshire list. 13476

HASWELL'S Calendar, or Vermont Almanack for 1794. Bennington: Anthony Haswell. Spargo. 13477

LYON'S Vermont Calendar: or, a Planetary Diary for 1794. Rutland: J. Lyon. DLC (8 ll.) 13478

The VERMONT Almanac and Register for 1794. Rutland: James Kirkaldie. [Morrison] 13479

HASWELL'S Calendar, Or Vermont Almanack for 1795. By Adam Astrologist. Bennington: A. Haswell. 12 ll. MWA (10 ll.); ICHi; InU (10 ll.); VtHi; Spargo. 13480

LYON'S Vermont Calendar: Or, A Planetary Diary for 1795. Rutland: James Lyon. 31 ll. MWA (27 ll.); PPPrHi; RPJCB. 13481

The VERMONT Almanac, and Register for 1795. Windsor: Alden Spooner. 30 ll. MWA; NN; NHi (23 ll.); MHi (impf); VtHi; Vt (ntp); M (impf); VtU; BritMus; Spargo. 13482

The VERMONT Almanack and Register for 1795. By Samuel Williams. Rutland: James Kirkaldie. [Cooley] 13483

HASWELL'S Almanack, and Register, for the State of Vermont for 1796. By Adam Astrologist. Bennington: Anthony Haswell. 18 ll. MWA; DLC (impf); ICHi; BritMus; Spargo. 13484

HASWELL'S Useful Sheet Almanack for 1796. Bennington: Anthony Haswell. Broadside. [Cooley] 13485

LYON'S Vermont Calendar: or, A Planetary Diary for 1796. Rutland: James Lyon. 31 ll. RPJCB. 13486

The VERMONT Almanac for 1796. Rutland: James Kirkaldie. 12 ll. [Evans] 13487

The VERMONT Almanac and Register for 1796. Rutland:

James Kirkaldie. 27 ll. MWA (26 ll.); Vt (impf);
VtHi (impf)   13488

HASWELL'S Almanack, and Register, for the State of Vermont for 1797. By Adam Astrologist. Bennington: Anthony Haswell. 18 ll. ICHi; Spargo.   13489

The VERMONT Almanack for 1797. Rutland: James Kirkaldie. 12 ll. VtU.   13490

The VERMONT Almanac and Register for 1797. Rutland: The Printing Office. 30 ll. MWA; NHi; Vt (ntp); VtHi; VtU (26 ll.); BritMus.   13491

HASWELL'S Federal and Vermont Register for 1798. Bennington: Anthony Haswell. 18 ll. Advertised in the "Vermont Gazette," December 26, 1797.   13492

The VERMONT Almanac for 1798. Rutland: [np] 18 ll. MWA (16 ll.); CtY.   13493

The VERMONT Almanac and Register for 1798. Rutland: The Printing Office. Advertised in the "Rutland Herald," December 18, 1797.   13494

FARLEY & Goss' Almanac, or Vermont Calendar for 1799. Peacham: Farley & Goss. 12 ll. DLC (impf); VtStjF.   13495

The GENTLEMEN'S and Ladies' Diary: and Almanac for 1799. By Asa Houghton. Putney: Cornelius Sturtevant. 24 ll. MWA; DLC (22 ll.); N (21 ll.); InU; VtHi.   13496

The VERMONT Almanac, and Register for 1799. Rutland: John Walker, jun. 22 ll. Vt; BritMus.   13497

The VERMONT Almanac, and Register for 1799. Rutland: John Walker, Jr. for S. Williams. 22 ll. DLC; Vt; BritMus.   13498

FARLEY & Goss' Almanac, or Vermont Calendar for 1800. Peacham: Farley & Goss. 12 ll. DLC. 13499

FARMERS Almanac for 1800. By Andrew Beers. [np:] Archibald Pritchard. Ct (10 ll.)   13500

The FARMERS' Almanac for 1800. By Andrew Beers. [np:] Archibald Pritchard. CtLHi (9 ll.)   13501

HASWELL'S Vermont and New York Almanack for 1800. Bennington: Anthony Haswell. 12 ll. MWA; NN; ICHi; VtHi; Spargo.   13502

SPOONER'S Vermont and New York Almanack for 1800. Bennington: Judah P. Spooner. CtY.   13503

The VERMONT Almanac and Register for 1800. Rutland: Printing Office. 18 ll. MWA; NN; BritMus.
13504
HASWELL'S Vermont and New-York Almanac for 1801. Bennington: Anthony Haswell. 12 ll. MWA.   13505

An ASTRONOMICAL Diary, or, Almanack for 1802. By Joel Sanford. Bennington: Collier & Stockwell. 12 ll. MWA; DLC; CtHi; CtLHi; CtY; OClWHi; VtHi; VtU.
13506
STAR Cross. By William Trescott. Peacham: Samuel Goss. 1802. 12 ll. MWA.   13507

The VERMONT Register and Almanac for 1802. Middlebury: Huntington & Fitch. [Gilman]   13508

The VERMONT Almanac for 1803. By Isaac Rice. Bennington: A. Haswell. 18 ll. MWA; NHi; CtY; VtBennHi (17 ll.)   13509

The VERMONT Register and Almanac for 1803. Middlebury: Huntington & Fitch. 48 ll. MWA; DLC; NHi; CtY; M; VtHi; VtU; BritMus.   13510

BEERS'S Calendar, or Vermont Almanack for 1804. By -- Beers [sic]. Manchester: W. Stockwell. 12 ll. MWA; DLC; VtHi.   13511

HUNTINGTON & Fitch's Vermont Almanac for 1804. By Eben W. Judd. Middlebury: Huntington & Fitch. 12 ll.

VtHi.   13512

NORTHERN Callendar [sic], or Vermont Almanack for 1804. By -- Beers [sic]. Manchester: W. Stockwell. 12 ll. MWA; DLC; CtY (3 ll.); VtHi.   13513

The VERMONT Register and Almanac for 1804. Middlebury: Huntington & Fitch. 48 ll. MWA; DLC; NHi; VtHi (impf); VtU.   13514

HASWELL & Smead's Calendar, or the Newengland & Newyork [sic] Almanac for 1805. Bennington: Haswell & Smead. 18 ll. MWA.   13515

The NEW-HAMPSHIRE and Vermont Almanack for 1805. Windsor: Nahum Mower. 24 ll. MWA; DLC; CtY; NhHi; VtHi.   13516

The VERMONT Almanac for 1805. By Eben W. Judd. Middlebury: Huntington & Fitch. 10 ll. DLC.   13517

The VERMONT Register and Almanac for 1805. Middlebury: Huntington & Fitch. 69 ll. MWA; DLC; NHi; VtHi.   13518

The CONNECTICUT, New-York and Vermont Almanac for 1806. By Eben W. Judd. Middlebury: Huntington & Fitch. 12 ll. MWA; CLU; Ct (11 ll.); InU (impf); NRMA.   13519

FARMERS' Calendar; or, New-York, Connecticut, and Vermont Almanack for 1806. By Andrew Beers. Manchester: A. Prichard. 12 ll. CtLHi.   13520

MOWER'S New-Hampshire and Vermont Almanac for 1806. By Amos Cole. Windsor: Nahum Mower; [etc]. 24 ll. MWA; DLC; NN; CtY; VtHi; VtStjF (21 ll.)   13521

The VERMONT Register and Almanac for 1806. Middlebury: Huntington & Fitch. 72 ll. MWA; NHi; VtHi; VtU.   13522

Vermont - 1807

FARMERS' Calendar: or the Vermont, Connecticut, and New-York Almanack for 1807. By Andrew Beers. Bennington: Anthony Haswell; Manchester: Archibald Prichard. 12 ll. MWA; DLC (impf); Ct; NRMA; VtBennHi; VtHi; VtU.   13523

MOWER'S New-Hampshire & Vermont Almanac for 1807. By Amos Cole. Windsor: Nahum Mower; [etc]. 24 ll. MWA; CtY; NhHi; VtHi.   13524

The VERMONT Almanac for 1807. By Eben W. Judd. Middlebury: J. D. Huntington. N (11 ll.); VtHi (8 ll.)   13525

The VERMONT Register and Almanac for 1807. Middlebury: J. D. Huntington. 72 ll. MWA; NN; VtHi.   13526

FARMER'S Calendar: or the Vermont, New-York, and Connecticut Almanack for 1808. By Andrew Beers. Bennington: A. Haswell. 12 ll. MWA (two varieties); DLC; ICU; NjMoW; VtBennHi; VtHi.   13527

FRANKLIN'S Legacy, or the Vermont and New York Almanac for 1808. By Eben W. Judd. Middlebury: J. D. Huntington. 12 ll. DLC.   13528

The NEW-HAMPSHIRE & Vermont Almanac for 1808. By Amos Cole. Windsor: Alden Spooner. 24 ll. MWA; DLC; NN (21 ll.); CtY; VtHi.   13529

The VERMONT and New-York Almanac for 1808. By Eben W. Judd. Middlebury: J. D. Huntington. 12 ll. MWA (10 ll.); VtHi; VtU.   13530

The VERMONT Register and Almanac for 1808. Middlebury: J. D. Huntington. 76 ll. MWA; DLC; NN; NHi; CtY; MB; VtHi; VtU.   13531

FARMER'S Calendar: or the Vermont, New-York and Connecticut Almanack for 1809. By Andrew Beers. Bennington: A. Haswell. 12 ll. MWA; DLC; NHi; VtBennHi; VtHi; VtU.   13532

The NEW-HAMPSHIRE & Vermont Almanac for 1809.
By Amos Cole. Windsor: H. H. Cunningham & C.
Spear. 24 ll. MWA; DLC; CtY; InU; VtHi; VtStjF
(23 ll.); Drake (21 ll.)   13533

The VERMONT and New-York Almanac for 1809. By
Eben W. Judd. Middlebury: J. D. Huntington. 12 ll.
MWA; VtHi.   13534

The VERMONT Register and Almanac for 1809. Middlebury: J. D. Huntington; [etc]. 72 ll. MWA; DLC; NN;
NHi; CtY; MB; MH; VtHi; VtU.   13535

The COMPLETE New-Hampshire & Vermont Almanac
for 1810. By Amos Cole. Windsor: P. Merrifield &
Co.; J. Cunningham, printer. 24 ll. MWA; DLC (impf);
NHi; CLU; CtY; InU; NBuG; NRMA; NhHi; Vt; VtHi.
    13536

The FARMER'S Calendar, or the Vermont, Newyork,
and Connecticut Almanac for 1810. By Andrew Beers.
[np, np] 12 ll. MWA; DLC; OClWHi.   13537

The FARMER'S Calendar, or the Vermont, Newyork,
and Connecticut Almanac for 1810. By Andrew Beers.
Bennington: A. Haswell. 12 ll. MWA (10 ll.); N;
CLU; VtBennHi.   13538

The FARMER'S Calendar, or the Vermont, Newyork,
and Connecticut Almanac for 1810. By Andrew Beers.
Bennington: Anthony Haswell. 12 ll. NRMA.   13539

The VERMONT and New-York Almanac for 1810. By
Eben W. Judd. Middlebury: J. D. Huntington. 12 ll.
MWA (10 ll.); VtHi (impf)   13540

The VERMONT Register and Almanac for 1810. Burlington: S. Mills; [etc]. 45 ll. MWA; DLC; NHi; MB;
VtHi; VtU.   13541

The COMPLETE New-Hampshire & Vermont Almanack
for 1811. By Amos Cole. Windsor: Merrifield, &
Cochran; J. Cunningham, printer. 26 ll. MWA; NHi
(impf); NNA (21 ll.); CtY; InU; VtHi; VtStjF

(23 ll.)   13542

The FARMER'S Calendar, or the Vermont Newyork and Connecticut Almanack for 1811. By Andrew Beers. Bennington: Anthony Haswell. 12 ll. MWA; DLC; CLU; CtY; ICN; KHi (11 ll.); NRMA; VtBennHi; VtHi; VtU.
                                                               13543
SWIFT & Chipman's Vermont Register and Almanac for 1811. Middlebury: Swift & Chipman; J. D. Huntington, printer. 54 ll. MWA; DLC; NN; MB.   13544

The VERMONT and New-York Almanac for 1811. By Eben W. Judd. Middlebury: J. D. Huntington, for Swift & Chipman. 12 ll. MWA; VtU.   13545

The VERMONT Register and Almanack for 1811. Burlington: S. Mills; [etc] 51 ll. MWA; DLC; NN; NHi; CtY; InU; VtHi; VtU.   13546

The COMPLETE New-Hampshire & Vermont Almanac for 1812. By Amos Cole. Windsor: Merrifield & Cochran. 26 ll. MWA; DLC (impf); CLU; CtY; VtHi; VtStjF.   13547

The FARMER'S Calendar: or the New-York, Vermont, and Connecticut Almanac for 1812. By Andrew Beers. Bennington: William Haswell. 16 ll. MWA (impf); MBC; NRMA; VtBennHi (11 ll.)   13548

SWIFT'S Vermont Register and Almanac for 1812. Middlebury: Samuel Swift; T. C. Strong, printer. 54 ll. MWA; DLC; NN; MB; MHi; VtHi; VtU.   13549

The VERMONT & New-York Almanack for 1812. By Eben W. Judd. Burlington: S. Mills. 10 ll. MWA; DLC; NHi.   13550

The VERMONT and New-York Almanac for 1812. By Eben W. Judd. Middlebury: Samuel Swift; T. C. Strong, printer. 12 ll. MWA; VtHi.   13551

The VERMONT Register and Almanack for 1812. Burlington: S. Mills. 52 ll. MWA; DLC; NHi (51 ll.);

Vermont - 1813

CtY; VtU. 13552

The COMPLETE New-Hampshire & Vermont Almanack for 1813. By Amos Cole. Windsor: P. Merrifield; J. Cunningham, printer. 24 ll. MWA; DLC; MB; NBuG; NhHi; CtY; VtHi. 13553

The FARMERS' Calendar, or the Newyork, Vermont & Connecticut Almanac for 1813. By Andrew Beers. Bennington: William Haswell. 12 ll. MWA; CLU; CtY; NNUT; VtBennHi; VtHi. 13554

The VERMONT & New-York Almanack for 1813. By Eben W. Judd. Burlington: S. Mills. 12 ll. Private collection. 13555

The VERMONT and New-York Almanac for 1813. By Eben W. Judd. Middlebury: Swift & Fillmore. 12 ll. Private collection. 13556

The VERMONT Register and Almanack for 1813. Burlington: S. Mills; J. K. Baker. 54 ll. MWA; DLC; NN; NHi; CtY; MB; MnU; N; VtHi; VtU; VtWinoS. 13557

The VERMONT Register and Almanac for 1813. Middlebury: Samuel Swift; T. C. Strong, printer. 63 ll. MWA; DLC; NN (impf) 13558

The FARMERS' Calendar, or the New-York, Vermont & Connecticut Almanack for 1814. By Andrew Beers. Bennington: William Haswell. 12 ll. MWA (impf); NBuG; NBuHi; CtLHi. 13559

The LADIES' and Gentlemen's Diary, and Almanac for 1814. By Asa Houghton. Brattleborough: William Fessenden. 24 ll. MWA; DLC; NN; MH; CLU; NBuG; NIC; NhHi; NRMA; ICU; InU; VtBennHi (23 ll.); VtHi; VtU; Drake. 13560

The VERMONT and New-York Almanac for 1814. By E. W. Judd. Middlebury: Swift & Fillmore; T. C. Strong, printer. 12 ll. MWA (10 ll.); VtHi. 13561

The VERMONT Register and Almanack for 1814. Burlington: Samuel Mills. 40 ll. MWA; DLC; NHi; MB; VtU; VtWinoS.   13562

The VERMONT Register and Almanac for 1814. Middlebury: Swift & Fillmore; T. C. Strong, printer. 54 ll. MWA; DLC; NN; OClWHi; NSyOHi; CtY; N; InU; VtU; VtHi.   13563

The FARMERS' Calendar, or the New-York, Vermont & Connecticut Almanack for 1815. By Andrew Beers. Bennington: Darius Clark and Co. 12 ll. MWA; DLC; CLU; ICHi; NRMA; VtHi; VtU.   13564

The NEW-ENGLAND Farmer's Diary, and Almanac for 1815. By Truman Abell. Weathersfield: Eddy and Patrick. 24 ll. MWA; DLC (impf); NN (impf); CLU; InU; NhHi; VtHi; VtU; VtStjF; Drake.   13565

The VERMONT and New-York Almanac for 1815. By E. W. Judd. Middlebury: Swift & Fillmore; T. C. Strong, printer. 12 ll. MWA (8 ll.); VtHi; VtU (11 ll.)   13566

The VERMONT & New-York Almanac for 1815. By E. W. Judd. Middlebury: Slade and Ferguson. 12 ll. DLC (9 ll.); NT (8 ll.)   13567

The VERMONT Register and Almanac for 1815. Burlington: S. Mills. 48 ll. MWA; DLC; NHi; NN; MB; N; CLU; VtHi; VtU; VtWinoS.   13568

The VERMONT Register and Almanac for 1815. Middlebury: Swift & Fillmore; T. C. Strong, printer. 48 ll. MWA; DLC; NN; NHi; NSyOHi; MHi; P; CtY; VtHi; VtU.   13569

The FARMERS' Calendar, or the New-York, Vermont & Connecticut Almanack for 1816. By Andrew Beers. Bennington: Darius Clark. 12 ll. MWA; DLC (impf); N; NSyOHi; CLU; CtLHi; CtY; NR; VtHi (impf)
   13570

The NEW England Farmer's Diary, and Almanac for

1816. By Truman Abell. Windsor: Jesse Cochran. 24 ll. MWA; DLC; N; NN (22 ll.); MB (23 ll.); MHi (impf); CLU; NhHi; InU; NBuG; VtU; Vt; VtStjF (21 ll.); VtHi; CtY. 13571

The VERMONT and New-York Almanac for 1816. By E. W. Judd. Middlebury: L. Fillmore & Sons; T. C. Strong, printer. 12 ll. MWA (9 ll.) 13572

The VERMONT Register and Almanac for 1816. Burlington: Samuel Mills; [etc]; S. Mills, printer. 48 ll. MWA; DLC; N; NHi; MB; CLU; CtY; VtHi; Nh; VtU; VtWinoS. 13573

The VERMONT Register and Almanac for 1816. Middlebury: L. Fillmore & Sons; T. C. Strong, printer. 54 ll. MWA; DLC; N; NN (impf); NHi; MHi; VtU; P; VtHi. 13574

ALMANAC for 1817. By Andrew Beers. Middlebury: Samuel Swift; T. C. Strong, printer. 8 ll. VtHi. 13575

BEERS' Almanac for 1817. By Andrew Beers. Burlington: Samuel Mills. 16 ll. DLC. 13576

BEERS' Almanac for 1817. By Andrew Beers. Printed for A. Pritchard. Burlington: S. Mills. 12 ll. MWA; DLC. 13577

The NEW England Farmer's Diary, and Almanac for 1817. By Truman Abell. Windsor: Jesse Cochran. 24 ll. MWA; DLC; NN (21 ll.); NjR (21 ll.); CLU; NhHi; InU; VtU; Vt; VtHi. 13578

The VERMONT Register and Almanac for 1817. Burlington: Saml. Mills; [etc]; S. Mills, printer. 56 ll. MWA; NN; NHi; MB; MHi; CLU; VtWinoS; VtU; MiD-B; VtHi; Drake. 13579

The VERMONT Register and Almanac for 1817. Middlebury: Samuel Swift; T. C. Strong, printer. 54 ll. NN; NHi; CtY; MH; VtHi; VtU. 13580

Vermont - 1818

The LADIES' and Gentlemen's Diary, and Almanack for 1818. By Asa Houghton. Bellows Falls: Bill Blake & Co. 24 ll. MWA; DLC; N; NN; CLU; InU; MH; NhHi; VtHi; Drake. 13581

The NEW-ENGLAND Farmer's Diary, and Almanac for 1818. By Truman Abell. Windsor: Jesse Cochran. 24 ll. MWA; CtY; MBC; NhHi; VtHi; VtU. 13582

VERMONT & New-York Almanack for 1818. By Andrew Beers. [np:] A. Pritchard. 12 ll. MWA; DLC; CtY; NHi; NRHi; NR; VtHi; VtU. 13583

The VERMONT & New-York Almanack for 1818. By Andrew Beers. Burlington: Samuel Mills. 12 ll. CLU. 13584

The VERMONT Register and Almanack for 1818. Burlington: Saml. Mills; [etc]. S. Mills, printer. 54 ll. MWA; DLC; N; NN; NHi; MHi; CtY; InU; VtBennHi; VtHi; VtU. 13585

WALTON'S Vermont Register and Almanac for 1818. Montpelier: E. P. & G. S. Walton. 66 ll. MWA; N; NHi; NNC; MB; P; Nh; InU; Vt; VtBennHi; M; MH; CLU; VtHi; VtU; BritMus. 13586

The GENTLEMAN'S Almanack, and Annual Register for 1819. By Zadock Thompson. Woodstock: David Watson. 24 ll. [Nichols] 13587

The NEW-ENGLAND Farmer's Diary and Almanac for 1819. By Truman Abell. Windsor: Ide & Aldrich for E. & W. Hutchinson, Hartford. 24 ll. MWA; MH; CLU; GU; NhHi; CtY; WHi; VtU; VtHi. 13588

The VERMONT Almanack for 1819. By Andrew Beers. Burlington: E. and T. Mills. 12 ll. DLC; VtHi (impf) 13589

The VERMONT Almanac and Farmer's Calendar for 1819. By Zadock Thompson. Woodstock: David Watson. 24 ll. MWA; DLC; N; VtHi; VtU. 13590

VERMONT & New York Almanack for 1819. By Andrew

Beers. [np:] A. Prichard. 12 ll. MWA; DLC; VtHi.
13591

The VERMONT Register and Almanack for 1819. Burlington: E. & T. Mills. 54 ll. MWA; DLC; NN; NHi; MHi; VtHi; VtU.
13592

WALTON'S Vermont Register and Farmer's Almanack for 1819. Montpelier: E. P. Walton. 64 ll. MWA; NHi; NNC; M; CLU; Nh; VtWinoS; WHi; VtU; VtBennHi; Vt; VtHi.
13593

-- Issue with no cut on titlepage. 64 ll. MWA; N.
13594

The FARMERS' Almanack for 1820. By Andrew Beers. Burlington: E. & T. Mills. 12 ll. [Gilman]
13595

The GENTLEMAN'S Almanack, and Annual Register for 1820. By Zadock Thompson. Woodstock: David Watson. 24 ll. MWA; VtU.
13596

The LADIES' and Gentlemens' Diary and Almanac for 1820. By Asa Houghton. Bellows Falls: Bill Blake & Co. 24 ll. MWA; DLC; MH; CLU; NhHi; InU; WHi; Vt; VtHi.
13597

The NEW-ENGLAND Farmer's Diary and Almanac for 1820. By Truman Abell. Windsor: Ide & Aldrich for Ebenezer Hutchinson, Hartford. 24 ll. MWA; DLC; CLU; N; GU; NhHi; CtY; InU; VtHi; VtU; Drake (21 ll.)
13598

The VERMONT Almanack for 1820. By Andrew Beers. Burlington: E. & T. Mills. 12 ll. MWA; CLU; VtU.
13599

The VERMONT Almanac and Farmer's Calendar for 1820. By Zadock Thompson. Woodstock: David Watson. 24 ll. MWA; DLC (impf); NHi (impf); CLU; VtHi; VtU.
13600

The VERMONT Register and Almanack for 1820. Burlington: E. & T. Mills. 54 ll. MWA; DLC; N; NHi; NN; VtHi; VtU.
13601

WALTON'S Vermont Register and Farmer's Almanack for 1820. Montpelier: E. P. Walton. 60 ll. MWA; N; NHi; NNC; MB; M; MHi; CLU; InU; Nh; VtWinoS; WHi; Vt; VtBennHi; VtHi; VtU.   13602

The FARMER'S Pocket Almanack for 1821. Montpelier: E. P. Walton. 18 ll. MWA; MH.   13603

The LADIES' and Gentlemen's Diary and Almanack for 1821. By Asa Houghton. Bellows Falls: Bill Blake & Co. 24 ll. MWA; DLC; NHi; N; InU (22 ll.); VtHi; Drake.   13604

The NEW-ENGLAND Farmer's Diary and Almanac for 1821. By Truman Abell. Windsor: Ide & Aldrich for Ebenezer Hutchinson, Hartford. 24 ll. MWA (two varieties); DLC; N; NHi (impf); MB (impf); MBAt; MH; CLU; GU; NhHi; CtY; WHi; Vt; VtHi; VtU.   13605

The VERMONT Almanack for 1821. By Andrew Beers. Burlington: E. & T. Mills. 12 ll. DLC; VtHi (imprint lacking); VtU.   13606

The VERMONT Register and Almanack for 1821. Burlington: E. & T. Mills. 54 ll. MWA; DLC; NN; NHi; MB; MH; OClWHi; VtU; VtHi.   13607

WALTON'S Vermont Register and Farmer's Almanack for 1821. Montpelier: E. P. Walton. 72 ll. MWA; N; NHi; NNC; M; MB; MHi; CLU; InU; P; Nh; VtWinoS; VtBennHi; VtU; Vt; VtHi.   13608

The FARMER'S Pocket Almanack for 1822. Montpelier: E. P. Walton. 18 ll. VtHi.   13609

The LADIES' and Gentlemen's Diary and Almanack for 1822. By Asa Houghton. Bellows Falls: Bill Blake & Co. 24 ll. MWA; DLC (impf); InU; VtHi; Drake.   13610

The NEW-ENGLAND and New-York Almanack for 1822. Middlebury: Copeland and Allen. 12 ll. VtMiS. 13611

The NEW-ENGLAND Farmer's Diary and Almanac for

Vermont - 1822   1299

1822. By Truman Abell. Windsor: Simeon Ide for Ebenezer Hutchinson, Hartford. 24 ll. MWA; DLC; NCH; WHi; NhHi; CLU; CtY; InU; VtU; NCanHi (22 ll.); VtHi.   13612

The VERMONT Register and Almanack for 1822. Burlington: E. & T. Mills. 54 ll. MWA; DLC (impf); N; NN; NHi; MH; MHi; MB; InU; VtHi; VtU; BritMus.   13613

WALTON'S Vermont Register and Farmer's Almanack for 1822. Montpelier: E. P. Walton. 72 ll. MWA; N; NHi; MHi; NhHi; OCLloyd; OO; P; NNC; M; CLU; Nh; VtWinoS; Vt; VtU; InU; WHi; VtBennHi; VtHi.   13614

The CHRISTIAN and Farmers' Almanack for 1823. By Andrew Beers. Burlington: E. and T. Mills. 24 ll. MWA (two varieties); CLU; VtHi.   13615

The FARMERS' Almanack for 1823. By Andrew Beers. Burlington: E. and T. Mills. 12 ll. MWA; CLU (impf); CtY.   13616

The LADIES' and Gentlemen's Diary and Almanack for 1823. By Asa Houghton. Bellows Falls: Bill Blake & Co. 24 ll. [Nichols]   13617

The NEW-ENGLAND Farmer's Diary and Almanac for 1823. By Truman Abell. Windsor: Simeon Ide for Ebenezer Hutchinson, Hartford. 24 ll. MWA; DLC (impf); N; NN; NNA; NjR; NhHi; MH; CLU; CtY; InU; Vt; VtU; VtHi; BritMus.   13618

WALTON'S Vermont Register and Farmer's Almanack for 1823. By Zadock Thompson. Montpelier: E. P. Walton. 72 ll. MWA; N; NHi; Ct; MHi; OCLloyd; OO; NNC; MB; M; CLU; Nh; P; InU; VtWinoS; VtHi; Vt; VtHi; VtU.   13619

The CHRISTIAN & Farmer's Almanack for 1824. By Andrew Beers. Burlington: E. and T. Mills. 24 ll. MWA; DLC; CLU; NIC; CtY; Vt; VtU; VtHi; MiD-B.   13620

The FARMERS' Almanack for 1824. By Andrew Beers.

Burlington: E. and T. Mills. 12 ll. MWA; VtHi. 13621

The LADIES' and Gentlemen's Diary and Almanack for 1824. By Asa Houghton. Bellows Falls: Blake, Cutler, & Co. 24 ll. MWA (impf); DLC; NhHi; VtHi.
13622

The NEW-ENGLAND Farmer's Almanack for 1824. By Truman Abell. Alstead, N.H.: Newton & Tufts; Windsor: Simeon Ide; Simeon Ide, printer. 24 ll. MWA; CLU; NhHi; MBC; InU (ntp); Vt; VtU; MDedHi.
13623

WALTON'S Vermont Register and Farmer's Almanack for 1824. By Zadock Thompson. Montpelier: E. P. Walton. 72 ll. MWA; N; NHi; MHi; NhHi; OCHP; OCLloyd; OO; NNC; MB; M; CLU; P; Nh; InU; VtHi; VtWinoS; WHi; VtU; VtBennHi; Vt. 13624

BEERS' Almanack, or, Connecticut, N. York, and Vermont Calendar for 1825. [np:] A. Prichard. 12 ll. MWA; N; NBuHi; NIC; VtHi; Drake. 13625

The CHRISTIAN & Farmer's Almanack for 1825. By Andrew Beers. Burlington: E. and T. Mills. 24 ll. MWA; DLC; N; NN; CLU; InU; VtHi; VtU. 13626

The FARMERS' Almanack for 1825. By Andrew Beers. Burlington: E. and T. Mills. 12 ll. VtHi; VtU. 13627

The NEW-ENGLAND Farmer's Almanack for 1825. By Truman Abell. Alstead, N.H.: Newton & Tufts; Windsor: Simeon Ide; Simeon Ide, printer. 24 ll. MWA; DLC (impf); NNA (23 ll.); NjR; Vt; MHi; CLU; NhHi; NbLM; CtY; WHi; VtHi; VtU. 13628

WALTON'S Vermont Register and Farmer's Almanac for 1825. By Zadock Thompson. Montpelier: E.P. Walton. 72 ll. MWA; N; NHi; Ct; MHi; MoKCM; NhHi; OO; OCHP; OCl; VtWinoS; NNC; MB; P; CLU; M; Nh; InU; Vt; VtBennHi; VtHi; VtU. 13629

The CHRISTIAN & Farmers' Almanack for 1826. By Zadock Thompson. Burlington: E. & T. Mills. 24 ll. MWA; DLC; N; CLU; CtY; InU; VtHi; VtU. 13630

Vermont - 1826

The FARMERS' Almanack for 1826. By Zadock Thompson. Burlington: E. & T. Mills. 12 ll. MWA; DLC (11 ll.)   13631

The FARMER'S Almanack for 1826. By Zadock Thompson. Woodstock: David Watson. 18 ll. MWA; VtHi; VtU.   13632

The NEW-ENGLAND Farmer's Almanack for 1826. By Truman Abell. Alstead, N.H.: Newton & Tufts; Windsor: Simeon Ide; Simeon Ide, printer. 24 ll. MWA; DLC; N; WHi; NhHi; CtY; InU; Vt; VtHi; VtU.   13633

WALTON'S Vermont Register and Farmer's Almanac for 1826. By Zadock Thompson. Montpelier: E. P. Walton. 72 ll. MWA; N; NHi; MHi; NhHi; OCHP; OCLloyd; OO; MB; M; NNC; CLU; NjJ; Nh; VtWinoS; WHi; VtU; VtBennHi; VtHi; P.   13634

The CHRISTIAN & Farmers' Almanack for 1827. By Zadock Thompson. Burlington: E. & T. Mills. 24 ll. MWA; DLC; OClWHi; CLU; MBC; VtHi; VtU.   13635

The FARMER'S Almanack for 1827. By Zadock Thompson. Woodstock: David Watson. 18 ll. MWA; VtHi; VtU; Drake.   13636

The NEW-ENGLAND Farmer's Almanack for 1827. By Truman Abell. Alstead, N.H.: Newton & Tufts; Windsor: Simeon Ide; Simeon Ide, printer. 24 ll. MWA; DLC (impf); N; NN; MHi (impf); WHi; NNC; NhHi; CLU; CtY; OFH (22 ll.); InU; NRMA; Vt; VtHi; VtU.   13637

WALTON'S Vermont Register and Farmer's Almanack for 1827. By Zadock Thompson. Montpelier: E. P. Walton. 72 ll. MWA; N; NHi; MHi; MSo; OCLloyd; M; P; OO; OClWHi; MB; NNC; CLU; Nh; InU; VtWinoS; WHi; VtU; VtBennHi; Vt.   13638

The CHRISTIAN and Farmers' Almanack for 1828. By Zadock Thompson. Burlington: E. & T. Mills. 24 ll. MWA; DLC; CLU; VtBennHi; VtHi (impf); VtU. 13639

The **FARMERS'** Almanack for 1828. By Zadock Thompson. Burlington: **E. & T. Mills.** 12 ll. MWA; DLC; N; NRMA. 13640

The **NEW-ENGLAND** Farmer's Almanack for 1828. By Truman Abell. Alstead, N.H.: Newton & Tufts; Windsor: Simeon Ide; Simeon Ide, printer. 24 ll. MWA; DLC; N; NCooHi; WHi; CLU; NhHi; CtY; InU; VtU; VtBennHi; VtHi; BritMus. 13641

WALTON'S Vermont Register and Farmer's Almanack for 1828. By Zadock Thompson. Montpelier: **E. P. Walton.** 63 ll. MWA; N; NHi; MHi; Mi; NhHi; OCHP; OO; OCLloyd; P; VtWinoS; NNC; MB; M; CLU; Nh; InU; VtU; Vt; VtBennHi; VtHi. 13642

The **CHRISTIAN** and Farmers' Almanack for 1829. By Zadock Thompson. Burlington: **E. & T. Mills.** 24 ll. MWA; DLC; CLU; VtU. 13643

The **COMPLETE** Vermont Almanac for 1829. By Marshall Conant. Woodstock: Rufus Colton. 32 ll. NHi; CtY; VtHi; VtU. 13644

The **FARMERS'** Almanack for 1829. By Zadock Thompson. Burlington: **E. & T. Mills.** 12 ll. MWA; DLC. 13645

The **NEW-ENGLAND** Farmer's Almanack for 1829. By Truman Abell. Windsor: Simeon Ide; [etc]. 24 ll. MWA; DLC (impf); NCooHi; WHi; MH; Vt; CLU; NhHi; VtHi. 13646

WALTON'S Vermont Register and Farmer's Almanac for 1829. By Zadock Thompson. Montpelier: **E. P. Walton.** 72 ll. MWA; N; NHi; MHi; NhHi; OCHP; OCLloyd; OO; P; NNC; M; MB; CLU; Nh; InU; VtHi; VtWinoS; WHi; VtBennHi; VtU; Vt; Drake. 13647

The **ANTI-MASONIC** Almanac for 1830. Woodstock: **D. Watson.** 18 ll. MWA; VtHi. 13648

The **ANTI-MASONIC** Almanac for 1830. By Edward Giddins. Danville: **E. & W. Eaton.** 24 ll. VtHi. 13649

The CHRISTIAN and Farmers' Almanack for 1830. By
Zadock Thompson. Burlington: E. & T. Mills. 24 ll.
MWA; DLC; VtHi; VtU. 13650

The COMPLETE New-England Almanac for 1830. By
Marshall Conant. Woodstock: Rufus Colton. 30 ll.
MWA (24 ll.); DLC; CLU; CtY; VtHi; VtU. 13651

The FARMERS' Almanack for 1830. By Zadock Thompson. Burlington: E. & T. Mills. 12 ll. MWA. 13652

The NEW-ENGLAND Farmer's Almanack for 1830. By
Truman Abell. Windsor: Simeon Ide; [etc]. 24 ll.
MWA; DLC; CLU; NhHi; NBuG; N; Vt; VtHi; VtU.
13653

WALTON'S Vermont Register and Farmer's Almanac
for 1830. By Zadock Thompson. Montpelier: E. P.
Walton & Co. 72 ll. MWA; N; NHi; MHi; Mi; NhHi;
OCHP; VtHi; OCLloyd; OO; MB; M; NNC; CLU; Nh;
InU; VtWinoS; WHi; Vt; VtBennHi; VtU. 13654

The CHRISTIAN & Farmers' Almanack for 1831. By
Zadock Thompson. Burlington: E. & T. Mills. 24 ll.
MWA (impf); DLC; CLU; VtHi; VtU. 13655

COLTON'S Vermont Miniature Register and Gentleman's
Almanac for 1831. Woodstock: R. & A. Colton. 60 ll.
[Nichols] 13656

COLTON'S Vermont Miniature Register and Gentleman's
Pocket Almanac for 1831. By Marshall Conant. Woodstock: R. & A. Colton. 60 ll. NN; MHi; VtHi; VtU.
13657

The COMPLETE New-England Almanac for 1831. By
Marshall Conant. Woodstock: R. & A. Colton. 18 ll.
MWA; DLC; CtY; MB; VtHi. 13658

The FARMERS' Almanack for 1831. By Zadock Thompson. Burlington: E. & T. Mills. 12 ll. MWA; VtU.
13659

The NEW-ENGLAND Farmer's Almanack for 1831. By
Truman Abell. Windsor. Simeon Ide; [etc]. 24 ll.
MWA; DLC; N; NjR; OClWHi; NhHi; InU; Vt;

VtHi. 13660

The **VERMONT** Anti-Masonic Almanac for 1831. By Samuel Hemenway, Jr. Woodstock: Hemenway & Holbrook, printers. 18 ll. MWA; DLC; NHi (17 ll.); VtHi; VtU. 13661

WALTON'S Vermont Register and Farmer's Almanac for 1831. By Zadock Thompson. Montpelier: E. P. Walton and Co. 72 ll. MWA; N; NHi; MHi; NhHi; OCLloyd; OO; M; MB; NNC; CLU; NjJ; Nh; InU; VtWinoS; WHi; VtU; Vt; VtBennHi; VtHi. 13662

The **CHRISTIAN** & Farmers' Almanack for 1832. By Zadock Thompson. Burlington: E. & T. Mills. 24 ll. MWA. 13663

COLTON'S Vermont Miniature Register and Gentleman's Pocket Almanac for 1832. By Marshall Conant. Woodstock: Rufus Colton. 64 ll. NN; NHi; VtHi. 13664

The **COMPLETE** New-England Almanac for 1832. By Marshall Conant. Woodstock: Nahum Haskell. 24 ll. MWA; NjR; MB; CLU; VtHi. 13665

The **FARMERS'** Almanack for 1832. By Zadock Thompson. Burlington: E. & T. Mills. 12 ll. MWA; VtHi. 13666

NEW-ENGLAND Comic Almanac for 1832. Woodstock: Nahum Haskell. 22 ll. VtHi. 13667

The **NEW-ENGLAND** Farmer's Almanack for 1832. By Truman Abell. Windsor: Simeon Ide; [etc]. 24 ll. MWA; DLC; MBUPH; NBuG; NhHi; N; VtHi; Vt. 13668

WALTON'S Vermont Register and Farmer's Almanac for 1832. By Zadock Thompson. Montpelier: J. S. Walton; E. P. Walton, printer. 72 ll. MWA (two varieties); N; NHi; NNC; VtHi; MB; CLU; VtU; Ct; MHi; NjJ; Nh; InU; M; VtWinoS; WHi; VtBennHi; NhHi; OCLloyd; OO; Vt. 13669

The **CHRISTIAN** & Farmers' Almanack for 1833. By

Zadock Thompson. Burlington: E. & T. Mills. 24 ll.
MWA; N; VtHi; VtU. 13670

EATON'S Antimasonic Almanac for 1833. Danville: E.
Eaton; Wells River: Capt. Ira White. 18 ll. MWA;
CtY; IaCrM; PPFM. 13671

The FARMERS' Almanack for 1833. By Zadock Thompson. Burlington: E. & T. Mills. 12 ll. MWA (impf);
DLC. 13672

The NEW-ENGLAND Farmer's Almanac for 1833. By
Truman Abell. Windsor: Simeon Ide; [etc]. 24 ll.
MWA; DLC; MH; NhHi; Vt; VtHi; VtU. 13673

VERMONT Miniature Register for 1833. By Marshall
Conant. Windsor: Richard & Tracy. 76 ll. NN; MH;
VtHi. 13674

WALTON'S Vermont Register and Farmer's Almanac for
1833. By Zadock Thompson. Montpelier: J. S. Walton; E.P. Walton, printer. 62 ll. MWA; N; NHi; NjR;
Ct; MHi; MeHi; NhHi; OCLloyd; OO; M; Vt; NNC;
MB; CLU; VtHi; NjJ; Nh; InU; VtWinoS; WHi; VtU;
VtBennHi. 13675

The CHRISTIAN & Farmers' Almanack for 1834. By
Zadock Thompson. Burlington: E. & T. Mills. 24 ll.
MWA (impf); VtHi (ntp); VtU. 13676

The FARMERS' Almanack for 1834. By Zadock Thompson. Burlington: E. & T. Mills. 12 ll. MWA. 13677

The NEW-ENGLAND Farmer's Almanac for 1834. By
Truman Abell. Windsor: Ide & Goddard; [etc]. 24 ll.
MWA; DLC; NjR; WHi (two varieties); Vt; NBLiHi (19
ll.); PPL; CLU; NhHi; NBuG; M; VtU; VtHi (two varieties); N. 13678

WALTON'S Vermont Register and Farmer's Almanac for
1834. By Zadock Thompson. Montpelier: E. P. Walton. 65 ll. MWA; N; NHi; Ct; MHi; MLoW; MBHM;
NhHi; OCLloyd; OO; M; Vt; OClWHi; NNC; VtHi; MB;

1306   Vermont - 1835

CLU; NjJ; Nh; InU; VtWinoS; WHi; VtU; VtBennHi.
13679

The CHRISTIAN & Farmers' Almanack for 1835. By Zadock Thompson. Burlington: E. & T. Mills. 24 ll. MWA; N; CLU; Vt; VtHi (ntp)   13680

EATONS' [sic] Antimasonic Almanac for 1835. Danville: E. Eaton; Wells River: Capt. Ira White. 18 ll. MWA.   13681

The NEW-ENGLAND Farmer's Almanac for 1835. By Truman Abell. Windsor: Ide & Goddard; [etc]. 24 ll. MWA (two varieties); CLU; NhHi; VtHi; Vt.   13682

WALTON'S Vermont Register and Farmers' Almanac for 1835. By Zadock Thompson. Montpelier: E. P. Walton. 65 ll. MWA (two varieties); N; NHi; MHi; MDeeP; NhHi; OCLloyd; OO; M; Vt; VtHi; NjJ; Nh; InU (64 ll.); VtWinoS; VtStjF; WHi; VtU; VtBennHi; NNC; MB; CLU.   13683

The CHRISTIAN and Farmer's Almanac for 1836. By Zadock Thompson. Burlington: Smith & Harrington, & E. Wellington. 24 ll. MWA (22 ll.); CLU.   13684

The FARMER'S Almanac for 1836. By Zadock Thompson. Burlington: Smith & Harrington, & E. Wellington. 24 ll. MWA; NBuG.   13685

WALTON'S Vermont Register and Farmers' Almanac for 1836. By Zadock Thompson. Burlington: Smith & Harrington & E. Wellington. 66 ll. MWA; M.   13686

WALTON'S Vermont Register and Farmers' Almanac for 1836. By Zadock Thompson. Montpelier: E. P. Walton and Son. 66 ll. MWA; N; NHi; InU (65 ll.); VtWinoS; Ct; WHi; MHi; Mi; NhHi; NjR; OCLloyd; NjJ; OO; MB; NNC; CLU; Nh; VtU; Vt; VtHi; VtBennHi.   13687

The FARMER'S Almanac for 1837. By Zadock Thompson. Burlington: Vernon Harrington, & E. Wellington; [etc]. 18 ll. MWA; VtHi; VtU.   13688

LITTLE Frank's Almanack for 1837. Montpelier: E.
P. Walton & Son. 10 ll. [On cover: "1839."] [Not
seen. This may not be an almanac, but a sort of
primer, as are earlier issues with this title from other
states.] MWA. 13689

The NEW-ENGLAND Farmer's Almanac for 1837. By
Truman Abell. Windsor: N. C. Goddard. 24 ll. MWA;
NhHi; Vt; VtHi; VtU. 13690

WALTON'S Vermont Register and Farmer's Almanac for
1837. By Zadock Thompson. Montpelier: E. P. Walton and Son. 66 ll. MWA (two varieties); N; NHi;
NNC; MHi; OClWHi; M; MB; CLU; NjJ; Nh; InU;
WHi; Vt; VtBennHi; VtU; VtWinoS; VtHi. 13691

The CHRISTIAN and Farmers' Almanac for 1838. By
Zadock Thompson. Burlington: W. R. and F. C. Vilas.
12 ll. VtU. 13692

The FARMERS' Almanac for 1838. By Zadock Thompson. Burlington: W. R. & F. C. Vilas. 12 ll. MWA;
VtHi. 13693

The FARMER'S Almanac for 1838. By Zadock Thompson. Whitehall: Y. D. S. Wright & Co.; Burlington:
H. Johnson & Co., printers. 12 ll. MWA; VtU. 13694

The NEW-ENGLAND Farmer's Almanac for 1838. By
Truman Abell. Windsor: N. C. Goddard. 24 ll. MWA;
NN (impf); NhHi; Vt; VtHi; VtU; WHi. 13695

WALTON'S Vermont Register and Farmers' Almanac for
1838. By Zadock Thompson. Montpelier: E. P. Walton
& Son. 66 ll. MWA (two varieties); N; NHi; NNC;
MB; PPL; MHi; CLU; NjJ; Nh; InU; Vt; WHi;
VtWinoS; VtBennHi; VtHi; Drake. 13696

The FARMER'S Almanac for 1839. By Zadock Thompson. Burlington: C. Goodrich. 12 ll. MWA; CLU;
InU; VtHi; VtU. 13697

The FARMER'S Almanac for 1839. By Zadock Thompson. Wells River: Ira White. 12 ll. VtHi. 13698

The NEW-ENGLAND Farmer's Almanac for 1839. By Truman Abell. Windsor: N. C. Goddard. 24 ll. NhHi; NjR; Vt; VtHi; VtU. 13699

The NEW-ENGLAND Farmer's Almanac for 1839. By Truman Abell. Windsor: Simeon Ide. 24 ll. NjR.
13700

WALTON'S Vermont Register and Farmers' Almanac for 1839. By Zadock Thompson. Montpelier: E. P. Walton and Son. 72 ll. MWA; N; NHi; NNC; M; MB; MHi; CLU; Nh; InU; VtWinoS; WHi; Vt; VtBennHi; VtHi; VtU. 13701

The FARMERS' Almanac for 1840. By Zadock Thompson. Burlington: Vilas, Loomis & Co. 12 ll. MWA; VtU. 13702

WALTON'S Vermont Register and Farmers' Almanac for 1840. By Zadock Thompson. Montpelier: E. P. Walton & Sons. 72 ll. MWA; N; NHi; NNC; M; MB; MHi; Nh; Vt; CLU; InU; VtWinoS; WHi; VtU; VtHi; VtBennHi. 13703

The FARMER'S Almanac for 1841. By Zadock Thompson. Burlington: C. Goodrich. 12 ll. VtHi. 13704

The FARMER'S Almanac for 1841. By Zadock Thompson. Burlington: Chauncey Goodrich. 12 ll. VtU.
13705

The THOMSONIAN Almanac for 1841. Bellows Falls: J. A. Martin; Moore & Fulton, printers. 18 ll. MWA; CLU; InU; MnU; VtHi. 13706

WALTONS' Vermont Register and Farmers' Almanac for 1841. By Zadock Thompson. Montpelier: E. P. Walton & Sons. 66 ll. MWA (two varieties); N; NHi; NNC; MB; M; MHi; CLU; Nh; InU; VtWinoS; VtHi; WHi; VtU; Vt; VtBennHi. 13707

The FARMERS' Almanac for 1842. By Zadock Thompson. Montpelier: E. P. Walton & Sons. 17 ll. MWA;

VtHi; VtU. 13708

WALTONS' Vermont Register and Farmers' Almanac for 1842. By Zadock Thompson. Montpelier: E. P. Walton & Sons. 72 ll. MWA (three varieties); N; NHi; M; MB; NNC; MHi; CLU; Nh; InU; VtWinoS; WHi; VtU; Vt; VtBennHi; VtHi. 13709

The FARMERS' Almanac for 1843. By Z. Thompson. Burlington: C. Goodrich. 16 ll. MWA; CtY; VtU.
13710

The FARMER'S Almanac for 1843. By Zadock Thompson. Montpelier: E. P. Walton & Sons. 16 ll. VtU.
13711

The VERMONT Almanac, Pocket Memorandum, and Statistical Register for 1843. By Hosea Doton. Woodstock: Haskell & Palmer. 72 ll. MWA; N; InU; MB; Vt; VtHi; VtU. 13712

WALTONS' Vermont Register and Farmers' Almanac for 1843. By Zadock Thompson. Montpelier: E. P. Walton & Sons. 64 ll. MWA; N; NHi; NNC; PPL; M; MB; MHi; CLU; Nh; InU; WHi; VtWinoS; VtU; VtBennHi; Vt; MiD-B; VtHi. 13713

The FARMER'S Almanac for 1844. Burlington: Chauncey Goodrich. 16 ll. CtY; VtHi; VtU. 13714

The FARMERS' Almanac for 1844. Montpelier: E. P. Walton & Sons. 16 ll. MWA. 13715

The VERMONT Almanac, Pocket Memorandum, and Statistical Register for 1844. By Hosea Doton. Woodstock: Haskell & Palmer. 72 ll. MWA; N; NHi; NjR; MB; MH; MHi; Vt; VtU; VtHi. 13716

WALTONS' Vermont Register and Farmers' Almanac for 1844. By Zadock Thompson. Montpelier: E. P. Walton & Sons. 64 ll. MWA; N; NHi; NjR (63 ll.); NNC; M; VtHi; MB; Nh; InU; VtWinoS; WHi; Vt; VtU; VtBennHi. 13717

The FARMER'S Almanac for 1845. Burlington: Chauncy

[sic] Goodrich. 12 ll. MWA; VtU.   13718

The **VERMONT** Almanac, Pocket Memorandum, and Statistical Register for 1845. By Hosea Doton. Woodstock: Haskell & Palmer. 73 ll. MWA; NHi (impf); NjR; MB; CtY; InU; Vt; VtU; MiD-B; VtHi.   13719

WALTONS' Vermont Register and Farmers' Almanac for 1845. By Zadock Thompson. Montpelier: E. P. Walton & Sons. 64 ll. MWA; N; NHi; OClWHi; NNC; PPL; MB; MHi; M; CLU; Nh; InU; Vt; VtWinoS; WHi; VtU; VtBennHi; VtHi; ICU.   13720

The **YOUTH'S** Almanac for 1845. By Truman H. Safford, Jr. Bradford: Asa Low. 24 ll. [Gilman]
    13721

The **CULTIVATOR** Almanac for 1846. By Luther Tucker. East Rutland: W. E. C. Stoddard. 16 ll. MWA.   13722

The **FARMER'S** Almanac for 1846. Fairhaven: A. Safford. CtY.   13723

The **FARMERS'** Almanac for 1846. By Zadock Thompson. Montpelier: E. P. Walton & Sons. 16 ll. MWA.   13724

The **FARMER'S** Almanac for 1846. By Zadock Thompson. Newbury: F. & H. Keyes. 12 ll. MWA; VtHi.   13725

GODFREY'S Almanack. Almanack for 1846. By Albert Godfrey. Brattleboro: Joseph Steen. 12 ll. MWA (5 ll.); CLU.   13726

The **GREEN** Mountain Almanac for 1846. By George R. Perkins. Montpelier: Clarke & Collins; Rochester, N.Y.: E. Shepard, printer. 8 ll. VtHi.   13727

The **VERMONT** Almanac, Pocket Memorandum and Statistical Register for 1846. By Hosea Doton. Woodstock: Haskell & Palmer. 72 ll. MWA; N; NHi; NjR; MB; VtU; Vt; MiD-B; VtHi.   13728

WALTONS' Vermont Register and Farmers' Almanac for

1846. By Zadock Thompson. Montpelier: E. P. Walton & Sons. 64 ll. MWA; N; NHi; NNC; PPL (62 ll.); M; VtHi; MB; MHi; CLU; Nh; InU; VtWinoS; WHi; Vt; VtBennHi; VtU.   13729

The YOUTH'S Almanac for 1846. By Truman H. Safford, Jr. Bradford: A. B. F. Hildreth. 24 ll. OMC (23 ll.)
   13730
The YOUTH'S Almanac for 1846. By Truman H. Safford, Jr. Bradford: A. Low; A. B. F. Hildreth, printer. 24 ll. MWA; DLC; N; NHi; OClWHi; MB; MH; VtHi; MHi; CLU; MoSW; InU; VtU; ODa.   13731

The CULTIVATOR Almanac for 1847. By Luther Tucker. Rutland: W. E. C. Stoddard. 16 ll. MWA; N; VtHi.   13732

The FARMER'S Almanac for 1847. Burlington: Chauncy [sic] Goodrich. CtY.   13733

The VERMONT Almanac, Pocket Memorandum, and Statistical Register for 1847. By Hosea Doton. Woodstock: Haskell & Palmer. 72 ll. MWA; N; MB; InU; MiD-B; Vt; VtHi; VtU.   13734

WALTONS' Vermont Register and Farmers' Almanac for 1847. By Zadock Thompson. Montpelier: E. P. Walton & Sons. 72 ll. MWA; N; NHi; NNC; PPL; M; MB; MHi; CLU; Nh; InU; WHi; VtWinoS; VtU; VtBennHi; Vt; VtHi.
   13735
The YOUNG Mathematician's Almanac for 1847. By Truman H. Safford, Jr. Boston: B. B. Mussey; Bradford: A. B. F. Hildreth, printer. 24 ll. MWA; N; MB; MH.
   13736
The YOUNG Mathematician's Almanac for 1847. By Truman H. Safford, Jr. Bradford: A. Low; A. B. F. Hildreth, printer. 24 ll. CLU; VtHi.   13737

The CULTIVATOR Almanac for 1848. By Luther Tucker. Brattleboro: Ryther & Platt; Albany, N. Y.: The Cultivator. 16 ll. VtHi.   13738

The FARMER'S Almanac for 1848. By Zadock Thompson. Fairhaven: A. Graves. 12 ll. N; VtHi; VtU.   13739

The VERMONT Almanac, Pocket Memorandum, and Statistical Register for 1848. By Hosea Doton. Woodstock: Haskell & Palmer. 72 ll. MWA; N; NHi; NjR; OClWHi; MBAt; MB; Vt; WHi; MiD-B; VtHi; VtU.   13740

WALTONS' Vermont Register and Farmers' Almanac for 1848. By Zadock Thompson. Montpelier: E. P. Walton & Sons. 72 ll. MWA; N; NHi; NNC; PPL; MB; M; MHi; Nh; CLU; InU; VtWinoS; VtU; VtBennHi; Vt; VtHi.
   13740a

The FARMER'S Almanac for 1849. By Zadock Thompson. Burlington: Chauncey Goodrich. 12 ll. VtU.   13740b

FREE Almanac, for the World, and Dr. Carter's Compound Pulmonary Balsam Advertiser for 1849. Newbury: F. & H. Keyes. 12 ll. VtHi.   13740c

The VERMONT Almanac, Pocket Memorandum, and Statistical Register for 1849. By Hosea Doton. Woodstock: Haskell & Palmer. Vol. II No. III 72 ll. MWA; N; NHi; NjR; MB; InU; WHi; MiD-B; Vt; VtU.   13740d

-- "Vol. II No. II" [sic] 72 ll. VtHi.   13740e

-- "Vol. II No. IV" [sic] 72 ll. NHi.   13740f

WALTONS' Vermont Register and Farmers' Almanac for 1849. By Zadock Thompson. Montpelier: E. P. Walton & Sons. 72 ll. MWA; N; NHi; NNC; MB; M; MHi; CLU; Nh; InU; VtWinoS; WHi; VtBennHi; Vt; VtHi.   13740g

The FARMER'S Almanac for 1850. By Zadock Thompson. Burlington: Chauncey Goodrich. 12 ll. VtU.   13740h

The VERMONT Almanac, Pocket Memorandum, and Statistical Register for 1850. By Hosea Doton. Woodstock: Haskell & Palmer. 72 ll. MWA; NHi; MB; InU; WHi; Vt; VtHi; VtU.   13740i

WALTONS' Vermont Register and Farmers' Almanac for 1850. By Zadock Thompson. Montpelier: E. P. Walton & Sons. 72 ll. MWA; N; NHi; M; MB; MHi; CLU; Nh; InU; VtWinoS; WHi; VtU; Vt; VtHi; VtBennHi.   13740j

VIRGINIA

GREW'S Almanack for 1735. By Theophilus Grew. Williamsburg: William Parks. Advertised in the "Maryland Gazette," November 22, 1734. 13741

The VIRGINIA Almanack for 1741. Williamsburg. DLC (14 ll., ntp) 13742

WARNER'S Almanack for 1742. By John Warner. Williamsburg: Wm. Parks. DLC (13 ll.) 13743

The VIRGINIA Almanack for 1743. Williamsburg. DLC (10 ll., ntp); ViW (7 ll., ntp) 13744

The VIRGINIA Almanac for 1744. Williamsburg. DLC (10 ll., ntp) 13745

The VIRGINIA Almanack for 1747. Williamsburg: Wm. Parks. ViWC. 13746

The VIRGINIA Almanack for 1748. Williamsburg: William Parks. ViWC (11 ll.) 13747

The VIRGINIA Almanack for 1749. Williamsburg: William Parks. 16 ll. CSmH (14 ll.); ViWC (13 ll.) 13748

The VIRGINIA Almanack for 1750. Williamsburg: William Parks. 12 ll. DLC (9 ll., ntp); ViWC (impf) 13749

The VIRGINIA Almanack for 1751. Williamsburg: William Hunter. 16 ll. DLC; CSmH. 13750

The VIRGINIA Almanack for 1752. By Theophilus Wreg. Williamsburg: William Hunter. 18 ll. DLC; CSmH; Vi (ntp) 13751

The VIRGINIA Almanack for 1753. Williamsburg:
William Hunter. 16 ll. DLC; NN (14 ll.) 13752

The VIRGINIA Almanack for 1754. By Theophilus
Wreg. Williamsburg: William Hunter. 16 ll. DLC;
PU; ViW (14 ll.) 13753

The VIRGINIA Almanack for 1755. Williamsburg:
William Hunter. 16 ll. DLC; Vi (15 ll.); ViU (15
ll.) 13754

The VIRGINIA Almanack for 1756. By Theophilus Wreg.
Williamsburg: William Hunter. 16 ll. ViHi; ViW (14
ll.) 13755

The VIRGINIA Almanack for 1757. By Theophilus
Wreg. Williamsburg: William Hunter. 16 ll. ViHi (12
ll.); ViW (14 ll.); ViWC. 13756

The VIRGINIA Almanac for 1758. By Theophilus Wreg.
Williamsburg: William Hunter. 16 ll. DLC (impf);
MWA; NHi; CSmH; ViHi (15 ll.); ViW (14 ll.); ViWC
(14 ll.) 13757

The VIRGINIA Almanack for 1759. By Theophilus
Wreg. Williamsburg: William Hunter. 16 ll. ViHi (15
ll.); ViW; ViWC (12 ll.) 13758

The VIRGINIA Almanack for 1760. By Theophilus Wreg.
Williamsburg: William Hunter. 16 ll. ViW (2 ll.);
ViWC ("appendix" only) 13759

The VIRGINIA Almanack for 1761. By Theophilus Wreg.
Williamsburg: William Hunter. 18 ll. DLC; ViHi.
13760

The VIRGINIA Almanack for 1762. By Theophilus Wreg.
Williamsburg: Joseph Royle, and Co. 16 ll. DLC;
CSmH (11 ll.); WHi (impf); VtU. 13761

-- Issue with 34 ll. ViWC. 13762

The VIRGINIA Almanack for 1763. By Theophilus Wreg.
Williamsburg: Joseph Royle & Co. 24 ll. [Morrison

Virginia - 1764

cites copy in DLC. Not found.] 13763

The VIRGINIA Almanack for 1764. By Theophilus Wreg. Williamsburg: Joseph Royle, and Co. 24 ll. MiU-C.
13764

The VIRGINIA Almanack for 1765. By Theophilus Wreg. Williamsburg: Joseph Royle, and Co. 24 ll. DLC; MiU-C; ViU (23 ll.); WHi. 13765

The VIRGINIA Almanack for 1766. By Theophilus Wreg. Williamsburg: Alexander Purdie, and Co. 12 ll. DLC; CSmH; MiU-C; PHi (10 ll.) 13766

The VIRGINIA Almanack for 1767. By Job Grant. Williamsburg: William Rind. 20 ll. MiU-C; PPAmP.
13767

The VIRGINIA Almanack for 1767. By Theophilus Grew. Williamsburg: Purdie and Dixon. 16 ll. CSmH (15 ll.)
13768

The VIRGINIA Almanack for 1767. By Theophilus Wreg. Williamsburg: Alexander Purdie & Co. 16 ll. DLC (impf); ViHi (14 ll., ntp) 13769

The VIRGINIA Almanack for 1768. By T. T. Williamsburg: Purdie and Dixon. 20 ll. DLC; CSmH; MH; ViHi. 13770

The VIRGINIA Almanack for 1769. By T. T. Williamsburg: Purdie and Dixon. 24 ll. DLC (22 ll.); CSmH; ViWC. 13771

The VIRGINIA Almanack, and Ladies Diary for 1769. By Merlin Rhymer. Williamsburg: William Rind. 24 ll. DLC (18 ll.); ViHi; ViU (20 ll., ntp) 13772

The VIRGINIA Almanack for 1770. Williamsburg: William Rind. 18 ll. DLC; ViHi (14 ll.) 13773

The VIRGINIA Almanack for 1770. By T. T. Williamsburg: Purdie and Dixon. 20 ll. MWA (impf); DLC; ViU (18 ll., ntp) 13774

The VIRGINIA Almanack for 1771. Williamsburg: Purdie

& Dixon. 24 ll. DLC; ViU; ViWC. 13775

The VIRGINIA Almanack for 1771. Williamsburg: William Rind. 16 ll. MHi; ViHi; WHi. 13776

The VIRGINIA Almanack for 1772. Williamsburg: Purdie & Dixon. 24 ll. DLC; ViHi; ViU (impf) 13777

The VIRGINIA Almanack for 1772. Williamsburg: William Rind. 16 ll. MWA; DLC; NN; MHi. 13778

The VIRGINIA Almanack for 1773. Williamsburg: Purdie & Dixon. 24 ll. MWA; DLC; Vi; ViHi (11 ll.) 13779

The VIRGINIA Almanack for 1773. Williamsburg: William Rind. 18 ll. DLC; ViHi (ntp) 13780

The VIRGINIA Almanack for 1774. Williamsburg: Purdie & Dixon. 24 ll. MWA; DLC; MHi; ViU; ViWC. 13781

The VIRGINIA Almanack for 1774. By Mr. Rittenhouse. Williamsburg: William Rind. 24 ll. MWA; DLC. 13782

The VIRGINIA Almanack for 1775. Williamsburg: John Dixon and William Hunter. 24 ll. MWA; DLC. 13783

The VIRGINIA Almanack for 1775. Williamsburg: Purdie & Dixon. 24 ll. ViWC. 13784

The VIRGINIA Almanack for 1775. By David Rittenhouse. Williamsburg: John Pinkney, for the Benefit of Clementina Rind's Children. 24 ll. ViHi (12 ll.); ViU (22 ll.) 13785

The VIRGINIA Almanack for 1776. By David Rittenhouse. Williamsburg: J. Dixon & W. Hunter. 24 ll. MWA; DLC; NN (23 ll.); ViHi (16 ll.); ViU; ViWC. 13786

The VIRGINIA Almanack for 1777. By D. Rittenhouse. Williamsburg: Dixon & Hunter. 16 ll. MWA; DLC; NN; CSmH; OHi; ViHi. 13787

Virginia - 1778

The VIRGINIA Almanack for 1778. By David Rittenhouse. Williamsburg: J. Dixon & W. Hunter. 12 ll. MWA; DLC; NN; ViU; ViW (10 ll.); ViWC (10 ll.); Wv-Ar. 13788

The VIRGINIA Almanack for 1779. By David Rittenhouse. Williamsburg: J. Dixon & W. Hunter. 12 ll. DLC; ViHi; ViWC. 13789

The VIRGINIA Almanack for 1779. By David Rittenhouse. Williamsburg: J. Dixon & T. Nicolson. 12 ll. MWA; DLC; ViU (11 ll.) 13790

The VIRGINIA Almanack for 1780. By David Rittenhouse. Williamsburg: J. Dixon & T. Nicolson. 12 ll. MWA; DLC; PHi; Vi (impf); ViU; ViWC. 13791

The VIRGINIA Almanac for 1781. By Robert Andrews. Richmond: J. Dixon, & T. Nicolson. 12 ll. MWA; DLC; ViWC. 13792

The VIRGINIA Almanack for 1782. By Robert Andrews. Richmond: J. Dixon, & T. Nicolson. 12 ll. MWA; NN. 13793

The VIRGINIA Almanack for 1782. By Robert Andrews. Richmond: Nicolson & Prentis. 12 ll. ViWC. 13794

The VIRGINIA Almanack for 1783. By Robert Andrews. Richmond: Nicolson & Prentis. 12 ll. DLC; PHi; ViU (10 ll., ntp); ViWC. 13795

The VIRGINIA Almanack for 1784. By Robert Andrews. Richmond: Dixon & Holt. 12 ll. MWA (impf); DLC. 13796

The VIRGINIA Almanack for 1784. By Robert Andrews. Richmond: Nicolson and Prentis. 12 ll. Vi; ViU; ViWC. 13797

The VIRGINIA Almanack for 1785. By Robert Andrews. Richmond: Dixon and Holt. 16 ll. MWA; DLC (14 ll.); ViU (15 ll.); ViWC. 13798

The VIRGINIA Almanack for 1786. By Robert Andrews.

1318   Virginia - 1786

Richmond: Dixon & Holt. 16 ll. ViHi.   13799

The VIRGINIA Almanac for 1786. By Robert Andrews.
Richmond: Thomas Nicolson. 12 ll. MWA; DLC;
CSmH; DeWint; NcD; Vi; ViU; ViWC.   13800

-- Issue with 20 ll. ViW.   13801

A NEW Virginia Almanack for 1787. Richmond: W.
Allen. 26 ll. DLC (25 ll.); N.   13802

The VIRGINIA Almanack for 1787. Petersburg: Miles
Hunter and William Prentis. [Evans]   13803

The VIRGINIA Almanack for 1787. Richmond: Augustine Davis. 18 ll. Vi.   13804

The VIRGINIA Almanack for 1787. By Robert Andrews.
Richmond: Dixon & Holt. 16 ll. CSmH; ViU (12 ll.)
                                                  13805
The VIRGINIA Almanack for 1787. By Robert Andrews.
Richmond: Thomas Nicolson. 12 ll. MWA; ViW (9 ll.);
ViWC.   13806

ELLICOTT'S Virginia, Maryland, and Pennsylvania Almanack for 1788. Winchester: Bartgis and Willcocks.
20 ll. CSmH (19 ll.)   13807

Der PENNSYLVANIA, Maryland und Virginia Calender
auf 1788. Winchester: Bartgis und Willcocks. [Evans,
my translation]   13808

The VIRGINIA Almanack for 1788. By Robert Andrews.
Petersburg: Hunter & Prentis. 24 ll. MWA.   13809

The VIRGINIA Almanack for 1788. By Robert Andrews.
Richmond: Aug. Davis. 24 ll. DLC (20 ll.); ViHi;
ViU; ViW (21 ll.)   13810

The VIRGINIA Almanack for 1788. By Robert Andrews.
Richmond: John Dixon. 16 ll. NcD.   13811

The VIRGINIA Almanack for 1788. By Robert Andrews.

Virginia - 1789

Richmond: Thomas Nicolson. 24 ll. MWA; DLC. 13812

The PENNSYLVANIA, Delaware, Maryland, and Virginia Almanack and Ephemeris for 1789. Norfolk: John M'Lean. [Evans] 13813

The VIRGINIA Almanack for 1789. By Robert Andrews. Richmond: Aug. Davis. 24 ll. MWA; DLC; ViRVal; ViU. 13814

The VIRGINIA Almanack for 1789. By Robert Andrews. Richmond: Aug. Davis. (Second Edition) 24 ll. [Evans] 13815

The VIRGINIA Almanack for 1789. By Robert Andrews. Richmond: John Dixon. 12 ll. ViU. 13816

The VIRGINIA and North Carolina Almanac for 1789. Petersburg. Advertised in the "Virginia Gazette and Petersburg Intelligencer," November 27, 1788. 13817

A PERPETUAL Almanack. Richmond: Aug. Davis. 1790. [Evans] 13818

The VIRGINIA Almanack for 1790. Norfolk: Prentis & Baxter. [Evans] 13819

The VIRGINIA Almanack for 1790. By Robert Andrews. Richmond: John Dixon. 16 ll. PHi. 13820

The VIRGINIA Almanack for 1790. By Robert Andrews. Richmond: Thomas Nicolson. 12 ll. NBLiHi. 13821

-- Issue with 24 ll. MWA (impf); InU. 13822

The VIRGINIA Almanack for 1790. By Benjamin Workman. Richmond: Aug. Davis. 24 ll. MWA; DLC; N; InU (22 ll., ntp); Vi; PHi (17 ll.) 13823

The VIRGINIA Almanack for 1791. By Robert Andrews. Richmond: Aug. Davis. 16 ll. MWA (14 ll.) 13824

The VIRGINIA Almanack for 1791. By Robert Andrews. Richmond: John Dixon. 16 ll. DLC; NBLiHi. 13825

The VIRGINIA Almanack for 1791. By Robert Andrews. Richmond: Thomas Nicolson. 24 ll. MWA (fragment); Vi (23 ll.); ViU (22 ll.); ViWC.   13826

The VIRGINIA Almanack for 1792. Petersburg: William Prentis. 16 ll. MWA.   13827

The VIRGINIA Almanack for 1792. By Robert Andrews. Richmond: Augustine Davis. 20 ll. DLC; GHi (14 ll.); NN; Vi.   13828

The VIRGINIA Almanack for 1792. By Robert Andrews. Richmond: T. Nicolson. 12 ll. NBLiHi; ViWC.   13829

-- Issue with 24 ll. DLC.   13830

The VIRGINIA Almanack for 1793. Norfolk: Baxter and Wilson. [Evans]   13831

The VIRGINIA Almanack for 1793. Petersburg: William Prentis. 18 ll. NcD; NN (impf)   13832

The VIRGINIA Almanack for 1793. Richmond: James Carey. 16 ll. DLC; ViHi.   13833

The VIRGINIA Almanack for 1793. By Robert Andrews. Richmond: John Dixon. 18 ll. MWA; CSmH.   13834

The VIRGINIA Almanack for 1793. By Robert Andrews. Richmond: T. Nicolson. 24 ll. MWA; DLC; GHi (19 ll.); ViU; ViW (22 ll.); ViWC.   13835

The VIRGINIA and Farmer's Almanac for 1793. Winchester: Richard Bowen. 16 ll. MWA.   13836

The VIRGINIA Almanac for 1794. Winchester: Richard Bowen. 18 ll. MWA (17 ll.)   13837

The VIRGINIA Almanack for 1794. By Robert Andrews. Richmond: John Dixon. 24 ll. MWA; DLC; InU (22 ll.)   13838

The VIRGINIA Almanack for 1794. By Robert Andrews. Richmond: T. Nicolson. 24 ll. DLC; NcD.   13839

Virginia - 1794   1321

The VIRGINIA Almanack for 1794. By Benjamin Banneker.
Petersburg: William Prentis. 18 ll. MWA (ntp); NN-Sc.
13840

The VIRGINIA Almanac for 1795. Winchester: Richard
Bowen. [Evans]   13841

The VIRGINIA Almanack for 1795. By Robert Andrews.
Lynchburg: Robert M. Bransford. 10 ll. Private collection.
13842

The VIRGINIA Almanack for 1795. By Robert Andrews.
Petersburg: William Prentis. 16 ll. MWA (8 ll.); NcD
(7 ll.)   13843

The VIRGINIA Almanack for 1795. By Robert Andrews.
Richmond: John Dixon. 24 ll. KyLoF; PHi (impf); Drake.
13844

The VIRGINIA Almanack for 1795. By Robert Andrews.
Richmond: T. Nicolson. 24 ll. MWA; DLC; ViRVal.
13845

The VIRGINIA Almanack for 1795. By Robert Andrews.
Richmond: Samuel Pleasants. 24 ll. DLC; ViHi. 13846

The VIRGINIA Almanac for 1796. Winchester: Richard
Bowen. [Evans]   13847

The GENTLEMAN'S Political Almanac for 1796. Alexandria: Ellis Price. Advertised in the "Columbian Mirror,"
December 19, 1795.   13848

The VIRGINIA Almanack for 1796. By Robert Andrews.
Richmond: John Dixon. [Evans]   13849

The VIRGINIA Almanack for 1796. By Robert Andrews.
Richmond: T. Nicolson. 24 ll. MWA; DLC; ViU. 13850

The VIRGINIA Almanack for 1796. By Robert Andrews.
Richmond: Samuel Pleasants, Jun. 20 ll. NHi; ViHi (impf)
13851

BANNAKER'S Virginia and North Carolina Almanac and
Ephemeris for 1797. Petersburg: William Prentis and
William T. Murray. 18 ll. MWA.   13852

BANNAKER'S Virginia, Pennsylvania, Delaware, Mary-

land and Kentucky Almanack for 1797. Richmond: Samuel
Pleasants, Jun. 22 ll. MWA. 13853

The VIRGINIA Almanack for 1797. Richmond: T. Nicolson. 24 ll. MWA; DLC; Vi; ViHi. 13854

The VIRGINIA Almanac for 1797. Winchester: Richard
Bowen. [Evans] 13855

The VIRGINIA and N. Carolina Almanack for 1797. Norfolk: Willett & O'Connor. [Evans] 13856

The VIRGINIA Almanack for 1798. Richmond: T. Nicolson. 24 ll. DLC; Vi. 13857

The VIRGINIA Almanac for 1798. Winchester: Richard
Bowen. MWA (19 ll.) 13858

The VIRGINIA Almanack, or Ephemeris for 1798. Richmond: Samuel Pleasants, jun. 18 ll. MWA; Vi; ViHi (impf) 13859

The VIRGINIA, and North Carolina Almanack for 1798.
Norfolk: Willett & O'Connor. NcD (22 ll.); ViU (15 ll.) 13860

The LOVER'S Almanac [for 1799]. Alexandria: Rev. M.
L. Weems. [Quenzel] 13861

The LOVER'S Almanac [for 1799]. Fredericksburg: T.
Green, for the Rev'd. M. L. Weems. 24 ll. ViW-RP; ViWC. 13862

The VIRGINIA Almanac for 1799. Leesburg: Bartgis and
Silliman. 18 ll. ICU. 13863

The VIRGINIA Almanac for 1799. Winchester: Richard
Bowen. 18 ll. MWA. 13864

The VIRGINIA Almanac for 1799. By Isaac Briggs.
Lynchburg: John Carter & Co. [Evans] 13864a

The VIRGINIA Almanack, or Ephemeris for 1799. By Isaac
Briggs. Richmond: Samuel Pleasants, Junior. 18 ll.
DLC; MBAt (impf); CSmH; Vi (ntp) 13864b

Virginia - 1799

The VIRGINIA Almanack or Southern Ephemeris for 1799.
Petersburg: William Prentis. 16 ll. MWA.   13864c

The VIRGINIA, and North Carolina Almanack for 1799.
Norfolk: Willett & O'Connor. 12 ll. MWA.   13865

The ANNUAL Register, and Virginian Repository for
1800. [Petersburg:] Blandford Press; Ross and Douglas.
102 ll. DLC; NN (61 ll.); WHi.   13866

The GOOD Old Virginia Almanack for 1800. Richmond:
Thos. Nicolson. 32 ll. ViHi (impf)   13867

The VIRGINIA Almanac for 1800. Fredericksburg: T.
Green, for the Rev. Mason L. Weems. 18 ll. MWA; ICU;
MiU-C; RPJCB; ViW-RP; ViWC.   13868

VIRGINIA Almanack for 1800. Lynchburg: John Carter.
15 ll. ViL.   13869

The VIRGINIA Almanac for 1800. Richmond: Merewether
Jones. [Evans]   13870

The VIRGINIA Almanac for 1800. Richmond: T. Nicolson.
Vi (ntp)   13871

The VIRGINIA Almanac or Ephemeris for 1800. By Isaac
Briggs. Richmond: Samuel Pleasants, jun. [Evans] 13872

The VIRGINIA & North Carolina Almanac for 1800. Fredericksburg: T. Green, for the Rev. Mason L. Weems.
18 ll. MWA.   13873

The VIRGINIA and N. Carolina Almanack for 1800. Norfolk: Willett & O'Connor. [Evans]   13874

The VIRGINIA & North Carolina Almanack [for 1800]. By
Isaac Briggs [and] Americanus Urban. Petersburg: Ross
& Douglas. WHi (10 ll.); BritMus.   13875

The VIRGINIA & North Carolina Almanack and Register
for 1800. [np, np] 48 ll. Vi (47 ll.)   13876

Virginia - 1800

The VIRGINIA & North Carolina Almanack and Annual Register for 1800. By Isaac Briggs [and] Americanus Urban. Blandford: G. Douglas. 54 ll. DLC (47 ll.); NBLiHi; BritMus.   13877

The GOOD Old Virginia Almanack for 1801. Richmond: Tho. Nicolson. 24 ll. MWA; DLC.   13878

The VIRGINIA Almanack, or Ephemeris for 1801. By Isaac Briggs. Richmond: Samuel Pleasants, Junior. 20 ll. DLC (8 ll.); Vi.   13879

The VIRGINIA & North Carolina Almanack for 1801. By Isaac Briggs [and] Americanus Urban. Petersburg: Ross & Douglas. 25 ll. MWA; DLC; NN; InU; MB; CSmH; NcD; WHi; BritMus.   13880

The GOOD Old Virginia Almanack for 1802. Richmond: Thos. Nicolson. 24 ll. MWA.   13881

The VIRGINIA Almanack for 1802. By Isaac Briggs. Richmond: John Courtney, Junior. 24 ll. Vi; ViRVal (21 ll.); ViWC.   13882

The VIRGINIA & North Carolina Almanack for 1802. By Isaac Briggs [and] Americanus Urban. Petersburg: Ross & Douglas. 24 ll. MWA; DLC; CSmH; MB; Vi (23 ll.); ViW (21 ll.); BritMus.   13883

-- Issue with added "Annual Register." 78 ll. MWA; PHi; Vi; RiRVal; ViU; ViW.   13884

The GOOD Old Virginia Almanac for 1803. Richmond. [Sabin 27835]   13885

The VIRGINIA Almanack for 1803. By I. Briggs. Richmond: John Dixon and John Courtney. 20 ll. MWA; ViWC.   13886

The VIRGINIA Almanack for 1803. By I. Briggs. Richmond: John Dixon and John Courtney, for Samuel Pleasants, Jun. 20 ll. DLC; Vi.   13887

The VIRGINIA & North Carolina Almanack for 1803. By Isaac Briggs [and] Americanus Urban. Petersburg:

Ross & Douglas. 24 ll. MWA; NcD. 13888

The VIRGINIA Almanack for 1804. By I. Briggs. Richmond: John Dixon and John Courtney, for Samuel Pleasants, Jun. 24 ll. NcD (23 ll.); Vi (20 ll.); ViWC. 13889

The FARMER'S Virginia and North-Carolina Almanack for 1805. By Benjamin Bates. Petersburg: John Dickson [sic] and Edward Pescud. ViL (7 ll.) 13890

The FARMER'S Virginia and North-Carolina Almanack for 1805. By Benjamin Bates. Richmond: John Courtney, Jun. 20 ll. Vi. 13891

The GOOD Old Virginia Almanack for 1805. Richmond: Thos. Nicolson. 24 ll. DLC; ViWC (23 ll.) 13892

JORDANS' Virginia & North Carolina Almanac for 1805. Norfolk: A. C. Jordan & Co. 20 ll. DLC. 13893

Der NEUE Nord-Americanische Stadt und Land Calender auf 1805. Winchester: Jacob D. Dietrich's Bucher-Stohr. [Title on leaf 3] 21 ll. MWA (impf); PHi. 13894

The TOWN and Country Almanac for 1805. By Abraham Shoemaker. Alexandria: Robert and John Gray. 18 ll. DLC; Vi. 13895

The VIRGINIA Almanack for 1805. By Benjamin Bates. Richmond: Samuel Pleasants, Jr. 24 ll. Vi; ViHi (23 ll.) 13896

The VIRGINIA & North Carolina Almanac for 1805. By Abraham Shoemaker. Petersburg: Somervell & Conrad. 24 ll. InRE. 13897

The GOOD Old Virginia Almanack for 1806. Richmond: Thos. Nicolson. 24 ll. MWA; NHi (22 ll.); ViWC. 13898

The JEFFERSON Almanack for 1806. By John Alexander. Alexandria: Cottom and Stewart, for John Gray. 18 ll. DLC. 13899

JORDAN'S Virginia and North-Carolina Almanac for
1806. Norfolk: A. C. Jordan & Co. 24 ll. DLC.
13900

Der NEUE Nord-Americanische Stadt und Land Calender auf 1806. Winchester: Jacob D. Dietrich's bucherstohr. 22 ll. MWA (two varieties); DLC; CtY; P; PPCS (18 ll.)
13901

The TOWN and Country Almanack for 1806. By John Alexander. Alexandria: Cottom and Stewart. 18 ll. Vi.
13902

The VIRGINIA Almanack for 1806. By John Alexander. Alexandria: Cottom and Stewart for John Gray. 18 ll. MWA; PHC.
13903

The VIRGINIA Almanac for 1806. By Benjamin Bates. Richmond: Cook & Grantland; Thomas Ritchie. 21 ll. DLC (impf)
13904

The VIRGINIA Almanack for 1806. By Benjamin Bates. Richmond: Samuel Pleasants, Jr. 20 ll. MWA; DLC (16 ll.); CSmH; Vi; ViHi.
13905

The VIRGINIA & North Carolina Almanac for 1806. By Abraham Shoemaker. Petersburg: Somervell & Conrad. 24 ll. MWA; InRE; InU (impf)
13906

The VIRGINIA Planter's Almanac for 1806. Richmond: Jacob Johnson. 24 ll. MWA.
13907

The ALEXANDRIA Almanack for 1807. Alexandria: Cottom and Stewart; Fredericksburg: J. Wescott; John Gray; Richmond: John Pumphrey. 18 ll. DLC. 13908

The FARMERS' Almanack for 1807. Alexandria: Cottom and Stewart. 16 ll. MWA.
13909

The GOOD Old Virginia Almanack for 1807. Richmond: Thos. Nicolson. 24 ll. MWA.
13910

JOHNSON'S Virginia Almanack for 1807. By Joshua Sharp. Richmond: Jacob Johnson. 24 ll. MWA. 13911

Virginia - 1807

The VIRGINIA Almanack for 1807. Alexandria: Cottom and Stewart. 18 ll. CSmH. 13912

-- Issue with added signatures. NcD (27 ll.) 13913

The VIRGINIA Almanack for 1807. By Benjamin Bates. Richmond: Samuel Pleasants, Jr. 18 ll. DLC; ViHi (12 ll.); ViWC. 13914

The VIRGINIA & North Carolina Almanac for 1807. By Benj'n Bates. Petersburg: Somervell & Conrad. 24 ll. MWA; NcD (impf) 13915

The VIRGINIA & North Carolina Almanac for 1807. By Benj'n Bates. Petersburg: Somervell & Conrad. (Second Edition) 24 ll. InRE. 13916

The VIRGINIA Farmer's Almanac for 1807. By Benj'n. Bates. Richmond: Seaton Grantland. 24 ll. NcD (21 ll.); Vi; ViW. 13917

The VIRGINIA Farmer's Almanac for 1807. By Benj'n Bates. Richmond: Seaton Grantland. (Second Edition) 24 ll. MiU-C. 13918

WASHINGTON'S Almanack for 1807. Alexandria: Cottom & Stewart. 18 ll. OMC. 13919

The FREDERICKSBURG Almanack for 1808. Alexandria: Cottom and Stewart. ViHi (17 ll.) 13920

The GOOD Old Virginia Almanack for 1808. Richmond: Thos. Nicolson. 24 ll. ViWC (23 ll.) 13921

JOHNSON'S Virginia Almanack for 1808. By Joshua Sharp. Richmond: Jacob Johnson. 18 ll. MWA; DLC; Vi. 13922

-- Issue with added signature. Wv-Ar (22 ll.) 13923

JORDANS' Virginia and North-Carolina Almanack for 1808. Norfolk: A. C. Jordan & Co. 21 ll. DLC (impf) 13924

Virginia - 1808

PLANTER'S & Farmer's Almanack for 1808. [Lynchburg:] Star Office. 12 ll. ViHi. 13925

The VIRGINIA Almanack for 1808. Richmond: Thos. Nicolson. ViWC. 13926

The VIRGINIA & North Carolina Almanac for 1808. By Benj'n Bates. Petersburg: Somervell & Conrad. 24 ll. MWA (22 ll.); InRE (18 ll.); NcD. 13927

The VIRGINIA Farmer's Almanac for 1808. By Benj'n. Bates. Alexandria: Robert Gray. 18 ll. MWA; NjMoW; PHC. 13928

The VIRGINIA Farmer's Almanac for 1808. By Benj'n Bates. Richmond: Fitzwhylsonn & Potter. 18 ll. DLC. 13929

The WASHINGTON Almanack for 1808. Alexandria: Cottom and Stewart. 18 ll. PHC. 13930

The ALEXANDRIA Almanack for 1809. Alexandria: Cottom and Stewart. 18 ll. MWA. 13931

BATES'S Virginia Almanac for 1809. By Benj'n Bates. Richmond: Seaton Grantland. 24 ll. Vi. 13932

JOHNSON'S Virginia Almanac for 1809. By Joshua Sharp. Richmond: Jacob Johnson. 24 ll. MWA (23 ll.) 13933

The MARYLAND & Virginia Almanac for 1809. Alexandria: Robert Gray. 18 ll. DLC. 13934

The VIRGINIA Almanack for 1809. Alexandria: Cottom and Stewart. 18 ll. ViHi. 13935

The VIRGINIA Almanack for 1809. By Benjamin Bates. Richmond: Samuel Pleasants, Jun. 18 ll. DLC. 13936

The VIRGINIA Almanack for 1809. By Benjamin Bates. Richmond: Samuel Pleasants for William Lowne. NcD (17 ll.) 13937

The VIRGINIA & North Carolina Almanac for 1809.

Virginia - 1809

Petersburg: Somervell & Conrad. 24 ll. MWA; NcD.
13938

The VIRGINIA Planter's Almanac for 1809. Alexandria: Robert Gray. 18 ll. DLC; Drake (12 ll.) 13939

The VIRGINIA Planter's Almanac for 1809. Richmond: Seaton Grantland for John Dickson, Petersburg. 18 ll. MWA. 13940

The VIRGINIA Planter's Almanac for 1809. Richmond: John Pumphrey. 18 ll. ViU (missing from shelves)
13941

The WASHINGTON Almanack for 1809. Alexandria: Cottom and Stewart. 18 ll. PHC. 13942

The FREDERICKSBURG Almanack for 1810. Alexandria: Cottom and Stewart. 18 ll. Vi. 13943

JOHNSON & Warner's Virginia Almanac for 1810. By Joshua Sharp. Richmond: Johnson & Warner. 24 ll. MWA (23 ll.); DLC; P; ViW (ntp); ViWC. 13944

The NEW Virginia & North Carolina Almanac for 1810. By Nathaniel H. Turner. Richmond: Manson & Minor. 18 ll. DLC. 13945

The VIRGINIA Almanack for 1810. By Benjamin Bates. Richmond: Samuel Pleasants, Junior. 18 ll. MWA; DLC; NcD; ViHi; ViRVal (17 ll.) 13946

The VIRGINIA & North-Carolina Almanack for 1810. Petersburg: Somervill [sic] & Conrad. 18 ll. NcU.
13947

The FARMER'S Almanack for 1811. Alexandria: Cottom and Stewart. ViW (17 ll.) 13948

The FREDERICKSBURG Almanack for 1811. Alexandria: Cottom and Stewart, for William F. Gray, Fredericksburg. 18 ll. Vi. 13949

The GOOD Old Virginia Almanack for 1811. Richmond: John O' Lynch. 24 ll. ViRVal (23 ll.) 13950

JOHNSON & Warner's Virginia Almanac for 1811. By
Joshua Sharp. Richmond: Johnson & Warner. 30 ll.
MWA; DLC; ViW (ntp)   13951

The VIRGINIA Almanack for 1811. Alexandria: Cottom
and Stewart, for R. Cottom, Petersburg. Vi (14 ll.)
    13952

The VIRGINIA Almanack for 1811. By Benjamin Bates.
Richmond: Samuel Pleasants, Junior. 18 ll. ViHi.
    13953

The ALEXANDRIA Almanack for 1812. Alexandria:
Cottom and Stewart. DLC (17 ll.)   13954

JOHNSON and Warner's Virginia Almanac for 1812. By
Joshua Sharp. Richmond: Johnson & Warner's Bookstore. 18 ll. MWA; DLC.   13955

The VIRGINIA Almanack for 1812. By Benjamin Bates.
Richmond: Samuel Pleasants. 18 ll. MWA; NjMoW.
    13956

The VIRGINIA Almanack for 1812. By Benjamin Bates.
Richmond: Samuel Pleasants, for Robert Gray, Alexandria. 18 ll. DLC.   13957

The VIRGINIA Almanack for 1812. By Benjamin Bates.
Richmond: Samuel Pleasants, for William F. Gray,
Fredericksburg. 18 ll. MWA; Vi.   13958

The VIRGINIA Almanack for 1812. By Benjamin Bates.
Richmond: Samuel Pleasants, for John Dickson, Petersburg. 18 ll. ViRVal.   13959

The VIRGINIA Almanack for 1812. By Benjamin Bates.
Richmond: Samuel Pleasants, for John Somervell,
Petersburg. 18 ll. MWA.   13960

The WASHINGTON Almanack for 1812. Alexandria: Cottom and Stewart. 18 ll. DLC.   13961

JOHNSON & Warner's Virginia Almanac for 1813. By
Joshua Sharp. Richmond: Johnson & Warner. 18 ll.
DLC; CSmH.   13962

Virginia - 1813

The VIRGINIA Almanack for 1813. By Benjamin Bates. Fredericksburg: William F. Gray. 16 ll. DLC. 13963

The VIRGINIA Almanack for 1813. By Benj. Bates. Richmond: Samuel Pleasants. 18 ll. ViU. 13964

The VIRGINIA and North Carolina Almanack for 1813. By Benjamin Bates. Richmond: Thomas Ritchie for John Somervell, Petersburg. 16 ll. MWA; NcU. 13965

COTTOM'S Virginia Almanac for 1814. Richmond: Peter Cottom. 24 ll. MWA (21 ll.); PHC; ViU. 13966

The FARMER'S New Virginia Almanac for 1814. By Meriwether Carpenter. Richmond: Ritchie & Trueheart. 18 ll. ViWC. 13967

JOHNSON & Warner's Virginia Almanac for 1814. By Joshua Sharp. Richmond: Johnson & Warner. 18 ll. DLC; CSmH. 13968

The VIRGINIA Almanack for 1814. By N. H. Turner. Richmond: Samuel Pleasants. 18 ll. MWA (16 ll.); DLC; CSmH. 13969

The VIRGINIA Calendar for 1814. Norfolk: Printed for the Purchasers. 18 ll. Vi. 13970

VIRGINIA Remembrancer for 1814. By Joshua Sharp. Richmond: Johnson & Warner. 24 ll. DLC; ViHi. 13971

COTTOM'S New Virginia Almanac for 1815. By D. B. Bullock. Petersburg: Richard Cottom. 18 ll. MWA; DLC; CSmH. 13972

COTTOM'S New Virginia Almanac for 1815. By D. B. Bullock. Richmond: Peter Cottom. 18 ll. MWA; NcD. 13973

The VIRGINIA Almanack for 1815. Richmond: Argus Office. 18 ll. MWA. 13974

The VIRGINIA Almanac for 1815. By D. B. Bullock. Alexandria: J. A. Stewart. 18 ll. PHC; Vi. 13975

Virginia - 1815

The VIRGINIA Almanack for 1815. By N.H. Turner. Richmond: Samuel Pleasants. 18 ll. DLC; CSmH.
13976

ALMANAC for 1816. Richmond: Frederick A. Maio & Co. NN (14 ll., ntp)
13977

COTTOM'S New Virginia Almanack for 1816. By David Richardson. Richmond: Peter Cottom; A. G. Booker & Co., printers. 18 ll. MWA; DLC (impf); Vi; ViRVal (17 ll.); ViWC.
13978

COTTOM'S New Virginia & North-Carolina Almanack for 1816. By David Richardson. Richmond: Peter Cottom; A. G. Booker & Co., printers. 18 ll. MWA.
13979

JOHNSON & Warner's Virginia Almanac for 1816. By Joshua Sharp. Richmond: Johnson & Warner. 24 ll. DLC (impf); PHi (impf); Vi (impf)
13980

The VIRGINIA Almanac for 1816. Fredericksburg: William F. Gray. 18 ll. PHC; Vi; ViHi (impf)
13981

The WASHINGTON Almanac for 1816. By David Richardson. Alexandria: John A. Stewart. 18 ll. NBuHi.
13982

The ALEXANDRIA Almanac for 1817. By David Richardson. Alexandria: J. A. Stewart; Benj. L. Bogan, printer. 18 ll. DLC.
13983

COTTOM'S New Virginia Almanack for 1817. By David Richardson. Richmond: Peter Cottom. 18 ll. ViHi; ViRVal (15 ll.)
13984

COTTOM'S New Virginia & North Carolina Almanack for 1817. By David Richardson. Richmond: Peter Cottom. 18 ll. MWA; DLC; InU; MBAt.
13985

The VIRGINIA Almanack for 1817. By David Richardson. Alexandria: J. A. Stewart. 18 ll. PHC.
13986

The VIRGINIA Almanac for 1817. By John Sharp. Petersburg: John W. Campbell. 20 ll. NcD.
13987

Virginia - 1817

The VIRGINIA Farmer's Almanac for 1817. Fredericksburg: William F. Gray. 18 ll. Vi.   13988

WARNER'S Virginia Almanac for 1817. By Joshua Sharp. Richmond: Benjamin Warner. 18 ll. MWA; ViW (11 ll.)   13989

COTTOM'S New Virginia Almanack for 1818. By Joseph Cave. Richmond: Peter Cottom. 18 ll. MWA; DLC; InU; OCl; Vi; ViW (16 ll.); ViWC.   13990

The NEW Virginia Pocket Almanack and Farmers' Companion for 1818. By David Richardson. Richmond: John Warrock. 18 ll. MWA; DLC; NBLiHi.   13991

The VIRGINIA Almanac for 1818. By John Sharp. Alexandria: J. A. Stewart; B. L. Bogan, printer. 18 ll. MWA; InU (fragment); PHC; ViU.   13992

The VIRGINIA & North-Carolina Almanac for 1818. By John Sharp. Petersburg: J. W. Campbell. 18 ll. NHi.
   13993

WARNER'S New Virginia Almanac for 1818. Richmond: Benjamin Warner. 18 ll. ViHi; ViW.   13994

COTTOM'S New Virginia Almanack for 1819. By Joseph Cave. Richmond: Peter Cottom. 18 ll. MWA; ViHi.
   13995

COTTOM'S North Carolina and Virginia Almanack for 1819. By Joseph Cave. Richmond: Peter Cottom. NcU (17 ll.)   13996

RICHMOND Directory, Register and Almanac for 1819. Richmond: Jno. Maddox. Private collection.   13997

The VIRGINIA Almanac for 1819. Alexandria: J. A. Stewart. 18 ll. MWA; InU (fragment); PHC; ViU.
   13998

The VIRGINIA Pocket Almanack and Farmers' Companion for 1819. By David Richardson. Richmond: John Warrock. 18 ll. MWA; DLC; ViU.   13999

The VIRGINIA Pocket Almanack and Farmers' Com-

panion for 1819. By David Richardson. Richmond: John Warrock for Frederick A. Mayo. 18 ll. MWA.
14000

WARNER'S Virginia Almanac for 1819. By Joshua Sharp. Richmond: Benjamin Warner. 16 ll. MWA; DLC; InU (14 ll., ntp) 14001

-- Issue with added signature. ViW (21 ll.) 14002

COTTOM'S New Virginia Almanack for 1820. By Joseph Cave. Richmond: Peter Cottom; Petersburg: Richard Cottom. 18 ll. MWA; DLC; NcD (17 ll.); ViU.
14003

COTTOM'S New Virginia & North Carolina Almanack for 1820. By Joseph Cave. Richmond: Peter Cottom. 16 ll. MWA; InU; KyBgW (ntp); NcU; ViW. 14004

The TOWN & Country Almanac for 1820. By John Sharp. Alexandria: John A. Stewart. 16 ll. MWA.
14005

VIRGINIA Almanack for 1820. By Joshua Sharp. Richmond: Benjamin Warner. 24 ll. DLC; N; PHi; ViW (19 ll., ntp) 14006

The VIRGINIA and North-Carolina Pocket Almanack and Farmers' Companion for 1820. By David Richardson. Richmond: John Warrock. 18 ll. NcU; ViRVal; ViWC.
14007

The ALEXANDRIA Almanac for 1821. By John Sharp. Alexandria: John A. Stewart. 18 ll. PHC; ViU. 14008

COTTOM'S Virginia and North-Carolina Almanack for 1821. By Joseph Cave. Richmond: Peter Cottom; Petersburg: R. Cottom; Lynchburg: Ward & Diggers. 18 ll. DLC; NcD. 14009

The FARMER'S Almanac for 1821. By John Sharp. Alexandria: John A. Stewart. 18 ll. NBuHi; PHC.
14010

The FRANKLIN Almanac for 1821. Richmond: N. Pollard. 24 ll. MWA; InU; Vi. 14011

VIRGINIA Almanack for 1821. By Joshua Sharp. Rich-

mond: Benjamin Warner. 18 ll. MWA; DLC; ViU;
ViW (13 ll.)   14012

The VIRGINIA and North-Carolina Pocket Almanack for 1821. By David Richardson. Richmond: John Warrock. 18 ll. MWA.   14013

The WASHINGTON Almanac for 1821. By John Sharp. Alexandria: John A. Stewart. 18 ll. MWA.   14014

COTTOM'S Virginia and North-Carolina Almanack for 1822. By Joseph Cave. Richmond: Peter Cottom; [etc]. 18 ll. MWA; DLC (impf); KyBgW; ViU.   14015

The FARMER'S Almanac for 1822. By Joshua Sharp. Petersburg: J. W. Campbell. 18 ll. MWA.   14016

The FRANKLIN Almanac for 1822. Richmond: N. Pollard. 24 ll. MWA; DLC; CoCC; CtLHi; ViW (16 ll.)   14017

TOWN & Country Almanack for 1822. By Joshua Sharp. Alexandria: John A. Stewart. 18 ll. PP.   14018

The VIRGINIA Almanack for 1822. By Joshua Sharp. Alexandria: John A. Stewart. 24 ll. MWA (22 ll.); PHC; Vi.   14019

The VIRGINIA Almanack for 1822. By Joshua Sharp. Richmond: Benjamin Warner. 24 ll. Vi.   14020

The VIRGINIA and North-Carolina Pocket Almanack and Farmers' Companion for 1822. By David Richardson. Richmond: John Warrock. 18 ll. DLC; ViHi; ViRVal.   14021

ALEXANDRIA Almanack for 1823. By Joshua Sharp. Alexandria: John A. Stewart. 20 ll. DLC.   14022

COTTOM'S New Virginia & North-Carolina Almanack for 1823. By Joseph Cave. Richmond: Peter Cottom. 16 ll. ViW.   14023

COTTOM'S Virginia and North-Carolina Almanack for 1823. By Joseph Cave. Richmond: Peter Cottom. 18

Virginia - 1823

ll. KyBgW (ntp); ViHi. 14024

The FRANKLIN Almanac for 1823. Richmond: Nathan Pollard. 24 ll. MWA; DLC; Vi (ntp); ViW. 14025

TOWN and Country Almanack for 1823. By Joshua Sharp. Alexandria: John A. Stewart. 20 ll. DLC.
14026

The VIRGINIA Almanac for 1823. By Joshua Sharp. Alexandria: John A. Stewart. MWA (missing from shelves) 14027

VIRGINIA Almanack for 1823. By Joshua Sharp. Alexandria: Julian A. Stewart. 20 ll. DLC. 14028

VIRGINIA Almanack for 1823. By Joshua Sharp. Richmond: Warner's Book Store. 24 ll. PHi (impf); PPi; Vi (20 ll.); ViRVal; ViW (22 ll.) 14029

The VIRGINIA and North-Carolina Pocket Almanack and Farmers' Companion for 1823. By David Richardson. Richmond: John Warrock. 18 ll. MWA; DLC; InU; N; ViRVal (15 ll., ntp); ViW; ViWC. 14030

WASHINGTON Almanack for 1823. By Joshua Sharp. Alexandria: John A. Stewart. 20 ll. DLC; PDoBHi.
14031

ALEXANDRIA Almanack for 1824. By Joshua Sharp. Alexandria: J. A. Stewart. 18 ll. PPL. 14032

The FRANKLIN Almanac for 1824. Richmond: Nathan Pollard. 24 ll. DLC; NN (22 ll.); ViHi. 14033

VIRGINIA Almanack for 1824. By Joshua Sharp. Alexandria: J. J. Stewart. 18 ll. DLC. 14034

The VIRGINIA Almanack for 1824. By Joshua Sharp. Richmond: Estate of Benjamin Warner. 35 ll. ViRVal.
14035

The VIRGINIA and North-Carolina Pocket Almanack and Farmers' Companion for 1824. By David Richardson. Richmond: John Warrock. 18 ll. MWA; ViHi; ViW.
14036

Virginia - 1824　　　　　　　　　　1337

WASHINGTON Almanack for 1824. By Joshua Sharp.
Alexandria: J. A. Stewart. 18 ll. DLC.　　　14037

COTTOM'S Virginia Almanack for 1825. By Joseph
Cave. Richmond: Peter Cottom. 18 ll. PHC.　14038

COTTOM'S Virginia & North Carolina Almanack for
1825. By Joseph Cave. Richmond: Peter Cottom. 18
ll. ViWC.　　　　　　　　　　　　　　　14039

The FRANKLIN Almanac for 1825. Richmond: Nathan
Pollard. 24 ll. MWA; DLC (impf); PPi; Vi; ViHi;
ViU; ViW.　　　　　　　　　　　　　　　14040

The VIRGINIA Almanac for 1825. Alexandria: John A.
Stewart; Baltimore: J. Robinson, printer. 18 ll. MWA;
DLC; N.　　　　　　　　　　　　　　　　14041

VIRGINIA Almanack for 1825. By Joshua Sharp. Richmond: Collins & Co. 30 ll. NcD; Vi.　　　14042

VIRGINIA and North-Carolina Pocket Almanack and
Farmers' Companion for 1825. By David Richardson.
Richmond: John Warrock. 18 ll. MWA; NBLiHi (16
ll.)　　　　　　　　　　　　　　　　　　14043

The WASHINGTON Almanac for 1825. Alexandria:
John A. Stewart; Baltimore: J. Robinson, printer. 18
ll. DLC; NBuG; NBuHi (17 ll.)　　　　　　14044

The FRANKLIN Almanac for 1826. Richmond: Pollard
& Goddard. 24 ll. MWA; MB (22 ll.); NBuHi; PPi;
Vi; ViHi; ViW; ViWC.　　　　　　　　　14045

The VIRGINIA Almanac for 1826. Richmond. 36 ll.
DLC (ntp)　　　　　　　　　　　　　　　14046

The VIRGINIA Almanack for 1826. By Joshua Sharp.
Richmond: Collins & Co. 18 ll. NcD.　　　14047

VIRGINIA and North Carolina Almanack for 1826. By
David Richardson. Richmond: John Warrock. 18 ll.
MWA.　　　　　　　　　　　　　　　　　14048

COTTOM'S New Virginia & North-Carolina Almanack for 1827. By Joseph Cave. Richmond: Peter Cottom; Petersburg: Richard Cottom. 16 ll. ViW (14 ll.)
14049

COTTOM'S Virginia Almanack for 1827. By Joseph Cave. Richmond: Peter Cottom. 16 ll. DLC. 14050

COTTOM'S Virginia & North Carolina Almanack for 1827. Richmond: Peter Cottom. 18 ll. ViWC. 14051

The FRANKLIN Almanac for 1827. Richmond: Nathan Pollard. 24 ll. DLC; NHi; Vi (impf); ViHi; ViW.
14052

The VIRGINIA Almanack for 1827. By Joshua Sharp. Richmond: Collins & Co. 18 ll. MWA; NcD. 14053

VIRGINIA and North Carolina Almanack for 1827. By David Richardson. Richmond: John Warrock. 18 ll. MWA; DLC; NcD. 14054

COTTOM'S New Virginia & North-Carolina Almanack for 1828. By Joseph Cave. Richmond: Peter Cottom; Petersburg: Richard Cottom. 18 ll. ViW (16 ll.) 14055

COTTOM'S Virginia & North Carolina Almanack for 1828. By Joseph Cave. Richmond: Peter Cottom. 18 ll. MWA; DLC; NcD (15 ll.); NcU. 14056

The FRANKLIN Almanac for 1828. Richmond: Pollard & Converse. 24 ll. MWA; DLC; NBuHi; PPi; ViHi (22 ll.); ViW. 14057

VIRGINIA and North Carolina Almanack for 1828. By David Richardson. Richmond: John Warrock. 18 ll. MWA. 14058

The CHRISTIAN Almanac, for Virginia for 1829. Richmond: American Tract Society. 18 ll. MWA; ViW.
14059

COTTOM'S New Virginia & North-Carolina Almanack for 1829. By Joseph Cave. Richmond: Peter Cottom. ViW (14 ll.) 14060

Virginia - 1829

COTTOM'S Virginia & North Carolina Almanack for 1829. By Joseph Cave. Richmond: Peter Cottom; [etc]. 16 ll. NcU; ViU; ViW (14 ll., ntp) 14061

The FRANKLIN Almanac for 1829. Richmond: Nathan Pollard. 24 ll. MWA; PHi; ViHi. 14062

The VIRGINIA Almanac for 1829. Richmond. DLC (22 ll., ntp) 14063

VIRGINIA and North Carolina Almanack for 1829. By David Richardson. Richmond: John Warrock. 18 ll. MWA; DLC; NcU; ViHi. 14064

The CHRISTIAN Almanac, for Virginia for 1830. Richmond: American Tract Society. 18 ll. MWA; ViHi. 14065

COTTOM'S Virginia & North Carolina Almanack for 1830. By Joseph Cave. Richmond: Peter Cottom; [etc]. 16 ll. MWA; NcD; ViW. 14066

VIRGINIA and North Carolina Almanack for 1830. By David Richardson. Richmond: John Warrock. 18 ll. MWA; NcD. 14067

The VIRGINIA and North-Carolina Pocket Almanack and Farmers' Companion for 1830. By David Richardson. Richmond: John Warrock. ViW (17 ll.) 14068

The CHRISTIAN Almanac, for Virginia for 1831. Richmond: American Tract Society; Collins & Co. 18 ll. MWA; Vi; ViU. 14069

COTTOM'S Constitutional Almanack for 1831. By Joseph Cave. Richmond: Peter Cottom. 18 ll. DLC; ViHi. 14070

COTTOM'S Virginia & North Carolina Almanack for 1831. By Joseph Cave. Richmond: Peter Cottom. 18 ll. MWA; DLC; ICN; NcD. 14071

VIRGINIA and North Carolina Almanack for 1831. By David Richardson. Richmond: John Warrock. 18 ll.

MWA (two varieties); DLC; NcU; ViHi; ViLxV. 14072

The VIRGINIA and North-Carolina Pocket Almanack and Farmers' Companion for 1831. By David Richardson. Richmond: John Warrock. 18 ll. ViW. 14073

The CHRISTIAN Almanac, for Virginia for 1832. Richmond: American Tract Society; R. J. Smith. 18 ll. MB; N; Vi; ViU. 14074

COTTOM'S Virginia & North Carolina Almanack for 1832. By Joseph Cave. Richmond: P. Cottom; [etc]. 18 ll. ViU; ViW (13 ll.) 14075

VIRGINIA and North Carolina Almanack for 1832. By David Richardson. Richmond: John Warrock. 18 ll. MWA; ViHi; ViRVal. 14076

The VIRGINIA and North-Carolina Pocket Almanack and Farmers' Companion for 1832. By David Richardson. Richmond: John Warrock. ViW (16 ll.) 14077

The CHRISTIAN Almanac, for Virginia for 1833. Richmond: American Tract Society; R. J. Smith. 18 ll. MWA; MB; Vi; ViHi; ViW (16 ll.) 14078

COTTOM'S Virginia & North-Carolina Almanack for 1833. Richmond: P. Cottom; [etc]. 18 ll. DLC; Nc; NcD; NcU; Vi; ViW (14 ll.) 14079

VIRGINIA and North Carolina Almanack for 1833. By David Richardson. Richmond: John Warrock. 18 ll. MWA; DLC; InU; NcD; ViHi. 14080

ALEXANDRIA Almanac for 1834. By Benjamin Hallowell. Alexandria: Gazette Office. 12 ll. MWA; DLC (11 ll.) 14081

The CHRISTIAN Almanac, for Virginia for 1834. Richmond: American Tract Society; R. J. Smith. 24 ll. MWA; NN; Vi (impf); ViU; ViW (23 ll.) 14082

COTTOM'S Virginia & North-Carolina Almanack for

1834. Richmond: P. Cottom; [etc]. 16 ll. MWA;
DLC (13 ll.); ViW. 14083

FRANKLIN Almanac for 1834. Richmond. ViW (15 ll.,
ntp) 14084

VIRGINIA and North Carolina Almanack for 1834. By
David Richardson. Richmond: John Warrock. 18 ll.
MWA; DLC; InU; NcD; ViHi. 14085

The CHRISTIAN Almanac, for Virginia for 1835. Richmond: American Tract Society. 24 ll. MWA; ViRVal;
ViU. 14086

VIRGINIA and North Carolina Almanack for 1835. By
David Richardson. Richmond: John Warrock. 18 ll.
MWA; IU; InU; NcD; ViHi; ViW. 14087

COTTOM'S Virginia & North-Carolina Almanack for
1836. By David Richardson. Richmond: Peter Cottom; [etc]. 18 ll. NcD; Vi; ViW (8 ll.) 14088

VIRGINIA and North Carolina Almanack for 1836. By
David Richardson. Richmond: John Warrock. 18 ll.
MWA; DLC; InU (ntp); LNHT; ViHi. 14089

The ALEXANDRIA Almanac for 1837. By Benjamin
Hallowell. Alexandria: William M. Morrison; Gazette
Office. DLC (17 ll.) 14090

COTTOM'S Virginia & North-Carolina Almanack for
1837. By David Richardson. Richmond: Peter Cottom.
18 ll. ViHi. 14091

The VIRGINIA & North Carolina Almanack for 1837.
By David Richardson. Richmond: Peter Cottom for
Yale & Wyatt. 18 ll. ViLxV (17 ll.) 14092

VIRGINIA and North Carolina Almanack for 1837. By
David Richardson. Richmond: John Warrock. 18 ll.
MWA; InU; LNHT; MoKU; NcD; ViHi; ViW (17 ll.)
 14093

COTTOM'S Virginia & North Carolina Almanack for

1838. By David Richardson. Richmond: Peter Cottom. 18 ll. MWA; NcD; Vi; ViHi (12 ll.); ViU; ViW (14 ll.)   14094

VIRGINIA and North Carolina Almanack for 1838. By David Richardson. Richmond: John Warrock. 18 ll. MWA; IU; InU; LNHT; MoKU (16 ll.); ViRVal; ViW (17 ll.)   14095

The CHRISTIAN Almanac, for Virginia for 1839. By David Richardson. Richmond: Virginia Tract Society; Yale & Wyatt. 24 ll. ViW.   14096

COTTOM'S Virginia & North-Carolina Almanack for 1839. By David Richardson. Richmond: Peter Cottom. 18 ll. MWA; DLC; NHi; ViW (16 ll.)   14097

The FARMER'S Calendar for 1839. By Charles F. Egelmann. Richmond: Smith & Palmer. 16 ll. MWA (10 ll.); ViU.   14098

The HUNDRED Years Almanac for 1799 to 1899. [Winchester:] Philip H. Spangler; Winchester Virginian Office. 1839. 28 ll. CLU; Vi.   14099

VIRGINIA and North Carolina Almanack for 1839. By David Richardson. Richmond: John Warrock. 18 ll. MWA; DLC (impf); IU; InU; LNHT; MoKU; NcD; Vi; ViW.   14100

COTTOM'S Virginia & North-Carolina Almanack for 1840. By David Richardson. Richmond: Peter Cottom; [etc]. 18 ll. MWA (ntp); DLC; Vi.   14101

The FARMER'S Calendar for 1840. By Charles F. Egelmann. Richmond: Smith & Palmer; [Baltimore:] S. Sands, printer. 16 ll. Vi; ViU.   14102

POOR Richard's Almanack for the Northern Neck, Virginia for 1840. By Richard Saunders, Jr. Richmond: Bailie and Gallaher. ViRVal (9 ll.)   14103

VIRGINIA and North-Carolina Almanack for 1840. By

Virginia - 1841

David Richardson. Richmond: John Warrock. 18 ll.
MWA; DLC; IU; InU (ntp); LNHT; NcD; Vi; MoKU
(17 ll.); ViHi; ViW (15 ll.) 14104

COTTOM'S Virginia & North-Carolina Almanack for
1841. By David Richardson. Richmond: Peter Cottom; [etc] 18 ll. DLC; MoKU; ViRVal; ViW (15 ll.)
14105

VIRGINIA and North Carolina Almanack for 1841. By
David Richardson. Richmond: John Warrock. 18 ll.
MWA; DLC; IU; InU (17 ll.); LNHT; NcD; Vi; ViHi;
ViW; WHi. 14106

COTTOM'S Virginia & North Carolina Almanack for
1842. By David Richardson. Richmond: Peter Cottom; [etc] 18 ll. MWA; MDedHi; NcD; NjP; Vi;
ViHi; ViRVal; ViW (15 ll.) 14107

The FARMER'S Calendar for 1842. By Charles F.
Egelmann. Richmond: Smith, Drinker & Morris. 16 ll.
MWA. 14108

VIRGINIA and North Carolina Almanack for 1842. By
David Richardson. Richmond: John Warrock. 18 ll.
MWA; DLC; IU; InU; LNHT; MoKU; Vi; ViHi; ViRVal;
ViW; WHi. 14109

COTTOM'S Virginia & North Carolina Almanack for
1843. By David Richardson. Richmond: Peter Cottom;
[etc]. 18 ll. MWA (two varieties); Vi; ViW (16 ll.);
NjR (13 ll., ntp) 14110

VIRGINIA and North Carolina Almanack for 1843. By
David Richardson. Richmond: John Warrock. 18 ll.
MWA; DLC; IU; InU; MoKU; NcD; Vi; ViHi (16 ll.);
ViRVal; ViW; WHi; Drake. 14111

COTTOM'S Virginia & North-Carolina Almanack for
1844. By David Richardson. Richmond: Peter Cottom;
[etc]. 18 ll. MWA; DLC; NcD; Vi; ViW (16 ll.)
14112

The FARMER'S Calendar for 1844. Richmond: Smith,
Drinker & Morris; [Baltimore:] S. Sands, printer. 16

Virginia - 1844

ll. ViU. 14113

VIRGINIA and North Carolina Almanack for 1844. By David Richardson. Richmond: John Warrock. 18 ll. MWA (two varieties); ICHi; IU; LNHT; NcD; Vi; ViHi (impf); ViW; WHi; Drake. 14114

COTTOM'S Virginia & North Carolina Almanack for 1845. By David Richardson. Richmond: Peter Cottom; [etc]. 18 ll. DLC; MoKU; NcD; Vi; Drake. 14115

ELLYSON'S Business Directory and Almanac for 1845. Richmond: H. K. Ellyson. 18 ll. NcD. 14116

The FARMER'S Calendar for 1845. By Edward Hagerty. Richmond: Drinker & Morris. 16 ll. MWA; ViW (ntp) 14117

RICHARDSON'S Virginia and North Carolina Almanac for 1845. By David Richardson. Richmond: Drinker & Morris. 18 ll. MWA; NcD; Vi; ViHi; ViRVal; ViW (17 ll.) 14118

WARROCK'S Virginia and North Carolina Almanack for 1845. By David Richardson. Richmond: John Warrock. 18 ll. MWA (two varieties); IU; MnU; Vi; ViHi; ViU. 14119

The AMERICAN Farmer's Almanac for 1846. By Edward Hagerty. Alexandria: Bell & Entwisle. 18 ll. DLC. 14120

COTTOM'S Virginia & North Carolina Almanack for 1846. By David Richardson. Richmond: Peter Cottom; [etc]. 18 ll. MWA; NcD; Vi. 14121

The FARMER'S Calendar for 1846. By Edward Hagerty. Richmond: Drinker & Morris; [Baltimore:] S. Sands, printer. 16 ll. Vi; ViU. 14122

The FARMER'S Calendar for 1846. By Edward Hagerty. Richmond: J. W. Randolph & Co. ViW (12 ll.) 14123

RICHARDSON'S Virginia and North Carolina Almanac for 1846. By David Richardson. Richmond: Drinker &

Morris. 18 ll. MWA; MoKU (14 ll.); Vi; ViHi; ViW
(17 ll.); WHi. 14124

WARROCK'S Virginia and North Carolina Almanack for
1846. By David Richardson. Richmond: John Warrock. 18 ll. MWA; IU; NcD; Vi (14 ll.); ViHi; ViL;
ViU. 14125

COTTOM'S Virginia & North-Carolina Almanack for
1847. By David Richardson. Richmond: Peter Cottom;
[etc]. 18 ll. DLC; NN; Vi; ViHi; ViW (16 ll.) 14126

The FARMER'S Calendar for 1847. By Charles F.
Egelmann. Richmond: Drinker & Morris; Baltimore:
Samuel Sands, printer. 12 ll. ViU; ViW. 14127

RICHARDSON'S Virginia and North Carolina Almanac
for 1847. By David Richardson. Richmond: Drinker
& Morris. 18 ll. MWA; Vi; ViHi; ViW (17 ll.)
14128

WARROCK'S Virginia and North Carolina Almanack for
1847. By David Richardson. Richmond: John Warrock.
18 ll. MWA; IU; InU (ntp); NcD; Vi (15 ll.); ViHi;
ViW (16 ll.) 14129

COTTOM'S Virginia & North Carolina Almanack for
1848. By David Richardson. Richmond: J. W. Randolph & Co.; [etc]. 18 ll. MWA; Vi; ViU; WHi.
14130

The FARMER'S Calendar for 1848. Richmond: Drinker
& Morris; Baltimore: Samuel Sands, printer. 16 ll.
ViU. 14131

The FARMER'S Calendar for 1848. By Charles F.
Egelmann. Alexandria: Bell & Entwisle. 16 ll. MWA
(impf) 14132

RICHARDSON'S Virginia and North Carolina Almanac
for 1848. By David Richardson. Richmond: Drinker
& Morris. 18 ll. MWA; NN; NcD (16 ll.); Vi; ViHi;
ViW. 14133

WARROCK'S Virginia and North Carolina Almanack for

1848. By David Richardson. Richmond: John Warrock. 18 ll. IU; NcD; Vi; ViHi (two varieties); ViW.
14134

The FARMER'S Calendar for 1849. Richmond: Drinker & Morris; Baltimore: Samuel Sands, printer. 16 ll. ViU.
14135

The FARMER'S Calendar for 1849. By Charles F. Egelmann. Alexandria: Bell & Entwisle. 16 ll. MWA.
14136

RICHARDSON'S Virginia and North Carolina Almanac for 1849. By David Richardson. Richmond: Drinker & Morris. 18 ll. ViHi.
14137

RICHARDSON'S Virginia and North Carolina Almanac for 1849. By David Richardson. Richmond: J. W. Randolph & Co. (Cottom's Edition) 18 ll. DLC; NN; Vi.
14138

-- Issue with added signature. ViW (22 ll.)
14139

WARROCK'S Virginia and North Carolina Almanack for 1849. By David Richardson. Richmond: John Warrock. 18 ll. MWA (two varieties); InU; NHi (impf); NcD; Vi; ViHi; ViU; ViW; Wv-Ar; Drake.
14140

The FARMER'S Calendar for 1850. Richmond: Adolphus Morris; Baltimore: Sands & Mills, printers. 16 ll. ViU.
14141

The FARMER'S Calendar for 1850. By Charles F. Egelmann. Alexandria: Bell & Entwisle. 16 ll. MWA (15 ll.)
14142

RICHARDSON'S Virginia and North Carolina Almanac for 1850. By David Richardson. Richmond: Adolphus Morris. 18 ll. MWA; ViW (17 ll.)
14143

RICHARDSON'S Virginia and North Carolina Almanac for 1850. By David Richardson. Richmond: J. W. Randolph & Co.; [etc]. (Cottom's Edition) 18 ll. DLC; NN; ViU; ViW (16 ll.); Wv-Ar.
14144

RICHARDSON'S Virginia, North Carolina, Maryland and District of Columbia Almanac for 1850. Richmond. [Sabin 70997] 14145

WARROCK'S Virginia and North Carolina Almanack for 1850. By David Richardson. Richmond: John Warrock. 18 ll. MWA; IU; NcD; Vi (three varieties); ViHi; ViRVal; ViU; ViW; Drake. 14146

WEST VIRGINIA

The FARMER'S Almanac for 1820. By Andbew [sic] Beers. Wheeling: S. Potter, & Co. [and Philadelphia] 16 ll. DLC; PHi; PPi (14 ll.)   14147

The VIRGINIA-PENNSYLVANIA Farmers' Almanac for 1822. Wheeling: S. Potter & Company. Advertised in the "North-Western Gazette," December 8, 1821. 14148

DAVIS & M'Carty's Agricultural Almanac for 1823. By John Ward. Wheeling: Davis & M'Carty. 18 ll. OClWHi; PWW (impf)   14149

DAVIS & M'Carty's Magazine Almanac for 1823. By John Ward. Wheeling: Davis & M'Carty. 30 ll. MnHi; NBuG; Matheny, Stutler.   14150

The FARMER'S Almanac for 1824. By John Armstrong. [Wheeling:] Davis & M'Carty. 18 ll. DLC; Ia-HA (16 ll.); Wv-Ar (14 ll.); Stutler.   14151

The FARMER'S Almanac for 1825. Wheeling: Davis & M'Carty. 18 ll. DLC; Ia-HA; Stutler.   14152

The FARMER'S Almanac for 1826. By John Armstrong. Wheeling: Davis & M'Carty. 18 ll. DLC; Ia-HA; IaHi; MWA; Wv-Ar (17 ll.); Perry; Stutler.   14153

The FARMER'S Almanac for 1827. By John Armstrong. Wheeling: William Davis. 18 ll. MWA; DLC; OMans; Perry; Stutler.   14154

AGRICULTURAL Almanack for 1830. By John Armstrong. Charleston: James M. Laidley & Co. 18 ll. Wv-Ar; Matheny.   14155

West Virginia - 1834   1349

The **FARMERS** and Mechanics Almanac for 1834. By John Armstrong. Wheeling: J. Fisher & Son. 18 ll. MWA; Perry; Stutler.   14156

-- Issue with added "Magazine." 30 ll. OMC.   14157

The **FARMERS** and Mechanics' Almanac for 1835. By John Armstrong. Wheeling: J. Fisher & Son. 18 ll. MWA; OMC; Wv-Ar; WvHu; WvWO; Norona.   14158

-- Issue with added "Magazine." 30 ll. WvU.   14159

The **FARMERS** and Mechanics' Almanac for 1836. By John Armstrong. Wheeling: J. Fisher & Son. 18 ll. MWA; OClWHi; Wv-Ar; Stutler.   14160

-- Issue with added "Magazine." 30 ll. MWA; OMC.   14161

UNCLE Sam's Comic Almanack for 1836. Wheeling: J. Fisher & Son. 18 ll. DLC.   14162

The **FARMERS** and Mechanics' Almanac for 1837. By John Armstrong. Wheeling: J. Fisher & Son. 18 ll. MWA; OClWHi.   14163

-- Issue with added "Magazine." 30 ll. MWA; OMC.   14164

UNCLE Sam's Comic Almanack for 1837. Wheeling: J. Fisher & Son. 18 ll. MWA; Drake (15 ll.)   14165

The **FARMERS** & Mechanics Almanac for 1838. By John Armstrong. Wheeling: J. Fisher & Son. 30 ll. [cover: The Farmers and Mechanic's Magazine Almanac for 1838.] OC; OClWHi; OHi.   14166

FISHER'S Farmer's and Mechanic's Almanac for 1839. By John Armstrong. Wheeling: Robert Fisher; John M'Creary, printer. 18 ll. OClWHi; OMC.   14167

-- Issue with added "Magazine." 30 ll. MWA; InU; OMC; PHi; Stutler.   14168

FISHER'S Farmers' and Mechanics' Almanac for 1840.

By John Armstrong. Wheeling: A. & R. Fisher; John M. M'Creary, printer. 18 ll. Norona (17 ll.) 14169

-- Issue with added "Magazine." 30 ll. MWA; OMC; PHi (29 ll.); Perry; Stutler (29 ll.) 14170

FARMERS' and Mechanics' Almanac for 1841. By John Armstrong. Wheeling: Stephenson & Garwood; John M. M'Creary, printer. 18 ll. MWA; OC; Stutler. 14171

-- Issue with added "Magazine." 30 ll. MWA; PHi. 14172

FARMERS' and Mechanics' Almanac for 1842. By John Armstrong. Wheeling: Robb & Stephenson; John M. McCreary, printer. 18 ll. MWA; OClWHi; OMC. 14173

-- Issue with added "Magazine." 30 ll. PHi (29 ll.); Wv-Ar; Stutler. 14174

FARMERS' and Mechanics' Almanac for 1843. By John Armstrong. Wheeling: William J. Robb. 18 ll. MWA; PPPrHi; Stutler (impf) 14175

FARMERS' and Mechanics' Almanac for 1843. By John Armstrong. Wheeling: Robb & Stephenson; John M. McCreary, printer. 30 ll. [cover: Farmers' and Mechanics' Magazine Almanac for 1843.] OMC; PHi. 14176

The FARMERS' and Mechanics' Almanac for 1844. By John Armstrong. Wheeling: William J. Robb. 18 ll. MWA. 14177

FARMERS' and Mechanics' Almanac for 1844. By John Armstrong. Wheeling: Stephenson & Haswell. 18 ll. OMC. 14178

FARMERS' & Mechanics' Almanac for 1845. By John Armstrong. Wheeling: William J. Robb; J. E. Wharton, printer. 18 ll. MWA; Norona. 14179

The FRANKLIN Almanac for 1846. By John Armstrong. Wheeling: John J. Haswell. 24 ll. Stutler. 14180

West Virginia - 1847

FARMER'S and Mechanic's Almanac for 1847. By John Armstrong. Wheeling: John Fisher. 18 ll. OC.
14181

FARMERS' and Mechanics' Almanac for 1847. By John Armstrong. Wheeling: J. E. Wharton. 18 ll. OMC.
14182

The FARMER'S Almanac for 1850. Wheeling: John H. Thompson; King & Baird, printers. 18 ll. MWA; OClWHi.
14183

WISCONSIN

KIKINAWADENDAMOIWEWIN or Almanac, wa aiongin obiboniman debeniminang Iesos, 1834. Bodjiwikwed or Green Bay: [Green Bay Intelligencer Office]. [Almanac in the Chippewa language.] DLC (7 ll.)   14184

WESTERN Almanac for 1844. By A. E. Hathon. Southport: Blish & Whitney; Wm. Harsha, printer. 12 ll. MoSHi.   14185

The **UNITED** States Farmers' Almanac for 1845. Milwaukee: P. C. Hale. 18 ll. WHi.   14186

BRISTOL'S Free Almanac for 1846. By George R. Perkins. [Milwaukee:] Wm. M. Cunningham. 16 ll. WHi; Drake.   14187

PRAIRIE Farmer Almanac for 1847. Milwaukee: I. A. Hopkins. 16 ll. WHi.   14188

The **UNITED** States Farmers' Almanac for 1847. Milwaukee. WHi (missing from shelves)   14189

AMERICAN Cultivator's Almanac for 1849. Racine: M. Miller; Beloit: Dr. Geo. Carey. 16 ll. NRMA.   14190

The **FARMER'S** Almanac for 1849. Milwaukee: John Nazro & Co. 14 ll. OClWHi.   14191

The **PEOPLE'S** Illustrated Almanac for 1849. Milwaukee: W. M. Cunningham. 16 ll. MWA.   14192

FARMERS' Almanac for 1852. Milwaukee: Henry J. Nazro & Co. 12 ll. WHi.   14193

GENESEE Valley Almanac for 1852. Fond du Lac:

Wisconsin - 1853

Boot & Partridge. MWA. 14194

BOOT and Shoe Almanac for 1853. Milwaukee: Bradley & Metcalf; Angell, Engel & Hewitt, printers. 12 ll. WHi. 14195

The WISCONSIN Almanac And Annual Register for 1856. By John Warren Hunt. Milwaukee: Rufus King & Co. 48 ll. MWA; DLC; C; IaHi; InU; MH; MHi; PPAmP; WHi; WM. 14196

STRICKLAND'S North-Western Almanac for 1857. Milwaukee: Strickland & Co. 25 ll. WHi. 14197

The WISCONSIN Almanac, and Annual Register for 1857. By John Warren Hunt. Milwaukee: Rufus King & Co. 63 ll. MWA; IaHi; MB; MH; MHi; PPAmP; WHi; WM; BritMus. 14198

NORST Folke-Calender for 1858. Madison: Chas. Erictson; "Emigrantens" Officin. 26 ll. PHi. 14199

STRICKLAND'S North-Western Almanac and Business Directory for 1858. Milwaukee: Strickland & Co. 48 ll. WHi. 14200

STRICKLAND & Co.'s North-Western Almanac and Business Directory for 1861. Milwaukee: Strickland & Co. 36 ll. WHi. 14201

STRICKLAND & Co.'s North-Western Almanac, Business Directory and War Record for 1862. Milwaukee: Strickland & Co. 38 ll. MWA; WHi. 14202

STRICKLAND & Co.'s North Western Almanac, War Record, & Business Directory for 1863. Milwaukee: Strickland & Co. 48 ll. MH; WHi. 14203

STRICKLAND & Co.'s Almanac, War Record, Tax Law and Business Directory for 1864. Milwaukee: Strickland & Co. 48 ll. WHi. 14204

STRICKLAND & Co.'s Almanac, Tax-Payer's Guide,

Post Office Directory and War Record for 1865. [Milwaukee: Strickland & Co.] 48 ll. NN; WHi; WM.
14205

STRICKLAND & Co.'s Almanac for 1866. Milwaukee: [Strickland & Co.] 36 ll. WHi. 14206

MILWAUKEE Business Directory, City Guide and Almanac for 1867. Milwaukee: A. Bailey. 81 ll. MnHi; OClWHi. 14207

POKROK; Kalendar savavny a poucny pro Cecho-slovany v Americe ne rek obycejny 1867. Od K. Boehma. Racine: I. L. Kober. 64 ll. [Almanac in the Bohemian language.] WHi. 14208

ROCK County Almanac and Business Directory for 1867. Janesville: Bailey & Wolfe. 48 ll. NN. 14209

STRICKLAND & Co.'s Almanac, Tax-Payer's Guide, and War Record for 1867. [Milwaukee: Strickland & Co.] 48 ll. WHi. 14210

BOOT and Shoe Almanac for 1868. Milwaukee: Bradley & Metcalf's. 12 ll. WHi. 14211

ROCK County Almanac and Business Directory for 1868. Janesville: Bailey & Wolfe. Advertised in issue for 1867. 14212

STADT-UND Land-Calender auf 1868. Milwaukee: J. B. Hoeger u. Sons; Philadelphia: King u. Baird, printers. PPG. 14213

STRICKLAND & Co.'s Almanac and Receipt Book for 1868. [Milwaukee: Strickland & Co.] 40 ll. WHi.
14214

BOOT and Shoe Almanac for 1869. Milwaukee: Bradley & Metcalf's. 12 ll. WHi. 14215

STRICKLAND & Company's Almanac for 1870. [Milwaukee: Strickland & Company] 40 ll. MWA; WHi.
14216

STRICKLAND & Company's Almanac for 1871. Mil-

Wisconsin - 1872

waukee: Strickland & Company. WHi.   14217

DANE County Almanac for 1872. By F. D. Lemmon. Madison: F. D. Lemmon. 20 ll. WHi.   14218

STRICKLAND & Company's Almanac for 1872. Milwaukee: Strickland & Company. WHi.   14219

WISCONSIN State Journal Almanac for 1874. [Madison:] Atwood and Culver. 30 ll. MWA; WHi (12 ll.)   14220

DEMOCRAT Almanac for 1875. Madison: Madison Democrat. 22 ll. WHi.   14221

CONFEDERATE STATES OF AMERICA

ALABAMA

B. B. DAVIS' Alabama Almanac for 1863. Montgomery: B. B. Davis. 30 ll. A-Ar; NHi; OClWHi (28 ll.); ViRC; Drake. 14222

J. B. CLARK'S Alabama Almanac for 1863. Selma: J. B. Clark. 30 ll. A-Ar. 14223

The CONFEDERATE States Almanac, and Repository of Useful Knowledge for 1864. By T. P. Ashmore. Mobile: H. C. Clarke. 60 ll. A-Ar; AB; CSmH; CU; DLC; InU; LU (48 ll.); MB; MBAt; MWA; MiU; Ms-Ar; NBuG; NHi; Nc; NcA (59 ll.); NcD; NcU; OCl; OClWHi; P; PP; ViHi; ViLxW; ViRC; ViU; ViW; WHi; Wv-Ar; Drake. 14224

The PLANTER'S Almanac for 1864. [Mobile:] 12 ll. MH; OClWHi. 14225

CLARKE'S Confederate Almanac for 1865. Mobile: H. C. Clarke. (Cheap Edition) 12 ll. A-Ar; AU; GEU; NcD. 14226

The CONFEDERATE States Almanac, and Repository of Useful Knowledge for 1865. By H. C. Clarke. Mobile: H. C. Clarke. 48 ll. AMob; AU; CSmH; CU; CtHT-W; DLC; GEU; MB; MBAt; MWA; Ms-Ar; NHi; NcA-S; NcD; OCl; PHi; PP; Vi (impf); ViHi; ViRC; ViU; WHi; Drake. 14227

-- Issue with 60 ll. OClWHi. 14228

ARKANSAS

MOORE'S Confederate Almanac and Repository for 1864. Arkadelphia: Messenger Publisher. 8 ll. Drake. 14229

GEORGIA

GRIER'S Southern Almanac for the States of Georgia, South Carolina, Alabama, and Tennessee for 1862. By Samuel H. Wright. Augusta: F. H. Singer. 12 ll. A-Ar. 14230

GRIER'S Southern Almanac for the States of Georgia, South Carolina, Alabama, and Tennessee for 1862. By Samuel H. Wright. Augusta: F. H. Singer; Arthur Bleakley. 12 ll. MBAt; NcD. 14231

GRIER'S Southern Almanac for the States of Georgia, South Carolina, Alabama, and Tennessee for 1862. By Samuel H. Wright. Augusta: F. H. Singer; Chichester & Co. 12 ll. NcD. 14232

GRIER'S Southern Almanac for the States of Georgia, South Carolina, Alabama, and Tennessee for 1862. By Samuel H. Wright. Augusta: F. H. Singer; Thomas Richards & Sons. 12 ll. GEU. 14233

GRIER'S Southern Almanac for the States of Georgia, South Carolina, Alabama, and Tennessee for 1862. By Samuel H. Wright. Augusta: F. H. Singer; Atlanta: J. McPherson & Co. 12 ll. NcD. 14234

GRIER'S Southern Almanac for the States of Georgia, South Carolina, Alabama, and Tennessee for 1862. By Samuel H. Wright. Augusta: F. H. Singer; Atlanta: J. J. Richards, & Co. 12 ll. G. 14235

GRIER'S Southern Almanac for the States of Georgia, South Carolina, Alabama, and Tennessee for 1862. By Samuel H. Wright. Augusta: F. H. Singer; Griffin: Brawner & Putnam; Macon: Jenkins & Hodges, printers. 12 ll. GU-De; NcD. 14236

GRIER'S Southern Almanac for the States of Georgia, South Carolina, Alabama, and Tennessee for 1862. By Samuel H. Wright. Augusta: F. H. Singer; Savannah: John M. Cooper & Co. 12 ll. GEU. 14237

GRIER'S Southern Almanac for the States of Georgia, South Carolina, Alabama, and Tennessee for 1862. By Samuel H. Wright. Augusta: F. H. Singer; Savannah: E. Knapp & Co. 12 ll. MBAt. 14238

HISTORICAL Register, and Confederate's Assistant to National Independence [for 1862]. By H. W. R. Jackson. Augusta: Constitutionalist. 48 ll. NcD (missing from shelves) 14239

GRIER'S Southern Almanac for the States of Georgia, South Carolina, Alabama, Tennessee, Louisiana for 1863. By T. P. Ashmore. Augusta: F. H. Singer; Milledgeville: Herty & Hall. 12 ll. GA; GEU. 14240

GRIER'S Southern Almanac for the States of Georgia, South-Carolina, Alabama, Tennessee, Mississippi, Louisiana for 1863. By T. P. Ashmore. Augusta: F. H. Singer. 12 ll. GU-De; MWA; NcD. 14241

GRIER'S Southern Almanac for the States of Georgia, South Carolina, Alabama, Tennessee, Mississippi, Louisiana for 1863. By T. P. Ashmore. Augusta: F. H. Singer; Thos. Richards & Son. 12 ll. NcD. 14242

GRIER'S Southern Almanac for the States of Georgia, So. Carolina, Alabama, Tennessee, Mississippi, Louisiana for 1863. By T. P. Ashmore. Augusta: F. H. Singer; Atlanta: Jas. McPherson & Co. 12 ll. G; GEU (11 ll.); MWA; T (impf) 14243

GRIER'S Southern Almanac for the States of Georgia, South Carolina, Mississippi, Louisiana, Alabama, Tennessee for 1863. By T. P. Ashmore. Augusta: F. H. Singer; Blackmar & Bro. 12 ll. A-Ar; AU; MBAt.
  14244
GRIER'S Southern Almanac for the States of Georgia, South Carolina, Mississippi, Louisiana, Alabama, Ten-

nessee for 1863. By T. P. Ashmore. Augusta: F. H. Singer; Macon: J. W. Burke. 12 ll. MBAt; NcD.
14245

GRIER'S Southern Almanac for the States of Georgia, South Carolina, Mississippi, Louisiana, Alabama, Tennessee for 1863. By T. P. Ashmore. Augusta: F. H. Singer; Savannah: John M. Cooper & Co. 12 ll. MBAt; NcD. 14246

CONFEDERATE States Almanac for 1864. Calculations made at University of Alabama. Macon: Burke, Boykin & Co.; J. W. Burke, Ag't. 12 ll. AU; GEU; LU; NcD. 14247

CONFEDERATE States Almanac for 1864. Calculations made at University of Alabama. Macon: Burke, Boykin & Co.; Atlanta: J. McPherson & Co. 12 ll. MB; MBAt; MWA. 14248

CONFEDERATE States Almanac for 1864. Calculations made at University of Alabama. Macon: Burke, Boykin & Co.; Greensboro': J. Russell. 12 ll. GEU. 14249

CONFEDERATE States Almanac for 1864. Calculations made at University of Alabama. Macon: Burke, Boykin & Co.; Mobile: S. H. Goetzel. 12 ll. A-Ar; CSmH; CtHT-W; DLC; GU-De; ICN; LU; M; MB; MBAt; MHi; MS; MWA; MnU; MoSM; NB; NHi; NN; NNC; Nc; NcA-S; NcD; OU; P; PHi; PPL; PPi; RPB; T; Vi; ViHi; ViLxW; ViRC; Drake; Hamner. 14250

-- Issue with 20 ll. GU. 14251

CONFEDERATE States Almanac for 1864. Calculations made at University of Alabama. Macon: Burke, Boykin & Co.; Savannah: John M. Cooper & Co. 12 ll. N.
14252

No entry 14253

No entry   14254

No entry   14255

No entry   14256

CONFEDERATE States Almanac for 1864. Calculations made at University of Alabama. Macon: Burke, Boykin & Co.; Tuscaloosa: D. Woodruff. 12 ll. AU. 14257

GRIER'S Southern Almanac for 1864. By T. P. Ashmore. Augusta: F. H. Singer; Blackmar & Bro. 12 ll. NHi; NcD.   14258

GRIER'S Southern Almanac for 1864. By T. P. Ashmore. Augusta: F. H. Singer; Chichester & Co. 12 ll. NcD.   14259

GRIER'S Southern Almanac for 1864. By T. P. Ashmore. Augusta: F. H. Singer; Thos. R. Rhodes. 12 ll. G.   14260

GRIER'S Southern Almanac for 1864. By T. P. Ashmore. Augusta: F. H. Singer; Thos. Richards & Son. 12 ll. GEU.   14261

GRIER'S Southern Almanac for 1864. By T. P. Ashmore. Augusta: F. H. Singer; Athens: Wm. N. White. 12 ll. CtY.   14262

GRIER'S Southern Almanac for 1864. By T. P. Ashmore. Augusta: F. H. Singer; Atlanta: Jas. McPherson & Co. 12 ll. DLC; GEU.   14263

GRIER'S Southern Almanac for 1864. By T. P. Ashmore. Augusta: F. H. Singer; Atlanta: J. J. Richards

& Co. 12 ll. MBAt. 14264

GRIER'S Southern Almanac for 1864. By T. P. Ashmore. Augusta: F. H. Singer; Milledgeville: Grieve & Clarke. 12 ll. GA; GU-De. 14265

The CONFEDERATE States Almanac for 1865. By T. P. Ashmore. Macon: J. W. Burke. 12 ll. AB; AU; DLC; G; MBAt; NPV (11 ll.); NcD; Drake. 14266

The CONFEDERATE States Almanac for 1865. By T. P. Ashmore. Macon: Burke, Boykin & Company. 12 ll. GU-De; NcD. 14267

CONSTITUTIONALIST Commercial Almanac for 1865. [Augusta: Constitutionalist Office] 16 ll. GEU (15 ll.); GU-De. 14268

GEORGIA and Carolina Almanac for 1865. [Sabin 27050] 14269

GRIER'S Almanac for the States of Georgia, S. Carolina, Alabama, Florida, Mississippi, Tennessee for 1865. Augusta: Geo. A. Oates. 12 ll. NcD (impf) 14270

GRIER'S Almanac for the States of Georgia, S. Carolina, Alabama, Florida, Mississippi, Tennessee for 1865. Augusta: Thomas Richard. 12 ll. OClWHi. 14271

GRIER'S Almanac for the States of Georgia, S. Carolina, Mississippi, Tennessee, Alabama, Florida for 1865. Augusta: Arthur Bleakley. 12 ll. GEU; MWA (impf) 14272

LOUISIANA

SOUTHERN Rural Almanac for 1862. By Thomas Affleck. New Orleans: Office of the "Picayune." 66 ll. Ms-Ar. 14273

WHITE'S Louisiana Almanac for 1862. New Orleans: Thos. L. White. 12 ll. DLC. 14274

The LOUISIANA Almanac for 1865. Mt. Lebanon: Office of the Louisiana Baptist. 8 ll. NBuG. 14275

The TRANS-MISSISSIPPI Almanac for 1865. Mt. Lebanon: W. F. Wells. 4 ll. MWA. 14276

MISSISSIPPI

The CONFEDERATE States Almanac for 1862. Calculations made at the University of Alabama. Vicksburg: H. C. Clarke. Drake (title-leaf only) 14277

The CONFEDERATE States Almanac, and Repository of Useful Knowledge for 1862. Vicksburg: H. C. Clarke. 88 ll. AU; CSmH; GEU; GU-De; InU; MBAt; MWA; MoSM; NBuG; NHi; NN; NcA-S; NcD; PP; TKL; ViRC; ViU; WHi; Drake. 14278

-- Issue with 54 ll. Ms-Ar. 14279

The CONFEDERATE States Almanac, and Repository of Useful Knowledge for 1862. Vicksburg: H. C. Clarke. (Second Edition) 40 ll. CSmH; DLC; MB; MBAt; MWA; NHi; NcU; OClWHi; PHi; ViHi; ViRC; ViU; WHi.
14280
CLARKE'S Confederate Household Almanac for 1863. Jackson: J. B. Morey. 12 ll. AU. 14281

CLARKE'S Confederate Household Almanac for 1863. Vicksburg: H. C. Clarke, bookseller and publisher. 12 ll. A-Ar; CSmH; DLC; GEU; GU-De; InU; MB; MBAt; MWA; N; NBuG; NHi; NNC; OClWHi; OU; PHi; Vi; ViL; ViLxW; ViU; WHi; Drake. 14282

CLARKE'S Confederate Household Almanac for 1863. Vicksburg: H. C. Clarke, Publisher. 12 ll. ICN; MBAt; Ms-Ar; NHi; Vi; ViW. 14283

The CONFEDERATE States Almanac, and Repository of Useful Knowledge for 1863. Vicksburg: H. C. Clarke. 51 ll. AU; CSmH; DLC (48 ll.); MB; MBAt; MHi;

Ms-Ar (50 ll.); NBuG; NN; NcD; NcU; NjR; OClWHi; PP; ScC; TKL; Vi; ViHi; ViRC; ViU.   14284

-- Issue with 56 ll. Drake.   14285

The MISSISSIPPI & Alabama Almanac for 1863. Vicksburg: H. C. Clarke. Advertised in Clarke's "Confederate States Almanac" for 1863.   14286

NORTH CAROLINA

BLUM'S Farmers' and Planters' Almanac for 1862. Salem: L. V. & E. T. Blum. 18 ll. CtY; MBAt; MWA (impf); Nc; NcD; NcU; Drake.   14287

TURNER'S North-Carolina Almanac for 1862. By David Richardson. Raleigh: Henry D. Turner. 18 ll. CtY; MBAt; MH; MWA; Nc; Nc-Ar; NcD; NcU.   14288

BLUM'S Farmers' and Planters' Almanac for 1863. By David Richardson. Salem: L. V. & E. T. Blum. 9 ll. CtY; MBAt; MWA (impf); NcD; NcU; Drake.   14289

TURNER'S North Carolina Almanac for 1863. By David Richardson. Raleigh: Henry D. Turner. 18 ll. CtY; DLC; MBAt; MWA; Nc; Nc-Ar; NcD; NcU; OClWHi.   14290

TURNER'S North Carolina Almanac for 1863. By David Richardson. Raleigh: Henry D. Turner. (Third Edition) 18 ll. NN.   14291

BLUM'S Farmers' and Planters' Almanac for 1864. By David Richardson. Salem: L. V. & E. T. Blum. 9 ll. CtY; KyU (8 ll.); MBAt; MWA; NcD; NcU; T; ViU; Drake.   14292

TURNER'S North Carolina Almanac for 1864. By David Richardson. Raleigh: Henry D. Turner. 16 ll. CtY; DLC; MWA; Nc-Ar; NcD.   14293

TURNER'S North Carolina Almanac for 1864. By
David Richardson. Raleigh: Henry D. Turner. (Second
Edition)   16 ll. MBAt; Nc; NcU.   14294

BLUM'S Farmers' and Planters' Almanac for 1865. By
David Richardson. Salem: L. V. & E. T. Blum. 9
ll.   CSmH (8 ll.); CtY; DLC; MBAt; MWA; NBuG;
Nc; NcD; NcU; ViU; Drake.   14295

NORTH Carolina Baptist Almanac for 1865. Rev.
Needham B. Cobb, compiler. Raleigh: [np] 20 ll.
NcD (impf); NcHiC (19 ll.); NcU.   14296

TURNER'S North Carolina Almanac for 1865. By
David Richardson. Raleigh: Henry D. Turner. 16 ll.
CtY; MBAt; MWA (impf); NNC; Nc; Nc-Ar; NcD;
NcU; OClWHi; PPL; RP; Drake.   14297

South Carolina

MILLER'S Planters' & Merchants' State Rights Almanac
for 1861: Being the... First of Southern Independence.
By Samuel H. Wright. Charleston: A. E. Miller.
(Third Edition) 25 ll. [Title page of earlier 1861 editions did not include the words "Southern Independence."]
MBAt; NcU; OClWHi; Sc; ScU-S.   14298

-- Issue with 30 ll. ScC.   14299

MILLER'S Planters' & Merchants' State Rights Almanac
for 1862. By Samuel H. Wright. Charleston: A. E.
Miller.   (First Edition) 24 ll. OCl; ScC; ScU-S;
ViU.   14300

-- Issue with 30 ll. GEU.   14301

MILLER'S Planters' & Merchants' State Rights Almanac
for 1862. By Samuel H. Wright. Charleston: A. E.
Miller. (Second Edition) 24 ll. GEU; MBAt.   14302

MILLER'S Planters' & Merchants' State Rights Almanac for 1862. By Samuel H. Wright. Charleston: A. E. Miller. (Third Edition) 24 ll. MWA; OClWHi; ScU-S. 14303

-- Issue with 30 ll. NHi (impf); NcD; Sc. 14304

The CONFEDERATE Almanac for 1863. Calculations adapted from the British Nautical Almanac. Charleston: A. E. Miller. [From a note in B. B. Davis' Alabama Almanac for 1863.] 14305

MILLER'S Planters' & Merchants' State Rights Almanac for 1863. By Samuel H. Wright. Charleston: A. E. Miller. (First Edition) 24 ll. GEU; MWA (22 ll., ntp); NcD; OClWHi. 14306

MILLER'S Planters' & Merchants' State Rights Almanac for 1863. By Samuel H. Wright. Charleston: A. E. Miller. (Second Edition) 24 ll. MBAt; ScU. 14307

MILLER'S Planters' & Merchants' State Rights Almanac for 1863. By Samuel H. Wright. Charleston: A. E. Miller. (Third Edition) 24 ll. OCl; ScC. 14308

MILLER'S Planters & Merchants' State Rights Almanac for 1863. By Samuel H. Wright. Charleston: A. E. Miller. (Fourth Edition) 24 ll. MH; NBuG; PPL; ScHi; ScU-S (impf) 14309

MILLER'S Planters' & Merchants' State Rights Almanac for 1864. By Robert Garlington. Charleston: A. E. Miller. (First Edition) 24 ll. L-M; OCl; OClWHi; Sc; ScC. 14310

MILLER'S Planters' & Merchants' State Rights Almanac for 1864. By Robert Garlington. Charleston: A. E. Miller. (Second Edition) 24 ll. GEU; MH; NcD; ScU-S (impf) 14311

MILLER'S Planters' & Merchants' State Rights Almanac for 1864. By Robert Garlington. Charleston: A. E. Miller. (Third Edition) 24 ll. InU; MBAt; MWA. 14312

South Carolina - 1864

The SOUTHERN Almanac for 1864. By Professor R. Garlington. Newberry C. H.: Houseal & Seig; Greenville: G. E. Elford's Press. 12 ll. ScU-S.   14313

MILLER'S Planters' & Merchants' State Rights Almanac for 1865. By Prof. Robert Garlington. Charleston: A. E. Miller. (First Edition) 24 ll. NcD; OClWHi; PHi; ScC; ScGrvF (22 ll.)   14314

MILLER'S Planters' & Merchants' State Rights Almanac for 1865. By Prof. Robert Garlington. Charleston: A. E. Miller. (Second Edition) 24 ll. OCl.   14315

MILLER'S Planters' & Merchants' State Rights Almanac for 1865. By Prof. Robert Garlington. Charleston: A. E. Miller. (Third Edition) 24 ll. DLC; MH; ScU-S.   14316

MILLER'S Planters' & Merchants' State Rights Almanac for 1865. By Prof. Robert Garlington. Charleston: A. E. Miller. (Fourth Edition) 24 ll. MWA; NBLiHi (21 ll.); NHi; NN; PPL.   14317

The SOUTHERN Almanac for 1865. By Professor R. Garlington. Greenville: G. E. Elford. 12 ll. DLC; MBAt; MWA.   14318

TENNESSEE

The CONFEDERATE States Almanac for 1862. Calculations made at the University of Alabama. By T. O. Summers. Nashville: Southern Methodist Publishing House. 16 ll. A-Ar; AU; CSmH; DLC; GEU; InU; MBAt; MWA; Ms-Ar; NHi; NN (impf); NNC; Nc; NcA-S; NcD; NcU; OCHP; OClWHi; OMC; PP; PPi; T; TMC; TN; TU; WHi; Drake.   14319

CUMBERLAND Almanac for 1862. Nashville: Bang, Baber & Co. 16 ll. NcD; T (impf); Drake.   14320

HILL'S Tennessee, Alabama, and Mississippi Almanac and State Register for 1862. By J. B. Hill. Fayetteville: E. Hill. 16 ll. T; THi (15 ll.) 14321

TEXAS

The TEXAS Almanac for 1862. Galveston: D. Richardson. 32 ll. CSt; DLC (31 ll.); MBAt; Mi; NH; NNA; Nh; Tx; TxDa; TxDa-N; TxDaM; TxF; TxGR; TxH; TxU; TxWB. 14322

TEXAS Almanac and Immigrants' Hand Book for 1862. Houston: J. Burke. [Raines] 14323

The TEXAS Almanac for 1863. Austin: D. Richardson. 32 ll. CSt; CtY; NH; NHi; Nh; Tx; TxDaM; TxF; TxGR; TxH; TxHi; TxU; TxWB. 14324

TEXAS Almanac and Immigrants' Hand Book for 1863. Houston: J. Burke. [Raines] 14325

The TEXAS Almanac for 1864. Austin: D. Richardson. 24 ll. CSt; DLC; Tx; TxAbH; TxDa-N; TxF; TxGR; TxU; TxWB. 14326

The TEXAS Almanac for 1864. Galveston: Richardson & Co., News Office. [Raines, probably in error]
14327

TEXAS Almanac and Immigrants' Hand Book for 1864. Houston: J. Burke. [Raines] 14328

The CONFEDERATE Almanac for 1865. Houston: O. Dietzel & W. Henry Eliot. 20 ll. MBAt; MS; TxGR.
14329

The TEXAS Almanac for 1865. Austin: D. Richardson. 32 ll. DLC; NH; Tx; TxAbH; TxDW; TxF; TxH; TxSa; TxU; TxWB. 14330

TEXAS Almanac and Immigrants' Hand Book for 1865. Houston: J. Burke. [Raines] 14331

VIRGINIA

CONFEDERATE Almanac and Register for 1862.
Lynchburg: J. P. Bell. 16 ll. CSmH; DLC; NHi; NjP;
PHi; Vi; ViL; ViU; ViW.   14332

[SHEET Almanac for] 1862 [Richmond: J. W. Randolph]
Broadside. Vi.   14333

POCKET Almanac for 1862. Petersburg: Evangelical
Tract Society. 12 ll. CSmH; MWA; NN; ViRC.   14334

RICHARDSON'S Almanac for 1862. By David Richardson. Richmond: J. W. Randolph. (Cottom's Edition)
18 ll. CSmH; DLC; GEU; InU; MBAt; MWA; NBuG;
NcD; PHi; Vi; ViHi (ntp); ViRVal; ViU; ViW; WHi;
Drake.   14335

-- Advertisement on last page: "Payne & Blackford."
18 ll. OClWHi.   14336

RICHARDSON'S Virginia & North Carolina Almanac for
1862. By David Richardson. Richmond: A. Morris;
Chas. H. Wynne, printer. (Wynne's Edition) 18 ll.
CSmH; LNHT; MB; MWA; NcD; ViW; Drake.   14337

RICHARDSON'S Virginia & North Carolina Almanac for
1862. By David Richardson. Richmond: West & Johnston; Chas. H. Wynne, printer. (Wynne's Edition) 18 ll.
CSmH; DLC; IU; InU (17 ll.); KyU; MBAt; MWA;
NBuG; NHi (impf); NN; NcD; NcU; PHi; Vi; ViRC
(impf); ViU; ViW; Drake.   14338

RICHARDSON'S Virginia & North Carolina Almanac for
1862. By David Richardson. Richmond: W. Hargrave
White; Chas. H. Wynne, printer. (Wynne's Edition)
18 ll. NcD; Vi.   14339

RICHARDSON'S Virginia & North Carolina Almanac for
1862. By David Richardson. Richmond: James Woodhouse & Co.; Chas. H. Wynne, printer. (Wynne's Edition) 18 ll. DLC; NNC; ViHi (impf)   14340

Virginia - 1863 1369

POCKET Almanac for 1863. Petersburg: Evangelical Tract Society; C. LeRoi, printer. 12 ll. NcU; Vi; Drake. 14341

RICHARDSON'S Virginia & North Carolina Almanac for 1863. By David Richardson. Richmond: George L. Bidgood; Chas. H. Wynne, printer. (Wynne's Edition) 18 ll. MWA; ViU; Drake. 14342

RICHARDSON'S Virginia & North Carolina Almanac for 1863. By David Richardson. Richmond: J. R. Keiningham; Chas. H. Wynne, printer. (Wynne's Edition) 18 ll. MBAt. 14343

RICHARDSON'S Virginia & North Carolina Almanac for 1863. By David Richardson. Richmond: A. Morris; Chas. H. Wynne, printer. (Wynne's Edition) 18 ll. MWA; Nc. 14344

RICHARDSON'S Virginia & North Carolina Almanac for 1863. By David Richardson. Richmond: J. W. Randolph; Chas. H. Wynne, printer. (Wynne's Edition) 18 ll. CSmH; DLC; MBAt; NHi; Vi; ViRC. 14345

RICHARDSON'S Virginia & North Carolina Almanac for 1863. By David Richardson. Richmond: West & Johnston; Chas. H. Wynne, printer. (Wynne's Edition) 18 ll. CSmH; NcD; NcU; Vi; ViHi; ViRC; ViRVal; ViU; WHi; Drake. 14346

RICHARDSON'S Virginia & North Carolina Almanac for 1863. By David Richardson. Richmond: James Woodhouse & Co.; Chas. H. Wynne, printer. (Wynne's Edition) 18 ll. ViW. 14347

RICHARDSON'S Virginia & North Carolina Almanac for 1863. By David Richardson. Richmond: C. H. Wynne, book and job steam printing presses. (Wynne's Edition) 18 ll. MBAt; MWA; NHi; NN; Vi; ViHi; ViRC. 14348

RICHARDSON'S Virginia & North Carolina Almanac for 1863. By David Richardson. Richmond: C. H. Wynne, plain and ornamental printer. (Wynne's Edition) 18 ll.

Virginia - 1863

DLC.   14349

The SOLDIERS' Almanac for 1863. Richmond: Soldiers' Tract Association; MacFarlane & Fergusson. 16 ll. MBAt.   14350

The SOLDIER'S Almanac for 1863. Richmond: Soldiers' Tract Association; Chas. H. Wynne, printer. 18 ll. DLC; MB; Vi; ViRC.   14351

The SOLDIERS' Almanac for 1863. By George B. Taylor. [Staunton: np] 12 ll. DLC (impf); MBAt; NcU; ViRC.   14352

The SOUTHERN Almanac for 1863. By C. A. Schaffter. Lynchburg: D. B. Payne. 16 ll. ViL; Drake.   14353

The SOUTHERN Almanac for 1863. By C. A. Schaffter. Lynchburg: Schaffter & Bryant. 16 ll. DLC; MBAt; MWA; NHi; NcD; NcU; Vi; ViHi; ViL; ViU; Drake.
        14354

ALMANAC for 1864. Lynchburg: D. B. Payne and H. C. Victor. 8 ll. MBAt; MWA.   14355

ALMANAC and Annual Diary and Memoranda for 1864. Lynchburg: Johnson & Schaffter. 48 ll. CSmH; NcD.
        14356

CLARKE'S Confederate Almanac for 1864. By T. P. Ashmore. Lynchburg: Bell & Co. (Cheap Edition) 12 ll. ViL; ViRC.   14357

[SHEET Almanac for] 1864 [Richmond: J. W. Randolph] Broadside. GEU.   14358

RICHARDSON'S Virginia & North Carolina Almanac for 1864. By David Richardson. Richmond: A. Morris. (Wynne's Edition) 18 ll. DLC; Vi; ViHi; ViRC; ViW.
        14359

RICHARDSON'S Virginia & North Carolina Almanac for 1864. By David Richardson. Richmond: J. W. Randolph: Chas. H. Wynne, printer. (Wynne's Edition) 18 ll. CSmH; NNC.   14360

Virginia - 1864

RICHARDSON'S Virginia & North Carolina Almanac for 1864. By David Richardson. Richmond: West & Johnston; Chas. H. Wynne, printer. (Wynne's Edition) 18 ll. DLC; LNHT; MWA; NN; OMC; ViW.
14361

RICHARDSON'S Virginia & North Carolina Almanac for 1864. By David Richardson. Richmond: Chas. H. Wynne. (Wynne's Edition) 18 ll. CSmH; DLC; KyU; MBAt; NHi; Vi; ViHi; ViLxW; ViRC (17 ll.); ViRVal; ViU; ViW; WHi; WvU. 14362

-- Advertisement on last page: "J. W. Randolph." 18 ll. Vi. 14363

-- Advertisement on last page: "West & Johnston." 18 ll. CSmH; DLC; GEU; MWA; N; NBuG; NcD; NcU; PHi; TxU; ViRVal (9 ll.); Drake. 14364

The SOLDIERS' Almanac for 1864. Richmond: Soldiers' Tract Association of the M. E. Church, South; Chas. H. Wynne, printer. 18 ll. NcD. 14365

The SOUTHERN Almanac for 1864. By David Richardson. Lynchburg: Johnson & Schaffter. 12 ll. DLC; MBAt; OClWHi; PYHi; ViU; ViW; Drake (impf) 14366

WARROCK'S Virginia and North Carolina Almanac for 1864. By David Richardson. Richmond: George L. Bidgood. 18 ll. ViHi. 14367

WARROCK'S Virginia and North Carolina Almanac for 1864. By David Richardson. Richmond: James E. Goode. 18 ll. CSmH; DLC; GEU; MBAt; MWA; NBLiHi; NHi; NN; NcD; ViHi; WHi; Drake. 14368

-- Advertisement on last page: "James Woodhouse & Co." 18 ll. NHi. 14369

[SHEET Almanac for] 1865 [Richmond: J. W. Randolph] Broadside. Vi. 14370

POCKET Almanac for 1865. Petersburg: Evangelical Tract Society; Petersburg Express Print. 12 ll. DLC;

MBAt; Drake. 14371

RICHARDSON'S Virginia & North Carolina Almanac for 1865. By David Richardson. Richmond: A. Morris; Chas. H. Wynne, printer. (Wynne's Edition) 18 ll. MHi; ViHi (16 ll.) 14372

RICHARDSON'S Virginia & North Carolina Almanac for 1865. By David Richardson. Richmond: West & Johnston. (Wynne's Edition) 18 ll. MBAt; ViRC (17 ll.) 14373

RICHARDSON'S Virginia & North Carolina Almanac for 1865. By David Richardson. Richmond: Chas. H. Wynne. (Wynne's Edition) 18 ll. CSmH; IU; MWA (impf); Nc; ViHi. 14374

-- Advertisement on last page: "T. C. C. Drewry." 18 ll. DLC; Vi. 14375

-- Advertisement on last page: "J. W. Randolph." 18 ll. DLC. 14376

-- Advertisement on last page: "J. C. Swan." 18 ll. N; NBuG; NN; NcD; NcU; PHi; Drake. 14377

-- Advertisement on last page: "West & Johnston." 18 ll. DLC; NHi. 14378

The SOUTHERN Almanac for 1865. By David Richardson. Lynchburg: J. P. Bell & Co. 12 ll. ViL. 14379

The SOUTHERN Almanac for 1865. By David Richardson. Lynchburg: Johnson & Schaffter. 12 ll. MBAt; NHi; NcD; NcU; PHi; Vi; ViU; ViW. 14380

WARROCK'S Virginia and North Carolina Almanac for 1865. By David Richardson. Richmond: James E. Goode. 16 ll. GEU. 14381

WARROCK'S Virginia and North Carolina Almanac for 1865. By David Richardson. Richmond: James E. Goode. (Fiftieth Edition) 18 ll. CSmH; MBAt; MH; MHi;

MWA; NHi; NN; NcD; Vi; ViL; ViRC; Drake. 14382

-- Advertisement on last page: "Joseph R. Keiningham." 18 ll. CtHT-W; F; MB; MWA; NBuG; NHi; ViU; Drake. 14383

-- Advertisement on last page: "West & Johnston." 18 ll. ViW; Drake. 14384

-- Advertisement on last page: "James Woodhouse & Co." 18 ll. OClWHi; ViW; Drake. 14385

Bibliography

Source materials, each entirely examined as a part of this project:

ALDEN, J.E. Rhode Island imprints, 1727-1800. New York, 1949
ALDRICH, N.W. Rhode Island books... in the library of N.W. Aldrich. Boston, 1915.
ALLEN, A.H. Arkansas imprints, 1821-1876. Bibliographical Society of America. New York, 1947.
---. Dakota imprints, 1858-1889. New York, 1947
---. [see also MC MURTRIE, D.C. & A. H. ALLEN]
ALLIOT, H. Bibliography of Arizona. Los Angeles, 1914.
ALTROCCHI, J.C. "Father Richard and his printing press." In: Thought, vol. 15. New York, 1940.
AMERICAN ART ASSOCIATION. Americana [catalog]. New York, 1923.
---. Illustrated catalog of Colonial and Revolutionary books. New York, 1917.
AMERICAN IMPRINTS INVENTORY. [United States Works Progress Administration, Historical Records Survey. Listed in order of Inventory Series Numbering]:
---. 1. Preliminary checklist of Missouri imprints, 1808-1850. Washington, 1937.
---. 2. Checklist of Minnesota imprints, 1849-1865. Chicago, 1938.
---. 3. Checklist of Arizona imprints, 1860-1890. Chicago, 1938.
---. 4. Checklist of Chicago Ante-Fire imprints, 1851-1871. Chicago, 1938.
---. 5. [McMurtrie, D.C. & A.H. Allen] Checklist of Kentucky imprints, 1787-1810. Louisville, 1939.
---. 6. [McMurtrie, D.C. & A.H. Allen] Checklist of Kentucky imprints, 1811-1820. Louisville, 1939.

---. 7. Checklist of Nevada imprints, 1859-1890. Chicago, 1939.
---. 8. Checklist of Alabama imprints, 1807-1840. Birmingham, 1939.
---. 9. Checklist of New Jersey imprints, 1784-1800. Baltimore, 1939.
---. 10. Checklist of Kansas imprints, 1854-1876. Topeka, 1939.
---. 12. Checklist of Sag Harbor, N.Y. imprints, 1791-1820. Chicago, 1939.
---. 13. Checklist of Idaho imprints, 1839-1890. Chicago, 1940.
---. 14. Checklist of West Virginia imprints, 1791-1830. Chicago, 1940.
---. 15. Checklist of Iowa imprints, 1838-1860. Chicago, 1940.
---. 16. Checklist of Tennessee imprints, in Tennessee libraries, 1793-1840. Nashville, 1941.
---. 17. Checklist of Ohio imprints, 1796-1820. Columbus, 1941.
---. 18. Checklist of Wyoming imprints, 1866-1890. Chicago, 1941.
---. 20. Checklist of Tennessee imprints, 1841-1850. Nashville, 1941.
---. 23. Checklist of Wisconsin imprints, 1833-1849. Madison, 1942.
---. 24. Checklist of Wisconsin imprints, 1850-1854. Madison, 1942.
---. 25. Checklist of New Mexico imprints and publications, 1784-1876. Detroit, 1942.
---. 26. Checklist of Nebraska non-documentary imprints, 1847-1876. Lincoln, 1942.
---. 31. Checklist of California non-documentary imprints, 1833-1855. San Francisco, 1942.
---. 32. Checklist of Tennessee imprints, 1793-1840. Chicago, 1942.
---. 36. Checklist of Utica, N.Y. imprints, 1799-1830. Chicago, 1942.
---. 38. [Townsend, J.W.] Supplementary checklist of Kentucky imprints, 1788-1820. Louisville, 1942.
---. 39. Checklist of Arkansas imprints, 1821-1876. Little Rock, 1942.

---. 40. Checklist of Massachusetts imprints, 1801. Boston, 1942.
---. 41. Checklist of Wisconsin imprints, 1855-1858. Madison, 1942.
---. 42. Checklist of Wisconsin imprints, 1859-1863. Madison, 1942.
---. 42a. Checklist of Wisconsin imprints, 1864-1869. State Historical Society of Wisconsin. Madison, 1953.
---. 44. Checklist of Washington State imprints, 1853-1876. Seattle, 1942.
---. 45. Checklist of Massachusetts imprints, 1802. Boston, 1942.
---. 52. Preliminary checklist of Michigan imprints, 1796-1850. Detroit, 1942.
ANDERSON GALLERIES. Western Americana [catalog]. New York, 1923.

BABCOCK, W.M. "The Goodhue Press." Minnesota Historical Bulletin, vol. 3. St. Paul, 1920.
BAER, E. Seventeenth century Maryland. A bibliography. Baltimore, 1949.
BALLOU, H.M. "History of the Hawaiian Mission press, with a bibliography of the earlier publications [1822-1840]." Hawaiian Historical Society Papers, no. 14. Honolulu, 1908.
BARNES, L. "Notes on imprints from Highland." Kansas Historical Quarterly, vol. 8. Topeka, 1939.
BARNSLEY, E.R. "Presses and printers of Newton, Pa. before 1868." Bucks County Historical Society Collections, vol. 7. Easton, 1937.
BASS, A.L.B. Cherokee Messenger. Norman, Okla., 1936.
BATES, A.C. Checklist of Connecticut almanacs, 1709-1850. Worcester, 1914.
---. "Part of an almanack." American Antiquarian Society Proceedings. Worcester, 1942.
---. Supplementary list of books printed in Connecticut, 1709-1800. Hartford, 1947.
BAUSMAN, L.M. A bibliography of Lancaster County, Pa., 1745-1912. Philadelphia, 1917.
BAXTER, C.N. & J.M. DEARBORN. Confederate lit-

erature... now in the Boston Athenaeum. Boston, 1917.
BAY, J.C. Rare and beautiful imprints of Chicago. Chicago, 1922.
BELKNAP, G.N. McMurtrie's Oregon imprints, a supplement. Portland, 1950.
---. McMurtrie's Oregon imprints, 2nd supplement. Portland, 1954.
BENNETT & MARSHALL. Four centuries of Americana, 1556-1954 [catalog]. Los Angeles. 1954.
BENTLEY, G.F. "Printers and printing in the Southwest Territory, 1790-1796." Tennessee Historical Quarterly. Nashville, December 1949.
BOSQUI, E. Memoirs of Edward Bosqui. Oakland, 1952.
BOSTON PUBLIC LIBRARY. "Almanacs, calendars,... in the Boston Public Library." Boston Public Library Bulletin, vol. 12, no. 2. Boston, July 1893.
BRECKENRIDGE, W.C. & F.A. SIMPSON. "Early Missouri imprints, 1808-1850." In: William Clark Breckenridge... bibliographer of Missouriana. St. Louis, 1932.
BRIGGS, S. "The almanac in America." Western Reserve Historical Society, Tract no. 69. Cleveland, 1887.
---. The essays, humor and poems of Nathaniel Ames. Cleveland, 1891.
BRIGHAM, C.S. An account of American almanacs and their value for historical study. Worcester, 1925.
BRISTOL, R.P. Maryland imprints, 1801-1810. Bibliographical Society of the University of Virginia. Richmond, 1953.
BRITISH ALMANAC AND COMPANION. "Almanacs." London, 1829.
BROWN, J.C. Library of John Carter Brown. Bibliotheca Americana. Providence, 1919-1931.
BYRD, C. & H. PECKHAM. "Bibliography of Indiana imprints, 1804-1853." Indiana Historical Collections, vol. 35. Indianapolis, 1955.

CAPPON, L. J. & I. V. BROWN. New Market imprints, 1806-1876. University of Virginia Imprint

Series, no. 5. Richmond, 1942.
CASSELL, A.H. "The German almanac of Christopher Sower." Pennsylvania Magazine of History and Biography, vol. 6. Philadelphia, 1882.
CASTANEDA, C.E. The beginnings of printing in America. Durham, 1940.
CHAMBERLEN, H.A. The first ten years of printing ... in Manchester [N. H.]. Manchester, 1948.
CHAPIN, H.M. Checklist of Rhode Island almanacs, 1643-1850. Worcester, 1915.
CLARKE, N.E. The Richard press, 1809-1823, with a bibliography. Detroit, 1951.
COLE, G.W. Catalog of the Wymberly Jones DeRenne Georgia Library. Wormsloe, Ga., 1931.
---. Library of E.D. Church. vols. 1-5. New York, 1907.
COLEMAN, J.W. John Bradford, esq., pioneer Kentucky printer and historian. Lexington, 1950.
COLLINS, V.L. Early Princeton printing. Princeton, 1911.
COOLEY, E.F. Vermont imprints before 1800. Montpelier, 1937.
COTTEN, B. Housed on the third floor... A collection of North Caroliniana. Baltimore, 1941.
COULTER, E.M. "California copyrights, 1851-1856." California Historical Society Quarterly, vol. 22. San Francisco, 1943.
COWAN, R.E. A bibliography of the Spanish press of California, 1833-1845. San Francisco, 1919.
COWAN, R.E. & R.G. Bibliography of the history of California, 1510-1930. San Francisco, 1933.
CRANDALL, M. Confederate imprints. Boston, 1955.
CROLL, P.C. Lebanon County [Pa.] imprints. Harrisburg, 1909.
CUNZ, D. "John Gruber and his almanac." Maryland Historical Magazine. Baltimore, 1952.
CURTIS PUBLISHING CO. The collection of Franklin imprints in the museum of the Curtis Publishing Co. Philadelphia, 1918. [Almanacs now in PU]

DAWSON, G. Southwest books [catalog]. Los Angeles, 1954.
---. West and Pacific [catalog]. Los Angeles, 1947.

DAY, A.G. "Pioneer presses of Hawaii." In: American Institute of Graphic Arts Journal, vol. 4, no. 5. New York, 1948.

---. Red letter days in the history of printing and publishing in Hawaii. Honolulu, 1949.

DE BOW'S REVIEW. A list of Confederate publications from DeBow's Review. Baton Rouge, 1937.

DE MORGAN, A. "On the earliest printed almanacs." In: British Almanac and Companion. London, 1846.

DORSON, R.M. Davy Crockett, American comic legend. New York, 1939.

DUKE UNIVERSITY. Checklist of Alabama pamphlets in the library of Duke University, 1823-1941. Durham, 1942.

EAMES, W. The first year of printing in New York. New York, 1928.

EBERSTADT, E.E. The William Robertson Coe collection of Western Americana. New Haven, 1948.

---. Alaska and the Northwest Coast [catalog]. New York, 1959.

EDDY, G.S. A work-book of the printing house of Benjamin Franklin and David Hall, 1759-1766. New York, 1930.

ELLISON, R.C. A checklist of Alabama imprints, 1807-1840. University of Alabama, 1946.

EVANS, C. & C.K. SHIPTON. American bibliography, 1639-1800. vol's 1-13. Chicago and Worcester, 1903-1955.

FARMER, S. History of Detroit and Michigan. 2nd edition. Detroit, 1889.

FITTS, J.H. "Memoranda enterred by William Thomas, father of Robert B. Thomas, author of the Farmer's Almanac." In: Essex Institute Historical Collections, vol. 14. Salem, 1876.

FORD, P.L. Bibliography of the issues of Hugh Gaine's press, 1752-1800. New York, 1902.

---. Franklin bibliography. Brooklyn, 1889.

FORD, W.C. "Broadsides, ballads, &c. printed in Massachusetts, 1693-1800." In: Massachusetts Historical Society Collections, vol. 75. Boston, 1922.

FOREMAN, C.T. Oklahoma imprints, 1835-1907. Norman, Okla., 1936.
FOREMAN, E.R. Proposed bibliography of Rochester publishers. Checklist of Rochester publishers, 1816-1860. Rochester, 1926.
FREEMAN, D.S. A calendar of Confederate papers. Richmond, 1908.

GEIGER BROS. [CO.] A historical treatise on the Farmer's Almanac. Newark, 1951.
GILMAN, M.D. Bibliography of Vermont. Burlington, 1897.
GILMORE, B. A Puritan town and its imprints, Northampton, 1786-1845. Northampton, 1942.
GRAVLEY, E. "William E. Woodruff, pioneer Arkansas journalist." In: Arkansas Historical Quarterly, vol. 14, no. 2. Fayetteville, 1955.
GREEN, S. & A. A list of early American imprints belonging to the library of the Massachusetts Historical Society. Cambridge, 1895-1903.
GREENLY, A.H. A bibliography of Father Richard's press in Detroit. Ann Arbor, 1955.
GREENOUGH, C.N. "New England almanacs, 1766-1775, and the American Revolution." American Antiquarian Society Proceedings, vol. 45. Worcester, 1935.
GROLIER CLUB. Catalog of books printed by William Bradford and other printers in the Middle Colonies. New York, 1893.

HALLOWELL, J.O. "Early almanacs." In: British Almanac and Companion. London, 1839.
---. "Historical notes on almanacs." In: British Almanac and Companion. London, 1840.
HAMMETT, C.E., jr. A contribution to the bibliography and literature of Newport, R.I., comprising a list of books published or printed in Newport. Providence, 1887.
HANNA, A.J. The Union Catalog of Floridiana. Winter Park, Fla., 1939.
HAPPER, E.F. "Seventeenth century American almanacs." In: Literary Collector, vol. 9, no. 2. Greenwich, Conn., 1905.

HARDING, G. L.   A brief history of the California
    Spanish press.   San Francisco, 1933.
---. "A census of California Spanish imprints, 1833-
    1845." In: California Historical Society Quarterly,
    vol. 11, no. 2. San Francisco, 1933.
HARGRETT, L.   Oklahoma imprints, 1835-1890. New
    York, 1951.
HARWELL, R. B.   Cornerstones of Confederate collect-
    ing. University of Virginia, 1952.
---. More Confederate imprints [supplement to Cran-
    dall]. Richmond, 1957.
HATCH, B. L.   Preliminary checklist of Waterville im-
    prints. Waterville, Me., 1952.
HAVEN, S. F.   "Catalog of publications in what is now
    the United States, prior to the Revolution." In:
    Thomas' History of Printing in America. Albany,
    1875.
HEARTMAN, C. F.   Cradle of the United States, 1765-
    1789. Metuchen, N.J., 1922, 1923.
---. Preliminary checklist of New Jersey almanacs to
    1850. Metuchen, N.J., 1929.
---. What constitutes a Confederate imprint? Hatties-
    burg, Miss., 1939.
HILDEBURN, C. R.   A century of printing. The is-
    sues of the press in Pennsylvania, 1685-1784.
    Philadelphia, 1885, 1886.
---. A list of the issues of the press in New York,
    1693-1752. Philadelphia, 1889.
---. Sketches of printers and printing in Colonial New
    York. New York, 1895.
HILL, F. P. & V. L. COLLINS.   Books, pamphlets and
    newspapers printed at Newark, 1776-1900. Newark,
    1902.
HILL, W. H.   A brief history of the printing press in
    Washington, Saratoga and Warren Counties [N. Y.].
    New York, 1930.
HOLMES, H. C.   Americana [catalog of the library of
    H. C. Holmes]. New York, 1923.
HOOLE, W. S.   Checklist of Charleston, S. C. periodi-
    cals, 1732-1864. Duke University, Durham, 1936.
HOWE, E. D.   Autobiography... of a pioneer printer.
    Painesville, Ohio, 1878.
HUFELAND, O.   "Checklist of books... printed in

Westchester and the Bronx." In: Westchester Historical Society bulletin, vol. 6. White Plains, 1929.

---. "The printing press in Westchester County, 1797-1860." In: Westchester County Historical Society bulletin, vol. 14, no. 2. White Plains, N.Y., 1938.

HUMPHREY, C.H. "Checklist of New Jersey imprints to the end of the Revolution." Bibliographical Society Papers, vol. 24. New York, 1930.

JERABEK, E. "Almanacs as historical sources." In: Minnesota Historical Society bulletin, no. 15. St. Paul, 1934.

JILLSON, W.R. "A bibliography of Lexington, Ky." In: Kentucky State Historical Society Register, vol. 44. Frankfort, 1946.

---. Rare Kentucky books, 1776-1926. Louisville, 1939.

KATZ, W.A. A historical survey of Washington [state] publishers and printers. Seattle, 1956.

KELLY, J. The American catalog of books published in the United States from January 1861 to January 1866. New York, 1866-1871.

KIMBER, S.A. Cambridge press title pages, 1640-1665. Takoma Park, Md., 1954.

---. The story of an old press. Cambridge, 1937.

KING, R.T. "The Territorial press in Missouri." In: Missouri Historical Society Bulletin, vol. 11, no. 1. St. Louis, 1954.

KITTREDGE, G.L. The Old Farmer and his almanack. Boston, 1920.

KNAUSS, J.O. "Territorial Florida journalism." In: Florida State Historical Society publication no. 6. Deland, 1926.

LEGLER, H.E. Early Wisconsin imprints, 1833-1849. Madison, 1942.

LEITER, L.Z. Rare Americana from the library of L.Z. Leiter. New York, 1933.

LERCH, A.H. "A printer soldier-of-fortune [Charles Fierer]." In: Bibliographical Society Papers, vol.

30. New York, 1936.
LICHTENSTEIN, D.G. The almanac as a record of life in Provincial America. New York, 1950.
LOY, W.E. "Some notes on the introduction of printing into California." In: Printer and Bookmaker, vol's. 25, 26. New York, 1897.
LUCKE, J.R. "Correspondence concerning the... first Arkansas press." In: Arkansas Historical Quarterly, vol. 14, no. 2. Fayetteville, 1955.
LUTRELL, E. "Arizona's frontier press." In: Arizona Historical Review, vol. 6. Tucson, 1935.
---. A bibliographical list of books, pamphlets... on Arizona in the University of Arizona library. Tucson, 1913.

MADISON, J. "Americana notes." In: Collectors Journal. Los Angeles, 1931-1934.
MALONE, R.M. Wyomingana: Two bibliographies. University of Denver, 1950.
MARBLE, A.R. "Early New England almanacs." In: New England Magazine, vol. 19. Boston, 1899.
MASONS, FREE AND ACCEPTED. "Masonic and antimasonic almanacs." In: Transactions of the American Lodge of Research, vol. IV no. 1. New York, 1944.
MATTHEWS, J.P. "Arkansas books." In: University of Arkansas Bulletin. Fayetteville, 1927, 1931.
MC CABE, J.D. "Confederate literature in the sixties." In: Southern Historical Society Papers, ns vol. 4. Richmond, October 1917.
M'CULLOCH, W. "Additions to Thomas' History of Printing." In: American Antiquarian Society Proceedings, ns vol. 31. Worcester, 1921.
MC GREGOR, S. "The Texas Almanac, 1857-1873." In: Southwestern Historical Quarterly, vol. 50, no. 4. Austin, 1947.
MC KAY, G.L. A register of artists, engravers, booksellers, bookbinders, printers and publishers in New York City, 1633-1820. New York, 1942.
MC KEON, N.F. Amherst, Mass. imprints, 1825-1876. Amherst, 1946.
MC MILLEN, J.A. The works of James D.B. DeBow. Hattiesburg, 1940.

MC MURTRIE, D.C. [Listed alphabetically by the State under study in each]:
---. A brief history of the first printing in the state of Alabama. Birmingham, 1931.
---. A note on P. Joseph Forster, pioneer Alabama printer. Hattiesburg, 1943.
---. Beginnings of printing in Arizona. Chicago, 1937.
---. "Early printing in Arizona." In: Arizona Historical Review. Phoenix, 1932.
---. Pioneer printing in California. Springfield, Ill., 1932.
---. The Delaware imprints of 1761. Metuchen, N.J., 1934.
---. "The beginnings of printing in the District of Columbia." In: Americana, vol. 27. Somerville, 1933.
---. The beginnings of printing in Florida. Hattiesburg, 1944.
---. The first printing in Florida. Atlanta, 1931.
---. A preliminary short-title checklist of books, pamphlets and broadsides printed in Florida, 1784-1860. Jacksonville, 1937.
---. "The first printing in Georgia." In: American Collector, vol. 3. Metuchen, N.J., 1926.
---. James Johnston, first printer in the Royal Colony of Georgia. London, 1929.
---. "Located Georgia imprints of the 18th century not in the DeRenne catalog." In: Georgia Historical Quarterly, vol. 18. Savannah, 1934.
---. The pioneer printer of Georgia. Chicago, 1930.
---. "Pioneer printing in Georgia." In: Georgia Historical Quarterly, vol. 16. Savannah, 1932.
---. "The beginnings of printing in Idaho." In: Gutenberg Jahrbuch. Mainz, 1932.
---. Bibliography of Chicago imprints, 1835-1850. Chicago, 1944.
---. Bibliography of Peoria imprints, 1835-1860. Springfield, 1934.
---. Early Illinois copyright entries, 1821-1850. Evanston, 1943.
---. The first printers of Chicago, 1835-1850. Chicago, 1944.
---. First printing in Indiana. Metuchen, N.J., 1934.

\-\-\-. "Indiana imprints, 1804-1849." In: Indiana Historical Society Publications, vol. 11, no. 5. Indianapolis, 1937.

\-\-\-. "Two early issues of the Council Bluffs press." In: Annals of Iowa, ser. 3, vol. 18. Des Moines, 1931.

\-\-\-. "Pioneer printing of Kansas." In: Kansas Historical Quarterly, vol. 1. Topeka, 1931.

\-\-\-. "Checklist of Kentucky almanacs, 1789-1830." In: Register of the Kentucky State Historical Society, vol. 30, no. 92. Frankfort, 1932.

\-\-\-. "Concerning a recently published supplemental checklist of Kentucky imprints, 1788-1820." In: Filson Club Quarterly, vol. 17. Louisville, 1943.

\-\-\-. John Bradford, pioneer printer of Kentucky. Springfield, Ill., 1931.

\-\-\-. "A supplementary list of Kentucky imprints, 1794-1820." In: Kentucky State Historical Society Register, vol. 42. Frankfort, 1944.

\-\-\-. Unlocated early Kentucky imprints. Louisville, 1931.

\-\-\-. Beginnings of printing in New Orleans. New Orleans, 1929.

\-\-\-. Denis Braud, imprimeur du roi a Nouvelle Orleans. Paris, 1929.

\-\-\-. Early printing in New Orleans, 1764-1810. New Orleans, 1929.

\-\-\-. Louisiana imprints, 1768-1810. Hattiesburg, Miss., 1942.

\-\-\-. Maine imprints, 1792-1820. Chicago, 1935.

\-\-\-. Early printing in Michigan. Chicago, 1931.

\-\-\-. Pioneer printing in Michigan. Springfield, Ill., 1933.

\-\-\-. "Les premières impressions Francaises à Detroit." In: Bulletin du Bibliophile, ns année 11. Paris, 1932.

\-\-\-. Pioneer printing in Minnesota. Springfield, Ill., 1932.

\-\-\-. A bibliography of Mississippi imprints, 1798-1830. Heartman no. 69. Beauvoir, 1945.

\-\-\-. The earliest extant Mississippi imprint. Hattiesburg, 1933.

\-\-\-. Checklist of St. Louis imprints, 1808-1830.

Chicago, 1931.
---. Early Missouri book and pamphlet imprints, 1808-1830. Chicago, 1937.
---. Montana imprints, 1864-1880. Chicago, 1937.
---. Pioneer printing in Montana. Iowa City, 1932.
---. The beginnings of printing in New Hampshire. London, 1934.
---. "A bibliography of Morristown, N.J. imprints, 1798-1820." In: New Jersey Historical Society Proceedings, vol. 54. Newark, 1936.
---. Beginning of printing in New Mexico. Chicago, 1932.
---. First printing in New Mexico. Chicago, 1929.
---. "History of early printing in New Mexico." In: New Mexico Historical Review, vol. 4. Santa Fe, 1929.
---. "Additional Buffalo imprints, 1812-1849." In: Grosvenor Library Bulletin, vol. 18, no. 4. Buffalo, 1936.
---. "Additional Geneva, N.Y. imprints, 1815-1849." In: Grosvenor Library Bulletin, vol. 18. Buffalo, 1936.
---. "Bibliography of books, pamphlets and broadsides printed at Auburn, N.Y., 1810-1850." In: Grosvenor Library Bulletin, vol. 20, no. 4. Buffalo, 1938.
---. "Bibliography of books... printed in Canandaigua, N.Y., 1799-1850." In: Grosvenor Library Bulletin, vol. 21, no. 4. Buffalo, 1939.
---. "Bibliography of books and pamphlets printed at Ithaca, N.Y., 1820-1850." In: Grosvenor Library Bulletin, vol. 19, no. 4. Buffalo, 1937.
---. A Checklist of books... printed at Schenectady, N.Y., 1795-1830. Chicago, 1938.
---. Checklist of 18th century Albany [N.Y.] imprints. Albany, 1939.
---. Imprints advertised in the Whitestone [N.Y.] Gazette, 1796-1798. Chicago, 1935.
---. Issues of the Brooklyn press, 1799-1820. Brooklyn, 1936.
---. "Pamphlets and books printed in Buffalo prior to 1850." In: Grosvenor Library Bulletin, vol. 16. Buffalo, 1934.

- ---. "Preliminary checklist of books... printed in Geneva, N.Y., 1800-1850." In: Grosvenor Library Bulletin, vol. 17, no. 4; vol. 18. Buffalo, 1935, 1936.
- ---. Rochester imprints, 1819-1850, in libraries outside of Rochester. Chicago, 1935.
- ---. Short-title list of books... printed in Ithaca, N.Y., 1811-1850. Buffalo, 1936.
- ---. Eighteenth century North Carolina imprints, 1749-1800. Chapel Hill, 1938.
- ---. "Pioneer printing in North Dakota." In: North Dakota Historical Quarterly, vol. 6. Bismarck, 1932.
- ---. "Antecedent experience of William Maxwell, Ohio's first printer." In: Ohio State Archaeological and Historical Quarterly, vol. 41. Columbus, 1932.
- ---. Early printing in Dayton, Ohio. Dayton, 1935.
- ---. Pioneer printing in Ohio. Cincinnati, 1943.
- ---. Oregon imprints, 1847-1870. Eugene, 1950.
- ---. First printers of York, Pa. York, 1940.
- ---. "The beginnings of printing in Rhode Island." In: Americana, vol. 29. Somerville, 1935.
- ---. The first decade of printing in the Royal Colony of South Carolina. London, 1933.
- ---. Beginnings of the press in South Dakota. Iowa City, 1933.
- ---. Early printing in Tennessee. Chicago, 1933.
- ---. "Pioneer printing in Texas." In: Southwestern Historical Quarterly, vol. 35. Austin, 1932.
- ---. Pioneer printing in Texas. Springfield, 1933.
- ---. The beginnings of printing in Utah, 1849-1860. Chicago, 1931.
- ---. Notes on early printing in Utah outside of Salt Lake City. Los Angeles, 1932.
- ---. Pioneer printing in Utah. Springfield, Ill., 1933.
- ---. The beginnings of printing in Virginia. Lexington, 1935.
- ---. The first printing in Virginia. Lexington, 1935.
- ---. Pioneer printing in Washington [State]. Springfield, Ill., 1932.
- ---. A record of Washington [State] imprints, 1835-1876, and some additional Washington imprints.

Seattle, 1943.

---. Was there a printing press in Washington [State] in 1844? Seattle, 1934.

---. The beginnings of printing in West Virginia. Charleston, 1935.

---. Early printing in Milwaukee. Milwaukee, 1930.

---. Early printing in Wisconsin. Seattle, 1931.

---. Early printing in Wyoming and the Black Hills. Hattiesburg, Miss., 1943.

---. Pioneer printing in Wyoming. Cheyenne, 1933.

---. Pioneer printers of the far west. San Francisco, 1933.

---. "The printing press moves westward." In: Minnesota History, vol. 15. St. Paul, 1934.

---. Westward migration of the printing press in the United States, 1786-1836. Mayence, 1930.

MC MURTRIE, D.C. & A.H. ALLEN. [See American Imprints Inventory, no.'s 5 & 6]

---. Colorado imprints not listed in "Early printing in Colorado." Denver, 1943.

---. Early printing in Colorado, 1859-1876. Denver, 1935.

---. A forgotten pioneer press of Kansas. Chicago, 1930.

---. Jotham Meeker, pioneer printer of Kansas, with a bibliography of... Baptist Mission Press... 1834-1854. Chicago, 1930.

MECHEM, K. "The mystery of the Meeker press." In: Kansas Historical Quarterly, vol. 4. Topeka, 1935.

METZGER, E.M. Supplement to Hildeburn's Century of Printing, 1685-1775. New York, 1930.

MILES, E.A. "The Mississippi press in the Jackson era, 1824-1841." In: Journal of Mississippi History, vol. XIX, no. 1. Jackson, January 1957.

MILLER, G.J. David A. Borrenstein, a biographical and bibliographical study. Chicago, 1936.

MINICK, A.R. A history of printing in Maryland, 1791-1800. Baltimore, 1949.

MISSOURI STATE HISTORICAL SOCIETY. "Missouriana." In: Missouri Historical Review, various issues. Columbia, 1936-1938.

MITCHELL, E.D. A preliminary checklist of Tennes-

see imprints, 1861-1866. University of Virginia, Charlottesville, 1953.
MIXTER, G.W. American almanacs. New York, 1947.
MOFFIT, A. "Checklist of Iowa imprints, 1837-1860." In: Iowa Journal of History, vol. 36. Iowa City, 1938.
---. Iowa imprints before 1861. Iowa City, 1938.
MOORE, I.H. "The earliest printing and first newspaper in Texas." In: Southwestern Historical Society Quarterly, vol. 39. Austin, 1935.
MORRISON, H.A. Checklist of American almanacs, 1639-1800. Washington, 1907.
MOSS, S.A. "The Low family of New York City publishers, 1795-1829." In: New York Public Library Bulletin. New York, February 1943.
MURNEY, N. "Book trails of Colorado." In: Collecting for profit. Los Angeles, 1931-1933.
MUNSELL, J. Bibliotheca Munselliana; a catalog of books... Albany, 1872.

NASH, R. Pioneer printing at Dartmouth. Hanover, N.H., 1941.
NELSON, W. Checklist of the issues of the press of New Jersey, 1723, 1728, 1754-1800. Paterson, 1899.
NEWBERRY LIBRARY. "Midwest bibliography." In: Newberry Library Bulletin [supplement]. Chicago, 1947.
NEW YORK ANNUAL REGISTER. "History of almanacs." In: New York Annual Register. New York, 1840.
NEW YORK PUBLIC LIBRARY. "List of almanacks, ephemerides, etc., and of works relating to the calendar, in the New York Public Library." In: Bulletin of the New York Public Library, vol. 7, no's 7 & 8. New York, 1903.
---. One hundred notable engravers, 1683-1850 [with a bibliography]. New York, 1928.
---. Printing from the 16th to the 20th century. New York, 1940.
NICHOLS, C.L. Bibliography of Worcester, 1775-1848. Worcester, 1899, 1918.

---. Checklist of Maine almanacs, 1787-1850. Worcester, 1928.
---. Checklist of New Hampshire almanacs to 1850. Worcester, 1928.
---. Checklist of Vermont almanacs. Worcester, 1928.
---. Notes on the almanacs of Massachusetts. Worcester, 1912.
NOLAN, J.B. First decade of printing in Reading, Pa. Reading, 1930.
NOURSE, H.S. Lancastriana: a bibliography. Lancaster, Pa., 1901.
NOYES, R.W. Bibliography of Maine imprints to 1820. Stonington, 1930.

OWEN, T.M. A bibliography of Alabama. Washington, 1898.
---. A bibliography of Mississippi. Washington, 1900.
OXFORD UNIVERSITY PRESS. The Oxford Almanack, 1674-1946. New York, 1946.

PARADISE, S.H. A history of printing in Andover, Mass., 1798-1931. Andover, 1931.
PARISH, J.C. "California books and manuscripts in the Huntington Library." In: Huntington Library Bulletin, no. 7. San Marino, Cal., 1935.
PARKER, W.W. "Printing in Gambier, Ohio, 1829-1884." In: Ohio State Archaeological and Historical Quarterly, vol. 62. Columbus, 1953.
PASCHAL, G.W. A history of printing in North Carolina. Raleigh, 1946.
PERRY, A. Some New England almanacs, with special mention of those published in Rhode Island. Providence, 1885.
PETTINGILL, G.E. Checklist of Franklin imprints in the Franklin Institute. Lancaster, Pa., 1948.
PHILLIPS, H. Catalogue of the almanacs of Henry Phillips, Jr. Philadelphia, May 25, 1863.
---. Certain old almanacs published in Philadelphia between 1705 and 1744. Philadelphia, 1881.
PIERSON, R.M. A preliminary checklist of Lexington, Ky. imprints, 1821-1850. University of Virginia Bibliographical Society, Charlottesville, 1953.
POLSCHER, A.A. Father Richard, notes on his print-

ing in early Detroit. Detroit, 1950.
PROUD, R. The Proud papers [auction catalog]. Philadelphia, 1903.

QUENZEL, C.H. Fredericksburg [Va.] imprints, 1778-1876. University of Virginia, Imprint Series, no. 4. Richmond, 1947.

RAINES, C.W. A bibliography of Texas... since 1536. Austin, 1896.
READY, J.K. A checklist of Vermont imprints, 1821-1835. Washington, 1955.
RECORDS, T.W. "The old printing office in New Harmony." In: Indiana Magazine of History. Bloomington, 1937.
REDWAY, V.L. Music directory of early New York City. A file of... music publishers..., 1786 through 1835 [and] 1836 through 1875. New York, 1941.
REICHMANN, F. Christopher Sower, Sr., 1694-1758, printer in Germantown. Philadelphia, 1943.
---. German printing in Maryland, a checklist, 1768-1950. Baltimore, 1950.
RICE, O.K. "West Virginia printers and their work, 1790-1830." In: West Virginia History, vol. 14, no. 4. Charleston, 1953.
RITCHIE, W. "Hand press printing in Southern California." In: Book Club of California Quarterly News Letter. San Francisco, Winter 1947.
ROACH, G.W. "Preliminary checklist of Batavia [N.Y.] imprints, 1819-1876." In: New York History, vol's. 24, 25. Cooperstown, 1943, 1944.
RODEN, R.F. The Cambridge press, 1638-1692. New York, 1905.
[ROSENBACH, A.S.W. COLLECTION]. One hundred and fifty years of printing in English America, 1640-1790. Free Library of Philadelphia, 1940.
RUDOLPH, E.L. Confederate broadside verse. Heartman, no. 76. New Braunfels, Tex., 1950.
RUGG, H.G. "Isaac Eddy, printer-engraver." In: Bibliographical essays. Cambridge, Mass., 1924.
RUSK, R.L. Literature of the Middle West frontier. New York, 1925.

RUTHERFORD, L. John Peter Zenger: his press, his trial and a bibliography of Zenger imprints. New York, 1904.

SABIN, J. Dictionary of books relating to America. Vol's 1-29. New York, 1865-1936.
SABINE, J. "Books and libraries in Newark to 1847." In: New Jersey Historical Society Proceedings, vol. 71. Newark, 1953.
SALLEY, A.S., JR. "The first presses of South Carolina." In: Bibliographical Society of America Proceedings, vol. 2. New York, 1907, 1908.
SARGENT, G.H. "The centenary of the Andover press." In: Granite Monthly, vol. 51. Concord, 1919.
SEALOCK, R.B. Publishing in Pennsylvania, 1785-1790. New York, 1935.
SEARS, J.H. Tennessee printers, 1791-1945. Kingsport, 1945.
SEIDENSTICKER, O. First century of German printing in America, 1728-1830. Philadelphia, 1893.
SEVERANCE, F.H. "Bibliography of the Niagara regions." In: Buffalo Historical Society Publications, vol. 6. Buffalo, 1903.
---. "Carrier's addresses." Buffalo Historical Society Publications, vol. 25. Buffalo, 1921.
---. "Story of Phinney's Western Almanack." In: Buffalo Historical Society Publications, vol. 24. Buffalo, 1920.
SHERA, J.H. "An eddy in the western flow of American culture. The history of printing... in Oxford, Ohio, 1827-1841." In: Ohio State Archaeological and Historical Quarterly, vol. 44. Columbus, 1935.
SHOEMAKER, A.L. "A checklist of imprints of the German press of Lehigh County, Pa., 1807-1900." In: Lehigh County Historical Society Proceedings. Allentown, 1947.
---. "Checklist of the imprints of the German press of Northampton County, Pa., 1766-1905." In: Publications of the Northampton County Historical Society, vol. 5. Easton, 1943.
SMITH, C.W. & I. MAYHEW. Pacific Northwest Americana. 3rd edition. Portland, Ore., 1950.
SNOWDEN, Y. "Confederate books." In: Charleston

[S.C.] Sunday News, August 9, 1903.
[SOUTH CAROLINA GAZETTE]. The South Carolina Gazette, 1732-1775. University of South Carolina, Columbia, 1953.
SPARGO, J. Anthony Haswell, printer, patriot, balladeer. Rutland, Vt., 1925.
SPIESEKE, A.W. "Almanacs printed by John M'Culloch." In: First textbooks in American history, and their authors. New York, 1938.
STAPLETON, A. "Researches in the first century of German printing in America." In: The Pennsylvania German, vol. 5, no. 2. Lebanon, Pa., 1904.
STEWART, KIDD CO. List of books and pamphlets... Confederate publications. Cincinnati, 1886.
STICKNEY, M.A. "Almanacs and their authors." In: Essex Institute Historical Collections, vol's 8 & 14. Salem, Mass., 1868, 1878.
STORKE, E.G. "History of the press of Cayuga County [N.Y.], 1798-1877." In: Cayuga County Historical Society Collections, no. 7. Auburn, N.Y., 1889.
STREETER, T.W. Bibliography of Texas. Parts 1-3, vol's 1-5. Cambridge, 1955.
SWASEY, J.H. "Rhode Island almanacs of long ago, 1727-1800." In: Newport Historical Society Bulletin, no. 92. Newport, 1934.
SWEM, E.G. "Bibliography of Virginia." In: Virginia State Library Bulletin, vol's 8 & 10, no's 2, 3, 4. Richmond, 1916-1955.
SWIFT, B. The Salisbury press; story of Buffalo's first printer. Buffalo, 1954.

TAPLEY, H.S. Salem [Mass.] imprints, 1768-1825. Salem, 1927.
TAYLOR, E.S. Supplement to Hildeburn's Century of Printing, 1776-1784. New York, 1935.
TERRY, R. Library of R. Terry [auction catalog]. New York, 1934.
THOMPSON, D.E. Bibliography of Louisiana books and pamphlets in the T.P. Thompson collection. University of Alabama, 1947.
THOMPSON, D.W. Early publications of Carlisle, Pa., 1785-1835. Carlisle, 1932.
THOMPSON, L. The printing and publishing activities

of the American Tract Society, 1825-1850. New York, 1941.

THOMSON, P.G. A bibliography of the state of Ohio. Cincinnati, 1880.

TINKER, E.L. "Bibliography of the French newspapers and periodicals of Louisiana." In: American Antiquarian Society Proceedings. Worcester, 1933.

---. Les ecrits de langue Francaise en Louisiane au XIXe siecle. Paris, 1932.

THWAITES, R.G. "The Ohio Valley press before the War of 1812." In: American Antiquarian Society Proceedings, ns vol. 19. Worcester, 1909.

TOOKER, W.W. Early Sag Harbor [N.Y.] printers and their imprints. Evanston, Ill., 1943.

TOWNSEND, J.W. [see American Imprints Inventory Series, no. 38.]

TRUMBULL, J.H. Catalog of the American library of George Brinley. Hartford, 1886-1893.

---. List of books printed in Connecticut, 1709-1800. Hartford, 1904.

TURNBULL, R.J. Bibliography of South Carolina, 1563-1950. vol's 1-5. University of Virginia, Charlottesville, 1956.

VAIL, R.W.G. "A patriotic pair of peripatetic printers... John Holt and Samuel Loudon, 1776-1783." In: Essays honoring Lawrence C. Wroth. Portland, 1951.

---. The voice of the old frontier. Philadelphia, 1949.

VANCE, L.J. "Dixiana." In: Bachelor of Arts, vol. 2, no. 1. New York, 1895.

VENABLE, W.H. Beginnings of literary culture in the Ohio Valley. Cincinnati, 1891.

WAGNER, H.R. California imprints, 1846-1851. Berkeley, 1922.

---. "Commercial printers of San Francisco, 1851-1880." In: Bibliographical Society Papers, vol. 33. New York, 1939.

---. "The New Mexico Spanish press." In: New Mexico Historical Review, vol. 12. Albuquerque, 1937.

WALKER, M.A. Beginnings of printing in the state of Indiana. Crawfordsville, 1934.

WALL, A.J. A list of New York almanacs, 1694-1850. New York, 1921.

WARDNER, H.S. "Alden Spooner, State Printer." In: The Vermonter, vol. 36. White River Junction, Vt., 1931.

WATERS, W.O. American imprints, 1648-1797, in the Huntington Library, supplementing Evans' American bibliography. Cambridge, 1933.

---. "Confederate imprints in the Henry E. Huntington Library." In: Bibliographical Society Papers, vol. 23. Chicago, 1929.

---. "Los Angeles imprints, 1851-1876." In: Southern California Historical Society Bulletin. Los Angeles, 1937.

WEBBER, M. Checklist of South Carolina almanacs to 1800. Charleston, 1914.

WEEKS, S.B. The libraries and literature in North Carolina in the 18th century. Washington, 1896.

---. The press of North Carolina in the 18th century. A bibliography of the issues. Brooklyn, N.Y., 1891.

WEGELIN, O. Books relating to the history of Georgia in the library of Wymberly Jones DeRenne. Savannah, 1911.

---. "The Brooklyn, New York press, 1799-1820." In: Bibliographical Society of America Bulletin, vol. 4, no's 3 & 4. New York, 1912.

WEINER, L. "Periodicals and almanacs." In: History of Yiddish literature. New York, 1899.

WEISS, D. "Printing in Hawaii." In: Inland Printer, vol. 72. Chicago, October 1923.

WEISS, H.B. Mahlon Day, early New York printer. New York, 1941.

WEMYSS, S. General guide to rare Americana. Philadelphia, 1950.

WENTZ, R. Eleven western presses. Los Angeles, 1956.

WESTERVELT, W.D. Journal of E. Loomis. University of Hawaii. Honolulu, 1937.

WEYGAND, J.L. Elihu Stout, printer to the [Indiana] Territory. Nappanee, Ind., 1955.

WHARTON, T.I. "Notes on the provincial literature of Pennsylvania." In: Historical Society of Pennsyl-

vania Memoirs, vol. 1. Philadelphia, 1826.
WHEAT, C.I. The pioneer press of California. Oakland, 1948.
WHEELER, J.T. The Maryland press, 1777-1790. Baltimore, 1938.
WHITE, N.H. "Printing in Cambridge since 1800." In: Cambridge Historical Society Publications, vol. 15. Cambridge, Mass., 1931.
WHITMORE & SMITH. Texas book list [catalog]. Dallas, 1935.
WICKERSHAM, J. A bibliography of Alaskan literature, 1724-1924. Cordova, Alaska, 1927.
WILEY, E. "Eighteenth century presses in Tennessee." In: Bibliographical Society of America Proceedings, vol. 2. New York, 1907, 1908.
WILLIAMS, J.C. An Oneida County [N.Y.] printer, William Williams... with a bibliography of the press at Utica, 1803-1838. New York, 1906.
WILLIAMSON, J. A bibliography of the state of Maine. Portland, 1896.
WINKLER, E.W. "Checklist of Texas imprints, 1846-[1862]." In: Southwestern Historical Quarterly, [vd]. Austin, 1943-1948.
WINSHIP, G.P. The Cambridge press, 1638-1692. Philadelphia, 1945.
---. A preliminary checklist of Cambridge, Mass. imprints, 1638-1692. Boston, 1939.
WISCONSIN STATE HISTORICAL SOCIETY. Catalog of books on the War of the Rebellion [1861-1865]. Madison, 1887.
WOOD, J.H. "Quaker imprints of Bucks County [Pa.]." In: Friends' Historical Association Bulletin, vol. 22. Swarthmore, Pa., 1933.
WRIGHT, M.H. "Notes on the life of Mrs. Hannah Worcester Hicks Hitchcock and the Park Hill press." In: Chronicles of Oklahoma, vol. 19. Oklahoma City, 1941.
WROTH, L.C. A history of printing in colonial Maryland, 1686-1776. Baltimore, 1922.
---. "The St. Mary's City press." In: Maryland Historical Magazine, vol. 31. Baltimore, 1936.
---. Source materials of Florida history in the John Carter Brown Library of Brown University. St.

Augustine, 1944.
WYATT, E.A. Petersburg imprints, 1786-1876. University of Virginia Imprint Series, no. 9. Richmond, 1949.
WYLLIE, J.C. Abingdon imprints, 1807-1876. University of Virginia Imprint Series, no. 1. Richmond, 1946.
WYNNE, C. "Origin of almanacs." In: Richardson's Almanac [Wynne's Edition] for 1862. Richmond, 1861.
WYNNE, T.H. Catalog of the library of T.H. Wynne. Richmond, 1875.

ZIEGLER, S.H. "The Ephrata printing press." In: Pennsylvania German Folklore Society Publications, vol. 5. Allentown, 1940.